D0822612

The Life That Ruth Built

●●●●●●●●●●●●●●●●●

A BIOGRAPHY

by Marshall Smelser

University of Nebraska Press
Lincoln and London

First Bison Book printing: 1993
Most recent printing indicated by the last digit below:
10   9   8   7   6   5   4   3   2

Library of Congress Cataloging-in-Publication Data
Smelser, Marshall.
The life that Ruth built: a biography / by Marshall Smelser.
p.   cm.
Reprint. Previously published: New York: Quadrangle/New York Times Book
Co., 1975.
Includes bibliographical references and index.
ISBN 0-8032-9218-x
1. Ruth, Babe, 1895–1948.   2. Baseball players—United States—Biography.
I. Title.
GV865.R8S62   1992
796.357′092—DC20
[B]
92-39757   CIP

Published by arrangement with Times Books, a Division of Random House, Inc.

To
Liz and Kate

Contents

Contents
ix

Preface

This is the story of a man greatly praised by the people, and of what their joyous acclaim did to him. He was a paid performer in an organized amusement. Mrs. Gradgrind, in Charles Dickens's *Hard Times*, told us circuses are not things to be learned about. I can add that circuses and similar enterprises aren't easy to learn about in a very exact way.

Writers, composers, artists, politicians, saints, business leaders, and warriors leave creations behind, whether letters, books, plays, musical scores, civil and canon laws, treaties, encyclicals, constitutions, meditations, orations, buildings, pictures, or situation reports, by which we may judge them. But actors, musicians, circus performers, and athletes, as a rule, leave only names, anecdotes, legends, press reports and criticism, and memoirs by necessarily biased friends. The job of writing the life of such a person known mostly for performance is to try to combine these hard-to-mix parts into a narrative which makes sense.

Most of what we know of Babe Ruth comes from the news stories of his day-to-day life in his public green-and-tan world, the baseball field. We know very little of his interior and private life. Myth and fable have rushed to fill the vacuum, much of it written rather lubriciously, as if between sniggers, and almost wholly undocumented. I don't deny Ruth's gluttony, but I tried to get it straight and explain it.

This is not a fan book. I broke into disorganized baseball at the age of eight and never have been a Yankee follower; as early as 1922 I mourned the failure of George Sisler and the Browns to turn back Ruth and the Yankee attack. And it is not a record book. Baseball statistics, delightful as they are to collect and study, are only a partial measure of the game, and they tell us next to nothing of persons. I have not written a book for baseball people; I prefer to think of it as a baseball book for people. I think it well to add here that the several books about Ruth which appeared in 1974 were available only after I had finished writing this book.

Finally, this is not an authorized biography. Only one member of Babe Ruth's family had anything to do with it. Mrs. Wilbur Moberly, his sister (born Mary Ruth and called "Mamie"), helped me in many ways. In return she laid one restraint on me: "Tell the truth!" I have tried to obey.

The following baseball players, who regularly batted against Babe Ruth when he pitched for the Red Sox, were very helpful: Lute Boone, George Burns, Jacques Fournier, Jack Graney, Baby Doll Jacobson, George McBride, Del Pratt, Larry Kopf, Sam Rice, George Sisler, Elmer Smith, Amos Strunk, Zeb Terry, and Sam Vick.

Each of the following played at least a full season with Ruth on the Yankees and was generous with answers to specific questions as well as those I should have asked: Sammy Byrd, Earle Combs, Ben Chapman, Jimmie DeShong, Bill Dickey, Cedric Durst, Mike Gazella, Truck Hannah, Chicken Hawks, Waite Hoyt, Henry Johnson, Arndt Jorgens, Mark Koenig, Lyn Lary, Ben Paschal, Roger Peckinpaugh, Jimmy Reese, Jack Saltzgaver, Joe Sewell, Bob Shawkey, Fred Walker, Pee Wee Wanninger, and Eddie Wells.

John Bertrand (Jocko) Conlan, articulate outfielder and umpire, played against Ruth, and also was a close friend of Brother Mathias. He is loaded with remembrance of time past and generous in sharing his recollections.

The following institutions and their directors earned my gratitude: the Boston Public Library, the British Museum, the Indiana University Libraries, the Library of Congress, the University of Minnesota Library, the University of Missouri Library, the National Archives, the National Baseball Library of the Baseball Hall of Fame, the Memorial Library of the University of Notre Dame, and the Xaverian Brothers Provincialate, Kensington, Maryland. My thanks go also to those who gave permission to use illustrations, who are acknowledged herein, to the Macmillan Company for permission to quote from Laurence S. Ritter, and to Charles Scribner's Sons for permission to quote from Ring Lardner, and to Harper and Row, Publishers, for permission to quote from Jim Brosnan.

I am also very grateful to the following:

The Baltimore Chamber of Commerce; Ann Banks of the *Baltimore Sun*; Darlene Barry of Lederle Laboratories; Charles Barker, St. Louis, Missouri; Mel and Ethel Berg, Newark, New Jersey; Dr. Lawrence Bradley of the Notre Dame Archives; Forrest D. Bradshaw, Town Historian of Sudbury, Massachusetts; Bob Broeg, sports editor of the *St. Louis Post-Dispatch*; E. S. Brother of the

New York News; Associate Dean Robert E. Burns, College of Arts and Letters, Notre Dame.

Peter P. Clark, Exhibit Curator of the Baseball Hall of Fame; Dr. Helen Cripe of the American Antiquarian Society, Worcester, Massachusetts; Professor Michael Crowe, Notre Dame; Bill Crowley, Director of Public Relations of the Boston Red Sox.

Dr. L. Robert Davids, Washington, D.C.; Ivan Dee, my original editor at Quadrangle; Patricia Dowling of the National Archives; John Duxbury of the *St. Louis Post-Dispatch.*

Dr. Dean R. Esslinger, Towson State College, Maryland.

Robert A. Fishel, formerly Vice-President for Public Relations, New York Yankees; Mike Flanagan, Knoxville, Tennessee; Dr. William Fowler, Northeastern University.

Marvin Gelfand, New York City; Emanuel Geltman, Quadrangle/ The New York Times Book Company; Donald C. Grant of the International Sports and Games Collection, Notre Dame; Stan Grosshandler, M.D., Hales Corners, Wisconsin; Professor William Gustafson, San Jose State College.

Alexander H. Hadden, Esq., General Counsel, Office of the Commissioner of Baseball; Kenneth M. Holt, Bloomington, Illinois; Joseph H. Huebner, Notre Dame.

Clifford Kachline, Historian of the Baseball Hall of Fame; the Reverend Thomas Hilary Kaufman, O.P. (Dominican), Grand Rapids, Michigan; John H. Kiers, Chicago; Bowie Kuhn, Esq., Commissioner of Baseball.

Marie K. Lawrence of the Notre Dame Library; Fred Lieb, St. Petersburg, Florida; William Loughman, Elmhurst, Illinois; Peter D. Lowenstein, Esq., New York City.

Pat McDonough, editor and publisher of *Sports Reporter and BPA Bowling*; Jack McGrath, Vice-President for Public Relations, Hillerich and Bradsby Company, Louisville.

Brother Bertin Manning, C.F.X., Kensington, Maryland; Georgia Mansbridge, London, England; Professor Eugene C. Murdoch, Marietta College.

Buck Peden, Director of Publicity, Chicago White Sox.

Edward W. Quill, librarian of the *Boston Globe.*

Chris Roewe of the *Sporting News*; Emil H. Rothe, Chicago; Harold W. Ryan of the National Archives.

Victor A. Schaefer, formerly Director of Libraries, Notre Dame; Arthur O. Schott, state baseball historian of Louisiana, New Orleans; Professor Samuel Shapiro, Notre Dame; Dr. Raymond Sickinger, Notre Dame; Jack Smalling, Ames, Iowa; Brother Thomas Spalding, C.F.X., Spalding College; C. C. Johnson Spink, publisher of the *Sporting News*; Red Smith, Harrison, New York.

Grover Tidell, San Francisco.

Professor David Quentin Voigt, Albright College.

Hilda Whitney, Sudbury, Massachusetts; Thomas Winship, editor, the *Boston Globe*.

Robert L. Zimmerman, the Curtiss Candy Company, Chicago.

Carmela Rulli and Marie Meilner of the Faculty Stenographic Pool at Notre Dame generously and intelligently converted my handwriting into typewriting with more zeal than anyone might think possible.

My wife, a first baseman's daughter, understood the importance of the book, at least its importance to me, and saw to it that it was possible (even necessary) that I write it.

MARSHALL SMELSER

South Bend, Indiana
1971–1974

The Life That Ruth Built

A BIOGRAPHY

1 · Rotten Start of a Bad Kid

George Ruth said he had "a rotten start" in life. Surely his early childhood was rather lawless. He lodged with his overworked and distracted parents in flats above several bars-and-grills, but most of his time was his own. He spent it on the streets and piers of Baltimore, where he learned freedom, profanity, and larceny. Young Ruth's Baltimore was peopled by longshoremen, sailors, street arabs, waterfront bums, railroad detectives, and wagon drivers armed with cracking whips. Risking the hazard of the whips, George and friends looted the passing drays like pirates, usually stealing garden truck to throw at other drivers. (A too zealous biographer has claimed George Ruth could throw a curve with a potato at the age of six.) He also found time for baseball before the age of seven, but we have no details of it.

A rotten start it may have been, but not unusual. Most city children of medium-poor parents grew up in the streets, unguided. Surprisingly few died of accidents. George's rotten start was typical of the 1890s, and if he had been maimed or black or retarded it would have been worse. He was white, splendidly endowed in body, and quick to learn what he wished to know. His early childhood was bleak but not crippling.

When Ruth was very young, Baltimore was the sixth largest city of the country. It was much the same kind of place it is now: a port to which ships brought raw materials to factories, and carried finished goods from foreign lands for Southern buyers. Its stuffy, self-coined slogan, "The Liverpool of America," fitted it well, except that sailors on shore leave called it a graveyard. Baltimore lacked both unspeakable vices and vigorous virtues.

Baltimore had built good ships since the eighteenth century. The waterfront was still busy when young George loitered, played, and pilfered there. Bulk-cargo schooners showed their forest of masts against clouds of black smoke from coal-fired steamers. Ships tied up at six great piers with cobble-paved lanes down their centers, past arcaded warehouses. The lanes were clogged with two- and four-wheeled horse-drawn vehicles, and among the carts and wagons darted men of trade dressed according to standing: entrepreneurs in top hats and cutaways, lesser men in shirtsleeves, vests, collars, ties, and derby or straw hats. These men and their equipment made a daily hubbub. The shouts, the cracking of whips, the rattle of iron tyres on cobblestones, the clop of hoofs, and the prospect of stolen fruit or just plain mischief usually drew troublesome numbers of tanned, fleet, idle street urchins such as George Ruth, out to raid the carts and drays, brave the wagoners' whips, and cheerfully enrage their elders and betters.

Near that part of Baltimore where George lived in his early childhood were the six great city piers and the terminals of eight railways and ship lines, all handy to the great Baltimore and Ohio Camden Station, a quarter of a mile long. Small boys take short views, and in the short run this neighborhood was a fine place to live the unsupervised life.

The Ruth family never lived in the grubbiest part of Baltimore. A slummy neighborhood of whites lay about a mile east of George's usual district, and a separate-but-equal black slum was a mile or so north, mostly in "alley homes." The Ruths, as small-business people, would rank at the top of the lowest class or, perhaps, at the bottom of the middle class.

Most Baltimore families of the kind the Ruths would be acquainted with had from two to five members; few had six or more. Three quarters of those who worked away from home were laborers, and a quarter of the men worked on the piers as longshoremen or wagoneers. Most of the wage-earning women shucked oysters, packed meat or fruit, or were in domestic service. More than half of the poor white women of Baltimore stayed home and kept their houses.

The poor of Baltimore were not prone to theft or gambling, but they often found themselves in trouble with the law for disorderly conduct (their No. 1 vice), assault and battery, and public drunkenness. Despite short-fused violence, the Baltimore proletariat had a stable family life: in the most disorderly, battered, and drunken police district, fewer than one seventh of 1 percent of adults were divorced.

The Germans made up the largest "ethnic group" in Baltimore. This gave the city a pleasantly beery, wurst-full, kraut-smelling life, later celebrated by H. L. Mencken. As the Ruths were of German descent, we may suppose they found it easy to think of making their living by working among beer taps and ovens.

All of the people here described were a cut below the Ruths, but

George Ruth, aged 3. He became George Herman
Ruth, Jr., in the next decade upon taking the
name Herman at his confirmation. Herman was his
father's middle name and the name of his friend at
St. Mary's Industrial School, Brother Herman, C.F.X.
(*Photograph courtesy of Mamie Ruth Moberly.*)

just barely. They were the people the Ruth family hoped to get its
living from, by selling food and drink. Such a modest restaurant
was a tough way to wealth. About half of Baltimore's wage earners
made from five to ten dollars a week. One family in ten owned its
own house. About the same proportion was able to save any money.
People don't usually get ahead by doing business with poor people
at just one stand, which was what the Ruths hoped to do.

The name Ruth may be from the low-German common noun
Rut, meaning "root" in English. Or it may be an Americanized
Rüthe, which means "wand" or "rod" and would be a good word in
Germany for "ball bat." Whatever it means, it is a German family
name. The present Ruth family believes George Ruth's paternal
grandfather was Peter Ruth, born in Bucks County, Pennsylvania,
in 1801, who married Kaziah Reager, born in Lancaster County in
1805. The strain is pure Pennsylvania Dutch. Young George was

supposed by some to have known a little German. If he did, he didn't get it from the Ruth side of the family. Pennsylvania Dutch resembles the German from which it degenerated, but it is Pennsylvania Dutch and nothing else. We don't know when the Ruths moved from Pennsylvania.

There were four Ruth families listed in the Baltimore city directory of 1855. George's grandfather was John A. Ruth, who went into the lightning-rod business in 1873. He also begat at least two sons, George Senior (1871) and John A. Junior. Excepting the Pennsylvania ancestor, all Ruths whose birthplaces are known were born in Baltimore. They have been a fertile tribe. Not counting business entries, the Baltimore telephone directory of 1971 listed ninety-two Ruths. Figuring that there must have been Ruth girls who married people not named Ruth, and that some of the clan either did not have telephones or had unlisted numbers, we may suppose there were about two hundred Ruth households in Baltimore in 1971.

George Herman Ruth, Sr., was a man of false starts in life. Before he settled down in the food-and-drink line at the age of twenty-four, he appeared in successive city directories as driver, agent, salesman, gripman, and, in 1895, the year of George Junior's birth, as in business with his brother, John Junior, making lightning rods. The lightning-rod listing was erroneously carried over from 1894; early in 1895 he was certainly in the restaurant business. George Senior was a man who tried to graduate from wagoneer to several unskilled white-collar jobs, fell back on the family lightning-rod business just before marriage, and then, when his wife was pregnant, somehow found the means to go into the restaurant business just before the baby was born. We may suppose grandfather John A. Ruth, Senior, sometime maker of lightning rods, stepped in to help. In 1895 John Senior, after passing the lightning rods to John Junior and George, had a grocery and saloon on Frederick Avenue. His connections with brewers, distillers, and wholesale grocers could have helped his needy bridegroom son.

George's wife was the former Kate Schamberger, also born in Baltimore. She had some Irish ancestry, but we don't know how much. The name Schamberger, like most German names, can be Americanized in many ways. The birth certificate of Kate's first child lists her as Kate Schamberg, on the authority of the attending midwife. But Kate's father is known, and he was the only Pius Schamberger in the city directory. He lived at 216 Emory Street (where Kate produced the baby) for a span covering at least the years 1887–1904. Emory Street qualified as an "alley." It had been laid out and built on before the Civil War. The house numbered 216 was a dwelling, not a saloon, not a workshop.

Accepting all variants as true Schambergers, we may notice George "Schaumburg," a "finisher," on Rayborg Street (mostly a row of whorehouses) in 1856, and George Schamberger, upholsterer, with a shop in downtown Baltimore in 1858.

That Pius Schamberger was George Schamberger's son is probable, but beyond proof. Pius was also an upholsterer, and a sufficiently respectable journeyman to serve as vice-president of Woodworkers Local No. 6. But he had that inner drive to qualify as a Baltimore German by starting out on West Brad Street in the 1860s and 1870s as a grocer and saloonkeeper. These sturdy kinfolk give the impression that no nineteenth-century relative of George H. Ruth, Junior, was ever much farther than arm's reach from knackwurst and lager. His father and both grandfathers at one time or other made their livings selling beer and what goes with beer.

George H. Ruth, Sr. (1871–1918) and Kate Schamberger (1875–1912) were married in 1894. George was Lutheran; Kate was Catholic. Kate was a small woman, like her surviving daughter who in the 1970s was four feet, ten inches tall. George was a strong young fellow, perhaps six feet tall or a bit less, with dark hair, brown eyes, a round head, and a broad nose. His first child, George Junior, looked just like him.

The elder Ruth is usually called a saloonkeeper. Where working-class Germans gathered, every restaurant owner sold drinks, every barkeeper (if there's a difference) sold food. H. L. Mencken was amused that every beer seller in that part of Maryland called himself a restaurateur, but it seems a fair enough name, if a little Frenchified.

It was hard work and paid little. People in that business in Baltimore in the 1890s made net profits of from five to a hundred dollars for a six-day week of 60 to 114 working hours. It would be proper to estimate George and Kate Ruth's joint profit at fifteen to twenty dollars a week, and their weekly hours at about a hundred each. Competition was keen. There was a licensed seller of legal beverages for each 105 Baltimoreans, the highest known ratio in the country. George and Kate worked very hard, Kate was not usually well, and her first child was left alone to run the streets and piers where he trained strenuously to be the champion of truancy when the crime should be invented.

George Ruth, Senior, did business in several places from 1894 until his death, usually under the name "Union Bar." H. L. Mencken's father, sketched by his son as a rabid union hater, avoided lunching at one of Ruth's "Union" bars, which was handy to his office, only because of the word "Union." A place on Camden Street, above which George Junior spent his unweaned and diapered days, was still open in 1968, operated by Vito Bludsens who

A gathering of cousins in the summer of 1896. George Ruth, aged about eighteen months, is with his mother in the front row, extreme left. His father is the leftmost of the three men seated on the bottom step, left center, wearing a bow tie, and holding pipe and mug of beer. (*Mamie Ruth Moberly.*)

had been in business there since 1923. The site is three blocks from Pius Schamberger's Emory Street house.

Shortly after the Camden Street restaurant opened, Kate Ruth brought forth a son in the house of her father. The date on the birth certificate is February 6, 1895. For years young George believed his birthday was February 7, 1894. On another occasion an elder friend of the family made affidavit that George was born on May 18, 1894. Of these dates, the one on the birth certificate would be most welcome in a court of law, but such vital statistics were officially reported by midwives, and who knows how carefully? Mother Kate might remember better than Minnie Graf the midwife. In any case, we can throw out the myth that George was an orphan, a myth, it is said, that he allowed to circulate in later years because he knew that to believe it would make orphans feel good. One important fact went unrecorded at the moment of his birth: the new kid on Camden Street was left-handed, but nobody knew it for awhile.

The mid-1890s were not easy years for young parents. The Ruth family's customers were badly hurt by the panic of 1893. Almost 40 percent of union members in Baltimore were out of work, and about half of the city's industrial workers were unemployed. The only response that Kate and big George could make was to lengthen their hours of work at the Union Bar. That left less time for bringing up children.

Altogether the children of George and Kate Ruth numbered eight. George was the eldest. There were four boys: George, John, and twins named Joseph and William. The four girls, Katherine, Annie, Elizabeth, and Mary, included a pair of twins of whom Mary was the survivor. Poor Kate Ruth! She died of tuberculosis when her eldest child was sixteen, and, before her own death, she buried six of her children. In 1900 the mortality rate in Baltimore for children under five years was 73.1 per thousand. Only George and Mamie lived to become adults. (George, by childhood mispronunciation, called Mary "Mamie," and so she is called today.) George was five years older than Mamie, which means that she, the only surviving contemporary, knows nothing of his pre-school years. But we can tell from his proudly posed studio portrait at age three that small George was loved by Kate Ruth. Pains were taken to slick him up so the Washington photographer would see him at his best.

The persistent tradition that these children spoke German before they knew English could be true if Kate Schamberger Ruth had been second-generation German-American and bilingual. But Mamie denies it, and says the only German they spoke as children were the scraps of slang that persist in German-American families for generations, usually as affectionate insults and good-humored put-downs.

Young George Ruth had a bulky criminal record in his first seven years, according to his own testimony. He started the story of his life with the remark "I was a bad kid," and his wife later quoted him as saying, "I was a bum when I was a kid." (Most children younger than seven "know" they are bad kids.) He appears to have spent a lot of time underfoot in the family bar where he learned to chew tobacco and to steal from the till. On the matter of the theft of money he stressed the fact that he stole only from his parents.

The climax of this life of crime came in 1902, when the Ruths were in business on Conway Street. As Ruth later told Johnny Evers (of Tinker to Evers to Chance), he stole a dollar from the cash drawer and bought a round of ice cream cones for the children of the block. For this, Big George took him down to the cellar and thrashed him with a horsewhip. Little George then defiantly stole more out of the till, proving himself too stubborn to bow to that kind of discipline. He soon passed from the custody of his father.

This story has the ring of truth. Evers was a matter-of-fact man. The date is right. Even the horsewhip fits the known facts of Big George's life—the city directory once listed him as a "driver." And there are plenty of well-founded stories of young George making

public splashes with large gestures of generosity similar to the buying of a round of ice cream cones.

But Ruth had a stain on his character worse than petty larceny
within the family. That was the crime of truancy. As sister Mamie
put it, "He did not like school." The threat of involuntary schooling
hung over him as a cloud all through his childhood. The Maryland
movement for compulsory school began in 1871, and in 1898 Big
Labor, Big Education, and Big Charity joined together to urge a
compulsory school law. They got it in 1902. The law required schooling from ages eight to twelve, and for the unemployed from twelve
to sixteen. H. L. Mencken explained that the new law was a try at
ridding Maryland of the "dirt pedagogy that had prevailed since
colonial times" and replacing it with "the new wizardries from
Teachers College, Columbia."

Ruth the Younger wanted neither dirt pedagogy nor wizardries.
He was one of the 25 percent of white children who were not in
school, and he hoped to keep it that way. Economics had been on
his side. It was well known in Baltimore that children were absent
because their parents were too busy making ends meet to find time
to supervise school attendance. This was certainly true of George
the Elder and Kate Ruth. The remedy was now to be coercion by
the state.

But George Junior, aged seven, said "No." He wasn't missing
much—unsanitary schools crowded in classes of from sixty to eighty,
and sometimes a hundred, taught by the lowest-paid teachers of
any Northern or Western city of comparable size, in a plant which
chronically had from 1,500 to 5,500 more pupils than seats. Perhaps
the mythical boy Lincoln would have profited in these conditions.
The real boy Ruth refused to try.

He thought his rebellion meant he was "a bad kid." The fact is
that the "high-absentee child" is likely to be the eldest child in a
low-income family and "a first-grader in an urban school." Such
children have more stresses than most. The description fits little
George exactly. And for stresses, his mother was chronically ill
(probably tubercular this early), and he had that series of illnesses
and deaths of younger brothers and sisters. If young George had
accepted the Baltimore schools with ease he would have been
abnormal. Nonetheless, his behavior met the Maryland description
of "incorrigible" and "vicious" for whom salvation by schooling was
at hand.

In 1882 the Maryland legislature had tried to help solve the
problems of the overworked parents of a truant boy.

AND BE IT ENACTED, That in addition to the classes of
minors, who, by existing laws, may be committed to said

St. Mary's Industrial School for Boys of the City of Baltimore, any justice of the peace of this State may commit to the care of said corporation every such white male minor as, on complaint of any parent, guardian, or next friend in whose custody such minor may be, and on proof taken before such justice, be adjudged by such justice to be a proper subject for commitment to said Institution by reason of the incorrigible or vicious conduct of such minor, and because of such incorrigible or vicious conduct to be beyond the control of such parent, guardian or next friend.

In the spring of 1902 Big George and Kate somehow arranged with St. Mary's Industrial School and with some willing justice of the peace to have Little George labeled "incorrigible or vicious" and "beyond the control" of his parents. Thereupon the magistrate committed him to St. Mary's. According to Mamie, the sole reason for sending her brother to St. Mary's was that "He would not go to school, and they did not have time to look after him as they should. . . ." Apparently they had tried to keep him in school even before the compulsory schooling act of 1902.

Big and Little George appeared hand in hand at St. Mary's on June 13, 1902, to enroll Little George, who wept and asked to go home with his father. The Xaverian Brothers were used to tears in such cases and took him in hand easily. Against his will, young Ruth had found a refuge from the kind of neglect that could have killed him, or worse.

At the risk of running ahead of the story, it is well at this point to explain that George did not live at St. Mary's continuously from 1902 until his last discharge in 1914. In that twelve-year span he spent about seven and a half years at the school. Several times he went home, usually at Christmas or for some family feast. While at home he was expected to attend the nearest public school, but he always flatly defied the School Act of 1902 and invariably went back to St. Mary's in the company of the St. Mary's "Visiting Officer," to the only school he could stand.

According to a cousin, Big George tried to rule his son by force. It did not work. When Young George was at St. Mary's, as long as Kate lived, Mamie and Kate visited him about once a month. He said his father never came. After his mother died, when Mamie was still a little girl, he came home to live for a year. As long as he worked—as he did then in his father's bar—he had reached the age at which he was safe from the school laws. He returned to St. Mary's in 1912 and never went home again. From 1912 until his discharge from the school in 1914 he had no visitors, ever.

for the family, not as something better than the family. They did not jam boys into a fixed curriculum. If brainwork became dull, a boy could switch to using his hands. And, as a graduate said, "Everything we did we had to do well." At St. Mary's Industrial School a boy could get a second chance. If he was like young George Ruth, he could even have a first chance.

The Xaverian Brothers also staffed Mount St. Joseph's College, up the road from St. Mary's Industrial School. Because the college was thought to be posh, some of the Brothers considered an assignment to St. Mary's as an assignment to the second team. Those who accepted a post at St. Mary's with satisfaction would be the best of the lot. And there was plenty to do. The ideal would be a ratio of one Brother for each eight boys, but they never had that many and made up the shortage by working longer hours.

The best remembered of the Brothers of that generation was Brother Matthias, who served as chief of discipline, dormitory prefect, classroom teacher, and assistant to Brother Herman, the athletic director. Brother Matthias was big, strong, firm, gentle. Ruth later thought he could have been anything he wished to be. The boys called him "the Boss." His room was a cubicle six and a half feet square, and he had to rehang its door to open outward because his specially built bed was as long as the room. The Grand Jury of 1919 liked the "great big fellow" who was so zealous for the boys. He did not rule by fear but by commanding respect. For example, he once put down a playground riot, which broke out during his absence, by standing at the highest part of the grounds and silently staring the boys to uneasy quiet.

This was the man who first took charge of the "baffled little bum of seven" when he came to St. Mary's. He attended to George simply because George needed attention. He measured young Ruth's talents and set about to develop them. For twelve years he was patient to perfection. He saw Ruth off into the world each time he left, and welcomed him back each time he was returned because of truancy from the Maryland school system. He tutored George in reading and writing (teaching the Xaverian style of handwriting, well shown in Ruth's handsome autograph), put him on the baseball teams that suited his successive stages of growth, got him started at learning the needle trades, and tried to explain the difference between right and wrong. Ruth believed Brother Matthias preserved him from the penitentiary, and later said flatly, "Brother Matthias was the greatest man I ever knew." Young Ruth very early showed a startling natural talent with a baseball bat, so Brother Matthias began to round him out by teaching him pitching and fielding.

Thus began a lifelong relationship of substitute-father and son. At any age thereafter, if Brother M. began a sentence with the words, "Now, George . . . ," Ruth knew he had lost whatever argument he hoped to win.

The Xaverians intended to take George Ruth and make him into a literate journeyman of a skilled trade. They taught him to read, to write, and to do arithmetic, and threw in some elementary grammar and a catechism of geography as well. The Brothers wanted him to get along well after leaving school, not merely to adjust to serving his time with them. To be a free man he had to have a salable skill, hence they taught him a trade.

The St. Mary's schedule was intended to keep the boys working at healthy tasks as busily as common sense permitted, whether academic, vocational, or athletic. George's schedule had something for him almost every waking minute. Up at six to wash and dress for Mass and breakfast. (The Brothers were up at five.) Classes— academic or vocational—from breakfast until ten in the morning. Recess from ten to ten-thirty. School or work from ten-thirty to eleven-thirty. Dinner and free time from eleven-thirty to one-thirty. School again until three-fifteen, after which there was a class in Christian doctrine, required of Catholics only. From then until supper at six the boys played, the small boys in the Little Yard, and the boys of fifteen or older in the Big Yard.

Academically, Ruth received a good elementary education.* Every day he had five hours of academic study and four hours in the shops. The school had two libraries, scaled to the ages of the boys, and encouraged the boys to read in bed from 7:30 until lights-out at 8:15. (Bedtime was postponed on evenings when dramatic or musical events were on the schedule.) Outdoor play at recess, in all weather except actual rainfall, was the rule. This might seem harsh, but after 1890 the school had a very good health record.

Trades were taught so well that the boys could compete in the world when discharged. Each boy chose his own. When Ruth was there the trades were printer, brushmaker, shoemaker, electrician, farmer, baker, bookbinder, carpenter, millwright, florist, launderer, knitter, and shirtmaker. The boys received token wages credited to their accounts in the school savings bank, which gave them drawing rights in the candy store.

George Ruth went to work in the tailor shop, learning to make shirts with about ninety other boys. He worked in a four-story stone building. Its first floor was the laundry. Its second floor was called Low City Tailor, and the third was Ruth's shirt shop, called High City Tailor. The boys worked by the piece, and the reward for

---

* The Brothers began a high-school course in 1922 which graduated its first class in 1929, but Ruth figured that having spent most of twelve years there made him a high-school graduate, or the equivalent.

dexterity was extra play time in the Little Yard or the Big Yard, according to age. Low City Tailor had a knitting mill with two thousand needles, which knitted all the stockings and underwear of the school. High City Tailor made all the shirts for a thousand or more boys.

The boys also did the housekeeping in the kitchen, dormitories, baths, dining rooms, power plant, and laundry. Some were porters; others were orderlies in the infirmary (a rather light duty, consider- ing the robust health of the place). Whether in shop or residence they served in organized gangs under capable teachers, some of whom were Xaverians and others laymen.

George Ruth learned how to make shirts. He claimed he could sew a shirt in less than a quarter of an hour. If he had stayed with his trade he could have made as much as twenty dollars a week in his prime.

The St. Mary's system did not neglect the arts, and of the arts music came first. It had practical value as well, because it kept the players out of mischief and was the perfect indoor amusement for foul weather. The band, dressed in uniforms from High City Tailor, usually played two concerts a week for the students. There was also a sixty-voice chorus, an orchestra, and a minor band for the smallest boys. The senior band often appeared in civic parades and other public rites, as, for example, the St. Patrick's Day parade of 1913, in which the band, with worldly presence of mind, struck up "Mary- land, My Maryland" opposite the offices of the *Sun*, which caught the notice of the photographers and got the band's picture in the paper.

It will be forever a question whether George Ruth profited directly from the music program. He certainly could sing in a melodious baritone, he *may* have mastered the harmonica, and he has been described as a snare drummer, a bass drummer, and a tuba player, but these assertions are wholly lacking in proof.

After music came the drama, and several ambitious dramatic clubs were active all the while George was in school. There was also swimming, and George either learned to swim at St. Mary's or improved on a skill he had learned near the Baltimore municipal piers. The recreation rooms had all the kinds of table games one would expect, including cards. Ruth's name has been associated with cards as a player more eager than wise. He excelled only at pinochle; from what we know of its social makeup, St. Mary's would be a good pinochle academy.

But music, dramatics, swimming, and cards faded in the fierce bright light of the highest-ranking recreation of all—baseball. Brother Herman was demigod of baseball, and Brother Matthias was his prophet. Herman and Matthias saw to it that this moon-faced little boy, who could hit like a magician, had a chance to play everywhere, and whenever time permitted.

Did St. Mary's do its job? The statistics say yes. The motivation was religious, but indirectly so. In George Ruth's day chapel was compulsory for thirty minutes a day, and a class in doctrine was required study for Catholic boys—again thirty minutes. For the other twenty-three hours the spiritual development of the boys was shaped by the example of grown men who were professionally religious and therefore in dead earnest. From a Catholic's point of view it worked, as shown by the figures on voluntary participation in public worship beyond the minimum of silent attendance. What of the state's interest? Some figures make it clear. In 1899 three of the 851 boys deserted; in 1905 there was not one desertion. In every year when George Ruth was a pupil there were a thousand to fifteen hundred boys who had been discharged under supervision and might be called "on parole." From 1902 through 1909, the years of complete figures during Ruth's stay, the grand total of "parole violators" was 252. More precisely, in 1904 there were 1,314 discharged under supervision, of whom only nine had to be returned to the school (the Visiting Officer did not blame *them* but their home conditions).

Altogether about nineteen thousand boys made a go of it after leaving St. Mary's, and fewer than a thousand failed to profit.

George Ruth enjoyed a postponed childhood at St. Mary's. The first seven years of neglect were survival years. We don't know what they may have done to the child deep down. The twelve years at St. Mary's brought out the kinds of traits we can see and describe.

He was one of the few who passed through St. Mary's who was proud of it. Most alumni despised and concealed their link with the place where Baltimore's bad boys went. George Ruth got on so well with his fellows and so enjoyed himself that he praised the school. He was always large for his age and he had a quick temper, but he was generally of a sunny disposition. With his size (and his father's violence) he had the makings of a bully, but there is nothing of that in his story; he seems to have preferred to be loved rather than feared. On visiting days he joked about his appearance, saying, "I am too big and ugly for anyone to come to see me." George was so much larger than the boys of his age that people passing out gifts at school parties tended to skip him, thinking him some kind of orderly or attendant instead of a pupil. On one such occasion someone made amends by giving him a very large box of candy for himself. It was common for these pauper boys to squirrel their gifts away for private pleasure, but George opened the box and "passed it around for everybody." A suspicious mind could ask, Was he buying something? And had his 1902 round of ice cream cones been the purchase of love his parents had no time for? But that kind of probe may be too hair-splitting. After all, he was a practicing Christian. How much of an average Catholic boy he was, for his time, he showed when like every other male Catholic adolescent he thought of becoming a priest. He took the question to Brother Matthias, who knew him pretty well by that time, and George quickly found himself back in the Little Yard working on the problem of how to play shortstop although left-handed.

The relationship with Brother Matthias was rooted firm. A friend once told Ruth that Matthias took him up only because Matthias was a frustrated ballplayer who could live a baseball life through Ruth. Ruth's angry reply was that the Brother liked him before he ever saw him near a baseball. George also was a fast friend of Brother Herman. The boy first received Communion in the old chapel of the school, and there, shortly after, he was confirmed. At confirmation he took the name "Herman" which, by nice coincidence, was also the middle name of his father. (His sister scoffs at the idea that George disliked his father.)

By age fifteen, an age when any employed Marylander was safe from the school board, George was a technically qualified shirtmaker. He got a job in Baltimore and the Brothers put him in their downtown hostel called St. James House, where boys went to live when they first left St. Mary's. George's departure surprised the small boys who could not believe that a right-thinking Xaverian would waste such a ballplayer in a shirt factory. George lasted two months in the sinful world. Accompanied by unprovable rumors of violations of St. James's discipline because of bad company, he returned to St. Mary's. The Brothers moved him to No. 1 Dormitory, which was also a transfer to the Big Yard. On his first day in the Big Yard three or four hundred boys cheered the recovery of their best ballplayer. He was not happy about his homecoming, but, well, they played much better baseball in the Big Yard than in the Little Yard.

He knew his trade as shirtmaker. High City Tailor made cheap workshirts of blue and gray cotton which brought a top price of about a dollar. Ruth was the best in the shop and proud of his ability to attach the collar properly, which was the most demanding part of the work. In view of later psychological findings about his coordination, the placing of George Ruth in the needle trades was a good stroke. If he had had the self-discipline to govern himself he could have been a self-supporting independent journeyman by the time he was sixteen. But he was still emotionally dependent on moral overseers. At this stage it was a real question whether he could ever be anything but a moral dependent.

During adolescence every young person begins to plan his or her life, and decides on an occupation, as George Ruth chose "shirt-maker." In many cases this first decision is changed because the young person learns of something else he or she can do better, or can get more by doing. In this matter George Ruth behaved normally. His "rotten start" had really been fairly common. His wickedness of truancy had been a normal reaction to the kind of life he lived at six. Now he was to change his occupational decision for the usual reason: he found something else he could do better.

3 · Oriole Magnate Signs New Bird

Ball players are born. If they are cut out for baseball, if
they have the desire and ambition, they will make it.
That's all there is to it.

—Walter Johnson

At St. Mary's Industrial School young George Ruth found himself
in a conservatory of the baseball arts. The Xaverian Brothers had
been boys themselves during the age when baseball drew far more
cash customers than any ·other sport and had no serious rival. The
Brothers were biased in favor of baseball. Any game which combined so much popularity and fun must be good for people.

St. Mary's had first won the city's school championship in 1897.
By 1909, when George Ruth was fourteen, it would have been foolish to bet against a St. Mary's baseball team. At peak strength the
school put forty-four uniformed teams in the field, all dressed by
High City Tailor. The umpires were elected officials of the student
body, paid by passing the hat at games. The administration of
St. Mary's was realistically shaped: the athletic director, Brother
Herman, ranked just behind Brother Paul, the superintendent, and
on a par with the prefect of studies and the head of the teachers of
trades.

After study, work, and prayer, sports and games were the life of
the place. The Brothers divided the boys into six sections, by age,
and each section was subdivided into three, for ease of management.
Each of these subsections had its own playing field, sleeping quarters, chapel pews, and athletic teams in inter-group play. For the
sake of interesting variations, there were baseball tournaments going
on from March through September—dormitory tournaments, section tournaments, and tournaments of teams representing trades.
The smallest boys' team was the Brownies, a highly popular group
in Baltimore and vicinity. Winners among these subsection teams

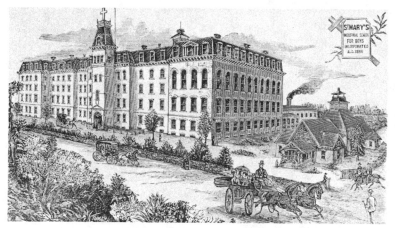

St. Mary's Industrial School, Baltimore, as it was when George Ruth entered in 1902. (*Xaverian Brothers, Kensington, Maryland.*)

Brother Matthias Boutier, C.F.X., George Ruth's best friend, of the faculty of St. Mary's Industrial School, Baltimore. (*Xaverian Brothers, Kensington, Maryland.*)

The faculty of St. Mary's Industrial School, Baltimore, about 1907 or 1908. Brother Matthias is the tall one, back row, center. (*Xaverian Brothers, Kensington, Maryland.*)

Where George Ruth learned to make finished work shirts from uncut cloth, in something less than fifteen minutes each. (*Xaverian Brothers, Kensington, Maryland.*)

Where George Ruth received his first Communion and was Confirmed. From 1910 until it burned in 1919 the old chapel served as the St. Mary's Industrial School auditorium. (*Xaverian Brothers, Kensington, Maryland.*)

The common room for older students of St. Mary's Industrial School, before 1914. (*Xaverian Brothers, Kensington, Maryland.*)

Brother Matthias presides over a class of older boys, 1912. If George Ruth is present, he is the boy in the left front row who is closest to Brother Matthias. (*Xaverian Brothers, Kensington, Maryland.*)

George Ruth slept and bathed here. Dormitory and shower room, St. Mary's Industrial School, Baltimore. (*Xaverian Brothers, Kensington, Maryland.*)

The old dining hall, St. Mary's Industrial School. (*Xaverian Brothers, Kensington, Maryland.*)

A typical elementary classroom at St. Mary's at about the time George Ruth entered. (*Xaverian Brothers, Kensington, Maryland.*)

George Ruth once thought (briefly) of becoming a priest. Here is a visual aid to believing that fantasy. (*Edward Fischer.*)

qualified for the intramural leagues. In intramural league play Ruth starred with the Red Sox, managed by Brother Matthias. St. Mary's had six other team sports in addition to baseball, and tag games for the small fry.

It is easy to justify this large sports program. It soaked up a lot of energy that could have been destructive; it was physically healthy, as proved by the infirmary figures, and for the winners, at least, it was psychologically healthy. It has been said that young people are much more likely to excel in sports than in anything else, and it is certainly true that there are thousands of great young athletes for every great young statesman. A sports schedule for all of the boys of St. Mary's could easily be approved on the principle that the program was humane, disciplined, and had a social function in the development of personality. But people in charge of such programs often dilute a theory of what's healthy by dragging in the nonsense that it is also morally virtuous. When Brother Paul was superintendent he unnecessarily said "play activities [are] an eighth sacrament without which it would be practically impossible to have a sound mind." A school set up on such a principle provided a perfect natural habitat for the young animal Ruth. And we will be kinder to Brother Paul if we know that he had been a satisfied college professor who received his appointment to be superintendent of St. Mary's with something like stage fright. But he began to like the place in his first week of service.

St. Mary's had a long playing season, sufficient team play, respect for skill, laurels for success, and good playing fields. Where these things have abounded in America ballplayers have appeared. There was only one *famous* player from this particular baseball hothouse. The school may have produced many other good players, but none is famous for his link with the school. St. Mary's had no alumni association and kept quiet about its Old Boys so as not to endanger their worldly success. Any ballplayer known to have come from St. Mary's must advertise the connection himself. Ruth always made much of it.

Within a few years after he came to the school George was on teams with boys three or four years older than he. By the time he was sixteen he was the best ballplayer of all. He finished the formal academic curriculum at fourteen. After that he kept on at his shirt-making trade, partly for the income. All possible playing hours went to baseball, weather permitting. And it took a lot of weather to stop baseball. On one Christmas morning he scraped the snow from the base paths and recruited seventeen other boys for a game.

For practice there were several routines. Brother Matthias would bunt to him by the hour in a corner of the Little Yard. There was also a game the boys called "Pokenins," which could be played by

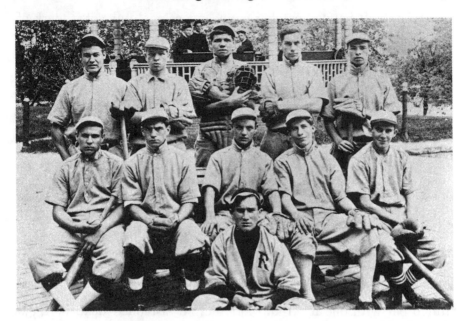

The St. Mary's Industrial School Red Sox, champions of the school, 1913, with their left-handed catcher, who also pitched well enough to strike out twenty-two in a game that season. (*Xaverian Brothers, Kensington, Maryland.*)

two boys, one pitching, one batting. The batter stood in front of a wall while the pitcher stood at pitching distance and pitched until he struck out the batter. Then pitcher and batter changed places and the game resumed. Ruth played the game often. If the players had talent, the game would produce pitchers who batted well. Obviously, Ruth was not falling into baseball by chance. He was getting into baseball in the way Vienna choir boys get into professional music, by well-paced, purposeful development.

Ruth was a "natural." Naturals become great without teaching, but not without practice. Muscular skills can be learned without conscious control (as all of us learned to say "Mama"), but there *is* learning. When certain skills work, there is a reward; when the skill fails, no reward. (The reward can be as slight as a warm glow of private satisfaction.)

The hard-practicing left-handed prospect began his defensive career as a catcher. He would catch the ball in the glove on his left hand, toss the ball straight up, drop the mitt on the ground, catch the ball again with his bare left hand and throw. George Ruth liked catching, mostly because he liked to be in the middle of that heavy traffic and rough play around home plate, where most of the game happens.

To be a left-handed catcher is unconventional but not a mark of folly. The only handicap of a left-handed catcher is that right-handed batters are in his way when he throws down to second or third. But a left-handed catcher is better for catching a right-handed pitcher than a right-handed catcher is, because he can more easily reach for the curves that break outside. In short, nothing in baseball itself bars left-handed catchers. As Al Lopez* once said, though, if a left-hander can throw well enough to be a catcher, they'll make him into a pitcher, which is precisely what happened to young Ruth. When he was sixteen and a well-established catcher on one of the teams of a four-team intramural league, his battery mate had disciplinary problems and was scratched from the roster. Ruth moved into the pitching job and pitched a two-hitter, winning 2–0. From then on he pitched often and well, though he often caught.

His admirable hitting did not suffer. From the moment we first hear of him he could hit. At St. Mary's he learned to hit the ball far. He said he copied Brother Matthias, who could swing a slender fungo bat with one hand and loft the old-fashioned dead ball 350 feet. Here was still another virtue to emulate, like receiving the sacraments or running the bases with mincing pigeon-toed steps, both of which were habits of Brother Matthias. Brother Matthias was such a powerful hitter that when he played ball with the boys he batted with but one hand, because he had once hurt a child fielder when he swung the bat with both hands. George Ruth used *both* hands and, with a fungo-type uppercut swing, he began to get distance.

As he neared manhood, George Ruth had found something he could do surpassingly well. It was pleasant to be No. 1 of more than a thousand boys, in one of the most admired of pursuits.

At the age of seven George Ruth had come to school from hard times. In twelve years his temperament was fixed. His life at St. Mary's was rather infantile, tightly governed by elders' rules, and at eighteen his responsibility for his own behavior was that of a free boy of eight who had not learned much about making prudent moral decisions in new circumstances.

During his last full year at St. Mary's Ruth was six feet, two inches tall and weighed 150 pounds. His body was built squarely with large bones and muscles. His eyes and hair were brown, and his skin tanned well. His friendly grin was of the kind that turns down at the corners of the mouth. During his mid-teens he was a homely boy. His laughter rumbled from deep inside. He had great energy, craved exercise, had blunt manners, guts, and a loud mouth. He

---

* Among other distinctions, Lopez, nineteen seasons, 1928–1947, holds the record for most games as a catcher.

George Ruth, aged 16, a left-handed shortstop of considerable promise. (*National Baseball Library, Cooperstown, New York.*)

was never broody. According to him, he was a physically hardy young man.

It takes some knowledge of the world for a youngster to model himself on a social stereotype. Christy Mathewson could act out the part of the ethical hero bucking for Eagle Scout. Herb Pennock could climb a horse and chase foxes all over southeastern Pennsylvania as though Queen Victoria were his aunt. But George Ruth's only models were Baltimore's waterfront slobs, at worst, and the Xaverian Brothers, at best. Would his life be a seesaw between those two roles?

George worked full time as a shirtmaker after he was fifteen and often worked overtime at High City Tailor to build his savings. His was an overflowing nature with a taste for rumpus that always revived in moments of high good cheer. He rarely returned to his dormitory with a whole shirt. His tears came almost as easily as his laughter, but he did not suffer from anxiety. He was "aggressive" in the sense that he liked to press advantages and make things happen, which is a fine way to win ball games.

Ruth's life at St. Mary's has left us a bouquet of uplifting memories, some of which may be true:

—he never used profanity unless no other word would fit;

—he never dodged a punishment by lying;

—he allowed no bullying of small boys when he was around;

—he used his overtime earnings to buy materials to make baseballs for the smallest boys;

—he once took the blame for breaking a window because the culprit was only eight years old and frightened;

—when he accumulated six or seven dollars in his account he used to spend it all on candy to give away;

—he received Communion two or three times a week, and many of the younger boys consciously followed his example.

That Ruth should have become a serious athlete was almost inevitable. Young men like to ally themselves in groups whose successes they can call their own. The St. Mary's sports program made that easy. In taking up baseball George learned more about his fellow citizens than he would have learned in nearly any other occupation. Ruth was never to feel ill at ease in any part of America or at any social level, as he might if he had been a boy wizard at, say, chess or music. He had taken up the only line for a gifted boy which prevented him from losing touch with his countrymen. Jacques Barzun's remarks on baseball and culture are often quoted without the qualifiers. The words about amateur baseball are a necessary part of the truism: "Whoever wants to know the heart and mind of America had better learn baseball, the rules and realities of the game—and do it by watching first some high school or small-town teams."

For a schoolboy, Ruth had a spectacular year in 1913. This very good ballplayer would have interested any major league scout, not so much with his obvious speed, throwing arm, and hitting, but for the less obvious absence of grave faults such as a bad stance, or an inability to hit a fast ball letter-high, or a genuine eagerness to get out of the way of a pitch high and tight. And the scout would have been interested to see him throw a fast ball, which is a natural talent that cannot be taught.

These virtues young Ruth was born with. All he needed to learn was the book of baseball rules. Systematic teaching might have hurt him, because he would have learned what people believed couldn't be done. Brother Herman and Brother Matthias gave him every chance to develop his inborn skills, but could they have taught him to hit a ball 425 feet (as alleged by a witness) at the age of seventeen? Or to pick men off first base when he had to wear a glove on his throwing hand? St. Mary's ballplayers had a stock joke: catcher Ruth would pick you off first unless you kept both feet on the bag.

Ruth didn't get much publicity in 1913, because the *Baltimore Sun* did not report St. Mary's Industrial School games. The *Sun* was very keen on amateur baseball, so we may suppose the Brothers kept their charges' names out of public box scores. Instead of telling about Ruth, the *Sun* played up Bill Morrisette,* a right-handed spitball pitcher at Mount St. Joseph's College. Morrisette made news, all right. In the spring of 1913 he pitched a no-hitter against Georgetown, a one-hitter against Holy Cross, and in a game against Seton Hall played on one of the St. Mary's diamonds, he struck out fifteen. Among his other triumphs were a five-hitter against Washington College and a three-hitter against Bucknell. But Ruth had a better year.

Superintendent Brother Paul, in his Annual Report for 1913 was moved to say, "One boy created a sensation by his excellent work." The word "sensation" was well chosen. In 1913 Ruth pitched and caught. As a pitcher he did not lose a game. He batted .537. His peak in intramural play came in the third week of September when, as a student paper reported, "Ruth, one of the 'Stars' star slabmen, allowed but one hit, that being a two base hit. . . . He also struck out twenty-two and issued but one pass." Ruth himself hit safely four times.

The game was the happy end of a season which had two weeks of alarm for Ruth. For Commencement Day at Mount St. Joseph's College, Ruth and St. Mary's were booked to play against Morrisette who would pitch for a pick-up team of graduating seniors. But Morrisette's catcher would be an undergraduate, Joe Morgan, who deserves a memorial as the true discoverer of Ruth. Ten days after the announcement of the game Ruth ran away from school. His close friend Fats Leisman thought the strain of waiting for the duel with Morrisette was too much to bear. Two days later he returned of his own accord. His punishment was to stand during play hours for five days on the road that divided the Little Yard from the Big Yard. After that the slate was clean, and his elders put him to work getting into shape for the big game.

Ruth need not have worried about the game. Unfortunately we

* Bill Morrisette (1893–1966), two trials with the Phillies and one with the Tigers, 1915–1920, was 3–1 in 51 innings pitched, with an earned-run average of 3.35.

St. Mary's Industrial School as it was in 1914 when George Ruth left. (*Xaverian Brothers, Kensington, Maryland.*)

do not have an exact score. What people remembered was that Ruth struck out fourteen and shut out the College. Off Morrisette the Industrial School scored either six or eight runs; it hardly matters which.

Eighteen-year-old George Herman Ruth, Jr., was the best amateur pitcher in that part of the world. Perhaps in the whole world.

In Baltimore there lived a man who had a business of developing promising young ball players. Jack Dunn,* chief owner of the Baltimore Orioles since 1910, had been a big-league fielder and pitcher. As a manager he had won pennants at Providence and Baltimore of the International League (earlier called the Eastern League). He is still remembered as a scout. Among his finds (all profitable to him) were Lefty Grove, George Earnshaw, Max Bishop, Ernie Shore, Joe Boley, Jack Bentley, and, of course, George Ruth. The eagle-beaked Dunn had judgment, tact, and audacity.

Dunn heard of Ruth as a matter of course. It was his purpose in life to listen to news of such promising youths. He seems to have had the word from Joe Engel, a Mount St. Joseph's alumnus who pitched for the Washington Senators, *and* from assorted Baltimore bartenders, *and* from George Herman Ruth, Sr., *and*, most persuasively,

* John Joseph Dunn (1872–1928), eight seasons, 1897–1904, infielder, outfielder, pitcher, Dodgers, Phillies, Baltimore (American League), Giants. Batting average .245. Won 64, lost 59, earned-run average 4.11.

from Brother Gilbert, the athletic director at Mount St. Joseph's who often found useful rookies for Dunn.

For reasons we cannot know, Brother Gilbert missed the commencement match between Ruth and Morrisette, and, in fact, doesn't even seem to have heard of it. Perhaps the participants scattered after the award of diplomas. But Brother Gilbert's catcher, the Joe Morgan mentioned earlier, urged Gilbert to go to St. Mary's in September to see Ruth play. Gilbert had heard many reports of amateurs who were overpraised, but he let himself be talked into it, probably on the principle that any excuse to see a ball game will do. He went with Morgan and his infielder Lewis Malone.* They sat in the bandstand near first base of the Big Yard, from where Gilbert could see a young fellow working out as catcher, "a tall, powerful, well-knit, dark-skinned carefree boy of 18 years, without a tight muscle in his body. . . ." But he was an oddity, as Brother Gilbert put it, "a fork hander," or left-handed catcher. Morgan said Ruth was not necessarily a catcher. "Never mind his catching —watch his hitting."

When Ruth's side came to bat, the leadoff man was safe on an infield single, and the next two batsmen struck out while the runner stole second and third. Then Ruth came to the plate, as Gilbert said, "one of the most graceful of big men that I have ever seen. There was ease in his manner and confidence in his gait." The opposing pitcher waved his outfield back. They were already retreating, and the right-fielder left the Big Yard, moved over to second base in the middle of a game being played in the Little Yard, and took his position about 280 feet from Ruth, a long way in the days of the dead ball. All of the younger boys stopped playing. The arrival of a right-fielder in the infield of the Little Yard always meant that Ruth was batting, and they watched to see what would happen.

The first pitch was a low curve inside. "With an easy grace" Ruth hit the old dead ball over the right-fielder's head and bounced it off the fence at the farthest point of the Little Yard. The fielder misplayed the carom or he might have held Ruth to a triple instead of the inside-the-park home run he scored. In his next two times at bat Ruth again hit home runs. In his fourth and last time up he struck out.

Brother Gilbert was ready to become a believer. Not only had he seen memorable hitting, but Ruth had sprinted for four bases like a deer, and had thrown to all bases as if he were firing rifle shots. His throws to the bases convinced Gilbert that he was a natural pitcher, and the Mount St. Joseph visitors went home knowing they

* Lewis Malone (1897–1973), four seasons, 1915–1919, Athletics and Dodgers, mostly at second and third base. Batting average in 133 games, .202.

had seen a great athlete. Because Gilbert wished to protect the scouting reputation he enjoyed among professional baseball people, he took the precaution of watching Ruth a second time. He took along his team captain and left-fielder, Porter M. Wamsley. Ruth hit two home runs. Wamsley thought the play of Ruth against the others was a comic mismatch. Gilbert, his own judgment confirming that of young Morgan, and supported by Malone and Wamsley, knew he had found something of value. He was haunted by the beauty of Ruth's throw to second which had no apparent arch, and which required no change of Ruth's posture.

During the rest of 1913 Brother Gilbert often had business with the St. Mary's printing shop. Whenever he came he asked for Ruth. Brother Alban, the master printer, went out of his way to praise Ruth and urged Gilbert to get Ruth a professional tryout. Gilbert once asked Ruth if he would like to play professional baseball. Ruth, overcome to the point of being almost speechless (a rare thing), said he would indeed like it. Would sixty dollars a month be enough? Yes, sir. Next Gilbert approached Brother Paul, the superintendent, who was completely receptive. Paul must have been wondering how he could dispose of Ruth in a Christian manner within the next couple of years. As he said, "George is a boy for whom I would like to do something." Considering what George was, it is hard to think what Paul could do better for him than start him on his way in organized baseball.

It is worth recording that both Gilbert and Paul were very high on George Ruth as a person in 1913. Paul said he was modest and sincere. Gilbert (writing fifteen years later) said he had known Ruth as "free from guile and deceit of any kind. He had implicit faith in the whole world: and he looked out on that world with the grave and solemn wonder of a child." Gilbert went on to quote Francis Thompson, "I hope one day to be sought for in the nurseries of heaven." The implication was that those nurseries were George Ruth's true home. These are strong moral recommendations from men who had high standards and who knew him well. It is clear that when he was around them Ruth put aside the waterfront scamp and put on the Xaverian Brother.

A chance for Brothers Gilbert and Paul to do something for George came indirectly from scouting pressure at Mount St. Joseph's. In the winter of 1913–1914 Jack Dunn signed Bill Morrisette but persuaded Brother Gilbert to promise him another player. Gilbert had a left-handed pitcher named Ford Bernard Meadows who had been looked over by the Giants, Yankees, Braves, Athletics, Senators, and Dodgers. Dunn wanted him, but Meadows didn't want to sign with anybody (nor did he). Brother Gilbert decided to do Dunn a favor and steer him to Ruth.

Jack Dunn and Fritz Maisel,* a Marylander who played with the Yankees and who came along for company, called at Mount St. Joseph's on February 14, 1914. Knowing Meadows would not sign, Brother Gilbert proposed to put Dunn onto the greatest left-handed pitching prospect in the world. Gilbert hadn't seen Ruth pitch, but he gambled that the left-handed catcher's throws in the infield foretold good pitching. Gilbert, Dunn, and Maisel drove over to St. Mary's and asked for Brother Matthias (who appeared in overalls). Gilbert wanted Dunn to meet Matthias because Matthias had managed the team on which Gilbert had seen Ruth play. When Gilbert told Matthias why they had come, Matthias said, succinctly, "Ruth can hit." But Dunn was after pitching. "Can he pitch?" "Sure he can do anything." (A sober statement of baseball fact.) Dunn and Gilbert now set out for Brother Paul's office, wading through a growing crowd of man-children attracted by news of professional ballplayers visiting in the yard.

When the news of visitors reached High City Tailor, Ruth came running to join the crowd. He was wearing faded blue overalls and was careful to slide on every patch of ice he came to. Gilbert nudged Dunn and said, "There's our victim." Dunn gasped at Ruth's size and muttered to Maisel, "Fritz, there is a Rube Waddell in the rough." (A Rube Waddell in the rough would have to be something pretty rough.) He saw an oddly shaped, gangling, full-grown man of nineteen, with obvious great strength in the swelling muscles of his chest and shoulders. Gilbert introduced Ruth to Dunn and told Ruth that Dunn had come to sign him for the Orioles. In later years Ruth said he was as surprised as if he had been invited to join the United States Senate. And one of the boys remarked, "There goes our ball club."

Dunn asked Ruth to throw some pitches. The two worked out in the Big Yard for perhaps half an hour, with Dunn, as Ruth said, "talking to me all the time, and telling me not to strain and not to try too hard." Then Paul, Gilbert, and Dunn talked for half an hour in Paul's office, while Ruth waited with a huddle of well-wishers. The elders sent for Ruth and told him of the legal guardianship question. Brother Paul was Ruth's legal guardian, by court order, until age twenty-one, but the Brothers had a routine for delegating the authority to employers so that Dunn could become guardian in fact. Dunn and Brother Gilbert arrived at a salary figure of six hundred dollars for the season of 1914 (forty dollars a month more than Gilbert's private minimum figure). It has been said, though it is hard to believe, that George was surprised to learn he would be paid money to play baseball.

* Frederick Maisel (1889–1967), infielder, five seasons with Yankees, one with Browns, 1913–1922, 591 games, batting average .242.

The very first news of Ruth as a professional baseball player appeared in the *Baltimore Sun* on February 15, 1914:

> The Oriole magnate signed another local player yesterday. The new Bird is George H. Ruth, a pitcher, who played with teams out the Frederick road. Ruth is six feet tall and fanned 22 men in an amateur game last season. He is regarded as a very hard hitter, so Dunn will try him out down South.

Use of the phrase "out the Frederick road" could have been a polite way to avoid saying that the new Bird came from the bad boys' school.

Immediately below Ruth's first press notice the *Sun*, coincidentally, carried a story of a development which was to have a great deal to do with Ruth's future. Its headline was IT'S UP TO BALTIMORE TO SUPPORT FEDERALS. Baltimore's support of the Federal League was to change Ruth's life.

For the present, George H. Ruth, pitcher, had started up the professional baseball ladder from near the top. The International League was accepted as ranking in merit immediately after the major leagues. Ruth was in a showcase where he would be seen by many shrewd baseball men. From old-time players' stories of how *they* broke into the big leagues we can believe it was not how you played the game but who happened to be in the park on the day you played. There were no obscure corners in this league.

Ruth was off to a good start in the only "work" he ever loved. A simple record at the school memorialized his leaving in the pupil books:

> George Herman Ruth, discharged Feb. 27, 1914—
> To join the Balt. baseball club.

It was farewell to shirtmaking. "He would have been a very good tailor, too," sighed Brother Clarence, "if Jack Dunn hadn't stepped in."

Outside the Park, 1914

BLIZZARD HEADED EAST

URGES FISH HOSPITAL

WILL TRY TO FLY ACROSS ATLANTIC

WILL DEBATE ON VOTES FOR WOMEN

TEACHER BEATEN WITH ROCK

NEW RULES FOR AUTOISTS

CARRANZA WILL
NOT EXPLAIN TO U.S.

HALF-BREEDS TROUBLE-MAKERS

4 AMERICANS DIE, 20 HURT
IN CAPTURE OF VERA CRUZ

"LOOK OUT! GREASERS SHOOT IN
THE BACK," WARNS OLD VETERAN

SHERIFF HALTS COXEY'S ARMY

ANTI-SALOON LEAGUE ELECTS

CROWD PURSUES NEGROES

TO GET NURSES READY FOR WAR

ALBANIAN THRONE SHAKY

SIX IN AUTO KILLED

ARMY NEEDS AVIATORS

PUDDING HASTENS HER DEATH

SHE TANGOES IN TROUSERS

ECZEMA PEELED OFF
IN GREAT FLAKES

4 · The Most Promising Youngster

The phenom will develop into a star.
—Jack Dunn, 1914

Despite a March blizzard which disrupted travel on the eastern sea-board, Oriole pitchers, catchers, and coaches left for spring training at Fayetteville, North Carolina, from Baltimore's Union Station at 8:00 P.M. on March 2, 1914. Jack Dunn stayed behind to bring the rest of the team a week later. The trip was a wholly new experience for George H. Ruth, Jr. He had never been on a train. Dunn added spice by giving him five dollars for pocket money, more than he had ever had at one time. George felt princely. How his world had broadened in just sixteen days after meeting Jack Dunn!

Catcher Ben Egan took charge of the recruits. Some he sent to their Pullman berths early so they would be well rested in case of emergency. Some were told to guard the shoes, which, Egan said, the Pullman porter would surely try to steal. Others were to call out the hours all night so that the Orioles would not ride past Fayette-ville by mistake. This kind of hazing was literally child's play to Ruth, and easy to take.

When the advance party reached Fayetteville, George was some-what surprised to find it much warmer than Baltimore. He also saw the immediate advantage of living in the Lafayette Hotel, where the Orioles paid the board bill. At breakfast he ate three orders of ham and wheatcakes. He might have tried four except he noticed his teammates silently watching him with the kind of wonder shown by visitors to the Grand Canyon. He rather enjoyed their attention, and he liked them as people.

Ruth had never seen an elevator until he checked into the Lafayette. The machine charmed him. He learned to operate it and came close to killing himself when he started it up while holding his head out of the door. Several Orioles saw him and shouted a warning in time. Off the field this big-city youth behaved like a legendary baseball rube. In Fayetteville he would go down in the morning to see the five o'clock train safely through town. Then it was time to go back to the hotel to be first in the dining room when it opened for breakfast. He also managed to get Baltimore press coverage as a basketball player. The Orioles played Fayetteville High. Three Orioles, including Ruth, had played the game before "and made some fine passes." The Orioles crushed the high school 8–6.

Now the sports pages were beginning to picture his face. He looked every day of nineteen, had hollow cheeks, and parted his hair in the middle. We know from other sources that he weighed 165 pounds. His uniform, probably left over from 1913, hung on him like old bags.

His movements while pitching and fielding lacked polish, but Ben Egan was working with him carefully. Ruth needed little formal teaching, but he needed plenty of controlled practice. One identifying trait caught everyone's eye: George had a theory that long strides slowed a runner. He ran in short, quick, flashing steps that made his socks blur like the spokes on a wagon wheel, whether he was running for a fly or stealing second. He would never change the style, which owed much to Brother Matthias, and yet he was properly rated a fast man.

Ruth got a nickname at Fayetteville. While veterans were baiting the rookies, Coach Sam Steinman warned them to go easy with Ruth. "He's one of Jack Dunn's babes." Roger Pippen, who covered the Oriole camp for a Baltimore paper, asked Steinman to explain. Steinman said Dunn had many very young players in camp but "Ruth is the biggest and most promising babe in the lot." Some of the players also had the mistaken idea that St. Mary's was a foundling home, so that anyone from there could be "Babe." The name stuck.

Babe Ruth.

Babe thought it was meant to be funny at first. If so, it soon lost its edge and became a useful proper noun.

After Dunn brought the squad to strength, the Orioles settled down to training-camp routine. The Lafayette Hotel was about a mile from the baseball field at Cape Fear Fairgrounds where the team worked out. The men walked to and from the grounds or rode in wagons. At first they ran the distance, but when they began to play in game conditions they saved their energies for the field. Fayetteville had unusually poor weather that spring—on one day, snow, rain, and hail in quick succession. Foul weather once kept the team loafing for three days, and the nearby fields were too muddy for cross-country hiking. In this season of boredom a "friend" dropped in with a roulette wheel and relieved the men of their pocket money.

When weather permitted, they shagged flies and played pepper in the morning, shagged flies and stretched the muscles of pitching arms in the afternoon. Unlike teams today, they had no special teachers, coaches, classes, blackboards, physiotherapists, mechanical pitchers, mass calisthenics, or videotape recorders. Teaching was oral and simple. Dunn, Steinman, and the catchers were the faculty. It was left to the individual player to improve himself and to get into condition. Rookies had to provide their own inner drive, because veterans ignored or even intimidated them.

Whether baseball's rites of spring have any physiological worth is doubtful. No studies prove it. Professors of physical education have done the scientific work on the effect of training, and they often use basketball players and track men because they are so plentiful around universities. In sports in which training has been measured, improvement appears in from four to six weeks. By a coincidence pleasant for baseball traditionalists, that's how long spring training lasts. In the days of Jack Dunn's Orioles the spring camp cost very little because profits from exhibition games paid most of the cost. Dunn could charge off any deficit as payment for the vast amount of newspaper publicity a training team received. In short, spring training cost little and seemed to do more good than harm.

What did spring training do for Ruth, beyond getting him his nickname? It did *not* give him confidence; he already had a world of it. Ruth did improve his stance at the plate by straightening his right knee, which he had a tendency to bend too much. He also abandoned a last-minute spiral of the bat which sometimes made him swing too late at fast balls. These two small batting changes are about the sum of his improvement at Fayetteville.

But Ruth had signed to *pitch*. When Dunn arrived in camp the pitchers, catchers, and Steinman were full of what Dunn felt must be "wild tales of Ruth's slugging ability. . . ." They turned out to be facts. The only time of the year when pitchers get much batting practice is that week of spring training before the hitters report. Then the pitchers have a festival of hitting, using the bats of players no longer with the club. In this batting orgy Ruth's skill had astonished the other members of the advance party. It is unlikely that any other rookie pitcher ever had so much publicity about his hitting. Only two weeks after Ruth had first climbed aboard a railway train the *Sun* of March 16 said:

DUNN PRAISES RUTH

JACK DECLARES HE IS MOST PROMISING

YOUNGSTER HE EVER HAD

The story had a direct quote from Dunn:

> Ruth has all the earmarks of a good ball player. He hits like a
> fiend and seems to be at home in any position, despite the fact
> that he is a left hander. . . . He is a whale with the willow, and
> some of the drives he is making in practice would clear the right
> field fence at Oriole Park.

What a man says for publication and what he writes in private to
a trusted friend may be different, but not in this case. Dunn wrote
to Brother Gilbert: "Brother, this fellow Ruth is the greatest young
ball player who ever reported to a training camp."

As soon as there were seventeen Birds in camp they drafted

Marker in Fayetteville, North Carolina, which com-
memorates Babe Ruth's first home run as a professional baseball player (in spring training). (*National
Baseball Library, Cooperstown, New York.*)

Ruth's roommate, the twenty-six-year-old sportswriter Roger Pippen, to make eighteen, and had a game. The date was March 7, 1914, and a memorable date it is. The Buzzards beat the Sparrows 15–9 in seven innings. The manner of the victory set off the Baltimore press like fireworks. Ruth had a two-column head in the next day's Sunday *Sun*: HOMER BY RUTH FEATURE OF GAME. "George Ruth, a pitcher Jack Dunn picked off the lots of Baltimore, is credited with making the longest hit ever seen by Fayetteville fans." With a runner on second, "the youngster landed on a fast ball and circled the bases before Billy Morrisette had picked it up in deep right field." Jim Thorpe, the famous Indian who was with the Giants in 1914, had held the Fayetteville record for the long ball, but "Ruth's hit was much longer than that made by Thorpe." Ruth started the game at shortstop, handled three chances well, batted fifth in the order, and ended as pitcher. He had two hits in three times at bat and scored twice. Ruth "can play any position."*

This was Ruth's first home run as a professional ballplayer. The pitcher who gave it up was a left-hander, Chick McKinley, who has no other claim to fame. The hit was made on a long-gone diamond at the Cape Fear Fairgrounds. (A survivor of that day, Maurice Fleishman, who served as bat boy, in 1952 promoted the erection of a marker to commemorate Ruth's hit.) After the game Roger Pippen measured the distance and found the point of impact to be 350 feet. Since then the distance has stretched, in some tellings, to more than 400 feet. The line score of this historic day was as follows:

| Buzzards | 174 | 000 | 3 | 15 | 14 | 1 |
| Sparrows | 101 | 150 | 1 | 9 | 7 | 1 |

Jarman, Ruth and Hurney. Cranston, McKinley and Potts. HR—Ruth, 7th (1 on).

Ben Egan went on record to say Ruth was more than a hitter. "Besides hitting to all corners of the lot, Ruth has shown up well in the box. He has a world of speed and handles himself like a veteran, although he has had no experience in professional ranks."

The Buzzards beat the Sparrows once more on March 9. Ruth played shortstop all the way, and very well.

The Buzzard-Sparrow series had been a pick-up series as much for fun as training. A week before any Oriole had left for camp,

---

* To add to the luster of the Baseball Writers Association of America, it ought to be recorded here that Pippen played the whole game at center field, was "two for three" with a double, a triple, two runs scored, and he drove in Ruth with the double. He made no error or putout in the field, but scored an assist.

Dunn had given out two lineups, the Regulars and the Yanigans. No. 14 on the list of Yanigans was "Ruth, p." By March 11 a Regulars-vs.-Yanigans series was underway. Ruth made some kind of news almost every day, striking out four batters in each of two three-inning stints, dragging a bunt for a hit, sharing a shutout with two other pitchers, making five assists and a double play in three innings as a shortstop, hitting in the clean-up spot while pitching, and other marvels.

Nine pitchers, including Babe Ruth and Bill Morrisette, survived the first cut of the Orioles squad on March 14. In the *Sun's* discussion of the pitchers remaining, Ruth got a paragraph to himself.

RUTH IMPRESSES DUNN

George Ruth has impressed Dunn most, and before he was at training camp a week he decided that he will be a regular whether or not he strikes his stride. The Oriole magnate predicts that Ruth will develop into a Rube Waddell, for he possesses every mark of a successful pitcher.

So far the Orioles had been playing only each other, but Babe Ruth had no fear of failure. As he wrote to Brother Alban, "I am making good in basket-ball, baseball and everything that they've got down here."

From mid-March to mid-April the Orioles played as many exhibition games as they could get in, nearly all against major-league teams. This series would provide a better test of Babe Ruth than the intrasquad contests. The Orioles took the first game of the exhibition series by beating the Phillies on March 16 at Fayetteville, but Ruth and other Yanigans were on the road humbling a nearby military academy 24–6. Two days later Dunn unleashed the Yanigans against the Phils. The Orioles won in the last of the ninth, 4–3. Ruth was the second of two pitchers and gave up two unearned runs; today's scorers would give him the "win." Two days later he worked against the Phillies in relief, coming in in the sixth inning to choke off a four-run rally. There was a man on and one out. Ruth struck out the next two batsmen and held the Phillies scoreless thereafter. As the *Sun* so well put it, RUTH SAVES THE DAY. He worked in two of the three games with the Phillies, faced twenty-nine batters, allowed two runs (unearned), and gave up six hits. He had earned a steady job.

Ruth got his first start as a professional against the world-champion Athletics at Wilmington, North Carolina, on March 25. He gave up thirteen hits in nine innings but won 6–2. Again the *Sun* rejoiced: "Ruth was the real hero." He had struck out Home Run

Baker twice and held Eddie Collins hitless. Later he said he had
not known who they were. Perhaps he didn't. Dunn remarked at
the time that when Ruth pitched to the A's he was as relaxed as
he would have been against "a local amateur club."

When the Orioles came home to Baltimore's Back River Park on
March 28, Ruth started against the Athletics again. They drove
him to his bath in the sixth inning, after he gave up seven hits and
four runs (the A's won it 12–5). Ruth showed a lack of fielding
polish by failing to cover first on a play which cost a run, but
attempts to steal bases proved to be hazardous when he was pitching (Stuffy McInnis was caught twice). Babe became the *Sun's*
"star southpaw" on April 5 by shutting out the Dodgers at home
on six hits, 10–0. He also tripled to drive in two runs. He lost to the
Yankees 4–0 on April 10, when the Orioles could hit only five
singles. Three days later the Giants beat a pitcher identified by the
New York World as "Baby" Ruth; score: 3–2. "Baby" gave up nine
hits, struck out seven, walked two, and plunked two with pitched
balls. In this game Egan came out to the mound and told his
pitcher to throw a "waste pitch" to Red Murray.* Ruth grooved a
fast ball, belt high, which Murray hit safely. Ruth told the annoyed
Egan that he had done as asked: thrown one "waist" high.

Baseball's spring prologue was drawing to a close. Babe Ruth
had pitched in seven practice games against major-league hitters.
He beat the Phillies and the Dodgers, split with the Athletics, and
lost to the Yankees and the Giants. (He also pitched four innings
against the Braves, but left the game with the score 2–2.) The
nineteen-year-old minor leaguer was accepted as one of the two best
Oriole pitchers. Dunn said, "I . . . picked up a great ball player, not
only a slugger, but a great pitcher. . . ."

Without his having anything to say about it, Babe Ruth was
conscripted to serve in the Federal League war. In the winter of
1913–1914 a group of would-be baseball magnates tried to establish
the Federal League as the third major league. Baltimore, as the
country's largest minor-league city, received a Federal League club
called the Terrapins. Baltimoreans believed major-league baseball
had come to town. The Terrapins had a park directly across the
street from the Orioles. Although the Federal League was warring
on the National and American Leagues, the International League
was the theater of operations. After August 1914 people called the
International League "the Belgium of baseball." In the spring of
1914 Baltimore talked more of Terrapins than of Orioles. Jack
Dunn's troubles were plain on April 13, opening day for the
Terrapins. The Federals drew twenty-eight thousand. Across the

---

* John Joseph Murray (1884–1958), eleven seasons as outfielder with Cardinals,
Giants, Cubs, 1906–1917. Batting average .270.

street the wonderboy Babe Ruth pitched for the Orioles in an exhibition against the Giants and drew a thousand. The Terrapins' three-game opening series drew forty-five thousand altogether.

The Orioles opened at home against Buffalo on April 21 and shut out the visiting Bisons. Babe Ruth started the second game. He stuffed a can of snuff under his lip, taking John Masefield's advice to "spit brown, my son, and get a hairy chest," and walked out to the rubber to begin the serious practice of his profession. Ruth's first inning of professional championship competition in organized baseball is worth notice. Ernest J. Lanigan reported it:

> Vaughn was thrown out by Ball; McCarthy walked and took second on a wild pitch; Murray flied to Cree; Ruth and Gleichman got mixed up on Houser's pop fly, the ball dropping safely for a hit and McCarthy taking third; Houser stole second; Jackson was hit by a pitched ball, filling the bases; Roach was thrown out by Ball. No runs, one hit, no errors.

That's about as much trouble as a pitcher can get into without letting the enemy score. Ruth went on to shut out Buffalo 6–0, giving up six hits. (Buffalo's McCarthy was *the* Joe McCarthy.)

But there were no fans. There were fewer than two hundred in the stands on opening day, the smallest crowd that ever saw an International League game in Baltimore. When the season was a week old it was plain that Dunn's team faced disaster. After three wins and a loss they had been seen by practically nobody.

Ruth ended his first week as a championship competitor by dropping the second game of a doubleheader against Rochester, 2–1, giving up but five singles while striking out six and walking two. He also received his first monthly hundred dollars. He bought a bicycle; for the first time in his life he owned something that somebody might think was worth having. He rode it wherever he went in Baltimore, including a visit to St. Mary's. In this way Ruth began his Big Spending, a practice encouraged by the fact that the more money he blew the more he made. The process began immediately. As soon as he bought the bicycle Dunn doubled his salary to twelve hundred dollars. In a month he raised it to eighteen hundred.

Dunn was a just man. He was trying to pay Babe Ruth what he was worth while the Orioles were going broke.

Ruth had a pretty good month of May. On the 1st he went into a game against Montreal in the tenth, shut out the Royals, then doubled home the winning run in the bottom of the inning. On the next day he pitched Baltimore to an 8–3 win over Toronto. Said the *Sun*: "George Ruth again was a hero." For once somebody saw him;

the Toronto match drew four thousand. After a five-day rest Ruth beat Buffalo again (at Buffalo) in eleven innings, 5–3. On a chilly day in Toronto before five hundred shivering customers Ruth lost a ten-inning game, giving up seven singles and losing by an unearned run. While still on the road he was bombed by Montreal, then by Rochester. He avenged the Rochester humiliation on the very next day as a pinch hitter, starting a three-run rally which won the game 8–6. In his next start, at Newark he was dismissed in the fourth inning of the first game of a doubleheader, but then started the second game and won it in eleven innings, 1–0. In those eleven innings he allowed five hits, walked three, and struck out *one*. The pitcher who wins by a score of 1–0 in eleven innings with but one strikeout is a frugal fellow who gets batters out by making them pop up or beat the ball into the dirt. He pitched successfully in relief at Providence on the 28th, and in the same series three days later took the worst clubbing of his short career, being unable to get through the second inning. On balance, despite three bad beatings, he had shown himself worthy of being an Oriole.

The Orioles had more serious troubles than those posed by the other teams of the International League. At the end of the first week of May the Orioles were second in their league, but the Terrapins were first in theirs. There was so little interest in Dunn's team that the Baltimore papers sent no writers on the Orioles' first road trip. Baltimore readers, if any, had to be content with brief wire-service summaries of International League games. It is all rather sad. The International League cities had grand baseball traditions, and their teams played ball just a notch below the major leagues. The race, after five weeks, was heated. Buffalo led Baltimore by a game; Baltimore (19–12) led Rochester by half a game. But to the people of Baltimore this was bush-league stuff. The Terrapins were accepted as major leaguers, loved, and supported.

Ruth worked eight times in June, getting all of the kinds of experience that minor-league play was supposed to provide for nineteen-year-old pitchers. He was twice batted from the mound, lost a five-hitter 2–1, twice won games in which he gave up two runs, won a game in which he gave up but one, and pitched a five-hit shutout. He also won a game in relief after five innings when the Orioles made up a seven-run deficit, and closed out the month as the winner of a sloppy 10–5 game in which the hits totaled twenty-six.

From the start of the season to the end of June, Ruth worked in twenty-one games; his won-lost record was 11–7. His frequent and regular appearances proved his strength and power of recovery.

Ruth's hitting records from April through June show a batting average slightly below .200, with eight hits in forty-one times at bat. Those eight hits included a double and three triples. Except for that odd proportion of triples, the rookie's batting foretold no bright future.

Meanwhile the Orioles' attendance figures were gloomy. Jack Dunn concluded that the high minor leagues could not survive the Federal League invasion without help. He would like to see the Double-A leagues (Double-A was then the highest minor-league classification) get major-league status. He was thinking of moving the Orioles to Richmond, out of the deadly shadow of the Terrapins. Attendance continued to shrink until it became microscopic. On June 25, on a day Ruth beat Toronto 13–8, the Terrapins were also at home, across the street. Although the press gave no attendance figure for that day, tradition says that Ruth pitched five innings in relief, to win, before twenty paying fans.

> I will not take a single man back who steps over the line dividing the American and Federal League. I hereby tell one and all of them that I will not even talk to them.
> —Ban Johnson, President, American League

The Federal League recruited boldly in the older leagues, using money for bait. The salaries of men who moved to the Federal League from "organized baseball" (which is the system topped by the older major leagues) increased from 33 percent to 200 percent.

The Terrapins played on land leased from a former owner of the Orioles, who let them have it on condition that the Terrapins not tamper with the Orioles; no Oriole went to the Terrapins. Ruth later said the Federals approached him in April 1914 with an offer of a ten-thousand-dollar bonus for signing and ten thousand a year in salary. It was a great temptation, but major-league officials had declared they would blacklist for life any player who went over to the Federal League. Ruth believed them, but when the Federals collapsed all the jumpers were forgiven. Nobody was blacklisted. With some bitterness Ruth said, "I just got jobbed out of twenty thousand dollars without a thank you from anybody and continued playing for my six hundred dollars." As a matter of law, he could not have signed *any* contract without the permission of his acting guardian, Jack Dunn, a point which did not occur to him.

Now that he had an income, Dunn required Ruth to bank part of his pay to be held until he came of age. Babe was becoming a public character, accepted in Baltimore both as pitcher and as person. "Too much can hardly be said in the youngster's favor," said the *Sun*. (We don't know where he lived in the spring of 1914; we may suppose he lodged with his father.) The name "Babe" was well enough known to appear at the head of a capsule biography in the *Sun* of July 10, 1914; the head is worth reprinting.

THE RISE OF BABE RUTH
Playing Hookey From School Starts Him on Brilliant Career
NOW BRIGHT BASEBALL STAR

Loves the Game, Plays Several
Positions And Is Making Big Salary
Through Natural Ability

The story that followed tells nothing we do not already know except that he had gained weight since the playing season started, and that Dunn was comparing him with Walter Johnson. Perhaps Dunn thought praise would raise his market value.

Terrapin rivalry was wiping out the Orioles. Back River Park set a new record for low attendance—seventeen fans, although the Orioles were still leading their league. Baltimore believed the Terrapins were big league and the Orioles were bush. Even the schedules seemed planned to kill the Orioles. On eighteen dates, scattered evenly from April 21 to September 26, both the Orioles and Terrapins played at home in Baltimore.

In self-defense Dunn began to sell players to support himself. He had already borrowed from Connie Mack and Joseph Lannin to meet his payroll. (Lannin owned the Red Sox and the Providence International League club.) Therefore Mack and Lannin had first call on Oriole talent. Mack was having money troubles, too, and was not buying anything. Lannin took nothing when the tray of *hors d'oeuvres* went around the first time. So Birdie Cree, for five thousand dollars paid to Dunn, went back to the Yankees from whence he had come after an injury in 1912. Deek Derrick and George Twombly went next, to the Reds; the sum of eighteen thousand dollars was mentioned but that is hard to believe. Cree and Derrick had been around for years; their leaving probably cut the payroll considerably.*

ALL ORIOLES FOR SALE
—*Baltimore Sun*, July 9, 1914

---

* William Franklin Cree (1882–1942), eight seasons, 1908–1915, Yankees, outfielder, batting average .292.

Claude Derrick (1886–1974), five seasons, 1910–1914, Athletics, Yankees, Reds, Cubs, infielder, batting average .242.

George Twombly, outfielder (1892–   ), five seasons, 1914–1919, Reds, Braves, Senators, batting average .211.

The auction brought Jack Dunn no abuse; he plainly had no choice but to realize the cash value of his players. The *Sun* ran a cartoon on the sports page which showed Dunn taking medicine from a bottle marked with a dollar sign and labeled "Sale of Players."

Lannin of the Red Sox now said he would like to buy pitchers Ruth and Ernie Shore. There were others of the same mind, among them John McGraw. Many able critics had seen these two competent young men in spring exhibitions.

Before Dunn went farther in breaking up his team he appealed to the meeting of the International League, called at New York by its president, Edward Grant Barrow, on July 2. He told his fellow owners he had lost twenty thousand dollars so far in 1914, and asked permission to move to Richmond. His stalling colleagues gave no firm reply.*

Dunn went to Washington, D.C., on July 3, giving no public reason, but a glance at the 1914 American League schedule suggests why. The Red Sox played the Senators in Washington on July 3. No doubt Bill Carrigan, the respected manager of the Red Sox, would like to hear for himself Dunn's account of the Oriole treasury of talent.

* The Orioles barely survived 1914 by playing their "home" games in Wilmington, Delaware, and finishing sixth. In 1915 league president Barrow moved the Oriole franchise to Richmond.

5 · Southpaw Displays High Class

He has come up really fast for a kid. Kept his confidence. Didn't get beat too often when he first came up. You got to have that early success in order to develop fast in this league.

—Jim Brosnan,[*] *Pennant Race*

Babe Ruth became an Oriole while wearing faded denim bib-overalls in the yard of St. Mary's Industrial School in Baltimore on February 14, 1914. On July 11, 147 days later, he was scuffing the clay in front of the pitching rubber in Fenway Park, Boston, getting ready to pitch to Jack Graney, the first batter. in the Cleveland lineup. The nineteen-year-old left-hander with the swelling shoulders pitched well against the Cleveland Naps[**] that day, though he had ridden a train all the previous night, and "the night before" is a nervous night for most rookie pitchers. Jack Graney later said of the game, "I remember it well. I was the lead-off man . . . and the first man to face Ruth in his debut with the Red Sox. . . . I had two hits that day." Graney[†] singled to open the game, but did not shake Ruth, who threw him out in a double play as he later tried to score.

RUTH LEADS RED SOX TO VICTORY

Southpaw Displays High Class In Game Against Cleveland
—*Boston Globe*, July 12, 1914

[*] James Patrick Brosnan (1929–   ), pitcher, nine seasons, 1954–1963, Cubs, Cardinals, Reds, White Sox, won 55, lost 47, earned-run average 3.54.
[**] The Cleveland American League club was known then as the "Naps," after Napoleon Lajoie, the fans' favorite player.
[†] John Gladstone Graney (1886–   ), outfielder, fourteen seasons, 1908–1922, Cleveland, batting average .250.

Other tones of voices in other news rooms:

Ruth Batted Out By The Naps
—*New York Times*, July 12, 1914

Ruth held Cleveland to five scattered hits and one run in the first six innings, while the Red Sox scored three times. In the seventh, Cleveland hit three singles which brought in two runs to tie the score. Duffy Lewis batted for Ruth in the seventh, which meant, of course, that Ruth left the game. Luckily for him, Tris Speaker drove in Everett Scott with the lead run in the last of the seventh. Dutch Leonard finished the game, saving the victory for Ruth, score 4–3. Tim Murnane, an able writer for the *Globe*—former player, former manager, former minor-league president—predicted a good future for the new left-hander, "a natural ball player" who "went through his act like a veteran" and who "will undoubtedly be a fine pitcher. . . ."

Thus, on July 11, 1914, Babe Ruth pitched and won the first big-league game he ever saw. The events of the previous weeks explain how he found himself pitching for the home club at Fenway Park.

Jack Dunn, the owner-manager of the near-bankrupt Baltimore Orioles, offered pitchers Babe Ruth and Ernie Shore and catcher Ben Egan to Connie Mack in June 1914. The great Athletics were in the process of losing $65,000 that year. Mack was planning to sell, not to buy. Joseph Lannin, owner of the Red Sox, had joined with Mack in helping Dunn to meet his spring payroll. Feeling obligated to deal with Mack and Lannin first (although John McGraw was also interested), Dunn offered Ruth and Shore to the Red Sox for twenty-five thousand dollars. Lannin countered with the figure of fifteen thousand. Dunn added Egan to the list and suggested nineteen thousand plus cancelation of Dunn's debt of thirty-five hundred to Lannin, and another loan from Lannin, the amount unknown. (This bargaining was done by telephone, a method novel enough to intrigue people in 1914.) Dunn's package was acceptable to Lannin, *if* the players suited his manager, Bill Carrigan.

On July 3 Dunn went to see Lannin and Carrigan in Washington. Freddie Parent, a retired shortstop who played for the Red Sox in Carrigan's first year, now worked for Dunn; Dunn took him along as a witness Carrigan would trust. Carrigan listened to Dunn's offer and asked Parent what *he* thought. Parent said Shore was surely ready for the major leagues now, and though Ruth lacked finish, "he can't miss with a little more experience." We know that Carrigan had great pitching in 1914, but no manager is likely to turn down good pitchers his owner will buy for cash. And because of the Federal League troubles there was no player limit that summer; in this Oriole deal Carrigan could not hurt the Red Sox. Dunn's offer, Lannin's money, Parent's advice, Carrigan's acceptance—and the deal was closed. Nothing remained but for Dunn, Ruth, and Lannin to pose for the standard photograph of player signing contract, an American conventional art form which has been well received for decades.

3 MORE ORIOLES SOLD

**Ruth, Shore and Egan Purchased
By The Boston Red Sox**

THEY LEAVE THE NEST TONIGHT

**More Than $25000 Said To Be Involved—Players Should
Be Big Help To Carrigan's Club**
—Baltimore Sun, July 10, 1914

Jack Dunn (L) of the Baltimore Orioles watches his legal ward sign to play baseball for the Red Sox of Joseph Lannin (R) during the season of 1914. (*National Baseball Library, Cooperstown, New York.*)

Of the three players in the deal, Shore was most wanted by Boston, Ruth next, and Egan* not at all. The Red Sox dealt Egan, Ruth's first professional tutor, to Cleveland almost as soon as he got off at South Station in Boston. Ruth was not a necessary part of a deal for Shore;** the Red Sox would have been glad to get Shore alone. Shore was a very good pitcher, but his career ended before he was thirty.

The Boston club was a going concern. From 1901, when the American League began play, through 1918 the Red Sox won six pennants and finished in the second division only twice. The club had been the "Americans," then the "Pilgrims," and in 1908 the "Red Sox," a fitting commemoration of the great old Cincinnati Red Stockings who migrated to Boston and became the nucleus of professional baseball in New England. The Red Sox settled in Fenway Park in 1912. (Tom Yawkey renovated and remodeled that most interesting of parks in 1933, but its basic shape is unchanged.) The thirty-five-foot-high left-field wall, only 315 feet away, was there to convert lazy flies to doubles all through Babe Ruth's Boston stay. (The first home run over that fence in 1912 excited awe.) Fenway has been a hostile environment for many left-handed pitchers. Could Ruth long survive there?

Joseph J. Lannin became the sole owner of the Red Sox in May 1914. In that year *Sporting Life* reckoned the Red Sox payroll to be the highest in baseball. The team certainly had talent. Its manager, Bill Carrigan, had been the first-string catcher since 1909, calling every pitch of every game. His firmness in denying his pitchers the command of their games brought him the dugout nickname of "Rough." Nevertheless, Babe Ruth always said Carrigan was the best manager he ever had. The outfield (Duffy Lewis, Tris Speaker, Harry Hooper) was great. Edward G. Barrow probably judged it correctly when he called it "the greatest defensive outfield the game has known." The infield was not as good as the Athletics' "$100,000 infield." The pitching was the best in the league.

Ruth came to these storied Red Sox with the reputation that he lacked respect for great men—that is, the elders thought he was a fresh kid. He was never ill at ease in any company, but in his youth he could be ill-mannered. Harry Hooper said his behavior showed he was "just a big overgrown green pea." He was pretty much like other rookies except that he hit the ball harder and he ate more. To reshape him, some of the Red Sox hazed him rather painfully until,

---

* Arthur Augustus Egan (1883–1968), catcher, four seasons, 1908–1915, Athletics and Indians, batting average .165.

** Ernest Grady Shore (1891–   ), pitcher, seven seasons, 1912–1920, Giants, Red Sox, Yankees. Won 63, lost 42, earned-run average 2.45. Perfect game 1917. World Series 1916, 1917, won 3, lost 1, earned-run average 1.82.

in fury, he challenged the whole team to fight. That lessened the abuse somewhat. On the material side, Ruth's last Oriole salary had been at the rate of eighteen hundred dollars a year. Lannin paid him at the rate of twenty-five hundred.

Lannin seemed to have made a good bargain with Jack Dunn. It seemed even better when Shore, on the day after Ruth's first appearance, beat Cleveland with a two-hitter, 2–1. Shore, a right-hander, fitted into Carrigan's rotation from the time of his arrival. Ruth stayed with the Red Sox for just five weeks, worked in four games, won two, lost one. In ten times at bat he made two hits.

The 1914 Red Sox made a good run for the pennant (they finished second), but they hardly needed pitching. Boston pitchers gave up the fewest runs, earned or unearned, of any staff in either league. Ruth seemed to be surplus, at least temporarily. About the time he joined the Red Sox they also acquired left-handed Vean Gregg* from Cleveland. Gregg had won more than sixty games in the past three seasons. In theory the team that had Gregg didn't need an untested left-handed rookie. Lannin and Carrigan decided to send Ruth to Lannin's Providence club of the International League for more experience.

Baseball law required that every other major-league team had to say it did not wish Ruth's services, thereby granting Lannin a waiver, before he could be sent to a minor-league team. August Herrmann, president of the Cincinnati Reds, refused to waive his claim to Ruth, which meant that if Lannin kept Ruth "on waivers" the Reds could buy him for a fixed price. Lannin asked Ban Johnson, the American League president, to try to persuade Herrmann not to block the transfer of Ruth to Providence. Johnson told Herrmann that only the Reds had refused to waive, and went on to explain that Lannin had spent a lot of money for Ruth, hoped to develop him, and would never let him go to another major-league club. "He is unable to give him the work at Boston, and by sending him to Providence he will have an opportunity to improve the team . . . and possibly make some money." Lannin told Herrmann he wanted to send Ruth down only to get experience. Herrmann yielded, and Ruth's name went on the Providence roster on August 15, 1914. Boston retained the option of recalling him on short notice, as a kind of insurance policy; for example, if Gregg broke a leg, Ruth could replace him in a day.

As a pitcher at Providence Ruth was a smashing success, winning eleven games and losing two, to make his combined Baltimore-Providence International League pitching record twenty-two wins

* Vean Gregg (1885–1964), pitcher, eight seasons, 1911–1925, Indians, Red Sox, Athletics, Senators. Won 89, lost 65, earned-run average 2.70.

and nine losses.* His manager was the original Wild Bill Donovan,** once a great pitcher, now a highly regarded teacher of promising young ballplayers. Looking back at Ruth's tour of duty with Providence we can see an event that looms larger now than then. On September 5, pitching at Toronto, he gave up but one hit, and won pleasantly, 9–0. In the sixth inning he came to bat with two men on base and hit the only home run he had ever hit in professional competition. It would be his first and last minor-league home run.

Providence won the pennant. There is a temptation to assume that Ruth won it for the team, but Ruth said Carl Mays's pitching was the chief reason Providence won. (On the day after the season ended, Ruth beat the Cubs in an exhibition game 8–7, pitching the complete game.)

Ruth matured as a pitcher in the seven months after he abandoned his career of shirtmaking in a Baltimore trade school. He faced more than a thousand batters, to whom he probably threw four or five thousand pitches. He certainly showed that he had control. He hit but eleven batsmen, threw only eleven wild pitches, and walked fewer than one in ten batsmen. For a pitcher, his International League batting was good. The average was .231. There was a curious warp or twist to the figures. He made twenty-eight hits, but thirteen were for extra bases: a home run, two doubles, and *ten* triples. The young lion was beginning to feel his strength. He was hitting the ball very hard. If the 1914 ball had been as lively as the 1920 ball, there would have been fewer than ten triples and more than one home run.

After the Providence season ended, Mays and Ruth traveled together to Boston, in a delayed train that could not feed them. Ruth shocked Mays by calling a cab (ninety cents) to take them from Back Bay Station to the Brunswick Hotel, across from Fenway Park. The American League season had a week to go. Ruth worked in one game, without decision.

When in Boston, during his short 1914 hitch with the Red Sox, Ruth usually had breakfast at Lander's coffee shop on Huntington Avenue. One of the Lander's waiters remembered him years later as "a big, lummockin' sort of fella." Counting out his days on the road with the major-league club, he may have breakfasted at Lander's as often as twenty times. His usual waitress was Helen Woodford, who lived with her family in South Boston. Sportswriters accepted the Woodfords as immigrants from Nova Scotia, but an

---

* G	IP	H	R	BB	SO	HB	WP	W	L	Pct.
35	245	210	88	101	139	11	11	22	9	.709

** William Edward Donovan (1876–1923), pitcher, eighteen seasons, 1898–1918, Senators, Dodgers, Tigers, Yankees. Won 188, lost 138, earned-run average 2.69.

affidavit says Helen was born in El Paso, Texas. The best known of her family was her brother William J., a failed South Boston politician who had moved to New York by the 1920s.

On one of his hypothetical twenty mornings at Lander's Ruth looked up from breakfast (according to him) and said, "How about you and me getting married, hon?" After a few minutes of grave reflection, Helen Woodford accepted the proposal. They went to Maryland after the baseball season where Ruth, a minor, got his father's written permission, and they were married in St. Paul's Church, Ellicott City, Maryland, on October 17, 1914. Helen Woodford Ruth gave her age as eighteen; she may have been as young as fifteen.

In the next several years this very pretty dark girl kept herself in the background of the Ruth scene, and was chiefly known as the only person in Massachusetts who habitually called Babe Ruth "George."

Ruth achieved much in 1914. There were about fifty professional baseball leagues. He had started just below the top and climbed to

Helen Woodford Ruth in 1919 or 1920. (*National Baseball Library, Cooperstown, New York.*)

one of the best teams in baseball in half a season. The Federal League's damage to the Orioles may have speeded his promotion to the Red Sox, but nothing could have put him on the Red Sox roster if he had lacked talent. It is reasonable to suppose that one in five hundred players was good enough to play in the International League. That is where Ruth *started*. His start was good, but he was far from famous. In the whole of 1914 he received but one piece of fan mail. It came from Brother Gilbert.

6 · Baseball Then

Baseball *is* Greek in being national, heroic, and broken up
in the rivalry of city-states.
— Barzun, *God's Country and Mine*

Babe Ruth broke into professional baseball at an exceedingly favorable time. In the first decades of the century baseball built on a solid foundation of popularity gained in the nineteenth century, and attendance grew at the same rate as the population. Paid admissions in 1903 were just below five million. In 1908 and 1909 attendance rose above seven million. Attendance declined a bit in Ruth's first two professional seasons, partly, of course, because of Federal League rivalry. (Every time the attendance figures drop a little someone weeps for the death of baseball. In 1915 a writer in *Harper's Weekly* said baseball was "rapidly receding toward the limbo of forgotten things.") The daily press made sure that baseball was not quickly forgotten. Sports coverage in leading papers of typical towns of 1890 was about one-twenty-fifth of the news. By 1923 it was one-sixth. Some of the added space went to newly popular sports and games, such as golf, but baseball increased its column inches. In 1913 the Associated Press connected all the big-league parks with all the principal afternoon newspapers and sent batteries, umpires, scores by half-innings, explanations of runs, key plays, and lineup changes. It was the broadest sports coverage ever, and more than is now available.

Baseball grew as Sunday baseball came to be accepted. Sunday games have always drawn the largest crowds. Laws barring Sunday baseball as indecent assembly, in all major-league cities except Chicago, St. Louis, and Cincinnati, had no visible effect on public morals except to oppress the poor. The rich could find recreation beyond the law on any Sunday, but slum children were jailed for playing ball in public parks on Sunday—three in Boston in 1911, four in Brooklyn in 1913. By 1919, however, baseball could also be played on Sunday in Detroit, Cleveland, and Washington. Thus eight of the major-league clubs could play at home on Sunday, five in the American League, three in the National League.

The growth of the city also made it possible for the major leagues to grow. There could be no well-paid athletes until the city concentrated ticket buyers in a small area. The streetcar, the telegraphic news service, the regular and predictable hours of factory work, the boredom of occupations which, unlike farming, had no work-changing seasons—all inclined city people to watch professional athletes.

Early in this century many city people came to have as much leisure time as an eighteenth-century nobleman who paid close attention to his farmlands. The earlier aristocrat pursued pleasures arranged for small groups, such as gambling, hunting, and fishing. Twentieth-century city people with the same amount of time to kill could not afford as much gambling, hunting, and fishing as a duke could. Uplifters hoped they would go to night school, buy opera tickets, overcrowd the art museums, and jam the public libraries, but they bought tickets to baseball games. It is no accident that the game of baseball, which has used so many farm boys and which still has a crossroads tone in its slang (a can of corn, a frozen rope), was perfected in New York city. People may have fled to the ball park to escape their factory jobs. But mass-attended sport in America is as much an aftergrowth of industry as it is a drug to kill the pain of a factory job.

Babe Ruth and the conditions of profitable baseball arrived on the American scene at the same time. The crowds could be in the park because of the rise of the city, the trolley line to the park, the free time of working people, the regular payment of city workers in cash. From Ruth's fifth birthday to his twenty-fifth, the rural American population increased six million while the city population grew twenty-four million. Not all of these urban people lived in cities with major-league franchises, but all of them were connected to baseball by the telegraph service to their daily newspapers. And all of them— it appeared later—seemed to be secretly yearning for an unknown American Siegfried, Hercules, or Beowulf whom they could cheer and richly reward.

In the front offices, unseen by fans, baseball was a business. Or, to paraphrase Jim Murray, if baseball wasn't a business, J. P. Morgan and Company was a sport. To call the owners "sportsmen" makes the language mean nothing. On the other hand, it overblows baseball to call it an industry, because a true industry uses a great deal more capital than baseball does. Baseball was and is a confederation of small businesses. In 1911 one could reasonably have valued all of the clubs and their parks at ten million dollars. (In the 1970s all twenty-four major-league clubs together are probably worth a fifth of the Harvard endowment, or a tenth of Exxon.)

As business, baseball has not been well run. Its popularity early in the century owed nothing to management, which has sourly and rightly been called "mediocre." Perhaps owners were content with mediocre executive performance because they took their gains as much in psychological income as in money. They seemed to enjoy ownership for the pleasure of being arrogant, as when the Pittsburgh management in 1909 scolded the customers for their failure to encourage the players (many such instances are available). Owners liked to treat their players as children at best and as domestic animals at worst. Perhaps owners were self-righteous because the sporting press usually sided with management on controversial questions. *Baseball* magazine, in 1914, warned players not to behave so that people would think them spendthrifts. "A very glaring instance of this among baseball players is the recent evil tendency to purchase and maintain automobiles." The writer could have been thinking of Babe Ruth. His bicycle had disappeared forever. In 1914 the police magistrate of Cambridge, Massachusetts, lifted his license after an automobile accident.

Recruitment of players was haphazard and leaned on tips from friends in the baseball business, as in the case of Brother Gilbert, coach, to Jack Dunn, owner-manager. The salary story of the best players shows how all players were rewarded at the time Ruth came. Honus Wagner* was one of the half-dozen best players ever. In 1909 his pay was ten thousand dollars; to get it he had to threaten to quit after the 1908 season. He played until 1917, and his salary remained at ten thousand. Ty Cobb** was even greater than Wagner (though there are arguments on that). In 1912 his salary was nine thousand. After a holdout he got a raise to $11,332.55, a fifty-dollar fine, and a public reprimand for being uppity. Since Ruth was a pitcher, it is worth noting that Christy Mathewson† made eight thousand dollars in 1911, and Walter Johnson's‡ salary in 1914 was ten thousand. The ten-thousand-dollar ballplayers of 1914 were much less numerous, in proportion, than the hundred-thousand-dollar players of the 1970s.

* John Peter Wagner (1874–1955), infielder, twenty-one seasons, 1887–1917, Louisville and Pittsburgh. Hall of Fame. Batting average .327.
** Tyrus Cobb (1886–1961), outfielder, twenty-four seasons, 1905–1928, Tigers and Athletics. Hall of Fame. Batting average .367 (all-time highest lifetime).
† Christopher Mathewson (1880–1925), pitcher, seventeen seasons, 1900–1916, Giants, Reds. Hall of Fame. Won 367, lost 188, earned-run average 2.13.
‡ Walter Perry Johnson (1887–1946), pitcher, twenty-one seasons, 1907–1927, Senators. Hall of Fame. Won 416, lost 279, earned-run average 2.17.

You know, baseball is a matter of razor-edge precision. It's
not a game of inches like you hear people say. It's a game
of hundredths of inches.

—Rube Bressler*

Baseball was a neater and tidier game before the First World War
than it was after. The single run had more value because it was
harder to get with the old dead ball. When Ruth came to play,
batters were hitting well below their averages of the 1890s. Players
won games by outwitting the other team and by trying to place
their hits. They even practiced getting hit by pitched balls. Survi-
vors think baseball was better then because shop talk was almost
continual when players spent so much time together in hotel lobbies
and on long train trips.

Defensive equipment was crude. The common fielder's glove was
hardly more than the kind of heavy glove a Northern farmer might
wear into wintry fields today. A one-handed catch was apt to cause
a sensation and be noticed in the news. Ball parks had grounds
which were little better than pastures, sometimes soft and porous,
at other times as hard as concrete. Spring-training exhibition fields
were often much worse. But the stands in the several home parks in
the major leagues were there only to seat and shelter the watchers
of baseball. Beloved shrines remaining—Wrigley Field, White Sox
Park, Tiger Stadium, Yankee Stadium, Fenway Park—and of the
new parks, that of Kansas City, show what ball parks can be when
they are built for baseball only. Nowhere but in these parks can a
spectator recapture the old-time pleasant intimacy of fan and game,
close to each other. Yankee Stadium, to be sure, isn't so very "inti-
mate," but it has no built-in abnormalities to serve the strange gods
of football.

The batters of 1915 struck out only two-thirds as often as the
batters of 1965. They swung large bats, up to three pounds in
weight. Two pounds is a common weight today. The old bat was a
club. The modern thin-handled bat has a whiplike character. The
old bat was for hitting singles and doubles. The new one is for
home runs.

All the pitchers in the league who had weak deliveries
suddenly began to have terrific stuff. . . .

—Eddie Collins**

* Raymond Bloom Bressler (1894–1966), outfielder, infielder, pitcher, nineteen
seasons, 1914–1932, Phillies, Reds, Dodgers, Cardinals. Batting average .301. Won
26, lost 31, earned-run average 3.40.
** Edward Trowbridge Collins, Sr. (1887–1951), infielder, twenty-five seasons,
1906–1930, Athletics, White Sox. Hall of Fame. Batting average .333.

Beginning about 1906 it became fashionable for pitchers to change the surface of the ball. Usually they wet a spot with spit, but some rasped a rough spot with a hidden piece of sharp or jagged metal, or with emery paper. Others polished spots on the surface with wax or talcum. When such a ball was pitched it moved in unexpected ways to make life harder for batsmen. Eddie Collins said the men who reworked the horsehide cover before 1920 were not so much pitchers as inventors. Pitchers worked faster, too. Games took less time because of a pitching manner now mostly out of style. The pitcher of 1915 felt it was good tactics to return the ball to the plate quickly in order to keep pressure on the hitter to be ready to swing the bat.

The ball was never the center of attention in baseball, as it is in most other ball games. In baseball, as Barzun said, "Man running is the force to be contained." Because a single run had great value, base stealing was important. In 1915 sixteen major-league teams averaged 164 stolen bases each. Fifty years later the twenty teams averaged seventy-two. To compare great hitters, for every five times Ty Cobb was on first base he stole second base once; for every eight times Tris Speaker was on first base he stole second base once. In a later time, Joe DiMaggio would steal second base every *seventieth* time he reached first.

This era of strong pitching, dead and doctored baseballs, primitive gloves, heavy bats, place hitting and bunts, base stealing, and playing for the single run is sometimes called the age of Cobb. It might better be named for John McGraw,* one of the most remarkable of players in the 1890s and for thirty-three years a much-copied manager. McGraw's team played a dashing, pressing game, always hoping to take the foe by surprise. It was a teachable strategy. When McGraw retired in the 1930s there were twenty-two ex-Giants managing in organized baseball. Ring Lardner thought the dead baseball gave intelligent managers and players, like McGraw and his best men, the advantage they ought to have. McGraw saw his job as getting the best out of good players. He insisted that they "think" and "anticipate"; mechanical errors could be overlooked, but not errors of judgment.

Some would argue that we tend to overrate managers. If the choice were between an average manager with great players, or a great manager with average players, we wouldn't need much time to choose the team with the great players. Nevertheless, when Babe Ruth was a rookie, managers were highly regarded for brain power.

---

* John Joseph McGraw (1873–1934), infielder, sixteen seasons, 1891–1906, Baltimore (American Association, National League, American League), Cardinals, Giants. Hall of Fame. Batting average .334. As manager of two Baltimore teams and the Giants he is seventh on the all-time won-lost list. His Giants won ten pennants.

Sportswriters compared them with military geniuses. Connie Mack was the Tall Tactician and John McGraw was the Little Napoleon (who was the Big Napoleon?). People accepted success at managing a ball club as proof of superior knowledge of psychology and of the Science of Baseball. Science had become a religion, but its novices got it mixed up with engineering and called the teams machines. In a jungle of figures of speech, conquering generals dominated baseball by directing their human machines to victory through the use of psychological warfare and the scientific principles of Inside Baseball. The workings of Inside Baseball were supposed to be beyond the ability of laymen to learn. The insiders of Inside Baseball knew that it was usually played indoors by men using typewriters.

In Ruth's early years in the major leagues, the watchers of baseball were fewer and more knowing than at any time since. The baseball crowd was a regular crowd, interested in no sport but baseball. After the First World War attendance grew, but the watchers were less intense. Although more people went to ball parks, they went less often. Today only among the bleacher regulars can we find the fan who resembles the typical fan of 1901–1917. These earlier and narrower fans knew the differing styles of their heroes in the way an art critic knows brushwork, or a music critic can recognize a brass section. They also delighted in villains, and when some great ill-tempered player came with a visiting team, joyous abuse was unconfined. It has been well said, "*Every crowd is 'against someone.'*" Heroes, of course, outnumbered villains. People want heroes. Most like them active; a few middle-class types prefer managerial heroes. Cobb, Mathewson, Wagner, and Johnson were active heroes, while McGraw would be the middle-class ideal (although nobody ever bought a ticket to see a man manage from the bench).

Young Ruth came into the major leagues when *the* great ballplayer was Ty Cobb, a hero in Detroit and a villain in the other seven cities of the American League. He was the measure of all baseball things. Leo Durocher once quoted Branch Rickey—as good a baseball scout as anyone—on five qualities to be considered in measuring a ballplayer (excluding pitchers): hits for a good batting average, hits with power, runs fast, throws well, fields competently. Fielding and hitting can improve with coaching; running and throwing are natural talents. Any player with two of the five virtues can be a major-league ballplayer. Any with four is a star. Cobb had all five.

It would have been a different game if Cobb had stayed in Georgia. Up to the First World War he personified baseball to both idolaters and ill-wishers. On the road he was a "sorehead"—an epithet thousand loved to chant in unison when he showed his frequent bad temper in an enemy park. Always appearing to play at peak ability, Cobb may not have been tense but he made the fans tense. That kind of performance is fairly called brilliant. Slender, light-skinned, with a face like a hawk under reddish-brown hair, Cobb was six feet, one inch tall and weighed 190 pounds, all of it gristle. He batted left-handed and threw right-handed.

Hitting against the spit, shine, and purposely roughened ball for sixteen of his twenty-four seasons, Cobb set the standing records for a lifetime batting average, for number of hits, and for runs scored (and stolen bases), and was twelve times the American League leader in batting. One could argue that his brilliant play was intended to glorify Cobb rather than to help the team. Often he took risks in situations when the club had more to lose than gain. But in the long run the team probably was the gainer, though that wasn't necessarily foremost in Cobb's mind from moment to moment. He was as mean as a junkyard dog. Hear what Davy Jones,* a well-liked teammate, said.

> Trouble was he had such a rotten disposition that it was damn hard to be his friend. . . . He antagonized so many people that hardly anyone would speak to him, even among his own team mates.
>
> Ty didn't have a sense of humor, see. Especially, he couldn't laugh at himself.

It has never been necessary to have a "rotten disposition" to be a great ballplayer. Cobb probably was just short of being psychotic. A historian of baseball, Harold Seymour, said it was "fortunate for baseball that he was maladjusted" or he wouldn't have been such a spectacularly great player. And great he was. Even before Cobb reached his peak, Charles Comiskey, the White Sox owner, in 1910 believed Cobb was the greatest player who had ever lived.

Cobb did not become young Ruth's model, though Ruth once said (in Detroit) that Cobb was the greatest. Ruth consciously copied Shoeless Joe Jackson,** who was, to Ruth, "the most natural and graceful hitter who ever lived." Jackson was slightly smaller than Ruth. His name Shoeless came from days of early poverty, and he may have been illiterate. At the age of thirty-three Jackson was barred from baseball for life after the 1919 World Series scandal.

* David Jefferson Jones (1880–1972), outfielder, fourteen seasons, 1901–1915, Milwaukee (American League), Browns, Cubs, Tigers, White Six, Pittsburgh Federals. Batting average .270.
** Joseph Jefferson Jackson (1887–1951), outfielder, thirteen seasons, 1908–1920, Athletics, Indians, White Sox. Batting average .356 (third highest all-time).

The life of the baseball player before the First World War, when the team was at home, was much the same as the life of any outdoor workman. But half the games, of course, were played on the road. On "getaway day" the players showered, dressed, and rode in a hack or coach to the railway station. Once aboard the train they gathered in the dining car. After dinner they settled down in the club car or Pullman cars to checkers, shop talk, reading, or cards. (Major leaguers traveled first class.) Poker was the chief pastime and leveler; a traveler with the White Sox said there was always at least one game going when the train was moving. After a few road trips even the rookie ballplayer became just another migrant worker. Even first-class passage could be tiring and boring. Trains lacked cooling systems, and many people never learned to sleep well in a Pullman berth. There being no Sunday baseball in New York or Boston, it was not unknown for a team to play in the northeastern corner of the country on Saturday, take a train to a midwestern game on Sunday, and return to the Atlantic coast for a game on Monday.

A surface difference of baseball then was clearly visible to the eye. In the past twenty-five years people have dressed brightly in ball parks. Earlier crowds wore black, dark brown, dark blue, relieved only by lighter shirts in warm weather when men took off their coats, and by the blouses and shirtwaists of the women. At a distance on a hot day the color of a baseball crowd was that of a rough salt-and-pepper tweed.

Ballplayers behaved as any sample of healthy American males would behave in the years 1869–1917. A California history professor and baseball scout said they had "all the graces and awkwardnesses of American society." There was talk of heavy drinking. Alcoholism was more often found in baseball before 1917 than after; probably all drug problems in American society were worse before the First World War than after. Very few baseball hopefuls were as poor in youth as Ruth. Most were villagers and lower-middle-class city lads. Baseball was a ladder to a more comfortable manner of living, but very few ballplayers came from the intolerably oppressed lowest tenth of the population, as some black and Latin players do today. Eccentricity was expected, not frowned on. The country did not yet have a mass culture to produce so many look-alike and think-alike young people. (Nowadays a colorful ballplayer is one who wears his cap on the side of his head, and the likes of Germany Schaefer who stole second, first, and second, in that order, in one inning, will never be seen again.)

Practically all players had as much schooling as Ruth. A surprising number had put in more school time. The Red Sox of 1909 had eight men (of seventeen) who had been to college, though not necessarily graduates. One had an engineering degree. Harry Hooper thought the college population was overrepresented in baseball. He believed that one player in five had at least gone to college for a time (in 1963 the figures were one in four of the coaches, two in five of the players, half of the managers). There was some foolishness written by diploma worshipers who thought college-tinted ballplayers would improve the language of the dugout and the manners and dress of the players. The reverse could as well be true. If college improved manners, speech, and dress (which is unbelievable), the collegians in baseball might find their polish dulling in the coarse and steamy life of professional sport.

When Ruth came, the American and National Leagues had become used to living in peace with each other. 1913 was the best box office year the sport had ever known. The Federal League hurt the owners in 1914 and 1915, but the competition helped the players by raising salaries. Business conditions were generally good. The national wealth increased by a hundred billion dollars from 1901 to 1920, and personal income was more evenly distributed than it would be later. Employment was high except for the two short depressions of 1907 and 1914, and *short* slumps do not hurt baseball attendance.

The cities had very good mass-transit systems, better than at any time since. Elevated railways, trolley cars, and subways carried crowds to ball parks cheaply and well. Suburban pioneers settled along rail lines by which they easily came back to the ball parks when they wished. Railroads promoted intercity baseball excursions at fares as low as half a cent a mile.

On the eve of the First World War baseball had the largest share of Americans' recreational spending. Its cut from 1907 to 1913 was greater than at any later time before the late 1940s. Other sports offered little competition. Boxing was disreputable. Horse racing was stained with open gambling. Football drew little attention off the campus. Basketball was not yet popular, tennis wasn't a spectator sport, and golf was not yet a rival. The serious competitor for the idle-hour dollar was the motion picture, the only mass amusement with the popularity of baseball.

The year 1915 promised well for a good pitcher working in front of the best defensive outfield ever put together. Given good health, the only question about Babe Ruth was the perennial question, whether a left-handed pitcher could succeed within a hundred yards of Fenway Park's monstrous left-field wall.

Outside the Park, 1915

BRITISH ROUT TURKS AND ASSAIL FORTS

"ABSTAIN FROM SMOKING"
DAY IN HUNGARY

ESKIMOS BECOMING THRIFTY

TELLS WHY U.S. IS HATED

AEROPLANES RAID
KARLSRUHE; 11 DIE

WOMEN RIDICULE
SECURITY LEAGUE

NEW GOLD COINS HERE

CARRANZA REJECTS
VILLA-ZAPATA OFFER

2000 BARRELS OF FLOUR
SOLD BY TELEPHONE!

GIRL OF 20 DESIGNS
A UNIVERSAL GOWN

HOPE FOR OLD WORLD
IN OUR EXAMPLE

SOCIALIST WRITERS
BLAME ROCKEFELLER

BATHTUBS TO COST MORE

FULL-TIME SCHOOLS AT SMALL COST

FILM PLAYERS CAST
INTO RIVER BY BLAST

7 · The Development of an Independent Artist (1915)

The Red Sox roster of 1915 included Babe Ruth's name. Never again did it appear on a minor-league list. Not only had he made it to the majors, but the young left-hander had moved on to the heavy side of an unbalanced league. From 1901 to 1919 four teams won the nineteen American League pennants: the Red Sox six, the Athletics six, the White Sox four, and the Tigers three. The Red Sox won the pennant in 1912, ranked fourth in 1913, and second in 1914. The player limit having been restored, Ruth was one of twenty-one 1915 regulars.

The Red Sox manager was the club's red-haired catcher, Bill Carrigan,* a quiet, well-liked, intelligent man who was self-made as a manager. Carrigan had many friends and made few enemies, even when he took over the Red Sox, a team regarded as unruly. He worked hard, thought carefully about baseball, and tried to have a relaxed and happy club. Ruth was in luck, for Carrigan was thought to be "a wise pitching coach."

The Red Sox had good material. McGraw once said the best possible American League outfield would be Cobb, Speaker, and Hooper. Carrigan had two of them. Defensively there never was an outfield better than his outfield of Speaker, Hooper, and Lewis.

Speaker** was a living example of the influence of Puritanism on American history. He might have been a Pittsburgh Pirate except for the fact that Pirate President Barney Dreyfuss lost interest in the otherwise promising minor leaguer when he learned that Speaker smoked cigarettes (he also ignored a tip on Walter Johnson

* William Francis Carrigan (1883–1969), catcher, ten seasons, 1906–1916, Red Sox, batting average .257. Manager, seven seasons, 1913–1916, 1927–1929, won 489, lost 500, two pennants, two world championships.
** Tristram E. Speaker (1888–1958), outfielder, twenty-two seasons, 1907–1928, Red Sox, Indians, Senators, Athletics. Hall of Fame. Batting average .344 (sixth on all-time list). Manager, eight seasons, 1919–1926, Indians, won 616, lost 520, one pennant, one world championship.

because it came from a cigar salesman). Speaker came to the Red Sox from the Little Rock team in 1908. Cy Young and catcher Lou Criger adopted the Texan, found him lodging, and generally eased his way. Speaker was twenty when he came up, weighed 180 pounds, and stood five feet, eleven inches tall. He had the cowboy's complexion, strong freckled hands, and bloodshot eyes that looked defective but were as sharp as an eagle's. Alfred Henry Spink, the patriarch of the *Sporting News* line, said, "He has a voice like rumbling thunder, and his softest words sound like the growl of a mastiff." Speaker read nothing but the box scores, and read them only to see that his hits were properly recorded.

This great ballplayer may have shortened his career by buying an automobile in 1910.

> . . . doubtless this same automobile has affected his batting eye. No one can guide an automobile for twenty miles without returning with a kind of squint in his eyes. . . . Speaker could easily bat for .400 if he would leave the automobile alone.
>
> —Alfred Henry Spink

Speaker was a rare and great hitter—one of the few who made three thousand hits—but today he is remembered as the measure of center-field play. He leads all outfielders in total chances, assists, putouts, and double plays.

Spink had a high opinion of right-fielder Harry Hooper,* calling him "one of the stars in the outer garden," and said Duffy Lewis** was "a worthy companion to Tris Speaker" and "has done some wonderful stunts in the fielding line. . . ."

The Red Sox infield improved in 1915 at the expense of the Athletics. Unable or unwilling to compete with Federal League salaries, Connie Mack broke up his team. He said he was short of money, that attendance was declining, but he could not bring himself to admit he was trying to economize. According to him, the players shared a bad attitude, rating their ability too high and Mack's too low. Mack's sell-off helped the Red Sox (and, as we shall see, the Yankees). After fifty-four games at shortstop with the 1915 A's, Jack Barry came to the Red Sox to play second base, spelling tired Heinie Wagner† who had missed the 1914 season because of

---

* Harry Bartholomew Hooper (1887–1974), outfielder, seventeen seasons, 1909–1925, Red Sox, White Sox, batting average .281.
** George Edward Lewis (1888–   ), outfielder, eleven seasons, 1910–1921, Red Sox, Yankees, Senators, batting average .284.
† Charles F. Wagner (1881–1943), infielder, twelve seasons, 1902–1918, Giants, Red Sox, batting average .250.

illness. Mack admired Barry and doubted that there was "an infielder in the game who can handle a ground ball like he can."

The best-remembered man of the 1915 Red Sox infield was the shortstop, Deacon Scott.* In his day he had the record for consecutive games played. Scott must have enjoyed baseball to play it so perseveringly, but he concealed his joy behind a solemn face which gave him the nickname "Deacon." Among other talents he ranked as "the smartest bridge player in baseball."

The Red Sox pitching staff also gained from Mack's cutback. All of the pitchers of the World Champion Red Sox of 1912, except Joe Wood, were gone by 1915, but the pitching was as good as ever. Boston then added the slender left-hander Herb Pennock** by purchase from Philadelphia during the 1915 season. Pennock was a Quaker of Scots-Irish ancestry and met the requirements for a proper Pennsylvanian by being descended from a seventeenth-century family that got rich in the nineteenth century (by making road-building machinery). His family wanted him to go to the University of Pennsylvania, but in prep school his chief interest was baseball. He signed with the World Champion Athletics after the season of 1911.

Pennock raised silver foxes at his country place near Kennett Square, Pennsylvania, and rode to hounds with the local hunt. He was tall and slight, and his endurance was less than Mathewson's or Johnson's, but he conserved energy by using a graceful, fluid delivery while substituting brain for muscle as much as possible. Ruth and Pennock would seem to have had little in common beyond their humanity and the fact of being left-handed pitchers, but they became fast friends for life. Ruth called him "a left-handed Mathewson."

Joe Wood,† the right-handed holdover from 1912, came into professional baseball after pitching for the high school in Ouray, Colorado, and, like Ruth, joined the Red Sox at the age of nineteen. The year 1912 was his peak: thirty-four wins, ten shutouts, and sixteen consecutive wins (paralleling Johnson's identical streak of the same year, and setting a record for the American League now shared by four pitchers). He won three games in the 1912 World Series. Never again did he have as great a year as a pitcher, so he later switched to the outfield with the Indians. With Ruth he may be one of the

---

* Lewis Everett Scott (1892–1960), infielder, thirteen seasons, 1914–1926, Red Sox, Yankees, Senators, White Sox, Reds, batting average .249.

** Herbert Jefferis Pennock (1894–1948), pitcher, twenty-two seasons, 1912–1934, Athletics, Red Sox, Yankees. Hall of Fame. Won 240, lost 162, earned-run average 3.61. World Series, won 5, lost 0.

† Joseph Wood (1889–   ), pitcher, eight seasons, Red Sox. Won 114, lost 69, earned-run average (including seven games with Indians) 2.03. Outfielder, six seasons, Indians, batting average (for all fourteen seasons) .283. His career: 1908–1922.

only two men to win as a pitcher in the World Series and to play on a world championship team in the outfield (1920).

Vean Gregg, the left-hander whose presence in 1914 made Ruth seem unnecessary, was, like Wood, fading as a pitcher and drawing an unpleasant amount of attention because of his decay. Ring Lardner created a character named "Has-Been" who said of Gregg, "We ain't got no way o' tellin' if it was just a slump or somethin' permerant."

Other Red Sox regulars of 1915 were Dick Hoblitzel, first base, Larry Gardner, third base, and pitchers Rube Foster, Ernie Shore, Dutch Leonard (the first), Carl Mays, and Ray Collins. It would take an unusual series of injuries, a train wreck, or a hotel fire to keep the 1915 Red Sox from being contenders for the pennant.

> . . . Rigid schooling in fixed rules is essential to the development of an independent artist, even if he makes no use of them, . . . it is only in this manner that freedom in workmanship can be achieved.
>
> —*Thayer's Life of Beethoven*

The 1915 Boston American League club was Ruth's final school. He had to see how polished professionals carried themselves and continually tried to improve. His five weeks with the Red Sox in 1914 had been crammed tight with new experiences: getting a car and a driver's license, having an accident, having his license suspended, meeting Helen Woodford, and proposing marriage to her. But none of these episodes was related to baseball. He had yet to settle in as a major leaguer.

First off, Ruth came up against clubhouse cliquishness which showed itself in a small way. The pitchers were loosening up, a ball tossed by Joe Wood got away from a catcher, Ruth rather crassly spread his legs and let it pass between his feet. Wood barked some resentful remark; Ruth replied in the same tone, inviting Wood off the field to defend his dignity. Carrigan enforced the peace at the moment, but Ruth had earned Wood's dislike, which meant Speaker didn't like him either, since Speaker and Wood were roommates and the closest of friends. Thereafter Speaker made it a point to ride Ruth. They were never friendly while both remained active players.

The incident was a symptom of the Red Sox condition. The club was split into two factions. Speaker and Wood headed one, Carrigan and Heinie Wagner the other. In this matter Ruth showed the kind of prudence he is never credited with: he joined Carrigan's legitimist group. Virtue and personal advantage luckily coincided. He needed Carrigan to teach him how to pitch in the American League.

Carrigan became the parent Babe Ruth had always needed. He

was only twelve years older than Ruth, but the title of manager added enough temporary age. Ruth worked hard to please him. Until early 1915 he had relied mostly on a fast ball and a change of speeds, but Carrigan taught him to study and remember batters' weaknesses and to improve his curve. Carrigan thus made him a big leaguer for which Babe Ruth was forever grateful. He always said Carrigan was his best manager. According to Carrigan, Ruth had the necessary natural talent but "he had to be disciplined to save him from . . . being his own worst enemy." Carrigan claimed he supplied only the discipline.

Ruth also learned by associating with good pitchers. He sensed their professional attitudes, saw how they forever studied opposing batters, and found them willing to help him.

During the season of 1915 it was plain to every watcher that Ruth was a good pitcher. People also saw him work at batting practice more than any pitcher they ever heard of. Carrigan had morning practices when at home early in the season. It was the only time a pitcher could get much hitting time (except on the days he pitched), and Ruth was always there with a bat. One spring day, when he was scheduled to pitch in Fenway, he took batting practice as the crowd filed in, and hit the squashy, dirty practice ball into the right-field seats. From then on, people took notice of batsman Ruth. He wasn't hard to see. At about six feet one and a half inches, Ruth stood four inches taller than the average major-league ballplayer and two inches taller than the average pitcher. Players referred to him casually as the big fellow.

At the beginning of the season, Ruth's salary was thirty-five hundred dollars, six hundred more than he had received in 1914. From April 1914 to April 1915 his successive salary figures were $600, $1,200, $1,800, $2,900, $3,500—five jumps in twelve months and almost a 600 percent rise from his Oriole starting salary.

On the eve of the 1915 season the usual forecasts appeared in print. Billy Evans, the umpire-writer, wrote a few hundred words on the prospects of the Red Sox, with special attention to the pitchers. Dutch Leonard, Rube Foster,* and Ernie Shore, identified as "secured from Baltimore in the middle of the season," had been among the top six in the American League in 1914. Joe Wood and Vean Gregg might also be valuable. He said nothing of Ruth.

By early May Ruth had won one and lost one. On May 6 he started against the Yankees in the Polo Grounds, opposing the

---

* Hubert Benjamin Leonard (1892–1952), pitcher, eleven seasons, 1913–1925, Red Sox, Tigers, won 138, lost 113, earned-run average 2.77. A later famous Leonard was also known as Dutch.

George Foster (1889–   ), pitcher, five seasons, 1913–1917, Red Sox, won 58, lost 34, earned-run average 2.35.

small right-hander Jack Warhop.* The game was scoreless for two innings. Ruth led off in the top of the third. As *The Times* reported (May 7), "He put his team in the running in the third inning by smashing a mighty homer into the upper tier of the right-field grandstand." Home runs down the foul lines into the lower stands of the Polo Grounds were cheap; one into the second deck was honest. Babe Ruth, the minor-league triples hitter, had finally managed to hit his first major-league home run.

But the Red Sox lost the game. The lead seesawed and then, in the bottom of the ninth, Danny Boone** —but let the rightly proud glove man tell it himself: "I doubled in the tying run and we went on to win the game, if I remember the score correctly, 4–3." The game went thirteen innings. Ruth pitched all the way, and very well. A New York writer was generous enough to say Ruth's play "was of high order, and it was only after the hardest kind of effort that the Yankees were able to break through his service" (*The Times*, May 7). Ruth walked three, struck out three, hit a batter, and threw a wild pitch. Only two Yankee runs were earned, the other two scoring as a result of errors by the Red Sox in trying to nail base-stealers. The Yankees had ten hits (and three stolen bases). Ruth himself had three hits in five at-bats, but failed in the clutch when he struck out in the eleventh with men on first and third and one out. The consensus was that he deserved to win and that the Red Sox catchers had lost it for him by bad throwing.

His behavior at the plate, according to Wilmot E. Giffin, was most unpitcherly. Giffin, who wrote for the *New York Journal* under the name "Right Cross," said "this ruthless Ruth" would someday play other positions in baseball. He added some verses on Ruth's bad manners, which began with these four lines:

A Social Error

When a pitcher meets a pitcher,
Should a pitcher clout?
When a pitcher meets a pitcher,
Shouldn't he fan out?

Heywood Broun was one of the sportswriters who watched Ruth's first game in New York. He remarked that he was "flagrantly left handed" and was "practically the only left-handed pitcher in the country not called Rube." Fred Lieb was another professional sports witness. The baseball writers of New York represented more than

---

* John Milton Warhop (born Wauhop) (1884–1960), pitcher, eight seasons, 1908–1915, Yankees, won 68, lost 94, earned-run average 3.09.
** Lute Joseph Boone (1890–   ), infielder, five seasons, 1913–1918, Yankees, Pirates, batting average .209. (Sometimes called Luke Boone.)

half a dozen dailies, plus wire services and feature syndicates. Ball-players had a better chance to get publicity in New York. What happened in baseball happened more loudly in New York.

Having finally made the home-run column of the official statistics, Ruth could also take pleasure in his batting average. Before the match with Warhop he was hitting .286. On May 6 he raised his average to .417. It never again fell as low as .286 that summer.

When the season was a month old Ruth had five pitching starts, with one victory and two losses. He and Carrigan could put up with that record for a moment. But the ratio of eighteen walks and nine strikeouts was intolerable. By the end of the season the rookie and his tutor had brought the ratio to an acceptable figure, 85 walks and 112 strikeouts.

> See how much fun this game is when you guys score runs?
>   —Jim Brosnan

Re-enter Warhop. Ruth pitched against him again in the Polo Grounds on June 2. Again in his first time at bat (second inning, two outs, man on first) Ruth lofted one into the second deck, ten feet farther than last time. Boston went on to win 7–1. Ruth gave up only five hits. He had now hit two home runs and was having fun. He hit another home run in St. Louis on July 21, by far the most sensational big-league hit he had yet made. Big Bill James* started for the Browns (and probably wished he hadn't). The *Sporting Life* carried the story:

> St. Louis, July 21—George Ruth hit the longest home run ever witnessed at the local American League park. Then he doubled twice and brought [in] three of the four runs with which Boston took the first of a seven-game series with St. Louis. Ruth's home run in the third went clear over the right-field bleachers across Grand Avenue and landed on the far sidewalk.

The ball did more than land on the sidewalk. It bounced off and smashed the display window of an automobile dealership. The St. Louis right-field fence was 315 feet away; this hit could be esti-mated at about 410 to 420 feet. And with a ball that said "punk" when hit, instead of "pock" as it says today.

The Red Sox found their groove that summer. As a team they led the American League in no category except games won. They didn't even have a twenty-game winner in a league that had five twenty-

---

* William Henry James (1888–1942), pitcher, eight seasons, 1911–1919, Indians, Browns, Tigers, Red Sox, White Sox, won 67, lost 71, earned-run average 3.20. Height 6'4".

game winners. Yet the Boston team finished two and a half games ahead of the Tigers and nine and a half ahead of the third-place White Sox. Opponents said the Red Sox did it with fielding, but the team ranked only second in fielding. Cobb explained it more precisely when he said Boston won the pennant by protecting narrow leads in late innings with shining defensive play, as when, according to Ruth, Duffy Lewis made a number of dumbfounding barehand outfield catches.

A four-game series between the Tigers and Red Sox at Fenway Park beginning September 16 settled the 1915 pennant chase, with a free Ty Cobb tantrum thrown in as a customers' bonus. Because Boston was angry at Cobb for rough play in an August series, the police assigned a special detail to protect him. Nevertheless he started a fight with Carl Mays, and the police had to escort him from the park for his own safety when the umpires threw him out. The Red Sox took three of the four games, Ruth winning one over Hooks Dauss,* 3–2. 1915 was a humiliating year for the Tigers. They fruitlessly won a hundred games—to Boston's 101. (On the 154-game schedule only the 1954 Yankees managed to surpass Tiger frustration; they finished second with 103 wins.)

In the World Series of 1915 between the Red Sox and the Phillies Ruth had little to do.

The Series opened with two games in tiny Baker Bowl in Philadelphia and then moved to Boston for two games. If more were needed they would be played in Philadelphia. For the second straight year the whole country had telegraphic links with the ball parks and everyone, as Thomas Wolfe wrote, had "a vision of the misty golden and October towers of the terrific city" where the championship was decided. The Boston games were played in new Braves Field, larger than Fenway Park, which had opened in August with a crowd of more than forty-six thousand.

For a few days it seemed there might not be a Series because of a quarrel over the allotment of tickets. In Boston a fan club called the Royal Rooters periodically marched from their favorite saloon to Fenway Park at the hour of the opening of the gates, singing as they went—usually the song "Tessie" from the musical comedy *The Silver Slipper*. At Series time they demanded four hundred seats in Philadelphia. All tickets had been allotted and sold. Negotiators feverishly compromised by taking two hundred of the tickets set aside for the National Commission (the governing body of baseball) and selling them to the Royal Rooters. The Bostonian fan club proudly marched into Baker Bowl singing "Tessie" and "The Song of Frightfulness," under direction of their leader, Boston's mayor

---

* George August Dauss (1889–1963), pitcher, fifteen seasons, 1912–1926, Tigers, won 223, lost 182, earned-run average 3.32.

"Honey Fitz" Fitzgerald, maternal grandfather of President John F. Kennedy.

After losing the first game by two runs, the Red Sox won the next four games by one run each. Foster, Shore, and Leonard did all of the pitching.

Although Ruth didn't pitch he got his winner's share, $3,780.80, which more than doubled his pay for 1915; in eighteen months his rate of annual income had risen 1,200 percent.

Ruth had one time at bat in the Series, as a pinch-hitter in the ninth inning of the first game, facing Grover Cleveland Alexander. Alexander had won thirty-one games in 1915, including twelve shutouts, and had held 1,274 batters to 250 hits for a season batting average against him of .196. When Ruth came in he had an eye for the close right-field fence and pulled a hard smash on the ground directly down the line. But the Philadelphia first baseman smothered it for an unassisted putout.

Carrigan didn't need Ruth to pitch in the Series. He needed right-handed pitching. The Phillies had only one regular left-handed batter. Carrigan planned to use his pitchers in the following order: Shore, Leonard, Foster, Shore, Leonard, Ruth, Shore. The Series didn't last long enough to get to Ruth's turn. He showed no impatience or annoyance. When it came to getting into a game he had other resources. Half an hour after one of the Fenway Park victories a reporter saw him in a vacant lot about a quarter of a mile from the ball park playing baseball with a group of boys.

Having made over seven thousand dollars in 1915, Ruth consulted some Xaverian Brothers about an idea he had. They also approved it, and he put up the money for his father to open a new bar and grill at the corner of Eutaw and Lombard Streets in Baltimore. Ruth Senior stayed in business there until his death.

> He was like a damn animal. He had that instinct. They know when it's going to rain, things like that. Nature, that was Ruth!
>
> —Rube Bressler

By the end of the season Ruth had found a home in the American League, as shown by the fact that opposing bench jockeys all knew him as the Big Monkey. He was relaxed on and off the field. The ball went farther off his bat than the bats of others, and people were beginning to believe that if he played every day he would be up there with the home-run leaders. (The home-run record in the American League in 1915 was seven.)

Because he batted too few times he couldn't qualify for a rating in the league batting championship, but he hit .315 in ninety-two at-bats which otherwise would have ranked him fourth in the league. His slugging average—which is the total of bases divided by the number of times at bat, and shows power if a player has it—was far above any other at .576. (The highest official slugging percentage was .491.) His twenty-nine hits included ten doubles, a triple, and four home runs. Thus more than half were for extra bases. That is not the way pitchers usually hit. The pitchers of sixty years ago hit no better than the pitchers of today. Yet Ruth was the second best Red Sox batter, for average, and the best slugger in all of baseball.

Was this man really a *pitcher*?

> It is a difficult task to get to first base safely in the face of effectual fire from a first-class club "battery" backed up by good support in the field.
> —Chadwick, *The Art of Batting* (1886)

The verb *pitch* has a small but interesting chapter of its own in the history of language. Without getting in too deep we may suppose that the word came into baseball when the only lawful delivery was underhand, as in pitching pennies and horseshoes. Ballplayers now distinguish between *pitching* and *throwing*. In pitching, today, one launches the ball with one of several motions which end with cracking the arm like a whip. In throwing, the arm aims the ball as in throwing darts. (Some pitchers call this *pushing*.) Throwing is all right for warming up, but in a game it is proof that the pitcher is tired.

There are two basic styles of true pitching. In one the leg is raised high in front and the pitching arm drops low behind. By bringing the raised leg down and the dropped arm up, the pitcher rotates arms and legs like spokes on a wheel and hurls the ball as if from a catapult. The pitching arm starts to move like a lever and ends like a whip. In the other basic style the pitcher gets his force entirely from the arm movement, pulling the arm around with muscle power until it becomes a lever itself. A coach once called this style the ripple-arm. How old that term is the writer doesn't know.

No modern pitching style is healthy. The slow overhand toss and the straight underhand pitch are the natural ways of throwing a missile. Pitching, as practiced since 1884 when a sidearm delivery became legal, is bad for the arm's joints, tendons, and cartilage.

Ruth was a ripple-arm pitcher, so far as we can tell from studying old photographs. George Sisler,* who had an engineering degree, said Ruth's delivery was a fling, from which it is clear that Ruth had

---

* George Harold Sisler (1893–1973), first baseman, fifteen seasons, 1915–1930, Browns, Senators, Braves. Hall of Fame. Batting average .340.

a quick motion of the arm rather than the accelerating arc of the rotating catapult.

Babe Ruth had a good fast ball, a good curve, a change of speeds, control, and knowledge of the batters. He used staple pitching techniques and he also, as Danny Boone put it, "kept the batters loose." When Carrigan was catching Ruth he would tell the batter when to get ready to go down. In one Red Sox-Yankee game of 1915 Ruth had a no-hitter into the sixth inning. He decked Boone twice in three pitches. As Boone said, "We had words. Then I broke it up with a two-base hit."

No one who batted against the young Red Sox left-hander has reported his use of a freak delivery—no screw, knuckle, fork, spit, emery, or palm ball. As the aggressive batter George Burns* later said, "He didn't need any." He simply came down overhand with what for some reason is called a three-quarter pitch (that is, if the top of his head is twelve o'clock, his arm passed through 1:30), using no deceptively jerky motion. Before the ball reached the plate his feet were on the ground side by side and he was in a position to field the ball, if necessary. Ruth was a very strong young man, and batters could not look forward to getting to him after he tired. Zeb Terry** said "he was strong enough," and Burns thought "he could pitch all day." If Burns had Walter Johnson and Babe Ruth on his team in a World Series, "The Babe would be my second choice, Walter Johnson my first. . . . That's all I would need in a four out of seven—they could pitch every other day." None of the surviving hitters thought he took pleasure in throwing at them. Sam Vick† said Ruth "figured him [the batter] as a professional ballplayer that could take care of himself."

As a pitcher, Ruth's fielding was good but not brilliant. Infielder-critics held him to a pretty high standard which he could not quite meet. Del Pratt,‡ a very competent critic, thought him "a little awkward. For a big man, would say good, but not quick in moving." A shortstop who played against him said he would have made a good first baseman, which sounds a little haughty.

For firsthand information on Ruth as a pitcher the writer con-

---

* George Henry Burns (1893–   ), first-baseman, sixteen seasons, 1914–1929, Tigers, Athletics, Indians, Red Sox, Yankees, batting average .307. An aggressive man at the plate, he was the batter hit-by-pitcher most often in 1914, 1918, 1919.

** Zebulon Alexander Terry (1891–   ), shortstop, seven seasons, 1916–1922, White Sox, Braves, Pirates, Cubs, batting average .260.

† Samuel Bruce Vick (1895–   ), outfield, five seasons, 1917–1921, Yankees, Red Sox, batting average .248.

‡ Derrill Burnham Pratt (1888–   ), infielder, thirteen seasons, 1912–1924, Browns, Yankees, Red Sox, Tigers, batting average .292. Led the American League in runs batted in with 103 in 1916, and in putouts at second base many times.

sulted fourteen men who went to bat in the American League at least two hundred times in one of the years 1915, 1916, or 1917, the years when Ruth was a full-time pitcher. (One of these fourteen, curiously enough, happened never to hit against Ruth.) The last request to each was to draft an imaginary scouting report on pitcher Babe Ruth, as if he would be an opponent in a forthcoming World Series. Several of these deserve publication.

DANNY BOONE: He is a good strong fast ball pitcher, good control, average curve, not much of a change up, free with a duster, and courage to back it all up. Not too good a fielder and an exceptionally strong hitter. Should not pitch him inside.

JACK GRANEY: Great competitor. Good stuff, fast ball, and curve. Great hitter.

LARRY KOPF:* Hit natural and hit the first good ball. He throws a fast ball, curve, and change of pace. Just a natural guy, nothing seems to bother him.

SAM VICK: I would say Ruth is a big strong pitcher with a fast ball, good curve, good change of pace, and good control. With that animal instinct telling him what a batter could and could not hit and with good control he worked the weak spots.

GEORGE SISLER: A great pitcher, good fast ball (alive), good curve and a good control. Knows how to pitch. A good competitor. . . . A natural.

This writer bows to all of these helpful, friendly, and wise players, but likes this report best:

SAM RICE:** Be ready to hit fast ball or curve, as he don't waste many.

Ruth had stuff and control, the natural physical talents that can't be taught. He had the craft to know what stuff to use and when. He had the poise to be able to use it regardless of pressure. Yes, this man was a *pitcher.*

By 1915 Babe Ruth had more money than any seven Baltimore cousins could make in a year. His appetite was good, and he wanted some fun to make up for fourteen years of delayed ripening in

* William Lorenz Kopf (1890–   ), shortstop, ten seasons, 1913–1923, Indians, Athletics, Reds, Braves, batting average .249.
** Edgar Charles Rice (1890–1974), outfielder, twenty seasons, 1915–1934, nineteen with Senators, one with Indians. Hall of Fame. Batting average .322.

St. Mary's School. He not only wished to learn what ballplayers did on the field, he was curious to know what they did after the game. In Boston this "born playboy" was like a fat pony let into tall oats. Ruth the Baltimore waterfront slob more often dominated Ruth the Xaverian Brother.

The reader should not prepare himself for a list of wild parties, drinking bouts, and specific orgiastic behavior. Of Ruth's vices we have only some traffic records and some generalized remarks by his second wife, sportswriters, and a few ballplayers, none of whom offers names, sites, or dates. We cannot even list the places he lived (no George H. Ruth in city directories 1914–1920; no auto registrations preserved from that remote time). There *are* reports of court actions following abuses of automobiles. Reckless driving is the positively proved vice of Babe Ruth. His other sins are known only from general descriptions.

Except for the simplehearted Christianity the boy Ruth picked up from the example of the Xaverian Brothers, he had no view of the world. When he emerged from his drawn-out boyhood in 1914 and 1915 he was, like most boys, a self-centered seeker of glee and zest. The delight of the moment moved him to action. (Luckily for his constitution, baseball gave him more glee, delight, and zest than did anything else.) The easiest type of playboy to tolerate is the celebrator. Ruth was a celebrator; John L. Sullivan was another. In Ruth's case there was so much to celebrate! But his parties glorified calories rather than whiskey. With his great appetite Ruth never dallied with food, and he was convinced that much beer went well with much food.

Seeking pleasure in food and in drink is not necessarily bad for a ballplayer. He can't play well when he is tense. Therefore he doesn't try to stay in peak condition for seven months. The playboy ballplayer hurts himself chiefly by losing sleep. It was claimed that rookie Ruth ate too much. Harry Hooper said that when some of the Red Sox were patrolling a city on the road, Ruth would flag them down to a stop, eat half a dozen hot dogs, drink half a dozen bottles of soda pop (all were six-ounce bottles then), "give a few big belches," and then shout, "Okay, boys, let's go." This would take the edge off his appetite for a couple of hours. In his defense one can only say he was not unique, and he *was* still growing.

> Between games I stuffed myself at the clubhouse lunch table. Two roast beef sandwiches, two cups of soup, a bottle of grape soda, three dill pickles, one olive, and a bar of ice cream. Then, plugging a chew of tobacco into my mouth I went, burping, to the bullpen, comfortable in

the knowledge that if I had to pitch in the second game I'd
die with a full stomach.

—Jim Brosnan

On the road we may suppose Ruth was easily bored. A traveling
major-league ballplayer has nothing to do for himself except pack,
unpack, tie his laces, button his clothes, and play baseball. Every
other detail is taken care of for him. All his games were played in
daylight, so Ruth made it a point to explore the world of the night
which was a foreign continent to a young fellow from St. Mary's
Industrial School. A man of much broader interest than his couldn't
expect to find a Shaw play or a symphony concert which synchro-
nized with every idle hour. On the other hand, a bar and a friendly
woman were always available.

Babe and Helen Ruth had a dimly glimpsed Red Sox social life in
Boston. They bowled regularly with other Red Sox couples and saw
much of the Jack Barrys. Mrs. Barry had been a schoolteacher.
We know no more. Perhaps she saw the obvious: George and Helen
had a lot to learn.

There was no malice in Ruth's pleasure hunt. He was not one
who sought evil. His way was the abuse of good things. His sins
were of the heart, not the spirit, and his urban hotel and Pullman
life would make it easy to fall into a pattern of self-gratification.

Nevertheless there lingers a gnawing suspicion that the saga of
Playboy Ruth includes a deal of myth. The group photograph of the
World Champions of 1915 shows Ruth lean and tough and with no
pudginess at all.

Ruth made no great publicity splash in 1915. All pitchers that
year were in the shadow of Pete Alexander* who pitched twelve
shutouts and did many other marvelous things. In the American
League young Ruth, who won eighteen and lost eight with an
earned-run average of 2.44, ranked fourth in percentage of wins,
behind his Red Sox teammates Wood, Foster, and Shore, who were
one-two-three, and show why the Red Sox won the pennant. Among
fifty pitchers who worked in two hundred or more innings, Ruth was
twentieth in earned-run average.

Spalding's Official Guide, 1916, sketched young Ruth at some
length, concluding that he was "a hitter of no mean ability" and "a
left-handed boxman" who "has ability in that position." Ruth had
played with spirit and fire. He was well known now. If Judge
Kenesaw Mountain Landis had ruled that baseball was in violation
of the antitrust laws, as claimed by the Federal League in a case he

---

* Grover Cleveland Alexander (1887–1950), pitcher, twenty seasons, 1911–1930,
Phillies, Cubs, Cardinals. Hall of Fame. Won 373, lost 208, earned-run average 2.56.

was hearing, there would have been a scramble for Ruth's signature on a contract.

THE ACCUMULATED BATTING FIGURES
BABE RUTH'S MAJOR-LEAGUE CAREER
1914, 1915

at bat: 102
hits: 31
home runs: 4
runs batted in: 23
batting average: .304

8 · The King of the Fenway Hill
(1916-1917)

The confident winning pitcher is king of the hill. To him breathing is a pleasure, eating is not just a habit. Smiling is easier, pitching is fun.

—Jim Brosnan

With the Federal League going broke and unable to start the 1916 season, there was to be a change in the Red Sox that, for awhile, alarmed some players. The salaries of a few had been raised to match the bait of the Federals. Now Lannin began to sharpen his pruning shears. During the winter he cut Tris Speaker's and Joe Wood's salaries so sharply they could never be content in Boston, and Speaker was dealt to Cleveland. Wood was a holdout through 1916. (Ruth's salary remained at thirty-five hundred, its 1915 figure.)

To Ruth and other pitchers, Speaker's departure was distressing, because it meant they no longer had the support of the greatest of center-fielders. When the season started Boston alternated Tillie Walker and Chick Shorten* in center field. The pitchers felt sorry for themselves for awhile. Ruth later said the memory of the lush winners' share of the 1915 World Series pulled him together.

Ruth proved his excellence by twice beating Walter Johnson in 1916, 1–0. (Johnson never beat Ruth in a 1–0 game.) On June 1, the day of the ceremony raising the 1915 pennant, Ruth beat Johnson on a three-hitter. Johnson gave the Red Sox four hits and a run. The Senators hit but one ball out of the infield, and no Senator got past second base. A Boston cartoonist celebrated the game with

---

*Clarence William Walker (1889–1959), outfielder, thirteen seasons, 1911–1923, Senators, Browns, Red Sox, Athletics, batting average .281, league home-run champion (tied with Ruth) 1918, 11.

Charles Henry Shorten (1892–1965), outfielder, eight seasons, 1915–1924, Red Sox, Tigers, Browns, Reds, batting average .275.

a cartoon in which Ruth had a perfectly round head, which was a correct rendering of Ruth's anatomy.

On August 15 Ruth repeated, but the job was harder.

RUTH OUTPITCHES JOHNSON

Red Sox Score Only Run of Game
With Senators in Thirteenth
—*New York Times*

It was a game of endurance. Johnson weakened first. After scattering four hits in twelve innings he let the Red Sox hit safely three times in the thirteenth.

Surprisingly, Ruth appeared to be declining as a hitter. He batted more often than in 1915, but hit one less home run and his average was lower. Carrigan, however, used his most effective pitcher as a pinch-hitter twenty-two times. During the season Ruth had looked enviously at the roof of the Polo Grounds where Shoeless Joe Jackson had hit the only home run ever hit all the way out. In midsummer, when he got the pitch he wanted, Ruth hit one over the roof at the same place. People who saw both hits said Ruth's was longer than Jackson's.

The Red Sox won fewer games in 1916 than in 1915, but finished two games ahead of the White Sox and four ahead of the Tigers. They gave up fewer runs than any other team, had the best fielding average, and made the fewest errors. Red Sox pitchers had twenty-three shutouts. It was a defenders' year. Not one of the Red Sox was among the top four in the league in any of the important batting categories. But their pitching was peerless.

> There is a world series with every revolution of the earth around the sun. And in between, what varied pleasures long drawn out!
>
> —Jacques Barzun

The Red Sox met the Brooklyn Superbas (yes, Superbas) in the 1916 World Series. Home games were again at Braves Field.

Metropolitan New York was gloomy about the chances of the Superbas hitting Red Sox pitching. It was believed that Ruth, Shore, Foster, Mays, and Leonard were "ready to tear through any team which the National League may send against them."

Shore won the first game on October 7, 6–5, but needed help from Mays* in the ninth when Brooklyn scored four times. They

* Carl William Mays (1891–1971), pitcher, fifteen seasons, 1915–1929, Red Sox, Yankees, Reds, Giants, won 207, lost 126, earned-run average 2.92.

had the bases full when Mays got them out with the help of a great fielding play by Deacon Scott. The Superbas had by no means disgraced themselves.

Ruth, "the Southern youngster," pitched the second game. The Sunday ban on baseball postponed the game until Monday the 9th, a moist, muggy day with the kind of low, gray, cloudy sky that helps pitchers. Brooklyn opened the game with a run in the top of the first. Hy Myers* looped a slow pitch into right center between Hooper and Walker. It should have been a single, but Hooper fell down and Walker slipped as he started for the ball, which rolled to the fence while Myers scored an inside-the-park home run. Boston came back with a run in the third when Scott tripled. Pinch Thomas** hit the first pitch on the ground to Cutshaw,† but Scott had to hold third while Thomas was thrown out. Ruth, next up, hit a bounding smash to Cutshaw who juggled it long enough for Scott to score before he could throw Ruth out. Ruth had a run batted in and, more important, a tied-up game.

Ruth struggled at the plate thereafter as the game went on and on in gathering gloom, with the score 1–1. He struck out in the fifth, eighth, and tenth innings (twice with men on base). In the twelfth, with two outs and a runner on first, he cockily dragged a bunt but was thrown out.

The Red Sox won it in twilight in the fourteenth when pinch-runner Mike McNally‡ scored from second on Del Gainor's§ single to right. Brooklyn had six hits, Boston seven. It was so dark in the last inning that some thought the fourteenth inning shouldn't have been played.

Babe Ruth had won the only World Series game he had pitched and set the still-standing record for winning the longest World Series game ever played. He had also pitched thirteen scoreless innings in a row. As art, his pitching was masterful. He walked three and struck out four, throwing but 147 pitches in fourteen complete innings—forty-seven strikes, fifty-four balls, six hits, twenty-three grounders, twelve flies, and five unplayable fouls. The most pitches in one inning were sixteen, the fewest, eight. In six of the innings he needed only nine pitches each.

---

* Henry Harrison Myers (1889–1965), outfielder, fourteen seasons, 1909–1925, Brooklyns, Cardinals, Reds, batting average .281.

** Chester Davird Thomas (1888–1953), catcher, ten seasons, 1912–1921, Red Sox, Indians, batting average .237.

† George Cutshaw (1887–1973), infielder, twelve seasons, 1912–1923, Brooklyns, Pirates, Tigers, batting average .265.

‡ Michael Joseph McNally (1893–1965), infielder, ten seasons, 1915–1925, Red, Sox, Yankees, Senators, batting average .238.

§ Delos Charles Gainor (1886–1947), first-baseman, ten seasons, 1909–1922, Tigers, Red Sox, Cardinals, batting average .272.

Sherry Smith* of Brooklyn obviously pitched well too.

The Red Sox took the Series four games to one, but Ruth did not appear a second time. Brooklyn fielded badly, making thirteen errors as compared with Boston's six. The winners' share was $3910.26 to each of what the *New York Times* rather thoughtlessly called "the ruthless Red Sox." One of the most respected of New York sportswriters, Hugh S. Fullerton, got broody and said the World Series should be abolished because the National League was too weak. (Fullerton knew baseball; he had correctly predicted the winning team in each of the five games.)

The World Series ended on Thursday, October 12. On the following Sunday most of the Red Sox played a barnstorming exhibition game against a semi-professional team in New Haven. Lannin had given permission and then withdrew it on Saturday. Such games were against a clause in the standard major-league contract which prohibited pennant winners from playing postseason games. The players nevertheless decided the arrangements were too far along to cancel. To punish the Red Sox, the National Commission withheld their World Series emblems—diamond-studded miniature gold baseballs worth about a hundred dollars each. The Commission also levied cash fines, but never said how much.

Quite apart from this episode, Manager Bill Carrigan said he was going to retire from baseball and go home to Lewiston, Maine. Carrigan had banking and motion-picture interests in Maine of more lasting value to him than baseball. Jack Barry succeeded him as manager. Carrigan's leaving shook Ruth. He had leaned on Jack Dunn, on Wild Bill Donovan, and, most of all, on Bill Carrigan. Ruth was twenty-one; Barry was a bowling friend of only thirty years. Could Ruth make it without an older man's support?

> **A young business executive gets no more pleasure seeing a title on his door than a young pitcher feels winning his twentieth game of the season.**
>
> **—Jim Brosnan**

Ruth's year was superb. At twenty-one years of age, in his second full season, he won twenty-three and lost twelve. His earned-run average of 1.75 was the best in the league. No Red Sox pitcher outdid him. Ruth's rankings among the record-setting American League pitchers of 1916 make an enviable list: first in earned-run average, shutouts, and fewest hits per nine innings; second in victories and innings pitched; third in winning percentage and strikeouts; fourth

---

* Sherrod Malone Smith (1891–1949), pitcher, fourteen seasons, 1911–1927, Pirates, Brooklyns, Indians, won 113, lost 118, earned-run average 3.32.

in complete games. If we score the pitching leaders as in a track meet, giving points for first, second, and third, the 1916 American League pitchers rank like this: Johnson 15, Ruth 13½, Shawkey 7½, Harry Coveleski and Cicotte* 6 each, trailed by a dozen more.

The American League was strong that year. The Federal League jumpers were back, and the First World War draft was yet to come. To the names of Shawkey, Harry Coveleski, and Cicotte can be added those of others to make a noble roster: Stan Coveleski, Red Faber, Pennock, Eddie Plank, and Big Ed Walsh. What did they have in common? Each pitched in the American League in 1916, each ranked below Ruth, and each has been elected to the Baseball Hall of Fame.

Ruth set an American League record in 1916 which still stands: most shutouts in one season by a left-handed pitcher, nine. He also got his first New York headline—in *The Times* of December 10: RUTH LED PITCHERS—the reference being to earned-run averages. A week later *The Times* rated him best in the league, all things considered: "Babe Ruth of Boston carried off the pitching honors of the league." A good measure of his success was the batting average of hitters opposing him, .199.

For a pitcher, Ruth's batting was very good but much below his earlier standards. He led the Red Sox in slugging percentage (.419) and that is all. He batted more often, hit only three home runs, and batted in fifteen runs as compared with twenty-one in 1915. His lifetime batting average slumped.

THE ACCUMULATED BATTING FIGURES
BABE RUTH'S MAJOR-LEAGUE CAREER
1914–1916

at bat: 238
hits: 68
home runs: 7
runs batted in: 38
average: .286

Every fan in that city considers that ball club his own, and the real owner is but [his] steward.

—Peter S. Craig

---

* James Robert Shawkey (1890–   ), pitcher, fifteen seasons, 1913–1927, Athletics, Yankees, won 196, lost 152, earned-run average 3.09.

Harry Frank Coveleski (1886–1950), pitcher, nine seasons, 1907–1918, Phillies, Reds, Tigers, won 81, lost 57, earned-run average 2.39.

Edward Victor Cicotte (1884–1969), pitcher, fourteen seasons, 1905–1920, Tigers, Red Sox, White Sox, won 207, lost 147, earned-run average 2.37, barred for life after 1919 World Series scandal.

The theatrical producer Harry Frazee, aged thirty-six, with a silent partner from Philadelphia, bought the Red Sox on November 1 for a price somewhere between four hundred and seven hundred thousand dollars, most of it to be paid in the future. At the age of seventeen Frazee had managed the Peoria team of the Western League and then bought the club. By 1916 he was a New Yorker and owned theaters in Chicago and New York. Because the top pay for actors was about eight thousand dollars, Frazee believed that would be a good ceiling for ballplayers. Edward G. Barrow, president of the International League, said Frazee "was a colorful and agreeable man, a good companion, and a good friend to me. He was better gaited to the theatrical business, however, than to baseball." That is the highest praise of Frazee the student of Boston baseball will ever find.

Frazee and his manager Jack Barry made some pitching changes early in 1917, selling the sore-armed Joe Wood to Cleveland as an outfielder, and sending Vean Gregg, the once-great left-hander, to Providence. In spring-training exhibitions the Red Sox and Brooklyn renewed the previous October rivalry. Brooklyn had the better of it, but Ruth worked nine innings against them in two games and gave up but three hits while his pitching colleagues were pounded painfully and lost both games.

Outside the Park, 1917

GEORGIA ACCEPTS BONE DRY LAW

DENIES GERMANS TOOK FRENCH RELIEF FOOD

DOUBLE-BRIMMED HATS COMING IN

WOULD BAR ALIEN TEACHERS

TORPEDO MISSED BY 20 FEET

WON'T PROMOTE PACIFIST

RED CROSS BANDAGES POISONED BY SPIES

BIBLE FOR LITERACY TEST

PUSH KINDERGARTEN BILL

SUFFRAGE FIGHT RENEWED

SERMONS BROUGHT UP TO DATE
TO LINK THE KAISER WITH THE
DEVIL AS AN ENEMY ALIEN

GINGHAM FROCKS AGAIN IN HIGH FAVOR

CARDINAL GIBBONS OPPOSES
NATION-WIDE PROHIBITION

ARREST GERMANS WITH 2-LB. BOMB

PARIS FEATURES BIG HATS

YALE ALUMNI WORK FOR 'DRY' REUNIONS

FOUR MILLION BOND BUYERS

QUEER PREDICAMENT OF THE MAYOR OF CHICAGO

HOW PATRIOTIC IS THE GERMAN-AMERICAN PRESS?

FIVE YEARS FOR WOMAN
WHO DENOUNCED DRAFT

Aggression thus may lead to success in sports, a successful business career, a one-way trip to San Quentin, or frequent trips to a psychiatrist.

—Arnold R. Beisser

Umpires are most vigorous when defending their miscalls.

—Jim Brosnan

The summer of 1917 saw the only outright unseemly act Ruth had yet committed on a baseball field. It brought him his second New York headline: SLUGS UMPIRE, INDEFINITELY SUSPENDED. What Ruth did was also the overture to a pitching performance now listed in the most respected group of entries in the record book.

Clarence B. Owen, a Chicago florist, better remembered as Brick Owen, the American League umpire, was behind the plate in the first game of a double-header between the Red Sox and Senators at Boston on June 23. Ruth started for Boston and walked the first batter on four pitches, three of which he thought should have been called strikes. After the fourth ball the Baltimore waterfront slob took over from Xaverian Brother George and loudly advised Owen to sleep more at night in order to be awake during the day. Owen recommended silence, or he (Owen) would put him (Ruth) out of the game. Ruth said that if Owen put him out, he'd slug him. Owen then ordered Ruth off the field and half turned away so that Ruth's fist, aimed for the jaw, caught him behind the ear. Barry and other players swarmed over Ruth and led him off the field. Ban Johnson, president of the American League, fined Ruth a hundred dollars and suspended him for ten days.

A typical pitcher believes four out of five *good* pitches should lead to outs. Here, in Ruth's opinion, were three good pitches called balls.

Umpire-phobia is worse in the early innings of a game because a bad call then can divert the whole course of events disastrously. On the other hand, as Clyde King said when he was pitching coach of the Reds, "The worst thing a pitcher can do is to get mad, at himself or anything else. It ruins his concentration." Nevertheless, pitchers (and other players, of course) often do explode. They can't help being what is called temperamental. No soprano ever had to work under the conditions facing a visiting pitcher who loads the bases in the bottom of the ninth, nor do crowds often shout for the failure of the pianist in a concert hall. All things considered, ballplayers discipline themselves pretty well. Before the First World War a single run seemed more valuable than it does now; a single ruling leading to a single run might well decide a game. We still see umpire baiting with ten-run leads, but that is cultural lag.

The umpire, to be sure, takes a different view. Several are said to be the author of the remark that the job requires the umpire to be perfect on the first day and to improve thereafter. And the plate umpire has a very tiring job, being liable for over two hundred quick judgments in nine innings (but Brick Owen had only to make four calls to shake down the thunder).

A few years before Ruth's outburst a player had been fined and suspended for the remainder of the season after striking an umpire. Just two weeks earlier John McGraw struck umpire Bill (Lord) Byron while leaving the field after a game. John K. Tener, president of the National League, fined McGraw five hundred dollars and suspended him for sixteen days. McGraw added oral aggravation and Tener, after another hearing, added another thousand to the fine. In two later cases, players who struck umpires received one-year suspensions. Ruth got off lightly.

For the Red Sox, and for Ernie Shore in particular, Ruth's flare-up ended happily. Shore replaced Ruth. The runner on first was thrown out trying to steal, and Shore allowed no one else to reach first base, thus forever enshrining himself in the list of eleven pitchers who have pitched perfect games, from Lee Richmond in 1880 to Catfish Hunter in 1968.

After his brief suspension Ruth's sharpness was still there. On July 11 he pitched a one-hitter against Detroit, winning 1–0 and putting Boston into first place; he also had two hits in three times at bat, one a triple. He walked four and struck out eight, getting five of the strikeouts when runners were in scoring position on second base.

By this time Ruth was such a confident pitcher that he did not care to go down the list of opposing batters before a game to sketch his proposed tactics. Instead he would give random answers with a solemn face until the inquirer realized it was a put-on.

Boston fell short of the pennant in 1917, finishing second, nine games behind the White Sox. The Red Sox again led the league in fielding and of all teams allowed their opponents the fewest runs. The pitching was great, with Ruth 24–13 and Mays 22–9, but the White Sox pitchers were greater. Ruth was first in complete games, second in games won, third in innings pitched and in fewest hits per nine innings. An entirely creditable record it was, and well worth his five-thousand-dollar salary.

There was no systematic selection of the outstanding players at the time, but the secretary of the Giants, who was also custodian of the official records, annually chose an all-star team. For 1917 he picked Eddie Cicotte as American League pitcher, because of his earned-run average of 1.53. (Ruth ranked ninth with 2.01.)

1917 was the first year in which no one had pinch-hit for Ruth. Only five players have ever had that distinction: Duffy Lewis, 1914

(Ruth's first game); Hick Cady and Del Gainor, 1915; Swede Henriksen, 1916; and Bobby Veach, 1925.* Ruth's hitting was much better than in 1916, although he had lost the knack of hitting home runs: four in 1915, three in 1916, two in 1917. But he was a walking puzzle for his managers. His batting average of .325 was the best on the Red Sox by far. Beginning in 1915 he led the Red Sox in slugging average each year. Boston had two precious metals in one vein, and each of them needed a different kind of mining. Was Ruth hitter or pitcher? Soon the Boston management would have to make a sober finding: which of Babe Ruth's talents was more valuable?

His cumulative pitching record, 1914–1917, follows:

Games	116
Games started	106
Complete games	74
Innings pitched	867⅔
Hits	640
Walks	311
Strikeouts	410
Shoutouts	16
Won	65
Lost	33
%	.663
ERA	2.02

THE ACCUMULATED BATTING FIGURES
BABE RUTH'S MAJOR-LEAGUE CAREER
1914–1917

at bat:	361
hits:	108
home runs:	9
runs batted in:	50
average:	.299

---

* Olaf Henriksen (1888–1962), outfielder, seven seasons, 1911–1917, Red Sox, batting average .269.

Forrest LeRoy Cady (1886–1946), catcher, eight seasons, 1912–1919, Red Sox, Indians, Phillies, batting average .240.

Robert Hayes Veach (1888–1945), outfielder, fourteen seasons, 1912–1925, Tigers, Red Sox, Senators, Yankees, batting average .310.

Babe Ruth had become well known around Boston. He put some of his money into a small Boston cigar factory which brought out the Babe Ruth cigar. He smoked it himself, and it sold well.

In the small hours of a November morning Ruth tried to drive his car between two trolley cars near Fenway Park. His car was a total loss. With him was a nameless woman. Ruth was unhurt, but his passenger needed hospitalization. And that is all of the story that appeared.

Outside the Park, 1918

WEATHER BLOCKS FREIGHT

CAN'T "CUSS" ARMY MULES

URGES ENLARGING
WOMEN'S WAR WORK

AMERICAN TROOPS NOW ON BATTLE FRONT

SUFFRAGISTS EXPECT
NATION-WIDE VICTORY

GERMAN MEDALS THAT APPEAL TO THE PASSIONS

BANDITS KILL AN AMERICAN
AND WOUND THREE AT TAMPICO

TAX LAW PUZZLES
WALL ST. BROKERS

HAIG REGAINS GROUND BUT LOSES IT AGAIN
MAKES STRATEGIC WITHDRAWAL NEAR YPRES

MAY REFUSE TRIAL TO SINN FEINERS

U-BOAT GIVES NO WARNING

PENALIZE BIG HOTELS
FOR SUGAR HOARDING

AMERICAN TROOPS LANDED AT ARCHANGEL

COST OF LIVING UP
50% IN FOUR YEARS

LONDON POLICE
WIN HIGHER WAGE

ARMISTICE SIGNED, END OF THE WAR!

9 · Ruth Puts Red Sox in Top Place Again (1918)

> I guess I just liked the game.
> —Babe Ruth

Babe Ruth was the first of the Red Sox to accept terms in 1918, signing a seven-thousand-dollar contract on January 15. Among other players there were holdouts because of salary cuts intended to prepare for any hard times that might be caused by the war, now in its tenth month. No one could be certain about it, but the Red Sox were going to be short-handed in 1918 when twelve men would go into the armed forces, including manager Jack Barry. The new owner, Harry Frazee, is remembered as a breaker-up of champions, but as these vacancies occurred, Frazee replaced some of the departing men with first baseman Stuffy McInnis, catcher Wally Schang, pitcher Joe Bush, and outfielder Amos Strunk,* a good job of patching. For the post of manager, Frazee picked Edward Grant Barrow.

> He was not a warm man who could inspire quick affection.
> —Arthur Daley [of Barrow]

Barrow was not liked by those who worked under him because he had a need for servility. His speech was overbearing, his physique impressive, and his bushy brows a memorable sight. When

---

* John Phalen McInnis (1890–1960), first baseman, nineteen seasons, 1909–1927, Athletics, Red Sox, Indians, Braves, Pirates, Phillies, batting average .307. He also signed on January 15, 1918.

Walter Henry Schang (1889–1965), catcher, nineteen seasons, 1913–1931, Athletics, Red Sox, Yankees, Browns, Tigers, batting average .284.

Leslie Ambrose Bush (1892–1974), pitcher, seventeen seasons, 1912–1928, Athletics, Red Sox, Yankees, Browns, Senators, Pirates, Giants. Won 196, lost 181, earned-run average 3.51.

Amos Aaron Strunk (1889–   ), outfielder, seventeen seasons, 1908–1924, Athletics, Red Sox, White Sox, batting average .283.

he lost his temper, which was often enough, he turned red and could not speak for choking. His nerves were brass. (After the 1941 season, when Joe DiMaggio hit .357 with thirty home runs and 125 batted in, Barrow, the Yankee general manager, suggested a pay cut.) Harry Frazee, his 1918–1920 employer, called him Simon, as in Simon Legree. Barrow enjoyed his reputation as a brawler who had many fist fights and never lost one. His statement that "boxing ranks next to baseball as my favorite sport" is unusual and unexpected from anyone who spent his life in baseball.

Barrow had a puritanical streak and would have stopped women from smoking in his ball parks if he knew how to do it. And he would allow no promotions to draw a crowd to a baseball park except baseball; for example, there would be no bicycle races before games in Newark, though the Newark fans liked bicycle races before games. His artistic taste had the restraint of a classicist. The standard Yankee uniform, clean-lined and free of tacky visual gadgetry sewed on as patches and labels, is his monument. He also had a certain acid wit, as when he spoke of Branch Rickey as "the only man . . . who can trade a five for two tens." And, to his credit, he *did* stop the Fenway ushers from warring with the customers over custody of baseballs hit into the stands.

Barrow was born near Springfield, Illinois, and grew up near Des Moines. After a job in Chicago before he was twenty, he worked with Harry Stevens on the concessions of the Pittsburgh ball park. (Had he stayed in business with Stevens he would have made ten times the money and had one-tenth as much publicity, power, and authority.) He was a minor-league manager and the discoverer of Honus Wagner. For two years Barrow managed the Tigers.

Jack Dunn, in 1910, led a group which made Barrow president of the Eastern League (later named the International League). The new league president skillfully commanded the defense against the Federal League and, after the threat passed, brought the players to heel. When they threatened to strike Barrow promised them a lockout in reprisal. How a man of his stormy temperament could have lasted as the employee of eight club-owners over eight years is a puzzle. In the end he had to leave his job as president of the International League after what he called "a loud and quarrelsome session." On that very day Harry Frazee hired him to manage the Red Sox.

The best of his players and least of his admirers was Babe Ruth. Barrow and Ruth had never met, though Barrow saw Ruth pitch for the Orioles and in the World Series of 1916. Their first meeting was on the occasion of signing the 1918 contract in January, in celebration of which Ruth and Stuffy McInnis lunched at Barrow's expense, and Ruth ate a whole custard pie for dessert.

Manager and player were bound to clash. Barrow expected to rule the Red Sox sternly and firmly; to him terror was a tool of management. We know now that personality traits are well fixed by the age of seventeen or eighteen, and only the passage of time or stiff military discipline changes them. Barrow and many other men who tried blustering manners and boot-camp discipline as ways of changing Babe Ruth into a meek, run-scoring machine were wasting their time, except that they may have avoided ulcers.

The first quarrel came when Ruth, without asking, got off a Philadelphia-bound train at Baltimore on an open Sunday to visit his sister Mamie. Barrow figured the truant had run away to commit excesses. A coach found Ruth, and they appeared in Philadelphia in time for the next game. But Barrow was enraged and railed at Ruth before the whole team. Ruth, annoyed, said he would leave to play with a shipyard team. In the private midnight hours Barrow talked him out of jumping the Red Sox. Barrow's singling out of the young pitcher for disciplinary attention was based on a feeling that a manager had to be a hard man in order to keep control; it had nothing to do with rational policy. Ruth had won forty-seven games and lost twenty-five in the previous two seasons. With the possible exception of the bizarre Rube Waddell, it is hard to imagine a pitcher of that ability hurting a team very much.

They arrived at a way of living together. Each disliked the other to the end. Their relationship showed—as many similar lasting dislikes have shown—that baseball success depends much more on skill at baseball than on friendship in the dugout.

With so many regulars going to war, the 1918 Red Sox were a kind of crazy-quilt team. They could field, and their pitchers, Ruth, Mays, Bush, and Sad Sam Jones,* were more than enough, but their hitting was lightweight, and they were short of left-handed batters. Where could the Red Sox get a good left-handed hitter? The 1917 league leaders, Cobb, Sisler, and Speaker, all batted left-handed, but were probably not available. The fourth-ranking batter in the league was a left-handed Red Sox pitcher who hit .325. But he pitched thirty-five complete games and won twenty-four! Yes—and he led the Red Sox in hitting.

Barrow took the risk. He asked Babe Ruth whether he could pitch in his regular turn and play as a fielder on the other days. Ruth said he could.

In 1918 Ruth pitched or played first base or played in the outfield when the opposing team's pitcher was right-handed. On other days he stayed in the bullpen chewing snuff, swapping lies, and

---

* Samuel Pond Jones (1892–1966), pitcher, twenty-two seasons, 1914–1935, Indians, Red Sox, Yankees, Browns, Senators, White Sox. Won 229, lost 217, earned-run average 3.84.

holding himself ready to go into the game as a relief pitcher or
pinch-hitter. First base was more fun for Ruth, but Stuffy McInnis
had that job when he was in good health. Ruth played mostly in
the outfield. In 1917 he had appeared in fifty-two games as pitcher
or pinch-hitter. In 1918, when the season was shorter, he played in
ninety-five games as pitcher, first baseman, or outfielder. His salary
stayed the same.

Baseball people aren't given to newfangled ideas. They usually
change their way of doing things only if they must. There are exceptions, such as Branch Rickey's farm system, Roger Bresnahan's shin
guards, Joe Tinker's defense alignment against the bunt, and the
Designated Hitter. But they are few. Ruth's translation to the outfield was a result of a manpower shortage. Barrow was candid: "It
was as much wartime necessity, as it was my own inclination. . . ."
It surely wasn't inevitable. Both Carrigan and Barry had seen Ruth
at his best, both ways, and had let well enough alone. In 1918 the
greater value of having Ruth at the plate as often as possible was
made clear by a national shortage of good left-handed hitters.

Despite what Fred Lieb called the "soggy lifeless ball" of 1918,
Babe Ruth found that being a batter improved his hitting, not so
much for average as for distance, and his long hits scared his foes
into walking him intentionally more often. On May 9 he chilled
pitchers' blood by getting five hits in five times at bat, including
three doubles and a triple. In the next seven weeks, home runs
began to rocket out of parks until he got his first New York headline
for a home run: RUTH GETS TENTH HOMER, which he hit in a game
at Washington on June 28. Two days later at Washington his headline writer needed more space:

RUTH PUTS RED SOX
IN TOP PLACE AGAIN

———————

BOSTON TERROR GETS ELEVENTH
HOME RUN OFF JOHNSON TO
BEAT WASHINGTON

The home run came in the tenth to win the game for Carl Mays.

What a surprise, then, that on July 3 Ruth jumped the Red Sox
to join the Delaware River Ship Building League as a member of
the team of the Chester Ship Building Company. Red Sox players
told reporters that he would soon be back, and they were right. He
missed the game of July 3 and the first game of the July 4 double-
header, and no more. What lay behind this escapade was Ruth's
discovery that hitting three days and pitching on the fourth day was

a lot of work. He got fame and glory for hitting, less notice for pitch-ing. Ruth explained that the shipyard league promised to excuse him from pitching and let him play every day, as was fitting for a pitcher who had hit eleven home runs. His return was prudent. Shipyard ballplayers were employees of the Emergency Fleet Cor-poration, and their pay was only for building ships. Assuming that he could have escaped from Ed Barrow, Ruth would have taken a painful pay cut.

What value league-leading Boston had in Babe Ruth shows clearly if one makes a journal for the next few days.

5th—Ruth pitched and beat the A's 4–3 in ten innings; at the plate he was hitless, but he walked in the tenth and scored the winning run. Ruth walked four, struck out eight, and gave up seven hits. Weather: unsettled, warm.

6th—Against Cleveland Ruth had a hit in two times at bat—a triple with two men on base; he then scored the winning run from third on a bad throw; Boston 5, Cleveland 4. Weather: cloudy, cool.

7th—Sunday in Boston, no game scheduled. Weather: partly cloudy, cool.

8th—In the first game of a double-header against Cleveland Ruth played right field, batted fourth, and in the tenth inning tripled to drive in the only run of the game; he had two hits in four times at bat. In the second game he went hitless and Boston lost 4–3. Weather: fair and cool.

On July 12 he enchanted an unnamed Chicago sportswriter who watched him hit two triples and a double, and score four runs in a game. Boston won it 6–3. The witness: "The more I see of Babe and his heroic hitting, the more he seems a figure out of mythology or from the fairy land of more modern writers. He hits like no man ever has, truly the master man of maulers. . . ."

From July 6 to 12, in seven games, this mauler was at bat twenty-three times, scored six runs, and made eleven hits, of which four were doubles and five were triples. His batting average for the week was .478, and his slugging percentage for the season thus far was .694.

On August 1 his batting average was .304 and, as a pitcher, he had won eight and lost five. By August 10 the Red Sox had played nine more games in the course of which their all-purpose star hit .312, raising his season average to .309. As a pitcher he now had

won ten and lost five. *The Times*, in a two-column head, put it well:
BOSTON BABE BUMPS BIG BATTING MARKS. But he had gone forty-one
days without a home run.

Ruth and the Sox made certain of the pennant in high style on
August 31 in the first game of a double-header with the A's. Ruth
pitched a three-hitter, winning 6–1. He had two hits in four tries
and scored a run. He walked four and struck out three. (The A's
won the second game, but no matter.)

As an outfielder, the all-around left-hander was adequate. He
claimed he had caught enough fungoes off the bat of Brother
Matthias to learn the job. Harry Hooper directed outfield play, usually from right field. Strunk was most often in center. By the end of
the season runners respected Ruth and were not trying to take the
extra base a runner can get from a bad throw. Against left-handed
pitching, and when Ruth was pitching, Barrow used George
Whiteman* in the outfield.

The 1918 season was uniquely short. Government did not stop
nor much discourage baseball beyond refusing to exempt ballplayers from the military draft. The owners stopped baseball when
income at the box office sagged badly. The final attendance count
(for about four fifths of a normal season) was slightly above three
million, a drop of more than two million below the count of 1917,
and the worst showing of the century. The owners bravely econo-
mized by stopping play and fearlessly releasing all players after ten
days' notice. This made every player a free agent! The owners then
generously conspired not to tamper with each other's players, saved
about two hundred thousand dollars in paychecks, and kept their
players in bondage. The effect of this squalid proceeding on the
Ruth story is that we don't know his exact income for 1918, anymore
than we do for 1914. The Red Sox played 82 percent of their games.
If they paid the same part of the payroll, they paid Ruth about
fifty-eight hundred dollars.

As a pitcher the all-purpose ballplayer appeared in twenty games
(166 innings); he won thirteen and lost seven, with an earned-run
average of 2.22. His name is not among the pitching leaders in the
usual pitching tables. But his name wasn't fading; it merely moved
over to the batting tables: first in slugging percentage and in home
runs (tied with Tillie Walker** at eleven), third in doubles and in
runs batted in. His pitching, however, was good enough to get him
on the *Spalding Guide*'s 1918 all-star team, along with Walter
Johnson.

* George Whiteman (1882–1947), outfielder, three seasons, 1907, 1913, 1918,
Red Sox, Yankees, batting average .272.
** Clarence William Walker (1889–1959), outfielder, thirteen seasons, 1911–1923,
Senators, Browns, Red Sox, Athletics, batting average .281.

The 1918 home-run record was all on one side of the calendar. All eleven were hit before July 1. While Ruth was hitting eleven home runs, all other Red Sox players of 1918 had five, and all other American leaguers hit eighty-nine. One of Ruth's "home runs" drove in a runner on base to win an extra-inning game and had to be recorded forever as a triple, under the rules of that era.

THE ACCUMULATED BATTING FIGURES
BABE RUTH'S MAJOR-LEAGUE CAREER
1914–1918

at bat: 678
hits: 203
home runs: 20
runs batted in: 116
average: .299

> The probability that the better team wins the World Series is estimated as 0.80. . . .
> —F. Mosteller, *Journal of the American Statistical Association* (1952)

The Red Sox opened the World Series against the Cubs in Chicago on September 4. The Cubs chose to play in Comiskey Park because it would hold more people than their own playground. The Red Sox were glad to play at Comiskey because they would be more at home there than the Cubs.

Everybody knew the Boston club was one of the best defensive teams ever, and very hard to score on, but the Cubs were favored to win over a team that ranked only seventh in hitting in the American League. And yet there was doubt. After all, "RUTH MAY BE A HERO" and might even be "the sensation of the series" unless the Cub pitchers could "subdue his wild hitting sprees." When the first game was rained out, the gloomy weather seemed to make both residents and visitors in Chicago more pessimistic, at least as seen in the think-pieces the writers had to contrive. It now seemed that "Chicago has an impressive respect for Babe Ruth's bat," or, to put it another way,

RUTH GAINS ADDED RESPECT
––––––––––
CHICAGO PLAYERS ADMIT THE BOSTON
PITCHER-HITTER IS DANGEROUS
MAN OF HIS TEAM

Pitching needs a positive, confident attitude; and when you
know how to pitch, you completely dominate the situation.
—Jim Brosnan

The Boston pitcher-hitter was the only double-threat man in
baseball. We might have to go as far back as the 1860s to find
another professional player equally feared for his bat as well as his
pitching arm. In batting practice in Comiskey Park he bounced the
ball off the right-field fence every time he took his turn. For a tactical surprise, Barrow named him the starting pitcher in the first game
against the Cubs' left-hander Hippo Vaughn,* which let Barrow
play his right-hand-hitting utility outfielder Whiteman. It worked.
Whiteman had two hits, and one was the hit that was needed: he
singled Dave Shean** from first to third, from where Shean scored
the only run of the game on a single by McInnis.

The Cubs left eight on base, having filled the bases in the first,
and having two on in the sixth, but had only the forlorn line of
zeroes for their day. Boston had five hits, Chicago six. Ruth walked
one and struck out four. Vaughn was so frustrated that he spoke
uncivilly to Red Sox coach Heinie Wagner; Wagner, bent on
revenge, alone invaded the Cub dugout where he fought the
whole Cub roster until forcibly evacuated, dripping water, mud,
and blood.

Nobody put the day's news more elegantly than the *New York
Times*:

BABE RUTH'S MIGHTY ARM HOLDS
CUBS SCORELESS THROUGH
NINE TORRID INNINGS

RUTH STAR IN TALE
OF BOSTON VICTORY
DETAILED PLAY, INNING BY INNING
SHOWS MASTERY OF BIG
RED SOX TWIRLER

The Cubs evened the Series by winning the second game 3–1.
Boston won the third game, also played in Chicago, 2–1. Ruth did
not play in either. For the fourth game, to be played on September 9, appearances during a war forbade special trains; both Cubs
and Red Sox rode on the same regularly scheduled train to Boston,
occupying five Pullman cars.

* James Leslie Vaughn (1888–1966), pitcher, thirteen seasons, 1908–1921, Yan-
kees, Senators, Cubs. Won 176, lost 137, earned-run average 2.49.
** David William Shean (1878–1963), infielder, nine seasons, 1906–1919, Athletics,
Phillies, Braves, Cubs, Reds, Red Sox, batting average .228.

Ruth pitched the fourth game and batted seventh in the order. Lefty Tyler,* winner of nineteen games that season, started for the Cubs. He had already won the second of the Series. In the fourth inning "the Tarzan of the Boston tribe . . . swinging his savage looking black bludgeon," put himself and the Red Sox ahead by tripling home two runs on a three-and-two pitch. This was Ruth's first World Series hit in eleven tries. The Cubs were scoreless going into the eighth inning, but then scored twice to tie the game. The Red Sox got a run in the last of the eighth to regain the lead. In the ninth, after the Cubs had a single and a walk, Barrow put Ruth in left field and called in Joe Bush to pitch. (Barrow kept Ruth in the game for his bat, in case the Cubs tied it.) Bush got three outs on two ground balls and saved the win for Ruth. In this game Ruth became the only World Series pitcher ever to bat seventh in the order, and the only player to start a World Series game as a pitcher and end it as a fielder. Since nothing in baseball is trivia, who shall say which fact is more important?

Ruth did not appear in the fifth game of the Series. It almost happened that nobody appeared. The magnates chose 1918 as the year to begin distributing 30 percent of the World Series players' pool to members of teams finishing second, third, and fourth, in order to maintain interest after the pennant races ended. The players did not learn of this split until the long train ride after the third game. It was a good idea whose time had not yet come, because attendance at the 1918 Series was poor and it was plain to see that the players' shares would be small. (Fewer than ninety thousand attended the first four games, from which the players' shares came.) The owners also kept ticket prices at regular-season levels as a kind of voluntary price control. Finally, as a way of washing off guilt for playing ball during a war, the players promised to donate 10 percent of their share to charity.

As the men learned how little World Series money they might expect, they decided they would not play unless they received a guarantee that winners would get fifteen-hundred dollars each and losers a thousand each. This balkiness came just before the fifth game. Ban Johnson came down to reason with the mutineers but couldn't because he was too drunk to talk. The players then realized there would be no negotiation. When Mayor "Honey Fitz" Fitzgerald made a speech from home plate saying the game would go on for the sake of the wounded in the stands, they started play, an hour late. Vaughn finally got a win over Boston, 3–0, giving up but five hits.

Ruth played in left field next day, in the sixth game, but only

---

* George Albert Tyler (1889–1972), pitcher, twelve seasons, 1910–1921, Braves, Cubs. Won 125, lost 119, earned-run average 2.95.

The established Red Sox left-hander, 1918, as much responsible as any man for Boston's world championship that year. (*National Baseball Library, Cooperstown, New York.*)

because Whiteman hurt himself making a great shoe-tongue catch for the first out in the eighth inning. Ruth did not bat. Carl Mays and the Red Sox won it 2–1 to take the Series four games to two.

I played with Ruth on the world championship team of
1918 and he was one of baseball's best pitchers.
        —Amos A. Strunk (1972)

Babe Ruth and Carl Mays beat the Cubs in the 1918 Series. The
statistics—except games won—favored the Cubs: more runs, more
hits, more runs batted in, more walks, fewer strikeouts, higher
batting average, lower earned-run average. Boston looked better in
errors (one, compared with five), triples (three to one), and games
won (four to two). The Cubs lost because Mays and Ruth each
pitched two games and each gave up only two runs. Mays's performance might be rated the better today except that Ruth had a
shutout and broke a pitching record during the Cubs' dark week
of the soul.

In the 1916 Series Ruth had pitched a fourteen-inning game,
giving up no runs after the first out. In 1918's first game he pitched
a nine-inning shutout. In the fourth game he went seven innings
before the Cubs scored. Thus in three games he had pitched 29⅔
innings of scoreless baseball, breaking Christy Mathewson's record
of 28⅓ set in 1905 and 1911.* Ruth thought he might have done
better except that the middle finger of his left hand was swollen
after he injured it in horseplay on the train from Chicago. A fellow
player ducked and Ruth hit his knuckles on the steel wall of the
Pullman car. The swelling made it hard for him to get the best grip
for his curve. Really, he could hardly have done better. His earned-
run average in his three World Series games was 0.87.

As it happened, Ruth's record-setting game of 1918 was his last
World Series pitching assignment. To rank pitchers for World Series
records it is usual to require twenty-five innings pitched. Ruth is
tied for first in won-lost percentage (three wins, no losses), he is
second in earned-run average, and fourth in fewest hits per nine
innings. He was not notable for stinginess in walks nor for large
strikeout totals. His World Series pitching record is the record of a
man with sharp intelligence, all focused on baseball and nothing
else.

The winning player's share in 1918 was $1,102.51, the smallest
winner's reward in the history of the World Series. The distribution
to charity was $18,319.51—all money withheld from the eight first-
division teams, from the umpires, and even from the official scorer.

During the argument before the fifth game of the Series the
players asked and got a promise of no reprisals. But during the
winter they learned that because of their threat to strike they
wouldn't get their championship emblems, and they never did.

* Whitey Ford of the Yankees broke Ruth's record with 33⅔ innings in the years
1960, 1961, and 1962.

Another curiosity of the Series is that it was the last to be played without a home run; the ball must really have been sodden in 1918.

About four weeks after the championship was settled, Bush, Schang, Strunk, and Wally Mayer* were punished in some undescribed way for playing postseason exhibition games, that is, barnstorming, in direct defiance of the National Commission.

The First World War was not terribly hard on Americans who stayed out of the armed services and did not speak against popular passions. Sooner or later all ballplayers registered for the draft. Before the war ended 227 major-league players were in the services; at least three were killed. Babe Ruth registered with a Baltimore draft board, received a deferment as a husband, and enlisted in the Massachusetts Home Guard, a reserve unit formed to replace the federalized National Guard. That was the total of his wartime military service. Some muscle-heroes—one thinks of Jack Dempsey—were widely condemned for absence from the forces. There is no trace of any abuse of Ruth. Sam Vick, Ruth's friend and teammate, who went to war himself, told the writer no one censured Ruth because "everybody seemed to like him" for his fund-raising work in good causes.

The Babe Ruth of 1918 was a fine looking athlete, trim waisted, strong, fast, a remarkably skillful base runner. . . .
—Edward Grant Barrow

Ruth was noticed wherever he went. People did not forget to introduce him at parties. And, as Vick said, people liked him. To Barrow his most remarkable trait was that he was "entirely without self-discipline," a statement plainly false in the light of his pitching record. Ruth was too much the perfect animal for Barrow's manichean taste. Barrow's trouble was that secretly he was the kind of man who would have preferred a cast-iron lawn dog to the real thing. Ruth was a healthy animal, too. He didn't make news with an illness until May 20, 1918, when he was hospitalized for a few days with an acute throat infection.

In the year 1918 the partnership of Ruth and son was dissolved by death. George Ruth, Sr., remarried after Kate Ruth died. His new wife Martha had a brother-in-law named Benjamin Sipes, a member of the Baltimore Fire Department. Sipes—nicknamed Doc —was a regular at the bar and grill on Eutaw and Lombard streets (which George, Jr., had financed). On the evening of August 27 Doc Sipes accused Ruth's bartender of dipping into the till. George sided with the bartender. Words became quarrel. We may suppose

---

* Walter A. Mayer (1889–1951), catcher, seven seasons, 1911–1919, White Sox, Red Sox, Browns, batting average .193.

that George tried to eject Sipes. However it happened, they went to fighting in the street outside, George fell to the sidewalk, fractured his skull, and died almost instantly.

Babe Ruth thereafter gave up his interest in the place.

Outside the Park, 1919

GAS OVERCOMES FIREMAN

GLASS ANNOUNCES
TREASURY PROGRAM

WAR FIGURES SHOW
PREPAREDNESS NEED

BARBER SHOT AND STABBED

BOLSHEVIST ORGAN
DENOUNCES LEAGUE

ONE KILLED, 8 HURT
IN EXCURSION CRASH

SUBMARINES TO STAY

300,000 GO TO CONEY ISLAND

REPORT KIEV TAKEN
BY THE UKRAINIANS

275 LEGION POSTS
IN NEW YORK STATE

LOS ANGELES NOW
WITHOUT TRAINS

GETS RADIO AT 4,366 MILES

ALL ITALY WAITS
DECISION ON FIUME

ANARCHIST LAWYER TESTIFIES

SYRACUSE STUDENTS
STRIKE FOR HOLIDAY

ARREST GIRL AS "RED" AGENT

KILLED IN ELEVATOR FALL

THREATS HASTENED MARRIAGE

10 · Ruth Stands Alone as Heavy Hitter (1919)

It's a gift.
—Babe Ruth (1919)

Harry Frazee again hired Ed Barrow to manage the Red Sox in 1919 but damped Barrow's hopes for an even greater year by sending three returning war veterans, Ernie Shore, Dutch Leonard, and Duffy Lewis, to the Yankees for fifty thousand dollars. Frazee's motive was to keep the payroll down.

Babe Ruth had a plan to keep the payroll up. In January he told friends he wanted more money, on the ground that he had been the standout of the World Series. He said the figure he would mention "may knock Mr. Frazee silly. . . ." The figure he had in mind was ten thousand dollars. (Frazee had once said he thought eight thousand was an absolute ceiling for anyone.) Neither budged for the next two months, and the Red Sox departed by sea for Florida on March 19 without Ruth. By this time Ruth had given Frazee a choice of two proposals: one year at fifteen thousand dollars, or three years at ten. The Boston fans sided angrily with Ruth against Frazee. There were published suggestions that other American League owners might chip in to make up the difference because Ruth filled their parks for them, or that Ruth's salary be raised by a public fund drive.

Ruth had by now become a celebrity and had acquired a manager (who signed himself "secretary") named John Igoe. Igoe thought Ruth could make money as a boxer. After the smallness of the World Series split, any income would be welcome. Ruth began to work out in a gymnasium in the winter and had an offer of five thousand dollars to fight Gunboat Smith. Barrow could see the folly of letting his most promising ballplayer get his brains scrambled in the prize ring. He took Ruth to Frazee's office and mediated the salary dispute.

The parties came to agreement on March 21: three years at ten thousand a year. Barrow then talked Ruth out of the boxing venture. Ruth, in excellent physical condition, left for Florida by rail. Obviously feeling full of beans, he told reporters he hoped to play two or three positions and be in the game every day, because life was perfect only when he came to bat with men on base.

Ruth had an extraordinary spring training. *Item*: In an exhibition game against the Giants at Tampa race track he hit a fair ball which traveled through the air to a point 508 feet from the plate and rolled until it was 579 feet away. (Reporters borrowed surveyors' measuring gear.) Barrow later said that particular home run was weighty in his decision to convert Ruth completely to an outfielder. *Item*: Against the Orioles in Baltimore on April 17 Ruth came to the plate six times, walked twice and hit four home runs. Stunned reporters asked him how he did it. The reply: "It's a gift." We don't know whether the tone was cocky or reverent. In his first two times at bat the next day he hit two more! *Item*: In six consecutive spring exhibition games he hit home runs.

Before spring training in 1919 it had seemed probable that Ruth would become a full-time pitcher again, but the sale of Duffy Lewis to the Yankees left a gap in left field. Should Ruth fill it? Frazee wanted to use Ruth only as a pitcher. Barrow was in doubt. To put him in the outfield was to cast aside the talent of the league's best left-handed pitcher, while to use him only for pitching was to deny the Red Sox the most powerful bat in the league. Frazee and Barrow had not made up their minds when the season started.

The Red Sox opened by beating the Yankees 10–0. Ruth played left field, was at bat four times, scored two runs, and had two hits, one a home run. In the next few weeks he pitched in turn and played the outfield on other days. When he complained of fatigue Barrow suggested he get more sleep. Meanwhile, Harry Hooper, the Red Sox field captain, had been working on Barrow.

> **I finally convinced Ed Barrow to play him out there to get his bat in the lineup every day.**
>
> —Harry Hooper

Coach Heinie Wagner and solemn Deacon Scott supported Hooper's advice to Barrow. Barrow's reluctance was partly for fear of snickers if the experiment failed and Ruth slumped as a hitter. But such a mistake could be corrected.

In May Ruth became a permanent outfielder. In his own self-interest it was a wise step. Even then hitters got the most attention. (No important national magazine carried a piece on Walter Johnson, greatest of pitchers, until he retired.) Fame sells tickets and pays high salaries. And, as it turned out, 1919 was the lucky time to switch. He *might* have been a great pitcher during the lively ball years after 1919; barring physical injury, he was *certain* to be a great hitter of the lively ball soon to be introduced.

Ruth's conversion to full-time hitter accompanied a historical curiosity: in 1919 when George Halas* tried to fill Duffy Lewis's place in the Red Sox outfield and failed, he made it more probable that Babe Ruth would change from the mound to the outfield. What would baseball and football be like today if Halas had made the team?

Johnny Sain, the respected pitching coach, once said it would be psychologically best if pitchers could keep sharp by working every day, but it is, unhappily, a physical impossibility. In the case of Ruth, batting every day made him sharper. His batting through 1919 brought a rising curve of public interest. By late July people were searching old home-run records and learned that Ned Williamson** had hit twenty-seven in 1884. Of all concerned, Ruth seemed least impressed.

On July 29, in a game against Detroit at Boston, he tied the American League record of sixteen, set by Socks Seybold† in 1902. The Tigers won it 10–8, but it wasn't Ruth's fault. He played left field, batted five times, scored three runs, and had three hits. So far in the season of 1919 he had hit a home run in each American League park. Some of his home runs were off knee-high pitches, others off pitches over his head.

On the day after he tied the league record he showed himself in his old role as a utility man. In a double-header against Detroit he played left field, first base, and pitched in relief in the second game, saving a victory for Boston. (He walked none and struck out three.)

His batting became steadily more interesting. By late summer the situation was as if written by a playwright. On September 20, before a capacity crowd at Boston in the first game of a double-header against the White Sox, Ruth tied the major-league record with a hit over Fenway's *left*-field wall. It not only tied the home-run record but, in heroic style, came in the last of the ninth with two outs to drive in the winning run. Something else had happened in that inning. For the first time, as he came to the plate, the crowd had roared for Ruth to hit a home run. Ruth had pitched for five and a third innings and then moved to left field. Determined to be

* George Stanley Halas (1895–   ), outfielder, one season, 1919, Red Sox, batting average (12 games) .091.
** Edward Nagle Williamson (1857–1894), infielder, thirteen seasons, 1878–1890, Indianapolis, Chicago (National League), Chicago (Players' League), batting average .255, home runs 63.
† Ralph Orlando Seybold (1870–1921), outfielder, nine seasons, 1899–1908, Reds, Athletics, batting average .294, home runs 51.

herculean, he also drove in the winning run in the second game. Almost alone, Ruth had postponed for a few days the clinching of the pennant by the Black Sox of 1919.

That home run number twenty-seven, which tied Ned Williamson's record, was a remarkable hit. The pitcher was Lefty Williams;* left-handed hitters rarely hit home runs over left-field fences off left-handed pitchers. Williams came to the Red Sox clubhouse after the game "to express his horrified disbelief." From that day on, the Red Sox usually knocked off work to watch whenever Babe Ruth took batting practice.

The day of all these heroics had been scheduled as Babe Ruth Day at Fenway Park, sponsored jointly by the city government and the Knights of Columbus; the K.C.'s gave him six hundred dollars in treasury savings certificates. A reporter asked Ruth what Frazee gave him for Babe Ruth Day. Answer: "A cigar." Everybody laughed except Frazee.

Ruth set a new major-league home-run record on September 24 at the Polo Grounds. As so often in Ruth's affairs, the hit had its own theatrical quality: the world-record home run tied the game in the ninth inning, 1–1. The New York crowd had jeered each of his appearances before. After the ninth inning, as the game went on, the crowd cheered him each time he came to bat. (With Hoyt** pitching for Boston and Shawkey for New York, the game went thirteen innings before the Yankees won 2–1.) *The Times* headline over its story said RUTH WALLOPS OUT HIS 28TH HOME RUN. The word "out" was carefully chosen. The home run went all of the way out, just like Ruth's and Jackson's hits out of the Polo Grounds in 1916. The record-breaking home run made all previous Polo Grounds home runs seem as "bunts compared to Babe's terrific smash," according to *The Times.*

His next home run, number twenty-nine, broke his own record on September 27 in Washington (where the Senators took both games of a double-header). Ruth sent the bat to St. Mary's Industrial School.

> . . . that rutting class of slugging batsmen who think of
> nothing else when they go to bat but that of gaining the
> applause of the "groundlings" by the novice's hit to the out-

---

* Claude Preston Williams (1893–1959), pitcher, seven seasons, 1913–1920, Tigers, White Sox. Won 82, lost 48, earned-run average 3.13. Barred from baseball after the World Series of 1919.
** Waite Charles Hoyt (1899–   ), pitcher, twenty-one seasons, 1918–1938, Giants, Red Sox, Yankees, Tigers, Athletics, Dodgers, Pirates. Hall of Fame. Won 237, lost 182, earned-run average 3.59. Among top seven pitchers in seven categories of World Series pitching.

field of a "homer," one of the least difficult hits known to batting in baseball, as it needs only muscle and not brains to make it.

—Spalding Baseball Guide, 1886

Ruth had set the record despite handicaps. A home-run leader's team ought to hit well so that he will get more times at bat, but the Red Sox batted sixth in the league. Furthermore, the magnates had shortened the schedule. Ruth appeared in only 130 games and had just 432 times at bat. It is worth noting that he did not set the record against short fences; on the average they were farther out than today's.

Ruth could not carry the Red Sox: they finished sixth. Barrow's group was not a happy one. Carl Mays was the unhappiest; when he refused to play, the Red Sox sold him to the Yankees for forty thousand dollars. Mays's defiance may have had an effect on the private thinking of Babe Ruth when he meditated on rendering unto Barrow what was Barrow's.

When Babe Ruth trotted out to Fenway's outfield, he was on hallowed ground where Duffy Lewis, Harry Hooper, and Tris Speaker had each averaged twenty assists per season. Many years later Harry Hooper downgraded Ruth's fielding. The Red Sox started 1919 with Ruth in right field, Hooper in center, and Braggo Roth* in left. Hooper said he feared they would run him down in wild pursuit of fly balls. He put Ruth in center and went to right field for his own safety. Hooper was surprised that Ruth and Roth never collided. If they had, he said, "the crash would have shaken Boston common."

Barrow had a different opinion of Ruth's ability. He thought Ruth was as good in right field as Speaker had been in center, with flawless judgment of line drives and flies, and a strong and accurate arm.

The figures support Barrow. Ruth played 111 games in the outfield and made 230 putouts. He had the startling total of twenty-six assists. He made but two errors. Hooper's dangerous galumpher, Babe Ruth, turns out to have been the leading defensive outfielder of the American League in 1919 with a fielding average of .992. (His fielding as a pitcher included two more errors and reduced his fielding average to .988, *still* the best for any player in the league.)

The Red Sox played only 138 games in 1919. After punishing financial losses in 1918 the owners feared more of the same in 1919. They timidly agreed on a schedule of 140 games to start on May 1, hoping to save money on spring training (Mack said the A's could

---

* Robert Frank Roth (1892–1936), outfielder, eight seasons, 1914–1921, White Sox, Indians, Red Sox, Athletics, Senators, Yankees, batting average .284.

train in Philadelphia). They cut the player limit to twenty-one from twenty-five, and secretly agreed to limit club payrolls. Colonel Tillinghast Huston, co-owner of the Yankees, said, "The players can sign at the salaries offered or not at all. . . ." In March Ban Johnson whistled loudly in the dark: "A thorough canvas [sic] of conditions has convinced me that baseball in 1919 will have its most prosperous year." Baseball did prosper, but Johnson, in March, did not really think it was healthy. The owners' fears probably cost them about six hundred thousand paid admissions. Baseball drew six and a half million paid; just as after previous wars, the game was booming and popular. Even the Phillies made money. With a schedule of 154 games baseball could have drawn another 10 percent. As for Ruth, he probably would have played 144 or 145 games and might well have hit thirty to thirty-five home runs.

Ruth had a splendid season. He batted .322, had by far the highest slugging percentage, set a new home-run record (hitting a dead ball), led in total bases, runs batted in, and runs scored. He also pitched often enough to win nine and lose five. More than half his hits were for extra bases (a new record). Although Ty Cobb had a much higher batting average, Ruth made more runs happen. Cobb had only half as many extra-base hits as Ruth. Put in another way, a fifth of all players' hits in that season were extra-base hits. A fifth of Babe Ruth's hits were home runs. Rogers Hornsby* led the National League with the same batting average Ruth had in the American League. (And of the forty-four regular American League pitchers, Ruth ranked twenty-fourth in earned-run average.)

All of this was enough to make one breathless, and the press responded.

RUTH STANDS ALONE

AS HEAVY HITTER

———

HIS REMARKABLE BATTING FEATS

PROVIDE GREATEST FEATURE OF

NINETEEN-NINETEEN BASEBALL SEASON

He was a "mastodonic mauler," "the greatest batsman the game has ever known," who "should shine for years to come as a home-run hitter." By the end of the season he was "the greatest individual drawing card. . . ." That total of twenty-nine home runs *was* a shocker. Since 1901 eight American League home-run champions

* Rogers Hornsby (1896–1963), infielder, twenty-three seasons, 1915–1937, Cardinals, Giants, Braves, Cubs, Browns. Hall of Fame. Batting average .358 (second on the all-time list).

had won the title with fewer than ten home runs. Sam Crawford and Braggo Roth had each won it with only seven. Furthermore, four of Ruth's 1919 home runs came with the bases full.* This man was making storybook heroes obsolete. The most the hero of a baseball thriller could do was to win the big game with a grand-slam home run. What author would dare allow his hero to go so far beyond credibility as to hit *four* home runs with the bases full while setting a new home-run record? Ruth's explosion was a surprise to the sporting public. The heroic age of home-run hitting had been from 1885 to 1900. As recently as May 1919 John McGraw had said, "The passing of the home-run hitter was a good thing, for it made the game faster and flashier." Some people thought the new record was a statistical freak, not likely to be repeated. But Grantland Rice pointed to the shortness of the 1919 season and said Ruth might hit thirty-five or more in 1920.

The rules makers began in 1920 to make baseball what it is today. A home run that drove in the winning run in the bottom half of the last inning would in the future count as a home run instead of the minimum hit needed to drive in the winning run. Ruth and several others had "lost" home runs because of the way the rule had stood. (In 1919 Ruth also lost a home run when umpire Billy Evans ruled that a fly ball dropped into the overflow crowd in the outfield for a double, when in fact it went into the stands and bounced back into the playing field where the crowd stood.) The rules also barred pitchers from spitting on the ball unless they had already begun to earn their bread as spitball pitchers. All the clues suggest an official but quiet attempt to encourage the fun Ruth had started with his bat.

People who found the home run coarse and unrefined hoped Ruth would reform. It was Barrow's opinion that the new champion would prove to himself that he could hit thirty or thirty-five and then, satisfied, would settle down "into a legitimate .400 hitter." Hooper agreed. *If* Ruth would sometimes shorten his grip on the bat and poke hits into left field "he will develop into one of the greatest hitters. . . ."

> **The fans would rather see me hit one homer to right than three doubles to left.**
>
> **—Babe Ruth**

If Babe Ruth had quit baseball after the 1919 season his record would still stand as excellent, lacking in greatness only because it

---

* At St. Louis, May 20; at New York, June 30; at Cleveland, July 18; at Detroit, August 23.

was short. In paging through the records of a century of professional baseball it is hard to find many that match or outdo Ruth's record for the years 1914–1919.

Ruth and Barrow had a collision in 1919. The Red Sox were staying in the Raleigh Hotel in Washington. Barrow waited up one morning for Ruth to come in; at four o'clock he gave up and went to bed. The next evening he tipped the porter to come and wake him when Ruth rolled in, regardless of the time. The porter roused Barrow at six in the morning. Barrow went to the room shared by Ruth and coach Dan Howley. When he knocked at the door the lights went out, but the night hawks had forgotten to lock the door. Barrow went in and found Ruth in bed smoking a pipe while Howley hid in the bathroom. A jerk at the bed clothes showed Ruth clad in street clothes. Barrow decided to save his words for the ball park.

The next day Barrow made a fiery clubhouse speech about training rules, provoking Ruth to offer violence. Barrow invited him to stay behind when the team went on the field and fight it out. Ruth left. (He was twenty-four and Barrow was fifty.) Barrow suspended him. The Sox went ahead and won without Ruth, which cheered Barrow somewhat.

That night on the train Ruth came to see that Barrow had imposed the worst possible punishment so far as he was concerned: denial of a chance to play ball. He went to Barrow's stateroom and apologized. They made an agreement that Ruth would leave a note in Barrow's box in the hotel every night when on the road, noting the time he came in. For the rest of the season that was the way they did it. Although Ruth always addressed Barrow in speech as "Manager," these notes saluted him as "Dear Eddie." Barrow said he never tried to verify the times Ruth noted.

> **I saw a man transformed from a human being into something pretty close to a god.**
>
> **—Harry Hooper**

While Babe Ruth was with the Red Sox he first dominated the American League in pitching, then in hitting. The hitting awakened more interest. As Ted Williams said, if you are outside a ball park and you hear the crowd roar it is probably because someone hit the ball. Even as a complete pitcher Ruth was a leader among Red Sox hitters. He batted over .300 each year except 1916 when he hit .272. In 1915 Tris Speaker outhit him, and in 1916 Larry Gardner.* Ruth led the team in 1917, 1918, and 1919. In 1916 he was the

* William Lawrence Gardner (1886–   ), infielder, seventeen seasons, 1908–1924, Red Sox, Athletics, Indians, batting average .289.

league leader in earned-run average and in shutouts. In 1919, as noted, he led the league in slugging percentage, home runs, total bases, runs batted in, and runs scored; he also was king of the outfield defense.

His pitching was as good in its way as his hitting was in its order, but the hitting caught more attention. In 1919 the Brooklyn manager Wilbert Robinson, the Yankee scout Joe Kelly, and Willie Keeler (who hit over .350 for seven consecutive seasons) agreed that Ruth was the greatest of all hitters. The sportswriter J. C. Koefoed studied all the batters from 1909 through 1919 who had hit five or more home runs in one season. Ruth led them all in slugging percentage but in no other category. (Cobb was not among the top seventy-five in slugging percentage.) Gavvy Cravath* led in home runs, but in comparing Ruth and Cravath, "as to which of the two is the better, time alone can tell."

Ruth had already shown a special quality that excited the public and brought them back to the park. Many players, some of them great, played baseball with care, with cunning, with artistry, perhaps even with science, but Ruth, above all other players, lived baseball with joy.

THE ACCUMULATED BATTING FIGURES
BABE RUTH'S MAJOR-LEAGUE CAREER
1914–1919

at bat:	1110
hits:	342
home runs:	49
runs batted in:	230
average:	.308

Some may think the odd shape of Fenway was a special help. Not so. Babe Ruth had hit eleven home runs in Boston and thirty-eight on the road.

* Clifford Carlton Cravath (1881–1963), outfielder, eleven seasons, 1908–1920, Red Sox, White Sox, Senators, Phillies, batting average .287, home runs 119.

11 · Strictly a Pitcher (1914-1919)

In fact, he was strictly a pitcher when I first played with
him, on the Red Sox. . . . It was hard to believe the natural
ability that man had.

—Sam Jones

In each of the three seasons from 1917 to 1919 the number of innings
Ruth pitched was less than in the previous year. His career as a
pitcher seemed to be drawing to a close. This is a good time to look
at his pitching record as a whole.

Pitchers are thought to be a breed apart from other ballplayers.
Some people say they are not really athletes at all. And they are
erratic—great in one outing, bungling the next, and for no clear
reason. Paul Krichell,* the Yankee scout, believed they had so much
time to think between jobs of pitching that it made them broody
and a little crazy. Of all these offbeat men in monkey suits, left-
handed pitchers are thought to be the oddest. Ruth's life disproves
this belief. On the baseball field he was wholly reliable. (Off the
field was another matter.)

Pitching needs more orderly thought than hitting does. Pitchers
consciously learn a set of muscle movements and have to think
hard about coordination while remembering the current strengths
and weaknesses of the hitters. A pitcher who lacks frightening speed,
who paces himself well through nine-inning games, and who wins,
has a keen intelligence. He may have only a narrow vision of the
universe—nothing but batters and home plates—or he may have a
kind of spotlight view of reality, illuminating only baseball. But it is
astute. Babe Ruth had that kind of brightness, something less than
wisdom, more than cunning. To most sympathetic watchers the

* Paul Bernard Krichell (1882–1957), catcher, two seasons, 1911–1912, Browns,
batting average .222.

pitcher is a tragic hero, as Thomas Wolfe said, "alone, calm, desperate, and forsaken" but possessed of "resolution, despair, and lonely dignity. . . ." On the mound Ruth was never desperate or forsaken, and he was rarely dignified in the sense of adopting a conscious pose. But he *was* alone, calm, and bulging with resolve.

Figures are not the man, they only measure him. Figures also bore many people, though people who are interested in baseball can swallow more figures than most. We need a *few* pitching figures here to take Ruth's measure. First, we should notice that he worked in a golden age of pitching, and belonged there. For the seasons 1915–1919 inclusive, Ruth's earned-run average was 2.02 in a period when American League pitchers *as a group* had annual earned-run averages ranging from a low of 2.66 to a high of 3.21. Some of the sparkle of pitching before and during the First World War may have been the reflection of sunlight from foreign substances added to the ball, but Ruth used no pitch of the kinds later outlawed.

The sportswriter Tommy Holmes once rated pitchers based upon some ideas of Branch Rickey, which intended to block out everything except the battle of pitcher and hitter.* It measured one season at a time. The effect is to overrate the strikeout (with an opponent on first most of us would rather have an easy ground ball), so that it is more correctly an index of strikeout kings. In order of rating, the top dozen were:

Index	Pitcher	Year
431	Koufax	1965
336	Johnson	1912
334	Walsh	1908
327	Mathewson	1908
313	Gibson	1968
312	McLain	1968
300	Alexander	1915
289	Feller	1946
265	Marichal	1966
256	Vance	1924
153	Grove	1931
144	Dean	1934

The writer applied the formula to Ruth's annual records. His 1916 index of 146 should displace Dean from the list.

Another index, modified (by the writer) from a scouting-report system devised by George Sisler and son, we will call the Solo

---

* A point for each inning in excess of hits, a point for each strikeout in excess of walks.

Index.* In this ranking, the lower the number the better. (Your average, no-more-than-adequate starting pitcher of those years invariably gets a rating of more than 1.00.) The writer applied it to the 1915–1918 cumulative records of all Hall of Fame pitchers working in Ruth's pitching years, and to the records of Eddie Cicotte and Ruth. It gets rid of an overemphasis on strikeouts and produces, it seems, a more sensible rate for Ruth.

Alexander	.45
Johnson	.50
Cicotte	.66
Ruth	.73
Rixey	.78
Faber	.81
S. Coveleski	.83
Plank	.89

Finally, for rating Ruth as a World Series pitcher, there is an infallible measuring machine, the scoreboard, which answers the really important question, Who won the game? Ruth pitched three World Series games and won them all. Each was a one-run game: 2–1, 1–0, 3–2. There is order, form, and shape in that index.

Another way of measuring Ruth the pitcher is to look at the results of his contests with the best. There may be some argument whether Walter Johnson was the best pitcher of all time, but there can be no quarrel with the claim that Johnson was accepted as the American League's leading pitcher when Babe Ruth was known mainly as a pitcher.

Ruth and Johnson pitched against each other nine times in the four seasons 1915–1919. Four of the games were in Boston. Ruth won six and Johnson three.

> "One to nothing" is as close to perfection as a game can be pitched.
>
> —Jim Brosnan

Ruth won three of these games by the score of 1–0. Johnson didn't win any by that score (he had a 6–0 shutout for one of his three wins). A great pitcher once said the main job of a pitcher is not to give up the first run. Ruth did the job. One other pitcher, Big Ed Walsh,** had the same record against Johnson: three 1–0 games, and no 1–0 win by Johnson.

* Walks (multiplied by 1.3), plus hits, less strikeouts, divided by innings pitched, equals Solo Index. "Solo" because it depends in no way upon manager or teammates.
** Edward Augustine Walsh (1881–1959), pitcher, fourteen seasons, 1904–1917, White Sox, Braves. Hall of Fame. Won 194, lost 130, earned-run average 1.82 (the best of all time).

In these near-perfect games the pitching statistics of Ruth and Johnson were as close as the scores. The three games had a total of thirty-one innings. In hits it was Ruth thirteen, Johnson fifteen; in walks, Ruth five, Johnson eight; in strikeouts, Ruth eleven, Johnson eighteen. The May 7, 1917, 1–0 game at Washington had a heightened interest because it was part of a Ruth winning streak.

RUTH WINS SIXTH IN ROW
Ruth Outpitches Johnson
and Red Sox
Beat Senators 1–0

That was a classic ball game. Johnson gave up four hits, Ruth two. Each walked a batter. Johnson had seven strikeouts, Ruth three. And Ruth drove in the only run with a sacrifice fly in the eighth.

What Ruth did is clear when we learn that Johnson was in sixty-four 1–0 games, winning thirty-eight and losing twenty-six. That is twice as many of these lean and tight games as any other pitcher—which tells us much about the Senators' scoring power. Before 1920 Johnson relied almost entirely on speed; in his whipcord and steel-spring days he had no need for foxiness. In most of the photographs of Ruth and another person in which the two are so posed that one can compare anatomy, Ruth's hands are larger than the other's. But not in the case of Walter Johnson, whose hands were the same width as Ruth's but half again as long. And he had arms to match.

> He had those long arms, absolutely the longest arms I ever saw. They were like whips, that's what they were. He'd just *whip* that ball in there.
> —Davy Jones, on W. Johnson

The duels of Johnson and Ruth were of a kind less likely to happen nowadays. Modern strategy holds that there is no point in starting your best pitcher against their best. The idea is to get one well-pitched game and hope their best man has a bad day. Of course, box-office promotional interest sometimes dictates setting headliner against headliner to sell that extra five thousand tickets.

Where does Ruth march in the parade of pitchers? Edward Barrow said he was as good as any left-handed pitcher he ever saw. And the record books show that he never had a losing season. But cool second thought tells us he hardly belongs among the pitching immortals. There is a kind of yearning to think he was a very great pitcher, but three years of full-time pitching is not enough time to qualify him. A way to set him in his proper place is to search for pitchers who had single years as good as his best (1916), and not much better, measured by earned-run average and ratio of walks to strikeouts. From this search we can report that he was a very good pitcher, as good as Johnson in 1914 or Mort Cooper* in 1942.

That much is certain. What might have been if he had pitched after 1919 is another matter. He was a durable, lasting pitcher. He finished almost two-thirds of his games. Starting pitchers of the 1960s (partly because of the importance of relief pitchers, of course) finished fewer than a third of their starts. Given his physical toughness, one might believe that Ruth could become one of the greats. His calendar age shows what the prospect was, *if* he had gone on. At the end of 1919 he had won eighty-nine and lost forty-six. He was twenty-four years old. At that age Pete Alexander was a beginner. Sandy Koufax was a loser. Neither Warren Spahn nor Lefty Grove won a major-league game before the age of twenty-five. With that start, and twelve or fifteen more years of pitching, Ruth would very likely have made it to everybody's list of the half-dozen greatest pitchers. But this is all moonglow. The hard fact is that in his brief respectable pitching career he firmly established himself to this time as the best *hitter* among all the thousands of major-league pitchers.

* Morton Cecil Cooper (1913–1958), pitcher, eleven seasons, 1938–1949, Cardinals, Braves, Giants, Cubs. Won 128, lost 75, earned-run average 2.97.

12 · Something for Their Money
(1919-20)

". . . You knew I was a Yankee fan before I married you."

"Yes," I sobbed. "But I did not think that you would drag your wife down with you. I never believed that you would humiliate me this way before my Flatbush friends."

"A woman's place in the bleachers is beside her husband," said John peevishly.

—*New York Tribune* (1916)

For a long time the Yankees (once called the Highlanders) had been paupers in New York where John McGraw and his Giants were princes. Starting as the Baltimore American League club in 1901, the franchise was taken to New York in 1903. In its nineteen seasons the club had never won a pennant. It finished in the second division a dozen times and in last place three times. Its best moneymaking year had been 1910—a profit of eighty thousand dollars. A Yankee team that draws badly at home is a liability to the American League, because the seven visiting teams need to profit from the visitors' share of the largest city's gate receipts.

In 1919 the Yankees belonged to Jacob Ruppert, a brewer, and Tillinghast l'Hommedieu Huston, an engineer. Each called himself "Colonel"; Huston had earned his rank. Ruppert's interest in New York baseball went back to 1900 when he tried to buy the Giants at the fair price of $150,000 but was turned away in favor of John T. Brush who got the team for the same figure. Ruppert had never seen the Yankees play before they moved into the new Polo Grounds in 1913 as tenants of the Giants, and he saw them only twice before he owned them (he went to see Ty Cobb and Walter Johnson). Ruppert had a chance to buy the Cubs in 1912 but turned it down, saying he wasn't interested "in anything so far from Broadway." Ban Johnson, the founding father and president of the American League, heard of this remark and made a mental note that Ruppert might be interested in something near Broadway. Joseph Lannin of Boston also hoped to lure Ruppert into American League ownership. Johnson told Ruppert in 1914 he could buy the Yankees, and then get Eddie Collins from the retrenching Connie Mack for fifty thousand.

The Yankee owners were Frank Farrell and William Bevery. Farrell was a gambling tycoon, and Bevery was a police officer who (it was said) found the secret of making crime pay. The organization headed by the two was thought to make about three million a year from prostitution, gambling, and civic corruption. A losing or break-even baseball team would not interest them for long. They were certainly not having money troubles, but the ball club was too small an operation to bother with if it was the source of any kind of annoyance; as it happened, the upward pressure of salaries during the war with the Federal League was annoying.

John McGraw of the Giants joined Johnson and Lannin in their attempt to attract Ruppert to ownership. McGraw did not like to share the New York scene with Farrell and Bevery. He also feared they might sell to someone of even worse repute.

Ruppert, who understood very well how to make money, looked into the records that passed for accountancy in the Yankee offices. They were a mess. Perhaps he ought to buy the Indianapolis minor-league franchise and move it to New York? At least the Hoosiers knew how to keep books. Ban Johnson advised against that, and helped Ruppert arrive at an understanding of the Yankees' money prospects. Ruppert made up his mind to buy the Yankees while vacationing at French Lick, the merry, laxative spa in Indiana where he spent several weeks a year. He bought the team in a spirit of play and invited his French Lick playfellows to share the fun. Colonel Huston thus became a New York owner in partnership with Ruppert. They each put up $225,000 for what Ruppert called "an orphan ball club, without a home of its own, without players of outstanding ability, without prestige." They took charge on January 11, 1915.

Ban Johnson had promised his influence to get five good players for the Yankees, but even Eddie Collins escaped them. By 1919 they had picked up only two first-rate players, Wally Pipp and Bunny High,* to show for about two hundred thousand dollars of added spending. They began to look on Ban Johnson and their fellow

* Walter Clement Pipp (1893–1965), first baseman, fifteen seasons, 1913–1928, Tigers, Yankees, Reds, batting average .281.
Hugh Jenken High (1887–1962), outfielder, six seasons, 1913–1918, Tigers, Yankees, batting average .250.

owners sourly. The Yankees had finished fifth, fourth, sixth, and, in 1919, third with the best attendance yet. Ruppert and Huston decided to rely on their own efforts to build a winner.

Jacob Ruppert's grandfather came from Bavaria, and by 1851 he ran his own brewery in New York. Jacob's father entered the brewing business in 1867, the year Jacob was born. The boy went to Columbia Grammar School and qualified for Columbia School of Mines, but, at his father's request, went into the brewery instead. When prohibition came the Ruppert firm had been turning out 1.3 million barrels of beer a year.

The brewery made rivers of money, more than enough to finance four successful campaigns for Congress by Jacob Ruppert, who ran as a Democrat in a nominally Republican district. He joined the Seventh Regiment, a militia unit for rich military hobbyists, and six other clubs. One governor made him an honorary colonel. He had a twelve-room town apartment and a house on the Hudson; his hobbies included a racing stable, two breeds of pedigreed dogs, and a herd of Percheron draft horses. The race horses were said to make a profit of fifty thousand dollars a year. There were also about twenty monkeys in the animal collection.

Ruppert's office was paneled in dark wood, had no curtains, and was ornamented by two bronzes of American Indians, a bronze eagle, and a tank of goldfish. Each of these decorations had its own marble pedestal. He never married, but lived at 1120 Fifth Avenue, sustained by butler, maid, valet, cook, and laundress.

Several people who knew Jacob Ruppert described him as aristocratic, which in twentieth-century America seems to mean that he inherited a great deal of money. He took himself very seriously and regarded his political colonelcy as a kind of knighthood. Perhaps in the beer or real estate businesses he behaved differently, but his baseball history makes him appear to have been the kind of man who took off his hat when he mentioned his own name.

Huston was an engineer and self-made rich man. Born in a small Ohio town in 1869, his first job was as city engineer of Cincinnati. When the Spanish-American War came, he went to Cuba as a captain in a volunteer regiment of engineers. He stayed on after the war to improve three major harbors, and while in Cuba met the Cuba-lover John McGraw. McGraw later introduced Huston and Ruppert in New York.

Huston was no dandy. He sometimes wore the same suit for many days, and he nearly always wore the same hard bowler hat. As co-owner of the Yankees he easily mixed with players and sportswriters, who called him Cap. His theory of baseball administration was simple: have a winner.

> ... I'd better put you in touch with some of the fellows I
> know who've lost money banking on civic pride to build
> their business in ball clubs. Baseball is not supported by
> civic pride. It's supported by interest in winners, a desire
> to see them perform or the hope that they'll get licked. ...
> Practically nobody will go, whatever his civic pride, to see
> a tail ender.
>
> —T. l'H. Huston

Up in Boston, Harry Frazee, the owner of the Red Sox, felt
harassed. He got along poorly with his players and lost a lawsuit to
a player who had filed his grievance against the Red Sox before
Frazee bought the club. Next he began a loud quarrel with Ban
Johnson late in 1918, hoping to replace the National Commission
with a single baseball commissioner, perhaps Judge Kenesaw Mountain Landis, perhaps ex-President William Howard Taft. Frazee
had many frictions and few profits.

His disenchantment with baseball sharpened the appetites of the
Yankee owners who behaved as if they endorsed *The Times*'s statement that "The Red Sox, as it stands today, is the greatest collection
of baseball talent in either league." This was the evaluation even
after the Yankees had bought Ernie Shore, Duffy Lewis, and Dutch
Leonard. When Carl Mays jumped the Red Sox in Chicago in July
1919, the episode ended in August with his name on the Yankee
roster. Baseball had just about lost its charm for Frazee, a man
always more interested in footlights than foul lines.

At the end of the 1919 season Babe Ruth made himself a bother
to Frazee. He let the sporting press know he thought his splendid
playing of 1919 proved that he deserved a raise from ten to twenty
thousand dollars. (*The Times* editorially noticed that Ruth's contract at ten thousand still had two years to run; he had taken a
capitalist risk, and lost.) To further trouble Frazee's sleep, Ruth
restated his alleged ambition to be a professional boxer, tracing it
back to his days as a preliminary boy in the Baltimore fight circuit
(pure flapdoodle, unless he meant that he boxed as a small boy at
St. Mary's School). Then again, if he did not choose to be a boxer,
perhaps he would become a full-time movie actor. The roads to the
silver screen and the prize ring crossed when Kid McCoy, former
boxer, and Al St. John, movie actor, announced that McCoy had
contracted to train Ruth for thirty days. Then, if McCoy said Ruth
was up to it, St. John would try to promote a match with—here it
comes—Jack Dempsey. This press release *may* have worried Frazee.
What it did for sure was to get Al St. John's name in the papers from
coast to coast, which was the true purpose.

A more certain torment of Frazee was Ruth's return (from California) of his contract, on Christmas Eve 1919, with a demand for a new contract at double the money. He added that it was no use trading him because he would play ball for no club but the Red Sox. When the reporters of Los Angeles County came hurrying to hear more, he told them he was "through with major-league baseball" unless the Red Sox paid him twenty thousand a year. After all, he had several pots boiling with deals, each worth more than ten thousand a year. No, he had decided not to become a prize fighter. Yes, he was still thinking of going into the movies. Meantime he was playing winter ball for money and golf for fun.

Yankee Manager Miller Huggins* had advised his owners that the best deed they could do would be to turn Ruth into a Yankee. Huggins's tastes were simple: he wanted the best ballplayer. Without knowing it, Ruth was helping Huggins. Frazee was loaded with debt and his notes held by Lannin, the former Red Sox owner, were due. The Red Sox had made money in 1919, mostly because of Ruth's home-run outburst, but Frazee lost more on Broadway than he made in Fenway. Ban Johnson was beginning to seek an eligible new owner for the Red Sox, just in case. On or about December 26, Frazee was trying to raise half a million dollars for some theatrical productions he had in mind. He called on Jacob Ruppert to ask for a loan. Ruppert suggested they talk about Babe Ruth. Then, on December 27, Frazee gave the press the magic words: the Red Sox were open to a deal for any player on the roster except Harry Hooper. That was three days after Ruth's ultimatum.

The rich but frustrated Yankees had looked at Boston as a warehouse of baseball talent since late 1918, when the Red Sox let New York have Ernie Shore, Dutch Leonard, and Duffy Lewis. That same year there was talk that the Yankees might buy Babe Ruth for $150,000. There had been no move in that direction by owners on either side; probably it just seemed logical. At the end of November 1919 Huggins let people know he expected to make some interesting deals in December, perhaps at the American League meeting in New York on December 10. It was during these weeks that Huggins advised Ruppert and Huston to try to get Ruth. Since the two owners were restless and fretful about the Yankees' years of mediocrity, Huggins's words were heard. Cap Huston was a convivial man who liked to drink beer and talk with engineers, writers, and ballplayers, and it was, perhaps, at some scientific, literary, and athletic symposium that he learned of Frazee's money shrinkage,

---

* Miller James Huggins (1879–1929), infielder, thirteen seasons, 1904–1916, Reds, Cardinals, batting average .265. Manager seventeen seasons, 1913–1929, Cardinals, Yankees, six penants, three world championships.

perhaps even from Frazee himself. It would round out the story neatly to say Huston craftily sent Frazee to borrow some money from Ruppert, but that is unknowable.

Earlier hypothetical conversations about selling Babe Ruth had always been treated as comic monologues, but when the possibility became real it was not difficult to close the deal. The talk between Ruppert and Frazee in the last week of 1919 is not recorded, but the results are public.

The price was $125,000, of which $25,000 was immediately paid as earnest money. No players except Ruth were involved, because Ed Barrow—who was angry at the deal—told Frazee the Red Sox management would look like fools if they pretended to believe the Yankees had any players fit to throw onto a scale to balance Ruth. In addition to the $125,000, Ruppert promised to lend Frazee $350,000, secured by a mortgage on Fenway Park. (This brought Frazee pretty close to the half-million he had started out to raise.) Huston balked at the idea of the Yankees lending money on a ball park, so Ruppert, a shrewd real estate operator, made the loan on his own. It was ten months before Ruppert's personal interest in the prosperity of the Red Sox was discovered. The conflict of interest probably would not be allowed in organized baseball today, but, in fairness to Ruppert, we may say he did everything he could to ruin the Red Sox. (Ruth was the fifth of the Red Sox to leave for the Yankees, and in Frazee's time the total would reach twelve; the great Yankee team of 1923 could well be called the New York Red Sox.) In spite of the destruction of the Red Sox, Ruppert still held the mortgage as late as 1931 and found it profitable.

Ruth's contract was conveyed in the usual legal form by adding baseball's uniform agreement for the transfer of a player. Surprisingly, the addition was dated December 26, 1919, two days after Ruth's ultimatum which demanded the doubling of his salary, and the day *before* the publication of the statement in which Frazee had said all Boston players were available except Hooper. The Ruth deal was signed and sealed at the time Frazee made that announcement. The Yankees were the first to know and obviously had the inside lane in any race to loot the Red Sox.

Ruppert and Huston laid out more money for Ruth than they had for the Yankee franchise and the club, though most of the money was a well-secured loan. Tris Speaker had cost Cleveland fifty-five thousand dollars, Eddie Collins was sold to the White Sox for fifty thousand, and the White Sox paid thirty-two thousand and two players for Joe Jackson. Ruth's price of $125,000 (quite apart from the Fenway mortgage) was easily a new record. It was also the best investment ever made by any club, and, in the long run, it turned out to be relatively frugal and thrifty. Furthermore it was the most glaring act in the demolition of one of baseball's greatest teams, the Red Sox of the decade 1909–1919: four pennants, four world championships, five finishes in second, third, or fourth place, and only two finishes in the second division.

> **Above all, get the fans a star whom they may worship, no matter what he costs, by trade or purchase. Give them something for their money.**
> **—Anonymous owner (1922)**

On the morning of January 6, 1920, the *New York Times* carried an eight-column sports-page headline: RUTH BOUGHT BY NEW YORK AMERICANS FOR $125,000, HIGHEST PRICE IN BASEBALL ANNALS. The story ran to one and a quarter columns, mostly a review of Ruth's career. Manager Miller Huggins was in California to give the new Yankee a better contract. Ruth was to be the New York team's regular rightfielder.

> **I believe the sale of Ruth will ultimately strengthen the team.**
> **—Harry Frazee (1920)**

Harry Frazee hurried into print to explain the sale of Ruth: the deal wasn't intended to weaken the Red Sox. Ruth's contract had been written just as he wished, but then he demanded a doubling of his pay. That made the idea of a contract meaningless; contracts were written just to prevent that sort of thing. Nobody was worth as much as Ruth was asking. The Red Sox were "fast becoming a one-man team," and one player didn't make a team, as proved by the sixth-place finish of 1919.

Boston's Royal Rooters were skeptical of all this. Their leader, Johnny Keenan, said "Ruth was 90 percent of our club last summer. It will be impossible to replace the strength Ruth gave the Sox." Frazee counterattacked: Ruth was "one of the most selfish and inconsiderate men that ever wore a baseball uniform." He added, "I could not get Joe Jackson for him in trade." This must be Frazee's relative evaluation of Ruth and Jackson. There is not a jot of evidence that he tried or wished to trade Ruth for Jackson. He needed money, not players.

> **. . . a tremendous blow to the army of loyal fans.**
> **—Boston Post**

The *Boston Post* predicted the Red Sox would be "crowding the Athletics for eighth place in 1920"; true, the Red Sox had survived

NOTICE All agreements, whether for the immediate or prospective release of a player, to which a Major League Club is a party, must be forwarded to the Secretary of the Commission for record and promulgation within five days after execution. (See Article V., Section 7, National Agreement, on back of this Agreement.)

UNIFORM AGREEMENT
FOR TRANSFER OF A PLAYER

NOTICE.—To establish uniformity in action by clubs when a player, released by a major league club to a minor league club, or by a minor league club to a major league club, refuses to report to and contract with the club to which he is transferred, the Commission directs the club securing him to protect both parties to the deal from responsibility for his salary during his insubordination by promptly suspending him. Payment, in part or in whole, of the consideration for the release of such player will not be enforced until he is reinstated and actually enters the service of the purchasing club.

TO OR BY A
Major League Club

WARNING TO CLUBS.—Many contentions that arise over the transfer of players are directly due to the neglect of one or both parties to promptly execute and file the Agreement. The Commission will no longer countenance dilatory tactics, that result in appeals to it to investigate and enforce claims which, if made a matter of record, as required by the laws of Organized Base Ball, would not require adjustment. In all cases of this character, the complaining club must establish that it is not at fault for delay or neglect to sign and file the Agreement upon which its claim is predicated. (See last sentence of Rule 10.)

This Agreement, made and entered into this 26th day of December 1919 by and between   Boston American League Baseball Club
(Party of the First Part)
and   American League Base Ball Club of New York
(Party of the Second Part)

Witnesseth : The party of the first part does hereby release to the party of the second part the services of Player George H. Ruth under the following conditions :

(Here recite fully and clearly every condition of deal, including date of delivery; if for a money consideration, designate time and method of payment; if an exchange of players, name each; if option to recall is retained or privilege of choosing one or more players in lieu of one released is retained, specify all terms. No transfer will be held valid unless the consideration, receipt of which is acknowledged therein, passes at time of execution of Agreement.)

By herewith assigning to the party of the second part the contract of said player George H. Ruth for the seasons of 1919, 1920 and 1921, in consideration of the sum of Twenty-five Thousand ($25,000.) Dollars and other good and valuable considerations paid by the party of the second part, receipt whereof is hereby acknowledged.

The parties to this Agreement further covenant to abide by all provisions of the National Agreement and by all Rules of the National Commission, regulating the transfer of the services of a player, particularly those printed on the reverse side of this Agreement.

In Testimony Whereof, we have subscribed hereto, through our respective presidents or authorized agents, on the date above written :

Witness :   BOSTON AMERICAN LEAGUE BASEBALL CLUB

(Party of the First Part)

AMERICAN LEAGUE BASE BALL CLUB OF NEW YORK

(Party of the Second Part)

Corporate name of Company, Club or Association of each party should be written in first paragraph and subscribed hereto. (See Rule 10.)

Club officials are cautioned to carefully read the provisions of the National Agreement and the rules of the National Commission, printed on the back of this Agreement, for their information and guidance.

The legal instrument by which Jacob Ruppert got Babe Ruth from Harry Frazee's Boston Red Sox, December 26, 1919. (G.S. *Gallery.*)

the departures of Cy Young and Tris Speaker, "but Ruth is different. He is one of a class of ball players that flashes across the firmament once in a great while."

> **I suppose this means I'll be sent to China.**
> **—Ping Bodie* (1920)**

Frazee, trying to win back angry customers, went too far in saying Ruth was a poor team player who was interested only in bettering his own records. Runs-batted-in were not then tabulated, but Fred Lieb, in the *New York Sun*, showed what nonsense Frazee spoke. Lieb extracted Ruth's runs-batted-in from the box scores. The Red Sox scored 565 runs in 1919. Ruth scored 103 of them and drove in 114. From 114 we must subtract the twenty-nine home runs, because they are counted both as runs and as runs-batted-in. With that adjustment, Ruth was responsible for a net 188 runs, or almost exactly a third of all runs scored by the Boston Americans.

All of Frazee's counterblasts were useless. He was a poor man— for a baseball magnate—who literally didn't know where his next half-million was coming from. People believed he sold Ruth because Ruth asked for a raise. To men and women unborn in the 1920s Frazee is not remembered with gratitude as the producer of *No, No, Nanette* but rather as the fiend of the fens whose greed broke up the Red Sox.

> **Ruth is the greatest hitter I have ever seen.**
> **—Jimmy Burke,** ** **Manager,**
> **St. Louis Browns (1920)**

> **Ruth has no particular weakness.**
> **—Eddie Cicotte (1920)**

> **In my opinion, Ruth is the greatest slugger of all times, and a dangerous hitter. He is a natural ball player.**
> **—Jack Dunn (1920)**

The *New York Times* preached a short sermon on the bad example set by all parties to the sale, which showed that a good player with a weak team could hold out "for an imposing salary" and "get somebody in New York or Chicago to buy his services."

---

* Frank Stephan Bodie (Pezzolo) (1887–1961), outfielder, nine seasons, 1911–1921, White Sox, Athletics, Yankees, batting average .275.

** James Timothy Burke (1874–1942), infielder, six seasons, 1898–1905, Cleveland National League, White Sox, Milwaukee American League (pre-Browns), Pirates, Cardinals, batting average .244. Manager, 1905, 1918–1920.

I was disgusted. . . . All Frazee wanted was the money.
He was short of cash and he sold the whole team down the
river to keep his dirty nose above water. What a way to
end a wonderful ball club!

I got sick to my stomach at the whole business. After the
1920 season I held out for $15,000 and Frazee did me a
favor by selling me to the Chicago White Sox. I was glad
to get away from that graveyard.

—Harry Hooper

The decay of the Red Sox: They finished fifth in 1920 and 1921,
eighth in 1922 and 1923. The club drew 417,000 in 1919 and 230,000
in 1924. To look at it another way, the 1919 Red Sox had one-ninth
of the American League attendance, and their share was never
again as high as one-tenth until Tom Yawkey bought the team in
the 1930s. The club drew but a twentieth part of the American
League attendance in 1923, the year when Frazee's sack of the Sox
was complete.

1920 1/6.   Contract increased $10,000 by agreement mak-
            ing total $20,000
            —New York Yankees Salary and Transfer File

A move to the Yankees in 1920 was no step upward nor a particularly desirable change for Babe Ruth, who had put down roots
in Massachusetts. Using Connecticut tobacco, his cigar factory made
the Babe Ruth cigar with his picture on every wrapper, selling at
five cents. Helen and he lived in rural Sudbury when at home. As
the most admired player of baseball's greatest team of recent years,
Ruth's standing in the New England sports world was agreeably
high.

At the time of the sale to the Yankees he was in southern California to play winter baseball. In a batting exhibition at a Los Angeles
ball park he set a curious record by batting continuously against a
relay of pitchers for an hour and hitting 125 balls over the fence.

The eleven-day delay between the agreement of Ruppert and
Frazee and the publication of the news was to give Huggins time to
get to California and see Ruth. Huggins found him playing golf at
Griffith Park in Los Angeles. He hadn't heard about the sale, but
the news Huggins brought came as no surprise, considering the
ultimatum to Frazee.

This first meeting suggested the poor relations that Huggins and
Ruth were to suffer. Huggins felt called upon to preach on the ethics
of life in New York, a place with many temptations for active, warm-

blooded young men in good physical condition, temptations which could lead to acts intolerable to the owners of the New York American League baseball club. Ruth listened, bored, and suggested that the only point to be talked about was his request for a raise. Huggins

Announcement of the homecoming concert of the St. Mary's Industrial School Band, after its tour with the Yankees, 1920. (*Xaverian Brothers, Kensington, Maryland.*)

Grand Musical Concert

—— By ——

"BABE" RUTH'S BAND

Fifth Regiment Armory

Thursday, September 23rd
8 P. M.

ADMISSION FREE

Doors Open at 7 P. M.

St. Mary's Industrial School Boys' Band having completed a successful and triumphant trip with the New York "Yankees" around the Western Circuit will help to celebrate "Babe" Ruth's Day by rendering a free concert for the citizens of the home town. "Babe" Ruth will positively appear in person at this entertainment. Here is your chance to get a "close-up" view of the "Home-Run King."

Remember "Babe's" Welcome Home

said it was all arranged: Ruth would get twenty thousand a year if he behaved himself.

Ruth looked on Huggins as a curious specimen who had been a player and manager in the National League and had recently moved over to the American League, displacing Ruth's friend Wild Bill Donovan, formerly the manager at Providence and more recently manager of the Yankees. Huggins was said to have been a good second baseman and leadoff man, but Ruth thought him pretty small, at five feet, six and a half inches and 140 pounds, to swing the old heavy bat and to come out ahead in the rough play around second base.

News of the Ruth-Huggins treaty cheered New Yorkers. And everyone knew that the Polo Grounds' right-field foul line measured only 257 feet from the plate to the wall—offering the cheapest home run in the major leagues for a left-handed pull-hitter. Ruth had always liked to play there.

The new Yankee finished his winter sports early in February and started east after saying he wouldn't sign a contract unless Frazee gave him part of the sale price. Fifteen thousand dollars would be about right. All he did was to show himself boyishly naive. A ball-player in Ruth's position has absolutely no leverage. *If* he wished to play baseball he had to play for the Yankees. He spoke acidly of Frazee, again bringing up Frazee's gift of a cigar (to George H. Ruth, cigar manufacturer) on Babe Ruth day in 1919, and adding that Mrs. Ruth had to buy a ticket to get into Fenway Park that day.

Ruth's arrival in New York was private. He didn't plan it that way, but all of the owners and writers were in Chicago at the baseball meetings.

Ruppert and Huston had not forgotten him, though. While baseball teams were insured as groups, one policy covering all the players on a roster, Ruth received special treatment. The Yankee owners had taken out a separate life insurance policy for him in the amount of $150,000. A fit sum for the most costly player in baseball.

13 · An Agreeable Guy

Upon earth there is not his like, a creature without fear.
—Job 41:33.

In the last week of 1919 the Yankees bought the best baseball player alive. What kind of man was Babe Ruth when near his prime?

There was nothing of angles about him. From head to foot he was all curves, including his fullmoon face and his stemware ankles. These curved lines did not make beauty. Paul Gallico, who knew him well, said, "He is one of the ugliest men. . . . A figurine that might have been made by a savage." Gallico thought his wide variance from the Greek sculptors' athletic ideal had its own appeal to the people. At first glance he seemed to be a barrel on bird legs, though his legs and ankles were strong enough to do their work. He was not fat during most seasons of play, but he showed a tendency to grow what was literally a beer belly. An anatomist at the University of Virginia tried to type Ruth's structure. From four categories—cerebral, muscular, respiratory, digestive—Professor R. Bennett Bean chose "muscular" for Ruth. Bean further divided "muscular" into long and short. Ruth was a short, a man built for heavy labors.

The anatomical ideal of the wedge-shaped athlete, broad in the shoulder and slim hipped, is an artist's generalization which we owe to ancient Greece. When a great player appears with a different form—Yogi Berra, Honus Wagner, Babe Ruth—people think him misshapen. Why the Greeks (and their Roman imitators) used the wedge for the shape of the athlete they did not say, but we may suppose that it was because their statuary was for public places and the wedge-man could be identified as male at a hundred yards. Thus the marble male athlete was a symbol of masculine beauty. Today we have no need for the stereotype.

Ruth's friends called him "the big fellow"; his few foes called him "the big monkey." How big was he? The twenty most frequently appearing players of the 1917 White Sox, 1920 Indians and Dodgers, 1921 Yankees and Giants, and 1922 Browns (all great teams) make a total of 120 players, of whom only nine stood taller than Ruth's six feet two. His weight in 1921 was 215. Weights change quickly among ballplayers, but Ruth was the heaviest of the 120 above—his belly was still almost flat. For his time he *was* a big fellow (or monkey).

His face was tough but not threatening. His lips were thick, his nostrils wide and flaring, his head as round as Charlie Brown's. As H. G. Wells said of one of his fictional characters, he had "a face like a carving abandoned as altogether too unpromising for completion." His shape—head, torso, legs—helped to make him a public figure because anybody in the ball park could pick him out of a group on the opposite side of the outfield. In the same way, anyone who had seen a picture of his face (and who hadn't?) would know him on the street at sight. In public the crowd could always identify him, a fact which had helped to make him its darling.

Except in the swing of his bat and the snap of his throwing arm, his motions were not graceful.

> **I went to the Yankee stadium one time to see Babe Ruth. He could bat, but his pigeon-toed stubbed little trot lacked beauty.**
>
> **—Marianne Moore**

Ruth ran pigeon-toed, it has been said, in imitation of Brother Matthias. Some track coaches believe it is the best way to run, because the runner can then push with all five toes.

His voice was preserved on many records, beginning with a 1920 Pathé. His baritone had a booming quality, but he was not a loud-mouth, unless he was in a celebrating mood or was answering opposing bench jockeys. He claimed his voice became huskier when he was burned with an overdose of silver nitrate on a Red Sox trainer's throat swab, but that was before the first recording. His laughter was called rolling. By all accounts it came easily.

Ruth's skill as a ballplayer was partly the result of relaxation, that is, the ability to stand uncommitted to any action and to be ready to do what was necessary at an instant's notice without adjustment. Thus he was almost never taken by surprise. Usually this ability to "hang loose" is very hard (but not impossible) for a thin-skinned front-rank player, because his job is always threatened by newer men. Ruth lacked that kind of feeling. Having no fear of rivals, Ruth was loose and ready to act at any moment as needed. He collected himself, so to speak, into one power of acting at his greatest competence, using his strength quickly and with great concentration. A player who can do this has much the same reaction-time as a healthy young cat; a first-rate infielder taking care of an unexpected pop bunt looks very much like a cat catching a house moth. The sudden spending of energy without reacting too quickly or too slowly is the mark of a great fielder, and shows a talent which is even more valuable to a hitter—because batting is harder than fielding. Tightness spoils form. Ruth was not shackled in movement. Marianne Moore said, "A gibbon in a flying leap seems to have no joints." Ruth at bat had that kind of looseness, as shown in many newsreel clips. His body functioned as a single unit which hung together perfectly.

When Ruth swung hard at the ball his energy exploded in all directions from a center just above the pelvis. The strongest parts of the body are the heaviest. Having the most inertia, their movements are slower. A player in a sudden burst of effort first uses the strongest muscles near his center of gravity (halfway through the trunk, an inch below the navel). Then come into motion the muscles of trunk and thighs, next the arms, calves, wrists, ankles, hands, feet. Force flows from the center of the body outward to the extremities. In 1919 Ruth had no rival in such explosions of energy. Even when he missed the ball, people gasped at the sight.

THE AUTHOR: Did Ruth ever show stage fright?
EARLE COMBS: * Never showed stage fright.
BOB SHAWKEY: Never.
JOE SEWELL: * * Always calm.

When Ruth became a New Yorker, psychologists Albert Johanson and Joseph Holmes persuaded him to come to Columbia University's psychological laboratories and take a battery of tests. Their findings deserve listing.

—The pitch he could hit hardest was just above the knees on the outside corner of the plate.

—When he hit the ball perfectly, in still air, with the bat moving at 110 feet a second, the ball would necessarily carry 450 to 500 feet.

—When a ball was pitched, Ruth inhaled sharply on the backswing of the bat and held his breath until after he swung or decided not to swing.

—Ruth could complete an electrical circuit by inserting a hand

---

* Earle Bryan Combs (1899–   ), outfielder, twelve seasons, 1924–1935, Yankees. Hall of Fame. Batting average .325.
* * Joseph Wheeler Sewell (1898–   ), infielder fourteen seasons, 1920–1933, Indians, Yankees, batting average .312.

tool into successive holes 132 times a minute with his left hand. The average score of other test-takers was 82 times a minute.

—He could complete a circuit by tapping a charged instrument on a charged plate 193 times a minute. The average score was 180.

—In a test of steadiness of nerve, by inserting a charged rod successively into small holes of different sizes, Ruth proved himself the best of five hundred who had tried.

—Ruth's eyes responded to briefly flashing electric bulbs in a darkened chamber 2/100 of a second quicker than the average person—very valuable for picking up the moving ball as it left the pitcher's hand.

—In responses to sound it took Ruth 14/100 of a second to react, and the average person 15/100.

—In reading groups of eight letters exposed for 1/50,000 of a second, Ruth could usually read six at a flash. Other persons could read four or five of the eight.

—Ruth could count twelve black dots of a group exposed on a card for 1/50,000 of a second. The average score was eight.

—In a test of the speed of recognition of arbitrarily numbered symbols his score was the average score.

—When given a card of printed matter and told to cross out the "A's" in a fixed period of time, his score was 50 percent above the average.

Babe Ruth's eyes, ears, brain, and nerves worked more quickly and accurately than those of the average person, and the coordination of all was "much nearer perfection than that of the average man."

Walter Hagen, the famous golfer, took the same tests. His reaction times were as much below the average as Ruth's were above it, but further testing showed it was a matter of a golfer's deliberation. A golfer's motion must be right the first time; he doesn't get three swings at the golf ball. When it came to identifying the arbitrarily numbered shapes and scratching out the "A's," Hagen showed greater concentration than Ruth. What was reported as a "Duel Between Champions" proved only that a baseball player swings during a fleeting moment while a golfer waits for reports from all of his nerves. There is no true comparison of the psychological requirements of the two games.

Peter Amondo, writing in the Berlin *Querschnitt*, reviewed Ruth's psychological test scores and concluded it was only faintly possible that the entire population of the United States could produce an equal to Ruth.

The tests show us that Babe Ruth did not become the leading American League pitcher of 1916, the leading defensive outfielder of 1919, and the leading slugger of all years up to and including 1919 by exerting his will power or cramming himself with facts.

> **Heroes like that man of muscle. . . . Without purpose, apparently, . . . [he achieves] that which most men, even those of exceptional intellect, could never attain if they followed every rule laid down in the book.**
> **—Bozeman Bulger**

Babe Ruth had five physical qualities which must be inherited: speed, endurance, strength, accuracy, and coordination. The least flashy and the most necessary was coordination. If you needed someone to thread a needle by dim light in a moving automobile, Babe Ruth would be your man.

Ruth played the ukulele and occasionally went ballroom dancing. It follows from what we know of the close alliance between his senses, nerves, and muscles that he should have been very good on the ukulele and at dancing. He wasn't. Obviously he wasn't really trying.

Babe Ruth did not divide his life into parts but lived it whole. Baseball, food, drink, sleep were all of a piece. Not for him a winter job to prepare for retirement from baseball. He behaved as if there was no life after baseball, no life apart from it. A home run and a prime sirloin were equally enjoyable, and in something of the same way.

Ruth resembled Charles Dickens's Major Bagshot who, "like some other noble animals, exhibited himself to great advantage at feeding-time." His digestive equipment was excellent, and his eating habits have been widely discussed. Some of the talk probably springs from envy. A look at remedies for indigestion in drugstores and on television screens hints that a large part of the population abuses its alimentary tubing as much as Ruth did, but is pitiably less able to cope. Cookery was not a fine art to this heavy eater; trash food, candy, hot dogs, the run of ball-park fare was as welcome as the work of New York's finest chefs. True, hot dogs were not main dishes but standard between-meals snacks. To accompany the trash food there was always the same heartburn remedy, sodium bicarbonate. Sometimes he ate it dry, a handful at a time. In the clubhouse he might take a swig of a saturated solution of bicarb and water which he kept in a jug in his locker.

People have expressed (or enjoyed?) shock at Babe Ruth's feeding habits, as though a ballplayer ought to set us an example of a spartan diet. But it is a fable that baseball players should keep rigid training. The season, from March through September, is too

long to allow a man to keep the kind of fine physical edge that a
boxer achieves on the eve of a match. Ballplayers can't obey the
stern training rules that are part of the mythology of athletics. They
need a different regimen. The average major-league player loses
from four to eight pounds a game (the pitcher loses even more),
which he usually makes up before the next game. The hotter the
weather the greater the weight loss, and the more beer and ice
cream are consumed. A player needs only to keep his muscles
stretched and supple, get enough sleep to stay alert during the
game, and avoid taking on so much weight that it slows him down.
Because of many reports of Ruth's overeating, it is worth noting
that when he joined the Yankees he had no double chin, no paunch.

Ruth consciously helped to create the fable of Babe the Glutton.
He often grossly overate when strangers or new friends were with
him, in order to keep alive his reputation as a greedy feaster. He
seemed to think he owed such a show to the spectators. Sometimes
it was a restrained and classic act, like the time he asked a waiter
to decorate his steak with a border of lamb chops. Usually it was
something gaudier. For Paul Derringer's* diversion Ruth once
arranged his own dining-car breakfast as follows: a pint of whiskey
mixed with a pint of ginger ale in a pitcher of ice, followed by a
porterhouse steak, four fried eggs, fried potatoes, and a pot of
coffee. He told Derringer this was his daily breakfast. During an
evening about New York (including Coney Island) with Harry
Heilmann, Fred Haney, and Joe Dugan,** Ruth refreshed himself in
the following style: (1) *Dinner*: two porterhouse steaks, a double
order of head lettuce with Roquefort dressing, a double order of
cottage-fried potatoes, a double order of apple pie a la mode. (2)
First snack at Coney Island: four hot dogs, four bottles of Coca-Cola.
(3) *Second snack at Coney Island*: the same. (4) *Late supper*: same
as dinner. All of this in five or six hours.

Unhappily, young players sometimes thought they could match
Ruth and began to eat their way out of baseball. When Huggins
caught on to Ruth's café showmanship he told young players they
would be wise not to run around with him.

Before the prohibition amendment, most players drank beer if
they drank anything alcoholic. Beer was Babe Ruth's drink. He

---

* Paul Derringer (1906–   ), pitcher, fifteen seasons, 1931–1945, Cardinals,
Reds, Cubs. Won 232, lost 212, earned-run average 3.46.
** Harry Edwin Heilmann (1894–1951), outfielder, seventeen seasons, 1914–1932,
Tigers, Reds, batting average .342.
Fred Girard Haney (1898–   ), infielder, seven seasons, 1922–1929, Tigers, Red
Sox, Cubs, Cardinals, batting average .275 (manager ten seasons, 1939–1959).
Joseph Anthony Dugan (1897–   ), infielder, fourteen seasons, 1917–1931,
Athletics, Red Sox, Yankees, Braves, Tigers. batting average .280.

never cared for bourbon, sometimes drank scotch, and drank beer as often as possible. Three shots of whiskey would leave him blurred and sleepy, but he could hold an awful lot of beer without visible signs.

> THE AUTHOR: Did he ever complain about trouble sleeping?
> JOE SEWELL: I never heard him complain.
> PEE WEE WANNINGER: Not in my presence.
> THE AUTHOR: Did he usually feel well in the morning?
> DEL PRATT: About eleven.
> SEWELL: Always ready to play ball.
> ART JORGENS: Didn't see him in the morning very often.
> TRUCK HANNAH: [He felt well] morning, noon, or night.
> THE AUTHOR: Did he care whether the weather was hot or cold?
> HANK JOHNSON: Never complained.
> BOB SHAWKEY: Liked it hot.
> BILL DICKEY:* Liked hot weather.
> THE AUTHOR: When he made up his mind was it hard to change it?
> SAM VICK: Nobody tried.
> SEWELL: He was very determined.

Babe Ruth's singing voice was better than he thought, and his musical taste was worse than he thought. In spontaneous song he was apt to bring out his favorite but now forgotten ballad, "My Darlin' Lou." From occasional mentions of what he liked in music it is plain he would prefer the fourth "B," Carrie Jacobs Bond, to Bach, Beethoven, or Brahms.

In the age of railroading, baseball players who did not read much were driven to cards. Ruth played vigorously, but not in the manner of a gambler. Excitement was his aim.

In hotels on the road he organized pinochle games in his room, which would run until the team's curfew. His poker playing suffered from his love of action. He would get into pots when he should

---

* Paul Louis Wanninger (1902–   ), infielder, two seasons, 1925–1927, Yankees, Red Sox, Reds, batting average .234.

Arndt Ludwig Jorgens (1905–   ), catcher, eleven seasons, 1929–1939, Yankees, batting average .238.

James Harrison Hannah (1891–   ), catcher, three seasons, 1918–1920, Yankees, batting average .235.

Henry Ward Johnson (1906–   ), pitcher, twelve seasons, 1925–1939, Yankees, Red Sox, Athletics, Reds. Won 63, lost 56, earned-run average 4.75.

William Malcolm Dickey (1907–   ), catcher, seventeen seasons, 1928–1946, Yankees, batting average .313. Hall of Fame.

have stayed out, and stay in after he should have thrown in his hand. He won very little because he took every risk. At bridge— auction bridge in those times—his style annoyed his partners because he tried to get the bid every time, whether he had the cards or not. The great talent for concentration shown in the Columbia tests did not carry over to cards. If people nearby were talking he followed the thread of their conversation until he became hopelessly confused in his play. Arthur Robinson said he played cards "the way he hits a baseball—wildly, freely, forcefully; and more often than not he loses."

There are three kinds of folk heroes: the holy hero, the tricky hero, and the muscle hero. In Ruth's time, baseball's holy hero was Christy Mathewson, the tricky hero was Ty Cobb, and the muscle hero was Babe Ruth. Folklore demands that the muscle hero live riotously and leave tales of revelry and sprees. Such stories cling to Ruth's memory. Almost none can be verified, but they lose no interest because they can't be proved. We can't prove much about Siegfried, Beowulf, Achilles, or Hercules, either.

If Babe Ruth were a statesman, biographers could not pin on him the label of lecher as can be safely done with, say, Aaron Burr. But, as a muscle hero Ruth *must* be a libertine, and that is his reputation, right or wrong. If true, it had no particular influence on baseball history nor could it make much difference to anybody else. But the muscle hero *must* be excessive. (For example: Ethan Allen drank so much whiskey that when a rattlesnake bit him it got drunk.) The folklore tells us that Ruth was a wencher, a boozer, a blowhard. Of course all true male folk heroes, from ancient strongmen to current pop-music stars, have been besieged by eager women. Legends in this field give Ruth powers worthy of Man o' War, but the stories are as wispy as fog and elusive to the grasp. Literary folk have compulsions to put down on paper their own secrets and their friends' secrets (and, lately, their parents' secrets), but athletes don't write much.

In some people envy and jealousy contend with love and admiration of public persons. They are full of affection for the memory of Babe Ruth but are anxious to believe their own standards of conduct are more rigorous in practice. At the same time they secretly feel they would have misbehaved splendidly if they had had his opportunities. They also are pleased at that secret guilty knowledge about themselves. One of the great pleasures Babe Ruth gave the world was that he became the idol of everybody who would like to flout every rule of conduct and still be a champion. It is common to hint and generalize about him as though to say, "After all, the Babe was only human, and barely that." It would be closer to the truth to say that in the struggle to command Ruth the Baltimore waterfront slob overcame Xaverian Brother George more often than not. The public record does not support the story of the great libertine. It may be the right description, but proof is lacking. The legend is collective wish-fulfillment.

Ruth was not vice-riddled, but his virtues had defects. There is a glimpse of reality in a press conference once held by a physician who was treating Ruth. The reporters hoped for a purple passage and asked whether the patient kept late hours or "dissipated in the winter." The physician laughed and replied, "He's very careless." This is the complete body of hard evidence in support of Ruth's reputation for high jinks.

But assuming that the reputation has some basis in fact, let us see what we can make of him. He was earthy and full of energy. In his departures from virtue there was nothing decadent. His lapses were because of appetite, not conviction. At any time he might bring forth admissions of guilt and simple resolutions to do better. He did not take up the vices of the aristocracy which have become democratically diffused in our century. He took up vices that most poor young Baltimore waterfront slobs would have liked to follow if they became rich. Suddenly having money to spend, Babe Ruth practiced working class excesses on a lavish scale. Not for Babe Ruth an intrigue with a duchess, but from him a call for madder ukulele music and colder beer. No other eminent man ever ate so much ketchup. In his most elegant depravity, assuming some truth in the legends, Ruth behaved like a plain-spoken, unpolished provincial general suddenly raised by his men to be Emperor of Rome in the last century of the Empire.

It is worth adding that Ruth overshadowed the other Yankees, but he was simply the most conspicuous high-liver in a rather wild bunch who, one spring, were described as "training on scotch."

Ruth limited his defects to hard-working animality. He grew up in a culture which enjoyed sin as illicit and did not, as we so often do, enjoin it as virtue. If he had been the leading haberdasher in a Three-Eye League town, a member of the board of directors of the local ball club, and a prominent Elk, his behavior would not have been much noticed except for amused comments on Monday mornings after memorable Saturday nights.

> . . . I know when I'm doing wrong. I'm still a Catholic.
> —Angus Wilson, *The Wrong Set*

Ruth had not given up his religion, though his practice of it was hit or miss. At intervals he imposed a revival upon himself to make up for neglect. Religion was taboo for argument, since that would cause "prejudice and hard feelings," but he made no effort to conceal his faith or his public worship. Once he agreed to a series of biographical pieces by his ghost writer Westbrook Pegler who caught up with him at Mass in St. Louis Cathedral. After a Saturday night out on some American League town Ruth would often take his non-Catholic companions to a dawn Mass. As Waite Hoyt told Bob Broeg, they would all put their dimes in the collection and see them covered by a fifty-dollar bill from Ruth, "the biggest tipper in town."

Ruth never met a Calvinist conscience in a place of authority until Barrow joined the Red Sox. He probably never heard a word of Freudianism, however disguised. This saved him a great deal of explanation and justification. He was a Christian hedonist, that is, a Christian who lived chiefly for pleasure. It is a common type among Catholics, though not viewed with favor by the Bishops of Rome. Considering the whole history of Christianity, Ruth can be matched often, and in every generation. Most people like him sin from lack of firmness of spirit rather than from malice. Members of the older religious groups in which faith is an intellectual concern can do wrong without trying to explain it away as a new kind of virtue. They can live in sin, know it, admit it. People from later traditions, or no tradition, believe a public sinner must have lost his faith or his sanity. Babe Ruth and Brother Matthias would think that a silly view.

Finally, let us note the occasional comparisons with Falstaff. While Shakespeare might have appreciated Ruth, Babe Ruth was no Falstaff. Falstaff could do nothing well. And he is the only important character in Shakespeare who was not what we call a marrying man. Ruth was a marrying man.

Babe Ruth managed to separate his public image from his real private life so that no matter what he did or was believed to have done, he remained a hero to the crowd. A muscle hero must be rated a champion carouser in order to make people believe he is the real thing. The myth of the heroic wastrel satisfies some primal appetite in humankind.

All of Babe Ruth's skill would have meant nothing if he lacked the will to win, but he was fiercely combative in the game. His coordination would have been useless at bat if he had a disabling fear of a fast ball (and nearly everybody fears it), but he was among the bravest of batters. Ruth had a drive to be great, and he liked the competition for mastery just as he plainly delighted in his remarkable deeds. Of all the world's pleasures, baseball was his favorite.

His joy in what he could do on a baseball field infected the fans, and they came to enjoy his triumphs as much as he did. (And those who came to see him fail could equally relish his setbacks.) Ruth was an aggressive player, not hostile but the kind who makes things happen instead of waiting upon happenings. A professional player must be determined. It is not money alone that pulls him. He learns to command himself, work hard, and overcome obstacles. It can't be done well if one doesn't like it. What Ruth liked most was to play baseball. In second place came winning. Only then came money. Like Ty Cobb, Dizzy Dean, and Ted Williams, he was supremely confident of his greatness. In a crowded railway smoking compartment he once announced loudly, "I can knock the head off any pitch that's ever been pitched." And he was tough enough to lose and then to bound back with extra effort at the next chance. He lacked some qualities that managers wanted him to have: conformity to authority without question, commitment to training rules, and —after he parted from Bill Carrigan—trust in his managers.

Ruth was inclined to take unnecessary risks, most of all when driving an automobile. Perhaps ballplayers come from a group of men who take death less seriously than most of us. The practice of bending over a slab of rubber with club in hand and facing a five-ounce pellet coming in at from seventy to ninety miles an hour may screen out those who put a high value on their lives. Among major-league baseball players, active and retired, the table of causes of death show three gross twists from normal when compared with American males as a group. Accidental deaths are seven times as numerous, suicides are also seven times as numerous, and twenty-seven times as many are murdered. The figures include all major-league players who had died from 1876 through 1953; and all explanations are merely speculative. Whether it is relevant we can't know, but Ruth had a taste for hazard.

The new Yankee outfielder was also as superstitious as any ballplayer. Some of his superstitions were almost universal, as, a hat on a bed brings bad luck. Some were widely held among baseball players generally; for example, the sight of a wagonload of empty barrels was a good omen. He also had some of his own. Hendrick Willem van Loon gave Ruth a silver dollar which he carried for years as his chief good-luck charm. The sight of a white or yellow butterfly meant something to him, but the meaning varied from mood to mood. When he had a good day he'd go into the hotel by the same door by which he had come out; if he had a bad day, he'd use any other door. Once he tried to lift the team out of a slump by pitching batting practice. They won, so he went on pitching batting practice until they lost. The same circumstance of winning after doing something out of the ordinary got him tours of duty warming up pitchers and hitting fungoes to the outfield. One of his favorite sports was hunting frogs at night with lights attached to the rifle near the sights; a good bag foretold base hits in the next game.

To those who smile it may be pointed out that fans are just as superstitious. A pitcher in a heated pennant race once received as gifts from fans two lucky pennies, a double acorn, a rabbit's foot, a buckeye, and several Japanese prayer scrolls.

> Baseball brains are not put into everyone's head. Babe Ruth . . . had baseball brains. . . .
>
> —Eddie Collins

One who uses his mind in every way possible, and all at once, thinks intuitively. That kind of use differs, for example, from the working through of long division. In baseball, and in nothing else, Babe Ruth used all his intellectual powers at once. He had facts to work on. He was no mental giant, but he knew more baseball than the average person, including the average sportswriter. His kind of baseball knowledge was soaked up from childhood and fixed fast in the memory by a kind of psychic obsession with baseball.

Outside of baseball Ruth was a commonplace man. He read practically nothing, though there are unconfirmed reports that he knew the Nick Carter detective stories and the Frank Merriwell boy athlete stories. Excluding baseball, his mind was variously estimated as equal to the mind of a child of nine, twelve, or fifteen years. Ruth as remembered is a colossal sculpture chipped out by the periodical press. The model for the figure was an intelligent man whose intelligence was narrowly focused on what he could do superbly on a baseball field. The model had almost no other life, and what other life he had was very ordinary. For example, his views on public questions were simpleminded opinions of the kind one might get from a not very thoughtful boy who lived before even the movies broadened people's views. Those of Ruth's opinions of public affairs which have survived sound like the opinions of anyone who glances briefly at the major headlines as he turns the pages toward the sports section. Except in baseball, language was to him a system of signaling situations or changes in circumstances rather than a way of exchanging and sharpening ideas.

Ruth, a true baseball genius, was a man who had a kind of microscopic mental world which was brightly lit, well ordered, and well understood. The development of a high order of intelligence in narrow scope may produce some kinds of instability. Was that true of Ruth? If so, it would explain his show-off gluttony.

He spoke his mind, most of the time.
—Joe Sewell

Babe Ruth had simplicity, a virtue which is not as much prized as it should be. As an Irish poet said of someone, "He lacked manners, but had manner." In Ruth that manner was directness. For example, in none of the thousands of surviving photographs is he shown consciously grimacing to express a heartiness he doesn't feel. In many of them he makes no effort to conceal the stupefaction of his boredom. He had a simple honesty in public relations.

His emotions were all on the surface. That let the crowd know and understand him. His sense of humor was pretty coarse. In stag company, according to one who knew him well, "He couldn't say five words without three of them being profane or vulgar." A kindly man called him "crude" and said protective sportswriters and friendly policemen concealed his occasional abusiveness. That he could be abusive is certainly not surprising. No celebrity has been more harassed by his public, and many who have been under much less pressure (for example, the Duke of Edinburgh) have reacted more explosively. Ruth's abusiveness was set free only by alcohol, so that the few recorded instances usually happened late at night with few witnesses.

Sometimes excessive swearing is explained as a substitute for the tears which are forbidden to men in our culture. Not in the case of Ruth. He was so obviously masculine that he never thought to assure it by hiding his occasional weeping. He used foul language for the simple reason that he was short of more exact words and phrases to express himself.

He had a short fuse and might explode very quickly, especially in dealing with owners and managers. His anger was rarely directed at ballplayers, and when it was it did not last long.

THE AUTHOR: Is it true that if he became angry he blew up quickly and it was soon over?

WANNINGER: Never saw a real show of temper in my stay.

COMBS: He was even tempered, wasn't overbearing.

ED WELLS: Never heard him blow up.

SEWELL: He never carried a grudge.

BEN CHAPMAN:* I should know!! But we became good friends.

---

* Edwin Lee Wells (1900–   ), pitcher, eleven seasons, 1923–1934, Tigers, Yankees, Browns. Won 68, lost 69, earned-run average 4.65.

William Benjamin Chapman (1908–   ), outfielder, fifteen seasons, 1930–1946, Yankees, Senators, Red Sox, Indians, White Sox, Dodgers, Phillies, batting average .302 (stolen bases 287).

Since sport has lately received specific psychiatric attention, it is well to add that studies of madness in sport nowhere connect with the kind of behavior that was Ruth's. With the possible exception of his flagrant public gluttony, he was an emotionally undisturbed man.

> He was no intellectual, you know, but an agreeable guy. He really liked baseball and he liked people. And he tried to be agreeable.
>
> —Marshall Hunt (of Ruth)

Ruth was as far from being a loner as it is possible to be. Had he lived on an island by himself, he would have died of being alone. He seemed totally dependent on the appreciation and admiration of others. Even on the baseball field it was said of him, "The bigger the crowd, the bigger the Babe." Rare is the player who does not play for applause as well as money, and Ruth was no exception, as he proved by his every gesture on the field. All his signs to the crowd, whether direct or indirect, were attempts to share with them the pleasure of the running catch or the home run.

Some have thought Ruth was an aloof person because he was so poor at remembering names. It wasn't indifference, it was laziness. It has been heavily emphasized in memoirs of the times, because his ignorance of names led him to blame any sportswriter for any sports report he didn't like. That made a weak memory memorable, to sportswriters.

Close friends and the distant crowd found Ruth frank, easy, and natural. He knew that people liked him, and he showed that he liked them. This mutual trust between star and public let him become "probably the best extemporaneous talker in sports," according to Joe Williams, very much in demand for conventions, men's clubs, benefits, and Communion breakfasts. His vital spirit swelled everybody with what Paul Gallico called the "magnificent afflatus of the Babe." He had the common touch that politicians need; in fact, Ruth had nothing but the common touch. There is no evidence to show that he was ever shy. His manner was the same to the box-holders and the bleacherites. As the leader in his chosen line of work he felt no need to defer to any other person's rank. His honest indifference to social standing may not have pleased people of status, but it delighted the crowd.

There was nothing childlike about Ruth's baseball records, but there was something boyish or at least youthful about the attitude he brought to the field when he played ball, and about everything else he did. Most professional athletes have a boylike strain in their temperaments, but few so much as Ruth. When things go well they are full of laughter, practical jokes, and hoaxes; when things go badly they may sulk, fight, get drunk, or jump the team. Ruth practiced the crude japeries of baseball vigorously, smashing friends' straw hats on sight at the end of the straw hat season, and pulling off many not especially clever practical jokes. When Barrow came to manage the Red Sox he proved to be bold and smart about baseball, but he was insensitive to Ruth's emotional makeup.

There is no need to create a psychological mystery about Ruth's degree of maturity. The plain fact is that he was oriented to childhood. He was a hero to the whole world of children with whom he had a "fine, soft touch." He had a quality for which there is no name: a heroic tolerance for and empathy with children. He might sometimes be curt with elders, but he never protected his privacy and comfort from children. He was photographed with sick or crippled children so often that cynics thought it was crude press-agent hokum; but Bill Slocum, friend and ghost writer, said he made fifty visits to children's institutions for each one that was photographed. The photographers would be there if the institution called them, not otherwise. The kids liked him. When they learned his tough face masked real kindness they leaned toward him, not away.

Babe Ruth played baseball with the feelings of a youth. It is almost the mark of a grizzled veteran that he does *not* run into the wall while chasing a fly ball; he saves himself and his earning power for tomorrow. But Ruth took the chances that amateurs take, the kinds of chances that can lead to accidents which keep players from ever playing again. Heywood Broun said Ruth played "gleefully" and yet needed no cheering section, no coach exhorting him to die for dear old club owner. For example, when he shifted fielding position as a new man came to bat, he ran. And Gallico saw that "his impish streak" doubled his pleasure in a home run because it upset the pitcher. Gallico thought his style showed the mind of a nine-year-old.

The thought of illness, suffering, aging, and death depressed him. His visits to the ill and the handicapped were often followed by hours of melancholy. After visiting a hospital in Asheville he left with tears on his cheeks, saying, "... I could be in there." This is a typical feeling in youth-oriented people who highly value health and energy and who think of childhood as the golden time of life. A sick child or a decaying adult sets order awry and is therefore cause for gloom. Ruth had very little experience of old age. He probably knew almost no old people when he was a boy. A grandmother of forty-five would seem a hag to him in 1920 when he was twenty-five.

We may doubt that he could organize his feelings about death and disability into coherent thought. Free-spirited, open-hearted people are not much given to analyzing their own feelings. We rarely know what Babe Ruth thought about the aspects of the universe that we think important. Quite likely, he didn't know either. He was a man of feeling, not of logic.

Outside the Park, 1920

DRIVE OUT REDS,
PERSHING WARNS

SOLDIERS' BONUS TO BE VOTED ON
BY REFERENDUM IN THIS STATE

PAPER CO. REPORT
ACCUSES UNION

MAKING A JOKE OF PROHIBITION IN NEW YORK CITY

BILLS AIMED AT DISLOYAL TEACHERS

CAR ROWDIES ARE FINED

HARDING NOMINATED FOR PRESIDENT

FLOATING OIL LIGHTS SEA

COX NOMINATED FOR PRESIDENT

DRY AGENTS SEIZE SHIP

FIFTH PLAGUE DEATH AT BEAUMONT

POISON 'WHISKY'
MADE IN GARAGE

HOW WOULD YOU MAKE
THE MAN YOU LOVE
PROPOSE?

WASH YOUR SPATS AND COLLARS ANY COLOR YOU LIKE!

SHALL WOMEN PRACTICE PARTY REGULARITY?

MEN'S ALL WOOL SUITS AT $19

HARDING WINS; MILLION LEAD HERE

"HOW DO YOU GET THIS WONDERFUL
FRUIT FLAVOR IN YOUR DESSERTS?"

WALL STREET EXPLOSION INQUIRY

IN A BOLSHEVIST DUNGEON

14 · New York Fandom
Has Surrendered (1920)

These reporters travel all round the country with the team all season and send in telegrams about the game every night. . . . Some of them are pretty nice fellows and some of them got the swell head. They hang round with the old fellows and play poker most of the time.

Ring Lardner, *You Know Me Al*

Thirteen reporters went to the Yankees' Florida training camp at Jacksonville in 1920. No one remembered a larger group of writers ever following a team. Even the *Morning Telegraph*, a horse-players' paper, sent a writer. The team and its retinue of authors assembled on March 2. Not only did the Yankees now have Babe Ruth, they had a new outfielder, Bob Meusel,* from the west coast. Meusel could also play third base. He hit very well, and, with Ruth, joined the group that cartoonist Robert Ripley had named "Murderers' Row" in 1919. They were Roger Peckinpaugh, Wally Pipp, Frank Baker,** Del Pratt, and Ping Bodie, who, as a group, had batted not quite .290 in 1919.

The spring exhibition series began riotously. The Yankees played the Reds in Miami and Palm Beach, both cities awash with liquor. Ruth, allegedly dulled by a hangover, ran into a palm tree in the Palm Beach outfield and knocked himself unconscious. Jacob Ruppert never forgot the trip; the Yankees did not again visit that part of Florida while he lived.

Ruth started the spring badly even when he felt well. The press platoon which had come to study him reported his failures at length.

---

* Robert William Meusel (1896–   ), outfielder, eleven seasons, 1920–1930, Yankees, Reds, batting average .309.
** Roger Thorpe Peckinpaugh (1891–   ), infielder, seventeen seasons, 1910–1927, Indians, Yankees, Senators, White Sox, batting average .259.
John Franklin Baker (1886–1963), infielder, thirteen seasons, 1908–1922, Athletics, Yankees, batting average .307.

When Ruth showed anger, Carl Mays suggested he do something worth praising and note the change in the writers' tone. But success was slow in coming. Ruth began to get edgier. In the third week of March a heckler at Jacksonville began jeering him continuously during a game against Brooklyn. After an hour Ruth climbed into the bleachers to quiet his tormentor but had to postpone the showdown when the heckler drew a knife and stood his ground. Yankee co-owner Tillinghast l'Hommedieu Huston hurried to protect his most valuable chattel from vivisection and was able to establish a peace. Up to this point the only really solid hit by Ruth had been a long but meaningless one in batting practice which cleared the Jacksonville fence thirty feet above the 428-foot mark. (Total distance estimated by the sportswriters: 478 feet.)

The New York press was growing skeptical. On March 29, after seven spring games with the Dodgers and three with the Reds, Ruth was batting only .264. He had seven singles and a double. Then, on April Fool's Day, he got the first olive out of the bottle, hitting his first home run while wearing a Yankee uniform, in a game at Jacksonville against the Dodgers. (Yankees 6, Dodgers 2.) That was in his eleventh game. In the remaining nine spring exhibitions Babe Ruth was almost his usual self: he hit no more home runs but raised his average to .314.

When the Red Sox had expected Ruth to play with them in spring training in 1920, they had scheduled nineteen one-day stands with the Giants to cash in on Ruth's new fame. Now the Red Sox and Giants were stuck with their contracts and wandered all over the South, as the Giant Secretary Ed Brannick said, "drawing flies and getting on each other's nerves." The Yankees played the Dodgers from point to point northward, partly on the same route used by the Red Sox and Giants, and made a great deal of money from eager Ruth watchers.

Spring schedule makers and promoters of exhibitions learned something. In dealing with the Yankees they usually wrote into the contracts a clause that Ruth would play. Thus he had few days off. For example, late in the summer of 1920 the Yankees had two successive open dates. They booked exhibitions at Indianapolis and Pittsburgh, filling the minor-league park and drawing twenty-nine thousand in Pittsburgh (where Ruth hit a home run). Major-league teams usually spent about fifteen thousand dollars getting ready for the scheduled season. In the spring of 1920 Ruth drew enough customers to Yankee exhibition games to pay the cost of spring training.

The Yankees opened the 1920 championship season against the Athletics at Philadelphia. Ruth made a fielding error which lost the game. Before the next day's game a body of Philadelphians marched to home plate with a gift for him—a boxed brown derby of the low-crowned style of the turn of the century, a stock symbol of the German dialect comedian. In baseball slang of the day, "to win the brown derby" was to make an important misplay. Ruth accepted the hat with good humor and posed in it for photographers. He thought it brought good luck, for he soon began to hit well.

The Yankees opened at home in the Polo Grounds (officially Brush Stadium) after winning but one of their first five games. In batting practice before the home opener Ruth, trying too hard, missed a ball and pulled a muscle as he corkscrewed in his mighty twist. He started the game but was in obvious pain and left after an inning. So far in the season he did not look like the highest priced of all players. During the rest of the home stand he played in right field. On the road he usually played in left. His aim was to avoid playing the sun field, that field where the late afternoon sun shone directly in the fielder's face. Huggins let Ruth have his way.

Babe Ruth did not hit a home run in the 1920 season until the twelfth game, and then, on May 1, he knocked it all the way out of the Polo Grounds into the first-base coaching box of an amateur game going on nearby. This was the third ball Ruth had driven completely out of the Polo Grounds; Joe Jackson was the only other player who had done it once. This was also Ruth's fiftieth career home run. The Yankees went on to beat the Red Sox 6–0. Ruth batted four times, had the home run, a double, and scored two runs. (In the seventh he grounded out with bases full.) Late in May the maintenance crew painted white foul lines vertically in right field, where possible, to make it easier to judge whether balls leaving the field were fair or foul. That month Ruth hit eleven home runs. Two went over the roof, four went into the upper deck, and there wasn't a cheap shot among them. One writer flatly said Ruth was "the greatest attraction in the history of the game." On Patriots Day in April the Yankees and Red Sox broke the attendance record at Fenway Park. The Yankees set a new attendance record at the Polo Grounds on May 31, when 38,688 persons paid to see the second game of a morning-afternoon double-header. Ruth did what they paid to see, hitting a home run (his only hit of the day) off Walter Johnson. Cleveland and St. Louis set new attendance records on successive Sundays when the Yankees came. Then on July 4 the Yankees-Senators game drew the biggest crowd in Washington baseball history.

In another double-header at home on June 2 Ruth hit three home runs, raising his total to fifteen, halfway to a new season record. In these two games Ruth had five hits in seven times at bat. During the home stand the Yankees and Senators drew eighty-five thousand people.

It wasn't all Ruth. The Yankees were a team. During the seven

The new Yankee, 1920. (*National Baseball Library, Cooperstown, New York.*)

games ending with the game of June 5 Bob Meusel, for example, had sixteen hits in thirty-two at-bats, while Ruth lagged behind with a puny average of .357. The Yankees hit thirteen home runs in that stretch; four were Ruth's. New York was half a game out of first place. In the first five days of June they drew 108,200 customers.

The New York fandom has surrendered to the Yankees. . . .
—*The Times*, June 7, 1920

Ruth's home runs continued to soar. Number seventeen came on the day of Cleveland's new attendance record (thirty thousand, June 13); Yankees 14, Indians 0. On a foul day in Comiskey Park, Chicago (June 17), he hit number eighteen, which very fittingly coincided with a clap of thunder; Yankees 7, White Sox 4. The next day was cold and blustery; Ruth hit number nineteen into the wind and all the way over the single-decked outfield seats; Yankees 7, White Sox 2.

Ruth's last home runs of June were numbers twenty-three and twenty-four in a double-header against the A's in Philadelphia on

June 30. That made it eleven for May and thirteen for June. His record of twenty-nine was obviously vulnerable. At the end of June he ranked fourth in league batting with an average of .372.

Nine dry days passed. On Knights of Columbus Day at the Polo Grounds, July 9, about a thousand K.C.'s paraded to the park from 144th Street and Convent Avenue and gave their Brother Knight Ruth a diamond-studded fob in the symbol of the Order. He reciprocated by hitting number twenty-five. On the 10th he hit another, to draw within four of a new record. Of the first twenty-six home runs of 1920, sixteen were hit in the Polo Grounds, and every one of them went into the second deck or out of the park. The home run of July 10 came in circumstances that showed the new respect for Ruth: one time at-bat provided the home run. He walked three times that day, but the walks availed the defense nothing, for Ruth scored twice and the Yankees won by one run.

The Polo Grounds' all-time attendance record was broken for the third time in the season when 38,823 came on July 13 to see the Browns and Yankees in a double-header. They split, and neither Ruth nor George Sisler did well. On the next day Ruth hit home run number twenty-eight, with another of his peculiar new box-score reports: one time at bat, one hit, two runs, three bases on balls. Batting .382 he was still fourth in the league, just behind his model Joe Jackson of the White Sox. And wonders refused to cease, for on the *next* day, July 15, with sixty-one games left to play, Ruth tied his twenty-nine-home-runs record with a home run which beat the Browns in the eleventh inning. Here he was at number twenty-nine; on the same day in 1919 he had but eleven.

He broke the record on July 20, in the last game of a four-day series in New York against the White Sox. This series drew 129,000, though on two of the days bad weather caused one-hour game delays. No other four-game series anywhere had drawn that many. And they kept on coming. A new major-league attendance record for a seven-game set was reached in the seven days ending on July 23, when more than two hundred thousand paid to get into the Polo Grounds.

The Indians used a Ruth shift on July 24, with three right fielders; he hit one to the wall for a double over their heads, and the next time singled between them. Number thirty-six came in a game when the Yankees took Sportsman's Park in St. Louis by storm, hitting for thirty-eight bases and winning over the Browns, 19–3. Ruth hit the ball over the right-field pavilion into Grand Avenue. He had four times at bat, scored four runs, had three hits, and, as a kind of ornament, had a neat sacrifice bunt.

The Yankees and White Sox drew a record-breaking crowd of

about forty thousand to Comiskey Park on August 1 to see whether Eddie Cicotte could keep his record clean of giving Ruth a home run. Before a crowd so large that many stood in center field, Cicotte beat Shawkey and gave Ruth no home run. Even though Ruth did not shine, a hundred or more boys worshipfully mobbed him. The novelist James T. Farrell marked this day as the end of the Ty Cobb era and the beginning of the age of Babe Ruth. Before this day Chicago fans had been enkindled by every chance to come out to 35th Street to hoot at Cobb; from now on more came to marvel at Ruth.

By setting a new attendance record in Chicago the Yankees increased to six the number of ball parks where they had set records.

Ruth hit number thirty-eight on the day after Cicotte overcame him. Cicotte's record may have been clear of Ruth, but not the records of the other White Sox pitchers, who had given Ruth nine home-run pitches so far. On August 14, in hitting number forty-two at Washington, Ruth repeated his 1919 feat of hitting a home run in each American League park. And, as so often, the home run gave New York the one run needed to win.

August 16, 1920, was a somber day in major-league history. Six clubs had the day off, and members of each came to the Polo Grounds to see the Yankees play Cleveland. They saw a pitch by Carl Mays strike Ray Chapman* in the head. Chapman died within twenty-four hours. Carl Mays, Ruth's teammate at Providence, was a great pitcher but was chiefly remembered for this accident. The pitch had been in the strike zone, and Chapman, confused by Mays's ground-sweeping delivery, had ducked into its path. (No other major-league player has died as a result of an injury received in a game.)

This Cleveland series was doubly fatal. Ruth hit his forty-third on August 19. It went all the way out of the Polo Grounds, and the excitement "killed Theodore Sturm of Bellrose, Long Island, who was sitting in the box in back of third base." On August 29 there was still another Polo Grounds record attendance, with fifteen thousand turned away for lack of room. Ruth did not play because of an infected insect bite which required lancing.

Telegrams from unknown persons in Pittsburgh, Cincinnati, Cleveland, and Chicago came to several Wall Street offices on September 9, saying that Ruth, Pratt, Meusel, and Lewis had been badly injured in an auto wreck while traveling to Cleveland. The first stories came on brokers' private wires, then over the news tickers. It took much telegraphing and telephoning to prove the

---

* Raymond Johnson Chapman (1891–1920), infielder, nine seasons, 1912–1920, Indians, batting average .278.

report false, probably a concoction of professional gamblers who were trying to affect the betting odds on the coming Yankee-Indians series.

Ruth's total of home runs rose slowly through the forties. Millions of people began to feel the suspense of waiting for number fifty. Then on September 24 he hit home runs number fifty and fifty-one in a double-header which the Yankees split with Washington. Number fifty-one also happened to be lifetime number one hundred. Ruth gave one of his bats to sell at auction for the benefit of Near East Relief (the ball club paid for the bats). The hitter had had a fine day: seven times at bat, five hits for nine bases, three runs scored. Number one hundred seemed a total worthy of celebration; *The Times* gave a visiting English cartoonist, Tom Webster, a four-column square to fill with sketches of Ruth. Number fifty-three beat the Athletics in Philadelphia on September 27, with Ruth driving in three runs as the Yankees won 3–0.

Two days later, on September 29, Ruth hit his fifty-fourth and last of the year as he broke the season home-run record by twenty-five. His final batting average was .376, fourth in the league after Sisler, Speaker, and Jackson.

By this time Cleveland had won the pennant, Chicago was two games behind, and New York three. The truth about the fixed World Series of 1919 came out shortly before the end of the 1920 season. Ruth said, "It was like hearing that my church had sold out." Cleveland benefited by the timing of the disclosures. The Black Sox had eliminated the Yankees from the pennant race by winning three straight games from them in Chicago just before the Chicagoans were expelled from baseball. If the Chicago men had left a week earlier, the Yankees would almost certainly have taken the 1920 pennant.

> Look at him now—(Wow).
> Look at him now.
> —"Batterin' Babe"

Babe Ruth saw to it that the Yankees had unusual companions during the last weeks of the 1920 season.

In April 1919 an accidental fire had destroyed all St. Mary's Industrial School buildings and their contents. The Baltimore Elks and the National Catholic War Council quickly revived the school's excellent band by gifts of four thousand dollars for music, instruments, and uniforms. The Brothers worked the band very hard as part of the drive for funds to rebuild the school, arranging for it to play benefits at places as far away as Long Island and Virginia.

In the summer of 1919 the Brothers also organized an exhibition baseball game on July 15 between a team of selected Philadelphia semi-professionals and the Baltimore Dry Docks, with Ruth pitching for the Dry Docks. This led to thoughts of larger projects for the school's most illustrious alumnus.

The goal of the fund-raisers was half a million dollars. By December 1, 1919, friends pledged about two hundred thousand dollars, and actually paid in $178,557. By late summer 1920 the goal had not yet been reached. Ruth then persuaded the Yankees to let the band travel with the team on the last swing around the American League circuit. Accompanied by Brothers Paul, Gilbert, Matthias, and Simon (the director), and by Father P. L. Ireton of St. Gregory's Parish, Baltimore, the band left Baltimore by rail on September 8 for a tour with the Yankees which included stops at Cleveland, Detroit, Chicago, St. Louis, Indianapolis, Pittsburgh, New York, Boston, Philadelphia, and, finally, Baltimore. There were fifty boys, aged nine to seventeen, although few were more than fourteen. At every stop men would unobtrusively drift over to talk with the Brothers. These were the purposely anonymous alumni who remembered the Brothers with affection, but—unlike Babe Ruth—did not wish to be known as graduates of a correctional house.

In each city the band paraded from its lodging to the ball park and played in the stands until the game started. Sometimes, but not always, they went through the stands and took up a collection before the game. They always displayed a large banner which read

BABE RUTH'S BOYS BAND

DO YOUR BIT TO HELP REBUILD THE SCHOOL

THAT MADE BABE RUTH FAMOUS

At night they played advertised concerts. On open dates they played afternoon concerts at places where crowds might be found—once, for example, at a race track.

Ruth appeared by prearrangement at each concert to plead for money. One of Ruth's fund-raising artifices was to say that he was often asked for an autograph. Anyone who wrote a check to St. Mary's Industrial School would get it back with his signature as an endorsement on the back. The musical program followed. The audience usually settled down tolerantly to listen with polite attention to a childish performance, and was pleasantly surprised. (This band later won the national high school championship in its enrollment class.)

A Babe Ruth song, which the band first performed on September 8 when marching past the *Baltimore Sun* building on the way

Few photographers of 1920 could resist posing Babe Ruth with a tuba during the fund-raising tour of the St. Mary's Industrial School Band, which made the last western road trip of the season with the Yankees. (*National Baseball Library, Cooperstown, New York.*)

to board the train for the tour, was titled "Batterin' Babe," composer unknown. The band boys sang the chorus in unison.

> Look at him now, and think of all the games that Babe has won—
> And how he whacks the homers when the Yankees need a run—
> We know he's broken records, we're sure he'll break some more—
> Can't you hear those bleachers roar—(Yow)—
> He hears the call and then the ball is sailin' in the sky—
> A mile away it kills a cow—(Vow)—
> And if a bandit on the border gets a baseball in the eye,
> Put the blame on Babe.
> Look at him now—(Wow). Look at him now.

This lyric invariably brought applause, which was Ruth's cue to enter holding up his hand for quiet. He then made his plea for money for the school. At every place the band played Ruth appeared with it for the local press. A favorite pose of the photographers was Ruth with the band, holding a tuba.

The tour opened at Cleveland where the boys had to watch four Yankee pitchers lose 10–4, but, to their delight, Ruth hit a home run. A spectator was so moved by their din that he bought them fifty bags of peanuts. Before any organized money-gathering began, Ruth had taken in $190 in checks from Yankee players and from Cleveland friends.

When on the move, the band had two Pullman cars. After an uproarious experimental stay in a Cleveland hotel the Brothers lodged the boys in various Catholic institutions in the cities they visited. They liked the hospitality of the Sisters of Charity at Lansdowne, Pennsylvania, the best. They passed from Cleveland to Detroit by ship, gave a concert during the passage, had Ruth make his pitch (this time he introduced all of the Yankees as well), and then passed their white sailor hats. Detroit was a good stand. At a concert sponsored by the Knights of Columbus the band took in twelve hundred dollars. In Chicago Mayor William Hale (Big Bill) Thompson received the suitably autographed bat with which Ruth had hit his forty-second home run of the season, and gave Ruth a check for the school. In Indianapolis the band paraded at the head of the Maryland delegation to the encampment of the Grand Army of the Republic. They also played a concert at the Claypool Hotel, where Ruth again acted as money-raiser, before the exhibition game against Indianapolis. The band had worked especially hard, so, on the way from Indianapolis to Pittsburgh, Ruth took the boys into the dining car to be his guests at an ice cream orgy. And he managed another home run for them in the exhibition game against the Pirates the next day.

In New York the boys toured the city in buses. At the Polo Grounds the baseball clown Nick Altrock was their drum major. In Boston they had a walking tour of historic sites. The boys even played at the Olympia Arena, the local boxing club of Philadelphia. To swell the crowd Ruth, of course, appeared.

The tour's climax was a benefit exhibition game in Baltimore on September 23 between the Yankees and the Orioles who had just won the International League pennant. The Knights of Columbus sponsored the game. Ruth went to a crowded Knights of Columbus meeting on the night of the 22nd. When he left, he was almost crushed by a loving mob. A friend pushed him into a shoeshine shop and closed the door. They waited until police came and cleared a path for a taxi to take Ruth away. On the next day the Knights practically concealed Ruth behind a bodyguard which, at game time, surrounded him and marched him to home plate where they gave him a flower construction in the shape of a bat ten feet long, of white and purple asters, and a gold-handled umbrella bearing the K.C. symbol. During the game Ruth played first base. The

Yankees had learned that Ruth could escape a crowd of worshipers more easily from first base than from right field.

The public seemed near-crazed by the man who had hit forty-nine home runs thus far, a figure as staggering in 1920 as a hundred would be today. People were in line for the Yankees-Orioles game by nine o'clock in the morning. All told, about fifteen thousand came. The Orioles won it 1–0. That night there was a mass fund-raising meeting at the Fifth Regiment Armory, where Babe Ruth made his pitch and added his own check for twenty-five hundred dollars.

That ended the tour. The band had traveled twenty-five hundred miles and played before four hundred thousand people, although, to be sure, most came to see baseball, not to hear the band. The gross income was $25,488.88. Expenses were $12,101.20, and net profit $13,387.68. This was a trivial fraction of the sum needed to rebuild the school, but we may suppose so much publicity in so many large cities (which was where the Catholics lived) had its value in raising more money. Babe Ruth showed himself at his best, and his personal cash contributions during the tour (exclusive of ice cream) added up to $4,100—a sixth of the gross take, a third of the net. And a fifth of his annual salary.

> When Truck Hannah hit one out to win a game the excitement was nothing unusual, but when Ruth then hit a home run with the game already settled the crowd was crazy with excitement . . . ready to tear up the stands.
> —Walter Johnson (1920)

In the year-end summaries of the sports history of 1920 the two leading characters were a man and a horse—Babe Ruth and Man O'War. Ruth and the Yankees, though they finished third, drew more people than any team in the history of the game. The big red horse and the home run were the leading facts of sporting life in 1920.

The Yankees outdrew the Giants by a hundred thousand, though the Giants finished second and the Yankees third. The Yankees' paid attendance figure was 1,289,422, which remained the American League record until 1946. First-place Cleveland drew 912,839, and second-place Chicago 833,492. True, New York was much larger than Cleveland and Chicago, but the margin of New York's attendance is so much greater that something must be allowed for Ruth's appeal. His presence also helped other teams, both in their share of receipts at the Polo Grounds and in their home parks where the assurance that Ruth would play drew more people to the games than usual.

Certainly the home runs did it. Ruth hit forty-nine in the years 1914–1919, and then fifty-four in 1920 alone. He admitted that the Polo Grounds was easier for him than any other park. He hit twenty-nine at home and twenty-five on the road. It is fair to say that few of his home-park home runs were at the minimum distance. Nevertheless, just to show off his gift, during batting practice he used to hit balls into the lower right-field deck with one hand (he did the same into the short right-field pavilion in St. Louis, just to have fun with the Browns).

Ruth hit one home run off Walter Johnson in 1920. Johnson said he doubted that Ruth had "a real batting weakness." He would swing at bad pitches, but his swing was the swing of a Joe Jackson plus thirty pounds. If a home run could beat you, said Johnson, Ruth was the worst hitter to face. But if a single could do it, Duffy Lewis or Roger Peckinpaugh were more dangerous.

Among Ruth's more remarkable 1920 record performances were his 150 bases on balls,* thirty-two more than any American League player had had in one season. Three times he was hit by pitchers. Thus he had 153 free passages to first base without a time at bat, which probably prevented him from setting a new record for runs-batted-in. Cobb's runs-batted-in record was 144 in 1911; Ruth had 136 in 1920. In two games Ruth walked four times; in eleven games he received three walks.

In 1919 seventy-five of Ruth's 139 hits were for extra bases, or 54 percent. He broke that in 1920 when 58 percent of his hits went for extra bases.

In comparing Babe Ruth with the leading American League hitters of 1920 in twelve usual classes of hitting and running figures, we find him first in slugging percentage, home runs, runs batted in, walks, runs scored, and percentage of home runs according to times at bat. All very impressive, but it seems likely that a person could as reasonably vote for George Sisler for Most Valuable Player, assuming the honor had been invented. If one scales the categories as a track meet, with points for firsts, seconds, and thirds, Sisler beats Ruth, 23–22 (and nobody else is close). Sisler leads in batting, Ruth in slugging. Ruth leads in home runs, Sisler in total bases. Ruth has most runs-batted-in, Sisler most hits. And Sisler is second in doubles, triples, and stolen bases—in which Ruth doesn't figure. At any rate, it is clear why there was a strong rumor that Ruppert and Huston tried to buy Sisler for the Yankees in October for two hundred thousand dollars.

---

* *The Baseball Encyclopedia* (1969) has it as 148, but the contemporary *New York Times* was insistent on 150. Where contemporary evidence contradicts the *Encyclopedia*, the *Encyclopedia* is less credible.

at bat: 1568
hits: 514
home runs: 103
runs batted in: 230
average: .328

Ruppert and Huston surprised nobody, on October 28, when they announced that Huggins would manage the Yankees again in 1921. But they surprised everybody with the news that Ed Barrow had arrived that day from the Red Sox to become the "business manager" of the Yankees.

Harry Sparrow, the Yankee "business manager" since 1915, died in May 1920. Ruppert and Huston found they needed someone to care for the details. Harry Frazee of the Red Sox is said to have recommended Barrow. (With Ruppert holding a big mortgage on Fenway we may at least suppose that Frazee offered no protest.) So Barrow took over the duties of general manager of the Yankees at age fifty-two after thirty-four years of experience at every level of baseball. He need not feel nervous in Huggins's presence, for he had won a pennant and a world series as manager of the Red Sox. The arrangement promised well for Barrow. The Yankees had the richest owners, and they were anxious to better the team. They had Babe Ruth. From now on Barrow could loot the Red Sox instead of being looted. It was a good time for him to leave Boston, because the fans and writers now loathed the ownership of the Red Sox.

Barrow came to New York like a Proconsul entering Rome in triumph with a procession of distinguished barbarian captives (all former Red Sox): Waite Hoyt, Wally Schang, Harry Harper,* and Mike McNally. The only mistake was sending to the Red Sox Muddy Ruel,** who might have handled Yankee catching until Bill Dickey came along. Barrow also brought Paul Krichell, aged thirty-eight, the baseball scout who became the greatest of Yankee scouts, which is no mean praise. Krichell remembered Barrow as Western Union's best customer. And every wire he sent included the words "immediately" or "at once." Barrow kept himself apart from team operations. He never stepped on a Yankee playing field and never went into the clubhouse unless the manager asked him in. Huston con-

* Harry Clayton Harper (1895–1963), pitcher, ten seasons, 1913–1923, Senators, Red Sox, Yankees, Dodgers. Won 56, lost 79, earned-run average 2.87.
** Herold Dominic Ruel (1896–1963), catcher, nineteen seasons, 1915–1934, Browns, Yankees, Red Sox, Senators, Tigers, White Sox, batting average .275.

tinued to call Barrow by Frazee's nickname for him, "Simon," as in Simon Legree. "Imperious" Ruppert called no employee by given or nickname. To him Barrow became, by mistaken pronunciation, Barrows. Some sportswriters called Barrow Cousin Egbert, others called him Cousin Ed.

The arrival of Barrow could have as much effect on the Yankees' future as the arrival of Babe Ruth. Ruth needed to be part of a team. Could Barrow arrange that the Yankees continue to be a team, and a better team?

15 · The Most Talked-of American

We have a wonderful press that follows us. Anybody should in New York, where you have so many million people.

—Casey Stengel

If Babe Ruth had spent his first five years of major-league baseball with the Dodgers, Giants, or Yankees, he would not have burst upon the world in 1920 as such a surprise. From 1914 to the end of 1919 he was in the traffic center of the communications network only when the Red Sox came to the Polo Grounds. At other times he was off on a branch line. When he moved to New York the press became his home-team press and puffed him up to his proper size. The admiration reflected in the daily papers was what we could expect if a harmless volcano had erupted and built a giant cone in the lower Hudson valley. The wonder is that anyone in New York City noticed the presidential election of 1920.

Many samples of writers' excitement in 1920 are available for illustration. The overwrought remarks of Benjamin De Casseres serve as well as any. In the first days of the season he threw off all restraint. According to De Casseres, the moons of Jupiter were five baseballs making nonstop home runs. Jupiter itself was "some Ruth of a planet." Getting drunker on metaphor, he then named Ruth "the John L. Sullivan of the diamond, Slugger Furioso." Ruth's origins were obscure; in point of fact "he was the super-slugger of the Inter-planetary League" who "used the parallax of Jupiter for a bat" and "the Pleiades for batting pills." Shooting stars seen by children were Ruth's long hits.

No writer could stay at that level of highfalutin comment for long without exhaustion. A briefer, less tiring literary art form was the coining of fanciful nicknames intended to be complimentary: The Sultan of Swat, The Colossus of Clout, The Behemoth of Bust,

The Bambino, The Slambino, The Babe. The Bambino has lasted longer than most, but was rarely used except in print (and later in radio). The Babe caught on. It is still so common as to be used in casual talk by people born since his death.

Yankee Fever required a shift in writers' assignments. When the Yankees went on the road before 1920 one sportswriter went along and sent back stories to six or more New York papers, while everywhere the Giants went a scribble of famous sportswriters was sure to go. All that changed when Ruth came. To John McGraw's disgust, the Giants, then at the peak of their great history, began to have trouble getting space in the papers. It was unpleasant for the Giants, but Babe Ruth increased the total coverage of baseball in the press and helped baseball to keep its lead in popularity over all other sports.

> Flying balls and flying runners weave over the diamond a brilliant net of interest, as if the stars should flash wildly about in the dark for an hour or so.
> —*The Nation,* December 1, 1920

The press was but reflecting the passion in the ball parks. The year 1920 was the opening of a decade in which sport came out into the daylight of classless acceptance. Baseball, in particular, was a running adventure story with new climaxes almost every day, and the players seemed mostly heroes or wizards. In the hot days of the summer of 1920 almost every move on the green and tan fields brought shouts from tens of thousands. That was the time, as Paul Gallico put it, of "a fantastic competitive cosmos in which nothing ever seemed more important than who won, what was the score, who did it, and how." William Wrigley, Jr., the owner of the Cubs, believed the sixteen major-league clubs needed forty stars among them to draw crowds. Of the players of 1920, more than thirty have been voted into the Baseball Hall of Fame. It was a vintage year. George M. Cohan loved baseball and knew why. When he was in New York he spent most of his summer afternoons in the Polo Grounds, secluded in the second deck to avoid notice. He followed the game, as he put it, to enjoy the experience of watching conflict in controlled circumstances, which is almost a definition of drama.

Baseball had an advantage in that the ballplayer, unlike, say, the jockey and the offensive lineman, stood out as an individual. Babe Ruth unconsciously gained by the visibility of the single player because he had an untaught natural showmanship that drew all eyes. And he was so plainly recognizable at a distance. As Jimmy Cannon once wrote, he seemed to have a basketball for a head and a baseball for a nose. He was a cartoonist's dream subject. Even his name helped. It is easy to say Babe Ruth, and the word Babe is just unlikely enough to be unforgettable. Ruth was the people's ball-player. When he hit a home run the Yankee fans were pleased with themselves and, for the moment at least, found peace of mind.

Ruth paid a price for the full-throated admiration of the crowd. By midseason 1920 he was so celebrated that the Yankee management had to stop giving out his home address. He could have no privacy if people knew where he was. In strange cities he might find it necessary to eat in small restaurants. The windows would be filled with the faces of boys and young men watching him eat. In one city a reporter flattened *his* face against the glass as well, and recorded what he ate and how much. Two or three times a week seeming strangers would approach, remind him of an alleged previous meeting (often said to have been in a hospital or the house of someone ill), and hope to be remembered. Ruth pretended to remember, and by practice managed to make the pretense convincing. All things considered, he was generous in treatment of his worshipers, but he was giving royal audiences. People came to him. He went to the people only in the ball park, hospital, orphanage, or prison.

> So he was praised and, without ever having been seen, was loved.
> —Confessions of St. Augustine, IV. xiv.

The novelist James T. Farrell described America as "a nation of frustrated ballplayers." Baseball does not hold aloft the shining ideal of fair play; its ideal is success. Babe Ruth was the most successful ballplayer yet seen. This had its effect on a people that said its ideal was the moral teaching of the Bible but which really lived by the Horatio Alger myth of the lucky and virtuous boy who overcame handicaps partly by his own efforts and partly with the help of well-placed patrons, until he achieved middle-class respectability and some hope of greater success to come. With a little effort Ruth's story could be twisted to fit that pattern, though he had, mistakenly, to be made into an orphan boy to give him the right start for his legend. He became the orphan boy who made it to the top. Baseball fans do not ask players to have more virtue than they have. They enjoy the sporting greatness of men who are in all other respects like themselves, or, more exactly, like their fantasies of themselves.

Thus Ruth was nationalized. *Current Opinion* called him "the most talked-of American." A large body of people worked together at great cost and by ingenious methods to tell the nation of everything he did as soon as he did it. Few world figures had their pictures published more often. His following was universal. Autograph hunters who knew and cared nothing about baseball begged his signature as if it were a holy relic of a tribal religion. Mink-clad ladies in chauffeur-driven cars spoke to him familiarly by the roadside. And all of this public veneration was spontaneous. His kind of following was too vast to be a claque. The pressure on him was heavy, but grace was the mark of his public response.

Ruth news stories, both routine and unusual, were always in the daily press. They included his bodily measurements, his alleged diet, and his daily baseball record under its own two-column headline. The peculiar stories he provoked may be illustrated by an August dispatch telling of the vacation plans of Judge Edward D. Dixon of the Court of Common Pleas in Cincinnati. The judge promised his son that he would see Babe Ruth hit a home run, so the two of them went on the road to follow the Yankees until they saw him hit one out. The other 399 men on the major-league rosters were in danger of becoming Babe Ruth's supporting cast.

It is a common belief that Ruth's 1920 eruption saved baseball from falling into contempt because of the Black Sox scandal. The fixing of the 1919 World Series wasn't known until near the end of the 1920 season. By that time the mighty figure of Ruth almost blocked the view of the shame of 1919. It is more precise to say that Ruth's amazing season of 1920 was so interesting to the people that they had less attention to spare for the Black Sox story as it came out in dribbles. In one column of a paper one might read the sour report of a Chicago player's confession and next to it find the heartening story of Ruth winning a game in late innings with a home run. Any reader could be excused for preferring to read of what could not be fixed—a game-winning home run.

Some have thought the idolizing of athletes has been harmful. Even Ring Lardner said such hero worship was a "national disease" which filled grandstands and emptied playgrounds. As early as 1904 a *Times* editorial writer said ballplayers were "merely Swiss mercenaries," and the energy spent in cheering them, if put to practical use, could make New York a model city. Such views (worthy of Cotton Mather) neglect a simple biological fact: people and populations age. During Ruth's playing career the number of Americans under the age of twenty-five increased by eleven million, while the number who were twenty-five and over grew by eighteen million. Millions were too old to use Lardner's playgrounds. Excepting golf —just then becoming a democratic sport—there is no sporting outlet for people much past the age of thirty-two. One can be a champion sports-car racing driver, a tall-yacht helmsman, a steeplechase rider, but those are the sports of the rich. To condemn the people in the

grandstand was a puritanic judgment. Most of the rain-check holders had a simple choice: go to the ball game or forget about sports.
The nation of frustrated ballplayers would rather go to watch
younger men play well at a game the elders had once played and
loved.

> ... whenever a player hits the ball out of the park I have
> a sense of elation. I feel as if I had done it. To me, every
> wall or fence is palpably an inhibition. Beyond the
> bleacher roof lies Italy....
>
> —Heywood Broun

The rage for Ruth was part of the shift from puritan values.
Americans had become a consuming people who hungered for
instant pleasures. These hedonists were never so sinlessly employed
as when they enjoyed the play of their athletic heroes and made of
them celebrities. It seems impossible to build lasting celebrity by
trickery. The people select durable heroes by mysterious ways. In
the case of Babe Ruth in 1920 he no doubt profited by war-weariness
and, coincidentally, from some technological aids to communications: the reflex camera for action photography, the Graphophone
for records of his voice, and the motion picture for newsreel clips.
Nevertheless, celebrity will not last without the consent of the
people. The people of 1920 were casting off restraints. Ruth, more
than any other, helped to make their national game less restrained.

Babe Ruth's smashing offensive style of play brought him popular
acceptance by acclamation. In the postpuritan age after the First
World War the great defensive play of the prewar years lost out.
The loosely constructed game with explosive scoring was the people's choice. The tightly disciplined play of the age of Cobb and
McGraw fell back before Ruth's bat. The seventeen-inning errorless
1–0 game, with the run scored by a scratch hit, a bunt, a steal, and a
suicide squeeze, had been a puritan delight from the days of the
fabulous Baltimore Orioles of the 1890s up to the First World War.
But the 11–10 game, with, say, four home runs, better suited the
mood of the people of 1920 and after.

16 · The Most Exciting Player to Watch

He was easy to like and was at his best in the clutch. To me he was the most exciting player to watch of all time.
—Bill Dickey

Although Babe Ruth was shaped like a barrel, he moved gracefully. Even his swinging strikes drew applause. His short-striding run *seemed* awkward to some people, but, in sports, awkward is as awkward does; this very large and thick outfielder stole fourteen bases in 1920. All opposing teams did not have the same views on Ruth as a base runner. Some tried to hold him on first base and some did not; it depended on the temperaments of opposing managers and pitchers. But Truck Hannah, who caught seventy-eight games for the 1920 Yankees and had to know something of base runners, said flatly, "He was a good base runner."

In the field Ruth used a cheap flat white glove which the average boy would not envy. Sliding pads did not appeal to him. He usually had two or three friction burns—the players call them strawberries —on his thighs and hips which the trainer would wash daily with rubbing alcohol and cover with taped-over gauze. He threw left-handed of course, though he usually, but not always, wrote with his right hand. "I get along just as well with either one," he claimed. When throwing from the outfield he used the whip-crack arm motion of a pitcher, with his throwing hand rising just before he released the ball at arm's length. He held the ball with the first two fingers on top, across the stitching if possible, and with the side of his thumb on the bottom. His throws were long and accurate.

Babe Ruth was a team player in every way except his refusal to play in that part of the outfield where the setting sun blinds the fielder. There is nothing at all to show that Ruth was reluctant to make the sacrifice or the hit-and-run play. Nor was his inability to remember the names of players a mark of toploftiness. He knew who they were but did not bother to clutter his memory with unnecessary proper nouns. On the bench he behaved as though among equals, though any newcomer, however famous, was apt to be called "Kid" for months or even years. When he went to the plate he usually exchanged some small talk with the catcher, but when at bat he rarely spoke to pitchers or umpires.

> A rabbit didn't have to think to know what to do to dodge a dog. Instinct told him. The same kind of instinct told Babe what to do and where to be. . . . I never heard anybody tell him anything to do on the ball field.
>
> —Sam Vick

Men who played with Ruth have very much the same explanations of his greatness.

EARL COMBS. Eyesight, good teaching, and perfect coordination made him a natural.

SAMMY BYRD. Great reflexes.

DIXIE WALKER.* Very relaxed, and wonderful coordination.

But there was more to Ruth's skill than a marvelously good physical arrangement. He had a keen mind for baseball.

To begin with, he learned the rules of the game at St. Mary's Industrial School, and knew them as professionals know them. Of twenty-two ex-Yankees who commented on the point, agreement was next to unanimous that he knew the rule book as well as he should.

Next, there is the accepted folklore that he never threw to the wrong base. The throw to the infield is the chief mental concern of the outfielder. He must make an instant judgment based on the speed of the runners, his own posture at the moment he gets his hands on the ball, the distance to throw, the state of the game, and the health of his arm. In a close game his decision may be decisive. If the outfielder can't get the lead runner but tries for him anyway, he may be giving the next man the extra base which puts him in position to score on a single, a fly, or even an infield out. No one has challenged Ruth's reputation for judging the outfield throw correctly.

A third point to consider is the contradictory tradition that he

---

* Samuel Dewey Byrd (1906–   ), outfielder, eight seasons, 1929–1936, Yankees, Reds, batting average .274.

Fred Walker (1910–   ), outfielder, eighteen seasons, 1931–1949, Yankees, White Sox, Tigers, Dodgers, Pirates, batting average .306.

often missed signs—those signals from manager to coach to batter (or base runner). Bob Shawkey, who later was his manager for a year, threw this charge out of court tersely: "No signs to *him*." Others have said he was almost always left to his own discretion.

A poll of teammates on the question of Ruth's mental powers as a ballplayer brought replies which are worth repeating.

JOE SEWELL. He knew the game of baseball and always played the percentage.

EDDIE WELLS. Ruth simply had the most natural equipment, physically and mentally, for a baseball player. . . .

BEN CHAPMAN. If he ever made a mental error, I can't recall it.

JACK SALTZGAVER. His baseball intelligence made him a natural.

CHICKEN HAWKS. He was a natural, smart, perfectly coordinated.

TRUCK HANNAH. He was a great student of the game, with natural talent and baseball smartness.

JIMMIE DeSHONG.* Perfect coordination, baseball smartness—a natural.

H. G. Salsinger, the Detroit sportswriter (who thought Ty Cobb the greatest), used to put Ruth to the test. Salsinger would ask why he made a certain play the way he did. Without hesitation Ruth would analyze the play, explain the several possible ways of making it, and justify his means, even though his way was not always the most obvious.

> "Get up and hit a home run," has never been a part of the usable technique of any manager. . . . In any home run there must be some element of good fortune as well as hefty shoulders.
>
> —Heywood Broun

Of course, the favorite tag of Ruth's fellows, "baseball smartness," does not account for the cannonade of home runs. But it has something to do with his batting averages of 1919 and 1920 which were .322 and .376. Jimmie Reese** told the author that after Ruth had batted against a pitcher just once, he had a pretty good idea of

---

* Otto Hamlin Saltzgaver (1905–   ), infielder, six seasons, 1932–1945, Yankees, Pirates, batting average .260.

Nelson Louis Hawks (1896–   ), outfielder-infielder, two seasons, 1921, 1925, Yankees, Phillies, batting average .316.

James Brooklyn DeShong (1909–   ), pitcher, seven seasons, 1932–1939, Athletics, Yankees, Senators. Won 47, lost 44, earned-run average 5.08.

** James Hymie Reese (1904–   ), infielder, three seasons, 1930–1932, Yankees, Cardinals, batting average .278.

how the pitcher planned to pitch to him, and reacted accordingly. The century-long table of averages shows us that pitching beats batting three out of four times. The reason is, in part, that the pitcher knows what the next pitch will be and the batter does not. Ruth, and a few dozen other great hitters, were able more often than most players to outguess the pitchers.

> **And the batter is one lone man playing the other nine men. . . .**
>
> —Paul Gallico

The batter has difficult and interesting problems. The pitched ball traveling at speeds up to 175 feet a second comes over the plate in from three-tenths to five-tenths of a second after it leaves the pitcher's hand. It gives no time for study. The hitter can reach it with his bat only in the last three feet of its passage. At that point he can actually hear it whizzing. That is why George Sisler said hitters must overcome fear of the ball, of the pitcher, and of the situation.

Physicists have said there are twenty-six possible mistakes a batter may make, any one of which will cause him to fail to hit safely. He must be perfect during a period of half a second or less, in noisy surroundings, and in physical danger. He must also have the bat which is right for him. He must also be lucky. Striking a sphere with a cylinder, intending to drive it to some place on a large plane (or off the plane) in the instant of time allowed to the batter, produces unexpected trajectories and bounces, some of which go for hits, but most of which don't. If it could be done in slow motion, it still would be harder than shooting pool or golf, because the ball is moving. As it is, the speed of the ball demands that successful batting be unthinking reaction. At first sight of the pitch the batter must decide in thirteen-hundredths of a second whether he will swing at the ball. If he intends to swing, he must start the bat, predict the velocity, the height, and the lateral location of the ball as it will be when it comes within reach of the bat, and then hit the ball within a quarter of an inch of the ideal spot on the bat. It would be impossible if it had to be done rationally instead of as a reflex.

Having mastered reflex hitting as much as possible, the long-ball hitter (as distinct from the short-swinging singles hitter) must find his groove—that is, the arc of swing that gets the best result. (Babe Ruth used the word groove, and it is in use today.) When a man has the feel of his groove he can wait longer before swinging and still put all of his power into the swing. No man can stay in his groove indefinitely. After a while he loses the feel and must recover it. Hence the slugger's summer season alternates between streaks and slumps.

We must remember that the pitch is not intended to be hit. The ball comes in hopping, sinking, sailing, or curving. The batter must find it with his eye, catch it on his bat at the right place, and then jerk it out of the park. As Roy Blount, Jr., put it, "This is comparable to picking off a runaway outboard motor and in the same motion heaving it up a flight of stairs."

An act of skill is one in which a man does more things at once than there is time to think about.

—John Ciardi

Having learned of the sale of Ruth to the Yankees, *The Times* of January 6, 1920, printed a description of his batting style.

Ruth's principle of batting is much the same as the principle of the golfer. He comes back slowly, keeps his eye on the ball and follows through. His very position at the bat is intimidating to the pitcher. He places his feet in perfect position. He simply cannot step away from the pitch if he wants to. He can step only one way—in. The weight of Ruth's body when he bats is on his left leg. The forward leg is bent slightly at the knee. As he stands facing the pitcher more of his hips and back are seen by the pitcher than his chest or side. When he starts to swing his back is half turned toward the pitcher. He goes as far back as he can reach, never for an instant taking his eye off the ball as it leaves the pitcher's hand.

The greatest power in his terrific swing comes when the bat is directly in front of his body, just half way in the swing. He hits the ball with a terrific impact and there is no player in the game whose swing is such a masterpiece of batting technique.

At the end of that 1920 season *Current Opinion* asked Ruth how he did it. He replied, "I swing every time with all the force I have and strike out just as often as others in the .300 class; but when I hit the ball, I *hit* it." Many years later he explained it again for Joe Reichler of the Associated Press.

What I did first was to get the proper stance. I'd shift my feet so I'd be well balanced. That was the most important thing. When I saw coming the pitch I liked, I'd take a swing. The very second that I felt the bat hitching onto the ball, I would give my wrist an extra twist, and give the ball the old golf follow-through—and that was that.

Less than a year before he died, speaking of a particular home run, he described his attack briefly: "I hit it as I hit all the others, by taking a good gander at the pitch as it came up to the plate, twisting my body into a backswing and then hitting it as hard as I could swing."

Grantland Rice summed up the sight as best a spectator could.

In lashing at the ball, Ruth put his big body back of the smash with as perfect timing as we have ever seen. There was no hurried motion, no quick swinging, no overanxiety to connect. It all happened with the concentrated serenity of great power under perfect control.

Ruth always said he thought Joe Jackson was the best of all hitters, and that he had consciously copied Jackson's posture and swing. (Jackson had it harder than Ruth because he batted against all of the trick pitches that were outlawed in 1920, and against pitchers using dirty, battered baseballs.) When at the plate Jackson aimed his right shoulder at the pitcher and stood with feet about twenty inches apart. Ruth changed the stance in that he held his feet about eight or nine inches apart, believing he could pivot better that way. Standing as he did, if he started to swing at a fast ball he had to go through with it. The completion of a powerful swing— if he missed—twisted him into corkscrew shape, as writers first noticed in print during his hitting spree of July 1918. (On a slow pitch he could check his swing.) The likeness of Ruth's and Jackson's styles was plain. Said Eddie Collins, "The Babe stands up there more like Joe than anyone else I have ever seen."

When a batter spun as Ruth did, he made the end of the bat move very fast, increasing its centrifugal force and the horizontal thrust of the ground under his feet. A long hit was thrown off Ruth's bat as water is thrown off a rotating wheel. And, when possible, he actually swung up to the ball from below its path. Stop-action photographs show the ball riding on the bat and coming around in an arc. It is at its lowest when directly over the plate, and it rises as it passes Ruth's body.

A writer in *Scientific American* in 1915 advised players not to hit fungo flies during pregame practice because it would lead to hitting flies during the game. If Ruth knew of this advice it would have been wasted on him, because he owed his success to copying Brother Matthias's experiments in hitting fungoes for distance. The uppercutting swing was certainly unorthodox and not to be copied by others. When Beethoven pointed out some breaking of the rules of music in the work of a young composer, the visitor said Beethoven had broken the same rules. Beethoven answered, "I may do it, but not you." Babe Ruth could have said the same. The uppercut swing intercepted the ball as it was about to reach the catcher. As the players say, Ruth took the ball right out of the catcher's glove. When other batters swing that way and connect, they foul on to the roof of the stand at best, or foul out to the catcher at worst.

> **If I tried to swing like Babe with my feet together and pigeon-toed and my back to the pitcher, I'd either get beaned on the back of the skull, or I'd strike out oftener than I do.**
> **—Hank Greenberg* (1947)**

Photographs of Ruth in action help us to know his methods. In a complete swing at a high fast ball the bat would rise, after hitting the ball, in a long follow-through which was much longer than the swing before bat met ball. When the bat hit a pitch knee-high in front of the outside corner (his favorite blow), the hitting swing was longer but so was the follow-through. Throughout his whole playing career he ended his swing with his legs crossed, weight divided between them, his right foot on its right edge and his left foot on its left edge. This put all of his weight on the ligaments and tendons of his ankles, and pretty well corrects the notion that he had spindly ankles. (Their thinness was an optical illusion; he was just a very big man with relatively small feet.)

When he came to the Yankees, Ruth batted from well back in the box. Once in the box he rarely stepped out. He liked to meet the ball in front of the plate. If that happened he could pull the ball to right field. He shocked many critics by holding the bat with the same grip regardless of the number of strikes. Moe Berg** said every great hitter he ever saw, except Ruth, moved his hands higher on the bat after two strikes (to make it easier to manipulate). But not Ruth. Because he was always ready to hit hard, he took very few called third strikes, though he struck out often. He had no consistent rule on whether to try to hit the ball when the count was

---

* Henry Benjamin Greenberg (1911–   ), infielder-outfielder, thirteen seasons, 1930–1947, Tigers, Pirates, batting average .313. Hall of Fame. 58 home runs in 1938.

** Morris Berg (1902–1972), catcher, fifteen seasons, 1923–1939, Dodgers, White Sox, Indians, Senators, Red Sox, batting average .243.

three balls and no strikes. Ruth (as most leading sluggers today) swung if he thought he could reach it.

> No one can tell you how to hit home runs. You either have
> the natural strength and reflexes, or you don't.
> —Hank Greenberg (1947)

Ruth resented the idea that his skill was merely the result of hereditary accident, so to speak. He always claimed he worked as hard for his success as anybody. If he learned how to hit, he probably taught himself. Baseball teams sometimes have hitting coaches, but they are pretty obscure functionaries in the baseball world, and none has been famous for improving his charges in the way that a dozen well-known pitching coaches are famous. What can, for sure, be taught about hitting is the strategy of the duel between batter and pitcher which relies on wise sayings, such as, when behind in the game it's a good idea to take the first pitch. But the muscle engineering needed to hit safely isn't taught. Advice on how to improve one's hitting is rarely in a language that makes for common understanding. It is rather like being instructed in the use of chopsticks by the conscious tension and motion of every needed muscle and tendon. Batting is a conditioned reflex. Great batting uses divinely given coordination and eyesight. Practice can improve the effective use of the gifts, but they have to be there before the practice starts.

Ruth changed people's minds about batting. Before he exploded into fame theory had it that a full swing lessened the batter's accuracy and helped the pitcher to the same degree, though there had been a few exceptions. Most of the great hitters—personified by Ty Cobb—used a short swing or chopped as if using an axe. They stepped forward to meet the ball in front of the plate. They not only feared to lose accuracy but thought the long swing would make them lose balance. Ruth changed that. His near-perfect eyesight, timing, and coordination let him get full power into the swing *with precision*. Others have since found it possible, but in 1919 and 1920 Ruth was thought to be a freak. If he had manipulated the bat in the pool-cue manner of Cobb he could have ranked higher than ninth in lifetime batting average as he does now. Henry Johnson said, "Babe has told me that if he had just gone for base hits he could have hit .450 or .500—and I believe him."

Ruth also changed the nature of the game as spectacle. When he came to bat the combat zone shrank to the ground between mound and home plate. He made the fans much more conscious of the war between pitcher and batter. For the minutes he stood there waving his bat the game was a contest between two men instead of eighteen.

And if Ruth hit the ball out of the park the pitcher was defeated, not by a team but by Ruth.

Ruth hit so hard, and got that bat traveling so fast, that when he nicked only a small piece of the ball, he had enough power to send a high, towering fly over the fence.
—Hank Greenberg

That Babe Ruth was strong there is no doubt. The hard question is, how strong? *If* we knew how fast the five-ounce ball moved after he hit it, and *if* we knew how much time elapsed during the swing of the bat before it met the ball, we could figure it as so many foot-pounds and convert that to horsepower. A dazzled Cleveland physicist estimated the speeds and times and thought that Ruth generated forty-four horsepower. But it was pure guesswork.

We can state Ruth's power another way, from reckoning based on the usual baseball statistics. Earnshaw Cook, in *Percentage Baseball*, explained a very useful and simple index he called the Power Factor, arrived at by dividing the player's total bases by the number of hits. If every hit were a single, the Power Factor would be 1; if every hit were a home run, the Power Factor would be 4. In practice, a Power Factor of 2 would be extraordinarily high. Applying it to Ruth's batting record for the years 1914–1917 when he was a full-time pitcher, we find his Power Factor was 1.53. In three of those four years Ty Cobb led the American League in batting average; for the four years his Power Factor was only 1.38. In the season of 1920 Ruth's Power Factor was the astonishing figure of 2.26; if the man's every hit had been a double, the Power Factor would have been but 2! Ruth was the most powerful hitter ever seen.

The very style of Ruth's home runs showed might. The word *towering* was very often used to describe them. Sam Vick told the author, "When he got one up in the air there was no park that would hold it." Some sluggers hit line drives and low-trajectory home runs. Ruth hit many like that, but his specialty was lofting the missile in the same parabola as followed by a mortar shell. His characteristic home run went so high and so far that it was dropping steeply when it fell beyond the fence. It was the kind of a blow that would be a long lazy fly out if hit by a lesser man. Such a ball can only go out if driven at an angle of about forty-five degrees to a great height—hence the adjective *towering*. Sometimes a Ruth pop fly would go so high that he was on second base when the infielder caught it (or lost his eye focus and, as the fielders say, gave up on the ball).

Before Ruth appeared in baseball, people accepted Ed Delahanty or Big Dan Brothers* as the most powerful of batters. Delahanty's and Brouthers' lifetime Power Factors were, respectively, 1.46 and 1.52.

In 1920 Brouthers watched Ruth from the press box at the Polo Grounds. He was almost as large as Ruth and still ranks eighth in triples, which is proof of power in the age of the dead ball. When asked his opinion of Ruth he said the liveliness of the ball didn't make the difference. "No matter what kind of ball you use, no one in the world could hit one as far as Babe Ruth." He thought Ruth's shape made it easy for him to pivot so that he could put great power into the swing.

That brings us to the question of the shapes and weights of sluggers. Weight would be an advantage only if the hitter held his arms so stiffly that the bat became an extension of them, but only toy ballplayers and hockey players swing that way. Of the truly great home-run hitters whose action photographs are easily available, Hank Aaron, Ted Williams, Mel Ott, Ernie Banks, and Al Simmons were wedge-shaped. All the others have a certain broadness of pelvis. We know that explosive bursts of muscular energy begin in the trunk of the body and flow out to the fingers and toes. A thickness of body is valuable to the long-ball hitter. Of course, not all players with thick torsos are leading home-run hitters. The difference, to judge by Ruth, is the speed of the explosion of energy. Ruth generated more muscular power *rapidly* than any other player of similar strength.

Ruth had certain advantages beyond his physique. The spitball was gone in 1920, though Ruth said the only thing he didn't like about it was that there were "germs in the spit and you catch disease." And new balls replaced battered and dirty balls more often, to the batter's advantage. (The policy began after Ray Chapman died in August.) Batting left-handed was a help to hitting safely, too, because Ruth could get to first base two- or three-tenths of a second faster, which amounted to a lead of four to six feet over a right-handed batter. Ruth also helped himself with his natural showmanship. He knew the way to please the crowd was to hit the ball far. While he was an unimaginative person, and usually lived entirely in the present, he once said that the man who starts something (read, slugger) usually stirs the crowd more than the man

---

* Edward James Delahanty (1867–1903), infielder-outfielder, sixteen seasons, 1888–1903, Phillies, Cleveland (Players League), Senators, batting average .346 (fourth highest all-time). Hall of Fame.

Dennis Joseph Brouthers (1858–1932), first baseman, nineteen seasons, 1879–1904, Troy, Buffalo, Detroit, Boston (all National League), Boston (Players League), Boston (American Association), Brooklyn, Baltimore, Louisville, Philadelphia, New York (all National League), batting average .342 (ninth highest all-time). Hall of Fame.

who stops something (read, pitcher). That faith helped a natural-born crowd-pleaser when he tried to hit one out.

The appearance of Ruth—a defector from pitching—made life more difficult for pitchers. They had been having things pretty much their own way in the first twenty years of the century, but Ruth seemed to bring witchcraft into the game. Rules of thumb were useless against him. Generally it is best to pitch low so that the batter will hit the ball on the ground, which gives five men a chance at it; Ruth loved to see a pitch come in knee-high. Generally it is best to pitch outside to a pull-hitter, because the usual pull-hitter likes to jerk the ball down the foul line; Ruth's favorite point of contact with the ball was in front of the outside corner. What could a pitcher do? The question still amuses Ruth's old teammates. Here are some answers.

MARK KOENIG.* Pitch and duck.

DIXIE WALKER. Pray for a single.

TRUCK HANNAH. Try to make him keep it in the park.

BOB McGRAW.** The only way to keep Babe from hitting would be for Ban Johnson . . . to give him a season pass to first base.

Some veterans who tried to answer the question with straight faces believed that a pitcher should work carefully, pitching curves high and inside at varying speeds. Eddie Wells, who pitched with and against him, warned, "Never throw him a fast ball over the plate." When Candy Cummings,† the presumed inventor of the curve, was in his seventies he watched Ruth and suggested the pitcher use a curve inside at the fists, a curve high on the outside, and then a curve inside at the knees. No two pitches should be at the same speed. Our 1920 scouting report on Ruth, then, shapes up like this: *curves high, in and out; curves low inside; waste the fast ball; change speeds on every pitch.* And despite the best-laid schemes of canny pitchers, Ruth batted .372 and hit a home run for every eight times at bat.

Ruth also gave fielders much to think about. A squarely hit ball bends the bat slightly and flattens itself momentarily like a soft-shelled egg. Then it moves away faster than it came. Ruth's blows

* Mark Anthony Koenig (1902–   ), infielder, twelve seasons, 1925–1936, Yankees, Tigers, Cubs, Reds, Giants, batting average .279.
  ** Robert Emmett McGraw (1895–   ), pitcher, nine seasons, 1917–1929, Yankees, Red Sox, Cardinals, Dodgers, Phillies. Won 26, lost 38, earned-run average 4.89.
  † William Arthur Cummings (1838–1924), pticher, two seasons, 1876–1877, Hartford and Cincinnati (National League). Won 21, lost 22, earned-run average 2.78. Hall of Fame.

were harder than any other batter's. Opposing infielders and out-fielders expected the ball on the right side of the diamond (though he could hit to all fields if he chose), and they played far back. Ruth did not bunt very often, but in 1920 his high batting average was owing in part to bunt hits against deep-playing infielders.

17 · The Emblem of the Game

Ruth's model . . . reflects the transition to the modern in
bat styling. Most notable is the handle size—smaller than
that of earlier models—and a larger barrel than those of
the periods immediately preceding. The bat pictured here
was used by Babe in the 1920 season.
—Jack McGrath, Hillerich & Bradsby Company

The modern baseball bat is a functional work of art as graceful
as the classic Grecian amphora. The symbol of ancient Hercules is
a club, of the Norse god Thor a hammer, of the American Hercules
a bat. Babe Ruth changed the play of the game and he changed
the shape and weight of the tool that is its emblem.

The bat is turned on a lathe. The following picture shows the
stages of shaping. From bottom to top there are:

—the "split," from a "bolt," which is a section of a small tree
trunk.

—the "round," turned from the split.

—the "square," a ripsawed piece of a very large tree trunk, used
just as the split is used.

—the "rough out," turned from a square or a round.

—the bat fresh from the lathe.

—the completely finished bat, in this case the model first named
for Ken Boyer and then for Ernie Banks. It is a rather light bat at
thirty-one ounces. Banks hit five grand-slam home runs in 1955,
the first year he used the bat.

The evolution of the bat has been from a rather graceless tapering
club, popular a century or more ago, through curious shapes. In the
picture on p. 185, from left to right, are:

—the maximum bat permitted by the rules, 42 inches long, 2¾
inches thick, and never used by any player.

Stages of Production of Louisville Sluggers

1. *Split*. After the trunks of the smaller trees are cut into sections called bolts 38″ to 40″ long, these bolts are then split.
From the "split" the "round" is turned—see stage 2A.

2A. *Round*. The round is turned from the split.

2B. *Square*. Bolts cut from trunks of large trees are rip sawn into squares instead of being split like those from the smaller trees.

3. *Rough-out*. Rough-outs are turned from squares and rounds.

4. *Bat* just off turning lathe.

5. A completely finished, genuine Louisville Slugger bat of Ken Boyer's model. (*Hillerich & Bradsby, Inc.*)

—the tipless cone, the earliest popular type, used from the 1850s through the 1870s.

—Willie Keeler's bat, 1892–1910.

—Heinie Groh's* bottle bat, 1912–27.

—the ball knob, 1895–1905.

* Henry Knight Groh (1889–1968), infielder, sixteen seasons, 1912–1927, Giants, Reds, Pirates, batting average .292.

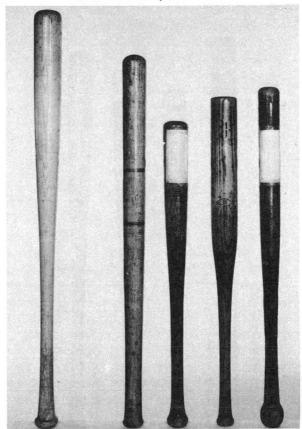

Unusual Bat Models

Big Bat—The "Big Bat" at the top is included only to portray legal maximum dimensions—2¾ inches in diameter and 42 inches in length—a length far beyond that used by anyone.

1. *Earliest*—The earliest type, long and heavy, has little shape—it simply tapers down gradually from a barrel that is relatively small to a very large handle. In contrast, the profile of the moderns (represented here by the Babe Ruth and the Ernie Banks, two of the most popular) is one of curves—from a large, but relatively short, barrel down to a long, medium-small handle.

2. *"Wee Willie" Keeler*, one of the most scientific batters in the history of baseball, used this diminutive Slugger—the shortest (30½") ever in the Major Leagues—to help compile his 19-year big league batting average of .345! Willie's famous motto was "Hit 'em where they ain't."

3. *The "Bottle Bat" of Heine Groh.* This unique bat, truly resembling a bottle in shape, has a long, large barrel that curves down abruptly to a small, relatively short handle. But Heine used it during 19 Major League seasons (and five World Series) for a very respectable .292 lifetime average.

4. *The "Ball Knob"*, conceived in 1895 by J. A. "Bud" Hillerich, who turned the first Louisville Slugger in 1884, enjoyed a moderate demand over a period of about ten years, but then dropped out of sight. (*Hillerich & Bradsby, Inc.*)

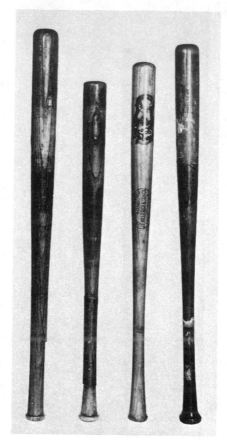

Left to right: Pete Browning's bat;
Hugh Duffy's bat; Ty Cobb's bat;
Babe Ruth's bat. (*Hillerich & Bradsby,
Inc.*)

Here are bats of great hitters. From left to right:
—Pete Browning's* bat. 1882–1894.
—Hugh Duffy's,** 1888–1906, with which he set the single-season
record average, .440.
—Ty Cobb's, which was 34½ inches long, and, at 42 ounces, a

* Louis Rogers Browning (1858–1905), outfielder, thirteen seasons, 1882–1894,
Louisville, Cleveland, Cincinnati, Pittsburgh, Brooklyn, St. Louis, batting average
.341.
** Hugh Duffy (1866–1954), outfielder, seventeen seasons, 1888–1906, Chicago
(National and Players Leagues), Boston (American Association and National
League), Milwaukee (American League), Phillies, batting average .329. Hall of
Fame.

heavy bat. He never used a bat weighing less than 36 ounces. With this first truly graceful bat he set the record lifetime batting average of .367 in twenty-four seasons.

—Babe Ruth's 1920 bat, almost as long as Browning's but thinner in the handle.

The batter intends to hit the ball with the barrel of the bat, the part that is cylindrical, which the players call "good wood." In all tools designed for men to swing there is a certain spot called the center of percussion. In a hammer it is in the head. In a baseball bat it is in the barrel, the exact location varying a little from bat to bat. A player knows he has hit the ball there when the bat follows through smoothly with no jar to arms or wrists. When a home-run hitter seems to pause at the plate to watch the ball climb, he has hit the ball at the center of percussion and expects it to go all the way. There are many action photographs of Ruth in that pose.

Ruth started the trend toward lighter bats. A heavy bat lets a man hit to all fields. In a way, it forces him to, because the weight makes it harder for him to get the bat around quickly enough to hit the ball when it is still in front of the plate and pull it down the foul line. Ruth was strong enough to pull the ball with a heavy bat, but when weaker players saw what profit there was in home runs they began to give up their heavy, chopping-style bats and to use lighter ones, so that the average weight dropped from more than 40 ounces to around 36 ounces. For example, Ted Williams in his prime used bats that weighed from 31 to 34 ounces. Neither Cobb nor Ruth ever used one that light.

Ruth's heaviest useful bat weighed 47 ounces. In 1920 he ordered several bats that weighed 54 ounces—for reasons unknown—but never repeated the order. The Babe Ruth model is still popular with players, but it has been turned down to a little less than 35 ounces while keeping the same graceful lines. In 1920 Ruth's usual bat weighed up to 44 ounces and was 35 inches long. It was a very modern design, with a thinner handle and thicker barrel than Cobb's.

From time to time Ruth would take a fancy to a particular bat and not let others use it. But when a teammate was in a slump Ruth was likely to press him to use one of his bats for good luck. Once, during an exhibition game, someone stole one of his bats. They cost but a few dollars, and the club paid that, but Ruth offered a reward of twenty-five dollars and a duplicate bat for its return, which shows that he could become strongly attached to a bat.

It is impossible to say how many he used. He broke few but he gave away many, and the Yankee management did not object. To strew relics of the hero among the people strengthens the cult.

18 · The Stitched Golf Ball

> . . . they fixed up a ball that if you don't miss it entirely it
> will clear the fence, and the result is that ball players
> which used to specialize in hump back line drives to the
> pitcher is now amongst our leading sluggers.
>
> —Ring Lardner

Babe Ruth had one advantage over all earlier hitters: a livelier ball,
which, many years later, he called "the stitched golf ball." After the
explosion of home runs in 1920, some said the ban on treating the
surface of the ball and the use of more baseballs made the change.
If that were true all hitting should have improved. Only the total
of home runs increased in a startling way. Batting averages were
higher but nowhere near in the same proportion. As for the frequent
issue of new baseballs, that began only in August 1920, after
Chapman died.

The makers of the baseball would not admit, and perhaps did
not know, that the 1920 ball had more resilience. Benjamin F. Shibe,
vice-president of the Athletics and an officer of the A. J. Reach
Company, denied in 1920 that there had been the slightest change
in the ball. But George Reach, in 1923, admitted its occasional
enlivening and deadening. Edward G. Barrow, the Yankee general
manager from 1920 on, believed a lively ball had been made especially for the Federal League in 1915. The only statistical comment
on the 1920 ball is that of Earnshaw Cook, who is convinced that it
was 16 percent more resilient than earlier balls. Cook also believes
that the ball used today is 12 percent more resilient than the 1920
ball, and suggests that with the present-day ball and a schedule of
162 games Ruth would have hit seventy-five home runs in 1920.

During the First World War the Bureau of Standards studied
baseballs to set rules for their purchase by the armed forces. The
services bought the kind which was made to last the longest. This

study of the ball would not make it lively, but for the first time the makers had all the facts they needed to make a ball with predictable performance. The makers' story is that in 1919 they got better machinery for winding yarn, and a better grade of Australian wool yarn. The new machines wound the new yarn more tightly and the ball bounded farther off the bat. The makers may have been honestly ignorant of a difference for a year or so.

The game changed. In 1919 there were 448 home runs in the major leagues; in 1920, 630. Runs came in clusters. Owing to the survival of players who grew up in dead-ball times, it would take ten years to complete the sluggers' revolution, but Ruth led the way, and the fans, as we have seen, broke attendance records almost everywhere the Yankees played in 1920. Baseball puritans were annoyed, but the style of baseball play is not, after all, a moral question. It is a matter of taste. It is also a matter of holding the fans' interest. In favor of the home-run epidemic it can be said that a team with a pair of heavy hitters is not beyond hope as long as they are trailing by no more than three or four runs. In 1901 or 1910 or 1917 a game was pretty well lost when a team fell that far behind.

Babe Ruth profited most by the stitched golf ball, so there is a certain comfort in knowing that the record he broke so awesomely in 1920 by hitting fifty-four home runs was not the record of some beloved but departed hero. Nobody's feelings were hurt, because it was his own record of 1919 that fell.

19 · The Center of the Crowd
of Kids

Boys worship the muscle hero. A boy can imagine himself a champion athlete much easier than he can imagine himself President.

Ruth accepted his half-god rank in the eyes of boys as gracefully as anyone possibly could. One ghost writer exploited the trailing crowd of boys by having Ruth say mawkishly, "I've always felt cleaner after a session with kids." We may suppose his tolerance of boyish clamors was an emotional consequence of growing up in happy regimentation at St. Mary's Industrial School where the people of his world were almost all boys and where he was a smashing social success. To surrender to boys was to return to their age, which he always felt was a good age.

Ruth was not the kind of public idol who unconsciously stoops when passing through any door less than ten feet high. He could be curt with grownups—though rarely—but never with children. He had no reason to fear a boy mob, because he treated them as Brother Matthias had treated the collected waifs of Baltimore. With boys he became Xaverian Brother George, and dockside Baltimore was forgotten. Ruth calmed crowding boys with smiling commands which they accepted with pleasure. Once in Canada police extricated him from a swarm of idolatrous boys and led him away on horseback. The unwanted rescue annoyed him because he felt he was in no danger. Everywhere possible, boys followed him like the tail of a comet, as though he were the heaven-sent leader of the young.

James T. Farrell's account of Ruth's mobbing by boys in Chicago in 1920 has been noted, as his evidence for the end of the era of Cobb and the beginning of the age of Ruth. His text is worth reading.

A crowd of over a hundred kids had him not only surrounded but almost mobbed. They pushed, shoved, scrambled, and yelled so that Ruth could scarcely move. Wearing a blue suit, and a grey cap, there was an expression of bewilderment on his moon face. He said nothing, rolled with the kids and a strange, hysterical and noisy little mob slowly moved on to the exit gate with Ruth in the center of it. More kids rushed to the edge of the crowd and they, also, pushed and shoved. Ruth swayed from side to side, his shoulders bending one way, and then the other. As they all swirled to the gate, Ruth narrowly escaped being shoved into mustard which had been spilled from an overturned barrel. Ruth and the kids left the park with the big fellow still in the center of the crowd ·of kids.

Thomas Wolfe wrote a similar episode, set in New York, in *You Can't Go Home Again*. It has every appearance of a sketch from life.

A crowd of young boys who had been waiting at the gate rushed upon them. They were those dark-faced, dark-eyed, dark-haired little urchins who spring up like dragon seed from the grim pavements of New York, but in whose tough little faces and raucous voices there still remains, curiously, the innocence and faith of the children everywhere.

In a moment they were pressing round him in a swarming horde, deafening the ears with their shrill cries, begging, shouting, tugging at his shirt sleeves, doing everything they could to attract his attention, holding dirty little scraps of paper toward him, stubs of pencil, battered little note books, asking him to sign his autograph.

Many boys venerated Ruth who never saw him, who, indeed, never saw a major-league game. They looked at newspaper photographs, studied Yankee box scores, and sometimes saw him in action in the newsreels. They persuaded their mothers to buy hundreds of thousands of fuzzy brown caps like the one the Hero wore. For many of them a visit of the Yankees to play an exhibition game in their part of the world, during the spring or on an open date in the summer, was a great affair. These exhibition games often remained unfinished. When such a game was in late innings a stray boy would run out on the field to get Babe Ruth's autograph. Ruth would take off his glove (he wrote with his glove hand), kneel on one knee while using the other as a desk, and sign whatever the boy brought. Emboldened, another would come, then others, then all, and the game would come to an end because the field was crowded. Sportswriters suspected that weary Yankees encouraged the disciples just to end the game, but the boys never really needed encouragement.

Ruth's mail was full of requests from boys for signed photographs. In the quantity he needed, photographs could be had from the best theatrical photographers for about eight cents each. In the winter after the season of 1920 he sent out five thousand of them—counting stamps and envelopes, an expense of about five hundred dollars. In his own characteristic response to pleas from boys, he paid the cost himself.

20 · The Skinny Little Scrap

The skinny little scrap of a fellow who did not seem to be able to find a uniform small enough to fit him.
　　　　　—Gerald Holland, on Miller Huggins

The man most closely linked to Babe Ruth's life in the 1920s was the small Yankee manager, Miller Huggins. In his playing days Huggins weighed about 140 pounds. He was five feet, six and a half inches tall. He had been a switch-hitting second baseman with the Reds and the Cardinals, and had managed the Cardinals before taking charge of the Yankees. He threw right-handed. His overblown nicknames were Little Everywhere and Rabbit. As a leadoff man, hitting from a crouch, he made his strike zone a small target and drew many bases on balls. In thirteen seasons he walked 1,002 times and had only 312 strikeouts. In 1910 he became co-holder of a record which still stands: six appearances at the plate in one game without a legal time at bat (four walks, two sacrifices). Folklore says he invented the delayed steal in 1903. He fielded well and ran the bases skillfully, stealing forty-one bases in 1906.

Huggins qualified for the practice of law before he became a professional baseball player. It is said that William Howard Taft knew him as a student and advised him to practice baseball.

The umpire-writer Billy Evans wrote a piece on the scarcity of second basemen in 1915, and listed the good ones—Eddie Collins, Johnny Evers, Nap Lajoie, Del Pratt, and Miller Huggins. Alfred Spink reviewed Huggins after his first season with the Cardinals (1910) and concluded that he needed "little boosting." Helene Hathaway Robison Britton, a militant suffragette, owned the Cardinals and acted as their general manager for eight years, but could not get along with her McGraw-trained manager, Roger Bresnahan.* Huggins became her manager in 1913.

When Jacob Ruppert and T. L. Huston bought the Yankees in 1915 they hired Wild Bill Donovan as manager. Donovan managed to finish as high as fourth once in his three seasons. Looking about for a new manager, Huston wanted Wilbert Robinson of Brooklyn, his good old hunting, singing, and drinking companion. Ruppert interviewed Robinson but wished to search further. Meanwhile Huston, a very fat man, had somehow conjured up a commission as colonel in the Corps of Engineers and had gone overseas with the army. Ruppert turned to Ban Johnson, president of the American League, for advice. Johnson nominated Huggins. Huston protested from France by cable. Actually, Ruppert had a distaste for Huggins before he knew him. He was repelled by Huggins' practices of wearing a cloth cap and smoking a pipe in public, which he considered marks of the working class. Ban Johnson urged that Ruppert at least talk with Huggins. No doubt averting his gaze from the cap, Ruppert listened to Huggins and decided that Huggins knew much about baseball if not about gents' wear. For his part Huggins had no wish to join the Yankees (their record was as bad as the Cardinals'), but J. G. Taylor Spink of the *Sporting News* bullied and coaxed him to take the job. Huston remained displeased and always felt that Huggins had slipped into the job while he was far away defending his country.

When Huston came home he made Huggins's life unpleasant. If players disagreed with Huggins, Huston would listen with sympathy. And during the last phase of the Yankees' last western trip of 1920, when they lost their weak grip on first place—and the pennant—Huston gladly explained to players and writers how Huggins had mismanaged the pitching. Huggins's position would have been intolerable except for his thick skin and the fact that Huston was waging war with Ban Johnson at the same time and had to divide his fire.

Huggins himself was an irritable man. He had chronic neuritis, which explains much, and enough dental trouble to sour his disposition. There is no doubting his knowledge of baseball, but his judgment of people was faulty. He did not know how to *lead* his star-spangled team. He tried to master them after the fashion of a lion tamer. Overrigid discipline has been a problem in baseball since the beginning. Managers try despotism, but if despotism fails then anarchy threatens. Huggins's despotism faltered from time to time,

* Roger Philip Bresnahan (1879–1944), catcher, outfielder, seventeen seasons, 1897–1915, Senators, Cubs, Orioles, Giants, Cardinals, batting average .279. Hall of Fame.

and he tried to reinforce it with temper tantrums. To his credit he did not resent the conduct of players who lost their tempers with him. In Cleveland, on the calamitous western swing of late 1920, he goaded Sam Vick with charges of timid play until Vick struck him. Vick believed he was through in baseball, but the next day Huggins told him he had behaved well, that he, Huggins, was glad to learn Vick had so much spirit.

However, Huggins was mean in small ways. During spring training in 1920 he borrowed Carl Mays's car almost nightly, used much gasoline, but never bought any. A few players have spoken of him with warmth, and he has been elected to the Baseball Hall of Fame, but Carl Mays was not alone in his final judgment of Huggins: shrewd, cold, selfish, and sometimes cruel. The same can be said of Napoleon, who was another small man commanding larger men.

The personalities of Miller Huggins and Babe Ruth could not blend. Ruth (and others) treated Huggins very badly. Ruth couldn't believe a little man could be of much account in baseball. And all of his life Ruth judged people by the way in which they tried to direct him. He liked those who persuaded and led him; he disliked those whose rules seemed arbitrary. Whether a manager or a magnate was a leader or a pusher was a judgment Ruth reserved to himself.

Waite Hoyt's memory of Ruth and Huggins in clubhouse quarrels preserved a scene which is much like a playground argument. Huggins rails at Ruth for staying out late. Ruth suggests that Huggins send him home. Huggins suggests that Ruth *go* home if he doesn't wish to play with the Yankees. Ruth caps him by saying that Huggins wouldn't be manager next year, when the choice would have to be whether to keep Ruth as a player or Huggins as manager. One gets the impression that if there had been only one baseball and one of them owned it, the owner would have gone home with it, pouting all the way.

When Huggins walked up and down in front of the bench, some of his men would slyly spit tobacco on his socks. Carl Mays quotes Bob Meusel and Ruth as calling Huggins "Little Boy." When a game reached a point of crisis, Ruth would ask, "What now, Little Boy? What do we do now, Little Boy?" Heywood Broun later said Huggins was wrong in his treatment of Ruth. "You can't make a Spartan out of an ancient Goth. . . ."

Miller Huggins has had much praise for spending his owners' money wisely when shopping for players. After all, it was his idea to buy Ruth. He was colorless and lacked showmanship, but he was good at scouting ballplayers, and his record for recommending good trades and buys is, on balance, very good. But for that same record it ought to be noticed that he made several big mistakes. He used Muddy Ruel very little and agreed to his departure. Jack Quinn* won 135 games after the Yankees decided he was too old to pitch. After the Yankees let Roger Peckinpaugh go he played on two pennant-winning Senators teams and was voted Most Valuable Player. And the year after Huggins benched Mays as a has-been, Mays won twenty and lost nine with the Reds.

Huggins not only had Huston and some boorish players to fend off, he also had a bad press. Before the start of the 1921 season, despite the national Yankee craze of 1920, the respected Hugh S. Fullerton wrote, "In the past Huggins has not shone as a leader of men."

The best we can say of Huggins—and it is pretty good—is that teams he managed won six pennants and three World Series. He had his tantrums and his small-mindedness, and was repaid in kind. Despite clashes of temperament which were discreditable to both sides, he was a winner on the field.

* John Picus Quinn, born, Picus (1884–1946), pitcher, twenty-three seasons, 1909–1933, Yankees, Red Sox, Baltimore Federals, White Sox, Athletics, Dodgers, Reds. Won 242, lost 217, earned-run average 3.27.

21 · The Real Town (1920)

> Al I told you Boston was some town but this is the real one.
> I never seen nothing like it and I been going some since we
> got here. I walked down Broadway the main Street last
> night. . . .
>
> —Ring Lardner, *You Know Me Al*

Babe Ruth didn't have to build a reputation in New York; he came
as the baseball king. His relations with players, owners, and fans
after he joined the Yankees differed from his relations with players,
owner, and fans in Boston where he had worked up from recruit to
greatest of sluggers.

When on the road with the Yankees he began to live in his own
suite, often in a different hotel from the rest of the team. He paid
his own hotel bills while the Yankee management lodged the other
players at club expense—three dollars a night plus four dollars a
day for meals. People have thought him wasteful for doing this,
but his gross income may have been as much as sixty thousand
dollars in 1920, and it is hard to see how his sixty-odd nights on the
road could have cost him much more than six thousand dollars,
which was not out of proportion in those years when the income tax
was a small matter. The figure of a hundred dollars a day is often
given as his hotel bill on the road. At the room rates of the time,
such a figure could be correct only if it included his overtipping
and a large quantity of food and drink for the throngs who visited
him.

It is true that Ruth's style of living was not typical of ballplayers,
who deserved their reputation as nickel-tippers. Most of them had
learned very early how to value a dollar. But from the time Ruth
received his first paycheck he had the welcome experience of learning that the more he spent the more he made. Once he left school
the money poured in as a river rising in flood.

For Ruth to lodge apart from the team did not hurt the Yankees. None of the players wished to room with him. He was a jinx of a roommate. Five players had shared his quarters briefly during the spring training and the early weeks of the 1920 season, and each of them had received his release. Furthermore, Ruth's distance cut the club's traffic flow. After a game Ruth often held court like a king. Clad in a red dressing gown and red slippers, smoking a sixty-cent cigar, he received his subjects in droves. Waite Hoyt said 250 came in one night. Helen Ruth was often with him. Neither of the Ruths knew many of their guests, nor were the guests well acquainted with each other. They shared only hunger, thirst, and regard for Ruth.

The king's subjects also wanted to speak with him when he was in the clubhouse. He had a pay telephone put in next to his locker at the Polo Grounds, and had an answering service made up of the other twenty-four Yankees who raced to answer the phone. Half the calls were from businessmen trying to force money on Ruth. The others were from unknown women. The answering-service workers disposed of the calls from women by identifying themselves as Ruth in each case and promising to meet the lady in the lobby of the Astor Hotel at eight sharp. One can only speculate on what may have happened in the lobby of the Astor on those nights. And on what would have happened if Ruth had absentmindedly strayed into the Astor to buy some cigars around eight o'clock.

When the club played on the east coast, moving between Washington, Philadelphia, New York, and Boston, Ruth drove his car from city to city, usually carrying four others. On July 7 he damaged the car (it was only three weeks old) while driving from Washington to Philadelphia. It was a one-car accident. Ruth failed to negotiate a sharp turn and ran off the road. With him were Helen Ruth, Coach Charlie O'Leary, Bootnose Hofmann, and Frank Gleich.* Rumor ran ahead of fact, and for awhile it was believed to have been a bloody affair, but Ruth telephoned the details to New York when he reached Philadelphia. No one had been hurt.

> He liked the night life, but was always at the park early the next day in time for batting practice and in good shape to play.
>
> —Roger Peckinpaugh

---

* Fred Hofmann (1894–1964), catcher, nine seasons, 1919–1928, Yankees, Red Sox, batting average .247.

Frank Elmer Gleich (1894–1949), outfielder, two seasons, 1919–1920, Yankees, batting average .133.

The Ruths liked Boston. At first sight the sale to the Yankees had only one advantage—the salary raise of ten thousand dollars which Ruth had asked. Otherwise he thought of New York as having a pleasantly close right-field fence and as being conveniently near the good beer of Hoboken. His uproarious welcome by Yankee fans in 1920 began to make him feel that New York could be home. The Ruths lived in the Ansonia Hotel for the next several years.

Ruth decided he ought to have a worthy car, so he bought a maroon twin-six Packard roadster for sixty-seven hundred dollars. The other Yankees called it "the ghost of Riverside Drive," and Waite Hoyt said Ruth drove it on Riverside Drive at ninety miles an hour. When the Yankees were playing at home his arrival at the Polo Grounds by car was sometimes made spectacular when the radiator boiled over and shot steam and water like a geyser.

That spring Ruth wore a flat-crowned, flat-brimmed straw hat. He was still lean enough not to look comic, but he soon reverted to his undeniable cap, in which he was seen everywhere and instantly recognized.

In social life the Ruths began to drift apart from ballplayers as a group. After a game Ruth was out of the clubhouse quickly because there was usually some one waiting for him. He was more in the public eye than players wished to be. So celebrated had he become that he could not walk or drive in the streets of any city without being pointed out. As Roger Maris was to say of himself later, the baseball field provided his only true privacy.

To use an old phrase, Ruth began to be taken up by society, by the people who lived in town houses on Fifth Avenue. They tested him by inviting him and his friends to parties, but usually not more than once. The Baltimore waterfront slob took over and drank champagne from the bottle while wading in private fountains. He never remembered the names of those who were entertaining him and, according to Hoyt, once spoke of the "hostess and . . . the hoster."

Ruth played golf once in a while. He had taken up the game (as well as bowling) while with the Red Sox. There are those who think golf is not so much a game as it is a trick played with balls and sticks, there being no goalies, fielders, guards, or linebackers, but Ruth was good at it. No doubt the temptation to hit a motionless ball during a polite silence was overpowering.

The money flowed in. The English may be a nation of shop-keepers, but Americans are a nation of consumers, and pretty gullible consumers to whom a baseball player's hired endorsement means something. A good part of Ruth's income came from renting his name to persuade buyers of consumer goods. For example, he received five hundred dollars in 1920 for sitting on two successive evenings at a conspicuous table in what must have been a conspicuously illegal beer garden in Chicago, and making an empty little speech to tell the customers he hoped they would have a good time.

Ruth also became a literary figure, in a sense. Late in the summer of 1920 the A. L. Burt Company published a children's book, *The Home-Run King; or, How Pep Pindar Won His Title*, by "Babe" Ruth (George H. Ruth). Burt advertised it with several juvenile series: The Boy Spies, The Navy Boys, The Blue Grass Seminary Girls, The Boy Scouts. The publisher brought it out in time to profit by the home-run storm in the Christmas trade. One can tell from the biographical sketch of the alleged author which was bound with the book that it went into production at the moment Ruth had hit fifty-one home runs. The true author is unknown, but it was almost certainly manufactured by the Edward Stratemeyer Syndicate which, beginning in 1906, produced hundreds of titles and sold millions of copies, including The Rover Boys, The Bobbsey Twins, and Tom Swift.

The Home-Run King is a boarding-school story and a typical product of the juvenile-fiction industry of that time. The characters include the town bully who pitches for the local team until he is run out of town; a runty wizard of sixteen with thick-lensed glasses who can brilliantly solve the problems of his peer group; some stouthearted, intelligent teammates; a distant but noble older boy who is captain of the school team; some angelically kind schoolmasters; a foppish sneak of sixteen who, with the town bully, arranges the kidnaping of the hero on the eve of the Big Game; a vaguely sketched girl (named Clara Sweet); the kindly manager McGilraw of the Blue Sox who played their home games in the Polo Grounds—and Pep Pindar (curiously named for a pre-Christian Greek poet), a hero modeled on Babe Ruth in size and baseball ability but in no other way. Anyone who read much children's fiction in the first third of the century knows this cast of characters and can guess the plot pretty well, given the school setting and the baseball props. And it probably pleased any bookish boy (the thicker his lenses the better) who was born in the years 1905–1910 and who found it under the Christmas tree in 1920. The profit of the book to Ruth is unknown, but it could have been large.

Ruth may have been no author, but he was a sure-enough movie actor. He made a picture called *Headin' Home.** Of course, ballplayers had ventured into the theater before, usually in vaudeville,

---

* Considine and Ruth, *The Babe Ruth Story*, mistakenly called this picture *The Babe Comes Home*.

though Mike Donlin,* after an enviable career as an outfielder, retired in 1914 and became a professional actor. Ruth made the picture without missing a game. The rumor around New York was that he was paid a hundred thousand dollars. The true figure was to be fifty thousand, but he received only fifteen of it before the film company collapsed. The producers made the picture in Fort Lee, New Jersey, across the river from New York. Ruth worked on the set in the mornings and played ball in the Polo Grounds in the afternoons. He missed batting practice for a week and came to the ball park every day still wearing his makeup, to the amusement of the other players and the annoyance of the stuffy Huggins.

The playbill of *Headin' Home* called it "that record breaking feature starring the great record breaker" and "a romance of youth and happiness. . . . It will make home loving people run to see it."

Headin' Home opened in New York on September 19 at Madison Square Garden, a house not usually given over to the movies. *The Times* review was shorter than its review of the latest Dorothy Gish, but longer than its notice of William S. Hart's new picture. In the reviewer's opinion, "The picture is really entertaining in places —and that's a lot to say for a production of its kind. . . . There are many excellent pictures of Babe Ruth—and he is an interesting person." The subtitles, by Bugs Baer, poked fun at Ruth, all in good humor. The story line had the tensile strength of a cobweb.

The movie had a happy ending (boy gets girl), but the business transaction ended badly. Ruth sued the film-makers on October 11 for his unpaid balance and asked for an injunction to block further distribution of the picture, surely an odd way to recover money from a sinking company. The producers calmed him with a worthless check. He put off depositing the check until the company had failed, and when the check bounced he was surprised that such things could happen. He carried the check around as an impressive souvenir and a good speakeasy conversation piece until it wore out from handling. According to legend, he claimed the fun of exhibiting the check was worth the amount of its face value.

Ruth agreed to make another picture in 1920 that didn't get started. Raoul Walsh, the movie director best remembered for *The Naked and the Dead*, promised Duffy Lewis a thousand dollars if he could talk Ruth into making a film solely about the way he hit home runs. Ruth said his price was forty thousand dollars. Lewis got his thousand and Ruth received an advance of ten thousand, but Walsh discovered he was too late in the market.

A group of operators who had filmed some of Ruth's home runs in

* Michael Joseph Donlin (1878–1933), outfielder, twelve seasons, 1899–1914, Cardinals, Orioles, Reds, Giants, Braves, Pirates, batting average .333.

The heroic ice man of "Headin' Home" (1920) roughs out his own baseball bat with a hatchet, in this still from the silent film. (*National Baseball Library, Cooperstown, New York.*)

the Polo Grounds, spliced them together and called the result *Babe Ruth in "Over the Fence."* Ruth sued them for a million dollars on the ground that the promoters had violated his civil rights. The defense argued that Babe Ruth was just as much a public figure as the President of the United States. (It is hard to disagree.) Ruth didn't expect to get the million dollars but he hoped to delay the distribution until he and Walsh could get a picture ready. The court issued a temporary injunction on Ruth's behalf but two weeks later accepted the defense argument with the comment that Ruth was a news subject, and the news was still of warm current interest. The makers of *Over the Fence* then brought out a second film

Helen Woodford Ruth at the Polo Grounds, June 3, 1920. (*National Baseball Library, Cooperstown, New York.*)

document which they called *Babe Ruth, How He Makes His Home Runs*. Walsh was stuck, and Ruth's screen appearances for the next several years were in newsreels only.

With new attendance records at the Polo Grounds, a stupendous new home-run record, the longest, reddest, speedingest car in town, a ghost-written book, a turkey of a movie, a theatrical lawsuit, and instant recognition at every street corner, Babe Ruth had become the most talked about celebrity in New York. In 1920 he and New York were beginning a love affair that lasted all his life.

> **Yes, you tell 'em I'm off the ponies for life, maybe.**
> **—Babe Ruth, January 1921**

Cubans were among Babe Ruth's biggest fans in 1920. The two morning newspapers in Havana carried the box scores of all Yankee games, and a movement was organized to bring Ruth to Cuba to play. Two Cuban sports figures, a promoter and a sportswriter, arrived in New York on August 6 to try to persuade Ruth to visit

Cuba for some exhibition baseball. John McGraw elbowed the Cubans aside; he had his own interest in such a visit. Because of the Prohibition Amendment, Cuba promised to become a winter refuge for thirsty citizens of the United States. McGraw and Charles A. Stoneham of the Giants happened to be in Havana when Oriental Park—a race track, gambling casino, and ball park—came up for sale. They bought it, with McGraw taking a 10 percent interest.

It was McGraw who organized the Cuban expedition, taking the Ruths and some other ballplayers from the United States. They left from Key West on October 27, planning to be gone a month. McGraw was to pay Ruth a thousand dollars a game.

The Ruths needed a passport; the application for the passport is one of the rare public documents Ruth left. It was in the handwriting of John J. Igoe, who had been Ruth's secretary in 1919. Igoe filled in his employer's occupation as "bal player" [sic]. In Babe's handwriting is an interlineation that Helen had been born in El Paso, Texas. Igoe described Ruth as twenty-seven years old (he was twenty-six), gave the physical distinctions all of us now know, and said he had no distinguishing marks. Unhappily, the application asked for no description of the passport carrier's spouse, which would interest us more.

The Cuban excursion was not a happy one. The fences were far away and Ruth hit only one home run. As usual, he was mobbed everywhere by boys, but these boys spoke no English and called him Bobbie, which he thought translated Babe into Spanish. He had a low opinion of the abilities of Cuban baseball players, partly because many were black. After leaving Cuba he gave an interview on the subject which reads strangely after half a century: "Them greasers are punk ball players. Only a few of them are any good. The guy* they calls after me because he made a few homers is as black as a ton and a half of coal in a dark cellar." To understand him (though not to excuse him) we must remember that St. Mary's Industrial School enrolled only whites, in accord with Maryland state law. After the age of seven, Ruth could not have known any black people except porters, waiters, and bellboys. His racism came from dockside Baltimore and was fixed in his character in boyhood.

At bottom, however, Ruth's distaste for Cuba was rooted not in race but in a swindle, of which he was the victim. Some confidence men, posing as rich playboys, let him see them win about a hundred thousand dollars at the race track. Although Ruth didn't know it, the races had been fixed solely to gull him. His new friends and the

* Cristobal Torriente (1895–   ), outfielder, seventeen seasons, Cuban Stars, American Giants (Chicago), Monarchs (Kansas City), batted .409 in 1922, *Pittsburgh Courier* All-Time All-Black team. ". . . A hell of a ball player."—Frank Frisch on Torriente in 1920.

bookies were agents of the fixers. When he asked for a tip they gave him a sure thing which brought him thirty-five thousand. He bet that on the next race and lost it. Thereafter he bet to try to recover his fleeting riches, until he was flat broke and his rich friends had vanished. He lost all he had made on the exhibitions (a sum unknown, but we may suppose it was about fifteen thousand dollars).

When the story was revealed in New York, Huggins remarked, "Poor Babe. He gets his in bunches." Huggins rather simplemindedly added the money lost by the failed motion-picture company, which was money Ruth never saw, to the thirty-five thousand Havana dollars, which was bait that the swindlers did not expect Ruth to keep, and concluded that he had lost more than seventy thousand dollars "in a few weeks time." But in dollars that he had actually received as truly his, and then lost, he was out only the amount of his exhibition game income and no more.

Ruth's trouble in Cuba caused Ruppert and Huston to try to take better care of him. Thereafter, when Ruth became friendly with suspicious characters, the Yankee management hired detectives to make inquiries to learn whether the strangers were suitable company (in money matters) for their most valuable employee.

Thus the glorious year of 1920 ended sourly. The *Sporting News* thought Babe Ruth was a spoiled child, worth a two-column searing summary of follies: failure to collect on the motion picture, and swindled in Cuba; all in all, "the old story about giants with the brains of a boy." And the writer added something that otherwise would have passed into oblivion: Ruth had appeared in a benefit basketball game after coming home from Cuba; he tried nine shots at the basket, missed them all, committed several fouls, and "was actually booed . . . out of the building."

Outside the Park, 1921

NEW RUM RING HERE
IN $1,000,000 FRAUD

UNION CHARGES PLOT
BY RAILS AND BANKS
TO END CLOSED SHOP

FATHER OF 34 CHILDREN
GETS MANY MESSAGES

FORBID GERMAN SECURITY POLICE
TO WEAR UNDEMOCRATIC MONOCLES

5 SOLDIERS KILLED
IN CORK REPRISALS

1921 CITY TAX RATE
HIGHEST IN HISTORY

ICE IS THE BEST PRESERVATIVE

METHODISTS URGE
MORE DRY LAW CURBS

ITALY REBELS AGAINST REBELLION

EINSTEIN EXPLAINS
FALLACY OF ETHER

U.S. STEEL REDUCES
WAGES OF 150,000
ABOUT 20 PER CENT

SHOT DOWN IN AISLE
OF MOVIE THEATRE

GIRL FLIER MAKES
199 LOOP THE LOOPS

MOB GOES TO LYNCH
GIRL'S NEGRO SLAYER
PRIEST OPPOSES VIOLENCE

DEMPSEY KNOCKS OUT CARPENTIER IN THE FOURTH ROUND

TRUCE IN IRELAND DECLARED

22 · A Strong Team Strengthened
(1921)

By 1921 it seemed that success had changed Babe Ruth. In Boston he had behaved as one surprised by it all, but now he carried himself as a professional. He had more poise and demanded respect. Evidence of his popularity pleased him. Waite Hoyt thought his conscience was less sensitive. Ruth looked into New York night life thoroughly and lived at a pace that might have wrecked the physical condition of a lesser man. After the Cuban swindle he trusted mankind less and got a permit to carry a pistol, because, he said, he had to carry large sums of money occasionally. On the other hand, he remembered his origins. He let James Cardinal Gibbons, or Brother Gilbert acting for Cardinal Gibbons, use his name in an appeal to rebuild St. Mary's Industrial School as "a national testimonial to Babe Ruth."

Unbelievably, in the first months of 1921 the Ruths were nearly broke. Ruth had to borrow from the Yankees to pay his federal income tax. He also lost his appeal from the court ruling in the case of the newsreel splicers who produced the Ruth home-run films. Then the Curtiss Candy Company of Chicago began a strong promotion of its "Baby Ruth" candy bar. After Ruth's protests to the company were rebuffed, he countered by founding the George H. Ruth Candy Company and trying to register the phrase "Ruth's Home Run" for a candy bar. The Curtiss company opposed it, and the patent office rejected Ruth's application. Nowadays the Curtiss Candy Company explains the matter in a way which deserves the reader's attention:

April 6, 1972

We have your letter of April 4th, requesting information concerning the origin of our trademark 'Baby Ruth'.

You will be interested in knowing that our candy bar made it's [sic] initial appearance in 1921 some years before Babe

Ruth, the ball player, became famous. The similarity of the names, therefore is purely coincidental.

Our candy bar was actually names [*sic*] after President Cleveland's daughter, Baby Ruth Cleveland, who visited the Curtiss Candy Company plant years ago when the company was getting started and this largely influenced the Company's founder to name the candy bar 'Baby Ruth'. . . .

Very truly yours,
Robert L. Zimmerman
Administrative Manager

Ruth Cleveland, born October 3, 1891, died of diphtheria on January 7, 1904.

[Bill Slocum] writes more like I do than anyone I know.
—Babe Ruth

At the time Babe Ruth was proving he couldn't manage money, a spirited, lean, and able promoter was coming to the rescue. Christy Walsh had been a sports cartoonist in Los Angeles before the First World War. He was quite capable of becoming a good sportswriter, but he was a gifted judge of the public taste and chose to make a career of pleasing that taste. In an age of mass consumption, Walsh saw that stories of great deeds in sports were a commodity which he could mass-produce. He began at the Indianapolis automobile race of 1919, which he covered as ghost writer for Referee-in-Chief Eddie Rickenbacker. Thirty-seven papers took the story, and seven of them asked for more. Walsh and Rickenbacker split $874 for an afternoon's work.

Walsh then started a syndicate specializing in sports. It was a wholesale business of buying professional prose and distributing it to newspapers under the bylines of famous sports figures. The first success was the sale of a biography "by John McGraw" to the North American Newspaper Alliance.

Babe Ruth really needed someone like Walsh, and needed him for more than selling his name to stick on top of other people's feature articles. The Ruths were harassed by promoters of every kind and were not wise enough to choose among them. To protect his privacy Ruth used the staff entrance to the Ansonia, had an unlisted telephone, and began to ignore his mail. Walsh got in to see him by replacing the bootlegger's delivery boy. Being very personable, he charmed Ruth into telling him that he was usually paid five dollars for each newspaper story with his byline. Walsh said he could get five hundred apiece, and Ruth, of course, was interested. Walsh left to draft a contract, rushed it to Pennsylvania Station where the Ruths were about to leave for Hot Springs, and got Ruth's signature with fifteen minutes to spare. The clincher of the deal was an advance to Ruth of a thousand dollars—which Walsh had borrowed from a bank for the purpose.

Walsh, having proved he could sell hack prose by the yard, had plenty of skilled help. During the life of his syndicate thirty-four baseball writers wrote pieces signed by baseball players, four of them for Ruth. Among Ruth's ghosts were Ford Frick, who made about ten thousand dollars out of it, Bill Slocum, who covered the Yankees for the *New York American* and wrote the most column yards "by Babe Ruth," and Westbrook Pegler, who later wrote as brutally of Ruth as he did of most people. Walsh's writers wrote sports pieces signed by Ruth, Lou Gehrig, Knute Rockne, Pop Warner, Rogers Hornsby, Bob Zuppke, Percy Haughton, Mickey Cochrane, Dizzy Dean, John McGraw, and Ty Cobb. Walsh also distributed the work of Hendrik Willem Van Loon, who became a firm friend of Babe Ruth.

The ghost-written sports story became such a staple that a sportswriter covering a World Series entered the press box and said it reminded him of a haunted house. But the ghosts, as Paul Gallico pointed out, never made the mistake of reporting any hard news under a player's byline. Walsh's conscience was clear because he looked on newspaper feature articles as entertainment only, and intended his ghosted stories merely as pleasant illusions, not deceits. Nothing went into the syndicate's stories which did not agree with the notions of the alleged author and at least roughly fit his temperament. If any other player's name would do as well for a byline, the writer had failed. It is a matter of taste, but nowadays those old essays seem full of slangy, false heartiness, and empty of content.

Walsh was good for Ruth, whose newspaper income rose from about five hundred dollars in 1920 to about fifteen thousand in 1921. And that was only a part of the benefit. From 1921 to the end of Ruth's career Christy Walsh played the part of a wise brother on all money matters. (He had no other influence.) When it was all over he said the association was often turbulent but never dull or unpleasant.

Barrow moved the Yankee's spring-training camp from Jacksonville, Florida, to Shreveport, Louisiana, in 1921. The Ruths and several others went first to Hot Springs to take the waters and play some golf. The move to Shreveport was not to encourage austerity, for Shreveport was what used to be called a wide-open town. The

Hot Springs detachment moved on to join the other Yankees on March 6.

ARRIVAL OF RUTH

STIRS SHREVEPORT

———

AWED MULTITUDE GREETS SULTAN

OF SWAT AT STATION—BABE

IS STILL OVERWEIGHT

—The Times, March 7, 1921

The crowd at Shreveport's Union Station numbered several hundred who stood in silent wonder. Ruth's smile was at its "widest expanse." He worked his way slowly through the people, stopping to shake hands with a retired ballplayer he recognized. He told reporters he had taken off ten pounds at Hot Springs but was still fifteen or twenty pounds overweight. Waite Hoyt and Harry Harper* were with the Ruths, but the crowd "paid no attention to pitchers."

When Ruth appeared at the Yankee training field attendance jumped fourfold. On his second day of spring practice, in an intra-squad game of which no box score was kept, he hit nine balls out of the park and bounced many off the fence.

The Shreveport worshipers responded with their best. The Commissioner of Public Safety allowed "His Majesty, Babe Ruth" to drive his green car without license plates, provided he put his name where the tags belonged. He used "Babe Ruth's Essex" which suggests that it was a dealer's promotional stunt. Ruth met and shook hands with every teacher and student of Shreveport High School; they gave him a bat five feet long made of flowers, which he arranged to hang from the ceiling of the lobby of the Yankees' hotel. Two days later, in an exhibition against the Shreveport minor-league team, Ruth, a temporary first baseman, hit three singles and three home runs in six times at bat, stole two bases, and scored four runs.

Miller Huggins was apparently the only grouch in Shreveport. The lively Yankees lived in a state of near anarchy in this hospitable and hedonistic city. Huggins fumed while Ruth speeded around town and Shreveport girls collected Yankees. The manager lived under the disapproval of owner Huston and feared to impose the discipline he would have preferred. The feverish training period at Shreveport in 1921 does not fit the notion that spring training

---

* Harry Clayton Harper (1895–1963), pitcher, ten seasons, 1913–1923, Senators, Red Sox, Yankees, Dodgers, won 56, lost 79, earned-run average 2.87.

should be austere. The Yankees never had more fun and rarely played better baseball. Exaggerated rumors of the Yankee revels drifted around the American League, half convincing the supporters of ascetic training that the Yankees must be supermen.

Jacob Ruppert and Huston had reason to be interested in this spring's results as measured in dollars. Spring training had usually cost owners ten thousand dollars or more. It had become the custom for major-league teams to pair off and play exhibitions on their way north. In 1921 the Yankees had already contracted to work their passage home in a long series with the Dodgers. But the number of tickets sold in small towns to people who wished to see Babe Ruth opened management's eyes. In future years they would also book local teams. With a promise that Ruth would play, the Yankees could get as much as 85 percent of the gate and show a spring-training profit. Ruth was paid extra for this extra strain.

Some new Yankees on the 1921 roster are worth notice. Frank (Home Run) Baker came out of his second retirement to play third base. Although bowlegged and awkward looking, he could make the risky plays, and he threw and ran well. Wally Schang* arrived in a shipment from the Red Sox to catch. Barrow said he was the strongest man he ever saw in baseball. Schang once picked Barrow up in jubilation at a victory and carried him around the clubhouse (Barrow weighed more than two hundred pounds). Waite Hoyt came as the key man in the Red Sox deal. Another former member of the Red Sox was Carl Mays, who had been with the Yankees before Ruth came. Mays was a perfectionist who lost his temper when fielders made errors. That was no more sensible than if fielders lost their tempers when pitchers threw fat pitches. Ruth, for one, resented Mays's attitude. Several times the two men were near blows. Mays probably backed off from a fight with Ruth because he knew that if the Yankees had to choose to keep Ruth or Mays, the choice would be easy.

While the Yankees were at Shreveport the Dodgers trained at New Orleans. The two teams played fourteen games on the way north. In 1920 the same two teams had played sixteen games, of which the Dodgers won ten. In 1921 the Yankees won nine of the fourteen games. It was and is a custom to rank the teams at the end of spring training, though winning games is not the purpose of the spring rites. In the ranking of 1921, the Indians and the Pirates were first with four wins each and no losses. The Yankees stood next with ten wins and five losses (they had played another game outside the Dodger series).

---

* Walter Henry Schang (1889–1965), catcher, nineteen seasons, 1913–1931, Athletics, Red Sox, Yankees, Browns, Tigers, batting average .284.

This was a most promising start for 1921. Ed Barrow, the general manager, and Huggins had strengthened the team as they thought proper, with the full cooperation of the owners. And the team they had strengthened had finished only three games out of first place in 1920. As opening day neared there was every reason for confidence.

23 · Golden Shod
and Dancing Days (1921)

Anxieties and difficulties afflict me, a fortunate fan, and
this baseball season has begun to happen after all.
— Roger Angell

The Yankees began the 1921 season explosively by getting seventeen
hits and eleven runs on opening day against the Athletics in New
York to win 11–1. Babe Ruth outshone himself with five hits in five
times at bat—two of them doubles—and a run scored.

Ruth's first home run came two days later on April 17 to beat the
Athletics 2–1. To get it he had to hit three out of the park succes-
sively, the first two veering foul just as they left the field. That night
Ruth appeared on the stage of the Hippodrome at an American
Legion benefit to have his mind read by the performer Dunninger.
Ruth wrote his unspoken thought on a scrap of paper. Dunninger
correctly read it as sixty. Ruth said that was the number of home
runs he hoped to hit in 1921.

Ruth continued to hit well. His home-run total reached three
and four on April 21 and 22 in Philadelphia. One of those days may
have been the day of the 1921 season that he popped one up so high
that he was on second base when it returned to earth, brushing
the glove of second baseman Jimmy Dykes* as it fell. The scorer
rated it an error; Ruth always insisted it was a double. The fifth and
last of his April home runs came in New York on April 25, off Walter
Johnson. At that date in 1920 he hadn't yet hit any.

Ruth had some legal difficulties early in May. A constable routed
him out of his bathtub in Boston to serve a paper saying he owed
the Commonwealth of Massachusetts $47.10 in automobile taxes for
1920 and 1921. Without breakfast Ruth went to the mayor's office

---

* James Joseph Dykes (1896–   ), infielder, twenty-two seasons, 1918–1939,
Athletics, White Sox, batting average .280.

and forswore Massachusetts citizenship. The assessor canceled the tax bill. Next a Chicagoan sued Ruth for four hundred dollars due on a ninety-day note given in part payment for a Stutz Bearcat automobile. Ruth said he had paid the debt, and no more was heard.

With legal entanglements overcome he began to hit the ball again. Walter Johnson served up home run number eight on May 7 in Washington before ex-President Woodrow Wilson, who was seeing his first ball game since 1916. Reporters agreed that it was the longest hit ever made in Washington. It started a rally which brought victory to the Yankees in the ninth inning. When the Yankees went to or from Washington Ruth often stopped at Baltimore to hit a few for the boys at St. Mary's Industrial School. Touching his native earth seemed to add to his strength.

Roger Peckinpaugh batted ahead of Ruth and was becoming a good-luck charm. He told the author, "[Ruth] used to say to me 'Come on, get on there, and I'll drive you in.'" On May 10 Ruth won a game at Detroit with a home run which scored Peckinpaugh, and two days later the Yankees beat the Tigers when Ruth drove Peckinpaugh across the plate twice, once with a home run, once with a triple (the score was 11–10). By May 14 Ruth had thirty-four hits, of which only fifteen were singles, with an average of more than two bases per hit.

Home run number twelve came in Cleveland, after Ruth had bumped Joe Sewell hard enough in a collision at second base to give Sewell a nosebleed. Tris Speaker, still hostile to Ruth, wanted to avenge Sewell on the spot and both dugouts emptied, but Ruth and Speaker were separated. Ruth was then put out in that most humiliating of ways, being picked off second. Number thirteen, on May 25, was the longest hit ever seen in St. Louis, a home run estimated at 550 feet. Even the Commissioners of the Southern Presbyterian Church Assembly felt the distraction of Ruth's presence and brought him to be introduced at their banquet. Number fourteen was hit entirely out of the Polo Grounds on May 29, in the presence of many of the Giants who had an open date. Number sixteen came in a loss to the Browns at the Polo Grounds on June 3. Ruth had dropped out of the listing of the five leading hitters, by average, in the American League, which was not at all embarrassing since the lowest ranking of the five was hitting .394.

Ruth was not alone in his home runs, though well ahead of rivals. After a fifth of the schedule of 1921 had been played the National League home-run total was a third of the 1920 total, and six of the eight American League clubs were ahead of their 1920 home-run rate. The slugging revolution was underway.

On June 8 Ruth paid a fine of a hundred dollars—with a single bill—for speeding at more than thirty miles per hour in his maroon Stutz. It was his second offense of the year, and the magistrate made him serve four and a half hours in a cell with four cellmates who became angry when he refused to join them at dice. He sent for his uniform and dressed in jail for the game. Forty minutes after his release he was in the batter's box at the Polo Grounds. Twenty news photographers, two newsreel cameras, and a thousand people welcomed him when he left jail. The magistrate was disappointed. When he jailed John L. Sullivan for an illegal prize fight, twenty thousand had come to greet the culprit on release. One of Walsh's ghosts, writing under Ruth's name, had him say witlessly that the judge should have excused him because "I love to put every ounce of strength into everything I do."

In the five days beginning on June 10, Ruth hit seven home runs off five pitchers, making at least one home run a day, and two each on the 13th and 14th (off Howard Ehmke and Hooks Dauss*) in Detroit. These were numbers seventeen to twenty-four. One of the home runs won a game; another tied a game which the Yankees then won.

The Yankees had no regular pitcher rested on June 13. Huggins put it to the team—who should pitch? Ruth volunteered, though he had pitched only four innings in 1920 and hadn't pitched at all in 1921. He started the game, hit two home runs, struck out Ty Cobb once, and gave up four runs in five innings. He quit pitching in the sixth, while still ahead, and finished the game as a center fielder. The Yankees held the lead and won 11–8, making Ruth the winning pitcher. If it were possible to feel sorry for Ty Cobb in a ball park, this would have been the day. He had just returned from a long illness to play in this disaster.

June was a great month for Ruth. He hit twelve home runs, won a game as pitcher, and was again among the top five batters in the American League. Of the home runs, one was a game-winner; three pulled the Yankees up to tie, and in each case they went on to win.

Manager Miller Huggins gave his endorsement to the campaign for better pitching and less slugging during a fanning bee at the Yankees' offices yesterday. Huggins believes that a letting down of pitching restrictions or the return to the less lively ball is imperative. . . .

—*The Times*, July 2, 1921

---

* Howard Jonathan Ehmke (1894–1959), pitcher, fifteen seasons, 1915–1930, Buffalo Federals, Tigers, Red Sox, Athletics, won 167, lost 166, earned-run average 3.75.

George August Dauss (1889–1963), pitcher, fifteen seasons, 1912–1926, Tigers, won 223, lost 182, earned-run average 3.32.

Ruth added eight home runs in the first eighteen days of July. Early in the month he had been two weeks ahead of his 1920 pace, but he slumped and got no more until he hit one on each of the last two days of the month, which left him just a day ahead of the 1920 gait. The home run of July 31 landed on the roof of the stands at the Polo Grounds.

In the first week of August the Tigers came to New York. Ruth phoned his friend Harry Heilmann, the Detroit outfielder, and asked that he meet Ruth in his hotel lobby at eleven in the morning. Ruth took him to Central Park where they hid behind trees. A woman passed, riding a horse very awkwardly. When she was some distance away, with her back to the men, Ruth threw a stone and hit the horse in the rump. The horse plunged and reared while the rider held on as best she could. Ruth was nearly helpless with laughter. When Heilmann asked what was going on, Ruth told him, between gasps, that the victim was Helen Ruth, who was trying to learn to ride. The horse seems to have been a more domesticated animal than Ruth was. That afternoon, strictly according to Greek tragedy, Ruth met retribution for his arrogance. He dropped a fly ball in the ninth inning which let Detroit score the winning run in a 9–8 game.

Ruth had fallen behind his 1920 pace but caught up by hitting two home runs on August 8, making his total forty-one. He needed only fourteen more to break his record, with fifty-four games remaining. On the 11th the Yankees moved into first place with a percentage of .618 to Cleveland's .617. That day, against the White Sox in Chicago, Ruth had a home run, then bunted for a single against the Sox infield which was playing deep and couldn't touch the ball before he reached first base. In the next few days the Yankees and Indians alternated in first place. The Yankees happened to be leading on August 15 when Jacob Ruppert, for no explained reason, announced that Huggins would manage again in 1922. Some have thought Ruppert was trying to lessen the pride of the anti-Huggins faction on the team, which was beginning to think the manager wasn't really necessary.

Ruth hit home runs entirely out of Comiskey Park, Chicago, on August 17 and 19 (the outfield stands were then single decks).

> Two or three hours in a ball park do not take anything off the waistline of the spectators or add anything to chest measurement.
>
> —*Chicago Tribune*, August 24, 1921

With both Chicago teams entombed deep in their second visions, the *Chicago Tribune* decided that professional baseball took up too much space in its columns. The publisher said the daily home game could have half a column while all the other major-league games would get space for box scores only. Space saved by this economy would go to local amateur sports which (according to the *Tribune*) improved people physically and morally. This was Puritanism's last stand against professional sports. In New York Colonel Huston, co-owner of the Yankees, put it wisely: if the daily press cut baseball coverage, local entrepreneurs would start local baseball sheets. The *Tribune* did not sacrifice itself for public virtue but went back to selling its readers the kind of paper they wished to read.

This proposed reform of the press was not aimed at Ruth specifically, though he got more space than any other sports figure. In the early 1920s the only paper not dazzled by Ruth's glitter was the leading baseball paper, the *Sporting News*, which regarded him as uppity and treated him pretty roughly.

Beginning on August 30 the Yankees played the Senators six games at the Polo Grounds in five days, and won them all, scoring fifty-nine runs in the series. Ruth contributed two home runs to this awesome display. By September 8 Ruth had fifty-three home runs and was batting .383 behind Cobb's .390. The Yankees were a full game ahead of the Indians.

Ruth tied his record with number fifty-four against the Athletics in Philadelphia on September 9, with the longest hit ever seen in Shibe Park. Back on the bench he told Peckinpaugh it would be a good idea to save the record-breaker for the home crowd in New York. It worked out that way, but Peckinpaugh is sure Ruth was swinging for a home run every time he batted (except for those annoyingly successful bunt singles). On September 16 he broke the record in a sloppy double-header (nine errors) against the Browns in New York by hitting one out in the first game. He knew it was going to be a home run when he saw the pitch coming. Elmer Miller, on third base, sensed it too, and began to jog to the plate as Ruth swung.

Ruth had not only set a new record for home runs in each of three successive seasons, but had some other records as well by the second week in September: most runs in a season—161, most extra-base hits—107, most total bases—412. The first two records broke his own records, set in 1920. The total-bases record broke George Sisler's record, also set in 1920. Ruth hit single home runs on September 10 and 11, to bring his total to fifty-seven.

The pennant would almost surely go to the winner of a four-game series at New York between the Yankees and Indians beginning on September 26. If either team won three games, that would practically end the race. Waite Hoyt won the first, 4–2. George Uhle*

---

* George Ernest Uhle (1898–   ), pitcher, seventeen seasons, 1919–1936, Indians, Tigers, Yankees, Giants, won 200, lost 166, earned-run average 3.99.

beat the Yankees 9–0 in the second. The Yankees took the third easily, 21–7.

By this time the Yankee pitchers were worn out. Huggins let the pitching platoon choose its own starter. They voted for Jack Quinn to start. This experiment in democracy failed. Quinn gave up three runs and left the game without getting a man out. The hitters would have to win this one. Thirty thousand frenzied customers saw a wild game which was not settled until the last pitch. Each pitching staff was a relay team. The Yankees won 8–7. Ruth hit two home runs and a double, drove in five runs, and scored three. Waite Hoyt, later a mortician, wrote, "It is an established fact that two spectators died in the grandstand. . . ." Ruth's barely credible manner of winning that fevered game verified Paul Gallico's observation, "The impossible was becoming the probable, and for the price of admission would take place before one's very eyes."

1921 was a year of economic depression. In July the Yankees admitted that attendance was 5 percent below the figure for the same date in 1920, but the decline was not to last. By mid-September the crowds became crushes. On September 11 forty thousand jammed the Polo Grounds, and the press claimed that sixty thousand had been turned away. At the moment the Yankees were a game and a half in the lead. The depression ended for Ruppert and Huston with the decisive Cleveland series, when 130,000 came to see the four games, which was thought to be a record for a four-game regular-season series.

The Indians were out of the race. They had won but eight of twenty-two games with the Yankees. Only two questions remained: on which day would the Yankees have the pennant for sure, and how many home runs would Babe Ruth hit?

The Yankees answered the first question quickly when they clinched the pennant on October 1 by winning the first game of a double-header from the Athletics in the Polo Grounds. They went on to win the second game as well, but it wasn't easy. Ruth came in from the outfield to pitch in the eighth inning with a six-run lead. The Athletics promptly scored six runs to tie the game, but Ruth held them scoreless for the next three innings until the Yankees could get a run in the eleventh to win, and to make Ruth a winning pitcher for the second time that season.

New York was joyful. The Giants had also won a pennant. The *Times* happily called Babe Ruth "the World-Child" of "these golden shod and dancing days." A New York broker, back in July when neither Yankees nor Giants were in first place, had bet twenty-five thousand dollars at 4 to 1 that New York would see all the games of the World Series. He spent part of his hundred thousand dollars to take a special train of friends to Atlantic City for a celebration.

Now he wanted to bet on the Yankees to win the Series, but not a gambler would do business with him.

The Yankee clubhouse was crowded and noisy with festival. Huston, his derby hat cocked over his eye, told Ruth he was worth every cent the Yankees had spent on him. Huggins, who had spent a miserable summer at odds with Ruth, Mays, Hoyt, and Meusel, wept for happiness. Enjoying the first of all Yankee pennants the team was, for awhile, a happy family, and Waite Hoyt coined the often retold line, "It's great to be young and a Yankee."

They couldn't have done it without Ruth, but they had Ruth in 1920 and finished third, so he didn't do it all. It was the strengthening of the Red Sox alumni association by enrolling Barrow, Hoyt, and Schang that made the slight difference between third place with ninety-five wins and first place with ninety-eight.

As for the second question of September—Ruth's home-run total —the world knows he hit fifty-nine. The last one came at home on October 2 against the Red Sox, with two men on base. Since the Yankees won 7–6, we can say Ruth won that one too.

The complete baseball reader needs even more numbers here, with the same hunger an addict needs drugs. Others may skip.

Babe Ruth ended the season with the third best batting average of the league, .378, behind Heilmann's .394 and Cobb's .389. Ruth led in slugging percentage (total bases divided by times at bat), home runs, total bases, runs batted in, bases on balls, and runs scored. Three years in a row, beginning in 1919, he set and then broke records for the proportion of hits which went for extra bases; his 1921 figure of 58 percent is still the record. His speed let him steal seventeen bases, and that same speed helped his batting average, because, with infields playing deep, he could get a bunt single almost at will. Only eight men have ever had as many as 420 total bases; Ruth's 457 of 1921 is still the record. In 1920 his slugging percentage was .847, still the record, and in 1921 it was .846.

We may grasp the meaning of these numbers more easily by comparing the records of his chief rivals. In 1920 Ruth had almost three times as many home runs as the next best total, and in 1921 more than twice as many. In 1921 he scored three runs for each two runs scored by the runner-up in that category. His 1921 slugging percentage was a third higher than the second highest. It is no wonder that his name is still used as a way to express the notion that something is extraordinarily big. In 1972 a CBS reporter described a Dakota animal fair as "one Babe Ruth of a swine show!"

Occasionally someone suggests that the short right-field foul line of the Polo Grounds made for cheap home runs, but the 113 home runs of 1920 and 1921 divide pretty evenly—fifty-five at home, fifty-eight on the road. In the American League the only other short right field was in Sportsman's Park, St. Louis, where Ruth played only twenty-two games in two years.

No doubt with some exaggeration, Ruth said about half of his home runs were hit off bad pitches, because the pitchers had quit trying to make him hit the ball to the fielders. If he could reach the ball with the bat, he swung.

This remarkable young man was twenty-six years old and had reached a new peak. His season of 1921 was a slight improvement over 1920, and there was no reason not to expect at least several more years of steady improvement before he reached a ballplayer's middle age, say twenty-eight to thirty-two years.

THE ACCUMULATED BATTING FIGURES
BABE RUTH'S MAJOR-LEAGUE CAREER
1914–1921

at bat: 2108
hits: 718
home runs: 162
runs batted in: 537
average: .341

24 · Giants Win Series (1921)

Nineteen seasons after the Yankees first began to play in the American League they won their first pennant. Now they would face the other Polo Grounds team, the Giants, in their first World Series.

By coincidence the opposing managers were the two men who had the longest unbroken service in the major leagues. Huggins had come to the Yankees in 1918. By 1921 only four Yankees remained from his first season (Roger Peckinpaugh, Wally Pipp, Bob Shawkey, and Aaron Ward*). Huggins was somewhat overrated in the public mind as a man who could direct bumptious stars. His talent was to resign himself to their boorishness. John McGraw hardly knew what patience meant. He was a tyrant, as Hugh Bradley wrote, with "florid imagination and colossal ego," who kept command by public humiliation of proud men. He resented the Yankees because they were tenants of the Giants and drew larger crowds. The 1921 World Series would be McGraw's chance to put them down.

The two teams seemed well matched for the best-of-nine series. The Giants were faster, but the Yankees had more batting power. The Giants might have better pitching, but the Yankees had Babe Ruth. Unless the Giants' pitchers overcame Ruth, the Yankees seemed likely to win. To the gamblers the match was even.

Lines began to form at the ticket windows at ten o'clock on the morning of Tuesday, October 4, the day before the first game. This early rush drew so much attention that people stayed home, despairing of tickets, and there were seven thousand empty seats on the day of the game. It was a chilly day, threatening rain.

When Ruth came to bat in the first inning with one out and Elmer Miller** on second base, the crowd fell silent for a moment

* Aaron Lee Ward (1896–1961), infielder, twelve seasons, 1917–1928, Yankees, White Sox, Indians, batting average .268.
** Elmer Miller (1890–1944), outfielder, seven seasons, 1912–1922, Cardinals, Yankees, Red Sox, batting average .243.

and then roared for about fifteen seconds. Phil Douglas* let go his first pitch. Ruth singled on the ground to center, scoring Miller for the only run the Yankees needed. The next time Ruth batted McGraw arranged an intentional base on balls. Ruth then struck out twice. As ball games go, it was satisfying. Carl Mays gave up five hits (four to Frank Frisch),** and the Yankees won, 3–0, though they didn't hit a ball in the air beyond the infield. Ruth played left field in this and the later games.

The day of the second game brought better weather, with the temperature in the high sixties. During batting practice Helen Ruth, a passenger in a flying boat, dropped three baseballs with a parachute from two thousand feet above the ball park (they landed near the main entrance). Her husband roused the crowd before the game by hitting a ball into the center-field stands, something nobody ever did during a game.

Waite Hoyt stretched the Giants' string of scoreless innings to eighteen by shutting them out with two hits. The Yankees made only three hits but scored three runs, two unearned. Ruth was hit-less but provoked the noisiest demonstration of the day by stealing two bases in the fifth inning. When he returned to the outfield everyone in the bleachers stood and cheered, though, on balance, it was a Giants crowd. *The Times* had to give up its play-by-play announcements at its office because the throng it drew blockaded traffic in Times Square. Irvin S. Cobb wrote that the Yankees "out-thought and out-gamed and out-played the Giants. . . ." The Yankees were now 4 to 1 favorites to win the Series.

The park was packed for the third game. The weather had improved so much that ice cream cones outsold hot dogs. It was warm enough for the Giants. They battered four Yankee pitchers for twenty hits (still the record), had an eight-run seventh inning, and won 13–5. Nevertheless the Yankees remained favorites at 5 to 3.

Ruth struck out twice, walked once, and drove in two runs with a single. A pinch-runner replaced him in the eighth inning. People who knew baseball knew something ailed him, but a few others jeered. He tipped his cap to the hostiles as he left the game. He had hurt his left arm when sliding in the second game and played the third game in pain. The arm had become infected. When that was known, the odds shortened to 3 to 2.

Rain on October 8 delayed the fourth game a day, though twenty-

---

* Philips Brooks Douglas (1890–1952), pitcher, nine seasons, 1912–1922, White Sox, Reds, Dodgers, Cubs, Giants, won 93, lost 93, earned-run average 2.80. Barred from baseball 1922.

** Frank Francis Frisch (1898–1973), infielder, nineteen seasons, 1919–1937, Giants, Cardinals, batting average .316. Hall of Fame.

five thousand people came to the park. The rumor was that Ruth was out of the series. He came to the Polo Grounds with an air of dejection and his arm in a sling. Dr. George D. Stewart, a Park Avenue surgeon, had lanced his left forearm just below the elbow and advised him not to play until healed. Nevertheless, when play resumed on the 9th, Ruth played. The Giants evened the Series by beating Mays 4–2. (There was a thoroughly investigated, groundless accusation that Mays threw the game.) With his arm still hurting, Ruth hit a home run which so moved the new grounds-keeper, who hadn't seen a Ruth home run, that he stared at the lofted ball and said, "It just ain't so." Heywood Broun, in the *New York World*, said the hit proved "The Ruth is mighty and shall prevail."

Despite his injuries Ruth also played in the fifth game. His wound was rigged with a tube for drainage, his left wrist was tightly bandaged, his legs were taped their full length, and he had a wrenched knee. In this condition and with the score 1–1 in the fourth inning he started the winning rally with a surprise bunt single and then scored from first base on Bob Meusel's double. He was exhausted from the running, and Huggins had to call time until Ruth could return to left field. The Yankees won the game 3–1 and now led in the Series three to two in games.

Ruth had played well. In sixteen times at bat he had four singles and a home run, and had scored three times. He drove in four runs. In left field he made no errors.

On Monday evening, October 10, after the fifth game, physicians examined him again. They warned him that he would probably cripple his arm if he played before it healed. Dr. George W. King, Ruth's physician, made a statement for the press.

> Ruth's injured arm is in such condition that he would be taking chances on further injury, possibly of a serious nature, if he were to take part in tomorrow's contest. The arm is swollen considerably from the work to which it was subjected during the afternoon and the wound is draining more than it had been earlier in the day. It is possible that we may have to make still another incision in the injured member. To play while the arm is in its present condition would be to invite a spread of the infection. We have ordered Ruth that under no condition shall he attempt to play ball tomorrow.

It seemed unlikely that he would appear again in the Series. The swelling had gone down by Tuesday morning, but his arm was so sore he could not drive his car. His plea to coach at third base met no favor, so he watched the sixth game from the press box.

In the press box was Joe Vila of the *New York Sun*. After the 1919 Series, before the scandal broke, the opinionated Vila dismissed rumors of the corruption of the White Sox. He said only "fools" believed such talk, because baseball was proof against stain, as all insiders knew. Now, two years later, he suggested in print that Babe Ruth had faked an injury because he could not take the pressure of World Series play. This may be the most doltish remark ever made about Ruth. Ruth came to the park the next day in an angry mood. The press box was then at ground level, and Ruth jogged toward Vila with purposeful strides. Vila thought Ruth planned to tear him to shreds and raised his typewriter to ward off violence. But his victim rolled up his sleeve to show his wound and challenged the *Sun* to print a photograph of his arm. There was no photograph, nor apology.

The Giants won the sixth, seventh, and eighth games. The Yankees played well, losing the last two by one-run margins, 2–1 and 1–0. In the eighth game Ruth batted in the ninth inning as a pinch-hitter. With visible pain, his left arm heavily bandaged, he fouled one, missed one, and grounded out to first base. We are permitted to think the story might have been different if Ruth had played all games. Even now, looking back, the Series seems to have been indecisive.

The Series drew 270,000 people, a new attendance record, though not every game was sold out. Huggins explained the Yankee loss not by Ruth's absence but by saying the Series was so long the Yankees were tired. (He didn't explain why the Giants did not tire.) Each Giant received $5,625, each Yankee $3,510.

Ruppert and Huston gave a dinner at the Commodore Hotel for players, scouts, and other employees. Ruth told reporters his arm was healing rapidly and should be well in a few days. He said he would like to play some exhibition games.

25 · The Commissioner or the Player (1921)

United States Judge Kenesaw Mountain Landis first drew the attention of major-league owners when the Federal League, trying to break the baseball monopoly, sued organized baseball in his court in 1915. The Federals thought Landis an enemy of monopoly (he had fined the Standard Oil Company $29 million, a showy gesture which the Supreme Court reversed). The major-league defendants believed he was a high-minded judge. Landis was neither, as it turns out. He was a ham.

The Federal League got cold comfort in Landis's court. He stalled the case for a year until the upstarts went broke and the older leagues were safe. He said he knew enough about baseball to know that a ruling in favor of the Federals would destroy or gravely hurt the game. He pretended shock at thinking of ballplayers as labor. In short, he acted not as a judge but as a fan.

Landis habitually wore a scowl. With his hawk nose and thick white hair he looked something like the American eagle or a beardless, bad-tempered Uncle Sam. His hats were battered, his language strong, his tobacco visibly chewed. He had a practice of jabbing listeners in the ribs for emphasis, which some found annoying. He was not really an ornament of the bench. Unwilling people found themselves before him without receiving subpoenas nor seeing warrants. Higher courts set aside many of his rulings. He sometimes prejudiced juries by remarks which he ordered stricken from the record. When defense lawyers objected, he threatened to punish them for contempt. Many of his charges to juries during the First World War were only patriotic speeches. He denied that free speech existed in wartime. He summoned Kaiser Wilhelm of Germany to answer in his court for the sinking of the *Lusitania*. Landis was honest, brave, arbitrary, bigoted, and he hoarded grudges carefully. Like the storied Englishwoman, he had a whim of iron.

... He appealed to the conservative, the traditional, the old-fashioned who found him a square bastion against the rioters, city slickers, and pay-off boys of megalopolitan life.
—Tristram P. Coffin, on Landis

For some years before 1920 organized baseball's three-man National Commission had been regarded as feeble and clumsy. The 1919 World Series scandal became public late in the season of 1920. The owners moved quickly to change the management of their monopoly to encourage the customers to believe baseball had cleaned its house. A single believable head was needed. Many names came up, but Kenesaw M. Landis had already proved his usefulness. The owners, meeting in Chicago, elected him Commissioner of Baseball at fifty thousand dollars a year, then trooped into his courtroom where he was trying a case. Playing his part of Ethical Hero for all it was worth, "the judge sharply banged his gavel and ordered them to make less noise." They had to wait in his chambers for forty-five minutes. Landis turned out to be a little greedy for status. He intended to stay on the bench while serving as Commissioner. This arrangement didn't work as well as Landis wished. Because he did not resign from the bench there was a movement in the Congress to impeach him. Would baseball's pilgrimage of penance begin with the congressional impeachment and trial of its purifying angel? Landis decided to resign his judgeship.

The public accepted Landis, literally, at face value. He *looked* the part of a crusader for manly virtue. Baseball had appointed its own policeman, which was good industrial strategy because it gave the appearance of reform without any check by outsiders. For the same reason Hollywood appointed Will Hays its czar. Rose C. Felt wrote that it "paid" to make a practice of "bolstering up the public confidence and treating it until it was sound. . . ."

His career typifies the heights to which dramatic talent may carry a man in America if only he has the foresight not to go on the stage.
—Heywood Broun, on Landis

Probably a majority of American males have envied Landis. He was the only successful dictator in American history, and he soaked himself in baseball the year round. He did not change the organization of baseball as much as he wished, because he could not legislate. But within the framework of the game he did what he wished. His employers dared not provoke him to resign. If he quit, his leaving would surely be theatrical, if not dramatic, and he would somehow manage to make them look sleazy and selfish. Unhappily for them, they came to wish they had set a time limit on his term of office. As it was, they grimly endured him.

Landis applied the laws of baseball to both great and small. For example, he banned two of the White Sox only because they had "guilty knowledge" of the 1919 fix and did not speak. He commanded Charles A. Stoneham and John McGraw to get rid of their race track and gambling casino in Havana, or get rid of the Giants. (They kept the Giants.)

One morning in the 1890s Ring Lardner and his father drove from Niles, Michigan, to South Bend, Indiana, to see an exhibition game between the Cleveland Spiders and a touring semi-pro team. For the Spiders the pitcher would be "positively Cy Young." Years later young Ring recognized the great infielder Bobby Wallace* as the man who had posed as "positively Cy Young." In 1910 baseball owners had to press hard to stop a Cincinnati promoter from taking major-league players on a postseason tour and thus making money out of "their" players.

Postseason touring is called barnstorming. From 1914 on, the uniform baseball contract barred its players from barnstorming in baseball and several other sports. Ban Johnson made part of the motive plain enough: "We want no makeshift Club calling themselves the Athletics to go to Cuba to be beaten by colored teams." (The Athletics won the World Series of 1913.) By 1921 the owners had refined the rule to bar only men who had played in the previous World Series.

The owners had several reasons. It hurt the owners' vanity when other promoters exploited major leaguers. Fakers salted a pick-up team with a few well-known names and pretended to present a famous team. Barnstormers often played against black or mixed teams (for example, the famous New York Cubans), and owners didn't want them to mix, for reasons that kept black men out of organized baseball from the 1880s to the 1940s.

When Babe Ruth was with the champion Red Sox they went barnstorming and received a light punishment.

> **If you keep telling a person he's a hero, he'll soon be telling himself, "By God, I *am* a hero."**
>
> **—Carl Becker**

Several men who played in the 1921 World Series received offers to go barnstorming. Landis refused permission. Those who guessed that Ruth would disregard Landis were right. The fine for breaking the rule would probably be no more than Ruth's World Series share,

* Roderick John Wallace (1873–1960), shortstop, twenty-five seasons, 1894–1918, Spiders, Cardinals, Browns, batting average .268. Hall of Fame.

and he could make that much in two days of exhibitions. It actually cost Ruth money to play in the World Series, since he could sometimes get thousands for a single exhibition game and in two games might net more than in the World Series. A tour could bring him as much as twenty-five thousand dollars.

One can easily imagine Ruth's feelings. At his age a man is usually self-centered. Young people feel one duty for each two wants or rights. Pennant-winning ballplayers would have a harder time than most of us when it came to weighing their duty, because they had so often been praised as heroes by public figures who are supposed to be experts on heroism.

Despite Landis's warning, Ruth went ahead. Carl Mays and Wally Schang had agreed to go, but a talk with Landis changed their minds. Bob Meusel and Bill Piercy* of the Yankees joined Ruth's defiance of the Commissioner and prepared to go on the road with the Ruth All-Stars, most of whom were New York semi-pros. After Ruth told Landis he would go barnstorming, the sportswriter Fred Lieb telephoned Yankee co-owner Huston at his hotel to advise him to try to stop the tour. Huston took a cab to Grand Central Station and talked with Ruth who told him the players had signed contracts and must go. The Ruth All-Stars then left for Buffalo and their first game.

Although the Buffalo International League club refused the use of its park, the Ruth team played the Polish Nationals on the 16th and won 4–2 before a crowd of several thousand. Ruth hit a home run. After the game, like a revolutionary citing the Higher Law, Ruth raised the plane of the argument: "We think that our action was for the best interests of baseball." He said he had tried to talk with Landis, but only by telephone. "He hung up on me twice."

Next the troupe appeared at Elmira on the 17th, where they drew about fifteen hundred and won 6–0. Ruth and Meusel each hit two home runs. At Jamestown, New York, the next day, Ruth played first base, Meusel pitched, and Piercy played center field. Ruth had two doubles in six times at bat, and his team won 14–10. It sounds like fun, and one has a suspicion that this was baseball as a true sport. Ruth felt pretty good and told local newsmen that he feared no punishment.

With more than half the exhibition schedule yet to play, the weather turned cold and wet. Minor-league clubs barred these outlaw vagabonds from their parks. The Ruth All-Stars, in a chill drizzle, lost at Scranton on October 21 by a score of 8–6. It was to be their last game together.

* William Benton Piercy (1896–1951), pitcher, six seasons, 1917–1926, Yankees, Red Sox, Cubs, won 27, lost 43, earned-run average 4.29.

This case resolves itself into a question of who is the biggest man in baseball, the Commissioner or the player who makes the most home runs.

—Kenesaw Mountain Landis (1921)

Before he left for Buffalo on the 15th Ruth had given reporters his brief for the defense in the case of Landis vs. Ruth *et al.* In previous years he had been able to count on barnstorming money and had received as much as three thousand dollars for a game. He had worked as hard as anybody to win the pennant and now was penalized for success. The rule was particularly unfair to him because he commanded much more money per game than any other player could ask. Because the career of a ballplayer is relatively short, the rules should not stop him from making any money he could, in any lawful way. Finally, organized baseball was applying the rule at a time when he was not under contract (his contract had expired). It would seem better to have made the plea to Landis instead of the public, but we know that Landis would not have budged.

The Commissioner had gone to his office in Chicago. His parting remark to reporters was that he would not fine the barnstormers, which left suspension as the only possible punishment. In his stagy fashion he conspicuously rode from New York to Albany in the locomotive's cab. Ruth had met his match. Landis was at least as much of a show-off as Ruth was.

Jacob Ruppert and Huston, when questioned by reporters, said the Commissioner had no alternative but to enforce the rule, unjust as it might seem in some ways. The owners had to muffle their voices. This was the first crisis of Commissioner-governed baseball, and a year before they had unanimously given Landis a mighty charter: they promised to accept his decisions "even when we believe they are mistaken" and not to weaken their support "by criticism of him or one another." Landis said no more until long after the barnstorm ended at Scranton.

The tour ended early because the Yankee management went into action. General Manager Barrow went to Chicago to try to melt Landis, Huston went to Scranton, and Ruppert stayed in New York to distract the press. Huston won the battle for Landis. Ruth surrendered in the dank cold dugout of the little park at Scranton. As Huston paid off the promoters for their trouble, Ruth said someone (unnamed) had offered him a hundred thousand dollars to play outlaw ball in 1922 if organized baseball expelled him. There was an understanding—or misunderstanding—that he would quickly go to see Landis (he didn't). Ruth claimed he had been "badly advised." He and most people thought Landis would be lenient. Huston, for the Yankees, said the owners would try to get the rule changed.

Ruth had not been badly advised. Every friend with an ounce of common sense told him not to defy the Commissioner. Landis had invited him in for a talk in New York, but Ruth told him he could talk only on the telephone because he had to catch the train for Buffalo. That was when Landis "hung up on" him—and then relieved his feelings by swearing at Ruth to his friends until he felt better.

After the Treaty of Scranton, Ruth still did not call on Landis. He went instead to shoot quail with Herb Pennock. He had quit the tour, but not because he feared or loved Landis. He quit because Huston made it plain he was hurting the Yankees, though the Yankees had no responsibility for his behavior. What sentence Landis would give Ruth, Meusel, and Piercy was long unknown, but on November 3, when the World Series checks went out of the Commissioner's office, theirs were not among them. Time dragged through November with only silence from Chicago.

Landis did not announce the punishment until December 5. He said he would hold back the World Series money and suspend each of them for thirty-nine days, beginning on the next Opening Day. Ruppert and Huston were satisfied because they expected worse. (Eventually the convicts got their World Series money, but, under the rules of baseball, men do not get paid while suspended, so each lost thirty-nine days' pay.) Landis's opinion went on to say the barnstormers had been "wilfully and defiantly" in violation of the rules of the government of baseball. It was more than a rule violation "but rather a mutinous defiance intended by the players to present this question: which is the bigger—baseball or any individual in baseball?" The only comfort for players and club was that Landis permitted them to take part in spring training and spring exhibitions, and to work out with the team each day before the regular season began. The punishment was generally viewed as surprisingly severe, and bore most heavily on the Yankees as a team. At the moment Ruth was touring in vaudeville. Reporters visited him in his hotel in Washington to get his comments. All he would say while they were in his suite was "Lots of potatoes," a remark addressed to the room-service waiter, not to the press.

Landis won much. He now had publicity to balance the popularity of Babe Ruth. Baseball thus had two poles: the hedonistic, swashbuckling Ruth and the righteous, incorruptible Landis who cast himself in an overblown melodrama as the Puritan Ethic incarnate. The Ethical Hero had handcuffed the Muscle Hero, and baseball was saved.

The president of the Pacific Coast League called Landis "the New Moses." Like Moses, Landis had detractors, even though his employers had gagged themselves. Within a year J. G. Taylor Spink, publisher of the *Sporting News*, called him "Landis the First" and said baseball didn't need an "erratic and irresponsible despot." The Commissioner put on his best scowl and said Spink was a "swine." The owners amended the barnstorming rule to allow any three World Series players, after getting formal permission, to play together on a tour lasting as late as November 10.

Baseball nonetheless remained a totalitarian country with an anointed Commissioner from whom there was no appeal. His subjects—whether owners or players—could easily defect if they were willing to get their bread in other ways. Did Landis really save baseball? He saved baseball as a monopoly business. His job was not merely to keep it honest but also to guarantee that the players were subject to the laws made by their masters. He did his job. There wasn't another overt mutiny against the tablets of the law until the players' strike of the 1970s. Landis was to the baseball business what chlorination is to drinking water, necessary but not satisfying in itself. It was reassuring to people who bought tickets to know that in this country you could drink the water and you could trust the baseball.

As for Babe Ruth's punishment, justice was on his side, but the law was on the side of Landis. Most people thought the penalty was too severe, but they also thought a penalty was well deserved.

26 · A Satirical Home Run:
That's Good

When Babe Ruth decided to defy the law of baseball and go barn-storming late in 1921, he also agreed to tour the Keith vaudeville circuit for fifteen weeks beginning on November 4, for which he would receive three thousand dollars a week. He was in rehearsal with his partners, Wellington Cross and a pianist, late in October. The Keith management put together a portable lobby exhibit of Ruth's baseball souvenirs to ship from theater to theater. The producer, E. F. Albee, wondered whether to bill Ruth as "The Super-man of Baseball." Tex Rickard, manager of Madison Square Garden, knowing of Bernard Shaw's play *Man and Superman*, suggested that Albee ask Shaw. Albee cabled: WOULD IT BE QUITE PROPER TO BILL BABE RUTH AS "SUPERMAN OF BASEBALL"? Shaw replied: SORRY NEVER HEARD OF HER. WHOSE BABY IS RUTH? Shaw had done Albee a real favor. The exchange appeared in papers from coast to coast.

Ruth & Cross, with an act by Thomas J. Grey, tried out in Mt. Vernon, New York, on November 3. They filled the house, the applause was spontaneous, and Ruth was at ease. Despite a cold, Ruth joined with Cross to sing "Little by Little" in "a not unpleas-ant baritone voice." The critic thought the most memorable gag began with the delivery of a telegram, said to be from Kenesaw Mountain Landis, Commissioner of Baseball, even then, as all the world knew, brooding on the punishment he would give Ruth for barnstorming.

CROSS: Is it serious?
RUTH: I should say it is! Seventy-five cents, collect.

They opened, in what Albee billed as "A Satirical Home Run: That's Good," in Boston on November 7 and moved to the Palace in New York on the 14th. Ruth & Cross had the best spot, next to closing, better even than Victor Moore who had to take the closing. They appeared twice a day.

Ruth found a flood of telegrams waiting in his dressing room on opening night in New York. Many came from baseball people and from politicos, but there were also best wishes from Eva Tanguay, Bennie Fields, Chick Evans, Gus Edwards, John Golden, Helen Keller, Francis X. Bushman, Irene Bordoni, Eddie Foy, William Collier, Buster Keaton, Eddie Rickenbacker, Benny Leonard, and John Ringling.

Ruth packed the house at the opening. The Standing Room Only sign went up early. The act went like this: As the orchestra played "Take Me Out to the Ball Game" Ruth entered in Yankee uniform. His entrance brought a full minute of applause before he could speak a word. Cross entered. The two did some two-line jokes, then sang the duet, and next did a parody of a mind-reading act. (Sample: CROSS—Tell me what this is, if you are *able*. RUTH—A cane.) They finished with another song.

The Times critic said it was unpolished but the best act put on by a ballplayer, and "entertaining." As the tour continued, reviews were generally favorable. A tabular record of all variety acts working in November, published for the professionals of vaudeville, scored Ruth and Cross well (only two places behind Victor Moore), noting two songs, a good start, a big finish, four bows, and a two-week run in New York. The most unsympathetic review appeared in the *New York World*, November 15.

All lip-rouged like a tight-wire lady, with a voice as sweet as a furnace shaker in action, hands that could not find a place on that whole wide stage to rest comfortably, a grace of carriage somewhere between John Barrymore and an elephant, Babe Ruth came out yesterday at the Palace. And the flappers flapped and the standees whooped her up until the poor chap stood on one foot, then the other, hoping they'd hurry and subside so he wouldn't forget his lines.

Albee's press man tied Ruth in with the well-reported visits of General le Baron Alphonse Jacques, commander of the Belgian army in the First World War, and Marshal Ferdinand Foch, commander of the Allied forces on the Western Front. General Jacques caught the show at the Palace and then took a batting lesson from Ruth in the alley behind the theater for the news photographers. The Knights of Columbus enrolled Foch as a member (Ruth already belonged) and posed the Marshal giving a brick to Ruth on the steps of St. Patrick's Cathedral to publicize the building of the K.C.'s new lodge hall. Legend says that on meeting Foch Ruth said, "I hear you were in the war." According to the press of the day, Foch made a speech in French and Ruth eloquently replied, "Oui." Later, when it came time to go back to France, Foch sent a farewell via reporters to the friend he knew as "l'enfant."

Babe Ruth's net profit from this excursion is unknown. The sportswriter Arthur Daley said Ruth told him he "spent fifty thousand dollars in expenses." Since Ruth was on stage each afternoon and evening, it wouldn't be easy to spend around five hundred dollars a day, unless, perhaps, he counted some otherwise unmentioned betting losses as "expenses."

Outside the Park, 1922

BODY OF POPE BENEDICT XV. LIES IN STATE

STRIKERS SHOT DOWN
IN PAWTUCKET RIOT

BOMB ROCKS CHICAGO LOOP

DEFENDS THE HORSE
AGAINST THE MOTOR

PLANS BIG SAVINGS
IN MILITARY COSTS

CORSET STAY KILLS SKIER

JERSEY DRY BILLS PASSED

PIERCE-ARROW LOST
$8,763,712 IN 1921

FOUR ARE KILLED IN BELFAST OUTRAGES

KU KLUX THREAT TO NEGRO MESSENGER

SHOT BY HIS FRIEND
TESTING STEEL VEST

SACCO AND VANZETTI FRIENDS
THREATEN LEGATION IN SOFIA

CARRIED LIQUOR IN WOODEN LEG

SMYRNA IN RUINS;
PROBABLY 2000 DEAD

UNITED STATES TO HAVE LARGEST AIRPLANE CARRIER IN WORLD

SEVEN KILLED IN AN ATTACK ON A NON-UNION MINE

TROOPS HUNT REDS
IN MICHIGAN WOODS

BRITAIN IS RUSHING
TROOPS TO ULSTER

SAYS ACTRESS KEPT HIM PRISONER 3 DAYS

27 · A Thousand Dollars a Week

In January 1922 Babe Ruth faced the unpleasant fact that the next baseball season would open without him. Ten thousand New Yorkers petitioned Commissioner Landis, but Landis didn't budge. When Ruth's vaudeville act reached Chicago he went twice to seek absolution in Landis's office, but the Commissioner was ill at home and Ruth could only leave word that he wished to plead his case. Ruth was temperate enough to say nothing about Landis in public.

Ed Barrow, the Yankees' general manager, visited Landis. He had to agree with the Commissioner when Landis said Barrow would have done the same when Barrow was president of the International League. Landis added that he knew he was, at the moment, the most disliked man in the country, but he intended to stand by his decision.

Huggins and Barrow strengthened the Yankees for the 1922 season by raiding the Red Sox again. They bought shortstop Everett Scott and pitchers Joe Bush and Sam Jones. With Ruth and Meusel suspended, they stiffened the outfield by getting Whitey Witt from the Athletics.

The team was to train in New Orleans, a rather distracting place for a training camp, especially in the prohibition years. Ruth and Meusel would train with the club by ruling of Landis who knew the Yankees expected to pay the cost of spring training by selling tickets to see Ruth play in exhibition games. Landis may have feared that if Ruth were barred from the plate during spring training he might not go south at all but instead try more vaudeville, or, God forbid, play outlaw baseball with a team out of Landis's reach. Huggins told Ruth and Meusel to train as hard as everybody else.

Barrow thought it would be good for players to prepare for spring training with light work at Hot Springs. Seven, including Ruth, took the advice. Ruth was in good physical shape but quieter than usual, probably not subdued by Landis but by deep reflection on his next contract. He played a lot of golf. Occasionally he and Marshall Hunt of the *New York Daily News* roamed the countryside looking for farmhouses which advertised country cooking. Surely these hominy hunts were symptoms of desolate boredom, almost suicidal.

The seven men of the Hot Springs detachment joined the Yankee advance party in New Orleans on March 2, arriving in a rainstorm, and moved into the Grunewald Hotel. The weather was unseasonably cold all the while they were in New Orleans.

Landis came down to New Orleans to polish his public image by making himself conspicuous at a charity game where he was successful bidder at $250 for a baseball autographed by Ruth. The Yankees beat the New Orleans Pelicans 10–3. First-baseman Ruth had three singles in six times at bat. That month Ruth dined frequently with several of the old families of New Orleans, who thus wasted the Western hemisphere's best cuisine on the world's most famous fancier of hot-dogs-with-the-works. No record tells us where Helen Ruth was in the early months of 1922.

Ruth had not yet signed a contract but said he and Huston had come to terms.

After the World Series of 1921, when Ruth's contract expired, gossips of the sporting press spread the story that he would get a colossal salary in 1922, paid jointly by all of the American League clubs. This plain balderdash seemed real enough to annoy the *Sporting News*, which scolded the race of sportswriters for writing nonsense in dull times between seasons. But it showed what an interesting topic Ruth's salary was. John McGraw was probably the best rewarded of all men in the game. His salary was forty thousand dollars a year, and he shared in the Giants' profits. The Cleveland Indians managed to get newspaper space by claiming that playing manager Tris Speaker was "without exception the highest paid man in baseball," but they gave no figure.

Huston went to Hot Springs to talk with Ruth about salary. He opened with a sermon, calling on him to repent his wastrel life and to stay away from the bright lights. Ruth eyed him with amusement and pointed out that Huston lived exactly as he lived. Round one was a draw.

Barrow kept a Yankee salary-and-transfer file on typewritten 4 x 6 cards, one to a player. The entries for Babe Ruth through 1921 were these:

1919   12/26   Purchased from Boston, A.L., $100,000. payable in four installments of $25,000 each.

1920		Cont. $10,000 as assigned by Boston (1919–20–21)
	1/6	Cont. increased $10,000 by agreement making total $20,000.
1921		Cont. $20,000
	2/18	Bonus for 1920—$5000
		Bonus for 1921—$5000

The bonuses of February 1921 could be called tips, for doubling the Yankee attendance in 1920. Ruth had a good case for a large raise.

Huston got down to serious talk in a Hot Springs bathhouse when he took the tub next to Ruth's and offered forty thousand a year for five years. (That was McGraw's deal with Charles A. Stoneham, to the dollar.) Ruth raised the figure to fifty-two thousand. Huston countered with fifty thousand for three years, and the club's option to renew for the next two years, and wanted to know why Ruth put on the extra two thousand. Ruth said he'd like to have a thousand dollars a week and suggested they flip a coin to settle the difference. There was a long wait while Huston telephoned New York and got Ruppert's approval of the six-thousand-dollar coin toss. Near midnight the coin arched in the air, Ruth called it, and won. Neither Barrow nor the owners would tell the salary, but Huston said they had flipped a coin and that Ruth would get five hundred dollars for each home run. This jocular tall tale became current myth and had to be denied repeatedly as late as 1925. The only reason for secrecy was that Ruth wished it secret.

Huston sent the terms to the office in New York, and secretaries prepared a draft for Ruppert's signature. When the paper arrived in New Orleans Huston called Ruth out of the Heinemann Park clubhouse to sign. Ruth borrowed a fountain pen from the groundskeeper, consulted no one, and signed it against a vertical post of the stands, as casually as if he were autographing a scorecard.

The agreement had some uncommon specific terms. Ruth was to get half his salary in fortnightly installments during the playing season. The other half of the year's money was due him at the end of the season. Christy Walsh, Ruth's financial adviser, told him he should put the postseason installment into a trust, but Ruth spent most of 1921's year-end pay to improve a piece of real estate. The document also regulated Ruth's private life. He was to "refrain and abstain entirely from the use of intoxicating liquors" and, during the season, to be in bed daily by one o'clock in the morning. If his behavior disabled him, the Yankees could cancel the contract and keep his withheld salary. Baseball people call this a contract, but a

Signing a contract in Jacob Ruppert's office while Edward Grant Barrow looks on, a standard public relations set-piece of the 1920s. (*National Baseball Library, Cooperstown, New York.*)

true contract is between freely bargaining parties. Ruth could sign, or quit baseball and look for a job making shirts.

Babe Ruth now had the written promise of a higher salary than any player had ever received. He also had one of the few player agreements that went beyond one year. The Yankees insured his life for three hundred thousand dollars and were to do so thereafter.

Along with the 59 percent pay raise he also got the title of captain. Thirty years earlier the title of captain had meant, roughly, assistant manager, but by the 1920s it was more honorary than real. Nevertheless it was pleasing because no player unpopular with his team would be named captain. No Yankee envied Ruth's salary. Right or wrong, they believed he was driving player salaries up. The Yankees, of course, were not paying him because of his skill. They paid him because he drew throngs. (If there were a true relation between playing skill and income, all international grand masters of chess would be rich.)

As soon as paydays came in April Ruth celebrated his raise by buying a Cadillac for St. Mary's Industrial School in Baltimore. It cost about five thousand dollars, or about 10 percent of his salary after taxes—a kind of tithe.

The Yankees set out in good condition to play their way northward to start the 1922 season. At a stop in Mississippi two thousand people stood long in the rain for an awed glimpse of Ruth getting off the train, and then tramped squishily to the Yankees' hotel where they stood and stared in hope of another glimpse of the demigod. When the Yankees came to an Oklahoma town so many boys clung to Ruth's open taxi that the driver had to crawl in low gear from the station to the hotel, no doubt expecting his tires to explode at any moment. As the philosopher Morris Cohen had recently said, baseball seemed to fit the usual definition of a religion.

28 · Wreaths of Wild Raspberry (1922)

As opening day neared in 1922, more and more people pressed Commissioner Landis to show mercy toward Babe Ruth and Bob Meusel by shortening their suspension.* Otherwise they could not play until May 20. American League owners told Landis he was penalizing *them*, and small boys loudly doubted Landis's ancestry as he walked the streets of Chicago. The Commissioner stood firm. We now know the suspension cost the Yankees about a hundred thousand dollars in gross receipts. In the seven years since 1915 every Yankee of the team that Jacob Ruppert and T. L. Huston bought had departed. The complete turnover of players meant a net expense for players of eight hundred thousand dollars, an eighth of it for Ruth. In effect, Ruth's suspension doubled his cost to the Yankees.

The 1922 Yankees could expect good pitching from Carl Mays, Waite Hoyt, Sam Jones, Joe Bush, and Bob Shawkey. The infield seemed improved. But with Ruth and Meusel banned for a quarter of the season, the outfield looked weak. The only regular from 1921 would be Elmer Miller in center field. By adding Whitey Witt the Yankees had a man fit to be a regular, and they would alternate Chick Fewster** and Chicken Hawks in the other place.

The Yankees opened on the road by losing to the Senators on April 12, but they did not droop. They won eight of their next nine games. By the 23rd they were comfortably in first place, leading the Indians by two games. They went right on as if Babe Ruth had never been born. The day before he came back to the lineup they had won twenty-two and lost eleven.

* Bill Piercy, the barnstorming Yankee pitcher, had gone to the Red Sox in a winter trade.

** Lawton Walter Witt, born Ladislaw Waldemar Wittkowski (1895–   ), outfielder, ten seasons, 1916–1926, Athletics, Yankees, Dodgers, batting average .287.

Wilson Lloyd Fewster (1895–1945), outfielder, eleven seasons, 1917–1927, Yankees, Red Sox, Indians, Dodgers, batting average .258.

In the early weeks of the season Ruth and Meusel were pretty bored. They couldn't play ball so they played in other ways which made it hard to stay in condition. They *seem* to have gone in for surgery on themselves as a way of killing time. Meusel had his tonsils out on opening day (tonsilectomies were a fad of the 1920s), and Ruth raised him one by having tonsils and adenoids removed at St. Vincent's Hospital on May 4. At the same place, day, and hour Helen Ruth underwent surgery for reasons unknown except that it was a repeat of a previous operation. On the next day "she was resting easily and would be in the hospital for another couple of weeks." Her husband left the hospital on the 10th, but she remained.

The suspension cost Ruth plenty in money. Players get all of the year's pay during the six months of the season. Thus each day's suspension cost Ruth about $285. He never had another clash with Landis.

During the time Helen Ruth spent in the hospital, Babe took up an employment that completely surprised all but his closest friends —baby-sitting. He appeared at the park before a game with a child he introduced as his daughter Dorothy. To eager questioners he said she had been born in Presbyterian Hospital on February 2. Interviewers then went to see Helen Ruth at St. Vincent's. Yes, the Ruths had a baby, born in St. Vincent's on June 7, 1921. Back to the husband. June 7 was right, he said; he had confused his own birthday with small Dorothy's, which was pretty lame since he had never claimed to be born on February 2. This exchange of contradictions has confused people ever since. But, as many who have adopted a child know, such families often think of two pleasant anniversaries to celebrate: the child's birthdate and the day the child came to live with the family. Circumstantial evidence says little Dorothy was born on June 7 and moved in with the Ruths the following February, which explains Helen Ruth's absence from spring training.

Helen's appearance had changed by 1922. Until 1920 the few newspaper photographs in which she appeared showed a pretty girl with slightly hollow cheeks and prominent cheekbones. In 1922 her cheeks were rounded and there was the beginning of a double chin.

By May 18 the Yankees had sold all of their reserved and box seats for the game against the Browns on May 20, the day of Ruth's return. On the 20th the crowds needed police control by ten in the morning. Early in the afternoon people began to fill the aisles in the upper decks.

For the Yankees the game was a disaster. The Browns scored seven runs in the ninth to win 8–2. Urban Shocker held the Yankees

Helen with Dorothy (aged sixteen months), September 23, 1922. (*National Baseball Library, Cooperstown, New York.*)

to three hits, and Baby Doll Jacobson* hit a home run with the bases full. The explosive rally began after two outs in the ninth when Sam Jones, covering first base on a ground ball, could not hold on to the toss. The umpire had already called the runner out and had to reverse his ruling. Thinking it a Yankee win, the crowd surged onto the field. It took twenty minutes to clear the grounds and resume play. By that time Jones had lost his coordination, and the Browns scored seven runs before the third out. (This shook Jones so badly that he lost his next ten starts.) Ruth's only sparkle was a "glittering" catch of a George Sisler foul fly while sprinting into the left-field corner. He also coached at third base to be continuously on display.

* Urban James Shocker, born Urbain Jacques Schockeor (1890–1928), pitcher, thirteen seasons, 1916–1928, Yankees, Browns, won 188, lost 117, earned-run average 3.17.
   William Chester Jacobson (1890–   ), outfielder, eleven seasons, 1915–1927, Tigers, Browns, Red Sox, Indians, Athletics, batting average .312.

The total attendance for the three-game series beginning on the 20th was about a hundred thousand.

> **The New York fans . . . haven't given me a square deal since I returned to the field.**
> **—Babe Ruth, May 26, 1922**

Ruth's return to form was too slow for impatient watchers. Before long the customers—in the baroque sports language of the day— began to "decorate the big slugger tastefully with wreaths of wild raspberry." He was holding his temper with an effort, and tipped his cap when booed.

On May 24 Ruth tried to stretch a single into a double. When umpire Hildebrand called him out, Ruth threw a handful of dust into the air, most of which hit the umpire in the face, and Hildebrand ordered him out of the game. He walked off the field in a rage. Two men behind the Yankee dugout had been giving him a hard time, and now one rose to shout, "Play ball, you bum!" Like a tiger Ruth sprang to the roof of the Yankee dugout and started for the heckler through a box filled with people. The tormentor fled, and the frustrated Ruth stood on the dugout to defy the unfriendly crowd. Then he jumped down and walked alone toward the clubhouse. Under the stands he said he'd do the same again.

Ruth's breach was to be judged by Ban Johnson, the league's president. Johnson took into account the strain of the Landis suspension and the pressure on Ruth after he returned to play. The punishment was a two-hundred-dollar fine and the loss of the captaincy of the Yankees after five days' tenure. Johnson said Ruth lacked the "mental strength and stability" to take the loss of public favor. Ruth said the Yankee followers were unfair.

> **The crowds that watch [baseball] average about as low in sportsmanship as a mass of human beings that can be found anywhere.**
> **—*The Times*, May 27, 1922**

In the eyes of those who buy the tickets, baseball is not played only by heroes. Many go to jeer, perhaps to satisfy a real need for visible villains. Far more players have been hurt by words from the stands than by sticks and stones. It may be more than coincidence that the suicide rate among major-league ballplayers is much higher than the national average. Even the certified saint of baseball, Christy Mathewson, hit a lemonade boy in the mouth—splitting his lip and loosening some teeth—for a slur against a Giant. In the old ball parks players and fans were close enough for words to have an effect. Abuse of a famous player is a great tonic for some.

Ballplayers tend to despise the crowd for its ignorance, for applauding results rather than form, whether the crowd is friendly or hostile. Players do not hear the well-informed watchers because they tend to be quiet in their contemplation of the game.

At the end of the first week in June, the ex-captain of the Yankees had hit four home runs and was eleven behind his 1921 pace. He gave up hope of setting a fourth consecutive home-run record. After two weeks of June he was batting only .259 with six home runs. On June 19 the Yankees stumbled numbly into a seven-game losing streak, teamwork shoddy, pitchers falling apart, hits not coming when hits were most needed. Since the return of Ruth and Meusel, the team had won thirteen and lost fifteen.

As the losing streak stretched, so did Ruth's self-control—until it snapped. On June 19 umpire Bill Dineen put him out of a game at Cleveland for "vulgar and vicious language" when called out. Ban Johnson suspended Ruth for three days. During the pregame practice of the next day Ruth hunted Dineen into the Cleveland dugout where the Indians protected the umpire physically, but all heard Ruth tell Dineen not to put him out of a game again or "I'll fix you so you'll never umpire again, even if they put me out of baseball for life. You're yellow!" He added what the witnesses called a "vile name."

On news of this uproar, Johnson lengthened the suspension to six days. The whole thing seemed to shake up the Yankees so that a paper could run the head: RUTHLESS YANKS BEAT INDIANS, 7–3, and the losing streak was over.

Ruth made the usual apology and then visited Dineen in the umpires' room, not to say he was really sorry but to tell Dineen this was the last time he'd ever be suspended for quarreling with an umpire. (He was mistaken.)

Ban Johnson, the League's founder and president, was "a man of ability" but not as much ability as he believed. By a letter to the culprit he added himself to the list of people who tried to push Ruth instead of leading him.

I was keenly disappointed and amazed when I received Umpire Dineen's report recounting your shameful and abusive language to that official. . . . Your conduct . . . was reprehensible to a great degree—shocking to every American mother who permits her boy to go to a game. . . . It is a leading question as to whether it is permissible to allow a man of your influence and breeding to continue in the game. . . . A man of your stamp bodes no good in the profession.

After a reference to Ruth's corruption of the Yankees, Johnson added,

It seems the period has arrived when you should allow some intelligence to creep into a mind that has plainly been warped.

Seven weeks later Babe Ruth showed what little effect Johnson's sermon had.

We can give you the best of service should you wish any member or members shadowed.
                                    —Circular of a detective agency to
                                    all major-league clubs, pre-1920

The Yankees of the early twenties were thought to be the all-time alcoholic team, a standing impossible to verify. Their reputation went back to the years before the First World War when two Yankees were said to drink more than a case of beer each, every day (which is hard to believe). Roger Kahn lumped most of Ruth's friends in a class headed "could take a drink." And that is what Ruppert, Huston, Barrow, and Huggins believed.

What could a management do when it believed its employees were short on the virtue of temperance? The answer is easy: spy on them. From an agency they rented a detective named Jimmy Kelly. For a cover he assumed the part of an ex-jockey and a baseball freak. Kelly won the players' confidence by giving them some horse-race winners. Then he followed the team on a western swing and became the conductor of Yankee tours of speakeasies.

This Judas betrayed them during a series with the White Sox. Ruth always enjoyed Chicago. With players of many teams he made Mrs. Elizabeth McCuddy's respectable bar and baseball boarding house (across the street from Comiskey Park) his headquarters. On rainy days he practiced with his golf putter on Ma McCuddy's parlor carpet. On hot bright days he would send a message across Shields Avenue: "Tell Ma to put six bottles of beer on ice—it's two out in the ninth." Jimmy Kelly lured Ruth and the others from this home-away-from-home into something more interesting.

Kelly arranged a tour of a large and illegal brewery at Joliet, Illinois, about an hour by trolley southwest of Chicago. He asked the Yankees to pose for a group picture in the brewery, had them autograph it individually, then mailed it to the Yankee owners. With a few beers visible and the authentic signatures scrawled all over the print, the tourists convicted themselves. Ruppert and Huston sent the picture to Landis, who was touring major-league club-houses preaching against games of chance and the evils of drink.

Landis met with the Yankees in Fenway Park and gave them a fierce scolding. The carefully rigged episode helps us to know the minds of a valid sample of American leadership in private affairs in the 1920s. A stuffy group. Perhaps, after that, the Yankees paid more attention to that proper old warning, don't take candy from strangers.

A careful look at the brewery photograph shows no one plainly gone in beer. Three mugs of beer can be seen for twenty-one men. The group is arranged in tiers in a way which required physical coordination. Any college class's summer reunion will produce more incriminating snapshots of beer fanciers.

July 1922 was the month of fists. At St. Louis Ruth spoke so sharply to Wally Pipp about his fielding that Pipp knocked him

Huggins and Ruth in 1921 or 1922. Ruth found it hard to believe that such a small man, five feet six and a half inches, 140 pounds, could ever have learned much about baseball. (*The New York Yankees.*)

over a bench in the dugout. Legend says each hit a home run in his next time at bat. On the very next day Aaron Ward and Braggo Roth fought in the same dugout. From St. Louis they transferred the bouts to Detroit, where there were two dugout fist fights in two days: Mays vs. Al DeVormer° and DeVormer vs. Bootnose Hofmann. Huggins restored a kind of peace by promising to fine the next who fought.

They also played baseball in July. On the 1st Ruth hit three home runs in a double-header with the Athletics, bringing his total to eleven, seventeen behind his 1921 rate. He was batting .267 at game time. The Yankees were in second place, two and a half games behind the Browns. Ten days later they had to deny a silly rumor that Ruth would go to the White Sox in a many-playered deal. All of those who were to go to the White Sox, according to this fable, were men who showed they found it hard to love Miller Huggins.

Despite his weak showing, Ruth was still a popular spectacle. When he caught a ball dropped off the George M. Cohan Theater in Times Square, to publicize a benefit for the police widows' fund, he drew a crowd of about fifteen thousand and stopped traffic for forty-five minutes.

July was also the month in which the Yankees outraged western feelings by another raid on the Red Sox. They bought Jumping Joe Dugan, a good third baseman, to the great anger of those who cheered for the Browns (or jeered at the Yankees). It seemed unfair to many people, since the Browns had a grave third-base problem of their own. Dugan was an established player in his sixth season, but when he joined the Yankees Ruth called him "Kid" and put him to work opening fan mail. (To anticipate a bit, the buying of Dugan probably won the pennant for the Yankees. The owners wrote a rule at the next winter meeting which still stands: no player transfers after June 15 except by asking waivers.)

Ruth hurt his right leg sliding at Detroit on August 9. An infection set in like the arm infection during the World Series of 1921. The unlucky accident happened at a time when he had lifted his batting over .300. Now he could not play again until late in August. Despite this rotten year, a Buffalo newspaper circulation promotion called the Babe Ruth Popularity Contest was highly successful.

Babe Ruth Is Suspended
For Third Time This Year
—*The Times*, September 2, 1922

° Albert E. DeVormer (1891–1966), catcher, five seasons, 1918–1927, White Sox, Yankees, Red Sox, Giants, batting average .258.

September started badly. On the 1st Ban Johnson suspended Ruth for three days to punish him for more "vulgar and vicious" language to umpire Thomas Connolly in a game at the Polo Grounds on August 30. Connolly put Ruth out of the game.

Ruth was of little direct help to the Yankees in September, but he scared the opposition. Although he was hitting poorly, pitchers kept walking him to get at Pipp who batted over .400 that month. The pennant race came down to the last series in St. Louis where the home customers were ferocious because of the Dugan deal and hungry for a pennant they had never won. (Whitey Witt was knocked unconscious by being hit on the head by a pop bottle.) The Yankees made the pennant certain in St. Louis by winning on September 30.

Babe Ruth, no question about it, had a bad 1922. And—except for the leg infection—it was his own doing. He had lost face by defying Landis. His behavior toward umpires Hildebrand, Dineen, and Connolly and toward Wally Pipp did not fit his previously relaxed character. He was tense. For the first time he heard unfriendly voices in places where he usually heard applause. It hurt. But he had more money than ever and as much fame as anyone could possibly expect. The papers gave him about twice the space they gave President Harding. On the road he was still in demand for public appearances off the field. He became a very popular speaker at parish communion breakfasts. Unexpected booing doesn't seem enough to explain his new angry mood.

What was at the bottom of his churlishness? The only basic change in his way of living was the arrival of the foster daughter Dorothy. When Helen Ruth appeared in Babe Ruth's public life, she trailed in the background as a minor supporting character. She clearly did not have the personal force to have much influence over her husband. And they were apart very often. The coming of Dorothy gave Helen's life a purpose it lacked. Babe Ruth had seen no model marriage in his early life which he could copy. He was a somewhat unsatisfactory husband, but Dorothy, on the other hand, was a wholly satisfactory child. He was not, of course, jealous of Dorothy, but he must have found himself disconnected from the main current of his family life. Helen was now able to give him only part of her attention. He would feel vaguely depressed. The first step from depression to normality is usually to grouchiness and bad temper. Thus for most of 1922 he bounced between depression and snappishness. Xaverian Brother George faded like a ghost; Ruth's other self, the dockside slob, ruled.

In that summer of 1922 two pitchers in the American League pitched to Babe Ruth without fear. One was George Uhle, a right-hander with the Indians. The other was Shucks Pruett, a left-hander with the Browns.

Uhle had a slider, according to Waite Hoyt who ought to know. The slider is a pitch that comes in like a fast ball but, if thrown with the right hand, breaks in toward a left-handed batter's fists. Ruth could hit a big bending curve, but he found it hard to hit the slider solidly. It was not used by many pitchers until after the Second World War. If Ruth's foes had used it often, his story would have been different.

Uhle battled Ruth on even terms, but Shucks Pruett was Ruth's master. He threw a screwball. When throwing the usual curve the pitcher rotates his wrist 180 degrees clockwise. When throwing the screwball the rotation is 180 degrees counterclockwise (which is harder on joints and tendons). The screwball breaks in the opposite direction from the way the usual curve breaks (for example, a right-hander's screwball breaks in toward a right-handed batter). When a left-hander threw it to Ruth it behaved just as the slider did when thrown by a right-handed pitcher. But the angle of a left-handed pitch, leaving the mound on the same side of the plate as the box occupied by the batter, made it even harder to hit. Pruett learned the pitch from Barney Pelty* who lived in his southeast Missouri neighborhood. Pelty had picked it up from Christy Mathewson who called it his fadeaway.

1922 was Pruett's first and best season. The first time he faced Ruth he came in in relief and struck him out with three pitches (he did the same to Cobb). Ruth struck out ten of the next twelve times he faced Pruett. On September 17 the Browns' catcher, Hank Severeid, insisted that Pruett throw a curve to Ruth. As Pruett said, "I hung the curve and Ruth hit the ball over the right-field wall." (He got just one more home run off Pruett, early in 1923.) Ruth was always feeble against young Shucks. He faced him thirty times, had four hits, fifteen strikeouts, eight walks, and a sacrifice. He popped up five times and grounded out twice. Lifetime batting average against Pruett: .182.

Pruett became a respected physician in St. Louis and a collector of ragtime music. He met Ruth in 1948 and thanked him for helping him through medical school, saying, "If it hadn't been for you, nobody ever would have heard of me." Ruth said that if there had been more like Pruett he couldn't have gotten by in the major leagues. We may wish that one of Christy Walsh's long-gone ghosts had been there to polish Ruth's reply and have him say, "If there had been more pitchers like you, nobody ever would have heard of *me*."

---

* Barney Pelty (1880–1939), pitcher, ten seasons, 1903–1912, Browns, Senators, won 91, lost 116, earned-run average 2.62.

Ruth finished the 1922 season about a fourth of the way down the list of American League batters with an average of .314. He hit thirty-five home runs, behind Rogers Hornsby of the Cardinals (42), Ken Williams of the Browns (39), and Tilly Walker of the Athletics (37). Only in proportion of home runs per time at bat, and in slugging percentage, did he lead his league. He was second —behind Witt—in bases on balls. In no other categories was he among the league batting leaders. His fielding had not suffered. He threw accurately enough to make fourteen assists, which ranked him ninth among American League outfielders.

THE ACCUMULATED BATTING FIGURES
BABE RUTH'S MAJOR-LEAGUE CAREER
1914–1922

at bat: 2514
hits: 846
home runs: 197
runs batted in: 633
average: .337

29 · Low On the Inside, Nothing Fast

The Giants won the National League pennant on September 25. Giant fans expected their team to win the World Series if they met the Yankees. Their optimism rested on the Giants' slightly better batting average and the claimed superiority of the Giants' infield. When the Yankees had *their* pennant certain, the betting odds favored them 7 to 5 on the theory that they had better pitching. (President Harding picked the Yankees.) John McGraw, manager of the Giants, had the best record of any manager at that time, with eight pennants and only one second-division finish. Miller Huggins was satisfied with himself. At age forty-three he had won two pennants in five seasons managing the Yankees. In all of the pleasant daydreaming about the coming Series the name of Ruth was not called in to weigh the balance on the Yankee side. His effect seemed doubtful. His season had been erratic, and in the 1921 World Series he had struck out eight times in sixteen times at bat.

On the evening before the first game *The Times* polled twenty-three wise men. Thirteen picked the Giants, six picked the Yankees, and four said it was too close to predict. But the wagerers made the Yankees favorites at 6 to 5.

By order of Commissioner Landis the World Series reverted to its original best-of-seven form. The nine-game series, as in 1919, 1920, and 1921, seemed longer than the public's span of attention. There was also fear that an intracity Series would lack appeal. Nevertheless advance ticket sales were larger than in 1921, and scalpers asked twenty dollars for $5.50 tickets before the first game.

The lines that usually formed in front of the ticket windows before the tickets went on sale were not as long as in 1921, but all reserved seats had been sold by the day before the Series opened. (And the best day's attendance in 1922 was higher than in 1921.) In those days fields of waving mink and pearl-pinned ascot ties marked the box seats, and the papers listed the celebrities present by the half-column. Of the notables best remembered today there were General John J. Pershing, Will Rogers, and Governor Al Smith, who threw out the first ball.

The Giants came from behind, scoring three runs in the eighth, to win the first game 3–2. Babe Ruth's day was hardly worthy of *The Times*'s box with its head *What Ruth Did at Bat*. He singled and drove in a run, and also struck out twice. After the first game the fickle wagerers made the Giants 5 to 4 favorites to win the Series.

I may not be the smartest person in the United States, but don't the damned fools think I know night from day?
—K. M. Landis (1922)

The second game of the Series had a disorderly end. Umpire Hildebrand called it on account of darkness at 4:15 P.M., with the score 3–3 after ten innings. Although the Commissioner of Baseball presides over the World Series, the umpires are in charge during actual play. Because Hildebrand had been seen talking with Landis a short time before he called the game, the crowd assumed he stopped the game because Landis told him to. About five thousand crowded around Landis's box shouting "Fake!"—the implication being that it was a trick to increase ticket sales. The Yankees were also suspicious. The Giants left the field so quickly that the Yankees believed they had advance knowledge. Babe Ruth came out of the clubhouse in trousers and undershirt to learn what the shouting was about. When told the customers were hooting the Commissioner he said, "I don't blame them." What particularly irked the crowd was that pitchers Jesse Barnes* and Bob Shawkey were making a beautiful game of it. Landis tried to quiet the near mob in order to plead Not Guilty, but they would have none of it. Police came to offer protection for the Commissioner and his wife, but he waved them aside and, with Mrs. Landis, plunged into the crowd to elbow his way to the right-field exit. Mrs. Landis wore a frozen smile. Near the exit people threw folded newspapers at them. "His face quivering with anger," Landis shook his fists and shouted "Cowards." There was no serious attempt to hurt the Landises physically.

According to the umpires, some of the Yankees had complained of poor visibility, so the umpires conferred at the end of the ninth inning and decided to call it off if still tied at the end of ten, mindful of complaints after the dusky end of the fourteen-inning World

---

* Jesse Lawrence Barnes (1892–1961), pitcher, thirteen seasons, 1915–1927, Braves, Giants, Dodgers, won 153, lost 149, earned-run average 3.22.

Series game at Boston in 1916 (which Ruth had won 2–1). It is true that Barnes and Shawkey were slow workers. The press-box consensus was that there was plenty of light, but nobody there would have to explain away a wrong decision on this question.

Once free of the ball park and its scoffing throng Landis neatly killed the charge of fraud by ordering the day's receipts—about $121,000—set aside for charity. Within two days he had a sheaf of begging letters. Three veterans' groups got half, and the New York ball clubs were told to give the other half to local charities.

In that futile game Ruth had a double and scored a run.

In the third game Jack Scott,* once cast off because of arm trouble, beat Hoyt and the Yankees 3–0, giving up only four hits and none of them to Ruth. The crowd's anger of the previous day was cooled by Landis's impoundment of the gate money, but it enjoyed booing Ruth in the fourth inning. Scott hit Ruth with a pitch. Once on first base, Ruth tried for third base when Frisch kicked a ground ball by Bob Meusel, and collided at full run with Heinie Groh at third. Groh made the putout but was upended. He and Ruth squared off to fight but umpires intervened. The crowd very noisily took Groh's side; after all, he was six inches shorter and sixty pounds lighter.

For the rest of the game the Giants bore down on Ruth with a piercing flow of taunts and jeers. He certainly had behaved badly and now became defensive about it. A consensus of seven Yankee veterans questioned on the point is that he did not usually start such exchanges, but he liked to give as much as he got; in this case he was plainly outnumbered. After the game he and Bob Meusel went to the Giants' dressing room in a quarrelsome mood. Ruth told the Giants that Johnny Rawlings** called him a name he would not take. The Giants seethed, and Barnes was about ready to use blows when some sportswriters and John McGraw came in. Frisch said Ruth was trying to get his name in the papers, and McGraw ordered him out of the room. Before Ruth left he told the Giants exactly which names they were not to call him, which his audience thought was a fine comic performance.

In the cigar stores, speakeasies, and pool halls of New York the Giants were now 1 to 5 favorites to win the Series. The feeling that Ruth was a bit erratic was justified. In three games he had a single and a double for eleven times at bat.

The Giants won their third victory on the 7th, 4–3, after having been two runs behind. Ruth was helpless when facing Handsome

---

* John William Scott (1892–1959), pitcher, twelve seasons, 1916–1929, Pirates, Braves, Reds, Giants, Phillies, won 103, lost 109, earned-run average 3.85.

** John William Rawlings (1892–1972), infielder, twelve seasons, 1914–1926, Reds, Kansas City Federals, Braves, Phillies, Giants, Pirates, batting average .250.

Hugh McQuillan:* a fly out, a walk, a foul out, and a pop-up to second base.

The Giants won the last game 5–3, again coming from behind by getting three runs in the eighth inning. McGraw's crisp and unquestionable defeat of the Yankees brought a mass demonstration of affection. This was only the third time in a score of World Series that the losing team failed to win a game. The Yankees seem to have fallen apart, with nerves shattered. When Huggins told Bush to walk a man intentionally, and Bush wished to pitch to him, Bush shouted a rude remark to his manager that was heard in the front boxes, including the press box. But Bush walked winning pitcher Art Nehf** twice, unintentionally. Ruth's only achievement with his bat in this game was a bunt sacrifice.

Ruth had never been as useless, even as a rookie pitcher. In seventeen times at bat he had a run, two hits, three total bases, a run batted in, and an average of .118. Since May 20 he had had one good month. The rest was letdown.

The World Series of 1922 saw the last victory of the old so-called Scientific or Inside Baseball over the power game. The bunting, running, stealing game was the legendary heritage of the Baltimore Orioles of the 1890s, generally accepted as the best team in history until the 1927 Yankees arrived. John McGraw, a sharp-tongued little grouch, learned his trade with the Orioles. His batting records are fragmentary, but he may have been in a class with Cobb, Wagner, and Ruth. He weighed about 110 pounds when he joined the Orioles, usually referred to himself in the third person, and was loved by almost no one except Alfred Spink of the *Sporting News*, Ring Lardner, and Mrs. McGraw, who wrote a useful memoir. In 1910 Spink had written of him: "Those who know McGraw best know him to be a thorough little gentleman, generous and kind to a fault and a prince of good fellows." Most sketches of him by his players say the opposite.

Individually the Yankees seem to have been better than the Giants, but everybody believed the Giants won the Series by superior team play. McGraw got the credit. He signaled every pitch and governed each of his batters. It was no secret. Everybody could see his catchers and batters look for his sign after every pitch. (McGraw is said to have once managed spring training in San Antonio by cables from Havana, before he sold his share of the Oriental Park race track and gambling hell.) The Giants' "book" on Yankee hitters appeared in print after the Series, and included this entry:

* Hugh A. McQuillan (1897–1947), pitcher, ten seasons, 1918–1927, Braves, Giants, won 89, lost 94, earned-run average 3.83.
** Arthur Neukom Nehf (1892–1960), pitcher, fifteen seasons, 1915–1929, Braves, Giants, Reds, Cubs, won 182, lost 120, earned-run average 3.20.

RUTH: low on the inside, nothing fast.

During the series, Ruth saw three fast balls (off the plate) and nine curves. All his other pitches were offspeed junk. To the credit of the Giants, be it remembered, they pitched to him. He walked only twice.

McGraw's value in the Series may be doubted. There is no way a manager in the dugout can get his team to hit .309 in five games. But the play-by-play stories of the Series show no bonehead plays by the Giants. The Yankees hit a wretched .203 and made several mistakes of judgment as base runners. For their clearheaded play the Giants received $4,545.71 each, while the losing Yankees got $2,842.86 apiece.

The Yankees had a flabby alibi: they were idle for four days between the end of the season and the Series, and lost their sharpness. A short-lived rumor said John Ringling, the circus master, was going to buy the Yankees. But the only change of Yankee policy was that Barrow finally persuaded Huston and Ruppert to stop coming down to the dressing room after losing games in order to ask Huggins why they lost.

As for Babe Ruth, he felt the pains of scorn, especially the scorn of the sporting press. Hitting erratically since May, and hardly at all in the World Series, the highest-paid ballplayer seemed unfitted for his job.

30 · It Is a Healthy Life

A change in baseball's regulations initiated by Commissioner Landis allowed as many as three World Series players to go barnstorming together. Babe Ruth and Bob Meusel booked a nineteen-game tour of Western states, with Ruth getting a thousand dollars a game and Meusel eight hundred. They played as opposing members of local teams. A scoffing sportswriter said Ruth denied he would lecture after each game on "How I Made Those Two Hits in 1922's World Series."

They were rained out of their two best sites, Kansas City and Denver. Elsewhere their reception was generally warm and they had good crowds, though Ruth wasn't allowed to forget his feeble hitting in the Series. They crisscrossed Oklahoma, Iowa, Colorado, Minnesota, and Nebraska. Ruth told Huston of the tour by telephone as soon as he came back to New York. He closed the conversation with an exclamation, "The baby's fallen out of the chair!" and then hung up.

The arm that Ruth hurt in the 1921 Series was reinjured in a barnstorming game, but his physician thought it would heal in a week. He weighed 215 pounds, his playing weight during the season but he began to expand as soon as he sat down in New York.

Ruth grossed seventeen thousand dollars on his exhibition swing, otherwise it was no fun. The playing fields were sometimes three or four hundred miles apart, and the players often had to travel by car for hours from the nearest railroad over primitive graveled highways. Ruth hit twenty home runs in the seventeen games, and he pitched one game, losing it because his right fielder made six errors.

Christy Walsh set to work to organize Ruth's money. The income since 1914 may have been as much as a quarter of a million dollars. At the moment he had, perhaps, fifty thousand, including what he netted from barnstorming. The half of his 1922 salary which was reserved for payment at the end of the season went mostly to buy a farm in Massachusetts. With help from Miller Huggins, Walsh persuaded Ruth to buy an annuity and to set up an irrevocable trust fund. The annuity premiums were to come from salary, and his "literary income" would continually add to the capital of the trust fund. They bought the annuity from the great Detroit hitter Harry Heilmann. Legend says that as Heilmann pocketed Ruth's downpayment he told the new annuitant he was a lucky man, to which Ruth replied, "But *you* got my money." The first annuity policy was for fifty thousand dollars. Walsh expected the trust fund would grow to about a hundred thousand by 1929. The income was not reinvested. Walsh arranged it so that Ruth could spend it, because the steady increase in the size of the checks would make saving fun for a man obsessed with keeping score. New literary income came immediately from the publication of Babe Ruth's All-American Baseball Team, picked by Walsh and his ghosts and sold nationally by Walsh's syndicate. Local papers gave prizes to readers who sent in lists most nearly identical with Ruth's selection. The All-American Baseball Team became an annual feature.

> Babe, a kid just stopped me on the street and asked me for a dime. He wanted to make up a quarter and buy a Babe Ruth cap. Don't you think you owe something to that kid and others like him?
> —State Senator Jimmy Walker, November 13, 1922

Because of Ruth's decline in 1922 the press treated him roughly. Walsh knew that a hero created by newspapers could be destroyed by newspapers. Taken together, the sports pages made up a kind of kangaroo court. Walsh and Helen pressed Babe into publicly throwing himself on the mercy of that court. It worked. Unlike the classic poets who could only report mythology, Walsh could make a myth on purpose and call it history.

The coolly written scenario called for the remorseful muscle hero of America to give a dinner in a private room of the Elks Club for his good friends the sportswriters of New York.

Walsh gave the dinner a theme, like a school prom. It was to be down-on-the-farm, that is, the cultivation of the mythic rural virtues during a winter in the country. The chief ornament of the dining room was a nearly life-size figure of a cow. After coffee Ruth told his guests that he regretted his lawless behavior of the 1922 season. He promised to quit drinking hard liquor for a year (we know he preferred beer anyway), to spend the winter on a Massachusetts farm shoveling snow and chopping wood, and then to go to Hot Springs for a time of intensive training in order to set a new home-run record in 1923. He said that when he made a mistake tens of millions read about it, but his only possible response to their stories was to swear at them in private. To revive his character as a frank and friendly ballplayer he asked for questions, any kind of questions. They pressed him hard and he handled himself well.

Finally came Senator Jimmy Walker, loved by all present because he was the author of New York's law permitting baseball on Sunday, which went into effect in time for the 1920 season. It was near midnight by the time Walker made his unrestrained sentimental speech about Ruth's duty to the boys of America. Ruth, according to himself and able witnesses, wept. Usually one reserves this steamy sort of scene for the privacy of a family. Ruth's public remorse made him everybody's wayward boy and everybody forgave him.

On the next day he left with wife and daughter by train for Sudbury, Massachusetts.

> **I won't deny it is a little lonesome sometimes, but I like the country, and so does Mrs. Ruth. It is a healthy life and no doubt good for us.**
> **—Babe Ruth, 1923**

One might almost think of Helen Ruth as a wraith who left no footprints where she walked. She materialized briefly from time to time, but never long enough for us to get a good look at her. The Ruth family's migration to rural Massachusetts was said to have been the result of one of several reconciliations of Helen and Babe, but we have no tales of quarrels.

Their home life in New York was feverish. Ruth kept open house in a suite at the Ansonia Hotel, just as he did in his hotels when on the road. The Ruths saw crowds of friends and strangers and could not always distinguish between them. Room service wore a path in the carpet to the royal presence. The baby slept irregularly. Ruth wandered from guest to guest, drink in hand, making promises never kept, starting business deals never closed. Apparently they had lived like this ever since Ruth was in the big money, say, 1919. Helen was in the background, getting a little thicker physically, not acting but acted upon. Her husband had become a kind of public utility, like the American Telephone and Telegraph Company, but not as much regulated and much more loved. There is no evidence that he was anything but kind to her, in his own fashion, but the days when the junior Red Sox had fun together when they went bowling in couples and in privacy were long in the past.

And then came baby Dorothy at the same time as the hostility of the sportswriters. Christy Walsh had misgivings about the effect of this disfavor. Helen very willingly joined him in coaxing her husband to set up a true household for the baby outside New York.

The Ruths had lived for short spells in borrowed or rented quarters in Sudbury as early as 1920. Babe had hunted quail and rabbits in Sudbury even earlier. A few days before the sticky 1922 dinner which was part of Christy Walsh's mythmaking program, *The Times* said Ruth bought a farm in Sudbury "last spring," which can only mean he took a lease with option to buy. (He acquired the freehold in June 1923.) The Ruth place, which he named Home Plate, was at the junction of Dutton and Hudson Roads. Home Plate was 190 acres of swamp, wood, pasture, and tillable land, most of it sandy loam.

The original house was probably square. The next addition was

The squire in full grouse shooting kit at an entrance to his country seat, Home Plate, in Sudbury, Massachusetts, 1923. (*Boston Globe.*)

a shed for wood and stock food, which later became a summer kitchen. At the other side of the house some owner had added an ell with its own kitchen for the family of a married son. Behind the ells were sheds dignified by the name carriage houses, which later became garages.

Ruth now had house, land, barn, pump house, garages, ice house, and ancient henhouses which he quickly replaced. He also owned a horse, a cow, a yearling, two pigs, ninety fowls, and furniture which came with the house. We can only wonder what the furniture may have been worth; the new owner hired a man to haul it away as junk. It is difficult to fix a value for Home Plate. Ordinarily one uses tax assessments multiplied by an accepted factor, but the Ruths may have been overassessed because the previous owner was not well liked and the town assessor rated him in part by his unpopularity. Ruth's assessment remained at the earlier figure. At a guess, he bought it for twelve or fifteen thousand dollars and spent five or ten thousand to renovate, replace the poultry houses, and buy animals. That would use up most of the twenty-six thousand the Yankees held back from his pay until the end of the season. The best acreage of Home Plate would sell in 1972 for about five thousand dollars an acre.

Sportswriters saw the withdrawal to Sudbury much as Napoleon's withdrawal to Elba and drew the obvious comparisons. One of them spoke of Ruth spending the winter of 1922–1923 "buried in the snow and seclusion of a little Massachusetts hamlet." Ruth didn't see it that way at all. He was going to the country in order to get in shape for the season of 1923. And he thought of himself as a kind of landed nobleman. His friend Herb Pennock, a genuine country squire, fox-hunting fur farmer, and his teammate with the Red Sox for four years, lived the kind of manorial life that Ruth seemed to be imitating. Ruth spoke of raising fur animals, too. He also had a tailor run up a very smart shooting kit, suitable for King George V in grouse-shooting time, and he posed in it for the *Boston Globe* photographer at the front door of Home Plate. It was a little fancy for your average middle-class American out after rabbits.

Babe and Helen refurnished the house, and Babe decorated it by nailing baseball souvenirs to the walls. They put up the new chicken house and stocked it with a thousand hens, most of which died at an epidemic rate. They had a boat and a shack for fishing gear at the nearby pond. Many noisy friends visited them and stayed up later than the sharp-eared neighbors. Babe intended to lose weight by chopping wood, a very good exercise for a batter, but Forrest D. Bradshaw, town historian of Sudbury who knew the Ruths, believes the wood Ruth chopped was more valuable for publicity than for

The house on Ruth's farm in Sudbury, Massachusetts. He called it Home Plate. (*Boston Globe.*)

heat. All the wood Ruth chopped could have been burned in a day or two. The farming operation was a flat failure, but it fooled some who should have known better. The *Country Gentleman* printed a piece on the subject which included this estimate: "Ruth's farm is not a play-thing, but a real farm. His stock is not fancy stock, but good dollar-earning stuff."

Babe Ruth was born near downtown Baltimore, one step above the poorest folk of the Baltimore slums. He knew nothing about country life; Grantland Rice said he called all flowers daisies. Home Plate could not be his true home. Except in the most countrified places he visited in spring training and while barnstorming, he never saw a farm animal unless through the windows of a Pullman car. He was a rootless man of the wardrobe-trunk culture. Like circus artists and touring actors, he lived his life in railroad cars and hotels, and it suited him well. We must sadly suppose the whole Sudbury venture was a short-lived victory of shadowy Helen Ruth, trying hard to live what she would think of as a normal life with husband and child. With a husband who had rarely been out of earshot of a city's hum, she may have chosen the worst possible site for the battle.

A girl that seemed to be lost.
—Forrest D. Bradshaw

The withdrawal to Sudbury gave the Ruths a smaller but more observant group of neighbors. Surviving acquaintances of the Ruths in Sudbury give the elements of a sketch of their life together.

Helen had auburn hair, was about five feet, six inches tall, and weighed about 130 pounds. Neighbors thought her attractive but would not call her beautiful. Catholics and Democrats were rare in Sudbury then so people remembered that Helen was both. She had a serious and brooding air, even tragic. The town historian of Sudbury, who knew her slightly, told the author she was "a girl that seemed to be lost." Rarely was she in Ruth's company among strangers, and, if she were, she as rarely spoke. A neighbor thought she seemed a little fearful of her husband. Usually when she came to the town center she came by chauffeur-driven car. Nobody saw her drive. She was pleasant in her dealings with townspeople. One of them told the author she seemed to be "married to someone that she had to live with and had to be at his beck and call. . . . She acted more like a servant or a slave than a wife. I don't know that Babe would have known how to treat a wife."

Babe left an impression of empty-minded frivolity. They still talk of his driving spikes in his walls to support souvenir baseballs, bats, and gloves, as though his rather elegant house was a cheaply built fishing lodge. He once asked the storekeeper to fill his car's gasoline tank, and let the puzzled man pump and pump with the old-fashioned hand crank until the tank took forty-eight gallons. He wouldn't tell where the fuel went. The explanation, from a third party, was that "Babe didn't want to have to stop for gas when he headed for New York, so he had a special gas tank that held about fifty-five gallons installed." One of the store windows of Sudbury had a heap of goods that seemed unsalable because shopworn, unlabeled, unacceptably exotic (as, pickled onions for martinis). Above was a sign: "10¢ each." Babe was delighted at the sight and bought about sixty dollars' worth.

About the only part of his country life that he took seriously was fishing through the ice at the nearby pond. He went at it as if it were a contest he must win, and he usually won.

Any irritation Babe showed was quick to rise and quick to pass. Boredom was his curse, and his attention frequently wandered, except when fishing. There is no surviving local tradition of Babe as a drinker. In dealing with people he was open and blunt, though he showed a suspicion that the local tradesmen had plans to take his money. He made Sudbury friends slowly but firmly; he got along most easily with the younger people. As everywhere, he liked to show off his great strength. Local politics and village life interested him not at all.

The Ruth household numbered five: Babe, Helen, Dorothy, Dorothy's nurse Fanny, and the chauffeur whose name is not recalled. The chauffeur did much of the shopping. Babe thought he spent too much and arranged with tradespeople to put a ceiling on the chauffeur's spending. Babe, on the other hand, indulged himself rather crudely. A local meat-seller described his shopping:

> Babe would come in and order two slices of top-of-the-round steak cut about three inches thick. These were for him. He would then order a pound or a pound and a half of hamburg [sic] for his wife and chauffeur.

Babe paid his bills promptly, sometimes complaining about what Helen and the chauffeur spent. He didn't like to wait his turn in a store but usually did unless he rushed in and said he was in a hurry. Then a storekeeper would ask other customers to wait a few minutes, "which they were glad to do just to tell the folks at home that Babe was in [the] store."

Helen did the housework and Babe answered the door when unexpected callers knocked; at least one such caller, collecting for a charity, got little and felt unwelcome. They "used to have great parties out here," both in the house and in the fishing camp by the pond. The guests were always strangers to Sudbury.

For no known reason, Babe thought the chauffeur was too attentive to Helen, not as a jealous husband but as a chief of the clan who wishes no one else to give orders.

The Ruths kept Home Plate for several years, but, as time passed, Babe's stays were shorter and Helen's longer.

Outside the Park, 1923

NEW YEAR IN WITH
MANY RUM RAIDS
AND MUCH SHOOTING

SOCIETY WELCOMES
MORE DEBUTANTES

KILL SIX IN FLORIDA;
BURN NEGRO HOUSES

TUTANKHAMEN TOMB
DAZZLES EGYPTIANS

12 SAILORS BATTLE
2 BROOKLYN POLICE

MADE HER LIVE ON $10 A WEEK;
COURT ORDERS MAN TO TRY IT

FRENCH FLIER BREAKS WORLD'S SPEED RECORD
IN FLIGHT AT MORE THAN 234 MILES AN HOUR

DENTIST SAYS WIFE
PUT HIM IN CELLAR

OVER NIGHT AIRSHIPS TO CHICAGO

BITES HIS WIFE AND SON

BOMB IRISH REBELS
IN SEASIDE CAVE

BOUND BROOK MOB
RAIDS KLAN MEETING

DRUG PROBLEM DISCUSSED

PRESIDENT HARDING DIES SUDDENLY

HITLER STORMS AT FOES

31 · Otherwise a Routine Spring (1923)

I have yet to hear a fan boo a home run.
—Sam Breadon, owner, St. Louis Cardinals

The shock of the home-run storm was wearing off in 1922 and 1923. Those who didn't like so many home runs began to speak out. John McGraw said, "The public does not like the lively ball. . . ." American League owners asked for a minimum distance requirement, say, three hundred feet. A *Times* writer joined the chorus with the remark "The home run is being overdone," and the *Boston Post* called home runs monotonous.

What was troubling the American League owners? Probably two facts. In the seasons of 1920, 1921, and 1922 the Yankees hit almost a fourth of all American League home runs, and Babe Ruth alone hit more than a tenth of the League's total. We may believe the movement to curb home runs was a movement to curb Ruth and the pennant-winning Yankees.

Commissioner Landis was in New York late in January 1923, as he put it, "eating his way" through the eastern banquet circuit. When asked about the alleged plague of home runs he merely pointed to the steady rise in attendance. As for fixing a kind of home-run zone in each park, he believed it would make the umpires' work too hard. The National League showed no interest in the proposal, and it died.

Ruth is a man of many infections.
—*The Times*, January 18, 1923

Babe and Helen Ruth came to New York by rail on January 16 for medical attention to the ring finger of Babe's left hand. Dr. Edward King lanced, cleaned, and dressed the finger at St. Vincent's Hospital on the 17th, and Babe went back alone to Sudbury where infant Dorothy had stayed "to watch over the place. . . ." Helen remained in New York for a few days.

Babe Ruth had become a regular surgical customer at St. Vincent's. From August 1920 to January 1923 he was operated on at St. Vincent's six times, once to have tonsils and adenoids out, and five times for infections of arm, leg, or finger.

He came back to New York a week after the finger dressing for an opinion on its condition. T. L. Huston, co-owner of the Yankees, said he was very pleased with Ruth's appearance, ". . . not exactly sylphlike and willowy, but he looks as if he was down to playing weight." Ruth stayed in New York at the Ansonia Hotel (Helen had gone back to Sudbury) until he left for Hot Springs on February 15 to join five other Yankees who planned to play golf and take the waters until spring training began in New Orleans on March 6.

In a week of Arkansas workouts Ruth reduced his weight to less than 210 pounds, his lightest since 1918. But from that day the Hot Springs venture was a total loss. On March 2, after thirty-six holes of golf, he was taken ill with influenza, his temperature rising to 104 degrees. He was in bed, too weak to sit, and cheered only by a stream of telegrams trying to confirm "a rumor that he was dead." He was up and about within the week, but the illness delayed his wobbly arrival at New Orleans by two days.

There were some new Yankees in the Grunwald Hotel in New Orleans. One was Benny Bengough* who would be around as a second-string catcher for the next several years, and who coined the nickname "Jidge" for Ruth, a frivolous contraction of George. Opposing players remained satisfied with The Big Monk or Monkey or Baboon, but his best friends called him Jidge for years. Bengough was one of several who later said Ruth liked to impress marginal players by showing his biweekly check for $2,166.66 (which was half his pay, the rest coming at season's end).

The Yankees also had more Red Sox plunder. The new specimen was Herb Pennock, a tall, spare, thin-faced, left-hander. He is still remembered for the grace of his pitching motion and for his durability. Although he was a self-contained and reserved man, he had liked Ruth since they played for Boston together. The life of this landed fox hunter and flower grower from the best prep schools illustrates a point about American sport in its social setting. Men born to Pennock's status who have great skill at team games can't find worthy competition as amateurs, since the best amateur teams can't play on even terms against even passable professionals. Because Pennock had a fierce passion for baseball he became a professional, pitched for twenty-two years, and entered the Base-

* Bernard Oliver Bengough (1898–1968), catcher, ten seasons, 1923–1932, Yankees, Browns, batting average .255.

ball Hall of Fame. In another time and place he might well have played amateur cricket for England and be remembered as one of the greatest of bowlers.

Pitcher George Pipgras* also joined the Yankees that spring but went back to the minors in two years; later he would be important to the Yankee pitching staff.

From mid-December 1922 until the following June the newspapers talked of a big New York–Chicago deal aimed at getting Eddie Collins away from the White Sox for as little as possible, but in the end the Yankees got a thirty-three-year-old utility infielder for cash.

> Ruth ought to have a better year.
> —Miller Huggins, April 15, 1923

Ruth, T. L. Huston, and infielder Mike McNally arrived at New Orleans together on March 8, to be met by Helen and Dorothy Ruth. Babe weighed only 202 pounds. He never weighed as little again at any time when he was not seriously ill. During the next several weeks he lived a regular life which proved that Xaverian Brother George was back in control. Apparently Jimmy Walker's mawkish speech had exorcised the waterfront slob. The Yankees used the ball park daily until the Pelicans took it over at one o'clock. After lunch the Yankee golfers, Ruth included, played their tricky game until dinner. Their general manager, Ed Barrow, said they were wasting strength. He may have thought his Yankees were disgracing him at what he would think of as a sissy game.

Once in shape the Yankees began to play a fifteen-game exhibition series with Brooklyn on their joint way home to New York. Ruth, as was usual in the spring, was running out of pocket money. This was probably the occasion when he borrowed fifteen hundred dollars from Waite Hoyt and Joe Dugan. He paid them back at the first April payday, with what he called 6 percent interest, that is, 6 percent of the whole, though he had the money only for a few weeks. They protested, but he had his way.

Ruth was short of something more important to him than money: base hits. He was in a real batting slump. One night on the road in the dimmed Pullman, Miller Huggins talked to him solemnly. Huggins said the falling off in 1922 may not have been a freakish thing; perhaps Ruth, at twenty-eight, was finished. This idea shook Ruth and stirred him to a serious effort to prove Huggins's theory wrong.

---

* George William Pipgras (1899–   ), pitcher, eleven seasons, 1923–1935, Yankees, Red Sox, won 102, lost 73, earned-run average 4.09. Tied with Ruth (among others) for first in percentage of World Series wins, at 3–0.

Otherwise it was a routine spring series. Ruth began to hit. Crowds in many brushy parks were so large that people were allowed to stand along the foul lines, which disturbed Ruth who feared he might pull a foul over first base and kill somebody. At Vicksburg he went seven miles with a stranger to spend an hour talking with a sick boy who idolized him. The troupe reached New York on April 8. The Yankees had won seven games, Brooklyn five. They resumed the series at Ebbets Field on the 14th, the Yankees winning 15–2. Ruth played right field and first base. In six times at bat he had a double and four singles. Perhaps he *wasn't* finished. Even Huggins said he thought Ruth would do more than in 1922. Two days later Connie Mack predicted that the American League race would be between the Yankees and the Tigers.

> **The whole thing is absurd. Mr. Ruth told me all about the case as soon as he learned of it. I am glad he is going into court and fight the case.**
> **—Helen Ruth, March 15, 1923**

Outside the Elks Club room on the night Christy Walsh staged the Cow Dinner of November 13, 1922, a man had thrust a paper into Ruth's hand. It was a legal document notifying him of a suit for fifty thousand dollars filed against him by one Barbara V. Escoe, as guardian of a minor, a Dolores Dixon, who claimed that Ruth was the father of her child.

Ruth's lawyer, Hyman Bushel, told the court Ruth would appear. Counsel for Escoe and Dixon filed his clients' detailed complaint while Ruth was in Hot Springs. Ruth did no more until March when, in New Orleans, he denied he ever saw the girl. Meanwhile the plaintiffs—as their lawyer later admitted—had been waiting for an out-of-court settlement. Bushel told reporters Ruth wished no secrecy.

Dolores Dixon's story was that she had done a lot of automobiling with Ruth in the summer of 1922, as often as four or five times a week, that she had met Ruth when she was working as a salesgirl in a department store, and that Mrs. Ruth knew her. Ruth replied, "It's blackmail!" (He meant extortion.) The girl appeared in court on March 16 and testified that Ruth had promised marriage, was guilty of statutory rape, and had fathered her child. The defendant, still in New Orleans, filed an answer through Bushel denying everything. There followed a six-week delay while Bushel organized a defense.

Apparently he also organized some research into the way of life of Escoe and Dixon. Late in April he moved to call a witness named Robert McChesney who, Bushel explained, would testify that the accusation was a "malicious conspiracy between the plaintiff and certain other persons."

Bushel was ready to produce McChesney on April 27, but before McChesney arrived that day the Escoes' lawyer withdrew the case "without cost to either party." Bushel was not surprised. He had talked with Dolores Dixon who admitted the suit was a scheme to extort money from Ruth. And it turned out that "Dolores Dixon" was a false name assumed by a girl never heard of before or since.

Some ballplayers have had to dodge predatory women as song-birds dodge hawks. Before Ruth's escape, Chick Stahl* committed suicide after harassment by a woman who claimed to be his pregnant wife, and Rube Oldring** of the Athletics was the object of a woman who claimed to be his wife, apparently trying to get his World Series money. For a time she had most of Boston believing Oldring wronged her.

Ruth came off well. The defense had offered no testimony. The name of its witness was alone enough to make the plaintiffs flee from litigation. Bushel gave the facts to Ferdinand Pecora, the District Attorney, who did not choose to prosecute.

But Babe Ruth did have some real legal trouble at the same time in another court. He paid a judgment of $583 for ramming a stranger's car at the corner of 86th Street and Broadway in the days after the World Series of 1922. That year 1922 had been a year when month followed month with woe.

Yankee Stadium was a mistake. Not mine but the Giants'.
—Jacob Ruppert

The election of Al Smith as Governor of New York in 1918 was a victory for Sunday baseball, which became legal in New York in time for the 1920 season. It probably swelled the potential market for baseball in New York by a third. Yankee attendance grew by two-thirds in 1920, and we may suppose that half the increase was because of Sunday baseball and half because of the excitement stirred by Ruth and company. Sunday baseball deserves part of the credit for the building of Yankee Stadium, though it may be going too far to call it The House That Sunday Baseball Built.

When Jacob Ruppert and T. L. Huston bought the Yankees, and for years after, the Giants were New York's darlings. Ruppert and Huston believed they would get a lease on the Polo Grounds in a form that would give them half the rights to its use, but in 1919

---

* Charles Sylvester Stahl (1873–1907), outfielder, ten seasons, 1897–1906, Braves, Red Sox, batting average .305.
** Reuben Henry Oldring (1884–1961), utility, thirteen seasons, 1905–1918, Yankees, Athletics, batting average .270.

Charles A. Stoneham bought a majority interest in the Giants and told the Yankees they could have only one-year leases as his tenants, at a hundred thousand dollars a year. Ruppert countered with an offer to put up half the value of the Polo Grounds, junk the structure, and join Stoneham in building an all-sports pleasure palace seating a hundred thousand people. Stoneham unwisely turned him down.

Legend says the Giants put the Yankees out in the street. Not so. Stoneham wished to have them as annual tenants at a rent he would fix. Ban Johnson, president of the American League, hoped Stoneham would evict Ruppert and Huston because they had gone to court to overturn one of Johnson's official rulings. Johnson intended to reclaim the franchise on the ground that the team lacked a playing field, then let Stoneham select a softer set of Yankee owners. That was folly. Ruppert, richest of owners, was unbeatable in that kind of scrimmage. He already had a vacant square block ready for such emergency, and planned, if necessary, to build a stand seating fifteen hundred which would give him a park to meet the League test (and where every ordinary fly would be a home run).

When Stoneham showed no interest in sharing permanent rights with the Yankees, Ruppert told him he would announce building plans if the Giants and Yankees had reached no understanding by a set date. When Stoneham was silent, the Yankees, on February 5, 1921, told the world they would build Yankee Stadium, as they named it from the first.

Stoneham may have been blind with jealousy. Before Ruth and Sunday baseball helped the Yankees they never drew more than six hundred thousand. Attendance in 1920 was more than a million. To look ahead a bit, the Giants won four straight pennants beginning in 1921, but the Yankees outdrew them, and most reporters who covered the Giants were reassigned to cover the Yankees.

> . . . the new playing field of Babe Ruth and his pals.
> —*The Times*, February 6, 1921

Ruppert took up an option on a parcel of land owned by the Astor Estate without consulting Huston, who didn't think much of the idea. Nevertheless Huston went along, and his engineering advice was valuable. It was an excellent site in the days before America reorganized its life around the automobile. It is sixteen minutes by subway from 42nd Street. Almost every rapid transit line went there or had a good connection leading to the place.

The builders intended Yankee Stadium to seat seventy-five or eighty thousand and to cost about two million dollars. The job was done in 284 working days in time for the season of 1923. Throngs of sightseers at the Stadium in March once reached a high of ten thousand on one day. They seemed most impressed by the great scoreboard in center field, made to show the course of all games in both leagues, with scores by innings and batteries at work. Before going to Hot Springs Ruth dropped in to hit a few but did not put one over the fence.

The Stadium in 1923 differed from its present form in a few ways. The outfield was surrounded by forty thousand square feet of wooden bleacher seats at about the present level. Part of the concrete grandstand along the third-base line had only the lower deck. (The upper decks were added after the season.) In 1923 no part of the grandstand curved into fair territory. One aim of the planners was to have better natural lighting than the Polo Grounds. The architects' preliminary drawings show the entire playing field enclosed by a three-deck stand, but it has not been done because it would lessen the daylight on the playing field.

Beneath the grandstand was an office building, a restaurant with several branches, and the clubhouses. Nearly everyone interested in baseball has seen the interior of the stands, if only on television. Some idea of the size of the Stadium can be had by noticing the scalloped ornamental frieze that hangs below the top of the grandstand: it is sixteen feet from top to bottom. The playing field has short foul lines to low fences, but left field deepens to 444 feet, and center field has an extreme depth of 461 feet.

Americans are like Romans in that smallness and delicate proportions appeal only to a few; most of them like bigness, magnificence, weight, and space. They have good taste in such matters. The voice of the republic is not a pontifical blessing from a high window or the cry of an imperial herald in a palace court. It is the voice of a crowd, best heard in its spontaneity in a ball park. Yankee Stadium suits the people. So does the World Series. So did Babe Ruth.

> On the whole it looks as if the shift to his new surroundings will be the least handicap Ruth will have to overcome if he hopes to surpass his present record of fifty-nine home runs for one season.
>
> —*The Times*, February 5, 1923

In the seasons of 1920, 1921, and 1922 Babe Ruth hit 148 home runs. Although the Polo Grounds had short foul lines, he hit only sixty-nine in his home park. It would seem that the shape of a playing field made little difference to him. But Dr. David Hewson of Oregon State University, who has looked long into the mechanics of home runs, figured that Ruth's slugging percentage in the home games of 1920 was an almost unbelievable .980. Hewson concluded: "If he had continued to play in the Polo Grounds, he surely would have hit more than 800 home runs."

Yankee Stadium was the first new park since the Braves opened theirs in 1915. Excepting the two in St. Louis, every major-league team now had its own ball park. The Giants added seats to the Polo Grounds while Yankee Stadium was being built, so the two New York teams had together a seating capacity of 119,000. Altogether, if schedules coincided to put all the teams in the largest parks, 265,000 people could watch big-league baseball at one time.

32 · The Peak Year

The House That Ruth Built
—Fred Lieb, April 18, 1923

On the American League's opening day in New York in 1923 the weather was cloudy, with temperatures in the forties. The gates of the new Yankee Stadium had to be closed half an hour before game time, and twenty-five thousand people were turned away. Of those who got in, a good many preferred to stand under the roof, three deep behind the seats in all three tiers, rather than sit in the uncovered bleachers. Photographers swarmed on the field before the game to record it all, including a pose of Ruth and the Yankee mascot, Ray Kelly. John Philip Sousa's band played before the game and for the flag raising. After the American flag reached the top of the staff, the 1922 pennant followed to the noisy joy of the crowd. Governor Al Smith then threw out the first ball.

Babe Ruth's hitting and Bob Shawkey's pitching won the game. The visiting Red Sox made just three hits. Ruth had a hit and a run in two times at bat. The hit was the first home run in the Stadium and scored the three runs that gave the margin of victory. (Ruth also made the only Yankee error.) Some of the fans ran out on the playing field to shake Ruth's hand before the game ended, which caused delay until the field could be cleared. They surged out again after the last out, making it hard for some of the Yankees to get to their clubhouse.

The standard line score shows the course of the game very well:

```
Boston        000  000  100—1   3   1
New York      004  000  00x—4   7   1
    Ehmke (8), Fullerton and DeVormer
    Shawkey and Schang
```

In his story of the game for the *Evening Telegram* Fred Lieb referred to the Stadium as The House That Ruth Built, and so it has been tagged ever since.

Edward G. Barrow, the Yankee general manager, toyed with the truth about the opening day's attendance. He gave out the figure 74,217, which reporters took without question and relayed to an interested world. They were properly annoyed when the truth came out in May at the time of a Milk Fund benefit boxing show. On Yankee advice the Milk Fund promoters put ten thousand temporary seats on the field and had 70,228 tickets printed for the whole capacity. Plainly, there could not have been many more than sixty thousand baseball seats. In its year-end summary of sports *The Times* gave the opening-day figure as seventy thousand, which made it the sixth largest crowd ever to pay its way to see a sporting event, and the largest baseball crowd ever.

Few watched a rival ball game in New York on the day Yankee

On the opening day of Yankee Stadium in 1923 Babe Ruth posed with the Yankee mascot, Ray Kelly. (*The Bettmann Archive.*)

Stadium opened. A young pitcher who batted third in his team's lineup made two hits, walked five, struck out seventeen, but lost his game for Columbia University, 5–1. The losing pitcher was Lou Gehrig.*

Despite his unsatisfactory 1922 season Ruth's popularity in early 1923 was as high as ever. The Lawyers Committee of the 1923 Salvation Army fund drive, headed by Fiorello H. LaGuardia, pledged three thousand dollars and promised to add another thousand for each home run Ruth hit in May. If they kept their promise, it cost them another nine thousand dollars.

Fan mail cluttered Ruth's clubhouse locker. He usually threw it on the floor. The trainer opened those letters which seemed to be from businessmen, and the players opened the rest, most of which were from women, often uninhibited ones. Once Ruth tore his mail to scraps. The trainer pieced together the business mail and found tatters of checks for endorsements and royalties totaling six thousand dollars.

In May Ruth unwittingly humbled his insurance man and friend, Harry Heilmann, the great Detroit outfielder. When Heilmann hit the longest home run in Detroit to that time, a grateful management commemorated it by putting a marker where it landed. The next day Ruth came to town and hit one fifteen feet farther. Heilmann's marker disappeared overnight.

> **I don't know what hotel you're at, so I'm sending this note.**
> **Will you have dinner with me this evening?**
> **—Babe Ruth to Claire Hodgson, May 1923**

Claire Hodgson, with her daughter Julia and her maid, came to New York from Georgia in 1920 to make a new start after an unwise girlhood marriage. Through mutual family friends she got a job as a model for Howard Chandler Christy, who watched over her small household like a father. She also posed for other popular illustrators and earned a modestly comfortable living. Her husband died flat broke in Georgia in 1922. When her father died in 1923 her mother and two brothers came to resettle the clan in New York.

Through Christy, Claire met Sigmund Romberg, and through Romberg she got a small part in *The Dew Drop Inn* which opened in Washington in May. The star was Jim Barton, a friend of Ruth's. When the Yankees came to Washington in the last week of May, Barton took Claire and her roommate to a ball game. Claire knew Ty Cobb and liked baseball for itself.

At the park Ruth came over to talk briefly with Barton who intro-

---

* Henry Louis Gehrig (1903–1941), first baseman, seventeen seasons, 1923–1939, Yankees, batting average .340. Hall of Fame.

duced him to the girls. The meeting was perfunctory. Claire had an impression of a sweaty face, a rough friendly voice, a gift for boyish small talk, a fat face, the beginning of a paunch, and legs like the legs of a chorus girl. He seemed of no particular interest, and showed none in her.

That evening Eddie Bennett, the Yankees' lucky bat boy (ten years, three clubs, eight pennants), brought a note to her at the theater. It was Ruth's invitation to dinner written in his graceful script. Claire wrote back accepting, provided she could bring a girlfriend. Soon Ruth was on the phone, approving the terms in a voice that "boomed." He gave her his suite number. Rather frigidly Claire suggested a restaurant. But, as he told her, he had to avoid restaurants to avoid mobbing. She needn't worry, he added, because his place would be full of people. "It always is."

At dinner he talked gloomily of that rotten year 1922. Gradually the suite became like the royal chambers of a Bourbon king, with a crowd attending on Ruth's dinner. He never left his chair. There was always a glass in his hand and somebody to fill it again. Claire told him he drank too much, which, he said, made her sound like Miller Huggins. As she left he said Huggins and sportswriters had told him to quit drinking but "you're the first dame who ever told me." On her way home Claire wondered just what the dames had been telling him.

Later Ruth saw her when the team and the show returned to New York. After the Yankees went on the road he phoned her frequently. That summer he spent much time with Claire, her mother Julia, and the brothers. By this time they were what used to be called serious. Marriage? He said no. He could not divorce Helen because he was a Catholic.

Their life was very private. He took the idolatry of American boys very seriously and wished to keep it. But in New York when he wasn't in his hotel he was at Claire's, amusing her mother, playing with Julia, arranging fishing trips with the brothers. Claire's household couldn't even display a photograph of him for fear a visitor would see it and talk. The sportswriters knew of the romance but never wrote a word. Whenever divorce and remarriage came up, the answer was the same: I'm married, I've got a kid, I'm Catholic.

Meanwhile, Helen and Dorothy Ruth were living alone at Home Plate in Massachusetts. Fablemakers have cast Helen in the role of banished queen. Nobody concerned left a written record of the matter, so we can only judge by events: Dorothy came to live with Babe and Helen Ruth. The Ruth royal chambers made a crowded, rackety, smoky home for an infant. Christy Walsh and Helen persuaded Babe to move to the country. Helen and Dorothy stayed there in 1923 except for Helen's brief visit to New York, and Helen and Dorothy's trip to New Orleans for spring training. Ruth was alone through the season of 1923. That arrangement seems to have been Helen's idea of what was best for Dorothy.

> I wouldn't go through the years from 1919 to 1923 again
> for all the money in the world.
> —Miller Huggins, 1923

Jacob Ruppert and T. L. Huston agreed to buy the Yankees in 1915 but did not agree wholeheartedly on anything important afterward. Each was a willful man, and they were often at odds. Ruppert had the stronger will and usually won out, because Huston wished to be liked and Ruppert didn't care for personal popularity in sporting circles. The two of them, by 1923, had spent more to build their ball club than any other owners.

Huston blamed Huggins for the loss of the 1922 Series. After the fifth and final game he told reporters, "Miller Huggins has managed the Yankees for the last time." That made Ruppert bristle. From that moment Ruppert worked to buy Huston's interest in the team. His first step was to tell the world that Huggins's job was safe. Those who knew the Yankees well began to say that any anti-Huggins people in the Yankee group would be leaving. Ruppert helped the prophets by saying the Yankees had some rebuilding to do and would trade any man.

REPORTER. Does that go for Babe Ruth?
RUPPERT. We'll trade any man on the team if it can strengthen the team.

Huston had his own press. When a writer publicly asked him a loaded question, to wit: since a manager is 40 percent of a team—a preposterous proportion!—how could the Yankees with Miller Huggins ever hope to win a World Series from John McGraw? Huston let the innuendo stand without rebuff.

In January 1923 Huston and Ruppert were near a sale agreement. The chief block was Ruppert's wish to bind Huston not to buy another club. Other owners enjoyed the Yankee split, hoping it would weaken the team. Huston began to entertain bids from all who wished to make offers. Finally, in May, the two came to terms. They closed the deal on June 1st (when the Yankees had an eight-game lead over the pack).

Ruppert met the best offer Huston had from outside—$1,250,000. Each had put up $225,000 to buy his half of the club in 1915. Now Ruppert owned it all at a total price of $1,475,000. Sunday baseball, Babe Ruth, and two pennants had raised the value of the Yankees.

Ruppert then let Barrow buy what Ruppert called a 10 percent interest in the Yankees for $300,000, which the general manager borrowed from concessionaire Harry Stevens. The Yankees sold for ten million in the 1970s; considering the depreciation of the dollar, the value of the club hasn't increased in fifty years even though New York has but two teams now instead of three.

Despite a rumor that Huston would buy the Red Sox, he said he was leaving baseball. That year he was the national commander of the Veterans of Foreign Wars and believed the office was worth his whole attention. He also felt his energy was lessening: "I'm old and tired. The Yankees are a good team and the Stadium is nearly finished. It looks as if my work is about done." Huston was Ruth's best (and only) friend in the Yankee front office. Their temperaments harmonized. Photographs of the two show that Huston, like Ruth, was hooked on the pleasures of the table. The scene in the Hot Springs bathhouse where they flipped the coin for the extra two thousand dollars a year showed how much alike they were.

When Huston signed away his share of the franchise the Yankees were in Chicago, where they received a telegram:

I AM NOW THE SOLE OWNER OF THE YANKEES. MILLER HUGGINS IS
MY MANAGER.

JACOB RUPPERT

Peace descended on Huggins. He now had undivided rule, and he became a better manager than when he had two masters, one of whom was hostile. It didn't, however, take away that certain meanness from his character. From 1919 to 1923 he developed calluses on his soul. With Ruppert's backing he was free to be tough and decisive.

Ruppert showed pride in his gang of peons. He immediately bought two extra sets of uniforms so the Yankees—against all baseball tradition—could start every game clean and sweet-smelling. For the rest of Ruppert's life they were the best-dressed team in the game.

[Gehrig is] the best college player since George Sisler.
—*The Times*, June 12, 1923

Things went so smoothly for the league-leading Yankees in June that the most stirring team news of the month came as a result of Paul Krichell's scouting:

YANKS SIGN GEHRIG,
COLUMBIA SLUGGER

The twenty-three-year-old recruit stood five feet, ten and a half inches and weighed 210 pounds. He was the most powerful hitter ever seen at Columbia; at the moment he was batting .440 with seven home runs. As a pitcher he had won six and lost three.

As for the most powerful hitter ever seen anywhere, Ruth was batting .355 (seventh in the league) with thirteen home runs and forty-seven runs scored. He was also getting an irksome number of bases on balls. For example, he had four intentional walks in a game at Cleveland on June 16.

Late in the month Ruth caused a flurry of alarm for his health. The Yankees scheduled an exhibition at New Haven on Sunday, June 24. Ruth missed the train and tried to get to New Haven by

Claire Hodgson as she appeared in "The Magic Melody" at the Shubert Crescent Theater in the early 1920s. (*National Baseball Library, Cooperstown, New York.*)

car before game time. When he failed to arrive the New Haven management had to refund about a thousand dollars. A telephone call to Home Plate roused only the caretaker who said Mr. Ruth hurt his foot, and then hung up. What the caretaker had in mind we can't know, but the fact—according to Ruth—was that he ran into heavy Sunday traffic which slowed him until it was too late to go on to New Haven. Huggins was grimly angry, but when the Yankees won over the Red Sox the next day, 14–3, with Ruth getting two hits in four times at bat and scoring two runs, it was hard to stay angry.

By July the Yankee success was lowering attendance all over the league. After seventy-five games Ruth was batting .378, second only to Heilmann who had .400. That month Ruth and Hoyt severed relations in a one-sided quarrel which was to last two years. Hoyt pitched the third game of a four-game series in Washington, the last series of a road trip. Huggins gave Hoyt permission to return to New York a day early. When the team reassembled Carl Mays told Hoyt, "Babe says not to talk to him any more." Ruth had taken Hoyt's early leaving as a personal affront. Since Hoyt refused to defer to the king, Ruth cut him off the list of loyal subjects.

About the same time, Huggins proved himself as small as Ruth and ten times as cruel. The manager wanted to send Mays to the minors after his so-so season of 1922 but could not get waivers. He nursed his grudge against Mays until it took fire. In Cleveland on July 17 he kept Mays in the game although Mays gave up twenty hits and thirteen runs, while rested Yankee pitchers sat and watched. His aim was the public shaming of Mays. Everett Scott and Wally Pipp refused to finish the game, as a way of protesting the treatment of Mays.*

In August all days were sunny. After the 111th game Ruth was batting .401. But perfection bores some people. The blasé *Herald-Tribune* ventured to speak for everybody: "The fans are tiring of long-drawn-out games with top-heavy scores, and those who are dyed-in-the-wool lovers of the game want something done to steer baseball toward better pitching." Because of more hits and more runs the games *were* longer, but the fans who objected the most were the writers in the press box, yearning for their dinners. *The Times* replied indirectly a week later with a sketch of Ruth's place in the game: "He is admittedly the greatest attraction at the gate that the game has ever known." The Yankees could hit, run, and field. Their pitching was so good that the six first-stringers were called "The Six Star Final."

In August Harry Frazee sold the gutted Red Sox. The Yankees

---

* Huggins was able to get American League waivers and Mays went to Cincinnati in 1924. He won 20 and lost 9 for the Reds, pitching fifteen complete games (two shutouts) with an earned-run average of 3.15.

were truly the Red Sox alumni association, with eleven former Red Sox players on the roster—five pitchers, a catcher, three infielders, and two outfielders. Frazee got more than a million dollars for what was left, which was probably more than it was worth.

Breezing through September the Yankees made certain of the pennant on the 20th, beating the Browns in St. Louis, 4–3. The club led the league by eighteen games. On the train after the game Ruth started what became the traditional form of Yankee pennant celebration by organizing a few players to go through the team's cars and rip the shirts off everyone's backs.

About ten days later Ruth turned his ankle while getting off a train in Boston, but on October 3 despite a limp, he put on an ill-fitting Giant uniform and played five innings of a benefit game at the Polo Grounds, batting against a minor-league pitcher whose nickname was Lefty and whose surname appeared in the New York papers as "Groves." In the fifth inning Ruth hit one all the way out of the park, the first time it had been done since he moved to Yankee Stadium. (The ankle healed before the first game of the Series on October 10.) Ruth completed his 1923 home-run total by hitting number forty-one on October 7. He had twenty-two on the road and nineteen at home.

> **Championship baseball teams are not founded on bats. They're built on a backbone of catching, pitching, a second-base combination and a center fielder.**
>
> **—Carl Mays**

In the twentieth century only three teams before 1923 had won pennants by wider margins than the Yankees' sixteen-game lead over Detroit.* The superiority of the Yankees was a team superiority. They gave up the fewest runs, their pitchers led the league in complete games, in strikeouts, and in earned-run average. Their fielders made the fewest errors by far and had much the best fielding average. Aaron Ward at second, Scott at shortstop, Joe Dugan at third, and Whitey Witt in center each led the American League in fielding at his position.

> **As Ruth goes, so go the Yankees.**
> **—The Times, 1923**

The American League race of 1923 was so lopsided it cut attendance to two hundred thousand less than in 1922, though business conditions were generally better. The Giants' attendance was also

---

* Pirates, 1903; Cubs, 1906, 1907.

Wearing a traveling uniform, and
in good trim, in the early 1920's.
(*National Baseball Library, Cooperstown, New York.*)

down 13 percent, perhaps owing to the attraction of the new Yankee
Stadium.

The baseball writers unanimously voted Babe Ruth the Most
Valuable Player. It was the first unanimous choice since Ty Cobb's
vote in 1911.

Ruth set a record for bases on balls, 170, which still stands.
Scorers did not tabulate intentional bases on balls until 1955; the
record since then is forty-five. Ruth, by careful unofficial count, got
eighty in 1923. He was safe on base more than half the times he
went to the plate. That astonishing record still stands (54.4
percent).

His final batting average was .393, second to Heilmann's .403. In addition to walks, Ruth led the American League in slugging percentage, home runs, total bases, runs batted in, runs scored, and proportion of home runs to times at bat. And nobody in the National League came near his figures except in home runs; Cy Williams* tied Ruth's forty-one. Although Ruth ranked only third in doubles in the American League, his forty-five were more than any hitter made in the National League.

There has been a long debate whether the seasons of 1920, 1921, or 1927 were Ruth's best. *He* believed 1923 was the peak year.

THE ACCUMULATED BATTING FIGURES
BABE RUTH'S MAJOR-LEAGUE CAREER
1914–1923

at bat: 3036
hits: 1051
home runs: 238
runs batted in: 763
average: .346

* Fred Williams (1887–1974), outfielder, nineteen seasons, 1912–1930, Cubs, Phillies, batting average .292 (home runs 251).

33 · A Splendid Series

I'd have hit eighty homers easily here this season.
—Babe Ruth, Polo Grounds, October 1923

For the third straight year the Yankees and Giants were to meet in the World Series. The Giants had a harder season, winning in their league by only four and a half games. But, as usual, the two teams seemed well matched. With Yankee Stadium open and the Polo Grounds made larger, it seemed likely the crowds would be the biggest ever. A few days before the first game the demand for tickets was heavy.

The Yankees' first baseman, Wally Pipp, cracked a rib two weeks before the end of the season. Young Lou Gehrig came up from Hartford to play first and batted .423 in thirteen games. The rule was that no player could play in the Series unless he was on the roster on September 1. Never short of gall, the Yankees asked permission to use Gehrig. Commissioner Landis said it would be all right if John McGraw agreed. John McGraw did not agree. The trainer wrapped Pipp in tape and he played well.

When Babe Ruth worked out in the Polo Grounds before the first game he looked fondly down the short 258-foot right-field line and said the fence was an easier target than the fence in the Stadium.

A great ball team beat a good one.
—*The Times*, October 11, 1923

The weather on Wednesday, October 10, was good for baseball —clear and with a temperature in the high sixties. The crowd in the Stadium was 55,307, a new Series record. Interest was so keen *The Times* begged people not to phone for scores during and after the game because the callers completely paralyzed *The Times's* phone system.

The first game went into the ninth inning tied. Then thirty-three-year-old Casey Stengel* hit an inside-the-park home run to win the game 5–4. Stengel gave a good dramatic performance in this most exciting of all plays, sprinting with one shoe half off, falling safe and panting on home plate. The Yankees on the bench loudly accused him of showing off. For the Yankees, Ruth also put on a good show in the fifth inning with a triple into the left-field corner. He was safe after what Grantland Rice described as a twenty-foot hook slide. Bob Meusel seemed about to drive him in to tie the game with a hit over second base, but Frank Frisch took it, running toward center field, and threw Ruth out at the plate without getting set to throw. After Stengel's theatrics, the Yankees had lost eight straight World Series games.

> For the first time since coming to New York, Babe achieved his full brilliance in a World Series game.
> —Heywood Broun, October 11, 1923

The weather for the second game was exactly as for the first. When Ruth went out to take his fielding position a fan promised him a new hat for each home run he hit. That was a costly impulse. Ruth hit two home runs in three times at bat, and he hit them in succession, a new Series record. Thus, with Herb Pennock who pitched well, he was responsible for the first World Series victory the Yankees ever had. The score was 4–2. Of the two home runs, one was a cheap one into right field, but the other went out of the park. He also had two bases on balls, neither intentional. As in 1922, the Giants did not cower before his reputation but pitched to him as if he were mortal man. His lone out was his longest ball of the game, driving Stengel to the wall in the Polo Grounds center field chasm, 475 feet away. Ruth was a merry man in the clubhouse after the game and promised more of the same.

> One of the daffiest guys I ever met.
> —Babe Ruth, on Casey Stengel

The games of this Series alternated between the Polo Grounds and Yankee Stadium. Thus the Series now moved back to the Stadium where it saw yet another attendance record, 62,430. Twenty-five thousand more were turned away. The game was the tight-

---

* Charles Dillon Stengel (1890–   ), outfielder, fourteen seasons, 1912–1925, Dodgers, Pirates, Phillies, Giants, Braves, batting average .284. Hall of Fame (as manager).

est since the last game of the 1921 Series, and had the identical score: Giants 1, Yankees 0. Art Nehf was the winning pitcher in each. Casey Stengel won the game with a home run into the right-field bleachers in the seventh inning. This time he could jog around the bases. To repay the Yankees for their derision of his first-game theatrics, he thumbed his nose at the Yankee bench as he rounded third base. Outraged, Commissioner Landis sent for him instantly, fined him fifty dollars, and said he would get no Series money if he misbehaved again. In this game Ruth played first base most of the time because Pipp had a strained ankle.

The Yankees crushed the Giants in the fourth game 8–0, getting thirteen hits off five pitchers to tie the Series at two games each. The attendance of 46,302 set a new record for the Polo Grounds. Ruth had a double in three times at bat and scored a run. Pipp played first. The sweating Giant pitchers threw 161 pitches in the game.

Back they went to the Stadium and to still another attendance record, 62,817, while fifty thousand people were turned away. The Yankees won 8–1, hitting safely fourteen times for nineteen bases against four Giant pitchers. Ruth singled and scored two runs. Joe Bush pitched a three-hitter. The Series now stood at three and two, in favor of the Yankees.

The Yankees won the sixth game and their first world championship on October 15 by beating the Giants 6–4. In the first inning Ruth hit one of his wondrous home runs over the right-field roof where the fence began to curve toward center field. The distance to the fence there was not less than 435 feet. The ball cleared the roof and landed among two teams of surprised West Indian cricket players. It was Ruth's third home run of the Series. Nehf held the Yankees scoreless from that point until the eighth inning.

As the Yankees came to bat in the eighth the Giants led 4–1. After Ward was out, Schang and Scott singled. Nehf walked two pinch-hitters, Hofmann and Bush, on eight pitches, forcing in a run. Ernie Johnson went in to run for Bush, and Rosy Ryan* came in to relieve Nehf. Ryan walked Dugan on four pitches, forcing in another run, and leaving the bases full as Ruth came to bat with the Giants leading 4–3 and with one out.

John McGraw had no place to put Ruth. Ryan had to pitch to him. First there was a called strike, then a foul strike, and next, counting on Ruth's eagerness, McGraw passed the sign for a waste pitch, ankle high. Ruth struck out. (Legend says the low pitch bounded in front of the plate.) As the players would put it, Bob

---

* Ernest Rudolph Johnson (1888–1952), infielder, ten seasons, 1912–1925, White Sox, St. Louis Federals, Browns, Yankees, batting average .265.

Wilfred Patrick Dolan Ryan (1898–   ), pitcher, ten seasons, 1919–1933, Giants, Braves, Yankees, Dodgers. Won 51, lost 47, earned-run average 4.14.

Meusel picked him up. He singled to right center. When Bill Cunningham[*] made the only error of the game, all three base runners crossed the plate, making the score 6–3 in favor of the Yankees, and that was the score when it ended. Briefly calming the gleeful frisks and frolics in the clubhouse, Babe Ruth made a stilted little speech —probably written for him—and gave Huggins a diamond ring, the gift of the team.

After twenty years of trying, the Yankees were champions of the world. At the moment they could even love Miller Huggins.

> Investigators of psychic phenomena must take note of the fact that Mr. McGraw's hypnotic powers work only on Mr. Nehf this year, and that after seven innings either Mr. McGraw's current is exhausted or he has burnt out the fuse.
>
> —*The Times*, October 16, 1923

Poor John McGraw. So much had been made of his success in calling every pitch in the 1922 World Series that people could not forego reminding one another of the claim to genius. McGraw masterminded the 1923 Series in the same way, but the Yankees got sixty hits in six games, scored thirty runs, and had twenty bases on balls. In 1922 Ruth walked only twice. In 1923 he was walked eight times, and never intentionally. McGraw's success in 1922 and his failure in 1923 were both exaggerated. The quality of pitching, as usual, settled the Series. When the Giants' pitching collapsed the Yankees became champions. That Ruppert was now sole owner and stood firmly back of Miller Huggins *may* have helped to make the Yankees better in 1923 than in 1922.

Writers who were alive at the time left us a sense that this was one of those World Series that leaves a glow of pleasure by giving us baseball at its most enjoyable, though the reasons are never the same twice. Many records were broken—playing records, attendance records, records for gate receipts, records for players' shares. The size of the crowds proved the wisdom of building Yankee Stadium and enlarging the Polo Grounds. And the game results proved that Yankee Stadium was an honest ball park, not tailored to the eccentricities of one team. The Giants won two of their three games in the Stadium, and the Yankees won all three they played in the Polo Grounds.

The Series changed the baseball current in New York. After 1923 the Yankees were more loved than the Giants. John McGraw had brought Huston and Ruppert together and advised them to buy the

* William Aloysius Cunningham (1895–1953), outfielder, four seasons, 1921–1924, Giants, Braves, batting average .286.

Yankees. Together they built a team that humbled McGraw. McGraw, in time, came to resent the Yankees.

Although the Series lasted only six games it grossed a million dollars, a new high. Attendance was 301,000, also a new record by a margin of thirty-one thousand. Each Yankee got $6,160.46, each Giant $4,112.88, record-breaking figures which stood until 1935. As a souvenir, each Yankee received a gold watch, the gift of organized baseball given out by the Commissioner's office. Colonel Ruppert added a gold fob to each watch.

Babe Ruth had a splendid series. He made seven hits in nineteen times at bat—four singles, a double, a triple, and three home runs— for an average of .368. He walked eight times and struck out six. He scored eight runs and drove in three. Thinking of the misery of 1922, Grantland Rice (in a parody of William Cullen Bryant) punned: "Ruth, crushed to earth, will rise again." His three home runs were a new World Series record, as was his total of nineteen bases.

And yet he did not much outshine the Giants' Casey Stengel. Stengel's two home runs won the two Giant victories. He batted .417 and drove in four runs to Ruth's three.

But Ruth sparkled in a winning cause, which made him remembered. A baseball star is made by newspapers, and he is more easily made when the competition is fairly even. When teams are evenly matched the single hero stands out sharply. Noting this, the press puffs him still larger and brings ever greater crowds to see and celebrate him. The great beast of publicity feeds on itself. We can believe Ruth's fame owed a lot to Stengel and the Giants who gave him good competition. A kind of fearful veneration was seen in 1923. Fans reached out to catch fouls off the bats of other men, but they tended to shrink away from Ruth's fouls as though they had in them something more than human. The muscle hero of America, like that ancient club-carrying Hercules, was becoming a demigod.

> . . . Baseball on the sabbath would keep young men away from crap games, card parties, and other forms of gambling.
> —Babe Ruth, *The Times*, October 26, 1923

As usual, Ruth went barnstorming after the World Series. In Scranton he came near to serious injury but escaped without a bruise. Six thousand boys brushed police aside and rushed to greet him on the field after his team had beaten the local team. Stepping carefully to avoid spiking any of them, he tripped and fell. The boys thought it was great fun and piled on him as he lay. It took four police to peel the boys off him. Ruth stood, brushed himself off, and wanted to throw baseballs into the mass of boys, but the police would not allow it. Probably every boy of them was a lawbreaker. They were admitted free, but the local sheriff said they could not come in until after school. Hundreds were there by noon, claiming they had a half-holiday to see the game. They probably took the same attitude toward compulsory schooling that their hero took when he defied the state of Maryland at the age of seven.

While in Scranton Ruth also spoke to all the amateur ballplayers in a group. He made a speech for Sunday baseball in which he proved that he had learned civic poppycock and claptrap from the best masters (who were numerous and able in that decade). He took the position that Sunday baseball would distract the young from even worse pursuits. That's true—at least for the length of time it takes to play nine innings, and assuming they don't bet on the game itself.

Outside the Park, 1924

COOLIDGE PRAISES
ANTI-SALOON LEAGUE

FIND DANCE HALLS
HERE 20% IMMORAL

BOB-HAIRED GUN GIRL
ROBS AS POLICE HUNT

LAST YEAR LOWEST
IN LYNCHING CASES
26 OF VICTIMS NEGROES

VOLLEY MOWS DOWN
29 BRITISH SOLDIERS
ON VISIT TO IRELAND

DANCE BY SIX GIRLS
HELD AT ST. MARK'S
DESPITE THE BISHOP

NEW YORK DEMOCRATS CALL FOR SMITH'S
NOMINATION FOR PRESIDENT

SMITH WANTS BEER

VON PAPEN IN LAWSUIT

FIND MISSING PASTOR
IN DELIRIUM, BRANDED
ON BACK WITH KKK

RISING FLOOD OF STUDENTS
OVERWHELMING THE COLLEGES

34 · It Wasn't Ruth's Fault (1924)

Babe Ruth, extra outfielder.
—Hans Wagner, January 1924

January 1924 was not an especially eventful month for Babe Ruth. In Massachusetts he paid fines for not registering his car for four years, for doing without a driver's license for ten years, and for speeding. Total: seventy dollars. Hans Wagner gave out his all-time all-star baseball team and listed Babe Ruth only as "extra outfielder." Ruth also spoke at the dinner of the New York chapter of the Baseball Writers of America (he was by now a fluent and popular after-dinner speaker).

Yankee General Manager Ed Barrow began to oversee the reshaping of the Yankee Stadium playing field. He moved home plate out ten feet and swung the foul lines a little to the catcher's right, which lengthened both foul lines, improved the lighting in the late months of summer, and gave the fans better views of the game around home plate.

Time came for Ruth's yearly attack on off-season fat at Hot Springs. He had ballooned to nearly 240 pounds. Helen and Dorothy saw Babe off at Penn Station on February 11. His leaving coincided with the arrival of President Calvin Coolidge to conduct the Lincoln's Birthday rites of the New York Republicans. A crowd of about two thousand cheered Coolidge's arrival in a snowstorm. Then ". . . many who had come to greet the President accompanied Ruth to the station gates in a sort of informal farewell" as he walked through the station carrying a golf bag on one shoulder and three-year-old Dorothy on the other.

Once in Hot Springs Ruth got down seriously to lowering his weight and his golf score. And then he got what he nearly always got in Hot Springs, a serious attack of influenza, with its companion fears of pneumonia. On March 1 his temperature was 104.2 degrees, but there were no complications beyond his impatience at being bedridden and his boredom with a steady diet of chicken soup. By March 5 he was on his feet, roaming his hotel in his bathrobe, back on solid food and cigars. By this time he weighed only 218 pounds, having lost about a pound a day since leaving New York. Three days later he said he felt weak, and on the same day played thirty-six holes of golf.

Umpire Bill Klem Raps Golf
As Pastime for Ball Players
—The Times, March 18, 1924

Many famous ballplayers liked to play golf. But in 1924 several of the best-known leaders damned golf as bad for players. Ty Cobb, manager of the Tigers, confiscated his men's golf clubs during spring training. Later he returned the pitchers' clubs, saying no pitcher had a batting eye to spoil. John McGraw forbade golf for the Giants from the start of spring training until the end of the season, fearing that in learning how to swing a golf club they would unlearn how to swing a bat, and, in any case, would talk golf instead of talking baseball. As for the Yankees, Ed Barrow continued to grumble about his serfs playing golf, but he did no more than grumble.

Huggins cut the length of spring training for the regulars from four weeks to three. The team would train in New Orleans again. For their annual trip north the Yankees scheduled four games with Rochester and ten with Brooklyn.

Ruth arrived in New Orleans on the 10th. Helen and Dorothy met him at the station (Helen carrying a bat), and the three checked into the Bienville Hotel. A writer asked Babe whether he would try for the batting or the home-run championship. Answer: "Both!"

There was a new center fielder on hand to spell Whitey Witt. He was Earl Combs, aged twenty-five, up from Louisville. His hair was prematurely gray, and he was prone to Bible-reading, hitting singles, throwing accurately, and making difficult catches.

Ruth began to take his swings on the 11th. Huggins thought spring training was mostly for practice in pitching and hitting. Each batter hit until put out, took his turn in the field, then returned to the plate to hit until out, and so on. Against the serious pitching of Joe Bush, Ruth hit the first pitch out of the park, but he struck out the next four times he had a turn, without even hitting a foul.

On the 18th Ruth did something that ought to go in the record book under the special heading: "Money Lost, Largest Denomination of Bill—G. H. Ruth, New York A.L., $1000." He had four one-thousand dollar bills in his pocket and lost one between the Bienville Hotel and a New Orleans bank. It was never recovered.

The Yankees played a few games with the New Orleans Pelicans. On March 23 the Pelicans looked feeble while losing 11–2. A watcher became so noisily scornful of their play that Ruth called time out, invited the man down to the field, gave him an autographed ball, and thus, by quieting him, made baseball fun again.

Lou Gehrig, called "the Ruth of the rookies," worked out at first base until the Yankees took to the road, then went back to Hartford for more seasoning.

When the exhibition series started Ruth set himself to ease the boredom of branch-line railway stations. He got a portable phonograph of the old spring-driven, bamboo-needle style (about as large as a modern portable typewriter case). With this he produced concerts in backwoods baggage rooms. His favorite record that spring was Moran and Mack's "Two Black Crows." He must have had several impressions of the shellac disk, because Red Smith, a completely trustworthy authority, said he sometimes played it a hundred times without intermission. When this became unbearable, even to him, he would organize a quartet to sing popular songs (he took the bass).

Jocko Conlan* was with the Rochester team in 1924 during the exhibition series. He gave an anecdote to the author which deserves to be printed in full.

> At Mobile there was a large crowd. After the game the teams went to their hotel and had dinner and Ruth still hadn't come back. He finally came in about eight o'clock without his cap; his shirt was torn, his fielding glove was tied to his belt with a cord, and his baseball suit was all muddy with Alabama clay up above his knees.
>
> The reporters asked Ruth, "Where were you?" Ruth said, "There were about seventy-five kids who stayed in the park and wanted to play ball. I spent all the time since the game hitting flies and shagging flies with the kids."

> . . . a good natured personification of brute force.
> —*Literary Digest*, 1924, on Ruth

The Yankees won their opening game on April 15 at Boston 2–1. When the Yankees were in Boston, Babe had Helen and Dorothy come in from Home Plate to his hotel. They had pleasant, playful

---

* John Bertrand Conlan (1899–   ), outfielder, two seasons, 1934–1935, White Sox, batting average .263. Hall of Fame (as umpire).

times. One writer said he saw Babe lose a boxing match with Helen in their Boston hotel room, and saw him "wrestled to the floor by his blond-haired three-year-old daughter Dorothy."

After winning early the Yankees slumped and began to lose their tempers. At Washington on the 25th umpire Billy Evans put Ruth out of the game for tossing his bat in the air when angered at a called third strike. At about this time of the season Waite Hoyt made it clear to Ruth that he thought Ruth loafed on a fly ball. The two had a fist fight in the clubhouse after the game. (Another year passed with only silence between them until Ruth impulsively offered Hoyt a beer and suggested they forget their quarrel.)

At about this time an alleged Ruthian debauchery occurred, of which we have a detailed narrative. Apparently some friends of Herb Pennock asked Pennock to come to dinner, bringing some autographed baseballs and his teammates Ruth, Joe Dugan, and Bob Meusel. Ruth drank enough to let the Baltimore waterfront slob take charge, and began to ogle one of the serving maids. A Philadelphian managed to get Ruth out of the house, and they spent the night on the town. As the sun came up he told Ruth they ought to get back to the hotel because the Yankees had a game with the Athletics at Shibe Park that afternoon. "Ruth was sitting in an easy chair, a girl on each knee. He held an open bottle of champagne upside down over his head . . ." and said he wasn't going to leave for awhile.

That afternoon at Shibe Park he said he felt great. Fred Merkle* said he didn't look it. Ruth bet him 2 to 1 he'd hit a home run. He hit two. The only names in the story are Pennock, Ruth, and Merkle. It *is* true that Babe Ruth hit two home runs in a game at Shibe Park on April 28, 1924.

Ed Barrow promoted the award of Ruth's Most Valuable Player certificate as Ruth Day at Yankee Stadium on May 14, when the Yankees were scheduled against the Browns. Ruth Day brought band music, armed men marching, the raising of the world championship flag, and victory for the Browns, 11–1. The Most Valuable Player of 1923 had a single.

To stir public interest in the Citizens Military Training Camps the Army arranged for Ruth to enlist as a private in the New York National Guard. We no longer think a man of six feet two and 215 pounds is a giant, but in 1924 the Army could not find a uniform big enough for him in New York, and sent him to Washington for a fit. While in Washington he met with General John J. Pershing for public-relations pictures. The enlistment on May 20 was as public as possible. Horses pulled a gun to Times Square where Ruth

---

* Frederick Charles Merkle (1888–1956), first baseman, sixteen seasons, 1907–1926, Giants, Dodgers, Cubs, Yankees, batting average .273.

climbed on one of the horses and sat for photographers while taking the oath amid the cheers of the crowd.

> ... a surging mass of bobbing straw hats and swinging fists.
> —*The Times*, June 14, 1924

The Yankees, Red Sox, Browns, and Tigers were closely bunched in the American League race when the Yankees went to Detroit for a series in mid-June. On Friday the 13th there were eighteen thousand hostile people in the stands. In the ninth inning, with the Yankees leading 10–6, Ruth told Meusel he saw Ty Cobb give Bert Cole* the sign to hit Meusel with a pitch. Meusel *was* hit, dropped his bat, and went to the mound to fight Cole. The umpires and Cobb converged on the mound, Ruth rushed out, both dugouts emptied, and Ruth and Cobb shouldered through the crowd to get at each other. Huggins and umpire Red Ormsby pulled Ruth away. Police in the stands jumped on the field and imposed a brief armistice. Umpire Billy Evans put Meusel and Ruth out of the game. They had to go through the Detroit dugout to leave. With police plainly pushing and shoving to force a passage for them, it seemed to the crowd that fighting had broken out. About a thousand came down on the field to join. Others tore up seats in the stands and threw them on the field. The police couldn't clear the grounds, having all they could do to get the Yankees safely into their clubhouse. Billy Evans then declared the game forfeited to the Yankees, 9–0. Police arrested about half a dozen of the fiercest fans, and the turmoil died.

One might defend the proposition that in Detroit from 1924 to 1934 nothing was more popular than ball-park rowdiness. On Saturday the 14th the game between the Tigers and Yankees drew forty thousand customers and an extra hundred police. The management hastily put portable bleachers in front of the outfield stands. Other ticket holders sat on the grass along the foul lines, where mounted police walked their horses. The fans booed Ruth, but that was the only demonstration. The Yankees won 6–2. Ruth had two doubles in four times at bat and scored two runs.

Ban Johnson then dealt out justice to Friday's bad guys. He suspended Meusel and Cole for ten days, and fined Meusel fifty dollars and Ruth a hundred. Ruth also had to buy a new glove. Someone stole his old one during the riot.

> Yes, he's a [censored], but he sure can hit. God Almighty, that man can hit!
> —Ruth on Cobb, *Sporting News*, July 12, 1950

---

* Albert George Cole (1898–   ), pitcher, six seasons, 1921–1927, Tigers, Indians, White Sox. Won 28, lost 32, earned-run average 4.67.

As late as thirty years ago you could get an argument on whether Ruth or Cobb was the greatest of ballplayers.

The style of play before the First World War fitted Cobb's cunning in overcoming tight defense. The style of the 1920s fitted Ruth. In Cobb's heyday the fans liked strong defense and liked offensive play to be sly and tricky. When Ruth came to his prime, tastes had changed. The big booming offense built attendance.

As Ruth first shone on the scene his chief rivals for public favor were Cobb and Tris Speaker. Both disliked Ruth, which proves nothing in Cobb's case since he carried so many grudges he was overstocked. In the case of Speaker it may mean that he felt inferior to the younger man. For his part, Ruth had no lasting distaste for Cobb and Speaker. In fact, he paid little attention to them. With Cobb's disposition what it was, we might expect to learn that he and Ruth came to blows. They never did, but not because of self-restraint. The umpires and their teammates were always awake to the possibility and took care to keep them apart. Cobb was ill-humored on and off the field. Ruth had short bursts of temper like summer thunder, soon over. Jimmy Austin* was rather emotional by today's standards in his description of Ruth, but he was doubtless sincere: "a warm-hearted, generous soul" with a heart "as big as a watermelon and made out of pure gold." That anyone should speak such words about Cobb is unthinkable.

In the field Ruth had a better arm, but Cobb covered more ground. Their leadership of the American League, season by season, in the important offensive categories has been tabulated. Cobb had fifty-eight season championships, Ruth had fifty-seven. If you were down three runs in the bottom of the ninth and had the bases full with two outs, you'd send Ruth up to bat. If the score were tied in the same circumstances, Cobb was your man. Fred Lieb's general conclusion seems sound: in the matter of runs Cobb was a retailer, Ruth a wholesaler.

In baseball's mythology Ruth is the muscle hero, Landis the ethical hero, and Cobb the foxy hero. There is a legend of Cobb's foxiness when he was a manager, to the effect that Cobb fooled Ruth into striking out. He ostentatiously signaled for an intentional base on balls. The pitcher threw a called strike. Cobb rebuked him. The pitcher threw another called strike. Cobb ran in, took out both pitcher and catcher, shouted that he would fine each a hundred dollars, and brought in a new battery. Then, as Cobb had planned, the new pitcher threw the third strike. But—we have no place, no date, no sure test of the story's truth.

After the riot in Detroit there was bad news immediately. Earl

* James Philip Austin (1879–1965), third-baseman, eighteen seasons, 1909–1929, Yankees, Browns, batting average .246.

Combs broke his leg. He would be out for the season. Ruth, however, was hitting extremely well. By the third week of June he was batting .368, ahead of Cobb's .359. The pennant chase was close; the first-place Yankees were only five games ahead of fifth place.

About this time Franklin D. Roosevelt asked Babe Ruth to endorse Al Smith for President. Ruth agreed, signed a hearty letter about poor boys rising from humble beginnings (very likely written by someone in Smith's headquarters), and accepted a nominal place on an Al Smith for President Committee. He had never voted in his life.

On July 4 the Yankees were in third place behind the Senators and Tigers. It wasn't Ruth's fault. He had twenty-one home runs and was batting .351. Ruth had a great July, hitting fourteen more home runs. In August he went on a safe-hit spree, raising his batting average, on the 18th, to .397.

August also brought a hint of domestic life. Whatever Babe Ruth and Claire Hodgson had going since May 1923 had not yet separated Babe and Helen Ruth, as we know from a report of a traffic case. (Such scant facts have we on Helen Ruth!) Ruth tried to do a work of mercy called ransoming the captive. A laundry driver crashed his truck into Ruth's car in New York on August 20. Helen Ruth had been driving, and Mrs. Mike McNally was her passenger. There were no personal injuries. The truck driver was fined fifty dollars. He had only thirty-five. The alternative was thirty days in jail. Ruth offered to pay the whole fine, but the grateful defendant would take only fifteen dollars.

According to legend, the hot months of 1924 also gave occasion for one of Ruth's most widely quoted phrases. President Calvin Coolidge went to see the Yankees play on a warm afternoon. The Yankees queued to meet the President. They filed by, shaking hands and mumbling greetings until Ruth's turn. He wiped his forehead on his handkerchief, thrust out his hand, and spoke, "Hot as hell, ain't it Prez?"

Whenever a mighty champion rises above the people there are always critics to wonder whether some overlooked challenger might not be even greater. F. C. Lane, writing in *Baseball*, nominated Rogers Hornsby as one who might have enjoyed the most fame if he had had the most press-agentry. He blamed Hornsby's relative obscurity partly on Hornsby himself, who neglected to fight umpires, spike infielders, and play dirty. (Hornsby would be well remembered today as a very sour and unloved man except that Cobb's much greater acid content drew so much more attention.) Comparing Ruth and Hornsby, Lane thought Hornsby the better hitter and more versatile fielder.

John A. Heydler, president of the National League, seconded the nomination of Hornsby. As Heydler pointed out, from 1920 through 1923 Hornsby had a higher batting average, more hits, more doubles, more triples. But Hornsby's home runs numbered 112 while Ruth in the same span hit 231. The crowds respected Hornsby. But they loved Ruth because he was *not* a beautifully classic hitter like Hornsby, but was a revolutionary slugger. As well tell the Mississippi to flow north as tell the fans to rate Hornsby above Ruth.

By mid-September the Senators led both the Yankees and the Tigers, their only remaining rivals. But it took two more weeks, in which the Senators won sixteen of their last twenty-one games, to make the first Washington pennant certain. They clinched it at Boston on September 29. Even the Boston crowd cheered the new champions. Across the country the Senators' feat was generally pleasing.

The Yankees finished two games behind. For the Yankees to have won a fourth pennant in a row was against the arithmetic of the game. (No American League team won a fourth consecutive pennant until the Yankees of 1939 pulled off the trick.) Many excuses for the Yankee failure are on the record. Combs broke a leg—but Combs was not a regular and appeared in only twenty-four of fifty games before the fracture. Ward was hurt—but Ward played 120 games in the infield. The truth is threefold.

Ex-Yankee shortstop Roger Peckinpaugh played furiously for the Senators, eager to beat the Yankees. Ex-Yankee catcher Muddy Ruel, while catching for the Senators, had a better year than Yankee catcher Schang. The third and most convincing part of the answer was the effect of Huggins's blind passion against Carl Mays. He sent Mays to the Reds on waivers and advised the Reds to cut his salary in half. Mays won his twentieth game of the 1924 season for his fourth-place club on the day the Yankees fell a game behind the Senators with eight games to play. They never caught up. In place of Mays the Yankees used Sam Jones, who won nine and lost six. The comparison of Mays's and Jones's records seems enough to explain the loss of a pennant by two games.

The Yankees players' 1924 Series share was roughly $81,000, while the Senators were dividing $331,000.

> . . . Baseball, the past few seasons, has been transformed from a scientific pastime to a contest of brute strength.
> —F. C. Lane, *Baseball* magazine, 1924

The brute Ruth had a good season in 1924. He hit forty-six home runs, well below his record, but enough to satisfy. In the seasons of

1919 through 1924 he had hit 10 percent of all the home runs in the American League.

Was it all brute strength? Well—he led the league in hitting in 1924 with a .378 average, far ahead of Cobb's .338. (Ruth had not ousted a decaying champion; Cobb hit .378 in 1925.)

Ruth also led the American League in slugging percentage, total bases, bases on balls, runs scored, and proportion of home runs to times at bat. He was a close second in runs batted in.

There was something else to notice in 1924. Ruth began to complain to his trainer of indigestion before every game. A frequenter of the clubhouse guessed that no other man alive had swallowed so much sodium bicarbonate.

THE ACCUMULATED BATTING FIGURES
BABE RUTH'S MAJOR-LEAGUE CAREER
1914–1924

at bat: 3565
hits: 1251
home runs: 284
runs batted in: 884
average: .351

Ruth covered the 1924 World Series with the help of a Christy Walsh ghost and then went barnstorming in the West.

It was the most successful tour yet. His party traveled eighty-five hundred miles to play in fifteen cities before 125,000 people. The Ruths won all fifteen games they played with the Meusels, helped by their leader's seventeen home runs. In the fifteenth game pitcher Ruth worked against the sentimental hero of the 1924 World Series, Walter Johnson, in Johnson's home town of Brea, California. Population of Brea: thirty-five hundred. Attendance: fifteen thousand. Both pitched the complete game. Pitching against the likes of Ken Williams, Ernie Johnson, and Jimmy Austin, Ruth won 9–1. He also hit two home runs.

Off the field Ruth autographed about five thousand balls, most of which were sold for charity. He made twenty-two scheduled speeches, headed four parades, refereed a boxing match, drove a golf ball 353 yards, visited eighteen hospitals and orphan asylums, ate four bison steaks at a sitting, and played a turn in a Los Angeles theater. He was back in New York on December 5, much richer and ten pounds fatter.

Christy Walsh kept up with a river of letters from confidence schemers, charitable societies, unknown beggars, and from clubs, schools, and churches which thought they would profit from hear-

ing Babe Ruth make a speech. And, to please individuals, to promote charities, or to increase newspapers' circulations, Ruth's name
was handwritten (by himself or others) on about ten thousand
baseballs and two thousand bats in 1924.

Outside the Park, 1925

FUTURE HAS BIG FOOD PROBLEMS

HOUSE HUNTERS LOOK FOR SITES
WHERE RADIO RECEPTION IS GOOD

STAGE CENSORSHIP ISSUE
ONCE MORE GROWS ACUTE

BOMB PUT IN CAR
KILLS DRY AGENT

TEA POT DOME DRAMA BRINGS OUT BIG CAST

BOY, 4, GIRL, 9, FOUND
INTOXICATED IN STREET

COOLIDGE NAMED 'BEAR RIBS'
BY INDIANS OF NORTH DAKOTA

ADVERTISEMENT SENT
BY TELEPHOTOGRAPHY

SIXTH EFFORT OF GIRL
OF 14 TO DIE IS FOILED

'WIFE KIDNAPED ME,'
SAYS RICHEST INDIAN

NEW YORK IS MECCA
OF RUNAWAY GIRLS

COOLIDGE SPEAKS
IN TALKING PICTURE

BRIGHT MEN WEAR BRIGHT COLORS

35 · Helen, I Feel Rotten

'Strongest Team I Ever Had,
Will Win Flag,' Says Huggins
—*The Times*, April 5, 1925

Baseball went on for eight months of every year of the 1920s, from spring training through the World Series. During the other four months the New York papers printed guesses, rumors, and dreams about John McGraw, Miller Huggins, the Yankees, the Giants, and Babe Ruth. Thus there was space for Huggins to tell the world in December 1924 what the Yankees needed. A short time later he had what we would think he needed most, Ruth's signature on a two-year contract at the old price, $52,000. Next he got Urban Shocker from the Browns. There was reason to think well of the Yankees' prospects that winter.

Ruth, with "portly form" covered by "a gaudy overcoat of startling hue," left on January 31 to join Bob Meusel and Aaron Ward at Hot Springs. He weighed 256 pounds, about forty too many. The Yankees were to train in St. Petersburg. Babe met Helen, Dorothy, and the Yankees in Florida in the first days of March. He was still much too fat. During the first workout, a rugged three-hour drill on a hot windless day, "the aldermanic stomach and chest were heaving slightly, as if under a great strain," which amused the watchers. (It was hard to feel sorry for the highest-paid ballplayer.) Huggins excused Meusel and Ward early, but not the fat man. Ruth looked poorly, and Huggins firmly meant to get him in shape.

The only fun Ruth had in Florida that spring was catching fish in the sea by lantern light, which he did night after night. Otherwise 1925 began to be a year cluttered with troubles. There was the lawsuit for seventy-seven hundred dollars filed on March 6 in New York for debts claimed by a bookmaker. There was a finger tip broken by a pitched ball on March 9, which would keep Ruth off the playing field for awhile. Could he force himself to get in "the well-known pink" by exercising on his own? There was the printed gossip that he was getting "old and fat" (at age thirty). There was the repeatedly overblown puffery of the rise to glory of Nick Cullop,* because of whom "Babe Ruth . . . may spend the season on the bench." (Cullop opened the season as an Atlanta Cracker.)

Late in March the Yankees and Brooklyn set out on the northward exhibition tour. They divided the first twelve games. Then, after a game at Atlanta, they went to play in Chattanooga. Ruth felt terrible and a physician advised him not to leave, but he put on several sweaters and caught the train, looking pale and strained. He slept most of the way and skipped batting practice. The field was muddy and rainsoaked, the base paths were buried in sawdust, and the skies threatened worse to come. But the crowd was at capacity, and for them Ruth hit two home runs. One went four hundred feet. They were to play again at Asheville on the next day (April 7). Ruth's batting average in exhibition games was .449. He had lost twenty-one pounds in twenty days; his weight was 235.

BABE RUTH ILL WITH GRIP, COLLAPSES; MAY BE SENT HOME

Collapsing on the station platform at Asheville, N.C., when he arrived there yesterday morning with the New York Yankees, Babe Ruth was rushed to an Asheville hotel and was attended by a physician and a nurse during the day. He has a bad case of the grip.

Last evening Ruth's nurse announced that he seemed considerably rested, but still was very sick. Manager Huggins of the Yankees, before departing with the team for Greeneville, S.C., made arrangements to send Ruth home this morning in care of Coach Paul Kritchell [sic], if he is able to travel.

It is not so certain that Ruth will be able to play in the opening game in New York next Tuesday.

—*The Times*, April 8, 1925

Since leaving St. Petersburg Ruth had been ill with a digestive or intestinal disorder. He made no change in his diet but treated himself with what he called a "bromide." In the game on Sunday, April 5, he hit a home run. On Monday, with a temperature of 102 degrees, he hit two home runs at Chattanooga. After the second

* Henry Nicholas Cullop (1900–   ), outfielder, five seasons, 1926–1931, Yankees, Indians, Senators, Dodgers, Reds, batting average .249.

home run he left the game in the fifth inning and took a cab to the team's hotel where he went to bed early but slept badly.

In the morning he breakfasted with sportswriter Bob Boyd, who said Ruth ate only toast and eggs, and not much. He was still running a fever on the train to Asheville. The train reached Asheville shortly before noon. While passing through the station Ruth collapsed and would have fallen except that Steve O'Neill* caught him. The players loaded him into a cab and hurried him to their hotel.

There seemed to be something abroad in the land that did not want baseball played. Sixteen players at the moment were ill enough to catch the eye of the press, including Ty Cobb, bedded down in Nashville with "flu," Howard Ehmke of the Red Sox, hospitalized in Rochester with a temperature of 103, and Rabbit Maranville** in Chicago with his ankle in a cast. Of the chiefs of the baseball tribe, Charles H. Ebbets, Brooklyn's president, was ill in the Waldorf-Astoria. In Charlotte, North Carolina, two days after Ruth's collapse, the Yankees' bus wrecked itself when its brakes failed, but, as *The Times* said, YANKS ESCAPE DEATH. Soon it was doubtful that Babe Ruth had escaped death.

"BASEBALL KING'S"

REPORTED DEATH.

BABE RUTH'S £20,000 FOR 20

WEEKS' WORK.

SNOW-SHOVELLING!

AMERICAN IDOL HAD A

BIG FALL.

It is reported in New York that "Babe" Ruth, the American champion baseball batter, has died in a train while on his way to New York, says a Central News telegram.

As a baseball king—he was the greatest player in the world—Ruth was infinitely more popular with Americans than any President could be.

His income as a player was, roughly, £20,000 for five months' work.

When the "Yankees" of New York bought him from the "Red Sox" of Boston they paid £25,000 for the transfer.

---

* Stephen Francis O'Neill (1891–1962), catcher, seventeen seasons, 1911–1928, Indians, Red Sox, Yankees, Browns, batting average .263.
** Walter James Vincent Maranville (1891–1954), shortstop, twenty-three seasons, 1912–1935, Braves, Pirates, Cubs, Dodgers, Cardinals, batting average .258. Hall of Fame.

Ruth, who was not more than 33, was brought up in a New York Catholic orphanage.

Smashing Hits.

He was equally successful at batting, fielding and pitching, but his smashing hits were his specialities.

His fame as a baseballer made him one of the most sought after men in the States. A visit from him brought honour and fame to the most insignificant township.

Ruth stood on the top of the highest pinnacle of fame for exactly two seasons.

He then thought himself more powerful than the baseball authorities, whose simple rulings have the force of a final court of appeal, and challenged their authority. He lost.

He was banished from the game for a time, got out of condition, and on his return had lost his form.

A few months later he was shovelling snow and sawing wood for a living; but he "came back" later.

Ruth was handicapped, however, by the fact that he was putting on fat.

"His obvious and growing waist line," wrote one critic recently, "is a matter of concern to all those financially interested in the pastime. It will not be long before his legs are unable to carry his body. He is expanding so much that he will soon have expanded out of the game."

Fashion In Braces.

Owing to his girth, Ruth discarded the popular belt and took to braces. This started the fashion for braces in the States.

A friend of Ruth's said to-day: "He was exceptionally strong. He was over six feet high and weighed some 15 stone. Last year he made more home runs—driving balls to the boundary—than any other batter.

"Two years ago he was given the much-coveted baseball medal, which is awarded for being the most useful man to a side."

—London *Evening News*, April 9, 1925

At Asheville it seemed best to ship Ruth to New York for medical care, with Paul Krichell for company. One reporter went along. While Ruth's train was in southwestern Virginia it missed a connection. He and Krichell did not reach Washington when expected. A Canadian wire service then reported his death. Before Ruth reached Washington, telephones were ringing in newspaper offices asking whether Ruth was dead. At the Washington station when he finally arrived he seemed better than expected, but his death was common talk in the streets. At all stops between Washington and New York crowds gathered to learn more about the dead or dying hero.

The Yankees were still on the road. Huggins had scores of telegrams of inquiry. When they played in Charlotte, Dazzy Vance* came to the press box to verify the local report of Ruth's death.

Ruth and Krichell played pinochle until they reached Newark. Krichell got Ruth up on his feet and into the washroom to tidy up before they came to Manhattan Transfer. Ruth sent Krichell back for a comb. Alone, he fell to the floor, struck his head on the wash basin, and knocked himself out. Krichell found him unconscious and had him carried to his berth. When the train reached Pennsylvania Station, messengers went for Dr. J. L. Murphy, staff surgeon of the railroad. There may have been as many as twenty-five thousand people waiting for news of Babe Ruth in the cathedral-like station.

Helen had returned early from St. Petersburg, avoiding the exhibition tour, to deliver Dorothy to Home Plate. There she heard of Babe's illness at Asheville and went back to New York alone in "bright spring attire." She thought it was the annual influenza attack, uncomfortable but not grave. When she heard that Babe arrived unconscious, "a little cry escaped her lips, her eyes filled with tears," and she rushed to the railroad car. Guards admitted no one but Helen, Dr. Murphy, and Yankee functionaries. The curtains were drawn. No announcement was made to the crowd. The Braves arrived from the south on the adjoining track, heard that Ruth was dead, and came for verification.

The stationmaster ordered an ambulance. Because a stretcher was too large to make the turn in the car's vestibule, the first problem was to get the senseless Ruth out of the Pullman car. The solution was to cut the side of the car to double the width of a window and pass him out. It took sixty-five minutes. When they got him out they used a freight elevator to take him down to the baggage room. Another delay followed. The first ambulance dispatched had a steering-gear casualty, so they waited for a second. Dr. Murphy flashed a light three inches from Ruth's open eyes, but they did not blink.

During this wait Ruth three times went into convulsions, "lashing out with arms and legs and muttering incoherently." He came to but once. As Helen leaned over him he whispered, "Helen, I feel rotten," and was unconscious again. It took six or seven men to hold him on the stretcher during the convulsions, and he had nine

---

* Clarence Arthur Vance (1891–1961), pitcher, sixteen seasons, 1915–1935, Giants, Pirates, Dodgers, Cardinals, Reds. Won 197, lost 140, earned-run average 3.24. Hall of Fame.

such fits, five in the station, three in the ambulance, and one at the hospital entrance. In the ambulance, when it came, the sobbing Helen rode with Babe while Christy Walsh sat up front with the driver on the way to St. Vincent's Hospital at Seventh Avenue and Eleventh Street.

At the hospital his usual physician, Dr. Edward King, looked him over, ordered an icepack for his bumped head, and said there seemed no danger from the head injury or the "influenza." By four in the afternoon Ruth was conscious, smiling, talking. Dorothy arrived from Sudbury about that hour. King's only doubt was whether Ruth could play in the opening game on the 15th. "Ruth's condition," he said, "is not serious. He is run down and has low blood pressure and there is an indication of an attack of the flu. What he needs is rest." Reporters pressed him for causes. "The big fellow doesn't take care of himself. He leads an active life and he eats heartily." Sniffing for sensation, one asked Dr. King to confirm that Ruth lived a life of "dissipation." Dr. King smiled. "He's very careless."

A subhead on *The Times*'s front-page story had read, in part, "Relapse Followed Fried Potatoes for Breakfast. . . ." There was not a word in the news story about his breakfast. But, because Babe Ruth was America's muscle hero, the legend sprang up and lived for years that he was ill because he tried to cure a bellyache by eating a double order of steak and french fries for breakfast on the train to New York. Sportswriters said he was "eating himself out of baseball." This legend came from the unsupported subhead in *The Times* and the remark of Dr. King about the carelessness of Ruth's hygienic practices. And from the legend came a popular name for his illness: The Bellyache Heard Round the World.

If proof of Ruth's popularity were needed it came from the people's response to his illness. The nation kept up with every bulletin. Every paper carried the story as though it was the report of a grave illness of a close friend. In some cities President Calvin Coolidge could not make the front page on the days when Ruth's life seemed to be in danger. Watchers stood outside St. Vincent's, some of them children with April flowers. Drivers of passing cars slowed to call out for news. The press kept a death-watch crew at the hospital. Brother Paul, the superintendent of St. Mary's Industrial School, telephoned every night from Baltimore to ask about the condition of his former pupil. *The Times* said Babe Ruth and Henry Ford shared the title of First Citizen (which was a little rough on Coolidge). People accepted the illness as "complications of acute indigestion and influenza," a "combined attack of many ailments."

Ruth was still bedfast on opening day, April 14, a week after the Asheville collapse, but got the score by innings. The Yankees, before fifty thousand, beat the Senators 5–1. Ruth's replacement, Ben Paschal,* hit a home run. Ruth said, "They don't seem to miss me very much."

On the next day a juvenile harmonica band came to serenade him but was turned away. He wasn't getting any better. Could influenza and indigestion keep him weak, feverish, and with a sharp abdominal pain for two weeks? To nearly everyone's surprise, the hospital scheduled him for surgery on April 17. His physician did not back off from the influenza/indigestion diagnosis, but now added that Ruth had a painful intestinal abscess which caused the fever. The operation would not be "serious" but "very painful." The surgery— Ruth said it was two incisions—took only twenty minutes under a general anesthetic. Dr. King thought his patient would be hospitalized for another ten days and unfit to play ball for two weeks after that. Thus his return to the field could not be before May 11.

On the day of the operation the Yankees were in sixth place, having won a single game and lost three. By an awkward coincidence a ghost-written feature article signed "by Babe Ruth" appeared on the day of the operation, as though dictated under anesthesia. It had been written in the Carolinas much earlier, but the timing embarrassed Christy Walsh.

Three days after the surgery it was plain that Ruth was on the mend.

> **The injured professional frequently is uncomfortable. His job is more in jeopardy when he can't work at all than when he's working badly.**
>
> **—Jim Brosnan**

From April 9 through May 1 only Helen and Dorothy Ruth and Ed Barrow could visit Babe. Friends and strangers strained the hospital's telephone service. Hospital administrators tried to satisfy the outside world with daily bulletins and tranquilize their famous patient with scores by innings. The scores were generally bad news, for the Yankees were floundering. On April 23 Dr. King judged recovery complete except for muscular weakness from lack of exercise.

At this point Helen's nerves cracked. She was hospitalized in St. Vincent's for a "nervous breakdown." The medical bulletins from now on featured a cast of two.

Days dragged on. After Ruth had been in bed for twenty days an interviewer put it to Dr. King bluntly: Will Ruth ever play ball again? King kept his temper. Nothing, he replied, has been hidden.

---

* Benjamin Edwin Paschal (1895–1974), outfielder, eight seasons, 1915–1929, Indians, Red Sox, Yankees, batting average .309.

In two or three weeks Ruth would leave the hospital. His progress was "satisfactory." He still used the word "influenza." Since most people had experienced the "flu," they doubted that it could lead to twenty days in bed.

The curious—and somewhat skeptical—press got to see Ruth in bed on May 2 when he held court for them in his flower-scented room. He told the writers he was weak, which they could see, and "felt like a featherweight." He agreed that he had "influenza"; he had it every spring. But "that indigestion stuff is the bunk!" He knew all about indigestion; he had lived with it for the past ten years. This thing he had now had given him the most painful time of his life. The thoughtful visitors believed he would need a pretty long time to get back in shape.

After a month in bed Ruth graduated to a wheelchair, which cheered him since he could not stand erect by himself. After a few days he could roll himself on to the elevator and take the air with Helen on the roof. She was publicly classed as a neurotic, so it occurred to some people to speculate that Babe was suffering a similar disability (no responsible person said it). A week after the May 2 press conference the weary hospital officials quit publishing predictions of the date of either Helen's or Babe's discharge. Twenty-five days after surgery Dr. King said Ruth was cured of influenza and indigestion. He was inactive only because he was recovering from the surgery. Thirty-six days had passed since Steve O'Neill caught him as he fell in Asheville. In mid-May the unofficial rumor around St. Vincent's was that he might swing a bat in mid-June.

Once recovery began for sure, Ruth's health returned as a snowball grows while rolling. His weight had dropped from 256 in February to 180 in April. Now he began to recover. A month to the day after his operation he left the hospital on foot to watch a police parade (Helen didn't feel up to it). On the next day his chauffeur, Thomas Harvey, took him for an auto ride. He walked to and from the car (again Helen wasn't up to it). That night he cheerfully hunted for the sounds of "about seventy-five" jazz orchestras on his radio. He also listened to the baseball scores. (The Yankees lost again; they had now won nine of their twenty-six games.)

Babe Ruth finally came back to Yankee Stadium on May 19, five weeks after opening day. He put on a uniform and hit a few pitches thrown by his chauffeur. The uniform hung like drapery, loose at the waist and baggy at the knees. After fifteen minutes he put one over the fence and knocked off, very tired. He was disappointed to be so weak, but Ruppert and Barrow were pleased at the workout. That night and for the next several nights Ruth slept at St. Vincent's. He intended to work out every day, increasing the time daily. In a few days he was able to jog around the warming track. The layoff had not hurt his batting eye at all, but his legs were slow in getting back their spring. He had thought of going up to Home Plate for recovery before joining the Yankees, but Helen was still in St. Vincent's so he stayed in New York.

After almost seven weeks in the hospital, Babe, without Helen, moved out on May 26 with a carload of accumulated gifts. That day he went out to the Stadium to see a double-header with the Red Sox. He got there early enough to take batting practice and hit some fungoes to the outfielders. The Yankees were going to Philadelphia for four days. Ruth would stay at home and work out every day at the park. Finally, Huggins said Ruth would be in the lineup on June 1. The Yankees that morning were in seventh place: they had won fifteen and lost twenty-five.

> . . . Ruth hadn't been drinking that much pop and it wasn't even a belly ache.
>
> —Roger Kahn

What ailed Babe Ruth in the spring of 1925?

The words of those who would talk were never very exact except for the phrase "intestinal abscess," and some of the things they said were flapdoodle. Ruth had not overeaten before his illness. (He had been losing a pound a day for three weeks before the collapse.) When Ruth was known to be gravely ill in 1947, *Life* revived the age of fable and said the 1925 illness had been a consequence of too many hot dogs and too much soda pop. The Detroit sportswriter H. G. Salsinger, who knew Ruth well, said in the 1948 obituary roundup that it was indigestion.

It hadn't been easy for outsiders to get the facts in 1925. Ed Barrow censored every scrap of sickroom news. His management of the story was out of character and stirred suspicion that he was hiding something. Dan Daniel, the New York sportswriter, said it was something "more than a stomach ailment" but said no more. Paul Gallico, sportswriter and novelist, made the most startling suggestion: "Ruth was suffering from something a little more sinister." That suggests attempted murder by poisoning. Perhaps by gamblers who had bet heavily against the Yankees in the winter book? Gallico may have stumbled on the perfect crime, since he was the *only one* who hinted at foul play. But, to a layman, it doesn't account for surgery, any more than "indigestion" and "influenza" do.

Ruth always ate too much, except during his antifat war every spring. In winter he always accumulated fat. He was easily bored, and eating was a pastime he could always arrange. But it is one thing to say he ate too much and quite another to say he ate the wrong things. Practically nothing is known about the relation of diet to athletic ability. Training-table menus are records of superstition. We also know next to nothing about the reverse effect, that is, the effect of exercise on the gastrointestinal tract. Most experimenters have used dogs and rats. As researchers have lately said, "It is regrettable that the supposedly chronic effect of exercise lacks an experimental basis." We can only suspend judgment on the relation of Ruth's diet and his ill health.

The explanation of the causes of his illness of 1925 has many blank spaces. Most people accepted the heroic bellyache as heroic indigestion. Many who were close to the case remained silent. Ruth himself spoke loosely, saying only that he always lived too high. The historian of the Yankees, Frank Graham, gave no plausible explanation.

There *was* a reason for the silence of insiders. They thought they knew the trouble, and they didn't wish it known. Ed Barrow's published autobiography ignored the matter entirely, but he believed Babe Ruth was suffering from syphilis and told it as a fact to one of the most respected of sportswriters. If Barrow told one, he probably told others. They said nothing. Barrow was not, of course, competent to judge. He must have made his own interpretation from a physician's guarded remark.

There is no way the lay writer can deal with this very technical medical question, especially since syphilis is called the great imitator and often briefly misleads able diagnosticians. A layman who went into a description of *S. meningitis* or *tabes* or *locomotor ataxia* or *symptomatic S.* would be out of his depth. But the Barrow diagnosis cannot be ignored. A Newspaper Enterprise Association story, written in New York in July 1972, said the illness of 1925 "was actually a case of venereal disease." The writer will leave it to his medical readers, if any, to reflect on the great performance of the season of 1924, the coma, the convulsions, the surgery, and the weight loss, to judge whether the facts are compatible with Barrow's statement. There is no doubt that Barrow said it, not merely that Ruth had the dread scourge but that this attack was its effect.

The best a layman can do is to put it like this: everybody who could have known the diagnosis in 1925 has skirted the question in a way that leads to a shallow conclusion that the illness was something shameful. Against that conclusion is the stone wall we run against when we try to get facts.

A cautious professional consulted by the author suggested several possible diagnoses of the *acute* condition. Ruth may have had peritonitis from an erupted inflammation of the intestine, although survival in the 1920s was rare. There could have been a localized intestinal infection from intestinal bacteria, or even an inflamed diverticulum which required surgery. It is possible he had an obstruction of the intestine, either mechanical or from an infection, which required a temporary colostomy and temporary drainage into a sack outside the intestinal wall. (The procedure was known before the 1920s.)

Of these possibilities only the last might seem embarrassing to the patient. And it is the one which would need convalescence from late April until the first of June.

To believe, we must have a reason, not a cynical guess. At the time there was one solitary statement of a precise condition: "intestinal abscess." There are many kinds of intestinal abscesses. Ruth's condition could have been something not shameful but embarrassing in that age. Perhaps the removal of a short length of gut? (The shortening of the intestine would be good material for abusive bench jockeys: "Hey, short gut!") The operation needs a period of recovery as long as Ruth's in 1925.

There we must leave the matter.

> . . . he just hadn't the necessary time to allot to the role of loving father.
>
> —Waite Hoyt

Helen Ruth was never in good health after 1920. She had several major operations and gradually became more withdrawn from the world. She spent more and more time at Home Plate while Babe spent less. He hadn't been able to put up with its loneliness for more than the winter of 1922–1923. When Babe fell ill in April 1925 Helen, as we saw, got the news at Sudbury. From April 9 until about the 23rd she spent as much time with him as was allowed. She bore up well until Babe was out of danger, then she herself toppled. As late as opening day she was sufficiently calm to go to the ball game alone and keep a scorecard of the game, but within a week she was herself a patient at St. Vincent's "in a nervous condition brought on by worry over the illness of the Yankee slugger."

What was she anxious about? We may wonder what Ed Barrow told her about Babe's illness. We may be practically certain Babe received mail from women in six American League cities, women unknown to Helen.

She stayed at St. Vincent's almost a month longer than her husband did. The diagnosis was always "nervous condition." They do not seem to have quarreled, ever, but on June 18 Home Plate was for sale. Babe hoped to get fifty thousand dollars for it, not for himself, for he was not pinched, but for Helen and Dorothy. He told inquiring newsmen the place was a nuisance and a burden, he spent only a few days a year there, and he found it hard to get a trustworthy caretaker. Helen stayed with Babe through June and then took Dorothy to live in Boston. She would expect Dorothy to start school in 1926. It would be easier in Boston.

That was the end of Helen's active partnership. When the Yankees came to Boston, Helen and Dorothy stayed with Babe at his hotel, on the friendliest terms, but he didn't see them much after the spring of 1925.

There was no divorce. It wasn't the sort of thing ballplayers did (until recent times), and, more important, they both had moral convictions firmly opposed to divorce. (The low divorce rate among ballplayers is a puzzle because, as Bernard Shaw described English family life, baseball life "is cut off equally from the blessings of society and solitude.")

As we shall see, during Helen's lifetime the separation was not good for them. Babe showed ill effects almost instantly.

36 · I Was a Babe and a Boob
(1925)

I might as well be 550 years old.
—Babe Ruth, June 29, 1925

The Yankees got off to a slow start in 1925. With Babe Ruth sick in bed they had to play the world-champion Senators in two of their first three series, of which the Yankees won two games. Ben Paschal, Ruth's replacement, hit a home run in each of the two victories, which showed what was needed. The team lacked dash and so did the fans. Attendance at Boston when the Ruthless Yankees first visited was down markedly. The Yankee slump and the absence of Ruth cost the American League clubs at least two hundred thousand dollars at the gate in the first seven weeks of the season.

Three weeks after the opening the Yankees and Red Sox were battling for seventh place. On that day, May 6, Huggins benched thirty-three-year-old Everett Scott, the Yankee shortstop, after he had set a record of 1,307 consecutive games.

At long last Ruth appeared in the lineup on June 1. The Senators beat the Yankees that day 5–3, but Ruth hit a ball out which was foul by inches, made a good fielding play, walked, and was thrown out at home trying to score from first base. He had to leave after six innings because of fatigue. It went unnoticed at the time, but that date became memorable for another reason: Lou Gehrig started at first base, the beginning of his record 2,130 games in a row. If Gehrig had not become a Yankee, Ruth might now be remembered as a first baseman.

In his first week Ruth hit well, fielded in a barely tolerable manner, and ran slowly. But Huggins seemed to think "half a Ruth was better than none," since the Yankees were playing too poorly to get along without him. It was clear that when Ruth had been absent he was not all that was absent from the Yankees. By mid-June they had clambered painfully to sixth place. Ruth had three home runs and a stolen base. When they slipped back to seventh place, there was talk that George Stallings, manager of Rochester who had managed the Yankees in 1909 and 1910, would replace Huggins. Three weeks after Ruth returned to play he fouled a ball into his left ankle during batting practice; the same ankle had been hit by a pitched ball a week earlier. The trainer had to strap and brace the joint. For awhile Ruth feared he might be out for the rest of the season, just when he was coming into form.

Huggins found it harder than usual to get along with Ruth that summer. Ruth's marriage was now only nominal, and he seemed rudderless. From February to June he had worked hard at playing the better of the only two manly roles he knew, the Xaverian Brother George. As a result he was alive. When the angel of death left him, the waterfront slob took charge and led him through a riotous and exhausting summer. A team buried in the second division gets red-eyed, frown-wrinkled, and slack unless it fears or loves its manager. Ruth despised his manager.

On the last day of June, in Boston, Huggins fined Ruth a thousand dollars for reasons unknown, very likely for causes more closely linked to blue laws than to baseball regulations. On the next day against the Red Sox the wrongdoer hit two home runs. Huggins threw up his hands in bafflement and remitted the fine. Later that month, on a western trip, Huggins began to scold Ruth and Meusel while the three stood on the back platform of their train. Ruth contemptuously "picked him up like a doll" and dangled him over the railing. They quarreled almost daily. When losing a game, which was more often than not, Huggins would ask, of no one in particular, how a team could win if the men weren't in shape. Ruth, to the air, would suggest they could win with changes in the batting order, wiser choices of pitchers, sounder game plans, and correctly chosen tactics.

The dreary season dragged on. Ruth wrenched his back in a fielding play in Chicago and had to leave the lineup (a sore back hurts worse in seventh place). Combs was laid up with indigestion. The pitchers were often used in quartets for each nine innings. Near the end of July Ruth had only eight home runs and, for him, a puny batting average in the .260s. He reached an all-time low on August 9 when Huggins sent Bobby Veach up to hit for him (Veach, in his fifty-six games with the Yankees, hit .353 that year). This catalog of misfortunes need go no further. It could be read with sympathy only in Philadelphia; middle-aged Yankee fans would be horrified. The failure of the Yankees in 1925 wasn't the fault of Ruth or Huggins—it was a team effort. The only cheerful thing that happened in Yankee Stadium that summer that was not outweighed by disaster was a campaign appearance by Jimmy Walker who was running for mayor. He very properly came to the Stadium to hear the cheers he deserved as the father of Sunday baseball in New York, and to be photographed with owner Jacob Ruppert and Babe Ruth.

> **Ball players are peculiar beings. First, they are caught young, as a rule; second, they are spoiled by overmuch praise if they make good; third, they have about twenty-two hours a day to think about themselves and their troubles, to nurse grievances, and to develop peculiar turns of mind.**
>
> **—Hugh S. Fullerton (1916)**

Having never played on a second-division team, Ruth wasn't getting much fun out of baseball in 1925. To him fun was necessary. He turned to other kinds of fun, chiefly to living it up after dark. Baseball became an obstacle to his social life. That summer he was something of a bore to intelligent teammates, what with bragging about his salary and behaving theatrically in public. Some who liked him were a little sad; they thought they were watching the disintegration of a man. He was one of the most conspicuous spendthrifts in the country. Since 1914 he had owned the nine most expensive cars he could find; during a hot spell in St. Louis he once wore twenty-two silk shirts in three days and gave them to the hotel chambermaid when he left town.

Huggins's job became steadily harder. His men were ill-tempered and so was he. His attempt to rule with a firm hand met resentment among bored players. On paper the Yankees seemed a very good team, but on the field they were a very bad one, and the frustration made their manager even more raspy than usual. Some of the senior players—including Whitey Witt, Wally Pipp, Wally Schang, Scott, and Ruth—were a hostile bloc which stood as one against Huggins. They were lax in discipline, and Ruth was supposed to be their libertine leader.

In August this mixture exploded. August is the month that tries players' souls. The schedule is a grind, the travel is boring, the out-of-town fans are wolfish, the umpires seem a criminal conspiracy. The best, most spirited players are the most unruly men of August.

RUTH FINED $5000:
COSTLY STAR BANNED
FOR ACTS OFF FIELD
—*The Times*, August 30, 1925

When the Yankees visited St. Louis in the last days of August, Ruth neither lived with the Yankees nor in his own hotel suite. He spent three nights in a row in the house of unidentified friends, but, unknown to him, Huggins had hired a detective to shadow him in Chicago and St. Louis. As Fred Lieb put it, "The report . . . indicated his companionship—mostly female—was of a rather dubious nature." Huggins phoned Ed Barrow in Saratoga and said he wanted to fine Ruth but had to be sure Barrow and Jacob Ruppert would back him. Barrow told him there was no need to bother Ruppert; Huggins would get full support. At the moment Ruth was vulnerable. In the thirteen games before August 29 his average fell to .245.

The afternoon of August 29 Ruth came to the clubhouse too late for batting practice. Only Huggins and Waite Hoyt were there. Huggins told him not to dress for the game: he was suspended and fined five thousand dollars. Ruth would have attacked him if Huggins had been anywhere near his size. He angrily told Huggins he would appeal to Ruppert, to which Huggins said he would like to be there when Ruth came in with a batting average of .245 and said his manager was picking on him. The enraged Ruth got a team railroad ticket from the club secretary and checked out of the Hotel Buckingham. His departure was known only by his absence from the field in the bottom of the first inning. After the game reporters stormed the clubhouse to quiz the reluctant Huggins. We can assemble his answers into one statement.

I absolutely refuse to discuss the circumstances which led to the fine and suspension except to say that Ruth was guilty of misconduct off the field. Of course it means drinking, and it means a lot of other things besides. There are various kinds of misconduct. Patience has ceased to be a virtue. I have tried to overlook Ruth's behavior for awhile, but I have decided to take summary action to bring the big fellow to his senses. He has forgotten all about the restrictions on this trip, hence the fine and suspension.

Huggins said the scourging was not for the way the big fellow was playing ball; Ruth had been wayward ever since his illness. Huggins also said the suspension was for an indefinite period, at his discretion. Later Huggins privately told a trusted writer (who never printed it) that Ruth had behaved worse in Chicago, by Huggins's lights, than in St. Louis. It wasn't the quality of Ruth's women that Huggins minded, it was the quantity.

It being a Saturday, neither Barrow nor Ruppert could be reached for comment.

A BITTER DOSE

— Sykes

(*New York Post.*)

The fine was forty-five hundred dollars higher than any ever levied on a ballplayer. (Fines have always been part of baseball; the first on record was for profanity among the amateur New York Knickerbockers in the 1850s—six cents.)

> **Confidentially—and you can print this—Miller Huggins is dumb.**
> —**Babe Ruth, August 30, 1925**

Ruth now behaved just as any other self-indulgent man in trying circumstances, that is, badly. Full of wrath from St. Louis to Chicago, he overspoke himself and kept his anger at white heat for about twenty-four hours.

After losing their eleventh game of the last fifteen, the Yankees boarded their direct New York Central train in St. Louis Union Station without Ruth. He had swapped his club ticket for a routing via Chicago with a dim notion of getting the almighty Commissioner of Baseball, Kenesaw Mountain Landis, to right his wrongs. At a stop before Chicago he said he got into the Hotel Buckingham only ninety minutes after Huggins's curfew—not mentioning three nights when he wasn't there at all. At Chicago he complained of Huggins's style; the manager could have fined him privately, but no! Huggins was shifting the blame for the team's poor showing from himself to Ruth. In the past the Yankees were so good they practically managed themselves. Only Huggins's bad management prevented them from finishing in first place by fifteen games over the Senators in 1924. "If Huggins is manager, I quit." *Question*: Had he ever disobeyed Huggins on the field? *Answer*: (Ruth was quite candid) Yes. Twice. He once bunted when ordered to hit away. Another time he was told to bunt and hit into a double play. But Huggins's judgment of what the situation called for was wrong both times. And five thousand dollars was an outrageously high figure: "Why, I know of guys killing people, and even bootleggers don't get that tough a fine. It ain't right."

By this time the writers had reached Ruppert who told them he supported Huggins; Ruth could quit if he wished. Ban Johnson, president of the American League (and no friend of Ruppert), cheered Huggins on for the good of the League. In Chicago Ruth learned of Landis's annual retirement to his Michigan lakeside place. He phoned the commissioner and received advice on which train to take if he were coming to call. But a suspension became the commissioner's business only after it had run more than ten days.

So Ruth rolled on to New York on the Twentieth Century Limited with his portable spring-driven phonograph and a vast suitcase containing, among other things, nine pairs of white flannel trousers. He was now calmed. He spoke no more to reporters. A crowd of about three thousand welcomed him to Grand Central Station. He took a cab to his suite in the Grand Concourse, followed by the press in a file of taxis. A crowd cheered his arrival at his hotel. Inside the hotel a process-server awaited him (in the interest of somebody suing Ruth about an automobile accident), and about a dozen reporters milled about. It was not a moment of triumph. Ruth shouldered the process-server over a piece of lobby furniture and plunged like a fullback through the clump of writers. When he reached his room he was at the lowest ebb of his life since age seven.

For some reason, frail jumpy Helen was there. He saw her alone briefly and then let in the writers to tell them he didn't wish to say anything except that he was sorry and was going to see Ruppert.

As soon as he could, he went to Ruppert's office. Ruppert was jovial but not alone. The Yankees hadn't detoured through Chicago, so Huggins was there first, but he left when Ruth came in. After a long talk with Ruppert, Ruth came away thoughtful. That afternoon he went to the Stadium to ask Huggins if he should dress to play. Huggins told him he was still suspended.

Huggins seemed physically afraid of Ruth—his "face was ashen white"—but there was no cause to be alarmed. He was now dealing with Xaverian Brother George who was perfectly contrite and filled with a firm purpose of amendment. The storm had blown out.

> **Ruth . . . has the mentality of a boy of 15.**
> **—Jacob Ruppert, September 3, 1925**

What Ruppert had told Ruth was what Huggins's detective told Huggins. He also said Huggins was the man with whom Ruth must make peace. Furthermore, the fine would stick. (And it did, for as long as Huggins was alive.)

Ban Johnson told reporters he had earlier asked Ruth to call on him at the League offices in Chicago where he intended to preach a sermon. Ruth never came, so Johnson gave his homily to the press: "He was ruining his own career and . . . he was a detriment instead of a help to the ball team." Joe Vila, the writer who once didn't believe a surgical incision when he saw it, because it was in Ruth's arm, wrote: "Ruth's punishment may bring the big fellow to his senses. He should realize his popularity is on the wane. . . ."

It took little courage to flog Babe Ruth. His teachers didn't know the future and may well have thought him absolutely finished. The shock-therapy Huggins gave him was a last resort. If he were finished it could be a bargain; he might get so angry he would quit and save Ruppert the fifty-two thousand dollars he was bound to pay Ruth in 1926. As it was, Ruppert saved three thousand dollars which he didn't have to pay Ruth during the suspension.

Just to make the most of the sensation, writers backed poor Helen into a corner by asking her if she were going to sue Babe for separate maintenance. Her answer was, "I have nothing to say," which was true. And she fled back to Boston.

Ruppert and Ruth remained on friendly terms all through the suspension. They even went to a ball game together. Ruth's job now was to apologize to Huggins and daily pray to him for a chance to play ball until Huggins thought he was sincere in his sorrow. He even argued passionately that he needed to play in order to stay in shape, which may have brought Huggins's only smile in weeks. The suspension was much worse than the fine, because Ruth was a machine designed only for baseball, and he was pleading for a chance to do what he could usually do better than anyone in the

Miller Huggins in the mid-1920s. A manager for seventeen years, 1913–1929, he finished below the first division only four times, won six pennants with the Yankees, and three World Series. (*The New York Yankees.*)

world. Huggins must have heard a sincere note in Ruth's voice on September 6, for he reinstated Ruth in time for the game of September 7.

Ruth was at the Stadium before the first ticket was sold, was first to dress, first on the field. Before four thousand fans, who cheered Ruth warmly, the Yankees dug themselves deeper into seventh place by losing to Howard Ehmke and the Red Sox 5–1, but Ruth had one of their five hits.

The amusement world tries to satisfy what people feel is a need to worship something larger and more dazzling than themselves. This feeling is not a bad thing. On the highest level the satisfaction takes the form of that virtue called religion. But when people worship a human being, they embolden him to puff himself like the frog in the fable until he bursts. And thus Babe Ruth burst in 1925. Huggins then taught Ruth a lesson he never forgot: don't be smug. After he returned to the game demigod Ruth came back to earth. (But the five-thousand-dollar fine bothered him for years.) There was no barnstorming profit likely in 1925 for a player who seemed in a state of decay, so Ruth didn't try it. The fine and the loss of postseason profits added up to about thirty thousand dollars, a high price for a short term of intemperate divinity.

There wasn't much left of the season of 1925. The Yankees did nothing important on the field, except that Ruth settled down to work and raised his batting average from .245 to .290. He then went to cover the World Series with his Christy Walsh ghost, but he took ill and had to return to New York before the end. He also lost the home-run championship of organized baseball when a shortstop of the Pacific Coast League named Tony "Lezarre" (as spelled by the Eastern press) hit sixty (in a two-hundred-game season).

After the wretched schedule was finished Ruth paid fifty dollars as out-of-court settlement of a hundred-thousand-dollar libel suit brought by a movie producer, joined the New York city police reserves (with some objection to the indignity of being finger-printed: "I thought it was the other fellows who got fingerprinted"), and went hunting moose in New Brunswick with Bob Shawkey, Joe Bush, Eddie Collins, and Benny Bengough. (Shawkey got a moose.) Ruth rode forty miles on horseback to the lodge, but after three weeks of regular hours he felt so good he insisted on walking the forty miles out to civilization. He then went duck hunting in Massachusetts for a week and said he intended to spend December and January at Home Plate in Sudbury.

The Times's annual review of sports gave Ruth a paragraph to himself, but not for playing baseball. He was notable in 1925 for his grave illness in the spring and his lost war with Huggins in the summer. The Yankees attendance in 1924 had been more than a million, but in 1925 it fell below seven hundred thousand. The American League prospered elsewhere, for the net loss was only sixty-eight thousand. Ruth's best work that year, really, was visiting orphanages in every league city and going with Pee Wee Wanninger and Bob Meusel to several prisons to show the convicts how they hit the ball. (He got along splendidly with convicts.) In championship baseball his only distinction was to finish second in the American League in home runs, with twenty-five, after Bob Meusel who had thirty-three.

THE ACCUMULATED BATTING FIGURES
BABE RUTH'S MAJOR-LEAGUE CAREER
1914–1925

at bat: 3924
hits: 1355
home runs: 356
runs batted in: 1110
average: .345

I was a babe and a boob.

—Babe Ruth (1925)

The Greeks had a formula for heroes of drama like Babe Ruth. First comes arrogance, then retribution, then destruction. But with Ruth destruction did not follow retribution, even though people were comparing his life with the legend of John L. Sullivan who was said to have drunk himself out of his heavyweight championship. Ruth did have a hard time financially, but that was nothing new. He counted the money he had forfeited since 1920 because of neglect of his own best interests at about a quarter of a million dollars: fees to lawyers and detectives, $25,000; a business failure (the candy bar? the cigar factory?), $100,000; gambling losses, $125,000. His comfort was the annuity which would begin to pay him five hundred a month at the age of forty-five. (Readers today might multiply those numbers by a factor of five or six to figure the 1970s' purchasing power he wasted.)

Huggins, after his anguish, came out well in 1925. With whip in hand he drove out the expendable soreheads of the Yankee roster (Ruth was not expendable). The Yankees of 1926 would start Lou Gehrig at first, Tony Lazzeri (alias "Lezarre") at second, and Mark Koenig at shortstop.

The year 1925 showed us Babe Ruth at his worse—swaggering, conceited, gluttonous of all sensual pleasures, a true slob wholly wanting in class. But he never forgot his origins. He wished to remember them, because to know how low he started made his present (if shaky) kingship all the sweeter. And he was never mean-minded.

What was Babe Ruth's future? When ballplayers are in their early thirties their careers usually decline. A few bounce in lively fashion back to their earlier heights, even to the Hall of Fame. Most fall dead, like pop flies on rain soaked sod. The season of 1926 would be the year of decision.

Outside the Park, 1926

QUERIES DUTCH PASTOR
ON BIBLICAL SERPENT

THREE DANCE 34 HOURS

FLORIDA ACREAGE
AT "BEFORE-THE-BOOM" PRICES

MOUSE ON OPERA STAGE
WHILE TENOR SINGS

STRIKE CHIEF HELD
SECOND DAY IN JAIL

PRIEST SAYS DRY LAW DEBAUCHES MINERS

MOB MAKES PRISONER
HANG SELF ON BRIDGE

PROFESSORS ASSAIL
COLLEGE FOOTBALL
AS A MORAL MENACE

FIRST PICTURE RADIOED FROM LONDON

CORNETIST TO QUEEN VICTORIA FALLS DEAD
ON HEARING OUR CONEY ISLAND JAZZ BANDS

WOMEN AND GIRLS
PARADE WITH KLAN

20 LYNCHINGS IN YEAR

WEAF MADE NUCLEUS
OF NEW RADIO CHAIN

FORD ESTABLISHES 5-DAY WEEK AFTER TEST

INDIANA VOTE HANGS
ON KU KLUX CHARGES

TELLS WHY WOMEN
EARN LESS THAN MEN

37 · Yankees Renewed, Ruth Reborn (1926)

He was as near to being a total loss as anyone I ever had under my care.

— Artie McGovern (1927)

A man who is contented only to play games until he wears out is hard to tell from an animal. To be a man he should use his mind to quicken and rule his body. In the winter of 1925–1926 Babe Ruth, in this sense, became a man. He formerly got hog fat between seasons, thinned down unsystematically in the spring, and then put on weight slowly through the playing season. He proved that sport and physical culture need have little in common—at least in a man's early career. His rhythm method of girth control would pass unnoticed if practiced by an anonymous corn-belt beer drinker, but not as the way of life of the most popular player of the most popular sport. He had not tried seriously to stay at his physical best. He rewarded himself for his jump from St. Mary's Industrial School to a job that paid a thousand a week by letting himself go at his second greatest pleasure, eating. (Baseball was first.)

At the end of 1925, aged thirty, he was in such poor condition that a less determined or lower-paid man in the same shape might have ended his playing career. A short list of flaws shows his problem: low blood pressure, rapid pulse, weight 254 pounds, chronic indigestion, flabby muscle tone, short breath. Instead of fading out of baseball he put himself in the hands of Arthur A. McGovern who ran a gymnasium for men and women at 42nd Street and Madison Avenue. McGovern, with medical advice but no medication, put Ruth on a regular scheme of physical improvement, strictly governing his diet and his rest, and working him physically four hours a day. It wasn't a program for the average man but one designed especially for this exceptional man. The sweetest-tempered Xaverian Brother might have snarled at McGovern's rules, but Ruth knew he

Back in condition in Artie McGovern's gymnasium, January, 1926. (*National Baseball Library, Coopers-town, New York.*)

had to salvage himself or quit baseball. McGovern figured that Ruth's erratic weight losses in ten years had added up to about two and a half tons of lard, all of it quickly replaced.

By mid-January Ruth's weight was down to 213 pounds. He bought a new supply of collars because all of his old ones were a full size too large. When he visited General Manager Ed Barrow at the Yankee offices people noticed that he bounded up the steps two at a stride. His blood pressure was normal, and his pulse was down from the low nineties to the high seventies. While building up Ruth's abdominal muscles, McGovern took almost nine inches off his waist-line and six inches off his hips. At the same time, Ruth's biceps, forearms, and calves were larger. For his build, Ruth's weight was exactly right.

Ruth and McGovern were so pleased with their human sculpture that they gave a three-round boxing exhibition at the annual dinner of the New York chapter of the Baseball Writers Association, just to show off the limber Ruth bounding about in tights. The audience found it entertaining and convincing. So satisfactory was the McGovern plan that Ruth would go through the same program with McGovern every winter as long as he stayed in baseball.

After 1925 Ruth was more responsible and more inclined to live his life privately. For example, Ruth's cars were just as costly but less flashy, his wardrobe just as large but better tailored. He ordered his baseball uniforms to his own taste; the caps had broader bills and higher tops, and his shirts and pants were cut more loosely to flow with his maturing figure.

Babe Ruth had not been a night-club playboy because he stayed away from the public who mobbed him affectionately in all public places. Now he abandoned his royal hotel-suite receptions. He went instead with small parties to private rooms in comfortable speakeasies owned by trusted friends who did not spread the news of his presence.

Why the change? Perhaps the fine and suspension of 1925 shocked him. Surely his mediocre figures in the 1925 record book could move a man to change his ways. And it is possible that the new Ruth was the work of Claire Hodgson. But there is no need to overcomplicate the matter. He had reached the age when most people become pretty well fixed in their attitudes. They usually still have plenty of energy, but they channel it more forcibly toward settled goals. As some psychologists have put it, a person achieves a "specification." Ruth at age thirty had his: to last as long as possible as a ballplayer.

The Yankees of 1926 began to take shape in Huggins's mind in December 1925 as he traveled busily to St. Petersburg, New York, Detroit, and Catalina Island, talking with baseball people about "this fellow Lazarre" and other prospects. Herb Pennock hinted of retiring from baseball until he got a raise. Catcher Pat Collins* was coming from the Browns. There were some rookies in addition to Lazerri: pitcher Garland Braxton and infielders Mark Koenig and Mike Gazella.** A successful knee operation assured that Joe Dugan would be back in good form.

Tony Lazerri,† whose name the writers found so difficult to spell at first, was the prize among the rookies. The Yankees bought him for cash from Salt Lake City on Paul Krichell's advice. He had never been east of the Rockies, nor, of course, had he seen a

---

* Tharon Patrick Collins (1896–1960), catcher, ten seasons, 1919–1929, Browns, Yankees, Braves, batting average .254.

** Edgar Garland Braxton (1900–1966), pitcher, ten seasons, 1921–1933, Braves, Yankees, Senators, White Sox, Browns. Won 50, lost 53, earned-run average 4.13.

Michael Gazella (1896–   ), infielder, four seasons, 1923–1928, Yankees, batting average .241.

† Anthony Michael Lazzeri (1903–1946), infielder, fourteen seasons, 1926–1939, Yankees, Cubs, Dodgers, Giants, batting average .292.

major-league game. With Koenig he became part of an excellent second-base combination, and, despite epilepsy, was to last for fourteen seasons. He was tall, thin, and square shouldered, with high cheekbones and a voice that always sounded angry and often was. He could be sociable, but he had a temper which led him to be harsh with anyone he thought a bother.

Henry Ludwig Gehrig, known as Lou, was the chief new regular in the 1926 lineup. Like Lazzeri, he was a Krichell find. Gehrig was a handsome, straight-nosed, dimpled Nordic type, broad in the seat and broader in the shoulders. His voice was tenor, and his speech was plain standard American. He was one of the three most powerful hitters who ever lived (Ruth and Ted Williams* being the other two). For all but two of his good years this great player lived in the shadow of Babe Ruth, known mostly as the man who followed Ruth in the batting order. When Ruth performed brilliantly, people roared approval. When Gehrig played as well, they took it as what they expected. But the great batters know who the great batters are; Jimmy Foxx once said Gehrig was a "more dangerous" hitter than Ruth.

Gehrig was born in 1903, three years after his parents came from Germany. His father was an ironworker. His mother was cook-housekeeper in a Columbia University fraternity house to help her son through college. The Yankees signed him in June 1923 before he graduated. At the 1924 training camp he had only ten dollars in pocket money, which he made last for ten weeks by tightfisted nickel-tipping. Such poverty had made Ruth a spendthrift, but Gehrig became tight. He and Ruth made a good contrast of ethical hero and muscle hero, the puritan and the hedonist, in their oversimple public images. Ruth tipped lavishly; Gehrig put his money in real estate. Before 1926 Ruth dressed whimsically; Gehrig could be counted on for coat and tie in the dining room. Ruth chewed tobacco, snuff, and cigars; Gehrig kept his pipe out of sight in photographs to avoid corrupting the youth of America. His biographers have made him a rather dull guy. We should remember that his best friends were Ruth, Benny Bengough, and Tony Lazzeri, and that his dugout nickname was "Biscuit Pants." His mother fed his friends at every chance, and Ruth gave her a Chihuahua which she named Jidge, after Ruth himself.

RUTH IN UNIFORM
ASTOUNDS CRITICS
—*The Times,* March 2, 1926

---

* Theodore Samuel Williams (1918–   ), outfielder, nineteen seasons, 1939–1960, Red Sox, batting average .344 (6th all-time). Hall of Fame.

The Yankees trained in St. Petersburg again in 1926. Huggins delayed the start until March 1, cutting a week off the usual time. Ruth, however, went to Florida a month early. He had all the indoor exercise he wanted; now he felt a need to work outdoors. Of the original Hot Springs golf-and-influenza pilgrims, only Ruth and Meusel were left, so Ruth gave up the annual pretense at getting fit on golf and hot water as a waste of time and money and went directly to Florida. He spent February watching his diet, playing golf, and studying major-league rosters with an expert eye. The roster-reading convinced him the Yankees would win the pennant and the Athletics would finish second. That was good handicapping; the Athletics finished third, a near miss.

When the other Yankees came to Florida in March they marveled at Ruth's figure. His cheeks and belly were flat, he was solid and compact, and he even seemed taller. His motions at play were easy and flowing. He had to tie his old uniform pants around his knees to stop them from flapping. He also affected the white eyeshade popularized by the tennis champion Helen Wills, "looking like a cross between a tennis star and a bookkeeper." The sight of him was cheering to the players, but the press was skeptical. The writers looked at the Yankees sourly, feeling somehow that the miserable record of 1925 shamed the New York writers' corps.

After preliminary drills the Yankees played two games in Florida with the Braves, losing both, 18–2 and 16–4. The sportswriters were horrified and angry. Westbrook Pegler, a former Babe Ruth ghost-writer, called the Yankees as the worst team he ever saw, a team convulsed by mutual hatreds, a team relying on a bogus reformation of Babe Ruth, a team sure to finish in last place. Both Ruth and Ed Barrow later said bitter reviews of the two games shook up the Yankees.

Something shook them up. Off they started on the northward campaign with eighteen games to play, eleven of them with the Dodgers. Like an army on the march they rarely knew where they were, leaving such details to Mark Roth, the traveling secretary. They knew only they would end their drive in New York. Meanwhile they won game after game after game. At Knoxville, Tennessee, Ruth hit a long one out of the park into a tree full of boys who dropped like windfall apples in hot pursuit of the ball. When they reached New York for the traditional final game with the Dodgers they had won all ten games with the Brooklyn team and the other seven as well. They put the maraschino cherry on top by taking the last game from the Dodgers, 4–1, in the Stadium. The future was there to see. Lazzeri had two singles. Koenig fielded with polish. Gehrig had two singles, a triple, and a walk. Ruth walked twice and scored a run.

After this eighteen-game winning streak the still-bruised New York writers—who knew, of course, that exhibition games don't win pennants—grudgingly granted that their fallen angels could finish in the first division. With our hindsight we can see that the Yankees were a functioning team once more.

> . . . terrific . . . hustling . . . sensational . . .
> —*The Times*, April 20, 1926, on the Yankees

Babe Ruth began the season of 1926 in the toils of the law of the Commonwealth of Massachusetts. Arriving in Boston for the opening game against the Red Sox, he was arrested for not paying his 1923 and 1924 local income taxes. Next he found a parking ticket on his car, became angry, refused to pose for photographers, and rode off to Fenway Park to wage baseball against Massachusetts.

Before a shivering crowd of only twelve thousand, the Yankees beat the Red Sox 12–11. Ruth had a single, two doubles, and three runs in six times at bat. Having humbled the Bay State he then paid its tax bill.

Ruth had other law business in Massachusetts. Home Plate had been for sale since the previous June. Babe had deeded the farm to Helen on October 20, 1925, subject to a mortgage of six thousand dollars held by a nearby bank. Lawrence Joyce of Waltham, the man who built the henhouses, had eight hundred dollars coming from Babe. When Helen found a buyer in February, Joyce hurried to cloud the title by attaching the place before the Ruths could leave the jurisdiction. Three days later, on February 28, Helen sold the farm but could not give an unclouded deed. Babe stepped in to clear the title. He paid Joyce and then appeared before the recorder of deeds in Middlesex County and swore that the statement of a mortgage as entered in the previous October transfer to Helen was a clerical error. The transfer to Helen was rewritten to omit all reference to a mortgage, signed again, and sealed under date of April 16, 1926, the day of the last Yankee-Red Sox game of that series. At the same time Helen closed the deal with the new buyer and a sad chapter had ended. Helen lived in Boston that year, at least as late as October.

April was a good month for Yankee fans. On the 20th Yankee power crushed the Senators 18–5 with twenty-two hits, the first of which was a home run by Ruth off Walter Johnson with a man on. Ruth had five of the Yankee hits. And they went on like that.

In the first week of May the Tigers came to town. Morris Markey of the *New Yorker* went out to see Cobb and Ruth. He sketched a typical Stadium scene with Ruth at bat:

Ruth came to bat. There was a man or two on base and the score was close. At first there was a throaty cheer from the multitude, but after a moment, as he stood there motionless at the plate, his bat poised at his shoulder, a dead hush fell. The air seemed to tighten, as if under some pressure which threatened to release itself in a moment with a terrific explosion. The outfielders drifted casually back against the fences. The pitcher glanced around to see that all was well. Even the peanut vendors paused in their shouting, and turned to watch.

At about the same time a German traveler, Dr. Gerhard Penzmer, saw Ruth and his idolaters and made a note for his forthcoming book: "The best ball player is, without doubt, a more popular man than the President of the United States."

Ruth had bounced back from 1925.

In May the Yankees ran up a sixteen-game winning streak which left them with a record of thirty wins and nine losses. Dour Ty Cobb, manager of the Tigers, conceded the pennant to the Yankees before the end of the month. In a late stage of that winning streak Ruth went to address the boys of the ten teams of the Fordham Juvenile League. (Young readers may be interested to know that "juvenile" then meant "youthful" not "delinquent," just as "adult" then meant "mature" instead of "obscene.") Ruth meant to tell the juveniles how to hit home runs, but the sight of him stirred "a vocal storm." He managed to tell them not to smoke but could go no further. New York was delirious about the renewed Yankees and the reborn Babe Ruth.

In June the Yankees went on their first western swing. Ruth was arrested at Howell, Michigan, on June 11, for catching "a few scrawny blue gills" five days before the fishing season. The game warden went to get a warrant, and Ruth quickly fled to Missouri as a fugitive from the game laws. A few days later, to bleach the stain of outlawry, he publicly volunteered to help the Reverend E. J. Flanagan of Boys Town, Nebraska, in his campaign against the misuse of orphan boys as farm laborers.

The first appearance of the Yankees in Chicago coincided with an international Eucharistic Congress which flooded Chicago with Catholics of every degree short of the Pope himself. Chicago was also the chief site of Babe Ruth's "conduct off the field" in 1925 which led to his great fine and suspension. Jocko Conlan told the author how the Yankees hoped to prevent a recurrence by inviting Brother Matthias to attend the Eucharistic Congress. Conlan had it from the Brother himself.

The Yankees stayed in Chicago at the Del Prado Hotel. . . . Somebody in the Yankee organization got the idea of sending for Brother Matthias. Brother came to the hotel and sat in a chair where he could watch everybody leaving the elevator. When Ruth came out for a night on the town he saw Brother Matthias, was very surprised, greeted him very cordially, and asked what he was doing in Chicago. Brother Matthias said he happened to be in town, wanted to see Ruth play, found out where he was staying, and came out to invite him to dinner. Ruth could not figure any way of getting out of the invitation. Brother Matthias kept him out until nearly 11 o'clock and said that by this time there would not be anybody waiting for Ruth wherever he might have been going, and that it was time to go to bed. During the dinner and afterward he gave Ruth a very strong lecture or sermon about how he should behave. This was the turning point in Ruth's behavior. Certainly he no longer after that time had the reputation for hell-raising that he had before.

On June 19, a chilly day, Patrick Cardinal O'Donnell of Ireland went out to Comiskey Park, met Ruth, gave him the ring to kiss, threw out the first ball, and saw the Yankees beat the White Sox 6–5. Ruth had two doubles in three times at bat, with a run scored and three runs batted in. The win put the Yankees ten games ahead of the league.

On July 4 the Yankee lead was eleven games. All through July they pounded out victories. On July 22, at more risk to himself than Barrow should have allowed, Ruth became the first to catch a ball dropped from an airplane. Dressed in his National Guard uniform, with the temperature at 97 degrees, he ran all over dusty Mitchell Field, Long Island, and finally caught the seventh ball dropped, from an altitude of three hundred feet. In July he also raised his total of 1926 arrests to three (perhaps a season record?) and paid a twenty-five-dollar fine for speeding on Riverside Drive at thirty-three miles an hour. The offense didn't require him to go to jail as before; jail was the penalty for the *second* offense in a calendar year. As he left the court a loving swarm of boys cheered their hero and made it hard for him to get into his roadster.

On the day after Labor Day, when Ruth's batting average was .374, the Yankees shamed themselves by losing a well-attended exhibition game to the Orioles in Baltimore, 18–9. Ruth, who played first base, had none of the Yankees' thirteen hits; in fact, he hit only one ball out of the infield. During the sixth inning, with the childish feeling that it must be somebody else's fault, Ruth stormed at Koenig, accusing him of loafing on several plays. When they returned to the dugout, Koenig, who was about forty pounds lighter, struck Ruth several times. Ruth didn't fight back but clinched and held Koenig's arms. People poured onto the field to see the struggle. Police had to herd them back to the stands.

In September the Indians gained, won four straight from the Yankees, and narrowed the lead to three games. But on September 19, before the largest Cleveland crowd to that time, the Yankees beat the Indians 8–3 with Gehrig as hero. He had three doubles and a home run in five times at bat, driving in five runs. Ruth had a home run and a single in four times at bat, scoring three runs. The Indian drive had been repulsed for that season. Less than a week later the Yankees certified the pennant by winning a double-header from the Browns, 10–2 and 10–4. Ruth hit three home runs off three pitchers, raising his season total to its final figure, forty-seven.

The Yankees certainly looked like champions, but New York was used to excellence. The victors arrived in New York to be greeted by a small group of idle old men, curious boys, and loving Yankee mothers and wives.

Just as the Yankee collapse of 1925 had been a team disgrace, so the Yankee glory of 1926 was a team triumph. The deeds of Ruth and Gehrig should not make us forget that well-balanced 1926 ball club. Earl Combs could cover half the outfield alone, and, as lead-off man, he could get on base. Bob Meusel, as Sam Jones said, "had an arm as long as this room, know what I mean?" The infield was great. The pitchers weren't the stingiest in the league, but they had the fourth best earned-run average. On offense the Yankees scored the most runs in the league, bettering their opponents by a run per game, which will win the pennant in most years.

Jacob Ruppert's checkbook also helped. During the season he acquired pitcher Dutch Ruether* from the Senators and catcher Hank Severeid from the Browns. Severeid was needed when Bengough broke an arm.

Babe Ruth hit forty-seven home runs. Al Simmons** in second place had only nineteen. Hack Wilson† led the National League with twenty-one. Ruth had more than 5 percent of all major-league home runs, and also began to use the sacrifice bunt. (Perhaps Huggins now dared to command it?) He had ten sacrifice bunts in 1926.

---

* Walter Henry Ruether (1890–1970), pitcher, eleven seasons, 1917–1927, Cubs, Reds, Dodgers, Senators, Yankees. Won 137, lost 95, earned-run average 3.50.

** Aloysius Harry Simmons, born Szymanski (1902–1956), outfielder, twenty seasons, 1924–1944, Athletics, White Sox, Tigers, Senators, Braves, Reds, Phillies, batting average .334. Hall of Fame.

† Lewis Robert Wilson (1900–1948), outfielder, twelve seasons, 1923–1934, Giants, Cubs, Dodgers, Phillies, batting average .307.

Of the dozen important offensive categories, Ruth led in seven (as in 1921, 1923, and 1924): slugging percentage, home runs, total bases, runs batted in, bases on balls, runs scored, and home runs as a percentage of times at bat. His margin over the second best in each category was wide except in runs scored; he scored 139, Gehrig scored 135.

THE ACCUMULATED BATTING FIGURES

BABE RUTH'S MAJOR-LEAGUE CAREER

1914–1926

at bat: 4419

hits: 1539

home runs: 356

runs batted in: 1110

average: .348

38 · Cards Show Best When Under Fire

The opposing teams of the 1926 World Series had season records much alike. St. Louisans and National Leaguers picked the Cardinals; New Yorkers and American Leaguers picked the Yankees. If the feelings of the fans matter, it is worth noting that New Yorkers took the pennant for granted. Not so St. Louisans. The city was in frenzy over its first league championship since 1888, and the people rejoiced so recklessly that when they came to count the cost they had two dead and thirty seriously injured. Would the Cardinals dare to lose the Series in such a setting?

James R. Harrison of *The Times* believed the Cardinals had a spark the Yankees lacked. The headline over his analysis read CARDS SHOW BEST WHEN UNDER FIRE. He believed the Cardinals were more competitive, cleverer, and better able to react flexibly to sudden changes.

The Series would be a fair test of pitching, because almost a week was to pass between the close of the season and the start of the Series. The pitchers would be rested.

So far as Babe Ruth was concerned, the World Series of 1926 was a domestic waypost. It was the occasion of the last public appearance of Babe, Helen, and Dorothy together. They posed for photographers before the first game, and Helen and Dorothy saw all of the games played in New York.

Herb Pennock beat the Cardinals and Willie Sherdel* at New York, 3–1, before a crowd of sixty-three thousand (held down by threat of rain) in the first game on Saturday, October 2. Pennock gave up only three hits. The new Yankee artillery was effective; Gehrig drove Ruth home with the winning run. All nine hits in the game were singles. The crowd welcomed Ruth with roars of delight whenever he came to bat.

---

* William Henry Sherdel (1896–1968), pitcher, fifteen seasons, 1918–1932, Cardinals, Braves. Won 165, lost 146, earned-run average 3.72.

Graham McNamee and Phillips Carlin described the game for a radio network of twenty-three stations, which was such a novelty that *The Times* published their narratives of all the games, word for word.

The hero of the second game was Old Pete Alexander. He was tall, knock-kneed, and deliberate in his motions. His eyes were gray, his face freckled, and the skin of his neck was wattled like a turkey's. The Cardinals got him cheap early in the season from the Cubs, because the new Cubs manager, Joe McCarthy, didn't find him meek enough and discarded him to show the other Cubs who was master. Alexander always tried to work so that no two pitches in a game arrived at the plate at the same speed; thus batters would not master his timing. (Contrary to legend he was no wreck; he would go on to win twenty-one games in 1927 and sixteen in 1928.)

On a summery day Alexander beat the Yankees 6–2, giving only four hits and striking out ten. The admiring crowd generously stood during the Cardinals' half of the seventh inning to honor Alexander. Neither Ruth nor Gehrig had a hit.

After a day of travel the Yankees won the third game in St. Louis on a wet day which required a thirty-minute rain delay. Little old Sportsman's Park had a record crowd of thirty-one thousand. Jesse Haines* won 4–0 and was doubly a hero — he not only shut out the visitors with five hits but had two hits himself, one of them a home run with a man on. Ruth had one single and Gehrig two. Thus far the Yankees seemed the lesser team.

The fourth game was a game of power. Each team made fourteen hits, but the Yankees made them longer and grouped them, so they won 10–5. Ruth set a new World Series record with three home runs, and even the St. Louis fans loudly cheered his work. The verbatim transcript of the radio description of the third home run shows the unnamed announcer (Carlin or McNamee) in a hyper-manic state:

> The Babe is up. Two home runs today. One ball, far outside. Babe's shoulders look as if there is murder in them down there, the way he is swinging that bat down there. A high foul into the left-field stands. That great big bat of Babe's looks like a toothpick down there, he is so big himself. Here it is. Babe shot a bad one and fouled it. Two strikes and one ball. The outfield have all moved very far towards right. It is coming up now. A little too close. Two strikes and two balls. He has got two home runs and a base on balls so far today. Here it is, and a ball. Three and two. The Babe is waving that wand of his over the

---

* Jesse Joseph Haines (1893–   ), pitcher, nineteen seasons, 1918–1937, Reds, Cardinals. Won 210, lost 158, earned-run average 3.64. Hall of Fame.

plate. Bell is loosening up his arm. The Babe is hit clear into the center-field bleachers for a home run! For a home run! Did you hear what I said? Where is that fellow who told me not to talk about Ruth anymore? Send him up here.

Oh, what a shot! Directly over second. The boys are all over him over there. One of the boys is riding on Ruth's back. Oh, what a shot! Directly over second base far into the bleachers out in center field, and almost on a line and then that dumbell, where is he, who told me not to talk about Ruth! Oh, boy! Not that I love Ruth, but oh, how I love to see a shot like that! Wow! That is a world's series record, three home runs in one world's series game and what a home run! That was probably the longest hit ever made in Sportsman's Park. They tell me this is the first ball ever hit in the center-field stand. That is a mile and a half from here. You know what I mean.

Each of the home runs had gone farther than the one before, but the third was not the longest ever hit in the ball park. Ruth had hit one in the same place on May 25, 1921.

The effect of the radio broadcast was to bring Ruth 813 telegrams, letters, and hand-delivered notes of homage. Inasmuch as the park's unscreened right-field pavilion was close to the plate, one should note that the first home run went over the pavilion roof, a few feet

The swing that drove the long home run to center in the 1926 World Series (October 6), as long a hit as ever was made in old Sportsman's Park. (*National Baseball Library, Cooperstown, New York.*)

fair, the second was also over the pavilion toward right center, and the third bounced out of the park from the center-field bleachers. They weren't cheap hits.

On the next day forty-three thousand jammed Sportsman's Park. They saw the Yankees win 3–2 in ten innings. The day's hero was Mark Koenig, who drove in the first run and, after Gehrig tied it up in the ninth, scored the winning run in the tenth. Ruth had two walks and a strikeout. The teams boarded their special trains for a day's ride to New York, during which the Yankees—with a three-two edge in games—could meditate on the prospect of facing Alexander again. The Cardinals' train reached New York in twenty-one hours and twenty minutes, setting a new record by nearly three hours.

The day of the sixth game, Saturday, October 9, was chilly enough to keep down the numbers in the Stadium. There were only fourteen in line for bleacher seats when the sun came up. For the Yankees the game was painful. Alexander held them to eight hits and two runs while the Cardinals had thirteen hits and ten runs. Ruth's line in the score showed only a walk, a stolen base, and an assist. The Series now turned on the seventh game. The Yankees might reasonably hope they wouldn't see any more of Alexander. They couldn't know that Rogers Hornsby, the Cardinal manager, told Alexander he might yet be needed in relief.

The final game of the World Series of 1926 was one of those few games that are talked of fifty years after they are played. The day was cold and drizzly, good pitcher's weather. During morning rain a rumor spread that Commissioner Landis had postponed the game. The uncertainty held the crowd down to 38,093.

Jesse Haines pitched well for the Cardinals until the seventh inning. Then, leading 3–2, he filled the bases and developed a blister on his hand. There were two outs, Lazzeri was coming to bat. Hornsby signaled Alexander to come in. Alexander, who could not stop at one drink, had been led astray by well-meaning friends into a night of celebration, but he knew his duty and had been warming up before Hornsby called. Bob O'Farrell,* his catcher, later said, "He'd been out on a drunk the night before and was still feeling the effects." Alexander strolled slowly to the mound, thinking how he would pitch to Lazzeri. Legend says Hornsby met him at second base and said, smiling, "There's no place to put him." Alexander knew Lazzeri was at least as nervous as he was. And Lazzeri had already struck out twice in the game, swinging at bad pitches.

---

* Robert Arthur O'Farrell (1896–   ), catcher, twenty-one seasons, 1915–1935, Cubs, Cardinals, Giants, Reds, batting average .273.

It wasn't Lazzeri's day. With two outs, an outfield single would have scored two runs and might have won the world championship. Lazzeri took a curve, a ball. Next he pulled a high inside fast ball down the left-field line, foul. Then he swung and missed two curves. No runs, three men left on base.

> **Let us suppose, then, that our batsman has reached, let us say, first base safely. He has then completed the first quarter of his journey to the home plate. The other three quarters still lie before him, filled with dangers for the unwary runner.**
>
> *—The Book of Knowledge: The Children's Encyclopedia* (1919)

In the eighth inning Alexander got the Yankees out one-two-three. In the ninth Combs and Koenig hit into fielding putouts. Then came Ruth, who already had three walks and a home run in this game. Another home run would tie the score. Hornsby went in from his post to tell Alexander to pitch to Ruth—but carefully.

In later years Alexander always insisted he struck Ruth out twice, in a manner of speaking. The count went to three balls and two strikes. Alexander thought the third ball was the third strike and started to walk off the field before the umpire's call. And he was certain the fourth ball was a strike, but Ruth jogged to first base with his fourth walk and eleventh of the Series. The crowd booed what it thought was an intentional base on balls.

If the Cardinals could get Meusel out they would be world champions; if the Yankees could move Ruth around they would tie the game. Meusel had a triple, a double, and three singles in twenty-one times at bat; as they say, he was "due." The defensive situation was this: O'Farrell had caught all seven games well, without error. Hornsby was an adequate second baseman. Babe Ruth had stolen eleven bases during the pennant season and had the only Yankee stolen base in the Series.

The last out of the Series came as a surprise to absolutely everybody. Let the unnamed radio announcer describe it:

> Ruth is walked again for the fourth time today. One strike on Bob Meusel. Going down to second! The game is over! Babe tried to steal second and is put out catcher to second!

Ruth tried a delayed steal which failed. O'Farrell threw perfectly to Hornsby. The Cardinals were champions of the world.

It depends on where I am. At third, it's "Be safe." That's because on a squeeze play it's better to leave too late than early. At second base I concentrate on one thing: "Be careful." I'm already in scoring position, and it doesn't make sense to take chances. At first it's "Be daring."

—Maury Wills (1972)

Ruth believed his daring attempt to steal second may have been "rash," but he hoped to surprise O'Farrell and be in a position to score the tying run on any solid hit. Ed Barrow, the Yankees' general manager, called it Ruth's only "dumb play." We know now that the hit-and-run play was not on, that Ruth was on his own. None of the Yankees ever blamed him. O'Farrell was curious enough to ask Ruth in 1928 what he had had in mind. Ruth said he thought Alexander was paying little attention to him; furthermore, as long as he stayed on first it would take two singles to score him. The way Alexander was pitching they probably wouldn't get two hits in a row, so it would be well to be where he could score on one hit. O'Farrell's comment was, "Maybe that was good thinking and maybe not. In any case I had him out a mile at second." Hornsby regarded his putout of Ruth as one of the great moments of his life.

One *can* say something for Ruth. If you are trailing by a narrow margin, and you have a chance to tie or win with your legs, you must run. You can't forget you're a major-league ballplayer, fall on your knees, worship the enemy's throwing arm, and say, You win.

Legend gives Ruth the last word.

"I wasn't doing any—————good on first base."

On Tuesday by airmail he promised a desperately sick boy in New Jersey to "knock a homer for you." The child's hero made it three.

—Radio description of fourth game,
The Times, October 7, 1926

John Dale Sylvester, aged eleven, son of Horace C. Sylvester, Jr., a vice-president of the National City Bank (which was *not* Jacob Ruppert's bank, as a cynic might suspect), was seriously ill at his home in Essex Fells, New Jersey, during the World Series of 1926. While following the games by radio he asked his father for a ball autographed by Babe Ruth. The elder Sylvester wired Ruth in St. Louis. Two baseballs autographed by several players of both teams came by airmail to Sylvester's house on the day of the fourth game, October 6, with a note of encouragement. There was no mention of a promise to hit a home run, but Johnny was pleasantly

The last put out of the 1926 World Series. With two outs, trailing by a run in the top of the ninth, Ruth tries to take second to put himself in scoring position. The play is scored 2–4 (Bob O'Farrell to Rogers Hornsby.) (*National Baseball Library, Cooperstown, New York.*)

stirred to hear the description of the record three home runs while clutching Babe Ruth's gifts. His father wrote proper notes of thanks to Huggins and Hornsby.

Johnny began to improve after that, and maudlin writers have claimed Ruth's gift cured him. The unnamed radio speaker invented the promise to hit a home run as a flourish to ornament his broadcast description of the three-home-run day. The press picked it up and pumped it large with gassy sentimentalism. Red Grange shamelessly climbed aboard the balloon and sent Johnny an unsolicited autographed football with the promise of a touchdown when he played in Yankee Stadium.

After the Series Ruth went barnstorming. His team was to play the Brooklyn Royal Colored Giants on October 11 at Bradley Beach near Essex Fells. On impulse, before the game, Ruth called on the Sylvesters without notice (which delayed the game two hours). Johnny was nearly stupefied by the visit of the demigod on whom he kept an up-to-date scrapbook, but after a halting start the two got along well. They didn't meet again for nearly twenty years. A year later Ruth didn't recognize the boy's name when it was mentioned.

The Johnny Sylvester story has been reworked in many ways to meet the needs of a young nation short of mythology. This author's favorite version has Ruth allegedly promising the home run on a visit *before* the World Series. When he kept his promise trebly, he saved the life of a worshiping boy who had but thirty minutes to live because of what was diagnosed as a terminal case of sinus trouble.

The winning team has the hero of the World Series—in this case Grover Cleveland Alexander. But Ruth had an excellent Series. He set ten new offensive records. And the ten are more than any batter ever set before, so that makes eleven. The Series drew the largest attendance—328,000—of any Series during Ruth's career. Because fourth-place teams received World Series shares for the first time, the individual player's shares were about six hundred dollars less than in the record year of 1923.

Ruth, Gehrig, and Shocker went barnstorming after the World Series. Ruth hired Gehrig at three hundred dollars a day, but when the tour proved highly profitable he raised Gehrig's share about 60 percent by paying him a flat ten thousand. The purpose was to entertain rather than compete. To illustrate: On a cold windy day in Canada before three thousand, Ruth began by hitting thirty-six balls out of the park in an exhibition of power before the game between the town teams of Guyburg and Beaurivage. Then he and Shocker played for Guyburg, with Ruth successively playing short-stop, first base, pitching, and umpiring. Guyburg won 4–3 as Ruth hit two home runs. They called the game in the ninth because they ran out of baseballs.

After the comeback of 1926 reporters liked to quiz Ruth about his next contract, to be signed in 1927. One writer suggested $150,000. Ruth said he "might accept it." Of course the writers carried the news to Ruppert who called the figure "preposterous," adding, "He won't get it." Both of them knew the decision was months in the future.

After the profitable barnstorming came vaudeville—twelve weeks as a single on the Pantages Circuit. *Rumor*: He would get a hundred thousand dollars. *Fact*: Sixty-five thousand. He opened in Minneapolis at the end of October and closed on the west coast. The Pantages people thought to get newspaper space by having Ruth in the receiving line in Minneapolis at a reception for Queen Marie of Rumania. Within earshot of reporters he was to tell her he was a king himself. Hardly a soul is now alive who could state a fact about that Queen whose royal progress was a temporary triumph of the ballyhoo of make-believe news, covered by the press in column feet. Ruth canceled a hunting trip to be there, but a minor-league pitcher came to his hotel to talk baseball and Ruth forgot Her Majesty. Looking back, his sense of proportion seems excellent.

The year-end review of sports in 1926 in *The Times* gave two paragraphs to the resurrection of the Yankees from the tomb of seventh place, with chief credit to the stronger infield and the rebirth of Babe Ruth.

Ruth won back the love of his countrymen who put their money where their hearts were. His income from early 1926 to the beginning of the 1927 season, from baseball, motion pictures (early 1927), vaudeville, barnstorming, syndicated ghost-written columns, and the usual unprincipled endorsements of advertised products—in days when income taxes were pleasingly low—was nearly a quarter of a million dollars.

Outside the Park, 1927

SAYS 'BOOTLEG LOVE'
PERMEATES NATION

10,000,000 HEAR
OPERA OVER RADIO

GIRL BANK ROBBER
SIGNS CONFESSION

RISE IN ALCOHOLIC DEATH RATES

ONE-WAY STREETS
FOR ALL MANHATTAN

HOOVER BEGINS NATION-WIDE ATTACK ON CHAOS IN RADIO

SAYS HIS TELEVISION
HAS SPANNED OCEAN

SCHOOLBOY, 13, HANGS HIMSELF IN HIS HOME

LINDBERGH SPEEDS ACROSS NORTH ATLANTIC

DEAN FEARS ONLY THE RICH
CAN GO TO COLLEGE SOON

IMMIGRATION QUOTAS FULL

RECORD OF THE WORLD FLIERS TO DATE

THINK BIG, HENRY FORD
ADVISES YOUNG MEN

STOCKS RISE, TOPPLE,
IN WIDE SPECULATION

SURVEY IS STARTED
OF DRUG ADDICTION

MARINE DIES FIGHTING
NICARAGUAN GUERILLAS

GOV. SMITH FLOODED
BY POLITICAL MAIL

39 · He Hit Sixty (1927)

Babe Ruth went on tour as a single in vaudeville, booked by Pantages for twelve weeks at sixty-five thousand dollars, starting in Minneapolis at the end of October 1926 and ending in southern California in January 1927. In the last week of January he was arrested in San Diego for breaking the child-labor laws. A deputy state labor commissioner brought the charge. Ruth put up five hundred dollars bail to appear on February 7. He did not appear in court but two lawyers answered for him. His dastardly deed was this: as part of his act he called children up on the stage without preparation, talked with them, and gave them baseballs. The judge agreed that every child in the house would be glad to take part. It cost Ruth his bail-bond fee and the fees of a brace of lawyers, part of the price of fame which made him a shining target for anyone who wished to share newspaper space with him—in this case a publicity-hungry public official who scored no political gain.

In the same week as his arrest in San Diego, Ruth signed to make a movie with Anna Q. Nillson called *The Babe Comes Home*. Shooting took twenty-two days. The film was widely ignored by the critics; the only person the author knows who saw it said it was rubbish. Making the picture was physically good for Ruth, because he took Artie McGovern, his trainer, to California. McGovern persuaded him to get enough sleep (bed at 9 P.M.; on the set at 6 A.M.) and had him run five miles a day. Harold Lloyd also cast Ruth for what would now be called a cameo part in *Speedy*, in which Ruth played a passenger in Lloyd's taxi.

At the end of this austere Hollywood career Ruth was in excellent physical shape. He was so pleased with his 1926 comeback that he stayed in condition. For example, his waistline was the same in early 1927 as it was in April 1926 (not quite forty inches). In California he and McGovern got it down to thirty-seven and a half inches.

Caught in his own mousetrap, a promotional still photograph, early 1927, for "Babe Comes Home," with Anna Q. Nilsson and Babe Ruth. (*National Baseball Library, Cooperstown, New York.*)

McGovern sent Ruth's measurements to owner Jacob Ruppert at the end of the California workouts, and the Yankee management was pleased at the figures. The physical report would be a trump card in the game of salary negotiation which was to start soon.

> **You fellows won't be able to play taps over Babe Ruth for five or six years yet.**
> **—Babe Ruth, March 3, 1927**

Ruth's new contract probably provoked more column-yards of newspaper stories than there were clock-minutes of negotiation. It was news for a month but discussed by the parties less than an hour. Early in February the Yankees sent him another fifty-two-thousand-dollar contract, which, as he told reporters, he would not sign because he wanted more money. He suggested he already had enough money to quit baseball if he didn't get a raise. And he might even open a chain of gymnasiums with Artie McGovern. A rumor that Ty Cobb was to get seventy-five thousand may have stiffened his backbone.

Until February 26 all Ruppert knew was what he read in the

papers, since Ruth grumbled only to reporters. Then Ruth returned the unsigned contract on February 22 (it reached New York on the 26th) with a letter giving his views on what he should get, and why. Ruppert had a convenient cold for the next few days and said nothing. Just before boarding the train from California to New York, Ruth said he wanted a hundred thousand a year; he spoke of how the Yankees made money out of him by playing exhibition games at every chance, and gave out Artie McGovern's favorable physical-condition report. A grievance which was news to all was that Huggins had collected, all told, seventy-seven hundred dollars in fines from him.

People didn't resent Ruth's attitude. W. O. McGeehan of the *Herald-Tribune* took a poll which showed agreement that the proper salary for Babe Ruth would be somewhere between a hundred and two hundred thousand dollars.

Ruth reached New York on March 2, met reporters and photographers at McGovern's gymnasium for three-quarters of an hour, and then went to visit St. Vincent's Hospital where poor Helen was ill again. Then he was off to settle his terms.

The Ruth-Ruppert treaty of 1927 was drafted in the Ruppert brewery offices at 91st Street and Third Avenue. Before getting down to words, the dickerers had to give up forty minutes to thirty news photographers. Once they got into the inner office they needed but fifty-five minutes to settle things. Ed Barrow opened the door to twenty writers and explained the terms: a three-year contract at seventy thousand a year (one imaginative reporter figured it, for a season of 154 games, at $454.54 per game, $56.67 per inning). Ruth told the newsmen he'd be around for years, and Jacob Ruppert, in a moment of uncharacteristic weakness, added the startling remark, "The Babe is a sensible fellow." To Ruth the important fact may have been that the contract kept him the highest-paid man in baseball. Two days later, at the formal signing, he wrote his name with his right hand and tried an *ad lib* joke: he batted left-handed and signed contracts right-handed, getting the best results that way in each case.

Barrow went into his own office, got out the little "New York Salary and Transfer File," and brought Ruth's 4 x 6 card up to date:

<pre>
1927)
1928)   Cont. $70,000 each season
1929)
</pre>

The table of Ruppert's baseball salaries in 1927 stood like this:

Name	Amount	Remarks
Barrow	25,000	
Huggins	37,500	
Ruth	70,000	Three years
Pennock	17,500	1000 bonus if won 25
Shocker	13,500	
Meusel	13,000	
Dugan	12,000	
Ruether	11,000	1000 bonus if won 15
Hoyt	11,000	1000 bonus if won 20
Shawkey	10,500	
Combs	19,500	
Lazzeri	8,000	plus round trip fare, California, for self and wife
Bengough	8,000	
Gehrig	8,000	
Collins	7,000	
Koenig	7,000	
Paschal	7,000	
Thomas	6,500	
Grabowski	5,500	
Gazella	5,000	
Giard	5,000	
Pipgras	4,500	
Durst	4,500	
Morehart	4,000	
Wera	2,400	
Moore	2,500	plus 5000 if lasted the season

Commissioner Landis and John McGraw each received sixty-five thousand that year. Rumor now said Ty Cobb was to get fifty thousand, and ten thousand more if the Tigers won the pennant. Rogers Hornsby's salary was forty thousand. Walter Hagen, the golfer, and Jack Dempsey, the boxer, were the only sports figures in the country who made more that year than Babe Ruth made.

Ballplayers like to think they are paid for skill, and management says its high resolve is to field great teams. The gritty facts are that ballplayers are paid for their drawing power, not their artistry, and management—at least in the days before television contracts and mysterious tax writeoffs—wished only to sell tickets, food, and drink at its ball parks. Was Ruth's salary too high? Those who thought not said Enrico Caruso packed the Metropolitan Opera House every time he sang and got three to five thousand dollars each time. Yan-

The New York Yankees of 1927, often named as the greatest team, certainly the most interesting. (*The New York Yankees.*)

BACK ROW LEFT TO RIGHT: Lou Gehrig, Herb Pennock, Tony Lazzeri, Wilcy Moore, Babe Ruth, Don Mills, Bob Meusel, Bob Shawkey, Waite Hoyt, Joe Giard, Ben Paschal, Walt Beall, and trainer Doc Woods.

MIDDLE ROW: Urban Shocker, Joe Dugan, Earle Combs, coach Charlie O'Leary, Miller Huggins, coach Art Fletcher, Mark Koenig, Dutch Ruether, John Grabowski, George Pipgras.

FRONT ROW: Julie Wera, Mike Gazella, Pat Collins, mascot Eddie Bennett, Benny Bengough, Ray Morehart, Myles Thomas, and Cedric Durst.

kee Stadium drew a lot more paying customers than the Met, and Ruth was paid much less per hour. Was a three-year contract prudent for the Yankees when Ruth was thirty-two? Huggins thought so: "He has the constitution of a horse."

THINKS GEORGE HERMAN WILL MAKE

TEAM IF HE WORKS HARD—

RUTHIAN WEIGHT 223 POUNDS

—*The Times*, March 8, 1927

Within a week of signing the new contract Ruth was in St. Petersburg. He played a round of golf in 92, asked sportswriter James R.

Harrison to test his abdominal muscles with his fists, hit several baseballs out of the park in batting practice, and loosened up by pitching to Benny Bengough. The very sight of his health and vigor cheered everybody.

Seventeen new Yankees came to camp, of whom the most important was the elderly rookie Cy Moore,* a balding, freckled cotton farmer from Oklahoma, aged thirty. He had a good sidearm sinker, a mediocre curve, no nerves, and, after six years in the minor leagues, a simplehearted view of life. The writers said Ed Barrow found him in the Sears, Roebuck catalog, but Barrow found him in the *Sporting News* in the pitching statistics of the South Atlantic (Sally) League. The Yankees scouted him in July 1926 and bought him in August from the Greenville, North Carolina, club; he won thirty and lost four in 1926, with an earned-run average of 2.86. He cost Ruppert thirty-five hundred dollars. As a hitter, he swung his bat beautifully, but always in the same arc. Ruth bet him three hundred dollars to a hundred that he wouldn't get three hits in 1927.

At the end of March the team headed north to play nine games with the Dodgers on the way home. John Kieran said Ruth was always the last man away from the park: "He has to autograph baseballs, score cards, and torn bits of paper for the ragged kids who waylay him outside the dressing room door." As usual the two teams played the last preseason game in New York. On a chilly day the Yankees beat the Dodgers 6–5. Ruth was an exploding sun. He drove in five runs including a home run with one on.

Now it was time for crystal-gazing. *The Times* thought Yankee pitching was weaker than in 1926, the rest of the team about the same, and believed other clubs had strengthened themselves. Huggins forecast "a closer race this time. Six clubs, with almost equal chance, must be considered as contenders." A poll was taken of forty-two experts. Nineteen picked the Pirates to win in the National League; nine picked the Yankees in the American League. Ruppert cast off caution and picked the Yankees because Ruth was "ready to have his greatest year."

Ninety-seven thousand people tried to see the opening day game, but twenty-five thousand had to be turned away. The Yankees beat the Athletics 8–3. Ruth had won a player popularity contest and received a silver loving cup from Mayor Jimmy Walker. But he went hitless.

Rogers Hornsby was now with the Giants and thus getting much more attention than before. Naturally he and Ruth were compared in every way. John Kieran decided Hornsby was a machine but Ruth

---

* William Wilcy Moore (1897–1963), pitcher, six seasons, 1927–1933, Yankees, Red Sox. Won 51, lost 44, earned-run average 3.69.

was a spectacle—"without doubt the most picturesque person the national pastime has produced. . . ."

At the end of April, Ruth had four home runs.

The Yankees took a western swing in May. By the 22nd they had won ten of thirteen road games and a total of twenty-three of their thirty-three games; they led the league by four and a half games. In Cleveland on the 22nd Ruth hit a homerun about six hundred feet in the air which cleared the fence by perhaps six inches. (He also accepted an Indian bonnet from a group of rodeo Indians sitting with the overflow crowd along the first-base foul line; he wore the bonnet for an inning.) Could the Yankees go on like this?

Ruth hit twelve home runs in May; his total was now sixteen.

In June the army had its annual Ruth-centered publicity for the Citizens Military Training Camps, with Ruth autographing balls and bats as prizes for the champion teams of the several camps. Ruth also introduced the German-American laborer's practice of wearing cabbage leaves under his cap on hot days. A leaf would last about three innings before wilting. Once he wore the leaf under his cap to the plate, hit a home run, and revealed the cabbage when he tipped his cap to the applause. Wits on the enemy bench claimed to see a connection between ham and cabbage. In Cleveland on

A strike, June 2, 1927 (he walked); typical posture after missing the ball. (*National Baseball Library, Cooperstown, New York.*)

June 11, after Ruth had hit two home runs, Luke Sewell, the Cleveland catcher, demanded an umpire's inspection of the bat. After a close look the umpire ruled it legal. Sewell may have made a good play: Ruth then struck out, to the pleasure of all Cleveland.

In June Ruth hit nine home runs, bringing his total to twenty-five.

> **It isn't a race in the American League, it's a landslide.**
> —John Kieran, *The Times*, July 6, 1927

On the Fourth of July the Yankees led the American League by eleven and a half games. They won a double-header that day from the Senators by scores of 12–1 and 18–1. The two games drew the largest crowd to that time—seventy-four thousand. Gehrig hit two home runs and briefly had a total greater than Ruth's. Ruth had five hits in seven times at bat. Thaddeus L. Boldon, a professor of psychology at Temple University, an institution much patronized by oppressed Athletics and Phillies fans, decried that record crowd and its human particles by saying that baseball fans were not well balanced because their love of sport excluded all sports but baseball. The headline over his views read BALL FANS LACK MENTAL POISE. The writer can only say that he has never met any baseball fans much concerned about their mental poise.

At Washington that month Ruth pulled an outside pitch on a line directly at startled pitcher Hod Lisenbee who leaped and let the ball pass between his legs for a hit over second base. Legend gives two reports: (1) it went over the center fielder's head, and (2) it went over the fence. In another generation it will have gone out of the ball park entirely.

In July Ruth hit nine home runs to make his total thirty-four.

During the winter of 1926–1927 Charles A. Comiskey, owner of the White Sox, added second decks to his outfield stands. Otherwise the grand park, the oldest in use, remains with its perfect dimensions just as it was in 1910 (including its primeval plumbing). On August 26 Ruth became the first batter to hit a ball completely out of the remodeled park. It traveled not less than 474 feet.* The Yankees were hitting so fiercely that Huggins praised his underrated pitchers to the press. He was especially generous to Cy Moore: "He is as cool as a cake of ice, has splendid control, and a deceptive delivery. . . . He is always ready . . . as nonchalantly as if he were going up to pitch to the batters in practice." In that month Ruth and Gehrig found themselves in a home-run contest which enlivened what might have been a less interesting season. Rivalry stirred both to hit more than they would otherwise.

* Dr. Michael Crowe made the calculations for the author, from measurements supplied by Mr. Buck Peden of the White Sox office.

In August Ruth hit nine home runs, making his total forty-three.

At the end of any season it becomes harder and harder to snap all the muscles into game condition.

—Jim Brosnan

Of course the Yankees weren't invincible. On a day in early September when they led the league by seventeen games, Lefty Grove* shut them out 1–0, the first time they were shut out in 1927. Grove gave the Yankees three hits, all singles; Ruth had two of them. And a week later, after beating the Browns twenty-one times in a row, they lost to the Browns 1–0, the loss debited to Cy Moore who gave up only seven hits.

But the 1927 Yankees were the next thing to invincible. If they won both games of a double-header with the Indians in the Stadium on September 13, they would win the pennant. They won both games by the same score, 5–3. Ruth hit his fifty-first and fifty-second home runs, his only two hits for the day, which shows he was trying to hit home runs. On the 24th the Yankees won their 106th game, breaking the American League record, and by the end of the season they had won 110, a record which stood until 1954.**

Off the field, the Yankees and Ruth had to correct two untruths in September, one trivial, one grave. *The Spectator*, an insurance trade paper, reported that the Yankees had insured Ruth's life for five million dollars; the truth: three hundred thousand. The graver matter was a charge that Ruth had struck a cripple on a New York street at 11 P.M. on July 4. (The plaintiff's manner of giving testimony made him seem somewhat disordered, emotionally.) Ruth proved he was in Newark or enroute from 7 P.M. until a few minutes after midnight.

After the Yankees had won the pennant, with weeks to play, the absorbing question was whether Ruth would break his 1921 home-run record of fifty-nine. He would have to hit eight in the next fourteen games. The whole nation began to count home runs.

In ten games Ruth hit four of the eight he would need, and on the 26th had four games to play in which to hit four home runs to total sixty. On the 27th he hit one with the bases full off Lefty Grove in New York. The next day was an open date.

On September 29 he tied the 1921 season mark when he hit two in a game at New York against the Senators, which the Yankees

---

* Robert Moses Grove (1900–   ), pitcher, seventeen seasons, 1925–1941, Athletics, Red Sox. Won 300, lost 141, earned-run average 3.06. Hall of Fame.
** The record had been set by the Red Sox who won 105 in 1912. The Indians won 111 in 1954. The standing major-league record was set by the 1906 Cubs, who won 116.

won 15–4. The first home run came in the first inning with the bases empty. The second he hit in the fifth with the bases full. In his life Ruth hit only sixteen home runs with the bases filled; here were two of them in consecutive games, a (shared) standing record yet. In the same game he had a triple to center which would easily have gone over the fence if hit to right field, and his last fly flattened Goose Goslin* against the right-field fence, falling inches short of a home run. Hod Lisenbee gave up the first of the two home runs. After the game he came around to the Yankee clubhouse in street clothes to get Ruth to autograph the ball he hit; Ruth signed it but didn't know who Lisenbee was.

With two games to play, Ruth needed one more to break the record.

Against the Senators on September 30, in the next to last game of the season, with the score 2–2 in the eighth and one out, Koenig tripled off the left-handed Tom Zachary,** who had already given up two home runs to Ruth that summer. Zachary thought himself clever; he used to kick dirt to hide the rubber and pitch from two feet in front of it. Ruth already had two singles and a walk in this game. Of his three bats, Black Betsy, with which he hit number fifty-nine, Big Bertha, an ash blond, and Beautiful Bella, a titian, Ruth carried Bella to the plate. With the score tied and one out it would have been wise to walk Ruth intentionally in hope of getting a double play, but the Senators pitched to him, which gave him a chance for number sixty.

The first pitch was a called strike. The second a ball, high. If witness be trusted, the next must have been a screwball, because it broke in, ankle high, about six inches inside. The reddish bat swung down and pulled the ball over Goslin's head halfway up the right-field bleachers, fair by a dozen feet.

The hit won the ball game and broke the season home-run record with a mark that stood until 1961. It also set the still standing record for most home runs hit in September—seventeen. Players and crowd joyously thumped one another, strewed scraps of paper, and sailed straw hats, but the glee was not as unbridled as might be thought. To Ruth the most interesting show of bliss was the sight of third-base coach Charlie O'Leary jumping on his cap, thus baring his bald head which he usually took pains to hide. (He was always out of sight when they played "The Star Spangled Banner.") Pete Sheehy, the Yankees' equipment manager, said, "There wasn't the excitement

* Leon Allen Goslin (1900–1971), outfielder, eighteen seasons, 1921–1938, Senators, Browns, Tigers, batting average .316. Hall of Fame.
** Jonathan Thompson Walton Zachary (1896–1969), pitcher, nineteen seasons, 1918–1936, Athletics, Senators, Browns, Yankees, Red Sox, Dodgers, Phillies, won 185, lost 191, earned-run average 3.72.

THE GREAT TURNSTILE WHIRLER

—Cassel in the New York *World*.

you'd imagine . . . he had already hit 59 another year and the feeling was that next year he would probably hit 62." But the author remembers the hot afternoon in a corn-belt town when a man burst out of the door of a cigar store which had the baseball wire service, shouted, "He hit sixty!" and ran down the street to carry the word.

In the top of the ninth the people in the right-field stands (Ruthville) all stood and waved handkerchiefs. Their hero grinned at his constituents and, as was his habit, gave them a series of well-snapped military salutes.

The Yankees won the pennant by nineteen games. They led in runs scored and held their opponents to fewest runs scored. They had the most triples, most home runs, best batting average, best slugging percentage, most bases on balls, and best earned-run average. They did this with little rest, for they played exhibitions on almost every open date. Always they drew baseball crowds, and they drew well at rural depots where stationmasters told the villagers when the Yankees' train was stopping for water or whatever. At such stops Ruth invariably went to the platform to make some friendly frivolous remarks, even if he had been asleep in his berth. The baseball writers voted Gehrig the Most Valuable Player (Ruth was ineligible because he won it before; a pretty silly rule).

Cy Moore had an earned-run average of 2.28 and the number of his wins was exactly the margin by which the Yankees won the pennant—nineteen. And he got five hits that season to win his bet with Ruth. With the three hundred dollars he bought a pair of mules to work his cotton patch, and named them Babe and Ruth.

Ruth's record, apart from the home runs, was not as spectacular as in some earlier years. Now he had Gehrig to contend with, and Cobb edged him out of the first five batters in the league by a margin of .001. Gehrig was third in batting and succeeded Ruth as leader in total bases and runs batted in. Ruth still led in slugging percentage, home runs, bases on balls, runs scored, and in home runs as a proportion of times at bat. Gehrig was close behind in slugging, bases on balls, and runs scored.

There has been some questioning of Ruth's 1927 home runs on three points. Ruth hit four home runs in St. Louis, but no one recorded whether any went into the nearby unscreened pavilion (310 feet).* Second, the rules then allowed a home run if the ball bounced out; but no Ruth home run in 1927 bounced out. Third, belittlers say that Yankee Stadium's short right field helped Ruth; but he hit thirty-two on the road, twenty-eight in Yankee stadium.

THE ACCUMULATED BATTING FIGURES
BABE RUTH'S MAJOR-LEAGUE CAREER
1914–1927

at bat: 4959
hits: 1731
home runs: 416
runs batted in: 1274
average: .349

---

* Home runs over the right-field roofed pavilion were long. Those into the pavilion stand were cheap. The front of the pavilion was screened a few years later. In 1932 Jimmy Foxx hit several against the screen (he hit fifty-eight home runs that year), which cost him the chance to break Ruth's 1927 record.

40 · Easily the Outstanding Figure

The Yankees were slight favorites over the Pirates as the World Series of 1927 opened. Their batting and fielding averages were practically the same, but the Yankees had three times as many home runs, scored many more runs, had more doubles, more triples. The Pirates were an old-fashioned singles-hitting, bunting, running, stealing team, matched against the leaders of the sluggers' revolution. National Leaguers argued that the Pirates' pitching would hold the Yankees and that the Yankees had won their pennant so easily they would be too relaxed.

The weather two days before the first game may have played a part in the outcome. On October 3, in Pittsburgh, Miller Huggins chose to take batting practice before the Pirates. Babe Ruth was first at bat, bunted a few times, lofted some very tall flies, and then hit two long ones into the right-field stands. Lou Gehrig, who followed, did the same. After forty-five minutes it rained, and the Pirates had to sit around the rest of the day, brooding. The Yankees played cards in their hotel. James R. Harrison's dispatch to *The Times* said, "This is the most blasé team we have ever seen go into a World Series."

During batting practice on the 4th Ruth hit five in a row over the fence, Gehrig hit two, and Bob Meusel, Ben Paschal, and Johnny Grabowski* also hit several out. Pirate followers in the stands "whistled softly." Pirates in the dugout apparently couldn't whistle because they watched "open mouthed. . . ." Wilbert Robinson of the Dodgers (or his Christy Walsh Syndicate ghost writer) said the Pirates weren't scared, just respectful.

Before the first game on Wednesday, October 5, Ruth posed for photographers, shaking hands with Huggins, with Jacob Ruppert,

* John Patrick Grabowski (1900–1946), catcher, seven seasons, 1924–1931, White Sox, Yankees, Tigers, batting average .252.

with Donie Bush,* with Barney Dreyfuss who owned the Pirates, with Mayor Jimmy Walker, and with Gehrig. After the photographers satisfied themselves, he made a thing of walking around shaking hands with himself. No brooder he.

In the first inning Ruth swung at the first pitch for a safe hit to right and scored immediately on Gehrig's triple. Ruth had three singles in four times at bat, which was half of the Yankees' hits, and he scored twice. The Yankees won 5–4. As for the old-fashioned running game, nobody stole a base.

The next day George Pipgras held the Pirates to seven hits, earning praise for his fast ball and winning 6–2. Ruth was hitless but struck out once in a spectacular manner greatly enjoyed in Pittsburgh.

The Series moved to New York on October 7, with Herb Pennock to pitch. The Yankee book on the Pirates said they murdered left-handed pitching, but Pennock was unimpressed. Before a crowd of sixty-four thousand he didn't give up a hit until the eighth inning, retiring twenty-two in a row with but one strikeout. By that time it was all over. In the seventh inning the Yankees had scored six runs on four hits. Three of the runs came from Ruth's home run with two men on. The final score was 8–1, Pennock giving only three hits. The Yankee book was wrong. The Pirates murdered only National League left-handers.

> We cannot imagine . . . anything more worldly or unreligious in the way of employment than the playing of professional baseball as it is played today.
> —Pennsylvania Supreme Court, 1927

The game of the 8th could end the Series, and it did, in a way no Pennsylvanian wished to remember. The final score was 4–3, Yankees; the winning run came in the last of the ninth inning. Early in the game the Pirates showed spirit, but when Ruth hit a home run in the fifth the team began to deflate like a tire with a slow leak. Ruth had already batted in a run with a single in the first inning to tie the game.

The last run deserves attention. With the score tied 3–3, the Yankees had men on first and second with no outs when Ruth came to bat. Johnny Miljus** was pitching. Since only the runner on third mattered, the Pirates decided to give Ruth an intentional base on balls. He shouted that Gehrig would hit if he didn't. When the

---

* Owen Joseph Bush (1887–1972), shortstop, sixteen seasons, 1908–1923, Tigers, Senators, batting average .250. Manager, 1923, 1927–1931, 1933.

** John Kenneth Miljus (1895–   ), pitcher, seven seasons, 1915–1929, Pittsburgh Federals, Dodgers, Pirates, Indians. Won 29, lost 26, earned-run average 3.92.

fourth ball came, Ruth hurled an epithet at Miljus and went down to first to fill the bases. Miljus then struck out Gehrig and Meusel, both swinging, and was on his way to getting a street named after him in Pittsburgh. Then came Lazzeri. Miljus got another strike. But the next pitch was a wild pitch and Earle Combs came in to score the run that won the game and the Series.

After the game the Pirate clubhouse was morguelike, but the Yankees had stopped being blasé and let cheerfulness break through. Ruth's "booming voice rang above those of the other players in that wild thunderous outburst of celebration. . . ."

The crowd was satisfied that Ruth was the hero of the Series. Three thousand waited for him outside the clubhouse, and it took a score of policemen to clear the way to his car on 157th Street.

Because of the quickness of Yankee victory, attendance at the Series was 126,000 less than the record attendance of 1926. Ruppert had to refund $217,000 for tickets bought for the unplayed Sunday game. Nevertheless the gate receipts were the highest ever for the players (who share only in the first four games). They had voted more shares than usual, so they did not break the 1923 player-share record.

Ending the Series early probably cost the owners two hundred thousand dollars apiece. Ruppert, at least, didn't mind. He was a fierce Yankee fan who liked to sweep every series and win every game by twenty runs. (And it is not fanciful to estimate his personal income at about fifty thousand dollars a week.)

Apart from Ruth's play, the Series set other marks. It was the first four-game sweep by an American League club. The third game had the highest gate receipts ever—$209,655.

Readers who like baseball numerals will press on; others may skip the next several paragraphs.

Gehrig tied the Series record for triples with two. Pennock won his fifth World Series game without defeat, also a new record. Paul and Lloyd Waner* of the Pirates, to their pleased surprise, found themselves the heroes of their happy Oklahoma home town where everybody had made money betting that the Waner brothers would, jointly, outhit Ruth and Gehrig. They did, .367 to .357. Mark Koenig led all hitters with .500. Urban Shocker, who won eighteen and lost six during the season, didn't get a chance to pitch, but Cy Moore pitched twice and got a hit, his sixth of the calendar year. Moore also had the best earned-run average of the Series—0.84. Fifty-

---

* Paul Glee Waner (1903–1965), outfielder, twenty seasons, 1926–1945, Pirates, Dodgers, Braves, Yankees, batting average .333. Hall of Fame.

Lloyd James Waner (1906–   ), outfielder, eighteen seasons, 1927–1945, Pirates, Braves, Reds, Phillies, Dodgers, batting average .316. Hall of Fame.

three radio stations carried Graham McNamee's and Phillips Carlin's descriptions of the games to about twenty million people.

I regard Ruth as easily the outstanding figure of the Series.
—Wilbert T. Robinson, October 9, 1927

Babe Ruth was the king of the field. True, Mark Koenig had a better Series batting average, but Ruth hit .400, had the two home runs of the Series, and was responsible for nine of the Yankees' twenty-three runs. He set nine records for lifetime World Series play: most runs (22), most Series (8), most Series batting over .300 (4, shared with Frank Frisch), most home runs (10), most total bases (63), most extra bases (36), most bases on balls (28), most runs batted in (22), and one not much sought after, most strikeouts (25). Even so there were people who still growled that he was the goat of the 1922 Series.

Ruth's outstanding play could cloud our understanding of the Yankee triumph. Although the Yankees in three of four games scored more runs in one inning than the Pirates did in the whole game, it was not a batters' victory. The pitchers beat the Pirates, giving them but eight earned runs in four games, striking out twenty-five and walking only thirteen. On their side, the Pirate pitchers gave up twenty earned runs. Yankee hitting was great, but it seems a sound opinion that Moore, Pipgras, Pennock, and Hoyt didn't need it all.

After the World Series the New York baseball writers gave Ruth a plaque as player of the year, to get around the foolish rule that a man could be Most Valuable Player only once in his life. The thirty-year-old rookie Cy Moore asked Ruppert for a pay raise. He thought about five hundred dollars would be nice. Ruppert multiplied the figure handsomely.

Christy Walsh arranged a barnstorming tour for Ruth and Gehrig after the Series. Ruth again paid Gehrig a flat sum greater than his Yankee salary for the year.

They opened at Trenton, New Jersey, against the Brooklyn Royal Giants, where Ruth hit three home runs and each time found himself wading through crowds of boys who ran out "to romp from third to home." The game had to be called in the eighth because they couldn't get the boys off the field after the third home run. On the next day, in New York against the Bushwicks, Ruth failed to hit one out. To make it up to the crowd of twenty thousand he tried to pitch the ninth inning. By that time the people had drawn ever closer until many boys were near enough to race the outfielders for balls hit beyond the infield. An outfielder made an error, one of the boys grabbed the ball, the crowd surged onto the field, and play had to be stopped before the end of the ninth inning.

Let us report one barnstorming day in detail to get the flavor. Ruth and Gehrig played the Brooklyn Royal Giants again on October 13, this time at Asbury Park, New Jersey. The law delayed the game because of a judgment against the promoter, and the sheriff attached the gate receipts. Ruth said he'd have to have the money in advance. A local judge took a cab, went calling all over town, raised the money, converted it to a cashier's check, and only then the game began. The police were unable to control the crowd of seven thousand as boys ran through police lines and fought to shake hands with Ruth. His only rest from handshaking was autographing. Older patrons fumed as the boys raced the fielders for batted balls and fled with the spoil. In one instance Ruth stole second and a boy snatched the ball so that he could not be put out, even though Ruth did not dare slide with a fountain pen in his pocket.

The game started with two dozen baseballs, most of which were stolen and then brazenly presented for autographing. When the supply was gone, another dozen were brought to the park, but Gehrig ended the game in the ninth by hitting the last of the third dozen (his second home run) into a lake beyond right field. As before, play had to be stopped before the game was complete.

During another game, boys so mobbed Ruth that he lost his footing. He put his cap in his mouth and held it with clenched teeth to keep it from being taken as a trophy.

The traveling heroes did not strongly resent these interruptions. They occasionally encouraged them, for the exhibitions could be dull. They usually played before overflow crowds loosely confined behind temporary rope barriers on all sides of the field. Late in a game Ruth might let the boys know their presence on the playing field was not unwelcome, by not rebuking the inevitable few show-offs who dashed out for autographs. Then would come groups and, finally, all of them, and the game would end.

That fall the barnstormers also played an exhibition in a prison (not named). Ruth could joke with convicts on even terms—calling a convict-umpire a robber, shouting for the cops when somebody stole second, asking the bleacher crowd what time it was, and then asking what difference it made to them, since they weren't going anywhere. All this he did without stirring anything but laughter. His ability to get on so famously with orphans, with the hospitalized sick, and with prisoners may have been formed by his own long years in St. Mary's Industrial School which was a blend of first-rate elementary school, orphanage, hospital, and prison, all of which have more in common than philosophers of education admit.

The travelers returned to New York on November 8 having played twenty-one games in twenty parks in nine states from Rhode Island to California. They had drawn 220,000 people, traveled eight thousand miles, and claimed to have autographed five thousand baseballs. Thirteen of their games ended prematurely because of fans swarming onto the field. Their largest crowd was thirty thousand, in old Wrigley Field at Los Angeles. Three California school boards closed their towns' schools to let the children see the game.

Ruth and Gehrig usually pitched to each other. At the plate they were about even; Gehrig batted .618, Ruth .616. Ruth had twenty home runs, Gehrig thirteen. Gehrig made ten thousand dollars. Ruth made a great deal more.

41 · The Talk of a Century

What had Ruth wrought in 1927? His total of sixty home runs was greater than that of any *team* in the American League except, of course, the Yankees. In both leagues together, twelve *teams* hit fewer home runs than he hit alone. And he hit them freely off right- or left-handed pitchers. Leaving out two pitchers who were in the league just long enough to let Ruth hit home runs off them, he hit fifty-eight off thirty-one pitchers. We can rank these pitchers by merit in three groups. The highest third gave up twenty-two home runs, the middle third twenty-four, and the lowest third gave up twelve. That grouping proves that enemy managers wisely saved their better pitchers for the Yankees, but the stratagem failed to thwart Ruth.

Ruth was helped by the superior hitting of the Yankees because it gave him more times at bat. At his home-run rate we may figure by arithmetic that he might have hit fifty-eight with the 1927 Browns. *If* he had played with the high-scoring 1950 Red Sox, and *if* they played a schedule of 162 games, he would have had sufficient times at bat for sixty-eight home runs.

He also improved on his use of the sacrifice bunt. He had fourteen in 1927.

The coming of Lou Gehrig may have given Ruth competition which spurred him to show off his power, though it did *not* lead to his getting fewer bases on balls than usual. Gehrig outdid Ruth in batting average and runs batted in. The friendly rivalry was surely good for the Yankees. One or other of them led the American League in doubles, home runs, runs scored, runs batted in, bases on balls, home runs as a proportion of times at bat, and slugging percentage.

Ruth was not deadweight in the outfield, either. Right field is the No. 2 position in the outfield, after center field. A right-fielder needs a better arm than a left-fielder because his throw to third is a longer one. The number of an outfielder's assists is one measure of his ability; errors are judgments by scorers, but assists are facts. More than ten assists is good. Ruth had fourteen in 1927. John Kieran saw a lot of Ruth that year: "In 1927 Babe Ruth was still one of the best outfielders in the league [and] had a marvelous throwing arm. . . ."

Six American League ball parks of 1927 favored left-handed home-run hitters. They were (lengths of right-field foul lines in feet): New York (296), Philadelphia (329), Washington (320), Cleveland (290), Detroit (325), and St. Louis (310). Boston had a curious right-field corner which angled out abruptly from 302 to 380 feet. Chicago was impartially hard on all long-ball hitters with both foul lines running 352 feet. But no hitter in history has consistently hit the ball as far as Ruth did, so comparisons are hardly worth pursuing further.

As for Ruth's home park, Ted Williams can speak with authority. He said Yankee Stadium had a bad batting background; he hit only thirty of his 521 home runs there. His favorite road park was Detroit's; there he hit fifty-five.

> **The older workers show the influence of growing experience, a greater familiarity with their tasks, and more uniformity in their work.**
>
> —Else Frenkel, "Studies in
> Biographical Psychology"

Folklore gives us a Babe Ruth whose personality was always that of a child. The reputation finds ground in such episodes as his borrowing a small-bore rifle in 1927 to shoot some squirrels whose chattering distracted him while putting on a golf course near Scarsdale. (He cooked and ate the squirrels). But he lacked an important childish trait: jealousy. Correspondents of the author often said they were grateful for Ruth's advice and coaching when they joined the Yankees as rookies. His tastes in 1927 certainly conformed to the class from which he sprang: baseball, food, beer, women, visits to people who were confined, applause, money, gambling, fishing, shooting, the saxophone, the acting of George Bancroft and Janet Gaynor—all in about that order.

But it is hard to define Ruth by drawing on such matters. We can be more precise about the maturing of his mind and body if we limit ourselves to his trade of baseball.

In sports that require only the activity of one's own body (running, swimming, and the like), champions peak at age thirty-two on the average. For those sports which need an implement or tool, the championship performer is usually better at eighteen than performers in other sports, and reaches his peak at about twenty-two. The skill stays at a declining but acceptable level until the late twenties. Then a curious thing happens, and it happens only in the tool-using sports. From thirty to thirty-five the *champion* tool-using athlete improves. After that, skill falls off at about the same rate as in other sports. The reason for the period of improvement is experience. When endurance is no longer at its highest level, experience more than makes up for the loss of strength. Who has not seen the useful pinch-hitter with the worn-out legs, the relief pitcher with a weaker fast ball and more cunning?

This fact of human development is behind the story of the sixty-home-run mark of 1927 and the superior record of outfield assists. Babe Ruth at thirty-two was surely older and, in baseball, surely wiser. The following graph illustrates the average career of a champion athlete in a tool-using sport. Ruth in 1927 was at the last peak of the line.

The public legend of Babe Ruth accepts 1927 as his best year because he hit the most home runs that year. The difference between fifty-nine home runs in 1921 and sixty home runs in 1927 hardly seems decisive, nor does the total of home runs alone settle the question, but the argument isn't worth much breath. The important thing is that from 1915 to 1927 he was the best ballplayer and had only two faltering years—1922 and 1925.

> **If the Old Baltimore Orioles are still talked of after thirty years, this team will be talked of for the next century.**
> —*New York World,* 1927

In the 1920s the Baltimore Orioles of 1896 were still the darlings of memory, the greatest of all teams. Who could forget a team batting average of .328 and *441* stolen bases? But in 1929 many decided the Yankees had succeeded to their place. The claim is still made.

The Yankees of 1927 didn't bat .328, but at .307 they hit the ball harder. Their special virtue was the clustering of extra-base hits to make a big inning. They scored more than six runs a game and held their opponents to fewer than four runs a game. Ruth and Gehrig hit a quarter of the home runs of the American League. Nor were they alone in their power. Of eight players in the league who batted in a hundred runs or more, four of them were Yankees. So often did they explode against a tiring pitcher (we shall see why that pitcher was so tired) that their attack came to be called "Five O'Clock Lightning." Every day a factory whistle near Yankee Stadium blew at 5 P.M.,* and it seemed that almost every day they

---

* The Yankees started weekday games late in hope of tempting office workers to knock off early to go to the ball game.

DISTRIBUTION OF RECORDS IN SPORTS USING IMPLEMENTS

According to Frieda Sack, from Charlotte Bühler, in, Else Frenkel, "Studies in Biographical Psychology," *Character and Personality*, V (1936-37), 11.

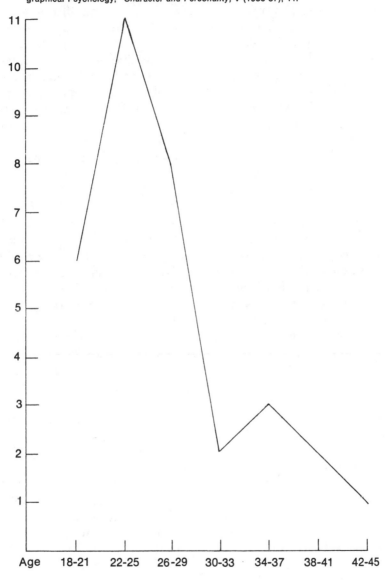

The vertical scale gives the number of records set
in the sports studied at the ages stated

scored as it sounded. (They even began to think factory whistles were lucky for them.)

But—if that great team had had a starting quartet of fourth-rate pitchers we would hear less of the 1927 Yankees. In the ranking of fifty American League pitchers by earned-run averages, Cy Moore and Waite Hoyt were first and second, Urban Shocker was fourth, Herb Pennock was eighth, and Dutch Ruether was thirteenth. These men allowed 109 fewer runs than were scored against any other team in the league. Considering those matters for which pitchers are alone responsible—hits, strikeouts, bases on balls—Yankee pitchers were about 7 percent more effective than the Athletics' pitchers and 25 percent better than the Senators' staff. Another point: the league leadership in double plays usually proves that the pitching is weak. As a result of Yankee pitching craft, the base paths were sparsely inhabited wastelands, and the Yankee infield made the fewest double plays in the league.

Who were all these impressive young men? In the years 1921–1923 the pennant-winning Yankees were loot from the sack of Boston and were a Red Sox Alumni Association. In 1927 only Ruth and Hoyt remained of that corps. The 1927 team owed most to Huggins and much to Paul Krichell, Ed Barrow, and Jacob Ruppert. After the 1925 disaster, Huggins cleaned out the soreheads (except Ruth). Then, with Krichell as chief scout, he found Lazzeri and Koenig, saw Gehrig's value, and with Barrow's advice and Ruppert's bottomless treasury filled out the team as needed. He also taught his younger men much, as when he spent two spring-training seasons teaching Lazzeri how best to make the double play.

Huggins called his team "the only team in history that didn't need the breaks." But he kept his superstition insurance. He would use no one but Mike Gazella to carry a message to the bullpen. When Ruth was up he would sit next to the same man he had sat next to when Ruth last hit a home run.

The 1920s was a decade of a go-to-college boom, and writers were careful to record the academic credits represented on the Yankee bench. The following colleges and universities sent men to the Yankees, not necessarily with degrees: Austin, Boston, Penn State, Niagara, Lafayette, Holy Cross, Columbia, St. Ignatius, Middlebury. The meaning is obscure. The three most valuable were Gehrig, the Columbia dropout, Ruth, from St. Mary's Industrial School, and Moore, from one or more one-room cotton-country schoolhouses.

Many have tried to rank the 1927 Yankees. What lawyers call an admission against interest came from Wilbert T. Robinson, once of the great old Orioles and always a National Leaguer, who said the 1927 Yankees were the greatest and drew scorn from National League followers as a traitor to his kind. Fred Lieb, who saw all but the Orioles, ranked these Yankees first. Joe McCarthy said they were inferior to the 1938 Yankees, and Connie Mack agreed. But when Mack came to write his memoirs he recanted and plumped for the 1927 Yankees (he could have made a case for his 1929 Athletics). John Kieran thought only two of the 1938 Yankees could have made the 1927 team: catcher Bill Dickey and third baseman Red Rolfe. Herb Pennock added Joe DiMaggio.* Ruth, in later life, picked the 1927 team; his second wife agreed.

Ed Barrow made an unexpected comment in his autobiography. He said the 1927s were the best of the Yankee teams, but the best of all teams was the 1919 White Sox.

The parade of expert witnesses ends with the academy of sportswriters, made up of a hundred sports editors of daily papers with at least a hundred thousand circulation. In 1963 they voted the 1927 Yankees the greatest of all teams. The voters wrote in the Yankees on 84 percent of their ballots; the Athletics of 1929 came second with 74 percent.

The people also voted on the question, by buying tickets. It was a dull pennant race in 1927, and that usually cuts attendance, but a record-breaking 2,246,096 paid to see the Yankees play. (And that doesn't include exhibition games.)

The Cubs of 1906 won more games, the Giants of 1930 had a higher batting average, the Giants of 1947 hit more home runs, but no baseball team ever stirred the American people as did the 1927 Yankees.

No one can know which team was best. A mediocre team in a weak league can look great. But the 1927 Yankees were surely the most interesting of all the teams there ever were.

What made the Yankees so striking was their formula for a winning team. Take acceptable fielding and hitting, add a pair of long-ball hitters and four distinguished pitchers, and you have the kind of team that won its pennant more often than not, from 1927 until the Second World War. After the sluggers and pitchers, most of the positions could be filled by a scientific random sample of players from other first-division teams.

The New Yorkers did have a hidden weakness: they depended on the thinly scouted open market for new players. The Cardinals were already raising a surplus of major-league players on their farms, but the Yankees hadn't a single farm club. With their few reserves and short roster they would soon find it hard to get good new players until Ruppert bought his own farms. Connie Mack's Athletics, who had first call on purchases from Jack Dunn's draft-exempt** Baltimore Orioles, had in effect the best farm club of the 1920s. The Athletics might soon be troublesome.

---

* Robert Abial Rolfe (1906–1969), third baseman, ten seasons, 1931–1942, Yankees, batting average .289.

Joseph Paul DiMaggio (1914–   ), outfielder, thirteen seasons, 1936–1951, Yankees, batting average .325. Hall of Fame.

** As compensation for losses in the Federal League war, Baltimore was exempted from organized baseball's minor-league draft rules. For example, Dunn sold Lefty Grove to Connie Mack for $100,500.

The sluggers' revolution of the 1920s had changed baseball in a way that could not be undone.

As an unforeseen by-product of a change in machinery, the ball was wound more tightly in the 1920s so that it became 16 percent livelier. A 300-foot fly-out of 1910 was a 350-foot home run of 1920. A ball darting through the infield moved seventy feet in 1920 in the time it would have moved sixty feet in 1910. The change gave batters an opportunity that Babe Ruth was first to seize.

The average of long hits per year shows what happened.

LONG HITS	1909–1916	1920–1927
Two-base hits	24,067	32,163
Three-base hits	9,579	9,660
Home runs	3,218	7,445

In comparison with the years 1909–1916, doubles in 1920–1927 increased from three thousand a year to four thousand, triples stayed at twelve hundred (longer ones became home runs), and home runs increased from four hundred a year to more than nine hundred. All safe hits increased, as batting averages rose from a range in the .240s to .260s (as today) to the level of the .280s.

Nowadays the totals of extra bases are even higher, but batting averages are down as relays of fresh pitchers strike out or pop up the fence-swingers. But in the 1920s if most teams increased *both* their total of extra-base hits and their batting averages, we must believe the tactics of pitching were outworn. Let us look at the state of the art of pitching in 1927.

Each team had from seven to nine pitchers (today they have ten, occasionally eleven). The whole body of major-league pitchers fell into three groups. About a fourth of them were called "first-string" pitchers, who almost never pitched in relief, and who worked about half of a season's innings. Half of the major-league pitchers were "journeymen," who worked as both starters and relievers, and who also pitched about half the innings. The other quarter of the major-league pitchers did almost nothing and may be called "strangers." They worked very few innings.

The following table shows the workloads of all major-league pitchers in a typical four-week span, August 4 to September 1, 1927. The thirty-six Strangers had life very easy.

	Games	Started	Relieved	Innings Pitched
38 First-string	231	215	16	1,486
58 Journeymen	260	119	141	1,481
36 Strangers	114	1	113	213⅔

Today, by contrast, a manager hopes not to let an opposing batter face a tired pitcher if he can avoid it. He uses specialized starters, specialized long relievers, specialized short relievers, and even "mop-up men" who come in to face the foe (and rest more valuable men) when the game has become hopeless. Batters thus face relays of fresh pitchers every day. In 1927 the Yankee starters finished eighty-three of the games they started; in 1973 Oakland starters finished only forty-six, and their schedule was eight games longer.

In practice the managers of the 1920s used only three-quarters of their pitching manpower. They kept the starter in until everybody knew he was tired. The fans usually saw three pitchers in a game, one for the winners and two for the losers, whether in 1910 or 1927. As a result, when the lively ball appeared the number of long hits and batting averages went up and so did earned-run averages. A manager could do nothing about the lively ball, but he could have used fresh pitchers in sequence to keep batting averages down. John McGraw used an honest-to-goodness relief pitcher, Doc Crandall, before the First World War, but Babe Ruth saw only one in the 1920s, Firpo Marberry* of the Senators. If every team had had a brace of Marberrys instead of pressing on with the tactics of 1910, home runs probably would have been just as numerous because of the lively ball, but the proportion of outs to times at bat would have been higher, and batting averages and scoring would have been lower.

As it was, with hits of all kinds more frequent, pitchers threw more pitches and tired sooner. Rested and rarely used pitchers watched the season roll by as daily spectators. The batting heroes of the 1920s looked even more heroic when they hit against so many weary pitchers. And that is why the lightning struck so often at five o'clock.

---

* James Otis Crandall (1887–1951), pitcher, ten seasons, 1908–1918, Giants, St. Louis Federals, Browns, Braves. Won 101, lost 62, earned-run average 2.92 (he averaged 5 innings per game).

Fred Marberry (1898–   ), pitcher, fourteen seasons, 1923–1936, Senators, Tigers, Giants. Won 147, lost 89, earned-run average 3.63 (he averaged 3⅔ innings per game).

Outside the Park, 1928

M'ADOO CHALLENGES
SMITH ON DRY LAWS

AIRPLANE MAKERS
RAISE DIVIDENDS

LOST GIRL, 12, RIDES
40 HOURS IN SUBWAY

CALLS BREADLINES
LONGEST SINCE 1916

RADIO UP 18 POINTS
IN RECORD MARKET

NEW NEEDS BESET COLLEGES FOR WOMEN

PEKING BLAMES FOE
FOR CONTINUING WAR

METHODISTS OF OHIO
BACK HOOVER AS A DRY

IS LOSS OF CHARM
THE PRICE GIRLS PAY
FOR SMOKING?

SPLIT IN TENNESSEE
ON SMITH'S RELIGION

SAYS OIL WILL LAST
WORLD 3000 YEARS

HOOVER REPUDIATES
'ANTI-ROMAN' LETTER
BY WOMAN LEADER

LISTS 28 SOCIETIES ON D.A.R. BLACKLIST

HOOVER WINS ALL BUT EIGHT STATES

42 · The Whole Ruth (1928)

Babe Ruth briskly pursued fun and fitness during the winter of 1927–1928. He played a fair game of bridge, better golf, and was a reckless automobile driver. It was hard for his magnificent muscles to remain immovable for five minutes when he was awake, but he so loved shooting that he could lie motionless in a duck blind for hours. In December he went fowling and brought Ed Barrow the gift of a goose, delivering it by hand to the Yankee offices.

He also took up the saxophone, practicing regularly all winter. He was again living in the Ansonia Hotel, which must have been the home of tolerant people. Just before Christmas he told reporters, "I can play two pieces now. By spring I'll be able to give you fellows a regular concert." Ruth's musical life included some conducting. The St. Mary's Industrial School band, now a national champion high school band, was on tour again to raise money for the school. Ruth took the baton (left-handed) in Jersey City and New York, and, of course, they played "Batterin' Babe."

Artie McGovern and Ruth worked together to get Ruth ready for the 1928 season. McGovern said Ruth liked boxing most, but McGovern held him to the proved calisthenics and the monkish diet.

It is hard to believe Ruth felt a void in his social life, but, for whatever reason, he joined the Elks in New York on February 12 in a ceremony that drew thousands. Changing social levels instantly, he became a country house guest of Herb Pennock at Kennett Square, where he joined the mounted gentry in fox hunting. He found the chase a good way to lose five pounds a day. From Kennett Square he went to Philadelphia to dance among brother Elks. He had the social mobility, up and down, of a jumping jack. When warmer weather came he would play golf in the high seventies.

In early 1928 he had a paid-up fifty-thousand-dollar annuity policy, an irrevocable trust fund of seventy thousand, a salary contract for seventy thousand (to start in April), and he was fifteen hundred dollars short of having enough cash to pay his 1927 income taxes. He borrowed the money.

Miller Huggins, as usual, traveled the country to add names to the Yankee roster. He wished to appear sphinx-like, parceling out facts grudgingly. In December he confessed to the signing of "a young catcher, William Dickie [sic] . . . who comes well recommended." Bill Dickey, who became the best of all catchers, got along well with Ruth whom he found "easy to like." They shared a taste for uncomplicated practical jokes and bird-shooting. Dickey talked so much about game birds that Ruth nicknamed him Pittridge, which is one way to pronounce partridge.

Huggins signed George Burns, a very good first baseman, on the theory that a club needed protection at its strongest positions, and Burns would be useful if Gehrig were hurt. There were doubts of the pitching when Hoyt became a holdout and Urban Shocker seemed too ill to play in 1928. Newcomers to the roster besides Dickey were pitcher Henry Johnson, infielder Ben Chapman, outfielder Sam Byrd, and infielder Leo Durocher.*

Hartford sold Durocher's contract to the Yankees for seventy-five hundred dollars in 1925, but he made only one major-league appearance that year. His first full season was 1928. Paul Krichell said he had "double-play hands," and Huggins called him "a mighty fine shortstop." He was the first recorded Yankee to appear in a Florida hotel lobby during spring training in formal dinner clothes. A day would come when Babe Ruth would think that only Durocher's hands were civilized.

> He is physically from five to ten years younger than he was two years ago.
> —Artie McGovern, February 9, 1928

By the end of the 1927 season Ruth had swelled to 237½ pounds, but McGovern's system had brought him down to 225½ when he finished the annual winter workouts. He told friends he wasn't going to Hot Springs: "Every time I go there I come away on a stretcher." As usual he went to Florida well before the start of spring training, accompanied this time by Gehrig. When he left, McGovern gave out his measurements.

* Leo Ernest Durocher (1905–   ), shortstop, seventeen seasons, 1925–1943, Yankees, Reds, Cardinals, Dodgers, batting average .247.

	1926*	1928
Weight	230	225½
Neck	16½	16
Chest	41	40
expanded	45	47
Waist	42	39
Hips	42	40
Thigh	23½	23
Calf	15½	14½
Biceps	14½	13¼
Forearm	12	10½

The reader will recall that the 1926 measurements were those recorded *after* the restoration of the wreck of Babe Ruth in the winter of 1925–1926. For a man of thirty-three he was preserving himself well. The old wallowing, beery days were long past.

On the train to Florida Ruth and Gehrig played a marathon of pinochle, interrupted by Ruth's royal audiences with flag-stop crowds. Wearing a gold and purple silk dressing gown, he always greeted them genially and promised every questioner that in 1928 he would hit sixty-one. In St. Petersburg the travelers received a bouquet of flowers, did some setting-up exercises for the newsreels, and then Ruth played golf, harassed by photographers until he begged them to go away. He lost two pounds that day. The next day he played thirty-six holes, disappointing a crowd which went to the ball park to see his first swings of the bat (admission was free in those days).

On his first appearance with bat and ball he wore a rubber sweatshirt and took off five pounds. He pleased the watchers by hitting the ball out of the park six times. The day's workout ended with Ruth pitching batting practice. Between golf and baseball he had by this time a painfully sunburned neck.

The spring-training exhibitions showed the unimportance of such games considered as victories or defeats. The Yankees won one and lost nine in Florida. Huggins didn't panic. He gave the team a holiday on the day before they started the northward migration.

Between seasons the seating of Yankee Stadium was enlarged by extending the left-field upper deck and mezzanine, and removing the boxes in front of the far end. The change enlarged the capacity to seventy-five thousand and lengthened the left-field foul line from 284 feet to 301.

As opening day approached only the Yankee pitching seemed

* From year to year there are discrepancies in the measurements published in the same papers. There is no way for the author to purify the tables; he is content to print them as they appeared at each publication.

doubtful. The Yankees made peace with Hoyt and released Dutch Ruether and Bob Shawkey. Urban Shocker voluntarily retired for reasons of health. Huggins replaced them with Stanley Coveleski, Al Shealy,* and Henry Johnson. Ruppert told friends only that the Yankees would finish in the first division. Huggins said they would be first or second, after a serious battle with the Athletics and Senators. Ruth, for his syndicated column, picked the Yankees. Huggins said the Pirates would repeat in the National League, but Ruth, wiser or luckier, said the Cardinals would win. The bookmakers had as much confidence in the Yankees as Ruth had. They made the Yankees odds-on favorites at 3 to 5.

> He's Irish, isn't he?
> —Patrick Dolan, Chief of Police,
> Weehawken, May 21, 1927

The Yankees opened in Philadelphia on April 11, a cold and shivery day, and they opened well. Lefty Grove was gone in the third inning. Herb Pennock gave the Athletics only seven hits as the Yankees won 8–3. Babe Ruth had a triple in three times at bat and scored three runs.

In the next thirty days the Yankees seemed certain to live in glory as they had in 1927. In twenty-one games Ruth hit eight home runs and Gehrig five.

Somebody in New York counted the appearances of public faces in the press to see which ones appeared the most. The leaders were President Coolidge, Mrs. Coolidge, that Queen Marie of Rumania whom Ruth had snubbed in Minneapolis, Lindbergh, Mussolini, Ruth, Mayor Walker, Gene Tunney, and Richard Jervis (the Secret Service man who was in most of Coolidge's photographs). Ruth had his picture in the paper in all seasons. Regardless of weather, mood, health, temporary occupation, or costume, his "phlegmatic, slightly puzzled expression peers out of Sunday supplements." If not in a baseball suit, he was usually wearing white flannels if in summer, and a camel's hair coat if in winter.

In the first week of May Ruth had another speeding ticket, this time in Weehawken for driving his eight-cylinder roadster at forty-two miles an hour. A crowd gathered on May 21 outside Weehawken police headquarters to see the culprit. When the charge was withdrawn there was "a wail of disappointment . . . from the lips of

---

* Stanley Anthony Coveleski, born Kowalewski (1889–   ), pitcher, fourteen seasons, 1912–1928, Athletics, Indians, Senators, Yankees. Won 217, lost 141, earned-run average 2.88. Hall of Fame.
  Albert Berley Shealy (1900–1967), pitcher, two seasons, 1928, 1930, Yankees, Cubs. Won 8, lost 6, earned-run average 5.71.

several score youthful admirers." They had waited for hours, but Ruth hadn't come to Weehawken. A reporter asked Police Chief Patrick Dolan why the quashing. With painful coyness the chief countered, "He's Irish isn't he?" (The correct answer: No.)

The Yankees rolled triumphantly into June. As of the 4th they had won thirty-six and lost eight and were eight games ahead of the Athletics. Ruth was third in the league in batting with .354, and Gehrig was close behind with .346. As always, when the Yankee train stopped in small towns there was a crowd crying for the sight of Ruth, who always came out to be seen. If it was daytime he'd wave his arm in a circle and ask, "Is everybody happy?" They always said they were. If it was dark he'd ask, "Why don't you folks go to bed? Don't you ever sleep around here?"

Ruth was fielding well, throwing accurately, and running the bases as if he weighed 175 pounds. Everywhere the Yankees went, his saxophone went. If time hung heavy in a ball park he'd nail one of Mike Gazella's pipes to the clubhouse wall, or slip into the opponents' clubhouse and nail a pair of shoes to the floor. On the field his cheek was round with a wad of dipping-snuff, and off the field he chewed cigars. Autographing was annually a greater burden. It became lighter when Ruth taught Doc Woods, the Yankee trainer, to forge his signature on baseballs. Because of the mass of autograph seekers, Ruth couldn't leave Yankee Stadium by the same exit as the other players. He'd peer out another door until it seemed safe, then dash to his car parked at the curbing. If mobbed by boys, he'd shout, "Wait a minute! Wait a minute!" they would fall back a bit, then he'd sign his name only for those who had baseballs and fountain pens. In this situation he never lost his temper, nor did the boys.

On July 4 the Yankees had won fifty-three of seventy games and were thirteen and a half games ahead of the Athletics. Ruth had thirty-one home runs. Later in the month he hit four home runs in three games with the White Sox (July 18–21), which made his total thirty-nine.

That week marked the peak of the Yankees' summer. They began to go downhill when they went on the road on July 25. Batting slumped. The cruel test that faces every team in August was too much for the Yankees. For example, Ruth hit only six home runs that month. The Athletics drew ever closer. Huggins believed the Yankees were too rich, too successful, too confident.

Ruth's popularity remained high. He had a fine time with a thousand Boston boys when an ice cream company brought them to Fenway Park, seated them behind the Yankee dugout, and stuffed them with free ice cream. The Red Sox won 8–3, but Ruth gained esteem in his favorite age bracket with a home run. After the game it took the police force to get him gently into the clubhouse through the happy throng of junior disciples.

Meanwhile the Athletics had become a true threat, surviving the August grind well and winning at a better rate than the Yankees. One reason Ruth didn't hit more home runs in August was that he began to hit for average, as the players say, and not for a home-run record. He told a friend a man could set a home-run record in last place, but he wanted to set a record of playing in ten World Series (he had already played in eight). He said he could hit .700 if he hit singles into left field (which he didn't).

In two weeks after the Yankees began that painful western trip they won six and lost ten while the Athletics won twelve and lost three. Thus the gap narrowed. From July 4 to August 31 the Yankees won thirty-one and lost twenty-nine.

Presidential politics briefly distracted Ruth that summer. He praised Al Smith publicly once in a while, and Herbert Hoover began to show an interest in baseball. When the Yankees came to Washington on September 1, Hoover went to the ball game and a photographer arranged to photograph him with Ruth. Only then did the photographer speak to Ruth, who casually agreed, until Joe Dugan said he would be helping Smith's opponent. Ruth then broke off the agreement to the outspoken annoyance of Clark Griffith, owner of the Senators, who did not explain what business it was of his; we may suspect him of being a Hoover partisan and of having arranged the tableau. One version of Ruth's words was "Nothing doing. I'm for Al Smith." The wording sounds like Ruth. Hoover could only say he looked forward "with pleasure" to meeting Mr. Ruth at some other time.

That day of high scheming for the presidency may have been the day of 1928 when it took four Senatorial assists to put Ruth out once. Combs was on second, Durocher on first, and Ruth at bat. Ruth hit a ball to right field. Combs and Durocher, knowing Goslin had a sore arm, tagged up to advance on the throw after the putout, but the ball went over Goslin's head. Ruth arrived at first base on a dead run, shoved Durocher toward second, and the three runners streaked around the bases toward home. Combs and Durocher scored but Ruth was out, Goslin to center to second to first (backing up the plate) to Ruel.

In September the American League struggle became taut. The Athletics gained steadily on the Yankees. They were to meet in a double-header in the Stadium on September 9. Police had to put down a riot at the Yankee offices on 42nd Street on September 6 when twenty-five thousand people tried to get in to buy eight thousand tickets. The subway system planned extra trains for the 9th, and the police department strengthened its Stadium detail.

On the 7th the Yankees lost a double header to the Senators and the Athletics won a double-header from the Red Sox. The teams were tied; the Athletics had picked up thirteen and a half games since July 4. On September 8 the Yankees beat the Senators, but the Athletics took another brace of games from Boston and went ahead of the Yankees by half a game.

New York scalpers asked twenty-five dollars for two-dollar seats and eight or ten dollars for $1.50 seats. Speculators were dealing with each other like brokers on the stock exchange. The attendance on the pleasant, summery 9th was a new record, 85,265, and the Yankees management believed a hundred thousand tickets could have been sold. An estimated five thousand watched from nearby rooftops.

> **We broke their hearts today.**
> —**Babe Ruth, September 9, 1928**

The Yankees took the double-header from the Athletics by scores of 5–0 and 7–3. Ruth had one hit in six times at bat and scored three runs.

The Yankees dressing room after the games was loud with joy. "The Yankees let themselves go, shouting . . . slapping one another on the back, pulling and tugging and hugging one another all over the place," wrote a witness. Gradually the din became a chant

> Same old A's!
> Same old A's!

> **It was the Ruth, the whole Ruth, and nothing but the Ruth at the Yankee Stadium yesterday.**
> —*The Times*, **September 12, 1928**

Monday the 10th was an open date, on which they might reflect on the news of the death of Urban Shocker, who had played in 1926 and 1927 with a heart ailment so distressing that he could not sleep lying down. In that condition he had won thirty-seven and lost seventeen for the Yankees.

The Yankees and Athletics met again on the 11th. Ruth broke a 3–3 tie in the eighth inning with a two-run home run which gave Henry Johnson a 5–3 win over Lefty Grove, who stayed in after he was tired, according to the principles of the day. The pennant was not yet guaranteed by the arithmetic of the standings, but, as Henry Johnson still says, this was the psychological end of the season. Johnson beat the Athletics five times in 1928. He told the

author: "I won fourteen games in 1928, beat Lefty Grove . . . to
clinch the pennant for us, for six thousand dollars."

The trouble with the Athletics was that they could beat everybody but the Yankees. Of twenty-two games between the two teams,
the Athletics won six. A split would have made the season end like
this:

	Won	Lost	
Philadelphia	103	50	—
New York	96	58	7½

Instead the final figures were:

New York	101	53	—
Philadelphia	98	55	2½

After the decisive series Ruth had a serious batting slump. H. G.
Salsinger, the Detroit sportswriter, said Huggins, who knew they
could still lose the lead, threatened Ruth with suspension unless he
was in bed nightly by midnight. In two weeks of regular hours he
made five hits, of which only one was a home run. In desperation
he stayed out all night in Detroit and hit two home runs the next
afternoon (September 27).

The Yankees clinched the pennant on September 28 by winning
in Detroit, 11–6. There were only two games left to play. Ruth hit
his fifty-third home run.

The Cardinals won in the National League by taking their game
of the 29th long after all their World Series tickets were sold. That
same day Huggins used a lineup at Detroit with only two regulars,
and the Tigers won 19–10. There was a feeling abroad that the
Yankees were a badly crippled team by the end of September.
(Their real weakness was a shortage of first-rate substitutes.) The
bookmakers made the Cardinals favorites to win the World Series at
6 to 5.

With the season ended the Yankees returned to New York to a
modest welcome by twenty red caps, a pair of New York Central
passenger agents, the gang in the baggage room, and several
commuters.

John McGraw said a great team is one that wins three pennants in
a row. If true, the Yankees of 1926, 1927, and 1928 were Huggins's
second great team, and it was of his own building. Critics rate the
1927 group as best of the three, but the 1928 men were very good,
even though slightly inferior in the batting statistics. (The 1928
pitchers had more shutouts and more strikeouts than the 1927 staff.)
Compared with other American League teams of 1928, the Yankees

were great. There were 1928 Yankees among the season's best five batters in batting average (2), slugging percentage (2), home runs (2), total bases (3), bases on balls (1), runs scored (3), doubles (2), and triples (1). The Athletics were not close behind in these matters.

Babe Ruth ranked tenth in the American League in batting with .323. His fifty-four home runs made him home-run champion of both leagues for the ninth time in eleven years. Through 1928 only Hornsby, Gehrig, Cy Williams, and Ruth had ever hit more than forty home runs in a season, and of these only Ruth ever hit fifty or more. Since Yankee Stadium opened, Ruth had hit five more home runs on the road than at home.

In fielding, however, he had become the least of Yankee outfielders. He was behind Combs and Meusel in assists, and he made no double plays.

A man is usually at his best when he is on the way to becoming what he is going to be. Ruth had arrived in 1927, if not earlier, but he was very good after 1927. Often a man will lose his sharpness when he reaches his personal peak. Ruth's decline after 1927 was not mental or emotional but wholly physiological, a result of aging. He played baseball not as a means to riches or power but simply out of joy. Because his only goal was to play baseball well, he played as well as he could as long as he could.

THE ACCUMULATED BATTING FIGURES
BABE RUTH'S MAJOR-LEAGUE CAREER
1914–1928

at bat: 5475
hits: 1904
home runs: 470
runs batted in: 1416
average: .348

43 · Triumph and Glee

The Cardinals were decided favorites to win the World Series of 1928 from the Yankees, at odds which lengthened from 6 to 5 to 5 to 3. Their pitching seemed better than the Yankees', and with good reason. The Yankee pitchers who ranked first and second in the American League in 1927 wouldn't be in the Series. Cy Moore fell off his barn during the winter and hurt his arm. He tried to pitch in 1928 but gave up after sixty innings and went home to Oklahoma to tend his cotton. Herb Pennock won seventeen and lost six in 1928, with the secondbest earned-run average in the league, but his arm became sore in mid-August and he never pitched again that year.

On the next to last day of the season Earle Combs ran into the left-field wall at Detroit and hurt his throwing wrist so badly it was clear he would be in the Series only as a pinch-hitter, if at all.

Thus the Yankees lost two front-line pitchers and one of the best center fielders there ever was.

There were other less hurtful injuries, enough to give the Yankees a squad of walking wounded. Mark Koenig hobbled about on a bruised heel. Joe Dugan had been on the bench for awhile late in the season with eye trouble. Lazzeri's arm was so sore he could not throw overhand. In ordinary walking, Ruth had a noticeable limp from an ankle strained in September. Gehrig, in the last game of the season, was knocked unconscious by a batted ball which struck him in the face, though he would recover by the start of the Series.

When the Series opened in New York on Thursday, October 4, the Yankees won 4–1, beating Willie Sherdel. Hoyt gave the Cardinals but three hits. The Yankees had seven hits, five by Ruth and Gehrig for eight bases. Ruth scored two of the four runs.

The second game was pleasant for the "lusty invalids" of New York as George Pipgras held the Cardinals to four hits while the

Yankees made thirteen to win, 9–3. Alexander started for the Cardinals but left the game in the third inning after the Yankees had six hits. Ruth had a double and a single in three times at bat, had a base on balls, and scored two runs. When asked if the Yankees would win four straight he replied, "Well, I hope we go right through them." He was still lame when baseball didn't distract him from the soreness.

After a day off for train travel to St. Louis, the Series resumed on Sunday, October 7. The radio broadcaster Phillips Carlin, surprised by color in a baseball crowd, tactlessly said the throng was as colorful as a football crowd. Many women were wearing touches of cardinal red and many men were coatless under the warm sun of a perfect day. John McGraw, who had seen most World Series, said the weather was the finest for a Series game he had ever known. The Cardinals had a Dixieland band in the stands before the game, which stopped only when the members watched Ruth or Gehrig take batting practice. They got to see Ruth hit three over the pavilion.

Sam Breadon, owner of the Cardinals, had enlarged the seating of his small park by building temporary boxes in front of the stands. This made the dugouts useless, so the teams sat in the open on country-style benches. This limited the foul area and thus cut down the possibility of foul fly-outs (an excellent idea, inasmuch as the only rule change baseball has really needed in this century is the abolition of the foul fly-out).

Tom Zachary, the left-handed pitcher who gave up Ruth's sixtieth home run in 1927, had joined the Yankees late in the season. He won the third game 7–3 with the help of two home runs by Gehrig. Ruth had two singles in four times at bat and scored two runs. He forgot his game leg when he scored with a sprint from second base on an infield hit, sliding into the plate with force enough to upend the catcher. After the third game anyone who wished to bet on the Cardinals to win the Series could get 20 to 1 odds.

> I said the National is a hell of a league. [Sherdel] said it sure is. I said put one right here and I'll knock it out of the park for you. He did, and I did.
>
> —Babe Ruth, October 9, 1927

The Yankees won their second straight World Series and eighth straight Series game on October 9, coming from behind with five-o'clock lightning to score six runs in the seventh and eighth innings. The score was 7–3, with Hoyt the winner and Sherdel the loser. The Yankees had five home runs, three by Ruth.

It was Ruth's day. In the first inning he hit into a double play. In the fourth he hit the ball out of the park. In the fifth he grounded out to first. The seventh inning opened with the Cardinals leading 2–1. When Ruth came to the plate the lightning bolt was gathering its energy (and Sherdel was losing his). As Joe Williams wrote: "The atmosphere takes on a strange tenseness, pulses beat faster, and your ears seem to catch the sound of distant thunder."

Sherdel got two strikes on Ruth. After the second strike he returned the ball to the plate without a windup for what would have been the third strike, except that it was called a quick pitch. The quick pitch was legal in the National League, illegal in the American League; Commissioner Landis had ruled it illegal for the Series. There was a stormy argument around home plate while players gathered in knots to discuss the ruling. Ruth walked from group to group clapping his hands in applause. When the umpire ruled the pitch null Ruth had another chance. He stood in the batter's box and exchanged some words with Sherdel. Then, pock! and the ball arched onto the roof of the pavilion to tie the game. The St. Louis crowd, uninformed on the subject of quick pitches, was furious. Gehrig followed with another home run and the Yankees led, 3–2.

Ruth took his place in the field (he played in left when in St. Louis) to a reception of boos and bottles from angry partisans. A bottle lit at his feet. He picked it up as if to throw it back into the crowd, which shrank as though Zeus had wound up to pitch a thunderbolt. Ruth smiled and tossed it lightly past the foul line.

He came to bat again in the eighth to hit against the new pitcher, Alexander. Alexander later talked himself into believing Ruth never hit a home run off him, but Ruth hit one now in a four-run inning, tying his own record for home runs in a World Series game. When he went to the outfield in the last of the ninth the bleacher crowd stood to applaud him. No bottles.

He ended Ruth Day by making a one-handed catch of a foul fly for the last out. He caught it while running in along the left-field line with his right hand over the temporary boxes. He had to run through a blizzard of scorecards and newspapers thrown at him, but he caught the ball at full run, waved it high, shouted, "How's that!" and kept on running until he passed from sight under the stands, "the picture of triumph and glee and kindly defiance."

Sportswriters foamed over. Examples: (1) "As he ran from the field his path was strewn with the invisible flowers of invisible persons who know real baseball greatness when they see it." (2) "Of all our baseball memories that shall be the clearest-etched and most unforgettable. Ruth, indomitable, unconquerable, triumphant."

The beer was cold, gorgeously, tastefully cold. It always is after you win.

—Jim Brosnan

Babe Ruth always thought baseball victories should be celebrated with festivals of which he was master of ceremonies. He delayed the departure of the victors' special train from St. Louis until he had overseen the stowing of a cargo of nourishment. Commanding a platoon of porters, he saw to the loading of beer, pickles, rye bread, ham hocks, and four bushels of spare ribs. It was a menu wholly fitted to one of the Ruth family's restaurants in dockside Baltimore.

Notified by telegraph from stationmaster to stationmaster, crowds met the train at every station as it rolled east through the night of October 9–10. If it stopped, as it often did, people would surge toward the sleeping cars chanting, "We want Ruth! We want Ruth!" He appeared every time, called for cheers for the Yankees, cheers for Lazzeri, cheers for Gehrig, cheers for Al Smith, and the response was loud. At Mattoon, Illinois, he added the Cardinals to the list but then checked the crowd with "No—they quit—to hell with 'em." And that remark brought a cheer. At Terre Haute, Indiana, he came out onto the observation platform in his undershirt, holding high a ham hock and a pitcher of beer. He got the usual cheers until he reached the name of Al Smith. Silence. (Indiana, Ku Klux bastion of the north in 1928; it figures.) Angrily he shouted, "If that's the way you feel, to hell with you!"

There were crowds at stations all the way through Indiana and Ohio, and crowds at Rochester, at Syracuse, at Albany.

Meanwhile the train was no place for a quiet man. Ruth went through the cars and smashed every straw hat that had survived the summer. Then, joined by others, he returned the way he came, seized on every Yankee or writer and, with plenty of help, ripped off his shirt or pajama top. Each victim joined the others on the destructive march. They even got Ruppert's pajama top. By this time Huggins was around the bend. At some time in the night, much taken in whiskey which he ordinarily didn't touch, he lost his false teeth.

When the revelers reached Grand Central Station about a hundred people saw them and sent up a shout, which drew another thousand. The greeters brushed the police aside when they saw the grinning round brown face topped by the undeniable plush cap. Shouting "There he is!" they rushed to kill him with love. Six policemen pushed and hustled him into the safety of the Biltmore elevator.

Only then the World Series of 1928 came to an end.

The Yankees had earned their night of revelry.

Winning two World Series in a row by four-game sweeps had never been done before. As a team they set new marks for a four-game series with thirty-four extra bases and nine home runs. As for the walking wounded whose pains had encouraged the oddsmakers to favor the Cardinals, limping Koenig made three double plays and sorearm Lazzeri made one. Dimsighted Dugan was in parts of three games. Ruth forgot his lameness in the delight of play. Moore and Pennock weren't missed because Hoyt, Pipgras, and Zachary did all of the pitching and gave up only eight earned runs while striking out twenty-nine and walking eleven.

The Yankee triumph won the heart of New York and made the city an American League stronghold until God breathed life into the Mets thirty-four years later. On the other hand, many of the millions who knew the Yankees only by the sound of their bats as broadcast over forty-five radio stations began to develop that holy and wholesome hatred of the rich Yankees who pressed down cruelly on the poor and won so often because they priced players out of the reach of other teams—or so it seemed to a whole generation of hinterland Americans.

Attendance at the 1928 Series was about the same as in 1927. The winners each received $5,813 and the losers $4,181. Because they voted more shares than in 1923, they did not outdo the record player-shares of 1923.

Ruth scattered new batting records through the book. He set a total of nineteen records for a four-game Series, of which eight still stand.* And he was more than a piece of artillery. In the field he made no errors, one assist, and nine put-outs, including the difficult catch which ended the Series and drove the sportswriters into a fine frenzy.

After the Series Ruth and Gehrig organized two. pick-up teams and went barnstorming. They called the teams the Bustin' Babes and the Larrupin' Lous. Their schedule began on October 13 in New York State and ended in a rainout at Denver on October 31.

Ruth also campaigned for Al Smith in October. Today he might be drawn into public life by political managers, not to run for office but to lend color to the group that comprises the tail of a glamorous political comet. But Al Smith wasn't in national affairs long enough

---

* Limiting the list to those set in 1928 for a four-game Series, which have not yet been surpassed, they are:
Highest batting average, .625.
Most runs scored, 9 (shared record).
Most hits, 10.
Most doubles, 3 (shared).
Most Series with three or more home runs, 3.
Most home runs in three series in three consecutive years, 9.
Most total bases, 22.
Most extra-base hits, 6.

to invent the celebrity retinue, and while Franklin D. Roosevelt used charm as a deadly weapon he had no use for glitter.

As soon as Ruth unpacked after coming back to the Ansonia from St. Louis, he went with Gehrig and Ruppert to call on Al Smith and his family in their suite at the Biltmore. He gave Smith the ball he caught in the last play of the Series and posed for photographs with Smith and Gehrig.

Ruth and Lazzeri spoke for Smith over WJZ on October 19. Ruth said he had received fourteen thousand letters and telegrams after the Series, and that in the past such letters had been only about baseball. (This was not accurate: generally, in the past, about two-thirds would be from men wanting to make money and women wanting to make love.) Now, he continued, half of his mail touched on politics. Of the first nine thousand pieces, seven thousand praised his trainside support of Smith on the night after the triumph in St. Louis and only two hundred protested. He said he was for Smith because of his ability to rise high from lowly beginnings.

Legend now claims the floor and adds that Ruth said most ball-players supported Smith; he then introduced his companion: "Here's Tony Lazzeri. Now, Tony, who are the wops going to vote for?"

Ruth joined John W. Davis, the Democratic presidential nominee of 1924, in accepting invitations from the Kentucky Democratic campaign committee to speak for Smith at a rally in Louisville on October 24. He and Davis were also on Louisville radio together on the 25th, and Ruth spoke that day to the boys of three high schools and to the Kiwanis Club. While in Louisville he took time to visit his batmaker, the Hillerich & Bradsby Company, which still produces the Ruth model of the Louisville Slugger. Jack McGrath, now vice-president of the company, remembers the visit: "He wore a brown suit and brown derby. But the thing I remember most was how strong he looked . . . he was really muscular." The brown derby, of course, was the symbol of Al Smith.

Al Smith, we know, failed. A very small part of the reason was that Babe Ruth didn't vote in 1928. On the day before the election he went to the New York city clerk's office to get a hunting license. (For once he didn't draw a crowd.) Where he was on election day we do not know, but we may suppose he lay motionless in a duck blind on Long Island.

Ruth bought "a new and shiny brown coupe" that fall (brown for Al Smith?). Returning alone from a visit to an orphanage near Paterson he stalled his engine at a Manhattan stoplight and couldn't restart it. Traffic jammed behind as he looked uselessly under the hood. Soon he was recognized and gathered a crowd of about fifteen hundred, not one of whom could help. He called the dealership for a tow. The dealer's people thought the call was a hoax, but Ruth had a total stranger identify him over the phone and the agency sent two cars, one to haul his car away and one to take him home. When he began to transfer a cargo of bats, gloves, and balls from his car, the assembled worshipers prayed to him for the holy relics until, in desperation, he gave them all away in order to escape.

In December the Baseball Writers Association of America chose an All-Star Team of 1928 for the *Sporting News*. Casting 233 ballots, they chose six players from the American League and five from the National. Babe Ruth's name led all the rest with 216 votes. No one could think a recount was needed.

Outside the Park, 1929

DEFENDS DR. BARNES
FOR DISCUSSING GOD

SENATE RATIFIES ANTI-WAR PACT, 85 TO 1

HOOVER IS SPEEDING
TO FLORIDA FOR REST

LOAN CURB HINTED
BY RESERVE BOARD

EARTHQUAKE HURT OPERA

SEES DRUG ADDICTION
MAIN CAUSE OF CRIME

SPECULATION RAISES RESOUNDING ISSUE

HIGH TIDE OF BROKER'S LOANS

SOUVENIR SEEKERS CUT ROSES
AT HOOVER'S PALO ALTO HOME

MOVING BANANA PILE YIELDS
MAN AND 200 BOTTLES OF RUM

WHOLESALE CRIME
ALLEGED IN INDIANA

FISHER DENIES CRASH IS DUE

THE CREATIVE MIND
DISCUSSED AT YALE

STOCKS COLLAPSE IN 16,410,030-SHARE DAY

44 · Widowed and Married (1929)

The winter of 1928–1929 brought little change in the Yankees' roster. Huggins would try for a fourth straight pennant with almost the same team. The Yankee management gave the press a list of 1929 Yankees, delicately printed in salmon and pink, which had four new names: catcher Arndt Jorgens, infielders Lyn Lary and Gene Robertson,* and outfielder Sam Byrd. The Yankees bought Lary from Oakland; in two seasons of spring training Huggins taught him how to make the double play, just as he had taught Lazzeri. Byrd was a good outfielder who replaced Ruth in late innings; he was an even better golfer and later became a respected professional. The sore arms of Pennock and Moore had healed, which made the Yankee pitching seem strong.

Among those let go to make room was one whom a truly super-stitious manager might have kept. Lucky Mike Gazella had played only with the Yankees and only in the pennant-winning seasons of 1923, 1926, 1927, and 1928.

The Yankees had the weakness mentioned before—no steady source of good players. While the Yankees were making these minor changes the Athletics added Jimmy Foxx and Mule Haas.** The Yankees planned to use rookies Gene Robertson, Leo Durocher, and Bill Dickey as regulars. Dickey was an excellent hitter, but the others would not help the Yankees' batting and slugging average. Neither Jorgens nor Byrd appeared in half the games. Lary played in eighty.

The Yankees had great front-line talent, but in 1929 they had

---

* Lynford Hobart Lary (1906–1973), infielder, twelve seasons, 1929–1940, Yankees, Red Sox, Browns, Senators, Indians, Dodgers, Browns, batting average .269.
  Eugene Edward Robertson (1899–   ), third-baseman, nine seasons, 1919–1930, Browns, Yankees, Braves, batting average .280.
** George William Haas (1903–1974), outfielder, twelve seasons, 1925–1938, Pirates, Athletics, White Sox, batting average .292.

what is called a shallow bench. Yet Ruppert had an example of successful recruiting plainly before him. The Cardinal farm system began in 1922. It soon paid for itself by producing more talent than the Cardinals could consume. The surplus was sold for cash to other clubs, or used to replace highly paid Cardinals who were themselves then sold, benefiting the club by the prices received and by the cuts in payroll. Ruppert and Barrow were too slow or too proud to copy Sam Breadon.

They were first in one matter, though. The 1929 Yankees wore numbers on their backs for ready identification (Cleveland numbered its sleeves in 1916 but gave it up). The numbers appeared according to batting order, thus Babe Ruth became No. 3 forever. Humorists had fun with the idea, suggesting, among other things, that Durocher and Ruth swap shirts and baffle the enemy pitchers.

Ruth weighed 234.6 pounds when he began his workouts with Artie McGovern on January 3, after some golfing and bird-shooting. When a rumor arose that 1929 would be his last year because of his bloated overweight, Ruth with some annoyance told reporters he hadn't weighed as much as 250 pounds since early in 1926. McGovern predicted Ruth would play another four or five years now that he took such good care of himself.

After the collapse of 1925 Ruth probably worked as hard as anyone ever worked to stay in condition. Here he was, hard at it, two months before spring training, wearing a rubber shirt to increase sweating, exercising to strengthen belly, arms, legs, shoulders, neck. On the third day of torment he hit a punching bag so hard he tore it loose from its support. He was down four pounds in the first nineteen days. McGovern would like him to lose another eight, down to about 222, being willing to let a man of Ruth's age add four pounds a year to his playing weight. By mid-January McGovern had Ruth walking five miles a day in Central Park, often in the unwanted company of news photographers.

The early weeks of 1929 were relatively newsless, there being no big-league hockey or basketball, nor any Super Bowl. Ruth moved three times in four days, trying to shake off reporters. One thing reporters wished to know was Ruth's opinion of the novel suggestion of John A. Heydler, president of the National League, that the pitcher not bat, but a tenth man of the team hit each time for the pitcher. That would give Ruth a lifetime job, but he was against it. He thought it would change the strategy of the game, and besides, every pitcher needed an easy out in the batting order or "he would never get off the spot."

By early 1929 Babe and Helen Ruth had been separated for almost three years. Their last public appearance together was at the World Series of 1926. The parting was cool rather than quarrelsome.

The New York press published rumors of divorce. One story had it that Ruth wanted a divorce but Helen insisted on a hundred-thousand-dollar settlement which Ruth couldn't make. Another said Helen wanted a divorce, and there is some truth to that. At least she thought about it, but a priest who was a friend of both Babe and Helen talked her out of it.

Helen put Dorothy in a private school in Massachusetts in 1927. Then she moved into the house of Dr. Edward H. Kinder, a widowed dentist of Watertown.

On the night of January 13 Dr. Kinder went alone to the boxing matches at the Boston Colosseum. After Helen had gone to bed the house caught fire from defective wiring. A passerby gave the alarm. A fire captain and a policeman found Helen face down in her nightgown on the floor of an upstairs bedroom. Although alive when they got her out, the woman known to the neighbors as "Mrs. Kinder" died of burns and suffocation before medical help came. (The "Kinders" were believed to have been married in Montreal.)

Police had Dr. Kinder paged at the Colosseum, leaving a message that his wife was injured. When he reached Watertown and learned of her death he was badly shaken. The death certificate gave her name as Helen Kinder. And the body had that identity until a few hours before her scheduled funeral.

Helen Ruth had a mother, a brother, and two sisters living in south Boston who knew Kinder and his late wife. Helen had lived with her mother briefly before moving in with Kinder. When her kin heard of Helen's death the identification of "Helen Kinder" could not stand. When they identified the body as that of Helen Ruth, Dr. Kinder panicked and hid out for twenty-four hours. He then voluntarily appeared at Watertown police headquarters where he and his lawyer talked with police for two hours. As he came out the press was waiting. The chief of police told reporters that Dr. Kinder, an old friend, had sheltered Helen Ruth when she was friendless and homeless. Why had Kinder told the medical examiner she was his wife? Dr. Kinder said he didn't remember doing that because he was so upset at the time.

After the story reached New York, Ruth instantly interrupted his gymnasium work, went to Boston, and took over the funeral arrangements. All in black, accompanied by his lawyer, John P. Feeney, he met the press and said he had seen Helen only a few times in the past three years.

There had already been a routine autopsy, and the Middlesex County district attorney said there was no mystery about the cause of death, but, at the strong urging of Helen's brothers, he ordered a second autopsy to be made in Boston which had better laboratory facilities and a trained pathologist who would help in making a search for poison. The brothers did not claim to suspect poisoning, but they wanted to scotch any rumors of a crime having been committed. The district attorney was already certain there was no arson. He also flatly denied a rumor that there was a knife wound.

The second autopsy confirmed the first. The family and Ruth arranged for funeral services in the house of Helen's family. Because of the public scandal of her relation with Dr. Kinder, her body could not be buried from a Catholic church.

The Reverend Richard A. Burke, curate of St. Augustine's, conducted brief services on January 17 at Helen's old home at 420 West Fourth Street, in company with her mother, three sisters, and Babe Ruth. Burial was in Old Calvary cemetery during a light snowfall.

An inquest, on February 2, brought together all the people concerned. Its finding was that Helen died of burns and suffocation.

Helen's mother temporarily took charge of Dorothy. Dorothy's origin had been a mystery to the public until her mother's death. Now it became clear that she was an orphan or a foundling taken in by Babe and Helen Ruth. Helen's will, made at the time of the separation, left five dollars each to Babe, to her mother, and to seven brothers and sisters. The remaining went to "my beloved charge and ward, Dorothy Helen Ruth . . ." (who turned out not to have been legally adopted). The estate was finally settled in 1934; it amounted to $34,224. By that time Babe Ruth had legally adopted Dorothy, as we shall see.

Helen Woodford Ruth, who married in a hurry and long repented, was the only person permanently hurt by close relations with Babe Ruth. She had been hospitalized for a "nervous breakdown" for many weeks in 1925. We don't know enough about Helen to know whether her lack of emotional balance was a cause or effect of the failure of her marriage. As for Babe, he hadn't been much help. He couldn't be, really. He had never lived a normal family life.

Four days after Helen's funeral Ruth and Barrow agreed that Ruth would go to spring training early, along with catchers Benny Bengough and Johnny Grabowski and some rookies. He was soon in Florida testing his weakening legs on golf courses. The legs go first, and his legs had shown it in 1928, both in the field and on the bases. He stayed in Florida instead of going to the Baseball Writers dinner in New York as he usually did. It was just as well, for he would have been traveling with Miller Huggins who was arrested as a hotel burglar in Daytona and jailed for eight hours before he could prove he was Huggins the Great.

Among the rookies who came early to Florida was Sam Byrd. Sunday baseball was illegal in St. Petersburg, so players who wished could play golf on Sundays. Byrd saw several Yankees leaving to play and asked if he could come along. He took every hole. They then hustled Ruth into a match with Byrd (Ruth had the best handicap on the team). Those who knew Byrd bet on him. Ruth took all bets and lost ingloriously.

Ruth used the same muscles for hitting baseballs and golf balls. At the end of his swing on the tee his feet were in the same position as when he finished his batting swing. Nearly any ballplayer can drive a golf ball far, but not necessarily with accuracy. Golf requires a steadiness of performance that baseball doesn't. A golfer doesn't get three swings, nor can he play so-so golf and still win the game with a long drive on the eighteenth hole. Ruth drove well, and his approach shots were good, but he was erratic on the greens. He kept up golf as long as he could, and his friends pleased him by gifts of golf equipment, to which he responded with gifts of auto-graphed baseballs.

Baseball training began in earnest on the day Herbert Hoover took his Quaker affirmation of office. Ruth drew crowds. He swung hard but didn't hit as many into the right-field lake of Crescent Lake Park as people expected. He seemed trim, so, inevitably, there was talk that age had caught him.

When the team took to the road they went to Texas, and Texas went frantic over Ruth. The invasion of Texas made more money for the Yankees than any earlier spring exhibition tour. They broke crowd records everywhere, and throngs stormed railway stations, hotel lobbies, and ball parks literally to mob Ruth. That spring the Yankees won sixteen and lost eight. In the twenty-four exhibition games they scored 201 runs. They looked like the team that had won eight straight World Series games.

When they came home for the traditional exhibition with the Dodgers, before only seventy-five hundred people on a very chilly day, they won 10–5 as Ruth hit two home runs and Lazzeri one.

The Associated Press polled sixty baseball writers on their choices to win the pennants. They chose the Yankees over the Athletics by a wide margin, the Giants over the Cubs more nar-rowly. The oddsmakers were cagier than the writers. As they saw it the Yankees were odds-on at 9 to 10, the Athletics were 11 to 10. In the National League one could take the Giants or the Cubs at the same price, 7 to 5.

Claire Merritt, daughter of attorney James Monroe and Carrie Lou (Rylle) Merritt of Athens, Georgia, at the age of fifteen mar-ried a widower, Frank Bishop Hodgson, aged thirty-three, son of a cotton broker and owner of a small hotel in Athens. Claire Merritt Hodgson later left the impression that Hodgson may have married her in order to lose his eligibility in the eyes of Athens matrons with marriageable daughters. When Claire was seventeen she bore a

Babe and Claire, early 1929, shortly before the wedding. (*The Bettmann Archive.*)

daughter, Julia, and Mr. Hodgson, though vaguely pleased at fatherhood, seemed to lose interest in the arrangement. Claire, a ripening beauty, brought her child and her maid to New York, and, with the proper introductions, became a self-supporting model for several no-nonsense professional artists, the best remembered being Howard Chandler Christy. She then became, with Sigmund Romberg's help, "a four-line actress." (Years later legend classed her as a "onetime *Follies* beauty." She *was* a beauty, but not for Flo Ziegfeld.)

As we have seen, she met Babe Ruth while in Washington on tour in 1923. Their friendship lasted. During spring training in 1925, though Helen was in Florida, Babe ran up a four-figures telephone bill calling Claire in New York. In 1929, after Helen's death, Ruth's Florida telephone bill for calls to Claire was nineteen hundred dollars. In New York City during baseball seasons after the parting of Babe and Helen, Ruth saw much of Claire, her mother, and her brothers, who all lived together. Claire's view of baseball was bounded by Babe Ruth's shadow. To her, Commissioner Landis was cruel and ruthless, and she disliked Ed Barrow, though Barrow —perhaps unknown to her—had gone along actively with all of Christy Walsh's schemes to save Ruth from ending his career flat broke. Ballplayers are creaky and old at an age when professional men are called promising. Without Barrow's help in withholding Ruth's salary on Walsh's plan, Ruth might have been a panhandling sponge at forty-five. But long-standing dislike of anyone who ever made Babe Ruth bend his stiff neck shows Claire's genuine interest in Ruth.

> You girls certainly got to get up early in the morning if you want to marry Babe Ruth.
>
> —Will Rogers

When Ruth returned to New York from Florida he wanted to marry Claire but feared it might be too soon after Helen's funeral. Claire suggested taking the advice of her friend the Reverend William F. Hughes of the Church of St. Gregory the Great. Father Hughes told Ruth to marry immediately, and it was done in a matter of days (after Ruth denied it to correspondents of Pittsburgh and Chicago papers). They were married at Mass at 6 A.M. in St. Gregory the Great on Wednesday, April 17, 1929, with Father Hughes presiding.

Until they came down the aisle no one knew they were there. By the end of Mass there were about 150 present, mostly the usual Ruth-worshiping boys on their way to school. Claire wore purple and, for once in history, the groom's clothes were described: "a blue serge suit, a mottled brown tie, white shirt, and tan shoes." When Babe put the diamond circlet ring on Clair's finger a flash bulb went off, to Babe's plain annoyance (his ears turned red). He had promised to pose after the wedding if the press would let them alone in church.

After the Ruths signed the register and returned to the sanctuary a dozen of the boys in church pushed against the Communion rail, reaching for Babe and alarming Claire. But Babe spoke to each and promised autographed balls to the altar boys. Then, after posing for the photographers, Babe took Claire's arm, said, "Come on, let's get out of this," and with skill from long practice snatched her from the growing crowd. It was raining as they left. It rained enough to wash out the opening day's ball game and give them a one-day honeymoon.

The "wedding picture," April 1929. (*National Base-ball Library, Cooperstown, New York.*)

They had a private wedding breakfast in their new apartment on the seventh floor at 345 West 88th Street—the building where Ruth's mother-in-law already lived—for the Merritt family and ten close friends, and every baseball reporter and photographer of the New York press. Peter de Rose, the composer and pianist, was there as was May Singhi Breen, the woman who scored the ukulele chords on practically every piece of sheet music published in this country for fifty years. It was a pleasant party, according to Red Smith, and it was a lucky day for Babe Ruth. He got a zealous wife who also was to him the only full-time mother he ever had. He needed both, very much.

Marriage made no sudden difference in Ruth the ballplayer, except, as W. O. McGeehan said, "he wore the conventionally silly expression of a bride groom."

The day after the wedding Claire sat in a left-field box on the postponed opening day. There were thirty-five thousand at this wedding reception. By the time she reached her seat, amid applause, she was frightened because her hems were shredded by

The Ruth family, April 1929. Left to right: Butch (Julia), Babe (George), Dot (Dorothy), and Mom (Claire). (*National Baseball Library, Cooperstown, New York.*)

souvenir hunters. Babe came over to pose for pictures. The crowd's usual loving demonstration seemed to her a riot. But she was ignored after the game started until Ruth hit an uncommon left-field home run that almost landed in her lap. As he rounded third base he blew her a kiss, with a silly grin. That evening Mrs. Ruth thanked him and began to take charge: she told him to knock off the public display of affection or the other players would have no mercy.

Jacob Ruppert was pleased. He said he knew what to do if Ruth slumped in midsummer—"have him get married again!"

45 · The Only Vital Spirit Left

Seeing a chance to steady Babe Ruth's life, Jacob Ruppert asked Claire Ruth to travel with the team on the road. Most team managements don't like to have wives along, even when the player pays the cost as Ruth did, because the wife wants to plan the player's life—shopping or sightseeing by day, going out at night—and the husband ends up playing ball games between more important events. But Claire's goal was to keep Babe playing at his best for as long as possible. It worked well. She also took his phone calls on the road and talked with many surprised females of the kind now called groupies.

Ruth went in for many public-relations stunts during the 1929 season. We may suspect the hand of his wife in this, as a way of showing the world that her husband was not wholly self-centered and self-indulgent. In May, much earlier than usual, he staged his annual patriotic ceremony of signing bats and balls as prizes for the Citizen's Military Training Camps baseball champions. And he was "wildly cheered" when he spoke for the *New York Telegram* program to choose the best schoolboy ballplayer in the city. (In his speech he came out against profanity.)

On May 16 the Yankees played an exhibition at Binghamton which drew ten thousand on a bitterly cold day and caused a two-hour traffic jam. The game broke up in the sixth inning when a crowd surged into right field to show its love for Ruth; running at full speed he barely made it to the dugout.

Worse was a panic in Ruthville in Yankee Stadium on May 19 when the crowd fled a sudden shower and jammed at a tight exit, killing two and injuring sixty-two. The piled bodies filled a cubic space ten by ten by eight feet. These were the very core of Babe's fans. He and Claire took baseballs and rainchecks to the hospitalized and sent personal notes and rainchecks to all the injured.

Still on the public-relations campaign he publicly sent a dozen signed balls to a boy in Chicago who hit a home run ball into the garden of a neighbor. The neighbor refused to give it back. The quarrel ended in court (the boy won), which is how the Ruths heard of the matter.

I see they have me dead up in Boston.
—Babe Ruth, June 15, 1929

Babe had a deep chest cold on June 1. Dr. Edward King, as usual, put him in St. Vincent's Hospital to guard against pneumonia, but after a day Babe went back to 345 West 88th Street and took to bed there. Instantly, on news of hospitalization there were rumors of death by heart attack, rumors which started in Boston.

Claire told reporters her hardest job was to keep Ruth quiet for ten days as Dr. King had ordered. "He would have all his friends here, too, if I hadn't set my foot down." The press got in to see Ruth on the 8th. He wore "an old rose dressing gown" for the audience. His news: he would play no more exhibitions, he would not play the second game of double-headers, he would try to avoid the crush of autograph-seeking crowds. "They mob you, meaning well enough, of course. I am always afraid of spiking some of them, and I generally end by spiking myself when I have fifty people on top of me."

On the next day Babe went to the Stadium to pick up some equipment for a vacation (and to eat a ham-and-cheese sandwich). He said he and Claire were going away for a few days so he could get his "nerves back in shape." They left by car on June 12 and refused to say where they were headed, but journalistic sleuthing traced them to a borrowed hideout on Chesapeake Bay. Claire learned they couldn't hide from the newshounds, so told them Babe would be in uniform by the 18th and would probably play on the 20th (which would be three weeks after the onset of his chest cold). Sure enough, Babe took batting practice on the 18th. He hit a ball out of the playing field to everyone's delight, and dropped one in center field about four hundred feet away.

While Ruth was ill his old employer Harry Frazee died in New York of Bright's Disease. Frazee was the man who sold Ruth because he needed the money. In 1925 his No! No! Nanette! was said to have made him three million dollars (and left us the standard "Tea for Two"). If he had had that kind of money when he bought the Red Sox, baseball history would be written in quite another way.

The Yankees appeared sluggish in July, and writers said they were in the race only because Ruth had recovered and was carrying the whole team. Their incredible popularity continued, however, and a ball autographed by Ruth and other Yankees brought fifty dollars at a charity auction (it would bring about five times that at any collectors' auction in the early 1970s). That month the St. Louis Browns raised the price of St. Louis home runs by screening the front of their right-field pavilion. It quickly cost Ruth. He batted balls against the screen on July 7 and 8 but cleared the pavilion on the 9th. He hit only three home runs in St. Louis in 1929 after the screen was up, but it seems to have made no difference in his overall totals. (His St. Louis home-run totals for these years were: 1927—4, 1928—4, 1929—4, 1930—2, 1931—4.) To stir some interest, the Associated Press polled all managers on the desirability of so many home runs. Fifteen responded. Huggins, Connie Mack, Joe McCarthy, and Emil Fuchs favored plenty of them. Ten didn't like the storm of home runs and blamed the ball. Lena Blackburne* suggested keeping a ball in play until lost, regardless of its condition.

At the moment (July 13) the Yankees led in home runs with seventy-three and were batting .303, but they were in second place, seven and a half games behind the Athletics. Critics thought the Yankees were rich, fat, and smug.

Ruth hit a fungo fly on July 31 in a try at bettering Ed Walsh's record of 418 feet, set in 1912. Ruth's went 447 feet. Witnesses also claimed he drove a golf ball 360 yards on August 2, but skeptical reporters went to the place and measured; the yardage was 325.

Ruth hit his five-hundredth home run in Cleveland on August 11, his thirtieth of the season. Since the Yankees lagged ten and a half games behind the Athletics, Yankee lovers made as much as possible of home run number five hundred. "Bells should have been rung when this thing came to pass, and fire-crackers set off, and traffic halted for one minute throughout the length and breadth of the land . . ." sang the *New York Evening World*, advising those who wished to see a monument to Ruth to take a look at Yankee Stadium, which "has the austere dignity, the quiet solemnity of the national bank, and for the same reason." Would anybody ever hit more than five hundred? *The Times* believed it could be done, because there were young men playing who were further along in their home-run totals than Ruth had been at their several ages. They always had had the lively ball to hit, which Ruth didn't get until 1920. (But none had hit near three hundred yet.)

Baseball attendance was less in August than in August 1928 in both major and minor leagues. Rochester, a Cardinal farm, was leading the International League but losing money. The rulers of baseball hoped the sag was owing only to dull, one-sided pennant chases. A seer might have seen it as a sign the customers had less disposable money.

---

* Russell Aubrey Blackburne (1886–1968), infielder, eight seasons, 1910–1919, White Sox, Reds, Braves, Phillies, batting average .214.

The Yankees also slumped. They disgraced themselves by playing three nine-inning games in St. Louis in late August without scoring a run.

> When they pick up a newspaper now, they turn to the financial page first and the sports page later. Those things aren't good for a ball club which is trying to beat a club like the one Mr. Mack has.
>
> —Miller Huggins, September 1927

Miller Huggins rarely called a clubhouse meeting, but early in September he gathered the Yankees together to try to stir them. The response was slight. He told Ruppert and Barrow the team was finished. He could not rouse them, he could not make them angry, he could not even make them laugh. As for himself, he said, he had insomnia.

They found somebody they could beat. They played the Sing Sing prisoners on September 5 and won 17–3. Ruth had three home runs, played first base while "exchanging witticisms" with the crowd of fifteen hundred, and pitched the last two innings. But outside, though Ruth had forty home runs and Gehrig had nearly thirty, the Yankees didn't have a batter in the top five and had no hope of the pennant. Huggins said their three pennants had them "glutted with success."

Miller James Huggins in all his life rarely felt well. He was troubled by "nerves," bad teeth, indigestion, sinus headaches, and insomnia. He also had a special reason for depression in 1929, because several friends lost money in the Florida land bubble by following his advice.

On September 22 he entered St. Vincent's Hospital suffering from erysipelas, a streptococcus infection of the skin which dissolves red blood corpuscles. (At first he got the all-purpose 1920s diagnosis of influenza.) Art Fletcher,* senior coach, took charge of the Yankees. Huggins's temperature rose to 105, he made his will, and he received daily blood transfusions. Babe Ruth made a pilgrimage to his Knights of Columbus lodge and asked for prayers for Huggins. On September 25, while the Yankees were playing in Boston, at a little after 3 P.M., Huggins died, aged forty-nine. The Fenway Park flag came down to half-staff and the game was stopped for a moment of silence. (The second-rate Yankees symbolically secured second place that day.) American League President Ernest Barnard canceled all league games on the 26th. Services were held on the

---

* Arthur Fletcher (1885–1950), infielder, thirteen seasons, 1909–1922, Giants, Phillies, batting average .277.

27th in New York, and a funeral in Cincinnati on the 29th. Eight Yankees, including Ruth, accompanied the body to Cincinnati.

Huggins was a Ruth-tamer who could only rule his best player by threats to keep him from playing. His relatives mourned him, but few others did who knew him. Eddie Bennett, the middle-aged hunchback batboy was an exception; he wept all through the evening of the day Huggins died. Huggins built great teams. It would be wrong to say money did it, because rich men have wasted much money in failures to build great teams. He used the money *wisely*. His relationship with Babe Ruth was always cold and often hostile. Huggins's sister and housekeeper Myrtle told the wife of a respected newspaperman, "Babe Ruth took five years off my brother's life."

There was absolute silence on the subject of a successor to Huggins, except to say he would be chosen after the World Series. Across millions of minds flitted the name Ruth.

> . . . Ball teams are like human beings. They are born, live, and die.
> —Edward Grant Barrow

The decade of the 1920s saw two great Yankee teams, the team that won the pennants of 1921, 1922, and 1923, and the team that won in 1926, 1927, and 1928. Both withered, but more of their players were chosen for the baseball Hall of Fame, five, than any other team of the 1920s. The Yankees of the twenties were the best of hitting teams, but the Athletics overtook them as pitchers and fielders. New York critics began to find baseball duller.

> Babe Ruth is the only vital spirit left in that circuit— where once there were a score of colorful personalities.
> —Jack Kofoed, *North American Review* (1929)

In 1929, for a third successive year, fifty or more men in the American League hit .300 or better. That was not unexpected, but fifteen were newcomers in their first or second years, a curious development.

Although Babe Ruth missed more than six weeks of play he had 499 times at bat and ranked seventh in the league with .345. He led in home runs with forty-six and also led in slugging percentage and in home runs as a proportion of times at bat. The names of Simmons, Foxx, and Max Bishop,* all of them Athletics, glowed in places of honor where once Ruth's name stood supreme.

* Max Frederick Bishop (1899–1962), second baseman, twelve seasons, 1924–1935, Athletics, Red Sox, batting average .271.

Ruth's legs, though failing, were still good enough. He had the second-best fielding average of his life in the outfield (he led the league in 1919). And in 1929 Ruth made more sacrifice bunts than ever before: thirteen.

> **Washington, 725 . . . Lincoln, 154 . . . Babe Ruth, 65 . . . Jefferson, 35 . . . Franklin, 19.**
>
> —Dixon Wecter

By 1929 Babe Ruth was a national heroic symbol above and beyond the baseball field. A poll of 8,813 urban schoolchildren on the question: Of all the persons heard, read about, or seen, whom would you most care to be like?, found Ruth scoring respectably among boys, with sixty-five votes. That was pretty far behind George Washington's winning total of 725 or Abraham Lincoln's third-place 154, but it did place Ruth ahead of Henry Ford, Thomas Jefferson, Theodore Roosevelt, and Benjamin Franklin (in that order).

Babe Ruth went to the World Series of 1929 as a member of the working press. It was the Christy Walsh Syndicate's most profitable Series. Seven ballplayers, seven ghosts, and Walsh split $43,252 for writing about the way the Cubs earned the contempt of a generation of Midwesterners by giving up twenty-six runs in five games, ten of them in one inning, to Mack, Foxx, Simmons, Haas, and friends. None of Ruth's World Series records were in danger because nobody in the Series was close enough to catch him. So many asked Ruth whether he was to be the next manager of the Yankees that he passed out a typewritten statement saying he and Ruppert agreed he had some good playing years ahead and "it would not be wise to take on the troubles and worries of a manager." But, he added, he hoped to be a manager some day.

After the Series the question of Huggins's successor was the first question of New York. Many names floated in rumor. Ruppert, at first, would only deny that it would be John McGraw, adding that McGraw could have it if he were available. One wonders if McGraw could have rekindled the Yankee fire, that McGraw of whom Fred Snodgrass* once said, ". . . I do believe he had the most vicious tongue of any man who ever lived. Absolutely!" That probably was not what the Yankees needed.

Art Fletcher, acting manager, would have been Huggins's choice, but he turned it down. Bob Shawkey became the manager, signing a contract on October 23.

* Fred Carlisle Snodgrass (1887–1974), outfielder, nine seasons, 1908–1916, Giants, Braves, batting average .275.

Meanwhile, Ruppert had finally noticed the Cardinal system of growing their own ballplayers. Connie Mack let Jack Dunn's home-owned Baltimore Orioles grow many for him while winning seven successive International League pennants. The Orioles being uniquely linked to Mack, Ruppert decided to have his own system. At the owners' meeting in December he said the prices of minor-league players were so high all major-league teams would have to buy minor-league clubs. (This was later to poise Ruth at a fork in his road where he may have taken the wrong turn.)

Babe and Claire idled out the remaining weeks of 1929 with commonplace distractions—another speeding ticket, an amateurish billiards exhibition for charity, the endorsement of a candidate for a New York state judgeship (by this outfielder who had never yet voted).

The waning of the second great Huggins team coincided with the market crash of 1929. Barrow warned the Yankees in advance to get out of the market. Most did, but Ruth hadn't been in the market. His assets were in the annuity and in the trust fund, which paid him twelve thousand dollars in 1929.

> **He had a heap of living to do to make up for the grim years of his youth. And he never thought there would be an end to his skills.**
> **—Claire Merritt Hodgson Ruth**

Babe Ruth never had a regular boyhood. He used his years with the Red Sox, and with the Yankees until 1925, to be a boy. The phase from 1925 until he married Claire we might call young manhood. After marrying Claire he became mature with her help.

Just as Christy Walsh had organized his income and his saving, so Claire now organized his spending. Except for the annuity and trust fund, Babe was broke in early 1929. Every year from 1920 to 1929 he had bought at least one Cadillac. Professional parasites knew him as an easy mark. He bought diamonds for ladies with whom he was only slightly acquainted. But most of it probably went to support bookmakers and touts who had long lists of slow horses. Slowly and gently, but firmly, Claire began to see that he changed his ways. She wasn't trying the impossible task of making him a miser. But she tried to change his typical lower-middle-class view that to have a large income was to be rich, and to spend it was the pleasant proof of riches. Her aim was to see that he got his money's worth, and to get him to think the unthinkable thought that he would not be a highly paid ballplayer forever.

THE ACCUMULATED BATTING FIGURES
BABE RUTH'S MAJOR-LEAGUE CAREER
1914–1929

at bat: 5974
hits: 2076
home runs: 516
runs batted in: 1570
average: .348

Outside the Park, 1930

TEACHER SEIZED IN POISONING OF TEN CHILDREN

NATIONAL PROHIBITION IS TEN YEARS OLD TODAY

BANS ANTI-WAR MEMORIAL

186 INDICTED IN RUM PLOT

LABOR SETS MARCH 19
FOR JOBLESS PARLEY

JURY FAILS TO AGREE
AT MAE WEST TRIAL

SCIENTIST VISIONS TRIPS TO MOON BY YEAR 2050

SAYS ADVERTISING
AIDS WORLD PEACE

EDDINGTON PREDICTS
SCIENCE WILL FREE
VAST ENERGY IN ATOM

INDIANA VENUS DE MILO
REMAINS UNCLOTHED

5,554 JOBLESS IN CAMDEN

POLICE DRIVE ON "ROAD HOGS"

HITLER WARNS PRESIDENT

URGES CHILD TRAINING
TO CURB COMMUNISM

SAY INFURIATED WIFE
SLEW SILENT HUSBAND

PRESIDENT ACTS TO SPUR EMPLOYMENT

SURVEY SITUATION
OF JEWS IN WORLD

REPUBLICANS LOSE GRIP ON CONGRESS

46 · I'll Take the Eighty (1930)

Babe Ruth's contract expired in 1929. In 1930, to get a raise, he staged his most renowned holdout.

Obviously Ruth's salary would never have been so high if there had been more men like him. In bars and around office water-coolers people compare what ballplayers make with what they could earn in some other kind of work. That overlooks the scarcity of players. About one in fifteen hundred American males aged eighteen, according to professional psychological testing, shows enough promise to be given a chance to start at the lowest minor-league level.

A better comparison of a player's salary is with the profits of baseball's owners. Since 1883 gross receipts of major-league clubs have grown eighty times while average salaries are only seven times higher. The players' share of the take was once half; now it is about a fifth. In the twelve years before 1927, by Jacob Ruppert's own calculation, the value of all clubs grew from something over twenty million dollars to fifty million.

From spring 1923 to fall 1927 the country had five prosperous years. Average major-league attendance rose 50 percent over the previous decade, a rate much faster than the growth of the population. Major-league baseball, looked at as one industry, made profits every single year of the 1920s, and only the deliberately wrecked Red Sox needed a great deal of red ink.

When Ruth joined the Red Sox in 1914 major-league attendance was 4,450,000; in 1927 it was 9,940,000, and it would reach 10,130,-000 in 1930. In 1929 the customers spent $66 million for spectator sports, mostly for baseball and college football.

A reasonable person could believe Babe Ruth's stirring play helped baseball to prosper as a whole. It is even easier to think he helped the Yankees make money.

In Ruth's first year in New York the Yankees' attendance doubled, and remained at or near a million annually for the decade (excepting the wretched season of 1925). The Yankees had a sixth of the American League attendance in 1919. After Ruth came it jumped to one-fourth (again excepting 1925). T. L. Huston, rumor said, would have sold his half of the Yankees to Ruppert for a hundred thousand dollars in 1919. We have seen how many times that number he got when he sold in 1923. In the eleven years from 1920 to 1930 the Yankees made more money than any club—$3,517,000— *after* paying the salaries of executives. Ruth's salary in eleven years was exactly six hundred thousand dollars. Whenever the Yankee management announced he was unable to play, they had a good many ticket cancellations, enough to notice.

For the first time a team financed its spring training from the tickets sold for scheduled exhibition games. In the years 1921–30 the Yankee spring exhibitions grossed $417,000 and cost $358,000, leaving a profit of $59,000. In pre-Ruth days there would have been a loss of roughly two hundred thousand dollars in the same period. The Yankees also scheduled exhibitions on every open date of the season. The behavior of the crowds proved they came to see Ruth. In all these years he missed only one such game, and that was because he underestimated his driving time from Sudbury to New Haven.

Here are the American League's profit-making teams of 1929 and the approximate profits: Athletics, $275,000; Yankees, $271,000; Tigers, $123,000; White Sox, $11,000; Browns, $5,000.

Did his reputation still stand high in 1929 and 1930? A most respected sportswriter, Hugh S. Fullerton, in the *North American Review* in 1930, rated him the best outfielder there ever was, "possibly excepting Speaker." More to the point, Grantland Rice, the writer most respected by players of the time, said that of all players from Cobb to Ted Williams, Ruth was the only one who could draw a capacity crowd in every city where the Yankees played.

In dealing with Ruth's bid for a raise, Ruppert had weaknesses and strengths. (To judge by the way many other owners talked of players, the owners' chief weakness was the Thirteenth Amendment which prohibits slavery.) The reserve clause, giving Ruppert sole right to Babe Ruth's services, was the trump card. In the end Ruth would play baseball on Ruppert's terms or he could set up as, say, a shirtmaker. The reserve clause was a term of a partnership called Organized Baseball, bound by a solemn covenant, the National Agreement. The owners worked together in private, sharing financial and tactical secrets on an exchange basis, while keeping players, press, and public in darkness.

Ruppert knew Ruth was worth plenty. But to give him more would spur the other Yankees to ask for more. Ruth's only true strength was the wish of Ruppert and Barrow to sign him early, because it made it much easier for them to deal with the other men on the roster. If Ruth stood firm, other Yankees might get balky at contract time.

Some cynics thought important holdouts were staged to get publicity. Not so in Ruth's case. He didn't need the attention. He was a living publicity stunt all by himself. The press covered holdouts at length, and Ruth may have enjoyed it, but Ruppert found it distasteful. Although he knew Ruth's great value to him, it irked him that a man who played games on summer afternoons cost him more than the best brewmaster.

Speculation about Ruth's next contract appeared in John Kieran's column in the *New York Times* in February 1929, eleven months before Ruth and Ruppert settled down to talk. In November Ruppert and Barrow went to French Lick, Indiana, where for several weeks they drank Pluto Water (the bubbly laxative spring water) to get in shape to argue with Ruth. Back in New York Ruth talked to his friends about motion-picture actors at two hundred thousand a year, of Jack Dempsey getting half a million for a fight while Babe Ruth had to play 154 games every year, half of them in a stadium specially built to hold the crowds he drew.

According to Stan Musial,* at contract time a player has to show the probability of great things to come. It does no good to dwell on the past; the owner has already bought and paid for the past. From others we know the three common elements of salary-bargaining are last year's playing record, the prospects of a better year to come, and (one that didn't apply in Ruth vs. the Yankees) the effect of low standing and poor attendance. Ordinarily the parties will let the talk roam over such points as the player's financial security—can we win the pennant?—the cost of living—the player's household budget.

Ruth, Ruppert, and Barrow settled down to talk in Ruppert's classic office at the brewery on January 8, 1930, the tenth anniversary of Ruth's first Yankee contract. It was friendly. Ruth smiled at an opening offer to renew the old contract for one year. Ruppert then suggested two years at seventy-five thousand. Ruth countered with three years at eighty-five thousand. Barrow said a three-year contract wasn't going to be written. The meeting adjourned. The issue really wasn't so much the money as the number of years.

Eight days later Barrow mailed all Yankee contracts as yet unsigned or otherwise agreed to. Ruth's was for two years at seventy-five thousand dollars a year. Silence followed for almost three weeks. Then Ruth (or Claire?) began a war of nerves by sending to each New York paper a financial statement which showed he could

---

* Stanley Frank Musial (1920–   ), outfielder, first baseman, twenty-two seasons, 1941–1963, Cardinals, batting average .331. Hall of Fame.

retire on an assured yearly income of twenty-five thousand dollars. He didn't have to play "for bread and butter"; if he wanted work for work's sake he had many offers from outside baseball, "even from a circus." Ruppert and Barrow responded with mixed solemnity and scorn, saying they hadn't gotten a copy and had some doubt of its authorship since the signature was typewritten.

Babe and Claire went off to Florida where Babe made believe he was more interested in bettering his golf than in the status of his contract. By February 19 he was the last player holding out, though he continued to work out with the team. Ruppert decided the time had come to go to Florida. In Yankee Babe-fighting, Barrow was only the picador. Ruppert was the matador who came out for the kill. Ruppert and Ruth had a friendly haggle in the clubhouse, during which Ruth made a concession: he would accept a contract for two years instead of three years. Ruppert made a concession, too. He would raise his figure to eighty thousand. Ruth still asked eighty-five. They broke off the talk, still friendly. Ruth asked friends why Ruppert would quibble about "a mere five thousand dollars."

> Well, I'll take the eighty.
> —Babe Ruth, March 8, 1930

The Yankees advertised that Ruth would play an exhibition game with the Braves. Ford Frick dined with Babe and Claire the night before. Frick said it would be folly to play, because if he were hurt he could not bargain. Babe saw the point and said if Ruppert would not agree by noon he would go home to New York. Frick told Dan Daniel the story, and Daniel sent it in fifteen hundred words to the *New York Telegram*. The next morning Babe told Daniel he had changed his mind and would play. He felt like playing ball and he liked Emil Fuchs, the owner of the Braves, who could use the money. Daniel, startled, told Ruth that to play without a contract would make Daniel seem a liar. Daniel was one of the Ruths' best friends, and this turn gave Babe pause. Daniel showed him a press description of a bread riot in New York, which surprised Ruth. He told Daniel he'd take the Colonel's offer.

To save Daniel by signing before noon, the Ruths came to St. Petersburg from their own headquarters to call on Ruppert at the Princess Martha Hotel at 11 A.M. Ruppert was at Crescent Lake Park where the Yankees trained. For forty minutes the Ruths waited in the lobby. When Ruppert came, he and Babe talked privately and at ten minutes to noon called in the reporters for the announcement. They then posed for photographers on the lawn. Dan Daniel had written his story, then made it come true. The actual signatures went on the contract a few days later. Babe usually signed himself "George H. Ruth" but this time signed the whole, "George Herman Ruth," which carries to this reader a sense of triumph.

Ruppert told the press no player would ever again get a contract for that much money. But it was a good deal for both parties. For two summers Ruth would get twelve checks totaling eighty thousand, drawn on the Yorkville office of the Manufacturers Trust Company and signed "Jacob Ruppert" (who was good for about 750 times that sum). Babe had to pay a uniform deposit, Claire's train fares, rent for his and Claire's hotel suites, and about five thousand a year in income taxes. Ruppert couldn't know it, but he was going to get the best year's attendance at Yankee Stadium of his lifetime.

With Ruppert's swordplay ended, picador Barrow got out his 4 x 6 card and added an entry:

1930   cont. $80,000

1931   cont. $80,000

On the side, Ruppert refunded the five-thousand-dollar fine Huggins had levied on Ruth in 1925, which had festered ever since in Ruth's heart.

We do not have a table of the highest-paid ballplayers of 1930, but the figures for 1931 are available.

Babe Ruth	$80,000	Yankees
Rogers Hornsby	40,000	Cubs (playing manager)
Hack Wilson	33,000	Cubs
Al Simmons	30,000	Athletics
Bill Terry*	25,000	Giants
Lou Gehrig	25,000	Yankees

In Connie Mack's memoirs he tells of paying Ty Cobb eighty thousand for one year, which would have to be 1927 or 1928. The only team to match the Yankee payroll was Mack's Athletics in their glory years of 1929–31. As the freeze of the Great Depression hardened, Mack couldn't keep pace and had to sell off his men piecemeal. Not all really good hitters were in the big money. Left O'Doul** made 254 hits in 1928 (a season record still shared with Terry) and batted .394 to lead the National League, for eight thousand dollars.

* William Harold Terry (1898–   ), first baseman, fourteen seasons, 1923–1936, Giants, batting average .341.
** Francis Joseph O'Doul (1897–1969), pitcher, outfielder, eleven seasons, 1919–1934, Yankees, Red Sox, Giants, Phillies, Dodgers, batting average .349.

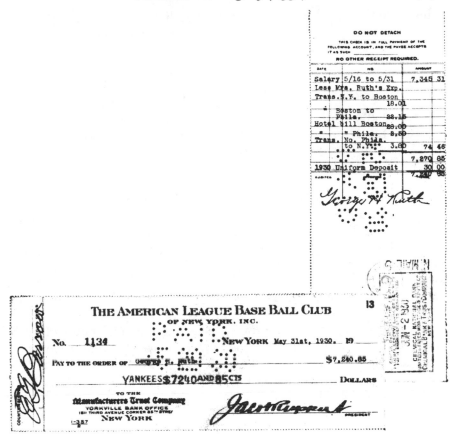

The take-home pay of Hercules. The fortnightly pay check for $7,240.85, May 31, 1930, with travel and hotel expenses for Babe and Claire, and the uniform deposit, in the sum of $104.46, already· taken out. Signed, Jacob Ruppert, countersigned, E. G. Barrow, endorsed George H. Ruth, canceled, June 2. (*G.S. Gallery.*)

His reward was a five-hundred-dollar raise. These were tough years for some owners. Emil Fuchs of the Braves had holdout trouble. Instead of paying salaries he proposed to divide all profits among the twenty-five players, leaving them to decide on the sizes of the shares. He got no takers.

As it turned out, Ruth's salary didn't hurt Yankee profits. The citizenry spent as much watching games in 1930 as in 1929, of which baseball got seventeen million dollars, a little more than in 1929. Ruppert privately told Grantland Rice he could pay Ruth two hundred thousand a year without overpaying him.

Just what did Ruth get? Today's $30,000 house cost $7,500 then, the $3,000 car sold for $750, the $4 watch (if one can find it) cost $1. His $80,000 equals $320,000 now; his annual income taxes then were worth what $20,000 will buy today. Another table may help:

Player	Salary	Year	1931 Value Before Taxes
Babe Ruth	$80,000	1930	—
Joe Dimaggio	100,000	1950	55,000
Willie Mays	125,000	1969	33,000
Dick Allen	225,000	1973	54,000

If Dick Allen could keep 60 percent of his income after taxes, a big *if*, he would need a salary of $307,133 to have Ruth's purchasing power after Ruth's puny five thousand dollars of income tax.

As of opening day before his new salary began, Babe Ruth, according to a *Times* estimate, had already collected $739,397 in salaries and World Series shares. The new salary was an annual wage five thousand dollars higher than the President's and fifteen thousand dollars higher than Commissioner Landis's.

The public generally approved. The big financial news of early 1930, measured by space in the papers, was Hoover's request to Congress to vote a hundred million dollars for farmers, the reduction of the English bank rate to 4 percent, the bankruptcy of Haiti, and Babe Ruth's salary.

47 · He Settled Down

A baseball player is attached to conventional worlds. An
entertainer isn't.

—E. Franklin Frazier

When Babe married Claire he was at an age when most ballplayers
are finished. Half the rookies of any season play only four seasons,
and the average of all players is six. The season of 1930 would be
Babe's seventeenth. Claire took it on herself to keep him playing
by keeping him healthy.

He ate too much. Just as Claire always carried lipstick, Babe
always carried sodium bicarbonate. He drank too much of whatever
was at hand—beer, whiskey, soda pop. He had many unsleeping
friends. Both his diet and his hours needed regularizing. Claire
found it could be done because she and Babe trusted each other.
Not for her the pushing and pressing of a Barrow or Huggins which
had made Babe mulish and angry. If he were to change he'd do it
himself, but he could use help. For example, he saw her logic when
she said fun in the third hour of the morning would begin to be
paid for in the third inning of the afternoon.

She began by barring hard liquor in the house during the playing
season. If a few teammates dropped in, a keg of beer could be
brought. Before marriage Babe's favorite mealtime was 11 P.M.,
preferably made up of a steak and beer. She persuaded him to
change to a club sandwich and milk, and that became the eleven
o'clock rite wherever they were. Breakfast remained a major meal,
often a steak or some mutton chops. Lunch was again a sandwich
and milk, before going to the ball park of the day. At the park he
was on his own—and sometimes undid the good work by a debauch
of hot dogs and soda pop because "I was hungry." Babe's life after
1919 was a war against fat, though he was always active. So the

Artie McGovern gymnasium tortures went on every January as they had since 1926.

Claire took special care of Babe to avoid his hurting himself: no heavy lifting, not even of his baggage; no using a can opener; no changing of razor blades (Claire did it). Babe began going to a barbershop for a daily shave in 1930. It was a nuisance, "but a fellow does hear a lot of funny stuff there."

During the rest of Ruth's baseball career Babe and Claire lived at the West 88th Street address. Of course they also lived in Florida during spring training, and they spent about seventy-five nights on the road each summer. They kept the same household hours and rites everywhere. Jimmy Reese sometimes visited the 88th Street place. The apartment took up the whole floor. There was a key for the elevator and one for the flat. Babe had a pool table where he played with guests "while Claire cooked dinner." (If Babe were twenty or thirty cents down, he'd try to hold up dinner until he could get even.)

Babe addressed his wife as "Mom" or as "Clara," indiscriminately.

Claire also cut back Babe's helter-skelter social life. People often used him as an ornament to their parties, not because of personal liking. Claire's response was to set a ten-o'clock curfew, saying that his true friends wanted him fresh and bright-eyed in the ball park. Those who objected weren't really his friends. This suited Babe well enough. He didn't like to be mobbed every waking hour. At his age it began to be more fun to settle in the flat and get into the beer, especially on nights of "The Lone Ranger," his favorite radio program.

Claire began to entertain quietly at home, and not exclusively sports people. There were artists, musicians, the family lawyer, the family physician, people from the business side of baseball, and newspapermen. Ballplayers like the Jimmie Reeses, the Lyn Larys, the Eddie Wellses, and the Henry Johnsons were there because they were friends, not because they were ballplayers. To all of these people Babe showed an unexpected skill: he had no superior at carving a roast. We may safely assume he learned how in the vast kitchens of St. Mary's Industrial School. His carving fretted Claire, however—those long sharp knife blades so near those eighty-thousand-dollar hands!

Two parts of Babe's social life were closed to her. She couldn't play golf well enough to play without spoiling it for Babe. She tried shooting and found it a masculine preserve, though she encouraged Babe to go, not knowing that hunters' shotguns and rifles have damaged far more ballplayers than have carving knives.

The quiet life between the World Series and the end of the year came to an end with Claire's annual New Year's Eve party, which she gave to prove she knew how to throw a party. It was also a final blast, like *Mardi Gras*, before Babe began the self-denying miseries of Artie McGovern's program for rendering lard from overweight sluggers. McGovern's drill became harder to take each year as Babe passed age thirty-five.

There is no record of Babe protesting his new way of life. Few ballplayers, after all, have gone out of their way publicly to outrage conventional morality, and the few who did usually took their fun in New York or Los Angeles show-business circles. (In fact, Claire had only a tenuous connection with the entertainment business.) This is not to say Babe's temperament changed. He simply had his first taste of orderly family life, and, like nearly all men, the older he got the better he liked it. The Saturday-night drunk is a common enough American middle-class figure. Babe always had more in common with him than with the purposeful sensualist. Babe had been playful rather than dissolute. Now with Claire navigating, he had found his social harbor.

Claire's guest list had the names of people who had two things in common: they were good company, and, excepting the transient young baseball couples she took up from time to time, they were somehow useful to Babe.

The other wives didn't like the idea of Claire traveling with the team, but Ruppert did, which cooled any heat on the subject. Claire's memoirs give us a good sketch of baseball travel in the railroad age.

All games were day games. After the Yankees finished the last game of a series they went directly to their train. Everyone but the Ruths headed for the dining car. Claire and Babe had to eat alone because their presence in any dining car or restaurant disrupted the place. (For the first evening of a New York departure she always brought a heavily loaded picnic basket.)

The club used three Pullman cars at the end of a scheduled train. The assignment of berths was strictly by convention. Senior players had lowers while junior players had uppers. The next day's starting pitcher, regardless of age, had a lower. The manager and traveling secretary each had a drawing room, the two coaches another, and the Ruths had one. About a dozen baseball writers had a third car to themselves, all in lowers. Once she was in her drawing room Claire stayed there, because the players didn't want to have to think of clothes on a baseball train. Sometimes Babe would wander out and get into a card game, usually poker at ten cents a hand; in a long game a very unlucky man couldn't lose more than three or four dollars.

In the city where they were playing the Yankees stayed at the best hotels, the other players two in a room and the Ruths in a suite (at

Babe's expense). They had their meals in the suite. In 1930 Bob Shawkey ruled that every player must be in the dining room by 9 A.M., including Ruth, but when Babe showed up service broke down and Shawkey gave way.

> Baseball makes broads aggressive.
> —Jim Brosnan

> The Babe brought out the beast in a lot of ladies the world over.
> —Claire Ruth

Claire took Babe's phone calls on the road and found it interesting work. Many were from women, some left over from the 1920s, others newly self-appointed friends. The fact that Babe Ruth was in town stirred many a woman to pick up a phone, even though the papers said his wife was with him, *even* though they published her picture with him. She talked with all who would talk and reported to Babe, who very much enjoyed pointing to the calls as overwhelming proof that she was the luckiest of women to have bagged him. There wasn't such a volume of communications traffic in New York because they changed their unlisted number so often they had trouble remembering the number of the moment.

Looking back we can see what Ruppert had in mind when he invited Claire along with the team. If, as some suggest, ball games are a fertility rite dating back fifty centuries (with the ball representing, perhaps, the sun or an egg), some of the ladies following Babe Ruth's career were in the same game. These women were more pitiable than amusing. They weren't tramps; a tramp need not wait until the Yankees came to town. They were lonely, and they fantasized about the Hercules of America, imagining a gaudy life of lower-middle-class splendor if only they could link his life and theirs.

Claire also began to work at money managing. She knew a bride could do more than a veteran wife, so she started early. The first step was to persuade Babe to let her take charge of the household spending. He could have a fifty-dollar check whenever he wished, but never a larger one. He seemed to need a great many of them, sometimes several a day. Claire decided it was worth writer's cramp to prevent what she had heard of: a hundred-dollar tip for a ham sandwich.

Babe was interested in money only so far as the flaunting of money proved he was a champion. He became a relatively rich man only because Christy Walsh and Claire coaxed him to let them make him so. Walsh and Claire became the paymasters. For example, Walsh came with an offer which could net as much as a hundred thousand, but Babe waved him aside, telling him to talk with Claire. He couldn't be bothered: it was time for "The Lone Ranger."

Claire saved money on automobiles. They had a small car in Florida and a sixteen-cylinder Cadillac in New York. When Babe wanted to buy a new car to celebrate the eighty-thousand-dollar contract, they didn't.

They budgeted the household at fifteen hundred a month, which was lavish at a time when middle-class income was fifteen hundred a year. Babe bought suits by the dozen at $250 each, and Claire encouraged him because she wanted him to dress like a champion. At the same time he practiced the petty economy of borrowing his mother-in-law's sewing machine to turn the frayed cuffs of his Sulka shirts, in order to use the shirtmaker skill he had learned at St. Mary's Industrial School.

Babe went along with the money policy because he wasn't a fool. He didn't like to think it, but Claire convinced him a day would come when the money would stop flowing.

Babe also became the father of a family almost instantly. He took charge of both of the daughters, Claire's Julia and his and Helen's Dorothy. To provide for Dorothy he had Helen's estate sue him for thirty-one thousand dollars, which he promptly paid, thus building up Dorothy's legacy to about thirty-five thousand, which grew to forty-two thousand by the time the estate was closed in 1934. Babe and Claire legally adopted Dorothy, and Babe legally adopted Julia, late in October 1930. Dorothy spent her next several winters at her Massachusetts boarding school. Julia went to school in New York.

> To our youth, most adults seem to be defined as adults by the very fact that the play has gone out of them.
> —Erik Erikson

Babe was not so hard for Claire to tame, though it was a full-time job. Most sane people wish to live orderly lives, and Ruth was surely sane. He achieved full manhood in his new station. Without Claire he would have remained generally kind, very friendly to small boys and to inmates of institutions, and sociable without regard to class, but the world is full of high-school freshmen with all those qualities. With Claire's help he struggled successfully to order his life. Babe became more than a friendly, loudmouthed adolescent who happened to be catlike on the baseball field. He became respected as a person.

Babe lacked a balancing femininity in his life before 1929; he had dominated Helen to the point of suppression. Such a one-sided life is rarely a balanced life except among intellectuals or very religious persons, and Babe, of course, was neither. Now Babe was fit to live in a world of men and women with a wife who was a match (or overmatch) for him. To use the baseball analogy, Claire became his manager, but not a blustering Barrow or nagging Huggins. She was the self-effacing manager who gets the best out of the star. As the Yankee equipment manager said, "He had some wild ways in his earlier days, but he settled down after his second marriage."

Xaverian Brother George had won—off the field. But the play hadn't gone out of Babe Ruth, since professional baseball was even more fun than stealing fruit from Baltimore waterfront drays. Between the foul lines the dockside slob in Ruth still had plenty of life and power.

At an owners' meeting after the 1929 season someone suggested screens in American League fields, arranged in such a way that home-run distances be the same in each park, and in such a way as to make them more difficult to hit. It failed of support.

Ruth was disappointed when Bob Shawkey became Miller Huggins's successor. Ruth had seen Ty Cobb, Tris Speaker, Rogers Hornsby, Eddie Collins, George Sisler, Ray Schalk, Bucky Harris, and Dave Bancroft* become managers. Was not Babe Ruth a pitcher, outfielder, and first baseman? He asked Ruppert for the job but was gracelessly told he couldn't even manage himself; he learned of Shawkey's appointment by reading it in the papers. Shawkey was Ruppert's fourth choice, which shows what Ruppert thought of Ruth as a potential manager.

Bob Shawkey had been a fireman on the Pennsylvania Railroad and became a professional ballplayer in 1911. He came to the Yankees in 1915 and pitched until 1927. In 1929 the Yankees made him one of the first of the specialized pitching coaches. Ruth liked him but thought his own claim was better than Shawkey's. The Shawkey promotion spurred Ruth's holdout in 1930.

Ruth weighed 233 pounds when he began the annual Artie McGovern grind. McGovern took off eight pounds in two weeks. At Ruth's age, 225 pounds was a satisfactory playing weight.

Babe and Claire left for Florida a little earlier than usual because Ruth had gotten his weight down quickly. They moved into the Jungle Country Club, eight miles from Yankee headquarters in St. Petersburg. For a week they were guests of pitcher Henry Johnson

---

* Raymond William Schalk (1892–1970), catcher, eighteen seasons, 1912–1929, White Sox, Giants, batting average .253. Hall of Fame.

Stanley Raymond Harris (1896–   ), second baseman, twelve seasons, 1919–1931, Senators, Tigers, batting average .274.

David James Bancroft (1891–1972), shortstop, sixteen seasons, 1915–1930, Phillies, Giants, Braves, Dodgers, batting average .279.

and his wife. Babe and Henry shared a taste for hunting, and Henry remembers Babe eating a dozen quail for dinner. Babe also filled the Johnson neighborhood with pilgrim boys flocking to their saint to get that sacred relic, his autograph.

La dolce Florida was pleasant enough. Golf with Al Smith, Bob Shawkey, and umpire Bill Klem; the baseball men were in the 90s, and Smith scored 119. Greyhound races. Dinners in the private dining rooms of Tampa's Cuban restaurants. An attempt to master the harmonica. A 325-yard drive on the eleventh hole of a tournament round at Belle Aire Country Club. The birthday party on February 7. A moment of grave danger on a quail hunt with Benny Bengough and George Pipgras when a rattlesnake bit their dog and Babe blew the snake's head off with his shotgun. The refereeing of a heavyweight fight between two unknowns in Tampa, with judges Edward Guggenheim, the copper tycoon, and Billy DeBeck, the cartoonist of Barney Google. A gift of a thousand autographed baseballs to be auctioned to help Father Flanagan rebuild burned-out Boystown. The last drinks of scotch before the opening of the season, when Babe would be on beer only.

Florida had become the spring baseball center with ten of the sixteen major-league teams training there. Of the new Yankees in camp, only fast Ben Chapman, as third baseman, would play regularly. Perhaps to stir up the holdout Ruth, the Yankees said they were going to try a rookie catcher, Bill Karlon,* in the outfield. Karlon, a recent high-school graduate, had a club of eager fans in Springfield, Massachusetts. Every night he had to phone them to tell them everything he had done. The other ballplayers always gathered to listen, derisively. He proved no threat to anyone's job. A more serious threat to Ruth was the danger of injury while training without a contract, as he learned when he spiked himself in an intrasquad game sliding into third base after a triple. The next day he came to the famous eighty-thousand-dollar agreement with Ruppert, and on the afternoon of the same day hit a home run in the game with the Braves. He had two hits in four times at bat and scored two runs. Evidently the price was right.

Barrow scheduled an exhibition tour in Texas for the second year. It was a triumph, just as in 1929. But Ruth hurt himself in the last game, a game at Dallas on April 6 which drew ten thousand. After a single and a double he walked. When Gehrig singled, Ruth tried to take third but pulled up lame with a charleyhorse between second and third, and was tagged out. He had to keep off his feet for three days.

Meanwhile Honus Wagner made his second try at picking an

---

* William John Karlon (1909–1964), outfielder, two games, 1930, Yankees, batting average .000.

All-American baseball team in *Collier's* in the first week of April. This time instead of listing Ruth as an extra outfielder, he chose him for the starting lineup, the only active player Wagner named.

On the eve of the season the bookmakers made the Athletics 5 to 3 to repeat and the Yankees 8 to 5 to win. The odds on the Yankees should have been a little longer.

> . . . It is a question whether Cobb in his best days was the equal of this great machine.
> —*New York World*, October 1930

When Bob Shawkey became manager, a friend sent him five rabbit feet. Opponents, unfettered by superstition, saw to it that the Yankees lost their first five games, one for each foot. Coach Art Fletcher, after the fifth loss, had a public funeral of his rabbit foot and asked others to do the same. The Yankees never recovered after the early stumble. Ruth, as always, publicly autographed his Citizen's Military Training Camp Trophies. That afternoon, April 26, he slid into Fenway Park's home plate, knocked himself unconscious, and had to be carried off the field (it took four to lift him). He not only had a slight concussion but painfully twisted the muscles of his left thigh.

With the Yankees doing badly it was time to put down Babe Ruth, and John B. Foster of the Consolidated Press came through with a finely tuned argument: although Ruth was hitting many home runs, other men were also hitting home runs. If other people could do it, he wasn't so much. The prosecution rested.

The Yankees finally pulled up to the .500 mark on May 18 by winning in Boston in a game played, for some reason, at Braves Field. Ruth hit the longest home run hit up to that time in that park. (It wasn't measured.)

Ruth made the only truly stupid play of his life on May 21 in Shibe Park, Philadelphia. For the first time in a regular season game he hit three home runs in one game. The third cleared the fence, crossed the street, a house, and two back yards, and landed on the roof of the next house. And he still had one more time at bat on a day when he was as hot as hydrogen fusion. Nobody had hit *four* in one game since Ed Delahanty did it in 1896. When Ruth came up in the ninth he faced the right-handed spitball pitcher Jack Quinn. Outraging reason, Ruth decided to bat right-handed against a right-hander. He took two called strikes in this unfamiliar batter's box, then crossed over to bat left-handed—and struck out. A case can be made for the attempt to steal which made the last out of the 1926 World Series, but not for throwing away a chance to hit four home runs in one game. It was his dumbest hour.

And he didn't seem very bright when he parted with Waite Hoyt early in the season (Hoyt went to the Tigers). For eleven of the past twelve seasons they had worn the same uniform. Said Babe in farewell, "Take care of yourself—Walter."

Ruth warmed as a batter through June. By the 28th the Yankees were two games behind the Athletics and had lost the same number of games as the A's (what is called "even in the loss-column"). Ruth hit home runs number twenty-eight and twenty-nine as the Yankees won both games of a double-header from Cleveland in the Stadium. The scores were 13–1 and 14–2. The Yankees had thirty-three hits that day and scored seven runs in the first inning of each game. At the moment Gehrig led the American League in batting with .399; Ruth was fifth with .380. Ruth's home-run rate was eleven days ahead of his record-breaking 1927 season, and New Yorkers were excited.

In a week the team cooled sufficiently to freeze itself permanently in third place. On July 2 Ruth tore off a fingernail on an outfield screen while trying to catch the second of Carl Reynolds'* three consecutive home runs. The American League standings that night were:

Team	Won	Lost	Pct.	Behind
Philadelphia	48	26	.649	—
Washington	44	25	.638	2½
New York	43	26	.623	2½

That was it. At season's end they were:

Philadelphia	102	52	.662	—
Washington	94	60	.610	8
New York	86	68	.558	16

Ruth finished at forty-nine home runs, eleven behind the splendor of 1927. But he had a destiny that regularly found him in a place of drama. The last game of 1930 was such an occasion. He pitched in Fenway Park and beat the Red Sox, 9–3. Boston did not get a runner past second base until two were out in the sixth inning. Through seven innings the Red Sox had only five hits, though they got six more in the eighth and ninth innings. Ruth walked two, struck out three, started two double plays, and made three assists. At the plate he had two clean singles, drove in a run, and scored

* Carl Nettles Reynolds (1903–   ), outfielder, thirteen seasons, 1927–1939, White Sox, Senators, Browns, Red Sox, Cubs, batting average .302.

Outside the Park, 1931

BUSINESS ILLS LAID
TO BIG GOLD RESERVE

PARIS INTRODUCES
SPORTS PAJAMAS

4,277,833 IN AMERICA
HAVE BEEN BOY SCOUTS

8 BANK HEADS GIVE BAIL

ALCOHOL POISONING KILLED 625 IN CITY IN 1930

ADMIRAL BYRD'S OVERCOAT STOLEN
AS HE POSES FOR FLORIDA PHOTOS

GOOD TIMES HERE
HENRY FORD AVERS

WEALTHY CAT DIES AT 19

56,000 ASKED TIME BY PHONE
AS DAYLIGHT SCHEDULE STARTED

SUIT FILED AT RENO
EVERY TWO MINUTES

WHOLE MARKET SLUMPS AS STEEL DROPS TO 99

HELP DRIVE TO HAVE
CHILDREN QUIT JOBS

LIVING COSTS HAVE DROPPED 15% SINCE 1925;
UNEMPLOYMENT SENDS PAYROLLS DOWN 40%

COLUMBIA STUDENTS
IN CLASH WITH POLICE

DRUNKEN DRIVING IN THE STATE
MORE THAN DOUBLED IN 4 YEARS

48 · Joe McCarthy and His Good Citizens (1931)

> Give a boy a bat and a ball and a place to play and you'll have a good citizen.
>
> —Joe McCarthy

Joe McCarthy, aged forty-three, a dark-eyed man who couldn't hit well enough to make a major-league roster, had become a successful minor-league manager. If he had not kept an iron grip on his strong temper he would be remembered as quarrelsome. He drove players hard but with perseverance rather than toughness. In thirty seasons in the minors and majors only one team he managed finished below the first division. McCarthy joined the Cubs after their last-place finish in 1925 under three managers. The Cubs finished fourth in 1926.

McCarthy wasn't happy in Chicago. Cub President William Veeck, Sr., seemed to interfere too much and to blame him personally for the loss of the 1929 World Series. McCarthy told a Chicago sportswriter early in 1930 he would leave the Cubs at the end of the season.

His ideal ballplayer was a team player with no personality. Huggins's joyous, angry, playful, brawling Yankees of the 1920s wouldn't pass McCarthy's tests of conduct. His good citizen was a man who wore a jacket and tie in the dining room and didn't raise hell on the train after winning the World Series. He had some quirky notions, for example, pipe-smoking ball players were too contented. (He may have changed his mind when he knew Gehrig better.) McCarthy and John McGraw must be named on every list of great managers. They were curiously alike in stuffiness. McGraw insisted on hats instead of caps; McCarthy insisted on woven shirts instead of knitted shirts. As for baseball making good citizens, well, it is hard to forget Ed Barrow's ranking of the 1919 Black Sox as the greatest of all teams, and he knew them well. It would be interesting to see long-term won-loss records of many prison baseball teams in play against outsiders.

From the time of Huggins's death Ruth hoped to manage the Yankees. When it was known that Shawkey was to go, Ruth asked for the job. Ruppert and Barrow knew that McCarthy was leaving the Cubs, and they wanted McCarthy. If he would not accept they had another candidate—not Ruth. Ruppert had claimed Ruth's lack of self-management barred him; but since 1926, and certainly since April 1929, Ruth had grown up. It is just possible that Ruppert and Barrow believed Ruth's new strength of will was Claire's will. Ruth wrongly believed that if McCarthy had not been available the job would have been Ruth's. He further believed they chose McCarthy over him only because he and Barrow disliked each other. They *did* dislike each other. But at no time did Ruppert or Barrow think of Ruth as a manager, not even long enough to have to dismiss the thought.

In October McCarthy declined an offer from the Red Sox, and by mid-month he was the Yankee manager. For the next two months there was no hard news about the Yankees except a public statement that McCarthy thought he needed a second-baseman and the Yankee management regarded Ruth as a fixture in the outfield. The fixture, for the rest of his life, thought he should be the manager.

> **Just as I believe Hans Wagner is the greatest ballplayer of all time, so do I believe Joe McCarthy is baseball's greatest manager.**
> —Barrow, *My Fifty Years in Baseball*

McCarthy had to put up with an anti-McCarthy clique among the Yankees, a group which thought Ruth should be the manager. Ruth was the senior man on the team, he was Babe Ruth, and, besides, McCarthy was a National Leaguer. After Ruth, Tony Lazzeri was the coolest toward McCarthy. McCarthy was intelligent. He knew he had to fight down his jealousy of Ruth. He was good at holding himself in check, though he never understood the public's love affair with Ruth. He knew a great ballplayer when he saw him, however, even though he didn't think Ruth was the greatest. A reporter, writing a story on the perfect composite player, asked McCarthy's opinion, and McCarthy told him it was too much trouble since Frank Frisch could do everything.

The new manager didn't like Southern ballplayers, because, he thought, they were so quick-tempered they defeated themselves, which wasn't the mark of champions. He let Ben Chapman and

Johnny Allen* go because of that prejudice. He may have thought of Ruth as a Southerner, which is a faintly funny characterization. But McCarthy's stereotyped vision could be comfortably blind; Bill Dickey was from Arkansas.

On the road McCarthy didn't run bed checks, but he had a rule that players must be in the dining room by 8:30 A.M., and he was there earlier, reading a newspaper and noting who arrived and in what condition. (The Ruths, of course, had breakfast in their rooms.) He banned shaving in the clubhouse; good citizens shave before they go to work. Out went the card table because a clubhouse was not a playroom. Players were to dress like champions, an idea carried to the field by having uniforms carefully cut to make the men look larger. He gladly carried on the standing Ruppert practice of starting every day of play with clean uniforms.

Ruth and McCarthy almost never saw each other off the field. Each was jealous of the other. Barrow was wholly on McCarthy's side. Where McCarthy thought Frisch was the greatest, Barrow plumped for Honus Wagner. Ruth couldn't finish better than third in any ratings by Yankee leaders.

Ruth's notion that McCarthy's lack of major-league playing experience disqualified him is clearly wrong. Some good managers never played in the major leagues. Barrow himself managed the 1918 Red Sox to a world championship. Pants Rowland did the same with the 1917 White Sox. Walter Alston had one time at bat with the 1936 Cardinals and struck out. The Braves under George Stallings won the World Series of 1914. Earl Weaver and Johnny Keane have also headed world-champion teams.

Great players have always been few, and fewer of them have been great managers. Of men elected to the Hall of Fame as players, fifty became managers. Twenty-three won more games than they lost; seventeen lost more than they won. Only three were famously good managers: Frank Chance, Fred Clarke,** and John McGraw (McGraw may have made it as a manager, but he belongs as a player, too). Great players, as managers, seem to lack patience with average players. Owning great skills, they don't see why lesser men can't learn more quickly.

Any rating of managers is subjective. But in order of their percentage of games won, they are: Joe McCarthy, Jim Mutrie, Charlie

---

* John Thomas Allen (1904–1959), pitcher, thirteen seasons, 1932–1944, Yankees, Indians, Browns, Dodgers, Giants. Won 142, lost 75, earned-run average 3.75.
** Frank Leroy Chance (1877–1924), first baseman, seventeen seasons, 1898–1914, Cubs, Yankees, batting average .296. Hall of Fame.
Fred Clifford Clarke (1872–1960), outfielder, twenty-one seasons, 1894–1915, Louisville Colonels, Pirates, batting average .315. Hall of Fame.

The classic posture after hitting one of his standard
"towering" home runs, about four hundred feet up
and four hundred feet out, at old Oriole Park,
Baltimore, 1931. (*Leroy G. Merriken, The Baltimore
Sunpapers.*)

Comiskey,* Frank Selee, and Billy Southworth.** Only Comiskey
and Southworth played in the major leagues, and they were journeymen, not stars. There is no comfort in these facts for anyone
who thinks Ruth should have been a manager. A manager thinks,

---

* Charles Albert Comiskey (1859–1931), first baseman, thirteen seasons, 1882–
1894, Browns, Chicago Players, Reds, batting average .264. Hall of Fame (as ad-
ministrator).
** William Harrison Southworth (1893–1969), outfielder, thirteen seasons, 1913–
1929, Indians, Pirates, Braves, Giants, Cardinals, batting average .297.

and thinks ahead. Except in specific plays, it doesn't matter what a player thinks. A manager is chiefly a leader of defense and mostly concerned with the use of substitutes who are mostly pitchers. Managers earn their living by worrying. Ruth was too much the extrovert. It comes down to this: he was passed over several times by those who knew him best.

Managing really isn't important enough to justify the anguish Ruth suffered over his failure to get the job. Anyone can see the relative value of a manager by considering one question: Would you rather have great players and an average manager, or average players and a great manager? The answer is easy. The payoff is rational. The manager is almost never the highest-paid man on the team.

Heavy snowfall in November and December kept Ruth off the golf course more than he liked, so he turned to the less pleasant conditioning indoors. The Artie McGovern torments of 1931 began on New Year's Eve 1930. Ruth weighed in at 233 pounds; his waist line was 42½ inches. Results were good.

When he could, he played golf during January. In a locker room discussion at the North Hempstead Country Club, Ruth named an all-star baseball team:

> Hal Chase,* 1b
> Larry Lajoie, 2b
> Honus Wagner, ss
> Jimmy Collins, 3b
> Joe Jackson, lf
> Ty Cobb, cf
> Harry Hooper, rf
> Ray Schalk, c
> Christy Mathewson, p
> Eddie Plank, p
> Herb Pennock, p

Excepting Chase and Jackson, who were banned from baseball for being bad citizens, every man Ruth named was later elected to the Hall of Fame. Ruth's friends argued against leaving Tris Speaker out of the outfield, but Ruth's answer was that nobody was a better

---

* Harold Harris Chase (1883–1947), first baseman, fifteen seasons, 1905–1919, Yankees, White Sox, Buffalo Federals, Reds, Giants, batting average .291.

Napoleon Lajoie (1875–1959), infielder, twenty-one seasons, 1896–1916, Phillies, Athletics, Indians, batting average .339. Hall of Fame.

James Joseph Collins (1870–1943), third baseman, fourteen seasons, 1895–1908, Braves, Louisville Colonels, Red Sox, Athletics, batting average .294. Hall of Fame.

Edward Stewart Plank (1875–1926), pitcher, seventeen seasons, 1901–1917, Athletics, St. Louis Federals, Browns. Won 327, lost 192, earned-run average 2.34. Hall of Fame.

natural hitter than Joe Jackson (whose batting style he had consciously imitated). Ruth spoke very harshly of Lefty Grove—"He's
good, but mainly he's just a thrower." There is always argument
about such lists, but Ruth's is defensible.

Near the end of the McGovern regimen the New York chapter of
the Baseball Writers, in the presence of nine hundred diners, gave
Ruth a plaque for service to the game. He and McGovern came on
stage to give a short burlesque of his training.

Babe, Claire, Julia, and Claire's sister, Mrs. C. G. Elliott, left for
Florida by sea on February 7, which Babe thought was his birthday.
He planned to play from thirty-six to fifty-four holes of golf daily
until the Yankees pitched camp. His weight was under control. The
Yankees began work on March 13 by dedicating Miller Huggins
Field and then playing a game between the Ruths and the Gehrigs.
A few days later Ruth returned to a favorite sport, night fishing. He
fell out of the boat, was pulled back in, and explained his soaking
cryptically, "My oar got away from me." As workouts continued he
told every interviewer he would hit sixty-one in 1931.

Most teams were cutting down on spring exhibitions as too costly,
but the Yankees could still pay their way by drawing crowds to see
Ruth and Gehrig. They scheduled thirty-three along the familiar
road north from Florida. Once out of Florida all of their games were
with minor-league teams.

On this tour the biggest story was a left-handed girl named Jackie
Mitchell, who claimed to be a pupil of Dazzy Vance. She pitched
for the Chattanooga Lookouts and struck out Ruth and Gehrig in
the first inning on six pitches. Her appearance was a promotional
stunt by Chattanooga owner Joe Engel,* who had once praised
George Ruth as a pitcher for St. Mary's Industrial School. Ruth and
Gehrig struck out on purpose. Lazzeri then walked. By that time the
watchers had lost interest, so Engel took out Ms. Mitchell.

Before the season began, Ruth had to disentangle himself from a
fruitless commercial endeavor. In the unpromising year 1930 a promoter had incorporated The Babe Ruth Shop, a men's clothing
store which was to pay Ruth a royalty based on gross receipts. Ruth
made a big deal of its grand opening on September 5, clerking for
his friends and the news photographers with a pencil behind his
ear and clowning with a hat four sizes too small. Knute Rockne,
Gehrig, Shawkey, and Graham McNamee helped to draw a crowd
of six hundred. After that hardly anybody came. On April Fool's
Day 1931 the shop was sold for the benefit of its creditors. Ruth was
a large creditor, for royalties. The buyer of the stock, to Ruth's

---

* Joseph William Engel (1893–1969), pitcher, seven seasons, 1912–1920, Senators, Reds, Indians. Won 18, lost 23, earned-run average 3.38.

Babe Ruth, aged about thirty-five. (*Mamie Ruth Moberly.*)

annoyance, advertised BABE RUTH QUITS and BABE RUTH QUITTING and BABE RUTH GOING OUT OF BUSINESS.

Ruth went to court and got an order barring the buyer from using his usually lucrative name, since the buyer had only bought the inventory.

> He once told me in these words, "When I become manager you won't be stealing bases at your discretion." My reply was, "When you become manager, send me to St. Louis."
> —Ben Chapman (1972)

The Yankees started the season of 1931 very well on the scoreboard but badly in the casualty list. In the top of the sixth inning on opening day in Boston, April 22, Ruth turned his ankle running between second and third. He then tried to score on a sacrifice fly. Catcher Charlie Berry* blocked the plate, but Ruth scored right through him. In the bottom of the sixth he ran to catch a ball and fell in a helpless heap while two runs scored. They carried him off. Claire went with him to the hospital where X-rays showed no fracture. (While in the game, which the Yankees won 7–5, Ruth had three hits and scored two runs.) A nerve center in his thigh was paralyzed as a result of the collision with Berry. He had feared his leg was broken.

While Ruth was on his back relearning to wriggle his toes, Myril

---

* Charles Francis Berry (1902–1972), catcher, eleven seasons, 1925–1938, Athletics, Red Sox, White Sox, batting average .267.

Hoag* filled in for him in the second game. (Ruth always called Hoag "Chinaman" for reasons Hoag never learned.) The Yankees won, but Hoag injured his ankle catching the fly that was the last out. The Yankees lost the next game with Dusty Cooke** in the outfield, and on the next day they lost Dusty, who slipped on soggy sod and broke his collarbone. Ben Chapman, an average infielder, moved to the outfield and became a good outfielder. By this time Jimmie Reese had become the No. 1 Babe Ruth fan and made a specialty of keeping track of the Ruths' luggage. Chapman called him Ruth's caddy, which angered both Ruth and Reese. Ruth and Chapman, the fastest Yankee since 1914, had some loud quarrels but settled into fast friendship.

When it came time to open in New York Ruth had to be wheeled in a chair to and from the train. A crowd of five hundred gathered at Grand Central Station, though there had been no public word of his arrival.

While Ruth was laid up the Yankees dropped to third place. Eleven days passed before he played again on May 3. Both he and Gehrig limped while in the game, a Yankee victory, 8–3, before a home crowd of thirty-five thousand. Ruth played only five innings, made two hits in two times at bat, drove in a run, and walked.

By the first day of summer it seemed clear it wasn't to be a great Yankee year. Although Ruth led the American League in batting with .390, the Yankees seemed firmly in third place.

The *Philadelphia Public Ledger* polled twelve veteran players, managers, and coaches in July, asking who was the greatest player in history? The jury included John McGraw, Walter Johnson, Connie Mack, and Joe McCarthy. The balloting for first place went thus: Ty Cobb 7, Honus Wagner 3, Ruth 2. (McCarthy tactfully listed Ruth first.)

Although the Yankees scored 1,067 runs in 1931, the most scored by any team between the year 1895 and the present, the Athletics (who scored 209 fewer runs) had pitching so much better that in each five games they gave up about four runs fewer than the Yankees did. The season doesn't need much more summary than that, considering that roughly a third of all major-league games are decided by one run.

Nevertheless Ruth's name was always in the baseball news and often in other news. He met the King of Siam (or vice versa), and they posed for photographers. He put out a hotel awning fire in

---

* Myril Oliver Hoag (1908–1971), outfielder, thirteen seasons, 1931–1945, Yankees, Browns, White Sox, Indians, batting average .271.
** Allen Lindsey Cooke (1907–   ), outfielder, eight seasons, 1930–1938, Yankees, Red Sox, Reds, batting average .280.

Boston with water from his bathtub as hundreds cheered in the street below. Then on the same day he took his bat and beat the Red Sox 4–1 getting two doubles, two runs batted in, and a run scored.

Home run number six hundred came in St. Louis on August 21. Ruth paid a boy twenty dollars to retrieve the ball from Grand Avenue. This home run stirred up a good deal of arithmetic which showed that Ruth hit nearly a third of his home runs off left-handed pitchers; it is most unlikely that he faced left-handed pitchers a third of the time. Further, he hit more home runs in July than in any other month, more in the first inning than any other inning, more with men on base than with bases empty, and more on the road than in New York. F. C. Lane, in *Baseball Magazine*, speculated on his possible lifetime total: "Seven hundred? That's a good bet. And maybe many more."

The Yankees ended in second place, never really alarming the Athletics who finished thirteen games ahead.

Before skimming the broth of records, it is well to note some 1931 changes in the rules and the ball, which changed the records.

—Home-run hitters got help from a rule change which said, "Home runs will be judged in both leagues at their point of departure from the playing field." Before that a ball that curved foul after leaving the field was ruled a foul ball. Ruth had lost unnumbered home runs that way.

—Home-run hitters lost on a new rule that the bounce-out home run became a ground-rule double. Ruth no doubt had hit some bouncers (but not in 1927).

—The sacrifice fly disappeared from scoring (to return in 1939). Thus a fly-out that drove in a run was a time at bat. The change (easily figured at the time) through June 1931 lowered the composite batting average of all players by six points (.006).

—The lively ball of 1930, "the lively ball at its liveliest," as Fred Lieb called it, was secretly deadened before the season of 1931. The reason is unclear since attendance in the high-scoring year 1930 was the highest ever. Whatever the reason, the rule lessened home runs by roughly a third in 1931.*

The American League season showed Ruth aging very little and Gehrig coming to his prime. Ruth was second in batting averages (.373) and Gehrig fifth. Ruth was first and Gehrig second in slugging percentage and in home runs as a proportion of times at bat.

	1929	1930	1931
* American League home runs	595	673	576
National League home runs	754	892	492
Totals	1349	1565	1068

Manager Joe McCarthy in the early 1930s. (*The New York Yankees.*)

Gehrig was first and Ruth second in total bases and in runs scored. Ruth was first and Gehrig third in bases on balls.

They tied for the home-run leadership with forty-six each.

Joe McCarthy beamed on Gehrig and was aloof from Ruth, noticing that crowds gave Ruth no peace in restaurants and railway stations while they were easier on Gehrig and they ignored McCarthy.

Crowd pressure could be seen at the World Series of 1931, covered with ghostly help by Ruth, McGraw, and Nick Altrock,* the professional baseball clown. Autograph seekers beset them. Skillfully Ruth shaped their signing to a mass-production technique. Ruth took all scorecards, notebooks, and other flat surfaces and signed with a pencil, giving McGraw and Altrock balls, bats, and other curved surfaces to be signed with fountain pens. On signal, they exchanged accumulated heaps and repeated, reversing the pens and

---

* Nicholas Altrock (1876–1965), pitcher, sixteen seasons, 1898–1924 (only fourteen games after 1912), Louisville Colonels, Red Sox, White Sox, Senators. Won 85, lost 75, earned-run average 2.67.

pencils. Counting scorecards only, Ruth signed at least four hundred in one session. This was public life as Babe Ruth had lived it for a dozen years.

And what he *really* wanted was to be the manager.

Ruth was getting fewer column inches of newspaper space in the early thirties, but that was the effect of the business sag, not a lessening of public interest. In the December summaries of the year 1931 he got little space; his tie with Gehrig for the home-run championship and his second rank in batting received attention, and that was all. A reporter asked him what he thought was his chief accomplishment of 1931. The reply: shooting a 73 on the St. Albans golf course in late December, which would be about the time he shed his usual all-brown ensemble and put on a Santa Claus suit for three hundred children gathered from city hospitals.

Strangers wrote twenty thousand fan letters to Ruth in 1931, which was about average for his peak years. Many were from boys. Mathewson and Ruth were the idols of American boyhood, but Mathewson, as the Ethical Hero, inspired awe, while Ruth, the Muscle Hero, inspired a kind of romping familiarity which Ruth enjoyed.

Ruth was in Los Angeles in October to make some movie shorts on how to play baseball. Stills were used to illustrate a book thrown together by Christy Walsh and signed by Ruth which came out in 1932.

While in Los Angeles he spoke of how success had limited his freedom. But it wouldn't be that way much longer: "I can't do anything. Not just yet. But wait. In two more years I'll be through with baseball, then I'm going to break loose—wide open. Not for long, but for awhile." This was the first hint of a schedule for retirement. Better to quit, he said, before people began to feel sorry for him. He claimed he was looking forward to the pleasures of anonymity. A day would come when he would walk down the streets of a great city and be unnoticed—for the first time since 1919—and he would not be pleased.

The Ruths did well financially in 1931, which is a good measure for any sports professional. They took in about two hundred thousand dollars in each year, 1930 and 1931, and managed to live on income other than salary. Claire said they had money from ghosted newspaper pieces, such as the annual All-Star Team, from radio and other personal appearances, and from endorsements of products they didn't necessarily use, such as five thousand dollars for praising cigarettes though Babe never smoked cigarettes. In recent years Babe had become the financial expert of the Yankee clubhouse, and visitors were stupefied to hear the legendary pleasure-seeker urging young players to think seriously about trust funds. By 1931 his funds reached $150,000 (not counting the annuity), and the goal of $250,000 seemed within reach before he retired. Then he would take sixty-eight thousand in cash and draw ten thousand a year.

But success, as he said, fettered him. He told the Los Angeles writers what he'd like to do but could not do: movies were said to be bad for the eyes, dancing bad for the legs, and speakeasies bad for the reputation. Reading on the train, where he spent so many hours, also hurt the eyes (he didn't *really* wish to read much). Public gambling starts gossip (and would probably start Claire, too!). The Yankees and the insurance companies banned flying. Swimming risked catching cold. The prolonged generous shaking of hands could bruise. High automobile speeds could injure him to the point of stopping his pay. Golf, the only safe and innocent pastime, drew swarms of autograph hunters who spoiled his game. A certain note of mischievous make-believe here hints that he was toying with the provincial press.

More authentic was his list of what had pleased him most: winning his first World Series game as a pitcher, striking out three heavy-hitting Tigers in one inning, holding the record for consecutive scoreless innings in World Series play, his total of home runs, and, most of all, telling the boys at St. Mary's Industrial School that he was going to play baseball for real money.

None of his alleged miseries and all of his real pleasures concerned baseball.

He also spoke of the future of baseball. Most big-leaguers of the future would come from the South, the Southwest, and California, he thought, where the climate let boys play long seasons. (He was right about California.) And anyone planning to be a big-league ballplayer must make up his mind to learn the game at about age four. Good citizens think ahead.

THE ACCUMULATED BATTING FIGURES
BABE RUTH'S MAJOR-LEAGUE CAREER
1914–1931

at bat: 7026
hits: 2461
home runs: 611
runs batted in: 1886
average: .350

Outside the Park, 1932

HOOVER ASKS SPEED ON RELIEF BILLS

SMITH WILLING TO ACCEPT NOMINATION

FORD WILL PRODUCE
AN 8-CYLINDER CAR

MISSING PAIR SOUGHT
IN LINDBERGH CASE

SCULPTOR COMPLETES HIS TASK
ON UNKNOWN SOLDIER'S TOMB

3 IN EVENING CLOTHES
ROB A PARK AVENUE CLUB

2,000 CANDIDATES
FILE IN ARKANSAS

OUR LARGER BANK NOTES GAINING IN POPULAR FAVOR

LEGLESS AMERICAN IS SWIMMING
ENGLISH CHANNEL TO RADIO MUSIC

TRAINED NURSE FOUND
STARVING IN WOODS

CRIMINALS AND REDS
IN BONUS ARMY LIST

SAYS CANCER CURES
ARE ON INCREASE

HALF OF WORLD'S RADIOS HERE;
TOTAL EXCEEDS 30,000,000

ROOSEVELT TO CALL
CONGRESS LEADERS
TO GO OVER PROGRAM

49 · The Legs Were Beginning to Go (1932)

Although major-league attendance in 1930 had been the highest ever, ticket sales fell off in 1931. After the season the owners took collective action by voting to cut salaries and to lower the player limit from twenty-five to twenty-three, aiming to lower their payrolls by a million dollars. The Giants asked Bill Terry, who hit .401 in 1930, and .349 with the deadened ball of 1931, to take a 40 percent cut. Commissioner Landis took a cut from sixty-five to fifty thousand while the league presidents and umpires also had their salaries lowered. Connie Mack said his payroll was higher than the Yankees'. He couldn't meet it and began to sell off his great team piecemeal.

The owners found their free lists swollen. In New York alone the Yankees, Giants, and Dodgers let in 250,000 people on passes in 1931, not counting schoolchildren. Passes were now sharply cut. The owners did not lower admission prices, arguing that they hadn't raised them during the good years. Around the leagues, from park to park, general admission tickets had gone from seventy-five cents to only a dollar in the past thirty years.

Baseball's chief treasure was its peerless popularity, ranking it well ahead of football and golf in that order.

In early December Ruppert, once more thirsting for Pluto Water, went to Indiana to swig his autumnal draughts and to plot a money battle with Babe Ruth. His first blow was a public remark that Ruth would have to take a cut. Ruth wasn't indispensable. He had played in many games "where only a few hundred fans came out. I guess that shows the fans don't jam the parks just to see him play baseball, doesn't it?"

Ruth believed he had had a very good year in 1931, good enough to earn a raise in normal times. The fair thing, he thought, would be to continue to pay him at his present figure.

Rud Rennie of the *New York Herald-Tribune* was having breakfast with all four of the Ruths on West 88th Street one January morning. Claire, in "pale green crepe pajamas and a green silk kimono," was seeing to it that Babe had a large ham steak before going out for golf. The mail came during breakfast, bringing a one-year Yankee contract for seventy thousand dollars. Babe asked Claire for a fountain pen. She feared he would sign it, but no, he needed a pen to send it back. He told Rennie he'd take the figure on a two-year contract but would have to get eighty thousand for one year.

> A disinterested statistician has figured it out that Ruth earned $3,500,000 for Colonel Ruppert in the last twelve years. That stupendous sum represents Ruth's personal box office drawing power over and above what the club would have taken in without him!
>
> —George Trevor, *Outlook and Independent,*
> January 27, 1932

The Detroit sportswriter H. G. Salsinger figured the extra income from Ruth's presence in exhibition games in the years from 1927 on was alone enough to pay his salary for those years. A writer remembered T. L. Huston's guess that Ruth drew an average of twenty-five hundred extra customers per game. Counting all games that would mean the Yankees grossed about $280,000 a year drawn solely by Ruth.

These suppositions are plausible. The Yankees' share of American League attendance from 1911 to 1920 was about 13.5 percent. From 1921 to 1930 it was 22 percent. The nation's Muscle Hero probably had a lot to do with the growth.

Ruppert's defense was to speak of a decline in Yankee receipts in 1931 of 12 to 15 percent—an oddly vague figure from a man who had to know exactly how much in order to pay his taxes.

The discussions of Ruth's salary brought forth a joke for which we have no date, no place, no straight man. Legend says someone told Ruth his eighty thousand was more than the salary of the President, to which Ruth replied, "I had a better year than he did."

As usual, the contract difference remained until spring training was underway. Ruth and Ruppert had two short talks at the ball field and another at the Roliat Hotel where Ruppert lived. The third talk was in the hotel foyer, in full view of reporters watching from a hundred feet away. After borrowing a fountain pen, Babe, Claire, and Ruppert composed a theatrical tableau of signing, in the hotel patio near a wishing well. With anguishing corniness each tossed a coin in the well and made a wish, audible to the reporters, of course. *Babe*: Another pennant so he could play in a tenth

World Series. *Claire*: More Yankee contracts in the family. *Ruppert*: The coins in the bottom of the well, in order to buy another minor-league club. Then Babe played in an eleven-inning exhibition game and went hitless.

Behind all the painful hokum was a real unpublicized touch of humanity. Ruth signed a blank contract, leaving it to Ruppert's sense of magnificence to guide him in filling in the amount. Magnificence is the only virtue reserved to the rich, and Ruppert was magnificent. He wrote in $75,000 *and* a percentage of the profits from exhibition games. It still stands on Barrow's worn 4 x 6 card:

> 1932   cont. $75,000 and 25% net receipts of ex.
> games

Before going to Florida Ruth had started work with McGovern in his best condition since the early 1920s. His chest, expanded, was forty-eight inches, the largest ever, and his waist was thirty-eight, the smallest in years. McGovern put him to calisthenics three days a week and golf the other three days, which suggests an interest in the legs of an old ballplayer.

So Ruth went at it, taking time off to be sworn in as a tenderfoot Boy Scout in full uniform, and very bored he looked. He led the cheering at the Baseball Writers' annual dinner when they gave Gehrig the award as outstanding player of 1931, and we may suppose he joined in talk of Ruppert's purchase of Newark and Ruppert's avowal that he would be as big a baseball farmer as Sam Breadon and Branch Rickey of St. Louis. (By May Ruppert was farming also in the Eastern, Middle Atlantic, and New York–Pennsylvania leagues.)

When Babe and Claire reached Florida the only Yankees left of the 1927 regulars were Ruth, Gehrig, Lazzeri, Combs, Pipgras, and Pennock. Hoyt and Koenig went to the Tigers. Dugan's knee finally failed, and Meusel went to the Reds. New faces were shortstop Frankie Crosetti,* and veteran third baseman Joe Sewell from the Indians, a wise batter who rarely struck out. Familiar faces from recent seasons were speedy Chapman and skinny Lefty Gomez** who explained his weight by saying "nobody can fatten up a greyhound." Pitcher Red Ruffing† had come over from Boston in 1931. A new pitcher was the short-tempered Johnny Allen from North Caro-

* Frank Peter Joseph Crosetti, (1910–   ), shortstop, seventeen seasons, 1932–1948, Yankees, batting average .245.
** Vernon Louis Gomez (1909–   ), pitcher, fourteen seasons, 1930–1943, Yankees, Senators. Won 189, lost 102, earned-run average 3.34 (height 6'2", weight 173 lbs.).
† Charles Herbert Ruffing (1904–   ), pitcher, twenty-two seasons, 1924–1947, Red Sox, Yankees. Won 273, lost 225, earned-run average 3.80. Hall of Fame.

lina who quarreled with anybody handy. And of course there was Bill Dickey, already on his broad plateau of excellence, the Dickey who introduced Ruth and the Governor of Arkansas and heard Ruth greet his new friend, "Glad to meet you, kid." Ruth was in his late thirties, at last a full-grown man, emotionally. All of these new men seemed like boys to him. As Jack Saltzgaver, another 1931 new-comer, told the author, ". . . The Babe ignored us completely. He never bothered to find out our names—just called us 'Kid.' When I went back over to New York in 1934, it was much the same."

On February 8 the Ruths celebrated what Babe thought was his thirty-eighth birthday with a party for twenty-eight guests at the Jungle Club. The table was laid as a baseball diamond, with base lines marked by flowers and a huge cake shaped to look like a base-ball. Babe played eighteen more holes of golf after the party. By this day he was burned a flaming red, as every spring. A few days later he talked to a troop of Boy Scouts at a dinner in Tampa. Afterward he told the scoutmaster he liked to talk to boys—"I want to be one of them." (There is a deeper psychological truth here than he knew.)

When Ruth (and Claire) and Ruppert came to terms for the 1932 contract the exhibition games started. For the trip back to New York the Yankees reduced their schedule from the more than thirty of 1931 to a week's play, laid out practically in a straight line from St. Petersburg to Philadelphia, where they opened on April 12 as the Depression was biting deeper.

In the opening week of 1932 Ruth had another of his disabling respiratory infections, with a fever and a sore throat. By the second week he was back in the game and doing well. On April 24 the Yankees were trailing 5–0 and vaulted back to win 16–5, Ruth getting his fifth home run before forty-one thousand people in the Stadium. The next day he joined in sponsoring a boys' baseball program for the police department.

Ruth also gave up golf during the baseball season because he needed to rest his legs, "especially since I have a little touch of water on the knee now and have to take care of that." He was hitting .394 at the moment, and the Yankees had won seven games and lost three. Some water; some knee. The Yankees had known of Ruth's flawed knee, from a cartilage tear, when they bought him from desperate Harry Frazee in 1919. Beginning in 1932 his knee hurt whether he played or not. For some years golfers had noticed that he usually played better on the first nine holes than on the second nine; we may suppose the pain of the knee upset his game. So, into storage went the heaviest driver known to his friends (17½ ounces) along with the rest of the golfing gear.

The manager thing came up again. A rumor said Ruth would

join Tom Yawkey in buying the Red Sox, becoming manager. There was enough talk to stir him to deny it. He said he saw a good chance to play in the 1932 World Series (which would be his tenth) and couldn't think of leaving the Yankees at the moment even if Ruppert would agree. He was batting .384 with eleven home runs (Jimmy Foxx had fifteen, an indirect sign of the aging of Babe Ruth).

On June 3 Gehrig finally did what Ruth once stupidly hindered himself from doing, by becoming the first since 1896 to hit four home runs in a nine-inning game.* It was a wild game with the Athletics, which the Yankees won 20–13. Ruth had one home run. The Athletics hit for twenty-seven bases and the Yankees for fifty, making a total of seventy-seven which is still the American League record.

By mid-July the Yankees were in first place by nine games with the Athletics second. On the 18th, in the seventh inning of a game with the White Sox, Ruth's right leg buckled under him while he was chasing a fly. He again had to be carried off the field, this time with "a rupture of the sheath of the extensor muscles in the rear of his right leg," that is, a charleyhorse. It was his first charleyhorse in the back of the leg. The legs were beginning to go.

Ruth was out for several days. When he came back he proved his eyes were still excellent. The Yankees went on the road, and Ruth had eight hits in his first ten times at bat, including three home runs and a double. Cautious pitchers walked him five times during this fiery streak. But of the first six road games he played only three in the field, appearing in two as a pinch-hitter. He had twenty-eight home runs on July 30. (Foxx had forty-one.)

Claire and Babe disappeared from Detroit on September 7 soon after the team had arrived to play the Tigers. Babe had symptoms of appendicitis so alarming that (without a word to the acting manager or the traveling secretary) he called Joe McCarthy, who was in Buffalo, and got permission to go to New York to see the club physician. Babe had seemed in perfect health the day before in an exhibition game at Binghamton where he hit a home run and fraternized with "the army of small boys who dogged his every step. . . ." Sammy Byrd filled in for him and hit two home runs that day.

The New York diagnosis was appendicitis, all right, but there was no emergency, so they buried him in ice packs and waited. The Yankees needed only four games to win the pennant, the World Series would open in eighteen days, and, all in all, it was an uneasy moment. Babe was batting third in the League at .348.

Ruth lived in glacial anxious idleness for three days. Then Dr.

---

* It has been done four times since 1932.

King said, "Babe Ruth was much better today and no operation will be necessary." The Yankees had to win two of their remaining thirteen games to be sure of the pennant. They did it without Ruth; Byrd and Chapman did the most. Dr. King defrosted Ruth on the 12th and said he could report for duty on the 21st. That would give him almost a week of play before the World Series.

> **They had me packed so deep in ice I don't feel thawed out yet.**
> —Babe Ruth, September 17, 1932

Weak and shaky, Ruth worked out at the Stadium on the 17th with scout Paul Krichell and some friends. He claimed he had lost eight pounds, but reporters were politely skeptical. By the 20th he could hit the ball into the right-field stands almost at will. John McGraw came out to watch, a ghost from the days when the game was hit and run, not slug and trot.

Ruth played the whole nine innings of the game of the 23rd, two days after the Yankees came home.

Babe Ruth knew in 1932 that his legs were going. He couldn't cover the outfield, and McCarthy was using Byrd and Hoag as runners for him as well as resting him in late innings if the team was ahead. In the outfield Ruth's great arm was outlasting his legs; he made a double play and ranked thirteenth in assists with ten.

Ruth finished the 1932 season fifth in batting average (.341) and second in slugging percentage and home runs (forty-one as compared with Foxx's fifty-eight). He was fourth in runs batted in and for the first time since 1925 failed to lead in home runs as a proportion of times at bat. But he was still undisputed king of the base on balls.

THE ACCUMULATED BATTING FIGURES
BABE RUTH'S MAJOR-LEAGUE CAREER
1914–1932

at bat: 7483
hits: 2617
home runs: 652
runs batted in: 2023
average: .350

another. He had much worse days back when he was baseball's leading left-handed pitcher.

Claire's domestication probably kept Ruth going. He had a very good year. In the American League he finished first in home runs, slugging percentage, bases on balls, and home runs as a proportion of times at bat. He was second in runs scored, third in batting average (.359) and total bases. But he dropped in the annual poll for Most Valuable Player, ranking tenth with only seven votes (Joe Cronin* won with forty-eight).

Bob Shawkey tried to lead the Yankees as a friendly elder brother. If he had won the pennant the manner would have drawn praise. By finishing third he smirched himself even though Yankee attendance broke all records. Late in September the Cubs fired Joe McCarthy after he finished in the first division five times and won a pennant once. There began to be talk that McCarthy might manage the Yankees. To Babe Ruth that was outrageous. In the International League he had pitched to McCarthy, an obscure minor-league second baseman who couldn't make it to the majors.

THE ACCUMULATED BATTING FIGURES
BABE RUTH'S MAJOR-LEAGUE CAREER
1914–1930

at bat: 6492
hits: 2262
home runs: 565
runs batted in: 1723
average: .348

---

* Joseph Edward Cronin (1906–   ), shortstop, twenty seasons, 1926–1945, Pirates, Senators, Red Sox, batting average .301. Hall of Fame.

50 · Chicago Isn't Like New York

> The fans ride Tiny pretty hard all over the circuit and
> they may shout things at him that will make you feel un-
> comfortable. Chicago isn't like New York. They're not
> cosmopolitan like us. They haven't got any manners.
> —Heywood Broun, *The Sun Field*

The World Series of 1932 was more of a grudge fight than most.
The Cubs had let Joe McCarthy go; now he was coming back to
attack them as manager of the American League champions. The
Yankees didn't fear the Cubs. When Ruth, with the help of his panel
of literary shades (whose advice he didn't always follow), picked
his 1932 all-star team for the Christy Walsh syndicate, he included
only one Cub, pitcher Lon Warneke.* But he had three Yankees—
Dickey, Lazzeri, and Gomez.

Before every World Series each team votes on the division of the
expected loot. In 1932 the Yankees were generous. They voted three-
quarter shares each to their trainer and their traveling secretary,
half a share to Charlie Devens, a rookie who came late in June
after school let out at Harvard and pitched only nine innings that
year, and half-shares each to a man who left for the Reds in June
and to another who quit baseball.

The Cubs surprised everybody by their stinginess. The front office
had fired manager Hornsby in August. The Cubs voted him nothing, on the ground that he got the whole of his forty-thousand-
dollar salary. They voted their traveling secretary and trainer
half-shares each, and quarter-shares to some late arrivals. What
particularly drew the eyes of the Yankees and the world was that
Mark Koenig, the former Yankee, joined the Cubs in August, played
the last thirty-one games at shortstop, batted .353, won praises from

* Lonnie Warneke (1909–   ), pitcher, fifteen seasons, 1930–1945, Cubs, Cardinals. Won 193, lost 121, earned-run average 3.18.

manager Charlie Grimm* for having made the pennant possible, and was awarded half a share. To the Yankee bench jockeys this was a red flag. Koenig told the author the Cubs could have voted him a full share at a cost of about fifty dollars apiece.

Newspaper speculation on the likely winner of the Series went through the usual exercises of weighing the season's earned-run averages and batting averages, but John Kieran spoke for the *volk* when he wrote, ". . . The Babe has managed to work his way into a record number of World's Series. There must have been some connection between the presence of G. Herman Ruth on a team and the presence of that team in a World's Series." The bookmakers made the Yankees favorites at 9 to 5.

The first game was played in the Stadium on Wednesday, September 28. Even before the game Ruth took off the new man, Xaverian Brother George, and put on the old, the Baltimore waterfront slob. For the rest of the Series he had a coarse and glorious time. There was more vituperation, invective, and abuse in this Series than in most, and Ruth was the prime mover. Usually he was a dugout-taunter only in self-defense or when trying out his heavy boyish humor, but this time he stung the foe. To get to their own dugout the Cubs had to go through the Yankee dugout. Ruth greeted Koenig with, "Hi ya, Mark, who are those cheapskate nickel-nursing sonsabitches you're with?" (or words much like that). Other Yankees joined their cantor and didn't let up on the Cubs until the Series ended. Bell-like shouts of "nickel-squeezers," "penny-pinchers," and "tightwads" stirred the Cubs to scoff at Ruth's ambition to be a manager, to question "grandpop's" legs and his ability to touch his toes, and to twist his origin from rebel-against-compulsory-schooling to bastard foundling. The tone of the New York contests was faithfully reported in Chicago before the Yankees arrived for the third game. Chicago was prepared. Westbrook Pegler, a man very easily vexed, took sides with the Cubs in print, using more elegant language.

As for the game, the Yankees made light work of it. After the Cubs scored twice in the first, Guy Bush** gave the Yankees neither a hit nor a walk for three innings, but the Yankees got three runs in the fourth and five runs in the fifth. They ended with a 12–6 win for Red Ruffing, though making only eight hits. The too careful Cub pitchers walked twelve batters.

In the second game the Cubs again started with a lead (a run in

---

* Charles John Grimm (1898–   ), first baseman, twenty seasons, 1916–1936, Athletics, Cardinals, Pirates, Cubs, batting average .290.

** Guy Terrill Bush (1901–   ), pitcher, seventeen seasons, 1923–1945, Cubs, Pirates, Braves, Cardinals, Reds. Won 176, lost 136, earned-run average 3.86.

the first), but the Yankees immediately scored two, and the Cubs didn't get the lead again. Gomez won it 5–2, beating Warneke.

> They were too careful. The way to pitch to the Yankees is not to be over-awed by their reputations but to throw caution to the winds.
>
> —Charlie Root's* ghost writer,
> *Chicago American*, September 30, 1932

The Yankees had an acid reception in Chicago. By introducing Ladies' Days that summer the Cubs had created a new breed of fans. When Claire and Babe reached the Edgewater Beach Hotel there was a narrow lane to the door, lined with "hysterical, angry" ladies who were fluent in strong language and had every intention of spitting on Babe and Claire, especially Claire.

On the day of the game, October 1, there was a strong wind blowing toward the outfield. Gomez came into the hotel and reported, "It's blowing sixty miles an hour. . . . Babe and Lou ought to hit a dozen." In batting practice Babe hit nine into the bleachers and Lou seven. When Ruth went out to left field to catch flies, customers threw an occasional lemon at him. He cheerfully tossed it back each time.

By game time the crowd, which included Franklin D. Roosevelt, neared fifty thousand. When Ruth came to bat in the first inning with two runners on base, more lemons. But he put the Yankees three runs ahead with a home run, his fourteenth World Series home run. When he went out to left field in the bottom of the first the bleacher people booed and waved him away. Ruth theatrically flung his arm out to point to the place where the home-run ball landed. When he came to bat in the second inning he was accompanied by rolling lemons. He flied-out to the satisfaction of the customers.

> BABE SILENCES JEERING CUBS
> —*The Times*, October 2, 1932

Ruth's next turn at bat came in the fifth inning with the bases empty and the score tied 4–4. Both starters, Pennock and Root, were still in the game. Sewell had just grounded out.

A single lemon rolled to the plate as Ruth stepped into the batter's box from the first-base side. In reply he looked around and

---

* Charlie Henry Root (1899–1970), pitcher, seventeen seasons, 1923–1941, Cardinals, Cubs. Won 201, lost 160, earned-run average 3.58.

then waved his right hand toward the outfielders. As the crowd booed, he took his place at the plate, pointed his shoulder at Root, Joe Jackson style, cocked his bat, and waited.

The first pitch was a called strike. Ruth held up a finger. Only the umpire and Gabby Hartnett* could hear him murmur the famous axiom, "It only takes one to hit it." The next two pitches were balls. The fourth pitch was a called strike. Ruth extended two fingers on his right hand as he swung his arm straight up. The Cubs were crowded on their dugout steps shouting slanders. Trainer Andy Lotshaw and pitcher Pat Malone** were the loudest. Ruth pointed his bat into the Cub dugout and told the Cubs he was spotting them two strikes. Privately he hoped he might foul a pitch into their dugout. Then he turned to Root and pointed a finger at him: "You still need one more, kid. I'm going to put the next pitch right down your throat!" Ruder words were scattered in this statement but haven't been preserved.

As the crowd booed angrily, Root collected himself and threw a slow curve into the strike zone, high and inside. Pock! Johnny Moore,† the center fielder started back, then stood to watch the ball fall. A home run.

Ruth trotted mincingly and mirthfully around the bases with a happy insult for every infielder. As he rounded second he repeatedly thrust the palms of his hands at the men in the Cub dugout in triumphant mockery, shouting "Squeeze the Eagle Club!" and, to Malone, "Meathead!" Ah, this was even better than life on Baltimore's wharfs and piers. Combs said the Cubs took cover "as if they were being machine-gunned."

When Ruth reached the Yankee dugout Chapman quickly asked him what he had been saying out there in the batter's box. "I called Charlie Root everything in the book," which is close enough for a happy man who was briefly short of breath.

It was the last of his record-making fifteen World Series home runs.‡ Over the years the ball was picked up by many people at many points outside the park behind center field. Actually it landed in the center-field bleacher ticket-sales booth at the far corner of the field, 436 feet from home plate. (The park has been remodeled, so the scene is not now the same.)

Hartnett grieved. "We tried every kind of pitch on Ruth in that

---

* Charles Leo Hartnett (1900–1972), catcher, twenty seasons, 1922–1941, Cubs, Giants, batting average .297. Hall of Fame.
** Pierce Leigh Malone (1902–1943), pitcher, ten seasons, 1928–1937, Cubs, Yankees. Won 134, lost 92, earned-run average 3.74.
† John Francis Moore (1902–   ), outfielder, ten seasons, 1928–1945, Cubs, Reds, Phillies, batting average .307.
‡ The record is now eighteen, held by Mickey Mantle.

series. It didn't make any difference." Root later said, "I should have wasted that pitch."

Legend has Ruth predicting a home run when he pointed to young Root. Only one witness, of the many who immediately wrote down what they saw, said Ruth had called the shot. When he first came to the plate he did wave in the direction of the outfield as a way of defying the unfriendly fans who greeted him with a lemon. Any hit, a screaming single, would have made good the gesture. The legend first appeared in print early in 1933. Babe, some weeks later, first told it at Claire's parties during spring training that year. By 1948 Babe believed there was a man on base when he hit it! Several writers who reported the game exhaustively on the day it was played didn't report the near miracle, but years later they were confident believers. Faith, we are taught, is a gift, and those writers should be grateful. The legend is harmless and is even comforting to some who need a Hercules.

The run put the Yankees ahead. Gehrig, lost in the glare of Ruth's sparkle, came up next and on the first pitch hit a forgotten home run which completed the two-run margin of the final score, 7–5.

Lou Gehrig in his prime, early 1930s. (*The New York Yankees.*)

After the game, in the clubhouse, Ruth explained the physics of the thing: "The wind was with us, that's all. Any time they let us hit it into the air, zowie, the wind did the rest."

With the Yankees leading three games to none, McCarthy decided there wouldn't be a fifth game. With the kind of cockiness Greek tragedy warns against, he passed the word to the traveling secretary who posted a notice that the train would leave for New York after the fourth game.

McCarthy (or Zeus) pulled it off. The Yankees closed down the World Series in four games by winning on October 2 before a sullen crowd of fifty-one thousand which saw the Yankees trail for awhile after the first inning, 1–4, and rebound to win 13–6. Ruth was hit on the right forearm by a pitched ball and probably couldn't have played in a fifth game the next day. When he came into the clubhouse after the game "he cut loose with a piercing yell. . . ." Art Fletcher started the team song, and they all joined in "The Sidewalks of New York." Landis and League President Will Harridge came in to shake hands all around. The team dressed hurriedly because their special train had steam up.

With Claire and McCarthy on board the return to New York was a joyous journey, but not a violent one as in 1928. A crowd jammed Grand Central Station, but Claire and Babe had left the train earlier at Hyde Bridge. Xaverian Brother George was in charge again.

> It was the tamest series since 1927, and even less entertaining.
>
> —*Spalding Baseball Guide, 1933*

The Yankees handled the Cubs so roughly that reviews of the Series as a work of art were cool. The Cub pitchers were afraid of the Yankee batters. They pitched so timidly they walked twenty-three men. It was a landscape with too many figures, and a few hits could bring in runs in bunches like grapes. The Yankees made eight errors, which dimmed *their* brilliance. The accumulated score of the thirty-six innings reads:

	R	H	E
New York	37	45	8
Chicago	19	37	6

We may say it was a mismatch. The erratic Cubs couldn't stand up to a steady team which had been in first place since the middle of May. What the Yankees could be proudest of was winning twelve straight World Series games (1927, 1928, 1932).

Joe McCarthy had the inner glow any man would feel who left off managing the Cubs, because, as Cub owner William Wrigley, Jr., put it, "I want a man who can bring me a world's championship."

The only stirring aspect of the Series as a whole was the size and fury of the crowds in Chicago. There were thousands of empty seats in New York; there was standing room only in Chicago. Attendance at the four games was slightly more than attendance at the five-game series of 1929, in which the Cubs lost to the Athletics. But the games at Yankee Stadium in 1932 drew even fewer than the first two games of the 1931 Series, which were played in the small St. Louis park. The Depression was getting tougher. As an editorial writer said of the New York attendance, "Even that is a better showing than our steel production figures or our car-loadings."

Ruth is now remembered as the hero of the 1932 Series. The part played by poor bland Gehrig, who did most to win it, is forgotten. To put Ruth's share in proportion we need some more baseball numerals:

	Ruth	*Gehrig*
at bat	15	17
hits	5	9
home runs	2	3
runs	6	9
runs batted in	6	8
average	.333	.529

Gehrig, like Uriah, was in the van of the battle.

This was Ruth's last series. In forty-one World Series games he had collected a barely believable set of World Series records, as they stood in 1932, leading all men in World Series home runs, total bases, extra bases, bases on balls, runs, strikeouts, runs batted in, most times batted .300 or more, and many more single-Series and single-Series-game records. The records aren't the man, any more than the collar size is the man, but they help to take his measure.

As mentioned before, Westbrook Pegler, a good builder of sentences who later graduated from writing knowledgeably about boxing to writing ignorantly of public affairs, joined the lemon-tossers and booers of Chicago. A malicious example: "One of their outfielders is a fat, elderly party who must wear corsets to avoid immodest jiggling, and cannot waddle for fly balls, nor stoop for grounders." Anyone who knows about athletic equipment can tell from photographs taken in 1931 and 1932 that Ruth wore an athletic supporter with a wide waistband, say six inches. Such a support can be had in any sporting-goods store. When Ruth wore it, it pushed his late-summer paunch up a bit. And a well-etched picture like Pegler's doesn't fade. The Pulitzer Prize-winning historian William E. Leuchtenburg picked it up and imprisoned it in the amber of his book *The Perils of Prosperity, 1914–1932*, describing Ruth as "a pathetic waddling figure, tightly corseted, a cruel lampoon of his former greatness. . . ." (We might add that Ruth also wore an elastic bandage on one thigh during the 1932 Series.) Ruth in 1932 had what a Wilkie Collins character called "an autumnal exuberance of figure."

He was also on base that season, by hits and walks (not counting errors), 286 times in 587 trips to the plate, or 48.7 percent—still impressive at bat. Of the twenty-four regular American League outfielders, however, only three made fewer putouts and only eight made more errors. The mighty Ruth had fallen to the rank of a journeyman major-league outfielder.

A good deal of what has been written about Ruth—like the called-shot home run in the 1932 World Series—is something like creative art. The artists have a purpose other than to inform. Most often they wish to entertain, sometimes to shock. To try to learn about Ruth from such sources is possible, but it is something like trying to learn the public morals of a foreign nation by visiting its graveyards, temples, and civic monuments. It is a hard way to get the inside story.

Babe Ruth was no longer the greatest. Lou Gehrig surpassed him. It was an open question whether Ruth would ever again be so honored in his generation, such a glory of his time.

Outside the Park, 1933

SEA WASHES SAILOR
OVERBOARD AND BACK

RELEASED BY KIDNAPPERS
ON HIS PROMISE TO PAY
$2000 IN INSTALLMENTS

REV. BROWN SAYS
F. D. ROOSEVELT
IS CHOICE OF GOD

UNEMPLOYED MINER SHOOTS MINE CHIEF

DOLLAR BREAKS SHARPLY

FAMILY TREES POPULAR GIFTS IN GERMANY

GROUP TO ASSIST GERMANS
SUFFERING UNDER HITLER

KILLS BROTHER-IN-LAW AND SELF

URGES ORGANIZATION
OF SOCIAL WORKERS

COL. R. R. MC CORMICK
URGES BUSINESS MEN
TO GO INTO POLITICS

PREDICTS FALL OF NAZI REGIME

BRANFORD RIVER SET ASIDE
EXCLUSIVELY FOR WOMEN ANCLERS

RETURNS FROM CANADA TO WED
AFTER FIFTY-YEAR BETROTHAL

FRENCH PRESS ANGERED
BY SUGGESTION TO REPAY
WAR DEBT WITH ART WORKS

51 · At Bat in the Gloaming (1933)

They'll have to raise the ante to get me to sign.
—Babe Ruth, *The Times*, January 17, 1933

The business depression deepened. Baseball attendance in 1932 was the lowest since 1920 by almost three million; it was almost four million below 1930. In the American League only the Yankees, it was said, made a profit. Other industries could lay off workers, but baseball needed a minimum number of them to make up eight games a day. As in most businesses, cutting the payroll offered the surest savings. Babe Ruth had stopped being a growth industry.

Ruth in mid-January was working mornings in McGovern's gymnasium and playing golf every afternoon. When his Yankee contract came in the mail on January 16 it was for fifty thousand dollars. Ruth mailed it back unsigned and went to a movie. He was in good condition, a pound or two above his playing weight. Reporters soon knew that all Yankees had been cut except a pair of newcomers who didn't make enough money to make any difference.

It had become the custom to have an annual press morning at McGovern's which drew writers and newsreel photographers and made for baseball talk. In 1933 it fell on January 19, three days after Ruth returned his contract. To questions he said he might take a 10 or 15 percent cut, but not one of twenty-five thousand dollars. That much "at one smack is no cut. That's what you fellows might call an amputation." Then, for the newsreels, he boxed a round with daughter Julia.

The January publication of the eighth annual selection of an all-star team by the *Sporting News*, which took a poll of sportswriters, weakened Ruth's bargaining strength. For the first time he failed to make the team. The voters elected Chuck Klein* their right-

* Charles Herbert Klein (1904–1958), outfielder, seventeen seasons, 1928–1944, Phillies, Cubs, Pirates, batting average .320.

fielder, giving him 111 votes to 63 for Ruth. It was the proper choice. Klein had led the National League in home runs (38) and stolen bases (20) while batting .348.

Thus matters stood until the scene shifted to Florida in March.

In Florida, on the day President Roosevelt closed all the banks, Ruth again said he would take a 10 or 15 percent cut. What about fifty thousand dollars? BABE: "Absolutely not!" CLAIRE: "No!" Doesn't the closing of the banks make any difference? Well, said Babe, here turned economist, the banks wouldn't be closed forever.

Ruth joined the Yankee workouts but made no counter-offer to Ruppert. On the day Ruppert came to Florida he wouldn't see reporters, but he talked fruitlessly with Ruth the next day. After that Ruppert was available to reporters. He wanted them to know that reports of a Yankee profit in 1932 were incorrect, and he hoped they realized that fifty thousand dollars would buy as much in 1933 as a hundred thousand would buy in normal times. The next move, he said, was Ruth's. Ruth was not stirred. "If it is fifty thousand dollars, and the next move is up to me, there is no move. . . ."

And there things stalled, briefly.

Only two days after his firm defiance Ruth told a friend he *might* take fifty-five thousand. The beginning of an exhibition series with the Braves may have weakened his will. Ruppert took up psychological warfare on March 18, saying Ruth must sign by Saturday the 29th or the offer would be reduced. Ruppert made a reasonable point; part of Ruth's salary was for drawing exhibition-game crowds to pay the cost of spring training. On one day during the holdout the attendance was only a hundred.

Ruth then suggested fifty-five thousand. Meanwhile, back in Manhattan, the Salvation Army polled 1,171 destitute men living in the army's shelter called Gold Dust Lodge, at 40 Corlears Street, citing the Ruth-Ruppert argument and asking what Ruth should get. Each man wrote down a figure. The range was from ten cents to a million dollars. The mean was $48,999. On the next question, whether anyone was worth eighty thousand a year, the division of the house was 599 aye, 572 no. The 599 then listed those who were worth eighty thousand. The results were: any U.S. President, 185; Babe Ruth, 140; President Roosevelt, 97; Al Smith, 12. Nobody else got as many as five votes. All this during the toughest winter in American history since the first winter endured by the Plymouth Pilgrims.

On the same day Ruppert and Ruth agreed to the figure of fifty-two thousand after ten minutes of talk. Then they came out for the hokey rite of signing in front of the newsreel cameras. Ruppert had won, but Ruth surely didn't suffer, since the price of everything was falling fast. By cutting Ruth's salary Ruppert also cut Ruth's stature.

In earlier years people bought tickets to Yankee games partly to see a man who was paid so much to play baseball. As cut followed cut Ruth lost that value, but it was too late in his career for it to matter.

Ed Barrow added another entry to the 4 x 6 card:

> 1933   cont. $52,000 and 25% net receipts of Ex. games during championship season

> I have wanted to play in ten World's Series, complete twenty seasons in the big leagues, and hit 700 home runs. Next season will be my twentieth in the Majors. . . .
> —Babe Ruth, October 24, 1932

The Ruths had arrived in Florida early in February, so that Babe would have several weeks free for golf. (On March 2 he pleased himself with a hole-in-one on a drive of 185 yards with a No. 2 iron at the Pasadena Golf Club.)

Although unsigned to a contract he had begun to work out with the Yankees on the 8th, first posing for newsreels and signing autographs. He had gained five pounds in Florida. Attendance leaped from about 150 to 700 but thinned when he finished an hour's exercise. With Ruth a holdout in Florida, attendance at Crescent Lake Park remained poor. In the years just before 1933 the Yankees usually drew 125,000 paid admissions to exhibition games. Because of Ruth's absence in Florida the people didn't come. His self-exile ended on the eve of the annual barnstorm northward, when business might be expected to pick up. Instead they were passing through a stricken country where people hid themselves and could not be lured out even for a sight of Ruth and Gehrig.

When they reached New York they could concentrate on baseball instead of rural sociology. The Yankees had about the same roster for 1933 as they used in 1932. The bookmakers made them odds-on favorites in the American League at a prohibitive 2 to 5. The only hope for rivals, it was said, would be the absence of Ruth from the lineup.

As regular as the March equinox, Babe came down with his April cold just before the season opened. Claire nursed him at home for three days and then, as a present for his fourth wedding anniversary, astonished everybody by taking him to a tailor to be measured for a suit. He was as docile as when he got his suits from High City Tailor in Baltimore at age eight. The dockside slob had been exorcised, and was never heard of again.

For all the fears of the owners, the opening games of the 1933 season drew fifteen thousand more than the opening games of 1932.

The comparison is not exact because the games weren't played in the same parks, but ruin was not yet in sight. The Yankees played through April and May as though they deserved to be odds-on favorites. The War Department again used baseball to support nationalism by having Ruth autograph prize bats for the citizens' training camps. Some orphans at the Passaic Home and Orphan Asylum flagged down a train which was speeding toward a washout and Babe Ruth, still feeling as one of them, brought them Ruth caps, Ruth neckties, and an autographed bat each; he invited a couple of dozen of them to Yankee Stadium where they had a wonderful time. At the moment (May 20) the Yankees were in first place by two games. Ruth also posed for newsreels as the auctioneer at a horse sale to benefit the Federation of Jewish Philanthropic Societies. He played golf on open dates, once beating the professional at Rye Country Club.

In mid-June the White Sox were also playing well. A Yankee double-header at Comiskey Park on June 18 set a new park attendance record, for a double-header, of fifty-three thousand.* (They split.)

Thereafter, Yankee power slowly ebbed. The Senators had a game-and-a-half lead on July 4 after the Yankees lost a double-header to Washington before the biggest crowd which had ever seen a ball game in the United States, 77,365.** Ruth got his eighteenth home run in the last inning of the second game. John Kieran wrote: "With a crowd like that he couldn't miss. It got down to his last time at bat in the gloaming. One chance left to do right by his public."

The Yankees were playing .700 ball at the end of May, but now the Senators led, and the Yankees wouldn't catch them.

> Give him a crowd, a gallery worthy of his best effort, and the old warrior will put on his show. . . . He isn't what he used to be. But pack the stands, set the stage, turn up the lights, and who is it brings down the house with his act? The Babe!
> —John Kieran, *The Times*, July 8, 1933

The annual All-Star game between teams presumed to be made up of the best players of each league began as part of the Chicago World's Fair of 1933 and was promoted by Arch Ward, sports editor of the *Chicago Tribune*. Once convinced by Ward, the owners picked Connie Mack to manage the Americans and John McGraw to

* The record fell on May 20, 1973, when the White Sox drew 55,555 to a double-header.
** The present regular season record is 84,587, at Cleveland, September 12, 1954.

manage the Nationals—McGraw had retired in 1932. He was in poor health, and the Giants had lost much of their New York following to the Yankees. In a sense, McGraw quit because his fans quit. He had been a manager for thirty-three of his sixty years.

The choice of players was left to popular vote. In the voting for all positions on the American League team, Al Simmons led Ruth 346,000 to 321,000. Simmons was batting .367, Ruth .313.

Comiskey Park was crowded on July 7 with every seat taken. (Autograph seekers were most interested in Ruth.) The Americans scored first, and Ruth arranged their victory in the third inning by hitting a home run with a man on base. The Nationals never caught up. In the eighth inning, with Frisch on base, Ruth made a spectacular catch of a ball hit by Chick Hafey* which could have been a home run to tie the game. (Ruth had earlier seemed unfit trying to field a Lou Warneke triple in the sixth inning that a fleeter man might have caught for a fly-out.) McGraw marveled at the catch of Hafey's ball—"That old boy," he said, is "marvelous." (That old boy was twenty-two years younger than McGraw and had, in effect, driven him out of baseball with a bat.) Ruth had two strikeouts, a single, a home run, and batted in two runs in four times at bat. The score was 4–2. Ruth had given the Americans the winning margin.

John Kieran, most intelligent sportswriter of the day, had been unlimited in his praise of Ruth for several years. The All-Star game performance transported him. He said he began to believe people who said the difference between the American and National Leagues was Babe Ruth, and he quoted Eddie Collins as saying people in the National League didn't know what it meant to have a man like Ruth around: you could strike him out three or four times and he would still beat you by knocking your team out of the park the next time he came to bat. The remark is illustrated by the career of the National League's Frank Frisch, whom Joe McCarthy thought was the perfect ballplayer (before McCarthy knew Gehrig). In the All-Star game of 1933 Ruth and Frisch had identical batting records, but in fifty World Series games Frisch hit not a single home run. Ruth, in forty-one World Series games, hit fifteen. Ruth batted in thirty-three World Series runs, Frisch ten.

The people loved the All-Star game, and, of course, we still have it. The 1933 profit was $46,506, which went to the players' fund as the base for today's pension fund.

While Ruth was knocking the Nationals out of Comiskey Park, the wise money was on the move, making the Senators 4 to 5 favorites to win the American League pennant and offering the Yankees at even money.

---

* Charles James Hafey (1903–1973), outfielder, thirteen seasons, 1924–1937, Cardinals, Reds, batting average .317. Hall of Fame.

After the All-Star game the baseball business went on slumping. William E. Veeck, Sr., president of the Cubs, proposed interleague play along the same lines broached forty years later. Five National League owners said it was an interesting idea, and none opposed it, but only one American League owner approved. Bill Cunningham of the *Boston Post* thought there would be no changes: "There hasn't been a new idea in a quarter of a century. . . . [Baseball] with the sole exception of Babe Ruth, who was a fortunate accident, has offered nothing especially novel." (Cunningham might have noticed the accidental enlivening of the ball in 1920 and its deliberate slight deadening in 1931.)

Lefty Grove shut out the Yankees on August 3. It was the first time the Yankees had failed to score in 309 consecutive games; their record in *The Little Red Book* (forty-sixth annual edition) still reads "Most consecutive games, scoring—308. New York A.L., Aug. 2, 1931–Aug. 3, 1933." Ruth was hitless.

Then the Yankees went on the road and came back eight games behind the Senators. Their homecoming drew no crowd. The only Yankee-talk among the fans was speculation about the 1934 roster. Would Ruth play next year? His batting and his fielding were both declining. Because of injuries he missed six of the games on the road and "like a tired man after twenty seasons, he took relief regularly." When he left games in late innings Sammy Byrd played right field. But Ruth was batting .307 with twenty-seven home runs. (Gehrig had but twenty.)

> A tired arm that isn't sore often will operate just as you expect it to and not give you too much when you want just enough spin or power on your pitch.
>
> —Jim Brosnan

On the last day of the season, when the Senators had long been certain of the pennant and the Yankees were assured of second place, Ruth earned his last great ovation. To draw a crowd, Barrow arranged that Ruth pitch against the Red Sox in the Stadium for a share of the receipts. He had pitched only one game in the last twelve years.

Before twenty-five thousand people he shut out the Red Sox for the first five innings. Then his arm began to stiffen. He could have left the game with the certainty that he wouldn't be the losing pitcher, but he stayed on to win 6–5, allowing twelve hits. All Red Sox runs were earned. His arm may have been stiff, but he walked nobody and struck out three. Babe Ruth marvels are almost too much. Going nine innings and winning would be enough. But, being Ruth, he had to provide the winning margin with his thirty-fourth home run of the season. As Tristram P. Coffin said, if this game had been played outside the walls of Troy, Ruth would loom large in the *Iliad*.

After the game he was so tired it took him an hour to dress, but a crowd of five thousand waited outside to cheer. His arm was so stiff he couldn't raise his left hand to his head, and he tipped his cap with the right.

The Yankees finished in second place, seven games behind the Senators but far ahead of the third-place Athletics.

Ruth's popularity was still great, and he still had the admiration of masses of boys. Xaverian Brother George was wholly in charge now, and the Lyn Larys showed their respect for him in an unexpected way. Lary told the author: "Babe was my son's godfather. Both my wife and I consider it a great privilege to have known him. He was a *great* man. . . ." An invitation to sponsor a child's baptism could not have been predicted as late as 1925.

Of the four leading sports heroes of the 1920s, Bill Tilden, Bobby Jones, Jack Dempsey, and Babe Ruth, only Ruth was still among the kings of his game in popular favor, but he was falling out of sight of his professional critics. The Associated Press poll of eighty-nine editors to choose an all-star team of 1933 drew eighty-eight votes for Joe Cronin but only three for Ruth.

As for the records of the year, it is well to note what Dan Daniel wrote in the *World Telegram*, and what Fred Lieb confirmed—that the owners further deadened the ball in 1933, with greater effect on the National League. A short table of runs scored by year shows it:

RUNS SCORED

	American League	National League
1931	6355	5537
1932	6436	5680
1933	6080	4908

One effect was to make pitchers look stronger while making sluggers look weaker. In comparison with 1932 Foxx had ten fewer home runs, Gehrig two, and Ruth seven. Ruth was among the first three batters of the American League in slugging percentage, home runs, and home runs as a proportion of times at bat, but ranked first only in bases on balls. His batting average was .301, the lowest since 1925. In the field his legs were failing but his arm was still among the best. He made nine assists and four double plays. Fourteen outfielders made more assists, but only two had more double plays.

Ruth covered the 1933 World Series as a working journalist, which meant he gave his ghost, Ford Frick, a running commentary on the game. In Washington the visiting press called on President Roosevelt. As they filed through the Red Room the President singled out Ruth for a greeting. Roosevelt told of arriving in Rochester in 1920, when he was campaigning for Vice President, and finding an unexpectedly large crowd in his hotel lobby. He thought the people were waiting for *him*, but the people had come to see the soprano Galli Curci and Babe Ruth.

Christy Walsh had booked Ruth for two exhibition games in Hawaii. A few days before the season ended Bucky Harris quit his job as manager of the Tigers after five straight finishes in the second division. Frank Navin owned the Tigers. Ed Barrow described him as a "cold, uncommunicative man with a poker face" who bet on horses a lot. Navin got Barrow's permission to talk to Ruth about managing in Detroit. Just when Ruth learned of this we don't know, but he put off meeting Navin although the World Series ended on October 7 and Ruth didn't have to be in California to board ship for Hawaii until about the 15th. Ruth believed he could talk with Navin when he came back from Hawaii and, in spite of Barrow's warning against delay, didn't go to Detroit. But when he reached San Francisco he telephoned Navin to say he was leaving for Hawaii and would like to have a yes or no answer. It was 3 A.M. in Detroit, and the annoyed Navin said "No." Navin thought anyone so casual about a managing job had too much arrogance or too little responsibility. (He hired Mickey Cochrane and won the pennant in 1934.) As late as 1948 Ruth was trying to explain his puzzling behavior. The real mystery is, why didn't Claire get him to Detroit sometime between October 7 and 14 (leaving time enough to get to a California port)?

Before the end of the World Series the President of Mexico and Ambassador Josephus Daniels together invited Ruth to play baseball in Mexico. They seemed to think it a social invitation. There was no profit talked of.

The Ruths' ship *Lurline* docked at Honolulu on October 19, and ten thousand people cheered their arrival. Babe paid a formal call on the governor and placed a wreath on the grave of Alexander Cartwright, the man who laid out the baseball diamond as we know it. The schools were let out for the second game.

In the first game, attended by fifteen thousand, Ruth, sweating in leis, started in right field but went to first base and then to pitch in order to escape from joyful boys of all ancestries who streamed out for autographs. All other players were Hawaiian. He had a single and a home run. After the game Babe was overheard to say to Claire, "I guess I'm getting too old. Another year and I'll have to quit."

Ruth not only played a two-game baseball series in Hawaii for profit but also played golf for charity, once shooting the Waialae course in three over par. He peddled the golf-match tickets on the beach himself.

Back home there was unfounded talk in the papers in November that he would manage the Yankees' farm club in Newark in 1934. At the moment, farm-system manager George Weiss and Yankee owner Ruppert were toasting each other in Pluto Water out in Indiana. Weiss told reporters the rumor seemed "terribly far-fetched." And so it turned out to be.

THE ACCUMULATED BATTING FIGURES
BABE RUTH'S MAJOR-LEAGUE CAREER
1914–1933

at bat: 7942
hits: 2755
home runs: 686
runs batted in: 2126
average: .347

Outside the Park, 1934

COURT INQUIRY SET
ON INSULL RECEIVER

PRESIDENT PLANS 50 TO 60-CENT DOLLAR

FORD CALLS NRA A STEP
TOWARD AN ERA OF JUSTICE

SHOOTS CAT AND HIMSELF

DRY LAW FINES IN CHICAGO
$3,060,054 IN 14 YEARS

DILLINGER RAIDS BANK IN SOUTH BEND, IND.

ROCKEFELLER, AT 95,
TO PASS QUIET DAY

JAIL TWO NEWS MEN
ON CONTEMPT CHARGES

DEATHS FROM HEAT
INCREASED TO 1,213

QUINTUPLETS GET SUN TAN

POLICE IN STEEL HATS
ROUT SILK STRIKERS

RELIEF FROM 'HANGOVER'
FOUND IN RADIO WAVES

EX-SLAVE DONATES
$1,000 TO COLLEGE

HARVARD ENDS BEER SALE
AS STUDENTS FAIL TO BUY

52 · The Superfluous Veteran (1934)

A rumor in the last week of 1933 said Babe Ruth might manage the Cincinnati Reds in 1934. The public story is this: Donie Bush had left the Reds. Larry MacPhail, the Cincinnati general manager, thought Ruth's presence in Cincinnati would raise attendance and asked Jacob Ruppert whether the Yankees would let the Reds have Ruth on waivers. Ruppert refused. He said he would let Ruth go to another American League club but not to the National League. In the light of Ruth's later brief and painful career with the Braves of the National League, the statement credited to Ruppert makes no sense. It seems the kind of incongruity that tips off the alert reader of detective stories. And so it was.

Ruth believed the public story. But Cincinnati was the front for a covert operation. Bob Quinn, the new general manager of the Brooklyn Dodgers, found his board of directors dissatisfied with their manager, Max Carey.* Quinn wanted Ruth but dared not hope to bring him straight from the Bronx to Brooklyn. Quinn had a friend sound out Ruth about managing an unnamed team, and Ruth believed it was the Reds. He said he would prefer an eastern club and would play out the season of 1934 waiting for something to turn up. Thus it follows that Quinn arranged the waivers approach to the Yankees through MacPhail. If it worked, MacPhail could then transfer Ruth to Brooklyn where he would become manager. (The Dodgers were surely eastern enough.) But Ruppert balked. Perhaps he smelled a plot, perhaps there was a leak. He surely wouldn't wish to see Babe Ruth a hero in Brooklyn.

At the same time the Yankees refused MacPhail, Bob Shawkey, who had been managing in Jersey City and Scranton, became manager of Newark, proving the Yankees were more interested in using Newark to develop players than to make Babe Ruth happy.

* Max George Carey, born Maximilian Carnarius (1890–   ), outfielder, twenty seasons, 1910–1929, Pirates, Dodgers, batting average .285. Hall of Fame.

Autographing baseballs for Babe Ruth's Radio Boys Club, 1934. (*National Baseball Library, Cooperstown, New York.*)

A suspect in the Lindbergh kidnaping case was arrested after a scuffle with police in a Chicago barber shop when detectives found in his basement a complete account of the Lindbergh case and records of the earnings of Jack Dempsey and Babe Ruth. One sheet had a picture of Ruth with the suspect's notation, "Will present this." Ruth had received no threats, but the news, since he had two daughters, plainly upset him. It turned out that the prisoner had nothing to do with the Lindbergh murder, but the police had caught a live one. He had successfully staged two bloodless kidnapings which together netted him seventy-two thousand dollars. Police believed Dempsey and Ruth were to have been next.

Ruth and the Standard Oil Company of New Jersey collided with Harold Ickes when Ruth contracted to help the company with a radio prize contest to promote the collection of coupons to win prizes at Standard stations. The contest plainly violated the Petroleum Industry Code of the NRA, as Ickes pointed out in asking for an injunction. By that time the oil company claimed it had enlisted more than half a million boys in "Babe Ruth's Boys Club." By agreement Jersey Standard gave up on the contest and Ickes withdrew the suit.

Babe Ruth, a clay model for a heroic bronze by
Reuben Nakian, as exhibited at the Downtown
Gallery, February 1934, an Associated Press photo-
graph. (*National Baseball Library, Cooperstown,
New York.*)

Reuben Nakian did a colossal eight-foot tall Ruth in clay (a ton
of it), cast it in plaster, and exhibited the cast in the Downtown
Galleries in February and then in Rockefeller Center in March. The
figure is of a batter completing a successful swing in the moment
before he begins his ceremonial four-base trot. No one ever put up
the money to have it cast in bronze, which is a pity. It belongs in
Cooperstown, Baltimore, or the Bronx.

Ruth had some not very flattering offers from people who thought
he wouldn't be playing with the Yankees in 1934—a one-year contract for thirty-five thousand to play for the San Francisco team of
the Pacific Coast League, and a curious suggestion that Ruth tour

all the minor leagues as designated hitter for every pitcher in every minor-league game he attended.

The American League, before 1933, had not suffered as much from the Depression as had business in general, but in that year its income was 31 percent below normal while the overall business index was down 25 percent.* *Good* teams were now losing money. The Pirates, second in 1932 and 1933, lost money both years. The Cubs lost money when they won the pennant in 1932 and lost much more in 1933 and 1934 with third-place finishes. The Senators won the pennant in 1933 and had to part with Goose Goslin because they couldn't pay his salary. The players' share of the 1933 World Series receipts was the smallest pool since 1922. After the Series Will Harridge, president of the American League, said owners would have to cut both salaries and overhead. They cut overhead by shortening the 1934 season a week, though the number of games remained at 154. As for the Yankees, their 1933 attendance was about three-quarters of the average attendance from 1920 to 1930.

For a change, in 1934 Ruth was not a holdout. He and Ruppert met at the brewery and signed a one-year contract for thirty-five thousand dollars on January 15, two months earlier than usual. They were so agreeable that some people believed it was the first stage in a palace revolution which would depose Joe McCarthy. Baseless rumors that Ruth was to be manager were, as they say, rife. Ruth grumpily observed to his sportswriting friends that Ruppert had given Admiral Richard Byrd a quarter of a million dollars to go to the South Pole (Byrd named his flagship *Jacob Ruppert*) and let Ruth help underwrite the exploration with a seventeen-thousand-dollar pay cut. The average cut of major-league payrolls was about 25 percent in the years 1932–33. Because Ruth signed so quickly, other players signed easily.

The highest seven salaries of 1934 were:

Babe Ruth	$36,696
Mickey Cochrane**	30,000
Chuck Klein	30,000
Bill Terry	27,500
Lou Gehrig	23,000
Carl Hubbell†	17,500
Rogers Hornsby	15,000

* The calculators used conditions of 1915–16 as "normal."

** Gordon Stanley Cochrane (1903–1962), catcher, thirteen seasons, 1925–1937, Athletics, Tigers, batting average .320. Hall of Fame.

† Carl Owen Hubbell (1903–   ), pitcher, sixteen seasons, 1928–1943, Giants. Won 253, lost 154, earned-run average 2.97. Hall of Fame.

(Cochrane and Hornsby were playing managers.) These figures were sharply lower than the same men would have gotten in the 1920s, but the average ballplayer, because of deflation, actually had about 4 or 5 percent more purchasing power than in the 1920s.

In any event, Ruth wasn't living at poverty level. He began to collect an annuity of $17,500 in February 1934, bringing him up to about fifty thousand. No American of the mid-1970s with three hundred thousand a year was as well off.

Barrow's entry for the year was:

> 1934   Cont. $35,000 and 25% net receipts,
> Ex. games during season.

Ruth had been the senior Yankee for some years but not the senior ballplayer. Herb Pennock, whose first season was 1912, outranked him in time. He and Ruth had been together since Ruth had become a Red Sox regular (except for the years 1920–1922). After the 1933 season the Yankees released him. When reporters asked the spare, hawk-nosed fox hunter how he would describe the Yankees' treatment of him, he said, "Royal."

At the beginning of 1934 there was a change in Ruth's public statements. Always in earlier years he talked of how many home runs he might hit. Now the question was how many games he might play, and he hinted that a hundred would be about right. He started the McGovern grind on January 3 at 235 pounds, not quite a fat man. The writers and photographers (and troops of small boys) were there. He asked them not to bring up the manager question again, and in reply to a question said he couldn't go back to pitching regularly because, after beating Boston in 1933, "I had such a sore arm I had to eat with my right hand for a week." At the end of the month he was on his back with his annual influenza. The temperature in New York dropped fifty-two degrees to zero in a day, and it wasn't a bad time to be confined to the twelve-room flat at 345 West 88th Street. On January 29 Claire, acting as press secretary, said, "It will be at least a week before he will be able to go out again."

> **His popularity is undiminished, his good nature inexhaustible.**
> —*The Times*, March 13, 1934

He didn't get outdoors again until, heavily packaged in wool, he went with Claire to take the train for St. Petersburg on February 8. He said he had lost about fourteen pounds. Perfunctorily genial with the press, he remarked, "Pretty cold, this, for an old man, eh kid? pretty cold." In Florida he soaked himself in golf for a solid month. The team of Babe Ruth and former United States Open Champion Billy Burke won the Tampa Professional-Amateur Tournament on February 15 with a best-ball score of 35, 31——66.

After the golfing he began baseball training with the usual ceremonial photography on March 12. His hour-long workout that day drew five hundred idolaters of all ages. If he had lost fourteen pounds in New York, he had gained them back at many nineteenth holes; he was on the pudgy side. He was hitting them out of the park well and beat the Braves on the 17th with a home run that made the score 6–5. His measured weight was now 226, about right.

On the northward tour he and Sammy Byrd leapfrogged ahead of the team to get to Atlanta (where the Yankees would play the Crackers) early enough to play golf with Bobby Jones. The foursome was completed by adding P. Hal Sims, the bridge champion. They had time enough for only nine holes. The scores were: Sims 41, Ruth 39, Byrd 37, Jones 36.

The spring was a success. There had been some doubt that Ruth would be worth special attention, but in the thirteen exhibitions he batted .429 with six home runs and led the team in both batting average and runs batted in. In right field, though, he seemed a little sluggish.

Opening day brought the usual gathering of prophecies. Rogers Hornsby, who had moved from the Cardinals to the Browns, said the American League teams were pretty evenly matched: "None of them looks super to me." The Associated Press poll picked the Senators first, the Yankees second, by a vote of 49–33. The bookmakers made them both 6 to 5 and take your choice. *The Times* gave two columns to prospects for the baseball season of 1934, with a paragraph or more for every team. It didn't mention Babe Ruth.

> . . . What is worrying Babe's legion of admirers is whether he will weather the hot days that seem to be here a little bit ahead of schedule.
>
> —Sam Murphy, May 1934

Opening-day attendance in 1934 was the best since 1931, so baseball was not becoming extinct. When the Yankees opened in the Stadium on the 24th they drew forty thousand.

Claire and Babe had Gertrude Musier as their guest on opening day. Miss Musier, age nineteen, was a polio victim who had recovered her sight after fifteen years of blindness. The Ruths sent their car to Flushing for her and posed with her for photographers. This sounds like hokum, and it is, if it is possible for the press to be hokey and the characters sincere. Ruth really meant it. In his relations with the young, infirm, and dependent, it was impossible to make it so corny that Babe Ruth was false to his nature. It was during one of these late seasons of his baseball life that Babe, clad in white flannels, driving home in his car with all of his family after a warm double-header, stopped by a traffic light at a park, was mobbed by boy ballplayers, got out of the car, and hit flies and grounders for his disciples for half an hour. No writers. No photographers. No publication until fifteen years after he died.

When the White Sox fired their manager, Lew Fonseca,* in May, the Chicago club privately pondered the question of Ruth as successor but silently passed him over. That same month the Yankees played an exhibition in Rochester. Rabbit Maranville, whose first season was 1912, lay in a Rochester hospital with a broken leg which he suffered in a Florida exhibition. He was grateful when Ruth took Gehrig and Byrd to visit him, telling his friends, "I knew Muscles would come."

But the Yankees weren't moving through their schedule like champions. On July 1 the bookmakers moved the Tigers up as contenders, lengthening the odds on the Yankees a little and on the Senators a lot. The Yankees' right-fielder didn't resemble the right-fielder of 1921. Ruth was below the American League median at .289 with twelve home runs. But he was still a nationalist symbol and autographed his annual quota of War Department prize bats and balls. He also was still worth money to advertisers. Beginning in April he had thirteen weeks on CBS radio, Mondays, Wednesdays, and Fridays, pushing dry breakfast cereals by selling souvenirs for coins and box tops. He wasn't very good at reading broadcast scripts, but it didn't matter; boys would listen to Babe Ruth if he were trying to teach Esperanto.

In popular balloting for the All-Star games there have been two biases, one in favor of the voter's home club and one, rather more defensible, in favor of long-established players who may not be as good at the moment as some younger, less famous players. Babe Ruth was elected in 1934 because of remembered glories stretching back to 1916. In 1934, though he was just barely of major-league ability, he got only six thousand votes fewer than Bill Terry who led everybody. When the starting lineups were settled, Ruth was the second weakest hitter of the list at .285. Just for contrast, the baseball writers polled themselves. Their all-star teams differed from the popular choices, but even they kept Ruth (and dropped Lefty Grove).

* Lewis Albert Fonseca (1899–   ), infielder, twelve seasons, 1921–1933, Reds, Phillies, Indians, White Sox, batting average .316.

The Americans won again, this time by a score of 9–7, but at the beginning the Nationals seemed invincible because of Hubbell's pitching. In the first inning the first two Americans got on base, one by a walk and one by a single, and then worked a double steal. Thus Ruth came to bat able to drive in two runs with a sharp single. But he took a called third strike, and hearts, as they say, bowed down. It was a screwball, and at Ruth's best, in 1921, Shucks Pruett had baffled him with screwballs. But then Hubbell struck out Gehrig, and then Foxx. Ruth didn't look so inept after all. In the second inning Hubbell struck out Al Simmons, struck out Joe Cronin, gave up a single to Dickey, and struck out Lefty Gomez.

In the remainder of the game Ruth went hitless but walked twice and scored a run. Those walks were marks of respect.

> **I'm getting out of this game before I'm carried out.**
> **—Babe Ruth, July 18, 1934**

One of Ruth's goals was to play twenty seasons. He hit home run number 699 on the twentieth anniversary of his first appearance, July 8, in Washington. Another goal was to hit seven hundred home runs. Number seven hundred came at Detroit on July 13, a hit that carried 480 feet over the right-field wall. At the moment only Gehrig and Hornsby had as many as three hundred. Ruth paid Lennie Bielski twenty dollars for the ball and gave him two new autographed balls and a box seat for the rest of the game. On the 17th, at Cleveland, he was walked for the two-thousandth time. Of contemporaries only Gehrig, with 1,508, ever received as many as fifteen hundred. Two thousand bases on balls add up to almost thirty-six miles of jogging down that ninety-foot base path.

Still at Cleveland, on the 18th, a line single off Gehrig's bat disabled Ruth when it struck him on the right shin. Three men carried him off. X rays showed no fracture, but he was out for a week. When he came back the Yankees had fallen a game behind the Tigers, and Earle Combs was out for the season after breaking his collarbone and fracturing his skull when he ran into the concrete left-field wall in St. Louis.

Walter Johnson was in St. Louis and composed an all-time all-star team for the writers. He put Ruth in right field.

Ruth was very talkative with Joe Williams of the *New York World* in Boston on August 10. "I'm definitely through as a regular player at the end of this season," he said, citing ankle and knee troubles. He'd like to stay on as a manager, active enough to pinch-hit when it might draw a crowd or win a game. He was going to play in Japan in the fall. "After that trip I'll be listening to offers—if any." At the moment his home-run total was 704.

The remarks moved *The Times* to an editorial appreciation: "He appeals to . . . [a] deep-rooted instinct in his public, as literally a Man of Might." (So did Hercules.) Ruppert was in Nashville. He told the *Nashville Banner* Ruth would be with the Yankees in 1935. "He has many more years up there as a pinch-hitter. Besides, I doubt if anyone could pay what he is worth to us."

Ruth had done himself no favor. He gave Ruppert and Barrow months to think of a way to solve their very burdensome Ruth problem. But he had spoken out in a moment of vexation. Relations with Joe McCarthy were always strained, and made copy even for the gossip columnist and broadcaster Walter Winchell. Ruth also did his best friend among sportswriters a bad turn. Bill Slocum knew how Ruth felt but kept quiet, and now Ruth had given Williams a scoop. Ruth had no sense of press-agentry at all. After the conversation with Williams he talked about retirement with anybody who asked, sometimes in gummy language, as, "If I find that things are sort of boring, there are always enough vacant lots around that I can go out and have a game of ball with a bunch of kids."

Matured in wearying bones, Ruth struggled on through this wretched season. He was booed in Yankee Stadium, which was a shock to the press box. ("Tear down Faneuil Hall. Rip up the Constitution. They hooted Babe Ruth yesterday.")

A reporter asked most of the Yankees if Ruth was finished, and Chapman told him, "If we had his money and his reputation we wouldn't take abuse from the fans." When a version of this came out in print Ruth was furious with the whole team until Chapman said it was meant as helpful advice and support from friends. Humiliations piled up. He ranked eighth in home runs in the American League and eleventh in both leagues. He didn't get a single vote in the Associated Press poll to choose a 1934 all-star team. And in the voting for Most Valuable Player, thirty-eight players were mentioned, but not Ruth. It was the first time he had been completely ignored.

Ruth made his last home appearance as a Yankee on September 24. It was a perfect day for playing baseball—partly cloudy, temperature in the mid-seventies, light breezes. He started in right field where he made an easy catch. He had a base on balls in the first inning, limped to first base, and left for a pinch-runner. A crowd of two thousand spattered its thin applause, and that was it. The Yankees lost the game, and that day the idle Tigers backed into the pennant, as they say.

Ruth's last game of the season was in Washington and rather more festive. The St. Mary's Industrial School Band came down to divert

Babe Ruth aging in the 1930s. (*The New York Yankees.*)

the crowd of fifteen thousand. Thousands of local residents, including President Roosevelt, had signed a testimonial of their love.
When he received it, Ruth spoke his thanks over the public-address
system and said he'd like to stay in baseball "as long as I can do
anybody any good," perhaps as a manager. He was hitless in three
times at bat but scored after a base on balls. Chinaman Hoag
finished the game in right field. The Senators won. Ironically, the
winning pitcher was a man for whom this game was the only victory of his major-league career, a career which lasted for twelve and
two-thirds innings.

Ruth covered the World Series (Cardinals over Tigers) for the
Christy Walsh Syndicate. This time he didn't scoop Bill Slocum,
he scooped himself. Thinking over Ruppert's hint that his future
lay in pinch-hitting, he told three sportswriters that he wouldn't
play in 1935 unless he was a manager. Every service except the
Christy Walsh string carried the news, to the great annoyance of the
Hearst chain which was Walsh's best customer. Ruth had spoken
most imprudently: he said he went to see Ruppert and asked,

"Colonel, are you satisfied with McCarthy for next year?" The Colonel replied that he was and I said "That suits me—that's all I wanted to know." I did not say that it was a case of McCarthy or me.

> Superfluous lags the veteran on the stage.
> —Samuel Johnson

The Yankees finished in second place, seven games behind the Tigers. A prime Ruth would probably have brought the pennant, but he was far from prime. He went to the plate fewer times than in any year since 1925 and batted only .288. He made the fewest assists of any of his full seasons thus far, the fewest putouts since 1917, and his lowest fielding average to date. Even the great arm was gone. For the first time runners could defy Ruth and take the extra base. His only distinction as a batter was that he ranked third in the league in bases on balls with 103. He hit twenty-two home runs, thirteen at home and nine on the road. This is the record of a ballplayer worth no more than five thousand 1934 dollars.

Claire thought the Yankees had used Babe too much in exhibition games—"They wore him out"—but no player who has played in twenty-two seasons has been hurried to the end of his playing life, since only half the players last as long as five seasons. Ruth had never been among the "tougher" players if you figure the number of games he played each year. Many played in a higher proportion of games. Nevertheless he lasted longer than all but a handful. Claire earned much credit. After marriage at thirty-five he hit over .300 for the next four years, in which he annually batted in more than a hundred runs and hit from thirty-five to forty-nine home runs. He liked baseball better than beer, night life, and overeating. The monkish regimes of Claire and McGovern kept him at his happiest.

The bench time of 1934 was a depressing time. In 103 games that year the Yankees used more than three outfielders, mostly because of removing Ruth in late innings. He also sat out twenty-nine games. This let him see a lot more of McCarthy than either of them liked. Ruth was openly critical of his manager's policies. The historian of the Yankees put it this way: "Joe watched him silently, giving him enough rope, confident that he would hang himself in the end." Ruth should have quit in 1933, but nearly all great ballplayers have stayed around too long. If it is hard to admit to being old at sixty, how much harder at thirty-five or forty.

A. E. Housman's theme was that laurels grow early but roses last

longer. All baseball careers are sad. They end at an age when lawyers still hope for partnerships, when physicians are cramming to
pass their specialty-board examinations, when young college teachers are trying to secure tenure by writing articles on Shakespeare's
knowledge of Levantine laxative herbs. Baseball is the quickest way
by which a young man can show himself superb, but youth is necessary to success, and shades of mortality early close around the
golden boys. Their playing life is so brief they have little leverage
with their employers. A few owners have been active in their
eighties; a few, only a few, ballplayers have been active in their
forties. Here is a graph of the ages of champions which shows the
decline of skills.

AGES AT WHICH PLAYERS SET SELECTED RECORDS IN
PITCHING, BATTING, RUNNING, AND FIELDING WHICH
STOOD AS SINGLE SEASON BEST, 1901–68

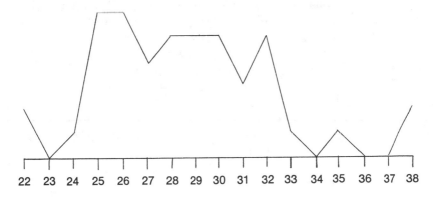

22 23 24 25 26 27 28 29 30 31 32 33 34 35 36 37 38

These are records which least depend upon the quality of the team
and little upon the judgment of the manager. The categories are:

Earned-run average, starting and relief
Strikeouts by pitcher
Strikeouts per nine innings pitched
Batting average
Slugging average
Hits
Home runs as a percentage of times at bat
Doubles
Runs batted in
Innings pitched
Fewest hits per nine innings pitched, starting and relief
Fewest bases on balls per nine innings pitched, starting and relief

Fielding averages of infielders individually by position, outfielders,
    catchers, pitchers
Total bases
Home runs
Extra-base hits
Triples
Stolen bases

Middle-aged people who followed Babe Ruth closely when they
were young have a tendency to believe he decayed rapidly, an
illusion caused by his compressing all of his public decline into the
seasons of 1933 and 1934. Through 1973 only sixty-three players, of
ten thousand, have lasted twenty seasons, and twenty of them were
pitchers. Of the men on major-league rosters in 1915, Ruth's first
full season, only three played after 1934 and none after 1935. Ruth
turns out to have been one of the most toughly knit of all. Whatever
his early gluttonous excesses, they didn't shorten his playing life.

Practically all ballplayers retire in good health, and many live to
a great age. Why must they stop playing ball so early?

Mentally and physically they are a very select group. Testing for
baseball aptitude among male high-school graduates with little baseball experience, the Kansas City Royals' psychologist, in the years
1970 to 1973, learned that only one in fifteen hundred had good
enough eyes, speed, intelligence, and reaction time to make it worth
the cost of trying to teach him to play professional baseball in hope
of finding major-league talent. From which it seems safe to say that
sometime before age forty nearly every major-leaguer slips enough
to become one of the 1,499 normal males.

Assuming that all organs stay healthy, the legs go first. If *injury*
bars a man from further play, it is usually an injury that hampers
throwing—in shoulder, elbow, wrist, or the tendons of the arm.
What happens to the leg muscles is what happens to any elastic
substance that is stretched many times: it loses the power of snap-
ping back. Babe Ruth illustrates how undamaged players decay
until they slip down to the level of us average people. His legs failed
several years before his arm; his arm failed before his eyes. Lee Allen
of the Baseball Hall of Fame put it well: "The batting eye is the
last to go—Rogers Hornsby, at fifty-seven, could still hit line drives."
Even the journeyman major-leaguer seems to retain that marvelous
coordination. It takes as good coordination to fall away from an
inside pitch as it does to hit the ball. All of us have seen the lame,
overweight, dead-armed designated hitter alternately hit the dirt
and hit the ball. Ruth in his last playing years could do both.

THE ACCUMULATED BATTING FIGURES
BABE RUTH'S MAJOR-LEAGUE CAREER
1914–1934

at bat: 8307
hits: 2860
home runs: 708
runs batted in: 2210
average: .344

53 · They Could Have Him
for Nothing

When Joe Cronin left the Senators to go to the Red Sox after the 1934 season, there was more talk of Babe Ruth becoming a manager. As such things go the rumors were rather detailed: the offer by Griffith of fifteen thousand a year and a part of the gate receipts, and the counter-proposal by Ruth asking thirty thousand flat. But Clark Griffith quieted the gossip: "Ruth has never been regarded as a managerial possibility here by me, nor will he be so regarded . . . so far as the management of my ball club is concerned." He tried to soften his words by blending in a remark that Ruth was "managerial timber," which must have been searing comfort.

In the next week a promoter said he had offered Ruth thirty-five thousand dollars to play with the House of David, a team which owed its drawing power—if younger readers can believe it—to the fact that all its players had long hair and most had beards. There is no echo of the offer in any record.

> . . . **The big guy has a big, loose mouth. He pops off too damn much about a lot of things.**
> **—Lou Gehrig (on Babe Ruth), 1932**

The years from age thirty to thirty-nine are more often than not critical years in which a person changes his or her attitude to self and surroundings. If the change is uncomfortable, as it often is, it leads to anger and frustration, called "midcareer crisis." Babe Ruth paradoxically reversed the usual pattern. He knew more peace of mind in that span than before or after. Jocko Conlan told the author Ruth was especially civilized in the early 1930s. Excluding the World Series of 1932 he was frank, open, polite, and uncomplaining (to all but Joe McCarthy, one must add). The only symptom that met the crisis norm was a split with Lou Gehrig.

In his first years with the Yankees Gehrig had been a leading

Ruth fan and almost an errand boy for his idol. While Lou was single, Babe spent a lot of time with the Gehrig family and later said, "It was one of the rare tastes of home life I ever had."

Lou married on September 29, 1933. The Ruths were not invited to the wedding reception, though, to be fair, it was a small party as Fred Lieb, the dean of sportswriters, remembers it. Perhaps Eleanor Gehrig thought Babe and Lou should part? Like Claire, she was a woman of strong will (in a short time she entirely revised Lou's style of dress).

Babe and Lou could only be close as long as Lou was fan and Babe was hero. As Babe decayed and Lou became the pride of the Yankees, the relation had to change. Babe became a little envious of Lou. As peers they weren't suited. Lou always wore a coat and tie in the dining car, scolded younger players who looked sloppy in public, and, all in all, seemed to become a stuffier man as he became a greater ballplayer. The first private notice of a potential rift came during a rainy-day bridge game in 1932 when Lou and Babe paired against sportswriters. Babe bid wildly, and they lost thirty-three dollars. When Babe left Lou showed anger. He hadn't liked a remark Babe made after going down five tricks—"Jeez, I sure loused that one. I butchered it, like McCarthy handles the pitchers." Lou, a team man, didn't approve of that kind of talk with reporters. But they weren't near breaking yet. In December 1932 Lou took up golf because he wanted "to play with Babe Ruth."

Lou signed a magazine article in early 1933 in which he quoted Babe as having said in 1927, ". . . There's a lot of fun in this thing but the money is the thing we're after. It's all over there . . . behind those fences! That's where the money is. The more balls we hit over the wall, the more world series we'll get. Suppose we forget each other and remember that." (Graceless, if true, but it doesn't ring true; World Series shares were a trivial part of Babe's income.)

A kind of counter was Babe's remark to a reporter that Lou was shortening his career by playing every day. Naturally the reporter asked Lou's view. Lou said he was paid to play every day.

Thus to the chill between Ruth and McCarthy, and silence between Mrs. Ruth and Mrs. McCarthy, was added a tension between the Ruths and the Gehrigs. Then came a complete break. Dorothy Ruth visited the senior Gehrigs frequently, usually wearing the same favorite clothes. Lou's mother unwisely remarked that Dorothy, Claire's daughter by adoption, wasn't dressed as well as Julia, Claire's daughter by birth. (The Gehrigs certainly had a thing about clothes.) The innuendo traveled from Yankee wife to Yankee wife until it reached and angered Claire, who angered Babe. Using an intermediary in the clubhouse, Babe sent an oral message to Lou: "Never speak to me again off the ball field." On camera they

Courtesy of New York *Evening Journal*

Old "Wagon Wheels"—Still Rollin'—Home!
Burris Jenkins, Jr., in the New York *Evening Journal*

were officially friendly; elsewhere they ignored each other. Ruth had behaved stupidly, and Claire doesn't come out of the scene looking well.

> Of course all Japan has gone wild over him. He is a great deal more effective ambassador than I could ever be.
> —Joseph C. Grew, *Ten Years in Japan*

A team of fourteen American major-leaguers toured Japan in 1931. Ruth had planned to go. The Japanese offered him twenty-five thousand dollars to come, but he found he was committed to making some short films during the weeks of the tour. In 1933 the joint meeting of the leagues gave the Athletics permission to take a team from the American League to Japan after the 1934 World Series. Ruth was very pleased to be asked. Plans were all made by the following July. Connie Mack would go, but Ruth would be the manager. As it worked out, the schedule set seventeen games in Japan in November, followed by a game in Manila. The Yankee players were Ruth, Gomez, and Gehrig. The team sailed from Vancouver for Japan on October 19; most of the married players took their families along.

Before they left Babe Ruth discovered his true birthday. He thought he had been born on February 7, 1894, but his sister Mamie, helping to make up his passport application, found that the date was February 6, 1895 (it had been and still is entered that way in the Baltimore birth records). Ruth had received a passport for the unlucky Cuba caper of 1920 with an affidavit of birth sworn to by a Xaverian who accepted the wrong date. Claire, many years later, said Babe's quick reaction to the truth was to say, "I can play a year longer." Up to this time they had been celebrating the birthday with a party every February 7. They decided to keep it that way.

An American engineer, it is said, introduced the Japanese to baseball in 1889 by teaching railway laborers to play. Visiting American professors in later years kept it up. As early as 1905 there were respectable Japanese amateur teams.

The Japanese welcomed the American team of 1934 warmly. Ruth described it:

> The Japanese people treated us royally. I had a tough time with the crowds. When we arrived in Tokyo I got a great thrill with the crowd around the station. We simply couldn't move. I had an American flag in one hand and a Japanese flag in the other, but our car couldn't move without knocking down a Japanese. Then they would bob right up again like rubber balls.

Ruth played as if it were 1921 in the Polo Grounds. The opponents were mostly college teams and collections of local baseball celebrities. They fielded and pitched well but hit poorly. The Americans won all games by lopsided scores before crowds that filled parks bigger than any in the United States excepting Yankee Stadium and Cleveland's park. Ruth once diverted the customers by playing first base while holding a parasol to keep off a drizzle, and the American infielders enlivened dead moments by going through the double-play on ground balls when there were no runners on base. Ruth was such a favorite that Beibu Rusu was the first American to make his name a household noun in Japan.

The Japanese had set up four prizes for the tour: for highest batting average, most home runs, most runs batted in, and one for pitching. Gomez won the pitching prize. Ruth won all three batting prizes over Gehrig, Charlie Gehringer,* and Foxx. In seventeen games he batted .408, with thirteen home runs, and played every inning. His hosts heaped gifts on him, including two large vases with his Japanese batting feats worked on as ornament. (Ruth

---

* Charles Leonard Gehringer (1903–   ), second baseman, nineteen seasons, 1924–1942, Detroit, batting average .320. Hall of Fame.

destroyed all of his Japanese souvenirs except these two vases on December 7, 1941.)

There was, naturally, golf. With Lefty O'Doul, Ruth played in a foursome at Osaka against Ambassador Joseph C. Grew and Shiro Akaboshi, the champion of the Tokyo Golf Club. They managed fourteen holes before cameramen drove them to cover.

Ruth is still remembered in Japan. The baseball park at Osaka has a plaque comemorating his visit, the annual baseball day to encourage boys' baseball is called Babe Ruth Day, and about twenty years later the tally of a newspaper poll to discover the most famous persons in Japan in the previous four decades listed only one foreigner, Babe Ruth.

But there was an unpleasantness, according to Connie Mack: "We knew our rooms were constantly being searched and that they shadowed us wherever we went."

From Japan the team went to Manila. The Americans suggested

Ruth's face alone was enough of a symbol to advertise the Japanese tour of 1934. (*National Baseball Library, Cooperstown, New York.*)

dividing the professionals so that each team would be half Philippine. The crowd wouldn't have it that way and angrily threw litter on the field in protest. So the Americans played the locals and won 24–1.

The tourists were ready to come home by December 13. Most of them recrossed the Pacific, but the Ruths, the Gehrigs, and others came home by way of Europe. The Ruths and Gehrigs traveled separately. Of all Asiatic sights Bali impressed Ruth most, "but when you see those women, billed as the most beautiful in the world, walking down the street chewing red tobacco—."

Once arrived in Europe the Ruths visited Switzerland where Babe managed to ski without breaking an ankle and enjoyed bobsledding. Thence to Paris where he might have had a memorable time in the early 1920s. In 1935 he said, "Paris ain't much of a town." There was something of vanity in it; nobody recognized him in the streets. He was angry when the United States Consulate listed his name in its unclaimed-mail column. At home, he said, people could get a letter to him merely by pasting his picture on the envelope. He passed up night life and much of the tourist round, finally fleeing from obscurity to visit an American school. It was depressing. The children knew who he was, but many of these disinherited small people had never seen a ball game, never learned how to hold a bat. To add to depression, Claire fell ill with influenza for twelve days.

Babe talked with a Paris correspondent of *The Times* about the prospect of managing: "Club owners can be awful funny when they want to. A ballplayer's supposed to be dumb and know nothing. When they get a ballplayer who thinks, they get suspicious." The relevance of these words is so dim they hardly seem worth a cable. The Paris writer had a rumor that Babe would join the 101 Ranch Wild West Show, but Babe couldn't imagine what he'd do in a circus. If he left baseball he'd play golf, shoot, and take life easy. And then the recurring theme from long-gone Baltimore poverty: "I've got enough money. I don't have to worry."

I could make one of the world's greatest batsmen out of him.

—Alan Fairfax, cricket teacher (1935)

Claire recovered in time for the February 6 birthday party, and then they flew to London where Babe perked up. He found a cavernous underground cricket school where his name was known. He took lessons. Clad in the pads he hit two fast bowlers to all fields. Rejecting the classic cricket stance, he hit as a baseball player, breaking wood off the edges of the flat bat and finally breaking the bat at the handle. He then bowled for fifteen minutes with no

Taking lessons in cricket, Thames House, London,
February 9, 1935. (*National Baseball Library, Cooperstown, New York.*)

success. All present enjoyed an argument on two points: whether a
bowler bowled faster than a pitcher pitched, and whether a cricket
batsman could really hit the ball six hundred feet on the fly. Babe
took the negative on both. When he heard that a really good professional player made as much as forty dollars a week he was shocked.
"What a racket that is! What's chances of me buying into one of
those football or cricket clubs?"

They sailed for America in mid-February. Exiled ex-mayor
Jimmy Walker and others of the American colony saw them off.
Julia said sadly, "I was in museums all the time," but Babe had
more fun in London than anywhere else on the trip.

The ship *Manhattan* brought the Ruths into New York harbor on
February 20, 1935, with the orchestra playing "Take Me Out to the
Ball Game." They had been gone four months. Artie McGovern
went down the bay to meet them. His expert eye told him Babe
weighed about 240 pounds. ("I've cut out using bread and butter
and that has aided me a lot.") Babe said he had a great trip and
wouldn't do it again for half a million bucks.

Getting down to serious matters he told the ship reporters he wouldn't sign a contract to play. "I think I'm entitled to a manager's job, or a try at it anyhow." If he were to sign as a player he would be no more than a pinch-hitter.

Then the reporters gave him *their* big story. Ruppert and Barrow had mailed him a contract at one dollar a year.

Did the junket actually achieve anything? There were some visible results.

Ruth's pay was twelve thousand dollars and expenses, or a third as much as his season salary from the Yankees. His comment on the pay of British professionals led to a movement to raise their salaries (with no famous results).

Lou Gehrig, who reached New York before the Ruths, carried himself as a man who had put off a great weight. He was now, for sure, the ranking Yankee.

The Japanese organized four professional teams in 1934 and 1935, and had a professional league going by 1936.

And what of the international good will such tours are supposed to further? The "Monthly Political Report for the Foochow [China] Consular District for November, 1934" arrived at the Department of State on January 3, where it was stamped CONFIDENTIAL and read and initialed by an Assistant Secretary of State, seven persons in the Division of Far Eastern Affairs, the Legal Adviser, and the Economic Adviser. Copies went to Military Intelligence and the Office of Naval Intelligence. Under the heading "Miscellaneous," Vice-Consul Gordon Lee Burke wrote:

Many local Americans and Japanese alike speak with enthusiasm of the good will that Babe Ruth and his team mates are creating with their baseball in Japan. The feeling is that Babe and his colleagues will do much to offset the talk of war machines at the London Naval Conference.

That was blither. Earlier foreign junkets had encouraged the export sale of sporting goods, as their organizers intended. Ben Shibe was the original mover of the 1934 tour. The Shibe family had interests in both the Athletics and in the sporting-goods business. The tour opened a new market.

Matsu Taro Shoriki, the publisher of the third largest Tokyo newspaper, had sponsored the tour in Japan and saw every game. A member of the Warlike Gods Society stabbed him not quite to death on February 21, 1935. The would-be assassin, after his arrest, said Shoriki was unpatriotic in promoting the baseball exhibitions which took money out of Japan during hard times. The New York office of a Japanese steamship line apologized to Babe Ruth, saying the tour was "one of the best means of promoting the Japanese nation's understanding of true Yankee spirit." If that meant New York Yankee spirit, it was correct.

> If Connie Mack or anyone else wants him as manager, the Babe can have his release.
> —Edward G. Barrow, October 27, 1935

The Athletics were in money trouble in 1934. The club owed seven hundred thousand dollars to a bank which needed four hundred thousand of it to stay liquid. Mack got the four hundred thousand by stocking the Red Sox with players for whom Tom Yawkey paid over a period of three years. It was all very gloomy for Mr. Mack who was seventy-one years old. He was finding it impossible to show his once-famous patience with young players, but as late as August 1934 a writer went out of his way to say he was "the only Big League manager whose possible retirement is never mentioned in sport-page gossip." (Mack owned part of the Athletics.)

To everybody's surprise the Associated Press photographed Mack and Ruth together on the oriental tour and captioned the picture with a guess that Mack would retire to his front office and let Ruth manage his team. Doing our own guessing, we may suppose Shibe and Mack asked Ruth to manage the tourists to see whether he *could* manage. Ruth, on arriving in Japan, was wholly ignorant of the rumor, but Ruppert told quizzical reporters the Yankees wouldn't stand in Ruth's way if another club wished to have him .as manager, and Barrow added they could have him for nothing. In Japan Mack said only that he hadn't thought about it because he hadn't believed he could afford the price. Before Mack left for Japan he told people in Philadelphia he would manage until he was eighty. A new group of reporters brought it up when the wanderers came to Manila, but the only statement they could cable was Ruth's —he would not sign a contract as a player. Everybody noticed that the Athletics hadn't discussed the question of Ruth's status with the Yankees, as baseball law required before they could talk with Ruth.

Mack came home the way he went and was tracked across the country by reporters. He gave them all the same testy answer—he'd manage the Athletics until he was eighty.

We know now that Mack had thought of hiring Ruth as field manager. He even said Ruth, if he were a manager, would be the only manager anybody would buy a ticket to see.

What put Mack off was the Ruth-Gehrig feud which split the shipload of baseball travelers into two chilly parts. And he blamed Claire for it. During spring training in 1935 Mack told Joe Williams that Claire was too strong an influence. "I couldn't have made

Babe manager. His wife would have been running the club in a month."

Babe Ruth never knew he had a real chance to manage the Athletics. The episode was quietly buried. Neither Mack, in his memoirs, nor his two ablest biographers mentioned it.

Thus passed Ruth's third chance to be a major-league manager. He lost Detroit because he didn't take time to meet with the owner. The finesse to bring him to the Dodgers by way of the Reds failed, though he wasn't informed of the scheme. Now he missed a chance with the Athletics because the senseless break with the Gehrigs made so many people uncomfortable. Babe and Claire's trouble was that they thought a managership should, of right, come to Babe on a silver tray.

Perhaps Claire wasn't really warmed by the idea of being a manager's wife. Most managerial careers have been nasty, brutish, and short. Better for Babe to be a retired hero than a fired failure—or so she might have thought. In any case, few good things come without effort. There would be a day when Leo Durocher, by example, would teach the Ruths the art of becoming a manager.

As to Mack's feelings, if Claire *had* run the Athletics she couldn't have done much worse than Mack did in 1935—five and a half games behind the seventh-place Browns.

Outside the Park, 1935

AARD-VARK ARRIVES
AT CENTRAL PARK ZOO

1 OF 3 MARRIED COUPLES CHILDLESS

S. S. PRESIDENT HARDING
SAILS WITH 96 DEPORTEES

HOARE AND LAVAL UNITE
ON ETHIOPIAN PEACE PLAN

WILLIAM BOYD LOSES $19,200
AT POKER ON S. S. EUROPA

PRES. CONANT RULES FACULTY
MUST SIGN MASS. TEACHERS OATH

MAKING PRIME LOANS
AT RATE OF 1% YEARLY

SOUTH AFRICAN LEADER
SUPPORTS GERMAN DEMAND
FOR COLONIES IN AFRICA

U.S. SKATING TEAM
SAILS FOR OLYMPICS

DEVELOPS NON-EXPLOSIVE SOLID GASOLINE

$2000 IN GOLD COINS DUG UP

HOOVER ATTENDS
ALUMNI REUNION

GETS $25 IN SUIT
FOR CURLS BURNED
BY BEAUTY OPERATOR

JEHOVAH'S WITNESSES REFUSE FLAG SALUTE, EXPELLED

54 · To Get Rid of a Demigod
(1935)

I've always been a big leaguer.
—Babe Ruth, January 1934

Babe Ruth's unwillingness to quit was discomfiting to Jacob Ruppert. How do you get rid of a demigod who won't go quietly? The Newark club of the International League offered a possible exit. In the winter of 1933–34* Ruppert offered Ruth the job of managing Newark, which nowadays seems a fair offer. He could prove his ability and could live at home. Newark was the Yankees' senior farm club, stocked with promising players, but Ruth thought it would be a step downward. Ed Barrow hinted that success in Newark could lead to higher things. Ruth was firm. Barrow tried to enlist Claire, but she told Babe he'd been in the major leagues for so many years he should stay in the majors. Christy Walsh also advised Babe not to go to Newark on the ground that the Yankee job would fall to him if he would only wait. Walsh later regretted his advice.

On press day at McGovern's gymnasium, early in 1934, Ruth told the reporters he found the offer wounding. It would be the same, he said, "as to ask Colonel Ruppert, one of the foremost brewers in the country, to run a soda fountain."

Babe was here unpleasantly childish, and so encouraged by the two people he most trusted, Claire and Walsh. It is interesting to speculate on what Ruppert might have done for Babe if he had been a smashing winner at Newark. McCarthy had yet to make his great reputation. Writers called him Second-Place Joe.

In Ruppert's mind, Ruth's scorn for the Newark job was clinching evidence that Ruth would thereafter be useless to the Yankees.

---

* Claire and Babe both dated the offer wrongly in their memoirs. Claire makes it 1932 and Babe 1935. Babe mentioned it to reporters as a recent offer on January 3, 1934 (*The Times*, Jan. 4, 1934).

After Ruth's pitiable season of 1934 his future career was a matter of common talk, with sense and nonsense mixed. Nearly every club had its manager by November. An unnamed owner said few owners would gamble on Ruth's "ability to maintain discipline," and there were doubts that he had the patience to try to rebuild a weak team. Colonel T. L. Huston, former co-owner of the Yankees, said he'd like to buy the Dodgers and make Ruth the manager. There was a rumor that the Yankees would trade Ruth to the White Sox for Al Simmons, and Ruth would manage the Sox.

A few days after the White Sox rumor fluttered and died, the Ruths came home from their world tour to find the one-dollar contract. Babe went to see Ruppert. Was Ruppert satisfied with McCarthy? Yes, wasn't Babe? No, we could have finished closer in 1934. Ruth was asking for McCarthy's job. Ruppert found the conversation distasteful, but he was already nearing the final solution of the Babe Ruth problem. He advised Ruth to have a talk with Barrow, which turned out to be interesting to both.

> **I don't get a cent out of it.**
> **—Jacob Ruppert, February 26, 1935**

Babe went away to shoot pheasants. To surprised reporters (there were *always* reporters) he said he had talked with Barrow and would continue as a player. The writers called Barrow who diverted attention by saying all he knew was that Babe phoned him, claimed he weighed only 238 pounds (not 260 as charged), and would bring Barrow a couple of pheasants. Claire denied knowing anything. Such denials are often tips that the yeast is working.

The Yankees invited the press to Ruppert's offices at the brewery on the very next day. It was dark, rainy, sleety, and snowy. Ruth, Ruppert, and Emil Fuchs, chief of the Boston Braves, all three dressed in somber blue serge, met them. The purpose of the meeting was to tell the world Babe Ruth was going to the Braves as player, "assistant manager," and vice-president. Ruppert made a speech, recalling that Ruth once said he looked on Ruppert as a father. Ruth interrupted: "I shoulda said Santa Claus." Ruppert added that Fuchs wouldn't have to pay anything for Ruth.

A reporter asked Ruth what a vice-president of the Braves would do. He didn't know. Fuchs answered for him. "Advisory capacity; be consulted on club deals and so forth." Ruppert tried to lighten the mood: "A vice-president signs checks. Everybody knows that."

The reporters figured that Ruth would some day succeed the Braves' veteran manager Bill McKechnie. "It is expected," wrote *The Times* man, "McKechnie will be promoted to an executive berth with the club." Looking back, we can see that was as happy a forecast as saying McKechnie was to become vice-president of Penn-Central.

Ruth's journey back to where he came from was no sudden happening. We need to go back some months to see the preparation for the blue-serge show of February 26, 1935.

Emil Fuchs had been a New York City magistrate, and before that he was the lawyer for Arnold Rothstein, the man at the top of the pyramid of gamblers who fixed the 1919 World Series. Fuchs must have been no knave, since Commissioner Landis made no objection when he and his associates, including Christy Mathewson, bought the Braves for four hundred thousand dollars in 1922. Fuchs tried for awhile to manage the Braves. George Sisler knew him well. He was "a nice man, but entirely out of place on the bench. Johnny Evers, coaching third base for us, would be looking in for a sign, and the judge would be telling jokes." In the whole period of Fuchs's control (1923–1935) the Braves sometimes rose to the level of mediocrity but not often.

Under Fuchs the club never made more than a hundred and fifty thousand dollars in a season and was having money trouble as early as 1928, the year when the books of marginal businesses began to predict the Great Depression. Fuchs survived 1928 by selling Rogers Hornsby to the Cubs for two hundred thousand. One trouble of both Boston teams was the city's ban on Sunday baseball. When the bankers thrust C. F. Adams into the Braves' front office to watch their interest, Adams bought the repeal of the Sunday prohibition ordinance from the City Council for thirty thousand dollars, paid a thousand-dollar fine for corrupt practices, and was well ahead.

The club's best season was 1933. It was in the pennant chase for awhile, drew half a million customers, and made a hundred and fifty thousand. Fuchs spent the money for ill-chosen players instead of paying debts. In 1934 the team slumped again and lost $44,038. At the owners' meeting in December there was talk that Fuchs would try to play home games at Fenway and make Braves Field into a dog track, but in January the use of Fenway was "firmly refused."

National League owners hoped Adams could take over the Braves, but he was too busy. He already owned the hockey Bruins and was helping in the building of Suffolk Downs. Adams said he was in the Braves' office only to oblige his banking friends. The National League had a thirteen-hour debate about dog racing on baseball diamonds and finally forbade it, knowing that Landis wouldn't tolerate such a mixture. Fuchs was eleven thousand dollars behind in his rent. The other owners were of a mind to tell him to solve his money problems or give the franchise back to the league, but they helped a little by leasing Braves Field itself and guaranteeing the rent for eleven years. The leasing was not so much to favor Fuchs but to repel greyhounds and the tote board. Fuchs set up a season-ticket sales committee made up of the governors of Massachusetts and Maine and forty Massachusetts mayors. They sold forty-three thousand dollars' worth of tickets by February 6. Fuchs said he had been offered cash for Wally Berger* and another player, but for sake of the fans he wouldn't sell. The obvious question: What about Babe Ruth? Fuchs said Ruth belonged to the Yankees, "and so I cannot make any comment . . ." (February 5).

As long as Ruth made no move, Ruppert had a burden. He hardly dared to throw a nation's hero overboard, so he tried to resign himself to the painful prospect of signing Ruth for 1935 at twenty thousand dollars. But the situation had dangers. Ruth had asked for McCarthy's job. It would be hard on McCarthy to have Hercules on the bench beside him most of the summer. A newspaper poll in New York showed that Ruth was still popular enough to stir vast sympathy. By himself Ruppert could do nothing except wait for the explosion. But Massachusetts forces, uncontrolled by the Yankee owner, were at work to save him.

When Tom Yawkey bought the Red Sox across town from the Braves, he seriously thought of getting Ruth as a manager. Eddie Collins, vice-president and business manager of the Red Sox, spoke against the notion; Ruth, he said, was too independent to work with the front office. On the last day of the 1934 season in Boston forty-six thousand people paid to say goodbye to Babe Ruth. Yawkey's feeling for Ruth reawakened. Collins won again, urging Yawkey to buy Joe Cronin for the job, which Yawkey did. In November 1934 James Michael Curley was elected governor of Massachusetts. His campaign manager was Emil Fuchs. Curley told Fuchs he should bring Ruth back to Boston with the Braves. Fuchs was so trapped in problems of cash and credit he wasn't free to move until February, when his stately commitee of governors and mayors sold enough tickets to wipe out the red ink of 1934.

Adams and Fuchs decided to humor Curley. There was a leak from the owners' meeting in December: Ruppert had told Adams the Yankees wouldn't stand in the way of Ruth going to the Braves as "assistant manager," but all concerned denied it warmly. In late January the rumors ran out like ripples in a pool: the Braves at home in Fenway Park, C. F. Adams president of the Braves, and, most interesting, Babe Ruth manager of the Braves.

Ruppert, who had been inwardly groaning against fate, sounded

* Walter Antone Berger (1905–   ), outfielder, eleven seasons, 1930–1940, Braves, Giants, Reds, Phillies, batting average .300.

out Fuchs in February. Fuchs was ready to be sounded out and told his caller that the Braves would take Babe Ruth if they could get him as a free agent.

The Ruths hadn't been back in the country ten days before Ruppert invited Fuchs down to settle for Ruth. Barrow immediately got waivers from all American League owners by telegraph and telephone. Ruth knew nothing of this. Fuchs played it sly. He wangled dinner at the Ruths on a Sunday evening, and his sketch of Boston possibilities stirred Babe to phone Ruppert at his country place. Babe innocently introduced Fuchs to Ruppert over the phone, and Ruppert asked that Ruth and Fuchs meet him at the brewery the next morning.

At the brewery Ruth, in forlorn hope, asked Ruppert whether he was still satisfied with McCarthy. Ruppert still was. Ruth finally gave up the idea of managing the Yankees, and they got down to the business which led to the public announcement of the Braves' new "assistant manager" and vice-president. Ruth was a lion on the baseball diamond but a mouse in dealing with Fuchs and Ruppert. He didn't know that Fuchs, once a millionaire, was teetering on the edge of bankruptcy, nor that the Braves were barely afloat. Worse, he didn't know Bill McKechnie had been kept in the dark.

He didn't know Emil Fuchs and Jacob Ruppert staged the playlet of Emil dining with Babe and Claire, tempting them with titles, and getting Babe to call Ruppert. Fuchs wanted to bring Ruth to Boston; Ruppert wanted to get Ruth out of New York. They both succeeded. Ruppert thus got rid of his demigod in a seemingly dignified way, and Fuchs satisfied the whim of Governor Curley, chief of his ticket-sellers. And it was faintly possible that Fuchs could still squeeze some profit out of Ruth's popularity.

Just what *was* Ruth to do as a Brave? Fuchs put it in writing three days before the press conference at the brewery. The letter has so many cloudy passages the reader should see it.

Feb. 23, 1935.

Mr. George H. Ruth, New York, N.Y.

My Dear George: In order that we may have a complete understanding, I am putting in the form of a letter the situation affecting our long-distance conversation of yesterday.

The Boston Braves offer you the following inducements, under the terms and conditions herein set forth, in order to have you sign a uniform contract plus an additional contract which will further protect you, both contracts to be filed.

1. The Boston club offers you a straight salary contract.

2. They offer you an official executive position as an officer of the corporation.

3. The Boston club offers you also the position, for 1935, of assistant manager.

4. They offer you a share of the profits during the term of this contract.

5. They offer you an option to purchase, at a reasonable figure, some of the stock of the club.

6. The details of the amounts agreed upon will be the basis of a separate contract which shall be a personal one between you and the club, and as the case may be, with the individual officials and stockholders of the club.

In consideration of this offer, the Boston club naturally will expect you to do everything in your power for the welfare and interest of the club and will expect that you will endeavor to play in the games whenever possible, as well as carry out the duties above specified.

May I also give you the picture as I see it, which in my opinion, will terminate to the best and mutual interest of all concerned.

You have been a great asset to all baseball, especially to the American League, but nowhere in the land are you more admired than in the territory of New England that has always claimed you as its own and where you started your career to fame.

The fans of New England have a great deal of affection for you, and from my personal experience with them are the most appreciative men and women in America, providing, of course, that you keep faith, continue your generous cooperation in helping civically and being a source of consolation to the children, as well as the needy, who look up to you as a shining example of what the great athletes and public figures of America should be.

I say frankly, from my experience of forty years interest in baseball, that your greatest value to a ball club would be your personal appearance on the field, and particularly your participation in the active playing of exhibition games, on the ball field in championship games, as well as the master-minding and psychology of the game, in which you would participate as assistant manager.

As a player, I have observed and admired your baseball intelligence, for during your entire career I have never seen you make a wrong play or throw a ball to the wrong base, which leads us to your ability to manage a major league base-ball club. In this respect we both are fortunate in having so great a character as Bill McKechnie, our present manager of the club, who has given so much to baseball and whom I count among my closest friends. Bill McKechnie's entire desire would be for the success of the Braves, especially financially, as he is one of the most unselfish, devoted friends that a man can have.

That spirit of McKechnie's is entirely returned by me, and I know by my colleagues in the ball club. They feel, as I do, that nothing would ever be done until we have amply rewarded Manager McKechnie for his loyalty, his ability and sincerity, which means this, George, that if it was determined, after your affiliation with the ball club in 1935, that it was for the mutual interest of the club for you to take up the active management on the field, there would be absolutely no handicap in having you so appointed.

It may be that you will want to devote your future years to becoming an owner or part owner of a major league ball club. It may be that you may discover that what the people are really looking forward to and appreciate in you is the color and activity that you give to the game by virtue of your hitting and playing and that you would rather have some one else, accustomed to the hardships and drudgery of managing a ball club, continue that task.

So that if we could enter into the spirit of that agreement, such understanding might go on indefinitely, always having in mind that we owe a duty to the public of New England, that I have personally learned to love for its sense of fairness and loyalty, and it is also in this spirit that I hope we may be able to jot down a few figures of record that will prove satisfactory to all concerned.

Sincerely yours,
EMIL E. FUCHS, *President.*

The numbered paragraph 2, which Fuchs told the press meant "vice-president," meant nothing at all. A "share of the profits" and a stock option *might* be valuable. Only time would tell. As time told it, the privileges wouldn't have been valuable until the late 1940s, long after Fuchs and Ruth left the Braves. Fuchs so hedged around the possibilities of Ruth becoming manager of the Braves that Ruth had no real claim to anything except a salary contract.

The letter is not evidence of ill will; it is just the work of the inexact and foggy mind of a desperate man who hopes that things will turn out well and that nobody will be angry.

Ruth replied with a gushy, empty letter. Among other things he would be pleased to play with Rabbit Maranville. He and Maranville, he said, were "the last of the two Mohicans."

What of McKechnie? It was all news to him. He could perhaps find some comfort in recalling a remark by Fuchs just five weeks earlier: "We feel McKechnie has been a very satisfactory manager for us and he can stay with me as long as he remains in baseball."

> **That act won the Yankees the John Wilkes Booth award by acclamation.**
>
> —Jim Murray (1972)

Ruppert's transfer of Ruth helped the Yankees as a baseball team. Joe McCarthy was in full command, Gehrig was a free spirit, and team morale was high. Shirt No. 3 passed to George Selkirk,* who heard himself booed when he first dutifully wore it. But many Ruth fans were wounded when Ruppert let Fuchs carry off their hero. Certainly the Yankees lost color and character. As late as 1972 an unforgiving admirer of Ruth said of the team he left, "They were as exciting as watching a master plumber tighten a joint."

Ruth probably made a bad choice. If he wouldn't leave while still a champion (and very few do), he would have been wise to take the advice of his close friend, the sportswriter Dan Daniel, to say nothing and let Ruppert stew. Daniel told him the Braves' finances were shaky and that if he stayed with the Yankees they would probably keep him for life. Another close friend, Bill Slocum, also advised against going to Boston.

But Ruth was one of nature's optimists who always figure the maximum profit instead of the minimum. He translated Fuchs's blurred promises as meaning he would certainly be a baseball executive, and he liked to accept the general belief that he would become the playing manager of the Braves.

---

* George Alexander Selkirk (1908–   ), outfielder, nine seasons, 1934–1942, Yankees, batting average .290.

As ballplayers would say, the Yankees got a lot of bad ink out of the deal. It would be useful to recapitulate the Yankee motives.

Ruth couldn't play well but was as popular as ever, which made him a nuisance. Ed Barrow had so much trouble getting along with him that he couldn't begin to think Ruth would ever be able to manage a ball club. Barrow was Ruppert's most trusted baseball adviser.

By asking for McCarthy's job Ruth brought on a showdown. McCarthy offered to quit in the winter of 1934–1935 if Ruppert thought it would help solve the Ruth Problem. But Ruppert wanted McCarthy, and if he had to choose between McCarthy and Ruth the choice was easy.

One solution would have been to play Ruth at first base. If Lou Gehrig hadn't been born Ruth might have played a season or two more at first base. But Babe was through as a player. Even Claire didn't like to see him play anymore, always fearing to see him leave on a stretcher. "He was hurt three times last season and I want no more of that."

The Ruth Problem was *not* a payroll problem. The Yankees drew a quarter of a million more in 1934 than in 1933. It was the problem of the discontented, worn-out star who despised his manager, made his manager think of quitting, and had to be sent away in some manner that seemed decent to the public.

Ruth and Fuchs worked out terms that satisfied both. The uniform baseball contract was for one year at a sum variously stated as twenty-five thousand and forty thousand. A separate three-year contract provided a share of the gross receipts above the average of the previous five years. Fuchs said he believed Ruth would make between forty and fifty thousand a year. The agreement was of doubtful promise to any but the most wishful thinker. The only real assets of the Braves were the preseason ticket sale, a very good ballplayer, Wally Berger, two or three adequate journeymen ballplayers, and a crumbling monument named Babe Ruth.

All the National League owners mechanically handed out praises of the deal, Mayor Fiorello LaGuardia and Bill Terry approved, and *The Times*'s ritual editorial said, "To have been a distinguished name in 1914 *[sic]* and to be still a great name in 1935 is a rare distinction in any field, including the outfield." Colonel T. L. Huston was bubbly: "The finest thing that could happen to baseball, especially the National League."

Lefty Gomez thought Ruppert and Barrow had made a mistake. Ruth had been the best of the oriental tourists and could still drive in runs. Further, he "managed the team during our trip and from what I saw I think he will make a good big league leader." Dizzy

Dean* looked on Ruth as a carpetbagger who had made all his money in the American League, getting a salary higher than any player was worth, and now was putting good ole Bill McKechnie's job in peril. Up in Buffalo Joe McCarthy was frosty: "I wish Ruth all possible luck, and that's all I will say about the deal." Through all the hullabaloo in the press the bookmakers stood firm. Before and after the news the Yankees were 5 to 2 to win in the American League, and the Braves were 40 to 1 in the National League.

With rather pathetic self-importance Ruth gave his views on how he would behave as a manager. He would be a disciplinarian without a whip.

You must have the good-will of men under you and you can never earn it by browbeating. A friendly slap on the back will do more than all the abusive criticism you can deliver, and that is the way I intend to work.

These words read as banal commonplaces unless we see them as Ruth's way of getting his own back against Ed Barrow and Miller Huggins.

Claire said she always loved Boston.

He will be plenty able to handle the job. Shouldn't I know?

—Claire Ruth, February 28, 1935

Fuchs and Adams hastily put together a civic feast of welcome in Boston at the Copley-Plaza Hotel on February 28. When Babe and Claire got off the train a milling crowd of thousands was out of control. Police formed a wedge and forced a path through the mass as Babe and Claire, sweating freely, walked to the hotel. Claire was pleased by the shrill uproar of hundreds of small boys at whom Babe, muttering "Jiminy! Jiminy!" waved his indisputable brown cap until his arm was sore.

At lunch a strange woman greeted them at their table. To Babe: "I hope you make a lot of touchdowns this year." The confusion was an eerie omen of the Boston venture as a whole.

Ruth told the press there would be no friction with McKechnie. "I will work with him in complete harmony." He would play in the outfield "wherever the sun isn't."

After-dinner speeches were the usual claptrap until C. F. Adams arose. Apparently having second thoughts about the whole thing, he

---

* Jay Hanna Dean (1911–1974), pitcher, twelve seasons, 1930–1947 (pitched five innings after 1940), Cardinals, Cubs, Browns. Won 150, lost 83, earned-run average 3.03. Hall of Fame.

spoke with a bluntness uncommon on such occasions. After advising the diners not to be too hopeful yet, he said:

> We must not forget that Bill McKechnie is frank, honest and correct when he says there can be but one boss.
> No one is fit to give orders until he can take them himself. Judging from Ruth's past career we can hardly consider him of managerial calibre now. I certainly hope he will merit promotion as manager of the Braves. He has much to learn within the next few months. He must prove himself to be a good soldier if he is not that already, and he must gain the loyalty of his team-mates.

Protecting McKechnie's interest, he went on to say that if Ruth became the manager, McKechnie would be

> my personal representative in the Braves organization, speak and act for me and have my unqualified proxy to carry on whatever official responsibilities and authority I properly should shoulder.

Talleyrand, Metternich, or Kissinger would have found a good deal to think about in Adams's stern speech, but simple hope is blind to the stark visions always in the mind of a Boston banker. We might expect resentment, at least, but there is no sign that anyone even listened carefully.

Claire and Babe cheerfully returned to New York on the midnight train to pack for the trip to Florida.

Getting Babe was a spur to the Curley ticket-selling machine. Within a week of the Babe Ruth dinner it was certain that advance sales would exceed a hundred thousand dollars. Fuchs and Adams also now managed to sell some stock in their baseball company.

In Florida Bill McKechnie* did his duty by praising the signing of Ruth. He was a thin-faced Scot whose looks fitted the adjective dour, but he is remembered as "good-natured, firm, sensible." He had an instant problem: his first baseman was too good to bench, and he was satisfied with his outfield, such as it was. Where to play Ruth?

He soon had a graver problem: Ruth's confidence that he would succeed McKechnie in 1936. Fuchs bumblingly said, "Ruth has an

---

* William Boyd McKechnie (1886–1965), infielder, eleven seasons, 1907–1920, Pirates, Braves, Yankees, Indianapolis Federals, Newark Federals, Reds, Giants, batting average .251. Manager, twenty-five seasons, 1915–1946, Newark Federals, Cardinals, Pirates, Braves, Reds, won 1,898, lost 1,724. Hall of Fame.

agreement that he will manage the club if certain conditions develop. The pledge is not definite in the sense that it is irrevocably binding." Perhaps Ruth wouldn't wish to manage. But he could be manager "if he wants it." Ruth was a lot more definite than Fuchs. Fuchs was plainly embarrassed and said that the letter to Ruth spoke for itself.

The Boston arrangement comes down to this: Fuchs tempted Ruth by stirring hope of a managership; Fuchs and Adams were not going to do wrong by McKechnie; Fuchs desperately hoped Ruth's ambition to be a manager was a passing caprice. If Fuchs had been brighter we could call him a villain, but the whole affair shows both Fuchs and Ruth as sufficiently dull witted to negotiate themselves into an impossible position. As for Adams, he was the agent of Fuch's creditors and concerned with nothing else except doing the decent thing by McKechnie.

Could the Braves possibly make Babe Ruth happy?

55 · Sore Smitten

The Ruths left Penn Station on March 3, bound for Florida on the Orange Blossom Special. Babe weighed about 230 pounds, and his tan matched his clothes—brown from head to foot. About three thousand people met the train at St. Petersburg, "the most tumultuous reception any individual ball player or ball club ever received here." It took fifteen minutes to get him out of the crowd and take him away through the freight terminal. All of the planned ceremonies of welcome were abandoned. When he was in a position to talk he said he was very happy. "I feel better than I have felt in four years." When Ruth and McKechnie met, Babe guaranteed his meekness: "Anything you say goes with me."

Ruth worked out the next day after borrowing pants and socks. He drew a crowd of thirty-five hundred. An ancient augur might have noticed that he hit a woman with one foul ball and dented a car top with another. People kept probing McKechnie's feelings until he was fed up and said,

> Ruth's title as assistant manager means nothing particularly. He will be called into conference as a member of the board of strategy . . . whenever anything comes up for discussion. Nothing will be held back from him. We'll get along all right, I'm sure. If any trouble develops between Ruth and myself you can be assured it will not be caused by me.

He thought Ruth could end some worries if he hit well. But exactly seven days later McKechnie felt he had to deny there was any strife among the Braves. His trouble was that Ruth was still sure he would be the next manager and chattered about it at will. McKechnie said only neither he nor Ruth would make *that* decision.

All of this was in the kingdom of private relations. Ruth's former ghost writer, Ford C. Frick, was now president of the National

League and, to promote *public* relations, twice during spring training called on all to witness how lucky the league was to have Ruth.
"Baseball needs color and Ruth will supply it. . . ." The president of
the American League, Will Harridge, manfully joined his peer by
predicting, "He'll fill every park. . . ." Frick saw Harridge and
raised him, saying Ruth would increase National League attendance
by half a million.

Dizzy Dean climbed on board the bandwagon and got some
more ink by saying he spoke out against Ruth only because he
feared for McKechnie's job. Ole Diz showed a houseman's flair by
taking all bets of people who believed that Ruth would get a home
run in his first four times at bat against Dean, at even money (the
arithmetical odds would favor Dean about 15 to 1). Dean and several other Cardinals then drove fifty miles across Florida to see
Ruth play. When Dean posed with Ruth for a fraternal photograph,
Mickey Cochrane of the Tigers rebuked Ruth for friendship with
those World Champion National Leaguers who had behaved so
badly in the 1934 World Series that they provoked a riot in Detroit.

In the first Braves intrasquad game Ruth played first base and
hit a home run. Attendance: about four thousand (paid). In the
first true exhibition, on a windy unpromising day, the Braves beat
the Reds 5–3. Ruth played six innings, all at first base. Attendance:
about thirty-five hundred. In a game with the Yankees the attendance of 4,726 broke the Florida record dating back to 1923. Ruth
played in the outfield (not well) and had a single in three times at
bat. On the next day the same teams drew about two thousand.
Ruth had a single in four times at bat. In the first eight exhibition
games the Braves drew twenty thousand, enough to pay for spring
training, perhaps enough to show a profit. At this rate they might
draw over a hundred thousand before they reached Boston. A game
against the Cardinals, with Dean pitching well enough to hold Ruth
hitless (and win all of those well-hustled bets), drew 6,467, breaking the new record with a crash. And Ruth home runs? Well, no.
Only in that intrasquad game. The best the sportswriters could
say was that two of his Florida fly-outs were long enough to have
been home runs in most major-league parks. On a day when Ruth
had to miss a Yankee game because of a stomach upset, attendance
dropped to twelve hundred.

The fans were not so much paying to see baseball as to see a
national historical monument. Babe Ruth himself was depressed.
The only fun he had was fishing in the Gulf of Mexico. He had
played well, the last guttering of the candle, in Japan, but now he
faced American pitching. "The kids were striking me out or making
me pop up. . . . It was a rotten feeling." He tried to do right by the
flattering big crowds, but "the harder I tried the worse I did." The

legs were gone. Having missed Artie McGovern's tune-up, working out in Florida for Ruth "just was torture." And what had never been thought since he played on the small boys' field at St. Mary's Industrial School: ". . . baseball was drudgery."

It's uncanny the way Ruth delivers when he is under pressure.
—Bill Terry, April 17, 1935

Twenty-five thousand people came to see the Braves open in Boston against the Giants on April 16. There was artillery fire, much military music, a parade to the flagpole, and a raising of the flag. Five of New England's governors and five mayors were in Governor James Michael Curley's box. The high temperature that day was 44 degrees, with a trace of snow.

Babe Ruth was the whole show. Although facing Carl Hubbell's screwball—and he usually had trouble with the screwball—he had a single and a home run in four times at bat, scored two runs, and batted in three. In the field he made one good play and no error. The home run went about 430 feet. The single was a pulled grounder past Bill Terry at first, who said he didn't even see the ball. The Braves won 4–2, and it was Ruth who won.

The next day Babe and Claire celebrated their sixth wedding anniversary with a party at the Ritz-Carlton, reading congratulatory telegrams from Lyn Lary, Lefty Gomez, and others.

The future was promising in the minds of wishful thinkers. Only Walter Johnson, who had been through the ballplayer's change-of-life eight years earlier, had it right. In a talk at St. Louis he said, kindly and calmly, that Ruth was through and didn't know it; it "is almost too much to believe" that he could be of value to the Braves. The bookmakers, by leaving the Yankees' and Braves' odds unchanged, showed the same thinking. Before opening day a poll of the baseball writers discouraged any dream that the Braves could finish much above sixth place.

The Braves and Giants played again for the Giants' home opening. The Giants won 6–5 in eleven innings before a crowd of forty-seven thousand, the largest opening-day crowd of 1935. Ruth played eight innings and had no hits but scored a run. In the field he made one very bad play and one very good play. He was cheered when he came and cheered when he left through an affectionate shower of torn paper.

But after that it was downhill. In the first ten days or so Ruth won two games with home runs and lost one by poor fielding. A Boston writer doubted he'd last the season, and predicted his share of the profits would be nothing because the Braves would lose money again. Then Ruth fell ill with his annual spring cold. When he returned to the field he played a mediocre game and had a continuing low-grade infection. In a moment of depression he said to someone, "I'm all washed up." When asked, he denied that he was quitting. "If I can break this cold I believe I can carry on without any trouble." McKechnie said Ruth would feel better when he had a few home runs and the weather was warmer.

After a swing as far west as St. Louis, the Braves came to Pittsburgh in the third week of May. Ruth was the main speaker at a testimonial dinner for Rabbit Maranville who was a promising young major-leaguer when Ruth began with the Red Sox. Ruth broke into tears when praising his friend, and the orchestra had to play for a bit until he recovered himself.

On May 25 Ruth started in a game in Pittsburgh. The Braves had won seven and lost nineteen. One of the Pirates, in their clubhouse meeting, said, "Don't worry about Ruth," but Waite Hoyt, a Pirate since 1933, interrupted. "I wouldn't say that." Surprised, they asked how to pitch to Ruth. Hoyt said there wasn't any way to pitch to Ruth.

Early in the game Ruth got his fourth home run of the season (number 712). When he came to bat again Guy Bush had come in to pitch for Pittsburgh. Thirty-nine years later Bush recalled the day. Ruth pulled a pitch with the bat handle, which barely cleared the fence, ten feet fair (number 713).

Well, it made me so mad that I thought to myself, "Is that the kind of home runs he's been getting?"

There was a big crowd and they were on Ruth. They were always on him, cheering him or riding him one. He was coming to bat again.

And, I said coming out of the dugout, "Well, that guy who hit the little bloop home run before will be up again in this inning, I'm going to throw three fast balls right by that guy and see what this crowd will do and get my laugh on him."

Well, that's what I started out to do. I got the first pitch in there for a strike and Ruth just watched it go by just as pretty, like he was looking at a softball. And, I didn't say a word.

I got a signal for another fast ball and I come through there with one, I mean, with everything I had on it. I hit the plate, maybe an inch or two inches off the plate, about halfway between his knees and his waist. Just where he could get that fat part of the bat on it.

He got ahold of that ball and hit it over the triple-deck, clear out of the ballpark in right-center. I'm telling you, it was the longest cockeyed ball I ever saw in my life.

That poor fellow, he'd gotten to where he could hardly hobble along. I ain't mad no more then. So, when he rounds third base, I just look over there at him and he kind of looked at me. I tipped my cap just to say, "I've seen everything now, Babe."

He just looked at me and kind of saluted and smiled, and that's the last home run he ever hit. We got that gesture of good friendship.

Ten thousand people warmly applauded number 714 and renewed their praise when Ruth left the game in the seventh inning. He had a single and three home runs in four times at bat and drove in six runs. (The Braves lost 11–7.) It was hard for a left-handed batter to hit a home run in Pittsburgh, but Ruth's last one was the first that ever went higher than the right-field roof.

He should have quit that day, but the Phillies had sold many tickets for the game with the Braves on May 30 and he felt he ought to play. Before going to Philadelphia the Braves lost three games in Cincinnati, where Ruth pulled a muscle in the outfield. He was batting about .180, still had a cold, and now a game leg.

In Philadelphia he played until he had a turn at bat. After grounding out to Dolph Camilli,* unassisted, he left, forty years old, lame, overweight, and with a bad cold. That was the end. The Associated Press story from Philadelphia didn't even mention his name.

With the Braves in twenty-eight games he had seven singles, six home runs, and a batting average of .181. His proportion of home runs to times at bat was normal, but his strikeouts were out of proportion. A short table is informative:

Year	Percentage of Strikeouts in Times at Bat
1921	15.0
1927	16.5
1934	17.0
1935	33.3

* Adolf Louis Camilli (1907–   ), first-baseman, twelve seasons, 1933–1945, Cubs, Phillies, Dodgers, Red Sox, batting average .277.

Spring training is hard at age forty. With the Braves at St. Petersburg, 1935. The catcher is probably Hank Garrity, a native of Jamaica Plain and former catcher for Holy Cross College. In this turn at bat, Ruth hit one out. (*The Bettmann Archive.*)

Emil Fuchs deserves our sympathy, too. He had been a million-aire in the early 1920s and now was to be flat broke. His policy had been to put all profits into buying players and meet all deficits by borrowing. It would take a World Series to break *that* cycle. He claimed in May 1935 to have declined a life-tenure judgship (no details). If so, it wasn't prudent.

Babe Ruth was dissatisfied (which was one of Fuchs's lesser troubles). Ruth's position was self-defeating. If he made money for the Braves, Fuchs could survive as owner and McKechnie would stay as manager. If things went badly, Adams would get the club and Ruth would have at least some chance of becoming manager, especially if Adams, distracted by hockey and horse racing, made McKechnie the president. Fuchs had a small note due to Adams in May which he was able to pay because of Ruth's early drawing power. He had a larger debt to pay to Adams in August. That would be the time of decision if Ruth was still around and available. Meanwhile, Fuchs suggested that Ruth buy fifty thousand dollars of Braves stock.

Ruth found the Boston sportswriters unpleasantly critical, which seemed absurd. As he told Claire, "If they were any good they'd be in New York." The desperate Fuchs used Ruth in every way to make a dollar, scheduling exhibitions on unkempt fields and once promising a retail clothier that Ruth would come to the store and give out autographs if the retailer would buy five hundred tickets (Ruth refused to go). Ruth told Fuchs he wanted to quit before the first western swing, but the harassed owner said he would have to "throw in the sponge" without Ruth.

When a ballplayer slumped, Ruth believed he ought to leave the park and have a party. The French Line invited Ruth to a promising party, the New York reception for the new ship *Normandie*, where Ruth would, in some mysterious way understood by press agents, represent Organized Baseball. When Ruth asked for a furlough for the party, Fuchs outraged him by refusing, after privately talking with McKechnie. Ruth argued that his knee had to be rested so he might as well go. Still the answer was no.

McKechnie had his own opinions and was becoming as dour as he looked. Since Ruth was of no help in winning games McKechnie advised Fuchs to get rid of him, but Fuchs believed the customers wanted him to stay. McKechnie then asked Ruth "to write his resignation." Fuchs advised Ruth to wait until he got over his cold and he could "leave while on top." On May 29, the day before Ruth's last appearance in Philadelphia, McKechnie told Fuchs Ruth simply couldn't go on; some action must be taken. The club couldn't play baseball with Ruth in the outfield. And Ruth demoralized the club, the pitchers especially (the weakest pitching staff in the league, we may note), by taking special privileges for granted. Fuchs had been patient with Ruth, but when the Kiwanis Club of Haverhill booked a Braves exhibition which drew only two thousand, Fuchs began to think McKechnie had a case.

The *Normandie* party was the fuse. On June 2 Ruth's fuming persistence wore out Fuchs, who had far greater troubles. After another refusal Ruth went away to think for awhile and then returned to Fuchs's office. Considering that Fuchs was drowning in IOUs, the conversation was friendly. Ruth understood that he had come to Fuchs to resign. When he went back to the clubhouse Fuchs passed out a release to the Boston writers in the press box: he was going to surrender the Braves to a group of "New England sportsmen" (read: creditors). He told the New York writers Ruth would see them in the clubhouse. *Question*: Why? *Answer*: He's fired.

So the New York writers told Ruth he had been fired before he could tell them he had quit. They wanted to know why. Ruth's explanation was, "Judge Fuchs won't let me go down to see the

Normandie." The New Yorkers trooped to Fuchs's office where they suggested that Ruth had made a lot of money for the Braves in spring training, but Fuchs evaded the point.

Ruth dropped by the front office to say goodbye to the secretary, giving her a hundred-dollar bill as a souvenir. He and Claire left Boston by car that day, leaving the Braves firmly in last place. The team went on to lose 115 games that season and could have made it 116 except for an unplayed rainout. No assistant manager and vice-president could have made much difference. McKechnie could as well have said they couldn't play baseball with Ruth *out* of the outfield.

On the way back to New York Babe wept, feeling hopeless, desperate, desolate. When the car pulled up in front of 345 West 88th Street, a group of neighbors and their children came out to say hello. In a small speech Babe put the best face he could on his situation. "I'm through as a day-in-and-day-out player . . . but I can still play a few days a week. I can pinch hit. I'm not through." And then a note of self-doubt: "At least I hope I'm not." He wouldn't talk about Fuchs, McKechnie, the Braves.

Three days later Fuchs said Ruth could have his Braves uniform as a keepsake if he wanted it. And free.

The final ruin of the Braves deserves some attention. Fuchs was out entirely by August 1; Adams took over Fuchs's stock and made McKechnie temporary president. In December the National League declared the franchise forfeited. With Adams's credit, new owners were found, and the Braves became the Bees for awhile.

Ruth might have taken a different line. The new owners got the club for about four hundred thousand dollars. Ruth might have pressed his way into the buyers' syndicate. It is just as well he didn't, because they made no money for many years.

> **By back ways they slink away, sore smitten by misfortune,**
> **nor does any sweet smile grace their return.**
> **—Pindar, on Olympic losers**

Being a hero is a temporary job, but most players have found it hard to quit the game, and none left it more reluctantly than Babe Ruth. Baseball was all Ruth knew. His mind was packed with baseball, its strategy, its tactics, but empty of everything else. He seemed built only for the game, and, after leaving St. Mary's Industrial School, no other demand was made of him. From the age of eight he had been fiercely competitive. In retirement there was no competition and no baseball, and nobody in the part of the world he once ruled seemed to remember him except in the past tense. Claire wrote that "From the end of the 1934 season until the day he died,

Babe Ruth, figuratively speaking, sat by the telephone waiting for a call everybody but he knew would never come." For awhile he went to ball games, but he didn't like to sit in the stands. So he played golf whenever he could and credited it with keeping him sane.

There was still a public interest in him, of the kind that stirs people to mow neglected cemeteries and repair historic houses. A press poll of major-league clubs found not one with an interest in using any of his skills. After a rumor that he had to pay his way into Yankee Stadium, his old ghost writer, Ford Frick, gave him a life-time pass to all National League ball parks. Ruth received a well-intentioned but not heartening invitation to manage the Palatka team of the North Florida League. *The Times*'s December review of sports in 1935 included a full column on baseball. The next to last paragraph read:

> The year also saw the final passing of the glamorous Babe Ruth as a player. Unconditionally released by the Yankees, the fading home-run monarch signed with the Braves. It proved an ill-starred venture, and after rumored differences with the club's owners the Babe resigned on June 2.

The words "final passing" make it sound as if he died. It was fitting. The paragraph was the obituary of a career. A Hearst cartoon showed him in ragged uniform walking away from The House That Ruth Built, with dogs labeled "ungrateful owners" and "jeering fans" barking at his heels. Ruth thought highly of that cartoon.

He joined Mayor Fiorello LaGuardia and Robert Moses in ceremonially opening parks and playgrounds, he had more publicity about a couple of minor traffic accidents than most people would get, he had an offer to promote baseball in England, and he clowned at his initiation into the Circus Saints and Sinners Club.

But his baseball life was meager. He played in a country-club picnic game and in a benefit game between the Minneapolis and St. Paul police teams which drew thirteen thousand (Ruth played four and a half innings for each team). In an exhibition at Dyckman Oval between the New York Cubans (blacks) and the pick-up All-Stars, which drew ten thousand, Ruth played first base and then, as an added attraction, batted for five minutes in which he hit six balls out of the park. There were no newsreels, no other cameras, no telegraph keys, no dignitaries—not even an alderman. But Ruth had a good time.

Christy Walsh used him again to cover the World Series that year, clad all in brown as usual. After the Series he went barnstorming, repeating the promotional device of a special exhibition of hitting balls over the fence. A fee of three thousand dollars for one appearance was common. At one of the games he used the public-address system to tell the crowd he was thinking of quitting baseball. That was pathetic. Baseball had quit him.

Golf remained. Ruth in 1933 had said he would try to become a golf professional when he retired. In the Westchester Country Club annual invitational tournament, among 226 players, he scored 81, nine over par on a rain-soaked course. The score was respectable; the 1934 winner had an 80. Ruth was all right as an amateur golfer, but his entry into open competition was disappointing. In the first round of the Acacia Country Club Open at Cleveland, in August, his score was 85. The leader in a field of 150 scored 65. Nevertheless Ruth had the largest gallery. Professional opinion was that his drives hooked too often and that his putting wasn't up to professional levels.

THE ACCUMULATED BATTING FIGURES
BABE RUTH'S MAJOR-LEAGUE CAREER
1914–1935

at bat: 8399
hits: 2873
home runs: 714
runs batted in: 2217
average: .342

56 · Waiting for the Phone to Ring
(1936-1937)

When Babe Ruth left baseball in 1935 he returned to something he hadn't known for thirty-three years—private life. Before retirement, as Tom Meany well said, "he had the happy faculty of wearing the world as a loose garment." How does a professional athlete get down, so to speak, from his special place? Young ones think it easy, but many veterans, like Ruth, leave the fields gracelessly, even painfully. In Ruth's case, considering the whole psychology of the normal life span, he never got beyond the emotional age of thirty-six or thirty-seven. Men in that age group aren't cutting back on activities as men in their forties begin to do. In finding the change unpleasant he wasn't alone. As previously noted, the number of deaths by suicide among major-league ballplayers is seven times greater than in the male population at large. That hints they have a hard time living in obscurity.

The only clear advantage of relative obscurity to the Ruths was that they could begin to go out in public in a year or two without having to push through a crush of idolizers, though they were always recognized and greeted by strangers.

Within a year and a half of leaving the Braves Ruth's usual weight was 240 pounds, with all dimensions larger except his biceps. His teeth were good. For Christmas 1936 Claire gave him a chair, a gift of unconscious irony.

When the Christy Walsh Syndicate went out of business in 1937 Claire took over the management of all the family money, though Walsh remained the agent for negotiating new contracts. To 1937 Walsh had accumulated a quarter of a million dollars in Babe Ruth's irrevocable trust fund. Because Babe was still in demand, Claire managed to run the family affairs wholly with income from endorsements, broadcasting, movie shorts,* and well-paid personal appearances.

* A clip from a short film for Warner Brothers (1936) is part of a Ruth documentary in a television series called "Biography," much used for local television

Ruth now had plenty of time to be a father to his daughters. The group of Mom or Clara, Butch (Julia), Dot (Dorothy), and Fadder, that is, Vater, was an entirely normal group. Perhaps the girls called him Fadder, or Vater, because the Anglo Julia and the Celt Dorothy thought it a little comic to have a heavy German father. The girls enjoyed being Babe Ruth's daughters because the family in a group was always a center of attention in public.

Like most fathers of daughters he alternated between bluntness and indulgence. When he told them to be home by 11 P.M. it was reason enough (for him) that "I'm a man; you're a girl." Or he could say to Julia, "You're a pretty girl, Butch, but you're too fat. Get yourself down." The girls took this sort of thing, as in the history of the race, easier from the father than the mother, especially as it was often soon balanced by some generous gift.

He could sacrifice for them. When Julia graduated from high school in 1934 Babe flew all night after a game in St. Louis to be there. When she needed a blood transfusion in 1938 he rushed from Ebbets Field with a motorcycle escort to give her five hundred cubic centimeters, which Claire thought saved Julia's life.

Young male visitors at the house, their faces always remembered, their names always forgotten, sometimes found themselves stuck in a bridge game with Babe, who played his usual wildly plunging style to the discomfort of more serious players. If he took a dislike to a young man—and he was suspicious of and bored by all of them —he simply banned further relations, which, luckily, worked. The girls had one fret. Were these youths calling to see *them* or because they were Babe Ruth's daughters? Dot was pleased when one obviously interested young man doubted that she was of the Ruth household.

Babe Ruth was a satisfactory father.

> **Oh, how I hated baseball and everything in it in those days.**
>
> **—Claire Ruth**

Most managers are hired in the fall, some in the winter. There was no good news in those seasons for Ruth in the three years after leaving the Braves. He kept busy by shooting birds and animals, catching fish, and, most often, playing golf. Always there was the hope that the telephone would ring, bringing an offer to manage. It

---

programming in the 1960s and 1970s. He appeared with Zez Confrey, composer of "Kitten on the Keys." The title of the song Ruth chanted for the film was "Home Run on the Keys."

never did. He shrugged off the silence with a false, devil-take-it attitude, fooling neither Claire nor himself. Occasionally he showed tears. Claire tried to get excited over small golf scores and large fish, but it was a game of let's pretend. Try as he would, Babe could not get used to the luxurious idleness of his life which was of the kind that sweepstakes ticket-buyers are hoping to win. He might better have gone into business. He knew sporting goods and gentlemen's furnishings, and Christy Walsh could have found men skilled in buying and accounting, but Ruth thought he would die in an office. So he remembered the magic of baseball as a dream of the future, and the dream was to end in gross humiliation.

Before baseball threw him off entirely, Ruth received one honor envied by thousands of ballplayers. In their wisdom the citizens of Cooperstown, New York, founded the baseball Hall of Fame in 1935 (and lately the excellent National Baseball Library). The demigods of this charming rural valhalla were chosen by the Baseball Writers of America, who held their first election in 1936.* There were 226 eligible voters, each of whom listed ten names. To be elected required 170 votes. The results of this first ballot were:

Ty Cobb	222
Babe Ruth	215
Honus Wagner	215
Christy Mathewson	205
Walter Johnson	189

The Ruths went to Florida for spring training in 1936 as spectators. It was dull, and only golf made the trip worth the trouble. More interesting was the offer of a player contract from Larry MacPhail of the Reds who intended to use Ruth as fifth outfielder, emergency first baseman, and pinch-hitter "at his own terms." But Claire convinced Babe his legs weren't good enough any more.

On opening day at the Stadium Babe was the hero of the crowd and the cameramen in the quarter-hour before game time. (To the photographers: "Grin? Sure I'll grin. What's that? You want me to look bewildered? Okay, anything to please.") When play started he was unnoticed. It was the same that fall at the World Series between the Giants and the Yankees, where Babe and Claire sat on the Giants' side.

During the World Series the Dodgers fired Casey Stengel, their manager. Insiders knew Stengel's successor would be either Burleigh

---

* Ruth's voice may be heard in the recording of the induction of the first members, which is part of the centennial-of-professional-baseball record widely sold in 1969.

GEORGE HERMAN (BABE) RUTH
BOSTON—NEW YORK, A.L.; BOSTON, N.L.
1915 – 1935
GREATEST DRAWING CARD IN HISTORY OF
BASEBALL. HOLDER OF MANY HOME RUN
AND OTHER BATTING RECORDS. GATHERED
714 HOME RUNS IN ADDITION, TO FIFTEEN
IN WORLD SERIES.

The Hall of Fame plaque. (*National Baseball Library, Cooperstown, New York.*)

Grimes* or Dutch Ruether, but naturally Ruth's name came up along with a rumor that T. L. Huston would buy the Dodgers and make Ruth the field chief. There was a month of suspense before the Dodgers said it was to be Grimes. Four weeks later Ruth talked with the owner of the Albany Senators about the manager's job, but he wasn't very much in earnest because he still believed minor-league baseball would demote him.

On opening day 1937 Ruth's arrival disrupted the flag-raising ceremony and drew all attention away from Mayor LaGuardia, Ruppert, Barrow, McCarthy, and Senators manager Bucky Harris, including the attention of the news photographers. But, again, when

* Burleigh Arland Grimes (1893–   ), pitcher, nineteen seasons, 1916–1934, Pirates, Dodgers, Giants, Braves, Cardinals, Cubs. Won 270, lost 212, earned-run average 3.53. Hall of Fame.

play started he was nobody except when he caused a flurry of interest by catching a foul ball. That year at the World Series autograph seekers mobbed him. By coincidence he again caught a foul ball, arousing louder cheers than any play of the first game.

Despite the owners' lack of interest in Ruth he was still a heroic national figure. The American Baseball Congress, the governing body of amateur baseball, was trying to get baseball accepted as an Olympic sport and would have sent Ruth to the Berlin Olympic Games with a team if it could have been arranged. The Sinclair Refining Company in 1937 advertised in 182 newspapers that Ruth would broadcast for them for thirteen weeks on sixty-one stations of the Columbia Broadcasting System, as the central figure in a baseball contest and running review of the season.

But these weren't things Babe Ruth really wanted—not opening days and World Series as a spectator, nor elections to a Hall of Fame, nor broadcasts, nor Olympic dignities. He wanted organized baseball to break its silence somehow, to answer his inner cry.

Ruth played golf as much as possible. In Florida he often played with well-known men: Dizzy Dean, Billy DeBeck, Billy Burke,

Following through after a drive, September 1938. (*National Baseball Library, Cooperstown, New York.*)

Lawson Little, Mickey Cochrane. At home his golfing friends were not as famous, mostly the members at St. Albans. From February 1936 through February 1938 he made a serious tournament campaign. He entered the following tournaments: New York Curb Exchange, Detroit Open, Leewood (Eastchester, New York), Melvin Open (New Hampshire), Bluff Point Invitational, and twice the Bermuda Mid-Ocean at Hamilton. He came close to winning only once, when he finished second at Bermuda in 1937. (In 1938 at Bermuda he didn't even make the first flight.)

Ruth's greatest golfing publicity came from a match on November 14, 1937, at Fresh Meadow, with Mysterious Montague. The affair was a promotion of the Hearst sportswriter Bill Corum for the benefit of Mayor LaGuardia's boys' camps. It was intended for eighteen holes.

Mysterious Montague was a legend out of California, where legend seems to blossom well and then to overblow. Montague was so strong he could hold up one end of a car while you changed a tire. He knocked birds off trees and wires with both wood and iron shots. He could putt even better. At Palm Springs, where the course record was 65, he went around in 58. Using a shovel, a rake, and a baseball bat he then went around in 80. During a nineteenth-hole argument he picked up George Bancroft and stuffed him into a locker. This was the stuff to give Hearst readers!

Ruth and Montague played a practice nine at Fresh Meadow on the day before the public match. Over the par 35 nine, Ruth shot 37, Montague 35. The public match was to be a mixed foursome, Babe, Montague, Sylvia Annenberg, and Babe Didrikson.

Twelve thousand paid a dollar a head to watch and get in the way. Many didn't know the difference between a driver and a chauffeur. They allowed lanes of ten or fifteen feet for driving, no room for backswings, and all somehow escaped without bloodshed or concussion. The first three holes took an hour, and the players had to quit at nine holes. Montague couldn't get through the gallery to play the sixth, and Annenberg had the same trouble on the seventh, so Ruth's and Didrikson's 38s, on a par 35 nine, were the only complete cards. The foursome netted five thousand dollars for LaGuardia's camps.

Ruth and Montague played again in private by match play, and Ruth won, five holes up, but didn't wish to brag (his medal score was 76).

The publicity did Montague ill. The sheriff of Essex County saw his picture. He wanted that mysterious golfer under another name for armed robbery and assault. When he was tried, Oliver Hardy, Bing Crosby, Andy Devine, and Johnny Weismuller appeared for the defense as character witnesses. The jury acquitted him, he entered the United States Open, shot an 81, and lost his celebrity.*

Ruth played golf on 240 days in 1936, and had a handicap of 3. His public scores in these years ranged from the high seventies to the low eighties. He wasn't good enough to be a pro.

Every fall Ruth and some friends went down east to kill deer and ducks. After one such hunt he drove through Manhattan with a deer across the front bumper, a buck over each front fender, and a bear in the rumble seat. For these Canadian kills the Minister of Highways in the government of the Province of Nova Scotia gave him a plaque at the National Sports Show in New York.

Heroes who win their glory in their youth, if they do not disappear from sight entirely, tend to take on the appearance of propriety and stability through ceremonial living in the public eye, never in the foreground but never wholly forgotten. This suited Ruth's favorite works of mercy very well. Three examples will suffice. He appeared at the American Federation of Actors Annual Benefit in the Metropolitan Opera House with LaGuardia, the massed bands of the Police, Fire, and Sanitation Departments, with Edgar Bergen, Henny Youngman, Ed Sullivan, Duke Ellington, and many others. The show grossed about $12,500 in all. As one of a cast of three hundred he helped to entertain four thousand children at a three-hour WPA circus in the Shriners' Mecca Temple, before Christmas; he was one of four clowns in a baseball grotesque. Paul Gallico staged a free water carnival for his paper at Jones Beach, which drew seventy-five thousand. Ruth came to hit long flies out over the water. Suddenly the sea was churned by more than a thousand children swimming after the batted balls.

A baseball hit by Babe Ruth was still a holy relic.

---

* He died in obscurity in Studio City, California, at the age of sixty-six.

57 · The White Elephant of Brooklyn (1938)

Leland Stanford MacPhail (a man who tried to kidnap the Kaiser after the First World War) had tried to finesse Babe Ruth into a manager's job in the early 1930s, introduced night baseball in the major leagues, and gave Babe Ruth his last job in organized baseball. MacPhail moved from the Reds to become executive vice-president of the Dodgers, a team which usually lost a great deal of money.

Babe Ruth attended the first night game at Brooklyn's Ebbets Field in June 1938 as a spectator. The crowd welcomed him with such uproarious admiration that MacPhail was moved to approach Ruth with an offer to be a coach. Ruth's heart leaped up, and he put the matter in Christy Walsh's hands. Walsh wanted twenty-five thousand dollars for Ruth, but Ruth might have done it for nothing, so MacPhail was able to get Ruth for fifteen thousand.

In his public statement MacPhail forestalled talk of Burleigh Grimes's leaving by saying he told Ruth he could not become manager. Grimes said Ruth was "a guy that really belongs in baseball." (It was commonly believed Ford Frick had a hand in the matter.) MacPhail settled details in his apartment in Columbia Heights at a meeting with Grimes, Ruth, and Leo Durocher, "captain and short-stop of the club." As the group parted, Ruth unwisely took Durocher aside (according to Durocher) and said, "I'll be boss around here before too long," to which Durocher replied that Babe had better get in line behind Leo.

There was much praise for Ruth's return to uniform, but a few farsighted people said it would be a replay of the Boston Braves disaster. As for Ruth, he was pleased, but, as he hinted wistfully to Claire, it could have been better—"it's not the Yankees."

> He's a white elephant . . . out here to drag in customers . . . nothing more.
>
> —Leo Durocher (on Ruth), 1938

As Durocher had warned, Ruth had better not discount Durocher in Dodger affairs. They had been teammates with the Yankees of the late 1920s. There is no record of Durocher or Ruth then singling out each other for unfriendliness; Durocher had unfriendly relations with practically the whole team. He also had a higher laundry bill than dandified Jacob Ruppert. In later years Ruth described Durocher as "the cockiest busher I ever saw. He didn't get that nickname Lippy for nothing." Durocher even went out of his way to anger Ty Cobb, which is like bouncing a ball of nitroglycerin. Branch Rickey, the puritan liberal, said of him that he was capable of "taking a bad situation and making it immediately worse." Durocher was many-sided in rousing anger; when he was with the Cardinals he managed to get the team's games picketed by union labor because he interfered in a garment workers' strike on the anti-union side. He came to the Dodgers from the Cardinals in 1937.

Durocher had many defenders. There were the owners who later hired him as manager for twenty-four seasons, all told. And when Jim Brosnan asked Marv Grissom* to name the best manager he had ever played for, Grissom was forcible in reply:

Leo! Durocher had them all beat. Nobody could touch him when it came to getting the best from a ball club. I could talk about him as manager for hours.

Grissom had also played under Eddie Dyer, Red Rolfe, Al Lopez, Lou Boudreau, Solly Hemus, and Bill Rigney.

Ruth joined the seventh-place Dodgers on Sunday, June 19, weighing at least 240 pounds, with his paunch hanging over his belt. The news photographers kept him busy for an hour. When he went out to the first-base coaching line there was an almighty cheer which said, in effect, We haven't got the best team, but we've got the best coach. The attendance was 28,013.

Actually Ruth's duties in Brooklyn were light: he was to hit balls over the fences during batting practice, and to do whatever first-base coaches do. He was a spare part and accepted his place.

But on the road he worked harder, at autograph sessions, in visits to hospitals and orphanages, and when, as if by magic, ten exhibition games suddenly appeared on the schedule. As Jimmy Cannon put it, they were going to move Babe Ruth around the country like a plaster saint in a religious procession. In pregame shows they used him in long-distance hitting contests (on September 27 in St. Louis he hit one all the way out of the park). He didn't help to win games, but he surely helped to sell tickets.

---

* Marvin Edward Grissom (1918–   ), pitcher, 10 seasons, 1946–1959, Giants, Tigers, White Sox, Red Sox, Cardinals. Won 47, lost 45, earned-run average 3.41.

Ruth played at least part of every one of the ten exhibitions, at first base. They brought in as much money as his salary. It was risky, because young pitchers wanted very much to strike out the baseball monument, and the vision in his right eye had weakened. All the exhibitions were at night, with minor-league lighting. It is marvelous that he wasn't hurt by a pitched ball. The exhibition schedule was not an abuse of the new coach; when he joined the Dodgers he said he'd be glad to play in exhibitions if he could help.

A clash between Babe Ruth and Leo Durocher was inevitable.

The first explosion occurred after a home game with the Cubs. The Cubs led 2–0 with two out in the ninth inning, Dodger runners on second and third, Cookie Lavagetto* at bat, Durocher on deck, Ruth coaching at first. Rather than walk the winning run, the Cubs pitched to Lavagetto who bounced the ball off the shortstop's leg into left field, driving in two runs to tie. Durocher relayed the hit-and-run sign to Lavagetto at second. Came a wide one, but Durocher threw his bat at it and got a weak single behind first base, enough to let the winning run score.

A young sportswriter innocently praised Babe Ruth for calling for the hit-and-run play. Grimes, the obvious author of the bold scheme, was annoyed, and Durocher did what he could to keep him annoyed, stirring Grimes up in the locker room with strong abuse of Ruth—all of which Ruth overheard. At the next clubhouse meeting the furious Ruth asked for the floor and verbally attacked Durocher, which led to a much-witnessed scuffle and a mark under Ruth's eye. When the team took the field reporters saw the bruise, heard of a fist fight in the clubhouse, noted that Durocher lagged behind under the stand, and drew the correct conclusion, though Durocher denied it, saying he was too little to hit Ruth (160 pounds vs. 240 pounds).

Contrary to his public statements, Larry MacPhail had once thought of Ruth as the manager of the Dodgers. Grimes suspected it but treated Ruth civilly and once prevented violence in the clubhouse when Ruth seemed likely to avenge himself after Durocher openly complained that Ruth forgot the signals in the time it took to get from the bench to the coaching box—"No wonder we're getting piled up on the bases." Durocher told the sportswriters the same. Doubts of Ruth on the signals killed Ruth's chance to manage so far as MacPhail was concerned. Durocher was prone to fury and fighting, but always in the direction of winning ball games. Ruth's temper, on the other hand, was aroused by hurt personal pride. More important, Durocher was right when he charged Ruth with carelessness about signals. H. G. Salsinger, a friendly, detached

---

* Harry Arthur Lavagetto (1912–   ), infielder, ten seasons, 1934–1947, Pirates, Dodgers, batting average .269.

observer, said of Ruth and signs, "He never remembered them." That was enough for MacPhail. In a way utterly beyond the imagination of Babe (or Claire), Durocher had campaigned very well for the managership of the Dodgers.

It was pretty certain that Grimes would be fired by the Dodgers at the end of the season. Ruth, of course, would like to be the new manager and so would Durocher, who regarded Ruth as an intruder. The blow to Grimes came on October 10. MacPhail named five possible successors, including Durocher but not Ruth. To entertain the press he made book for the sportswriters (with a twenty-five-cent limit). Durocher opened at 9 to 5, but betting drove the odds down to 4 to 5. Grimes himself had earlier nominated Durocher, but MacPhail masked his interest. Then, in Chicago during the World Series MacPhail called Durocher to his room in the Congress Hotel and told him he would be the manager. The public statement came in New York on the 12th, surprising nobody. Ruth, MacPhail added in reply to a question, was never in the running and declined to be "available" as a coach (which was just as well, since Durocher wouldn't have taken him).

Thus, finally and bleakly, ended the career of Babe Ruth in organized baseball, unproved as a manager in the minors, untested in the majors. He got the news while playing golf and sent best wishes to Durocher and "every member of the team." Then he went home to Claire and "sat in the kitchen, head in hands, crying again."

Since 1933 Babe had expected a job as manager to come as a reward deserved, not as a job to be competed for and won. Claire and Christy Walsh encouraged him in his vain attitude. European pleasure lands have many permanently exiled members of royalty and expelled chiefs of state who took the same position.

There has been sympathy for Ruth in his failure to get the only thing he wanted that he didn't have, but few of the sympathetic have been in a position to say with certainty that he would have been an able manager. The irrelevant reply to this is that he did a lot for baseball. But it was mutual. A hard-throwing, hard-hitting boy out of St. Mary's Industrial School made about two million from baseball, half from salaries and World Series shares, and half from the well-organized profits of his celebrity. It is not unreasonable to believe that Ruth would have been eagerly sought if those in a position to know thought he could do the job.

Ruth thought he had been abused and betrayed. He became chronically bitter, brooding on being passed over by the Yankees, Tigers, Braves, and Dodgers. After 1938 he wasn't seen so often in baseball parks, and Claire had a lively resentment of the Yankees.

He never showed the slightest talent for managing except on the Japan tour with a team that could only look superb. Tactics is for players; strategy is the work of managers. There is no strategy in the parts of a game, and there are no tactics for the whole. Tactics divides the game into steps, and the players are supposed to know what to do (no manager has to give a signal to catch a fair fly ball). But, in the trite phrase, the manager has to make a game plan. Players learn tactics by doing, the manager arrives at strategy by knowing the whole. Babe Ruth was tactically superb, but there is little in his life to hint that he had the strategic gift or any interest in game problems considered broadly.

If he could have bent to it he might well have been preserved as a symbolic coach, drawing ahs from the crowd as he hit fungoes before the game and teaching batting when it was possible (which usually isn't the case). But, again, he'd have to go job-hunting, and that he could not do. He had never sought a job in his life.

58 · A Living Shrine, a Walking Reliquary (1939-1946)

From the end of the 1938 season until late 1946 Babe Ruth's life was pretty much of a piece. Public interest in the part of his life he lived in open view relaxed a little, but only a little. His fame made life a little harder for news people, who had to cover well-intentioned but rather dull affairs to which Ruth lent his presence, and to check out frequent rumors of his death by assassination, automobile accident, or heart failure on the golf course.

In 1942 the Ruths moved to an eleven-room apartment on Riverside Drive. In place of the homespun practical jokes of baseball clubhouses, Babe made up some solo performances. If photographers came to the Ruths' place he collected their used flash bulbs and used them to bomb Riverside Drive from the roof. And he liked to drop bars of soap into the fountain in front of the building. These things he thought loudly laughable. No doubt they would have been reviewed very favorably at St. Mary's Industrial School or in any hotel used by ballplayers.

Every year he and Claire gave a birthday party to celebrate his completed year, inviting from forty to sixty people. The press was always on hand (leaving the used flash bulbs for Babe, of course). Every year his birthday photograph showed his face more like a full moon. His weight he always gave as 240, but that was probably low. Almost every year Babe and Claire were photographed at the World Series. With Gloria Swanson and other storied leftovers from the 1920s he endorsed and spoke for Thomas E. Dewey for President in 1944, and, with Joe Louis, endorsed Dewey again for governor in 1946. Newspapers often sought Ruth's opinions on current baseball affairs.

> It was the only time in his life he ever called me Babe to
> my face. I couldn't help crying when I went out.
> —Babe Ruth, January 13, 1939

Jacob Ruppert, owner of the Yankees, died on January 13, 1939, of a number of ills, the chief of which was an inflammation of the veins, called phlebitis. He was a bachelor. Except for brewery officials and relatives, Babe Ruth was the last to see him. Ruppert sent for him. When Ruth arrived he took the dying man's hand and said something encouraging; Ruppert smiled but could only say, "Babe." Ruth went out of the room in tears.

Ruppert left about a hundred million dollars. One looks in vain for a bequest to an old ballplayer. His will divided the estate equally between two relatives and a former chorus girl the press had absolutely never heard of, so discreet had the Colonel been.

> Damn it, I went over there because I had to, I wanted to
> laugh and cheer him up. I wound up crying like a baby.
> —Babe Ruth, July 4, 1939

During spring training in 1939 Lou Gehrig wasn't playing well. As time passed he worsened. In June he went to the Mayo Clinic where physicians found he was suffering from an always fatal nerve disease, amyotrophic lateral sclerosis. He was thirty-nine when he could no longer play.

The Yankees staged Gehrig Appreciation Day on July 4, inviting the surviving 1927 team. Babe Ruth, in a white double-breasted linen suit and brown and white wingtip shoes was much the widest and almost the tallest of the group around Gehrig on the field. With tears in his eyes he spoke extemporaneously in praise of the 1927s, saying they could beat the current Yankees. Gehrig then spoke. When finished he couldn't smile until Ruth came over, put an arm around him, and whispered the first words between the two since 1933. Both laughed, and the heretofore silent crowd cheered and cheered.

Gehrig lingered another twenty-three months until he died on June 2, 1941. Ruth immediately, at 1 A.M., went to the Gehrigs, ending a childish quarrel started by Babe who actively resented Lou's inability to control his mother's speech.

Hollywood decided to make a picture about Gehrig's life. Ruth was the first to sign, November 2, and would play himself. He was hog fat (267 pounds) at the time and spent the next sixty days dangerously taking off forty-seven pounds to fit the part. His trim figure astonished his fellow guests at a press party given by the producer early in January 1942. He was good in the picture. No actor he, but very capable of being himself. So warmly did he throw himself into the part that he hurt his hand by punching it through a Pullman window in the victory celebration scene.*

Thus passed Lou Gehrig, still in Ruth's shadow. Forever the record book has him batting behind Ruth in the lineup. Lifetime batting averages: Ruth .342, Gehrig .340.

Golf was absorbing. Ruth played in pick-up foursomes and in tournaments. Clubs had him as a guest in order to give him plaques which were something like valentines. In 1940 he got his second hole-in-one (on a 220-yard hole), this time at his home course, St. Albans Golf Club. In the White Mountain Open at North Conway, New Hampshire, he was mediocre on the course (an 82, well behind the three first-rank qualifiers who shot par 70s), but he won the amateur driving contest with three drives that averaged 260 yards. His standing as a golfer had a measure here; the professional winner averaged 278 yards.

Baseball blended with golf in the summer of 1941 when Ruth and Cobb played a golf series of three matches for the benefit of the Golden Rule Farm for children, the American Red Cross, and the USO. The sites were Commonwealth in Massachusetts (June 25), Fresh Meadow on Long Island (June 27), and Grosse Ile in Michigan (July 29). It was Cobb's idea and the sports editors loved it, knowing Cobb's fierceness in any game. Bette Davis put up a cup for the winner.

Cobb won the Massachusetts match, three and two, although Ruth had earlier been two up. Both were in the low eighties which was higher than their practice rounds (they finished the eighteen holes). At Fresh Meadow Ruth won, but the match went nineteen holes. They drew only 250 watchers at a dollar a head. The Detroit match was a foursome, with Ruth and Mysterious Montague paired against Cobb and Walter Hagen. Ruth and Montague won the foursome but only because Montague scored a par 71, five strokes better than Hagen. In Ruth against Cobb, it was Cobb 86, Ruth 89, and Cobb had it, three and two. It was a sweltering day, very hard on the two overweight ballplayers.

In medal play, so far as records survive, Ruth's scores in these years ranged from 75 to 89, with more in the eighties than in the seventies.

With the coming of the Second World War Babe Ruth played in his last baseball game on July 28, 1943, at Yankee Stadium, an Old-Timers game between a team he managed, called the Yanklands, and the University of North Carolina Pre-Flight Cloudbusters, man-

---

* The picture, *The Pride of the Yankees*, still circulates in the middle 1970s on television and offers a chance to see and hear Babe Ruth briefly in a condition approximating his condition in the early 1930s.

aged by Ted Williams. The Cloudbusters were all former major-leaguers training for naval flight commissions. The game was a benefit for the American Red Cross. Williams's team won, 11–5, by virtue of a seven-run seventh inning. Ruth was a pinch-hitter in the sixth and got a base on balls after a foul strike. He thus started a four-run inning himself. The pitcher who walked Ruth was Johnny Sain,* and the foul off Sain was the last time Ruth's bat hit a ball during a game. When the next batter drove him to second, he pulled up lame and called for a pinch-runner.

The game made about thirty thousand dollars for the Red Cross. Photographers saw to it that Ruth and Williams posed together. It was their only meeting.

Not all of Ruth's civic and ceremonial appearances were linked to the war. He posed congratulating New York Boy Scout number 350,000 as part of a Scout recruiting drive in 1943, helped celebrate Canadian Dominion Day at a New York border village, and gave a surprise Christmas party for thirty young polio patients of the Hospital for Joint Diseases.

Ruth's presence assured publicity for any civic event, and his presence in a baseball suit made it certain that people would buy tickets which profited an organized charity. In addition to the game with Williams's Cloudbusters, Ruth, with Walter Johnson, made money for Army-Navy Relief by increasing the attendance at a Yankee double-header to more than sixty thousand. Between games Johnson pitched to Ruth with the aim of entertaining the fans with long Ruth drives. Of twenty-one pitches, Ruth hit the third and the twenty-first out of the playing field. The second one went into the third deck a bit foul, but Ruth trotted around the bases anyway. Claire had sat through the whole thing with white knuckles, fearing he'd hurt himself.

Babe Ruth in his late forties had become a patriotic symbol, ranking not far below the flag and the bald eagle, invariably photographed promoting remote battles or the relief of the miseries that follow battles. He canvassed door-to-door for the Red Cross, umpired benefit ball games, gave baseball films to the Navy and the Red Cross for showing in ships and in overseas servicemen's clubs, sold war bonds in theaters and on the radio, lent his name and steadily fatter face to bond-selling contests. In the largest bond-selling contest, held in 1944, people voted for sports figures by buying bonds and naming their favorites. The rankings, in order, were Lou Gehrig, Ward Cuff, Mel Ott,** Babe Ruth, followed by nineteen

---

* John Franklin Sain (1917–   ), pitcher, eleven seasons, 1942–1955, Braves, Yankees, Athletics. Won 139, lost 116, earned-run average 3.49.

** Melvin Thomas Ott (1909–1958), outfielder, twenty-two seasons, 1926–1947, Giants, batting average .304. Hall of Fame.

ballplayers with fairly good showings. Figures from other sports (as the football player Ward Cuff) turned up, but ballplayers were much the most numerous.

Ruth's best-remembered tie with the Second World War was the use of his name by Japanese infantrymen. *The Times* told it all:

'TO HELL WITH BABE RUTH'

YELL CHARGING JAPANESE

Cape Gloucester, New Britain (Delayed)—Staff Sgt. Jeremiah A. O'Connor, a Marine Corps combat correspondent, reports that Japanese troops charged the Marine lines here shouting the strange battle cry
'To hell with Babe Ruth!' . . .

The Times ground out a rather heavy-duty industrial-grade editorial on Japanese terrorist societies, such as the Warlike Gods who tried to kill the 1934 baseball sponsor of the Ruth tour, hoping that when the end came for Japan there would be an end to terrorism.

A movement to have Babe Ruth tour the combat zones in charge of a pair of professional teams, to play exhibitions for the men in the forces, reached the floor of Congress. Ruth said the state of his health barred such a trip.

The once-great muscles were now usually used for bowling. Ruth took up bowling in 1915, let it go, and came back to it in the 1940s. He didn't care at all for competing; his interest was in trying by himself to improve his average. He often bowled alone at the lanes of the Riverside Plaza Hotel on 73rd Street. Photographs of Ruth the kegler show a fat man with apple-shaped cheeks separated by definite lines from an irrefutable double chin. Once he made his annual birthday party a bowling party. His average was about 175. Three times he went along with suggestions that he bowl in fund-raising exhibitions for the National Foundation for Infantile Paralysis. He went into these affairs wholeheartedly, making good-natured fun of the crowds for stinginess, ordering the collection taken up twice, and himself giving enough money to raise the amount noticeably. He felt he wasn't bowling well enough to repay these crowds, and had to be told that the crowds cared nothing at all about his bowling but came to see Babe Ruth.

Babe Ruth had two illnesses in the year 1942 severe enough to alarm his friends.

On January 2 Claire and his physician spirited him out of the apartment building at 1:40 A.M. and took Babe in an ambulance to an unnamed hospital. It turned out he had collapsed because of taking off so much weight so fast in order to be fit to play himself in *The Pride of the Yankees.* After twenty days of rest he was discharged to go hunting in upstate New York but instead had to take to his bed at home with a cold, sore throat, and fever. He was out of the house inside a week and then back in bed immediately with a sinus infection. He wasn't really well again until February 7. He had been disabled thirty-six days. It is a measure of public interest that *The Times* carried fourteen news stories on this illness.

While in California to make the Gehrig movie Ruth caught pneumonia. The studio people tried to calm him by saying they could "shoot around" him until he got well. His condition was critical when he left his hotel on a stretcher on April 8 to go to Hollywood Presbyterian Hospital. Only Claire was allowed to visit him. His temperature was above normal until the 13th, and he was able to have visitors only on the 14th and after. He was back at work on the picture on the 20th, having been disabled exactly two weeks. *The Times* felt that popular interest justified nine stories on the illness. A publicity picture, with Teresa Wright pressing a stethoscope to his chest, showed him with a jowly face, creased enough to show he had been under real strain. For the time being he quit cigars and alcohol, though he took up pipe-smoking. If hopelessly enslaved to nicotine, he would have been wiser to be the complete ballplayer and chew. Chewing tobacco is harmless to the pharynx; pipe smoke is not.

He was never emotionally disturbed enough to need psychiatric care, but in these years he was not a happy man. The many hokey photographs taken then show depression. Babe Ruth was no longer seen as useful in baseball except for ritual occasions which meant nothing in the records but could sell tickets. Ruth was a kind of ornament, a living shrine, a walking reliquary of baseball records. He found it very hard being a Grand Old Man in his early forties.

When he spoke at a baseball writers' dinner and said, "I gave twenty-two years of my life to big-league baseball and I'm ready to give twenty-five more," not one of the thousand baseball men there offered him a job. His only consolation was that the children still knew who he was. But this too had a drawback: they kept writing to him. And every time a sportswriter wrote a column on Babe Ruth (they still do, even in the 1970s) his mail increased. So long as he was able, he acknowledged all the mail.

If Babe Ruth had lived into his sixties he would have mellowed into the phase of a man's life when he puts aside many of this world's commitments. Consciously or unconsciously, old people usually adjust their demands to what is possible, in order to get peace of mind. Ruth never reached that age. He lived as do aging dandies, decayed professional beauties, forgotten child screen stars, and most of the ten thousand major-league ballplayers in the first years after eclipse, fretting and in pain until they link up with reality in a healthy way. Ruth was an unwanted man and didn't live to be old enough not to care.

A thunderbolt out of the sky.
—Larry MacPhail, June 1, 1946

In 1946 Babe Ruth, in his anguish, did something he had never done before. He asked for a job.

Since 1939 the Ruppert estate had operated the Yankees, but when the franchise earned only 5 percent of its estimated value in 1945 the executors decided to sell. It went for three million dollars to Del Webb, Dan Topping, and Larry MacPhail.

Ed Barrow left the club (and Joe McCarthy did not finish the 1946 season). At the end of the 1945 season the new owners signed Bill Dickey to a playing contract, killing a rumor that Dickey would manage at Newark.

Ruth gulped down his vanity and called MacPhail in January 1946 to ask for the job of manager of the Newark farm. MacPhail was staggered. He said it was a very interesting idea and he would call back. After a wait of two weeks Ruth called him again. Mac-Phail said George Weiss, the new general manager, was in Chicago, and MacPhail would call Ruth as soon as Weiss returned. There was another long wait. Ruth called a third time. MacPhail, full of regrets, said the Yankees had other plans and were getting somebody else. The whole story was in *The Times* on June 2, but the embarrassed MacPhail wouldn't answer reporters' questions. The final touch was a letter from MacPhail, dated October 8,° a polite brush-off, offering Ruth a job promoting amateur baseball in greater New York as agent of the Yankees. Babe knew it was bad news when Claire handed him the envelope. As he put it, good baseball news comes over the telephone; the bad news they drop into the mail. Once again he put his head on the kitchen table and cried.

Babe was now bitter against organized baseball. And Claire hadn't forgiven the Yankees at least as late as the mid-1950s.

Nobody really likes Jorge [Pasquel] but he's a national hero.
—Anonymous Mexican, *The Times*, May 16, 1946

Organized baseball had some legal problems in early 1946. There was talk of unionizing the players, and the Mexican League under Jorge Pasquel was raiding United States baseball. Pasquel invited Babe Ruth to visit him in Mexico City with all expenses paid, too good a thing to turn down. No, Babe said, they hadn't offered him

° Printed in Claire Ruth, *The Babe and I* (Englewood Cliffs, N.J., 1954), p. 194.

a job, but it would be a nice vacation. (The Ruths weren't in financial trouble; Claire ordered all the groceries from Gristede's, a fancy New York grocer, and she kept the balance in the checking account at more than a hundred thousand dollars.) Mexicans were pleased that Pasquel was baiting the *gringos*, defying their futile court orders, and entertaining their greatest baseball hero, if only as a guest. As Babe, Claire, Julia, and Julia's new husband boarded their plane, Babe enjoyed telling reporters how stodgily and negligently the United States baseball owners ran the game.

On arrival in Mexico City he shouted, "Que tal, amigos!" to the crowd and talked, as usual, with a crush of reporters. They told him how wonderfully a home run jumped off the bat at that altitude, to which he suggested jovially, "You could possibly bunt one."

Ruth sat with Pasquel in a crowd of fifteen thousand to watch a ball game on May 16 (he soon had a low opinion of the level of play). As it turned out, he saw little of his host who was a man of many interests, but he got in some golf and wasn't at all annoyed that Pasquel couldn't be pinned down. Ruth didn't really want a job with the Mexican League; he hadn't lost hope of an opening at home. The Ruths went to a bullfight and left early ("That first one certainly died hard—it took twenty-five minutes to kill him").

Mexicans asked him if baseball was a monopoly in the United States, as many judges had denied. Ruth called it monopoly, referring the judges to the uniform baseball contract with its reserve clause: "All they have to do is read it."

He and Claire went to another ball game, which so bored him he couldn't remember who won or by what score. He much preferred the golf, swimming, and fishing Pasquel contrived for the Ruths at Acapulco, where Babe was redly sunburned. Finally he got down to baseball, giving a fifteen-minute batting display during which he managed to hit two balls over the fence off easy pitching.

After two weeks they flew back. Pasquel had made no firm offer, was often invisible, but manfully picked up all the bills. Why he wanted Ruth to come is a question. It was good press-agentry for the Mexican League, since American newspapers reported the Ruths' doings almost daily. That may be enough to explain the invitation.

When the Ruths returned, Babe said he had a good time, and then he told reporters about his talks with MacPhail on the question of managing Newark and how he had been "getting pushed around for more than a month." *Question*: Why did he feel baseball owed him anything? In reply Babe reached way back into the past and dredged up the offer he once had to play in the Federal League. As a rookie he had been told that organized baseball would forever bar all Federal League players. He believed it and turned down an offer. But baseball welcomed the return of the Federal jumpers with no penalty. Thus, said Ruth, he was "jobbed out of $20,000" and baseball showed no gratitude.

It was just as well Ruth had no part in the Mexican League, for Pasquel overextended himself, lost about $350,000, and went off to shoot animals in Africa. Like the Federals of the previous generation, the outlaws who jumped from the United States were forgiven.

Back home, sour on baseball, Ruth went into golf as much as possible. As the summer passed his closest friends noticed that he didn't seem in very good physical condition. His voice was getting hoarser. Ruth noticed it himself but blamed it on the crude silver-nitrate treatment by the Red Sox trainer so many years before, or maybe it had something to do with his sinuses. He also was suffering from pains over his left eye, which he treated with aspirin.

59 · An Ability to Die Well
(1947-1948)

Babe Ruth's left-frontal headaches became rapidly worse in late 1946. He entered French Hospital in a wheelchair on November 26 for observation, with severe pains above his left eye. His face was so swollen that his left eye was closed. Thus far his treatment had been only aspirin and penicillin. (He weighed 278 pounds.) Three days later a hospital spokesman said Ruth was much improved (but the No Visitors sign was up). There wasn't much of a public flurry, though editors saw to it that his obituaries were brought up to date. X-ray examination showed no cause of his pain.

On December 14 there was ungrounded optimism that he would leave the next day, much improved from his "combination of ailments," but he was still there on the 16th. Dentists took out three bad teeth which Ruth himself blamed for his illness. A week later the hospital said he was "on the road to complete recovery" from his "sinusitis" but wouldn't be going home for Christmas.

Soon several muscles of his head were paralyzed and he was unable to raise his left eyelid, unable to swallow, and unable to speak without difficulty. Six specialists, on January 5, 1947, advised surgery to relieve "intractable pain" and added, "The outlook is considered serious." They set surgery for the next day.

That evening Paul Carey, Ruth's friend of eighteen years, asked him, "Don't you think you ought to set your house in order?" Ruth knew what Carey meant. He hadn't lost his faith, but his religious practice was hit or miss. Carey brought a priest, Ruth received the sacrament of penance, and the priest said he could receive Communion in the morning, before the operation, without fasting. But Ruth insisted on fasting (no foods or fluids from midnight, as church regulations then stood).

The operation on the 5th, by Dr. H. M. Wertheim and five others, lasted two hours. They didn't tell what they did, but we now know they tied off a main artery on the left side of the neck, and Ruth believed they purposely cut nerves to relieve pain. What was important, but unsaid, was that they proved to themselves Ruth had cancer. On the next day his condition was described as "fair," but as days passed there was no improvement. X-ray therapy proceeded until, as Ruth put it, "my hair came out in hunks when the nurses tried to comb it." They fed him intravenously. He lost 128 pounds. Although he told nobody, he expected to die.

But gradually he seemed to mend. A week after the operation he walked a few steps. And a week later a few more. Toots Shor sent in meals (which Ruth couldn't eat). Finally, on February 3, visitors were allowed. Among the first was the baseball commissioner, A. B. Chandler. Ruth pointed to his thin arms, and they both wept. Chandler, wiping his eyes, said, "Babe, you are Mr. Baseball," and left. Frank Stevens, the baseball concessionaire, came too. Ruth told him, "This is the last time around, but before I go I'm going to get out of here and have some fun." By this time Ruth was able to draft a public letter of thanks for all of the kind messages he had received.

Babe, Claire, Julia, and their large brown dog celebrated Babe's fifty-second birthday in the hospital. Babe seemed cheerful. There were a recording of the voices of Eddie Collins and Ted Williams, telegrams from Connie Mack and Jack Dempsey, a bottle of Lourdes water from an unknown admirer in Whiting, Indiana (Ruth sprinkled the water over himself), the equivalent of a florist's inventory to scent the room, and four gifts of birthday cakes. Connie Mack's wire read, in part, HOPE YOU HAVE MANY MORE BIRTHDAYS AND PASS MY 84 YEARS.

On February 15 Ruth left French Hospital, much shrunken. When he saw a hundred people waiting, the tears came. Walter Winchell, on the radio, had said he was down to a hundred pounds. Ruth said his bones alone weighed more than that! Actually his weight had fallen as low as 150 pounds and then rose to 186. This ballplayer, eleven years retired, had received about thirty thousand letters and telegrams while hospitalized, many of the letters coming from children unborn when he played his last major-league game. Before the flood of mail began he had sometimes wept in misery when alone, but here was Ruthville rebuilt and rustling with postal cheers. His favorite was this:

Dear Babe,
    Everybody in the seventh grade is pulling and praying for you. I am enclosing a medal and a holy picture which if you wear will make you better.

Your pal -
Mike Quinlan

P.S. I know this will be your 61 homer. You will hit it.

There was still time for the boys. Autographing at
Hotel Onondaga, Syracuse, New York, June 5, 1947.
(*National Baseball Library, Cooperstown, New York.*)

Babe wore Mike Quinlan's medal pinned to his pajamas the rest of
his life. May Singhi Breen, Melvyn Lowenstein (the Ruths' lawyer),
and Paul Carey organized a correspondence staff which answered
all of the mail that came to the hospital.

When first at home on Riverside Drive Ruth had three nurses on
eight-hour shifts. Claire said he was a "very sick man," but a week
later he went over to Newark to help station WOR celebrate its
twenty-fifth anniversary by broadcasting a few words. Hank Greenberg dropped in on a snowy day to ask whether Ruth would advise
him to sign a playing contract with the Pirates (Ruth said yes).

Physically he improved. He asked to be driven out to look at
Bayside Country Club, Queens, on March 11, and on the 22nd he
spent four hours there practicing his putting. Early in April he went
to a press conference at the Waldorf-Astoria where the Ford Motor
Company announced he had signed a life contract to help promote
American Legion junior baseball. At 194 pounds he was "gaunt and
drawn, but in good spirits"; his voice was markedly hoarse. On the
next day, April 8, he flew to Florida with Claire and a nurse to rest
and take the sun as the well-shielded guest of Raymond F. Kilthau
of Great Neck, a golfing friend of twenty years. Three days later he
caught a fifty-pound sailfish after a thirty-minute struggle which left
him feeling "whipped." His voice was but a hoarse whisper. Wherever he went children flocked and clamored. At the Bayshore golf
course he scored a 45 on the first nine but couldn't drive more than
150 yards. Pleased to have played, he said, "I haven't felt better
since I left the hospital." Photographers show him so thin that his

once fat cheeks had vertical wrinkles and his once round chin came to a point when he smiled. The group flew back to New York early in the third week of April. At least he had a tan to replace the hospital pallor. When they got home Johnny Sylvester, the promised-home-run-boy of the 1926 World Series, came to pay a welcome call, bringing the old baseball.

The occasion of the return from Florida was the setting of April 27 as Babe Ruth Day in every park of organized baseball by proclamation of Commissioner Chandler. It wasn't a commercial promotion; prices weren't to be raised.

In New York Babe Ruth Day had threatened rain, cleared up for the game, and afterward it poured. Attendance was 58,339. While Ruth waited for the start of the ceremonies, Yankee greats of 1947 asked for his autograph like schoolboys. Other autograph hunters were kept at a distance. As Ruth waited, temporarily gray of head because of X-ray treatment, we may suppose he thought of Lou Gehrig's halting trip to the plate on a similar day nine years earlier.

First on the program was Cardinal Spellman's prayer. Spellman wrote one for the occasion, being a man of literary confidence greater than his talent. Commissioner Chandler was next. He too had a prayer, but few heard it because the crowd booed him (he had recently suspended Durocher for a year). Boos turned to applause at Chandler's mention of Ruth's greatness. The league presidents had their say, presenting Ruth with a plaque and an autograph book signed by well-wishers. Mel Allen, the Yankees play-by-play broadcaster, then introduced Babe Ruth, who, in the pathetic hoarse and growly voice so often reproduced, gave his usual remarks on getting boys started early and closed with "I'm glad to have had the opportunity to thank everybody. Thank you." He coughed badly during his talk. This was a mercifully short program. There would have been more civic bunkum except that everybody knew Ruth was "still a mighty sick man." The chief guest stayed until the eighth inning when he left, very tired. Ed Barrow sat through it all in a mezzanine box, and nobody interviewed *him*. In Baltimore, St. Mary's Industrial School joined the Orioles in the ceremonies.

In the dugout, just after the speeches, where Ruth had another painful coughing spell, the Cardinal offered to bring Communion to him at home. Ruth replied, "I'll come down to your place." The Cardinal didn't stay for the game.

The next day there was a rumor that Ruth was dead of fatigue, but, as his physician said, "he just overdid yesterday."

One can't help feeling that the Japanese observed Babu Rusu Day (on the same date) more appropriately. Instead of gassy speeches about the ennobling religions of baseball and nationalism, they gave a thousand yen (about twenty-five dollars) to every professional player who hit a home run that day.

On April 28 Ruth went out again for a longing look at the Bayside fairways.

New York weather was foul that spring, and Ruth's health got no better. It seemed best to flee back to Florida with friend Kilthau, wife, nurse, and dog on May 10. The usual daily schedule at Kilthau's place was: up at 7:30 (Ruth was usually first), a swim off Kilthau's beach with the dog, breakfast, a reading of the sports pages, some practice with golf clubs or fishing from the pier, lunch at a nearby country club, and then a nap until late afternoon. Ruth and his host played much gin rummy. Bedtime usually came before 10 P.M. "The rest," he told friends, "is doing me an awful lot of good." The troupe went back to New York on May 23. Ruth found the return trip tiring.

Having rallied as much as he could, on June 4 Babe, Claire, a physician, and a nurse started forty thousand miles of travel for Ford Motor's American Legion baseball project, beginning with Syracuse. They traveled in relative comfort since the company bought half the seats on any flight they took, to give them room. Ford had spent a million dollars on junior baseball since 1943, had 5,891 teams playing, and the program was still growing. The routine was this: a motorcade from the airport to the hotel (with the route announced in advance), a civic lunch, another procession to the local park, a cameramen's session with Ruth and the boys as Ruth held a bat (and hit a few grounders until medical advice stopped it). The streets were usually lined with friendly crowds, and schools often set their children free to see the doings. The civic luncheons seemed to need climaxes, so people gave Ruth those civic awards that in a republic take the place of royal birthday honors: Sports Father of the Year (on Fathers' Day), Sports Award of B'rith Sholom (Philadelphia), Service Award of Boystown, Nebraska, National Civic Service Award of the Fraternal Order of Eagles, and lesser things. These decorations probably did the donors some psychological good.

The travel kept Ruth's mind off his physical miseries to some extent, but late in June he had to check into Mt. Sinai Hospital for four days of unexplained treatment.

The treatment Ruth received at Mt. Sinai was the injection of a substance called teropterin, a synthetic folic acid. Folic acid is one of the vitamin B complex. It had cured spontaneous breast cancer in mice. Ruth's case was one of several hundred experimental treatments. When used on human subjects who had every known kind of cancer, some showed improved appetite, a few gained weight but more lost, and about half of the anemia cases improved. More than a third had less pain, but opiates had a better score than that. People so treated usually felt better, but researchers knew they would feel better just because of the special attention. At least it wasn't poisonous, and there were no unwanted changes of pulse or respiration. All of the patients died of cancer sooner or later, so it must be scored as one of the blind alleys of cancer-cure research, and hopes raised by headlines "Vitamins for Cancer" were false.

After beginning the treatment Ruth settled down to helping Bob Considine extract notes from Ruth's memory for their book *The Babe Ruth Story*, which they had been working on together off and on since Ruth left French Hospital. Allied Artists bought the film rights for $150,000 in July and hired Considine to do the screen treatment.

After a physical examination at French Hospital on August 1, Babe, Claire, and retinue took wing again for Junior Legion ball. Claire said his physicians thought he was "getting along very nicely." Considering his racked appearance, that meant he was not wholly disabled. Hospitable San Franciscans almost killed him with kindness, even including some yachting on salt water (delightful, but only for people in perfect trim). The baseball show at Seals Park drew twelve thousand, free, and Ruth, in his wretched gravelly voice, spoke correctly on raising the young to do right.

> Just putting a ball and a bat in a boy's hands doesn't make him a player. You've got to start young and keep at it. I started when I was six years old.

Back in New York Ruth and Considine pressed on with the construction of *The Babe Ruth Story*, which the *Saturday Review* reported as coming along well. (Unknown to most, Fred Lieb was putting Considine's notes in book form for a flat fee, which wasn't the wisest deal for Lieb—the book made a lot of money.) The Ruths went to the World Series (Yankees over the Dodgers) where Babe posed with Ty Cobb and Tris Speaker (no one of them liked the other two). He looked positively ghastly.

He played Santa Claus at the Astor Hotel on December 10 at a benefit for the Sister Kenny Foundation, entertaining forty child polio victims. We may suppose he reflected on death in these weeks of the old year. Brother Gilbert died late in October of a cerebral hemorrhage, and at the moment when Ruth was ho-ho-ho-ing for the crippled children at the Astor, Walter Johnson died of a brain tumor. (Then Herb Pennock died in January.)

Ruth was a patient at the neurological institute of the Medical Center for a week beginning January 10, 1948. What was done was not announced. All that was said was that he was "doing nicely."

We now know there was surgery performed on his neck, but there are no details. To recover from his operation Babe, with Claire and male nurse Frank Delaney, went off to Florida on February 3. Reporters asked what he thought of his approaching birthday. He answered that the number of years meant nothing; it all depended on how you felt. He felt weak and said they "could put down 'ninety,' with this neck." But his weight was 212.

The train trip to Florida he reported as "not so good." A hundred and fifty people, including Paul Carey, met them at the station in Miami. Ruth was wearing a white camel-hair coat and matching cap. The Ruths checked into the Golden Strand Hotel in Miami Beach. Paul Carey told people the Ruths would stay until mid-March and then go to California where Babe would advise on the making of the picture based on *The Babe Ruth Story*, newly published. Six weeks later Ruth said he felt much better, but they didn't leave for California until late April.

The job of advising on the film was only public-relations gas. The Ruths wanted Paul Douglas for the lead; they got Bill Bendix, who, to Claire, was better cast in the title role of Eugene O'Neill's *The Hairy Ape*. She said it was "a ridiculous choice." Ruth's only advising was to pose showing Bendix how to hold a bat. The producers hurried production as much as possible and used Ruth only to get space for their press releases.

That charade finished, the Ruths again went on the road for Ford and Junior Legion baseball. A Ford vice-president said Ruth would be "high on a list of baseball's top money earners" because of this job, but wouldn't give the figure. (It was a thousand a month and all expenses.) By this time the Ruths could use money; cancer isn't a cheap disease. When Ruth gave the manuscript of *The Babe Ruth Story* to Yale in a ceremony at a Yale-Princeton ball game on June 6, he was very thin, very tanned, spoke steadily and well, but his voice had that gravelly, cracking quality.

The season of 1948 was the twenty-fifth season of play in Yankee Stadium. What a fit time to prop Babe Ruth up in public to draw a paying crowd! The scheme was to play a two-inning Old-Timers game on June 13 and then retire shirt No. 3 for all time by giving it to the Baseball Hall of Fame along with the 1927 bat that hit home run number sixty, and his glove and shoes. Claire was cynical about the way the Yankee management could see Babe's value in promoting sales and nothing else, but said Babe's feelings were "far purer than mine." On the day there were several rubbishy speeches and, more to the point, a laying of wreaths on the tombstone-like center-field monuments to Miller Huggins and Lou Gehrig.

Babe, in spanking-clean uniform, his hair brown again after the temporary graying, sat in the Old-Timers' sweltering dressing room

wrapped in his camel-hair coat, shivering. Then there was a deadly
fifteen-minute wait in the runway behind the dugout. Finally he
walked out on the field, posed with a bat (which he needed for
support) and stood in "the caldron of sound he must know better
than any other man." When he walked off he tottered to Ed Barrow,
finally making his peace with the icy man who, since 1918, thought
of him only as a batting machine. Ruth's picture, from behind as he
posed on the field, has a noble quality. Photographs of his face that
day are grisly.

After the June 13 show at Yankee Stadium Ruth was plainly failing. He said he wasn't "feeling very good at all." Nobody told him
what his illness was because they underestimated his ability to die
well. His physician took him to Memorial Hospital on East 68th
Street, a cancer center (as Ruth well knew), on June 26. Toots Shor
began his catering service again. A private detective was always at
Ruth's door to keep out strangers.

At Memorial Hospital there was a chaplain, an alumnus of St.
Mary's Industrial School who had been in the school very briefly, the
Reverend Thomas Hilary Kaufman, O.P. (Dominican). Sharing
both religion and the old school bond, he had Ruth's complete con-

Good-bye. June 1948. (*National Baseball Library, Cooperstown, New York.*)

fidence. Father Kaufman found him "thoroughly drained and wasted" but resilient, in good spirit, calm, resigned, lucid, patient. Ruth once told Bozeman Bulger that he valued his religion because it set a standard by which to measure oneself, like a batting average. In his case, in 1948, the standard, of course, was the crucifixion. While Ruth didn't go to his own Calvary willingly, hardly anybody does. He wasn't one of those who ignore death until the last minute. He thought about death for weeks and let himself die naturally. To help keep his mind on the game, so to speak, he had a statue of St. Martin de Porres, the black saint, at his bedside. As somebody once said, his religion was hard to live in but a good one to die in.

When word seeped out that Father Kaufman was with Ruth, the priest received a river of mail from children, thanking him, sending pennies for Mass stipends, and enclosing an enormous number of rosaries and similar sacramentals, all for Ruth.

Radium or X-ray treatments began on July 2, but no other anti-cancer medication. The hospital said Ruth was "resting more comfortably." The patient flew to Baltimore by chartered plane on July 13 to appear at some kind of outdoor ecumenical meeting, but it was rained out. In Baltimore he saw his diminutive sister, Mamie Ruth Moberly, and several Xaverian Brothers. As he drove through the Baltimore streets bystanders recognized him everywhere and boys trotted along shouting, "It's the Babe! It's the Babe!" To escape the telephone and the curious, Claire, Julia, Dorothy, and Mamie moved to a hotel near the hospital, not registering under their true names.

The Babe Ruth Story, the film from the Ruth and Considine book, was to open at the Astor Theater in New York on the 26th. Mayor O'Dwyer and a group of press people joined in the press-agentry and tormented Ruth with a well-noised call at the hospital on the 25th, where Ruth, in a chair, went through the form of inviting everybody to see the picture. Proceeds of the opening would go to a Ruth charity.

Claire and Babe went to the opening and endured half the picture before leaving. Bosley Crowther of *The Times* reviewed it (July 27):

It is hard to conceive that anyone—Babe Ruth's fans, least of all—will be entirely happy about this dreary succession of heroics and tears, passing for factuality. Granted that the Babe, as determinedly played by William Bendix, was a truly colorful figure and a man of human foibles, it is hard to accept a presentation of a great, mawkish, noble-spirited buffoon as a reasonable facsimile of Ruth. There is even a minimum of base-ball playing and most of that patently phony and absurd

Thirty days before death, July 16, 1948. (*National Baseball Library, Cooperstown, New York.*)

Arriving at Memorial Hospital, New York, August 1948, left to right, Mamie Ruth Moberly (Mrs. Wilbur Moberly), Claire Ruth, Julia Ruth Flanders (Mrs. Richard Flanders).

studio action. On the sidelines, Claire Trevor and Charles Bickford are wasted.

Crowther thought it was more like low-grade fiction than low-grade biography. *Time* said, "It turned out to be a mawkish tribute that left out everything that was robust about the man." Claire couldn't stand it; to her it was an "obscenity," a "ridiculous charade," a "masterpiece in mush." It is still seen in the 1970s on late-night television.

August opened with a heat wave that made Ruth uncomfortable in the uncooled hospital. His appearance at this time, according to Father Kaufman, was that of "a triangle standing on its point. Massive bone structure through and across the shoulders, with the skeleton tapering down to very skinny legs and ankles." Joe Dugan was admitted to call in the second week. Ruth took his hand. "I'm gone, Joe. I'm gone." On the 10th he had a cold and a slight fever. Word that he was dying began to spread, and boys, his chief link with the whole people, began to gather in groups outside the hospital. Now only Carey, the family, and Father Kaufman were admitted to the room. The hospital bulletin of the 12th said his condition was "critical." The switchboards were swamped with calls (as were police and newspaper switchboards), and on the 12th and 13th ten thousand pieces of mail arrived, including a note from President Truman. Altogether fifty thousand letters and telegrams came to the hospital during this stay. As yet the physicians had not told the people what exactly ailed their patient, but on the 14th they began to issue hourly medical bulletins on his condition.

Ruth made a mighty effort on the 16th and managed to sit in a chair for twenty minutes. His temperature rose all day. He told his womenfolk, "Don't come back tomorrow. I won't be here." By this time he seemed to have symptoms of pneumonia. That evening he made, so far as we know, his last remark. His male nurse, Calvin L. Holderman, R.N., asked him to autograph a copy of *The Babe Ruth Story*. Babe said, "If I don't do it tonight, I never will." He drifted into a light sleep. Father Kaufman, Claire, Mamie, Julia, and Dorothy left the room.

He never awakened. He died at 8:01 P.M., Eastern Daylight Time, August 16, 1948.

The announcement of his death named cancer as his disease for the first time. All three radio networks interrupted their programming for special programs on Babe Ruth. Claire's cousin, Johnny Mize,* left a game at the Polo Grounds in the fourth inning and joined the family. On the 17th the flag at the Baseball Hall of

---

* John Robert Mize (1913–   ), first baseman, fifteen seasons, 1936–1953, Cardinals, Giants, Yankees, batting average .312.

Fame in Cooperstown flew at half-staff. Moe Berg said, "Ruth isn't a man; he's an institution."

The postmortem showed that Babe Ruth's cancer originated in the upper part of the pharynx, that is, the top of the area between the mouth and the tube leading to the stomach. It is the place where the nose passages lead to the top of the throat. Surgery for cancer would have been useless there, even if surgeons had known that was the seat. A tumor growing there pressed on certain nerves leading from the brain, one of which was needed to move the muscles used for speaking and swallowing, hence his hoarseness and difficulty in swallowing. There were signs of the tumor in his neck which led to the operation of early 1947. The surgeons discovered cancer then, but there was no way to learn where it first started.*

> **His death . . . impoverished the public stock of harmless pleasures.**
>
> —Samuel Johnson

Ruth's body lay inside the main entrance to Yankee Stadium on the evening of the 17th for viewing by all who cared to come. The flags of the Stadium were at half-staff. People came dressed as if to see a ball game, lined four abreast all around the Stadium and a block more. Street vendors sold hot dogs, soda, and souvenir pictures of Ruth. The people passed his coffin steadily and respectfully until midnight and all the next day. Estimates of the number of mourners at Yankee Stadium range from seventy-seven thousand to two hundred thousand; there was no counting them.

About seventy-five thousand came to the funeral at St. Patrick's Cathedral on the rainy morning of the 19th. Some got inside by the power of black-edged tickets of admission (there were many empty seats), but sixty-five to seventy thousand stood under umbrellas, or wearing raincoats, or covered with newspapers in the rain outside, held back by police lines.

The nave of the cathedral was spattered with temporal dignitaries of all degrees from the worlds of politics, stage, screen, industry, commerce, and journalism, plus four plain old-fashioned ballplayers and one umpire. Altar boy Robert Kerby, now a professor of history, remembers the cathedral as unusually dark because of the driving rain of a heavy cloudy-black August shower. In the sanctuary was Cardinal Spellman, an impressive crush of forty-four auxiliaries and monsignori, and twelve altar boys. At the end of the prescribed Latin rite service the Cardinal *again* tried to improve on the ancient noble prayers with his own composition. (Cardinal Spellman may

---

* Cancer is Claire Ruth's special curse. It has killed her mother, father, brother, and husband.—*New York Sunday News*, July 29, 1973.

Part of the crowd which filed through Yankee Stadium at night, when Ruth's body lay there. (*National Baseball Library, Cooperstown, New York.*)

Part of the crowd which filed through Yankee Stadium on the second day that Ruth's body lay there. (*National Baseball Library, Cooperstown, New York.*)

Crowd on Fifth Avenue to see funeral cortege. (*National Baseball Library, Cooperstown, New York.*)

have been the only man who was programmed, as they say, always to be wrong in temporal matters and always to be right on eternal questions.)

After the funeral mass, as though this were fiction, the sun came out while the pallbearers jouncily carried the coffin down the steps. The cortege drove about thirty miles to Gate of Heaven Cemetery as another hundred thousand stood at curbs to watch it pass. The body was placed in a receiving vault until the grave could be prepared. Hundreds pressed around, and many took gladioli for remembrance. Final burial was a private ceremony on October 24.

Only Presidents who have died in office have attracted larger crowds of mourners to their funerals than Babe Ruth drew to his funeral. The only larger funeral in Ruth's lifetime was Franklin D. Roosevelt's.*

* One's mind turns back to the funeral of Rudolph Valentino in 1926, but Italian fascists, Italian antifascists, and self-important Hollywood people seized on the Valentino funeral as the chance to make public demonstrations to advance themselves or their causes. The result was a hundred injuries, the "irreverence of thousands," "disorder and rioting."—*The Times*, Aug. 25, 26, 31, 1926. Ruth's funeral was in every way a funeral and nothing else.

Babe Ruth left his family well off for money. His fourteen-page will, dated August 9, 1948, signed in shaky handwriting "Georgge* Herrman Ruth" [sic], initialed on every page with a firm "GHR," left his estate to Claire, for her life, and then to his daughters, less 10 percent after Claire's death to a charitable trust called the Babe Ruth Foundation. Claire, Julia, and Dorothy each received five thousand dollars immediately, and sister Mamie ten thousand dollars. The net value of the estate when closed in 1951 was $360,811, which would be about equal in value to twice or three times that much in the mid-1970s. When one realizes that Babe always lived well and had absolutely gambled away, lost in business, and been swindled out of about a quarter of a million dollars, the size of the remainder is imposing. Claire, Christy Walsh, and Babe's ability to see reason when presented in a friendly manner deserve equal credit.

The Babe Ruth Foundation was to help children in need. Babe hoped it would attract money of itself, but the largest contribution was a hundred thousand dollars from Sam Briskin, chairman of the Revère Camera Company. The trustees would not plunge into fund-raising in spite of many suggestions of such schemes, for fear the money would tend to go for overhead costs instead of to the children. At present the Foundation is dormant.

Babe Ruth's death brought a flood of proposals for memorials.

Here the author must confess a bias; he believes monuments should be monumental, and would never vote to take money intended for a tombstone and spend it on a useful object called a memorial, hospitals always excepted.

In this perhaps warped view there seems a certain shabbiness in the rush to finance pleasures, as a baseball academy ("the West Point of Baseball"), a polo trophy, and a Babe Ruth Stadium for Cardinal Spellman's current project—Archbishop Stepinac High School, intended as a three-hundred-thousand-dollar charitable contribution to rich suburbanites.

Only one man, Emerson Maxwell of Newark, is on record as urging that Yankee Stadium be renamed Babe Ruth Stadium. It was a splendid motion and died, so to speak, for want of a second. In September Baltimore named its new ball park Babe Ruth Stadium, and in December the Baltimore Park Board renamed it Municipal Stadium. There is no important baseball field today named for Ruth (or any other player). But, quite selflessly, Knoxville, Tennessee, named a new playground for Ruth, and York, Pennsylvania, named a new boys' baseball field Babe Ruth Field.

New York did something for Ruth's memory by naming the inter-

---

* He scratched out the second "g" in "Georgge" but no one noticed the second "r" in "Herrman."

section of 161st Street and River Avenue, in the Bronx, Babe Ruth Plaza, and also named a playground in McCombs Dam Park for him. The Yankees erected a third monolith in center field, next to Gehrig's and Huggins's, on which was lettered:

GEORGE HERMAN "BABE" RUTH

1895–1948

A GREAT BALL PLAYER

A GREAT MAN

A GREAT AMERICAN

ERECTED BY

THE YANKEES

AND

THE NEW YORK BASEBALL WRITERS

APRIL 19, 1949

There was also a sea of memorial writing (much of it, as a critic said, "incredibly mawkish"). In the four days after Ruth's death there were 490 columns of praise in New York newspapers alone. The British daily press also noted his death. In the next fifteen months there were thirteen articles in the *Saturday Evening Post, Recreation, Newsweek, Life, Time, Scholastic, American Magazine, Colliers, Science Digest,* and the *Saturday Review.* There were no doubt many more in less well-indexed magazines.

It is twenty-odd years since his death, but one with ears tuned and eyes alert will hear or read his name almost monthly. Even without any imposing monument his memory will last in this country till memory be dead.

The grave marker, Gate of Heaven Cemetery. (*National Baseball Library, Cooperstown, New York.*)

60 · What Did He Have to Merit This?

Babe Ruth's success depended on his constitution and his temperament, but it also owed much to the accident of timing. If he had come to New York before the First World War he would have played with a weakly financed team much less able and popular than the Giants. He came to New York when the Yankees had rich, ambitious owners who were able to make the most of the interest he stirred. The result was a rising zest for public spectacles, and Ruth rose with the flood, in just the right place. From 1920 to 1932 there was a stormy excitement over baseball unknown before or since. The only rival idols of baseball heroes were college football players and occasionally boxers. A career like Ruth's is no longer possible. Today baseball has the lively competition of professional football, hockey, golf, and basketball, which split the popular interest. Imagine concentrating the popular feeling for the darlings of basketball, hockey, and football entirely on baseball heroes, and mostly on Babe Ruth. That's the way it was in the 1920s. Where Ruth stood was the center of the world of games. As the most cursory reading of the 1920 sports pages shows, his feat of hitting fifty-four home runs in 1920 was deliriously exciting.

No one was more persistently popular, not even Lindbergh. The press used hundreds of tons of extra newsprint to tell of Lindbergh, but the story ran out in a few years. Ruth's story went on and on. He met an elemental need of the crowd. Every hero must have his human flaw which he shares with his followers. In Ruth it was his hedonism, as exaggerated in folklore and fable. If he were nothing more than an exceptional batter he would have been respected, but he attracted more than respect. The public love of Ruth approached idolatry. His reputed carnality was necessary to the folk-hero pattern. As Waite Hoyt said, he was "the kind of bad boy it is easy to forgive." He fit the public image of what a highly paid ballplayer *ought* to be, and, if he didn't really fit, the people wished to believe any legend that would shape the image. (They still do.) The combination of great skill on the field and a shared flaw off the field made him the most admired and theatrical man in the game.

He made money. Salaries, a bonus in the early twenties, and a percentage of club exhibition games paid him about a million dollars. World Series shares and barnstorming profits made perhaps another half-million. Many kinds of what we might call celebrity income also brought in about a half-million. In real purchasing power, a few heavyweight boxing champions and Pele, the Brazilian soccer player, are the only muscle heroes who have done better.

It is hard to think of Ruth as doing anything else with his life. If he could have started earlier in golf, say, as a caddie, he might have made as much as twenty-five thousand dollars a year, which was high for an annual income of a golf professional in his time. With his nearly perfect physical coordination he could, no doubt, have become a mechanically excellent pianist, but he showed no artistic tastes. Boxing had no money ceiling at the time, but the company and the game itself were dangerous, and he did not have the kind of killer spirit necessary. Football was not then profitable. It had to be baseball.

People like to think he would play even better if he were playing today, but the only advantage today's batters have is that American League fences, according to a calculation suggested by Cleveland Amory, are closer on the average by about twenty-four feet. This advantage is offset by all-night flying, less regular hours, the creation of the specialized relief pitcher, and the inferiority of the lighting for night games. Furthermore, Ruth didn't have to compete with blacks.

Ruth's last photographs have made him seem a freak carved out of blubber with no ability except to hit the ball a long way. Red Smith said what most expert witnesses felt: "The truth is that he was the complete ballplayer, certainly one of the greatest and maybe the one best of all time." Ruth seems almost to have been tailored to the game. We can list very few serious rivals for the adjective "best." Smith's word "complete" is the key word. Ruth could have been in the big leagues a long time at every position except second base, shortstop, and third base, positions at which left-handed throwers are handicapped. For example, only two pitchers in the Hall of Fame have better won-loss percentages than Ruth's (Whitey Ford and Lefty Grove). His many-sidedness was so dazzling that if it were supported only by oral tradition, apart from baseball's great heap of numbers called statistics, young people would snicker at the Ruth stories of the elders.

Every art form has its greatest practitioner. Every art form also has able men who say there is *one* way to perform (the *one* way

Babe Ruth monument, Koshein Stadium, Kobe, Japan, dedicated February 26, 1949. (*National Baseball Library, Cooperstown, New York.*)

changes from time to time), and they set down the rules. In each case the greatest practitioner first excelled according to the rules, then threw them away and soared above. Ruth pitched conventionally and as peer of the best in 1915, 1916, and 1917, but he found one position too confining. He went on to prove he could do almost everything else better than almost everybody else. The collaboration of Ed Barrow and Babe Ruth in converting a pitcher to a master of the whole game was the most influential single act in baseball history since the decision to pitch overhand instead of underhand.

To rate one player as the best is, of course, to place a high value on opinion. It is true that the pitching strategy of managers in Ruth's day differed from today's, and for the worse. But we can fairly contrast him to his contemporaries. After 1919, while in his prime, he was incomparable. There is no doubt at all that he was the best of his own age.

Ty Cobb's name comes to mind, of course, but Ruth could have done everything Cobb did, if he chose to do it, except to steal as many bases. Branch Rickey, perhaps baseball's only true intellectual, saw Ruth as "a rational conservative in play as compared to Cobb." Cobb would often risk games in order to shine, but Ruth never. Ruth's risks were risks to snatch victory. We don't much dwell on Ruth as man thinking. But thinking is not some kind of juggler's trick or a special exercise of the consciously literate. A man thinking is a man completely attending to something he is doing. In the ball game (though almost nowhere else) Ruth qualified as *homo sapiens.*

He was, even more, an instinctive player. The leaping spirit of life that animated Ruth's play can solve many a game-puzzle which reason is too slow to solve.

Hercules, the Greek patron of athletes, was usually pictured as a man carrying a club. Whether civilized man is man the tool user, man the timekeeper, or man the fuel burner (as anthropologists debate), the oldest graphic symbol of civilization is said to be the club-carrying man. That is what Ruth was. Despite his pitching and fielding records, we remember him as the man with the club, primitive but successful, the fundamental man who was victor over everything. Like Hercules, he satisfied the feeling of the people of his time that there was practically nothing a man couldn't do if he was strong enough and had a big enough stick.

There is an old saw which says: You can't win 'em all. Babe Ruth at bat seemed to be asking, "Why not?"

> **Ruth filled the parks by developing the home run into a hit of exciting elegance. For almost two decades he battered fences with such regularity that baseball's basic structure was eventually pounded into a different shape.**
>
> **—Lee Allen**

The explosive popularity of Babe Ruth in 1919 and 1920 marked the division between quite different styles of play. The characteristic elements of the earlier style were the bunt, the hit-and-run play, and the stolen base. In 1911 the total of stolen bases in both leagues was 3,394; in 1951 it was 863. The new idea was to clutter the bases with runners who waited for a long hit to bring them home in a group. Not only batting and running changed. Pitchers had to work more carefully, pitching to alleged weaknesses, preferring to walk batters rather than to chance the home run.

The earlier game was consciously dedicated to the nineteenth-century god Science. To bunt, to steal, to hit-and-run was explicitly called "scientific" baseball in the first decade of this century, by which time the religion of Science had trickled down to the popular culture. Babe Ruth, the iconoclast, showed the crowd they need not

The center-field monuments, Yankee Stadium. Left to right, Gehrig's, Huggins's, Ruth's. Ruth's was erected early in the season of 1949. (*The New York Yankees.*)

believe in the old god, that baseball was for fun not for a moral duty.

Ruth and those who tried to play as he played prompted changes in rules, equipment, and strategy. If one Ruth could fill a park, wouldn't sixteen Ruths fill sixteen parks? The ball became livelier and the pitcher was forbidden to spit on it. Even welterweight infielders now had bats with heavy barrels and thin handles. The successors of those pitchers who were kings of the diamond from 1900 to 1920 faced the painful fact that slight .220 hitters could wreck winning games in late innings by swinging for the fences.

The change was not universally welcome. It made the game too much dependent on strength for those who liked baseball as a game played with a sphere and a cylinder, which blended the sport of gymnastics with geometry. The new game has also somewhat lowered the standard of outfield play, since almost none of the annual three thousand home runs requires any response on the field. But the people, by buying tickets in greater proportion, showed they liked what had happened. It is still true that an advertised duel between two leading pitchers may sell an extra ten thousand tickets. But a 1–0 loss for the home team, pitched by a pair of journeymen, will please the crowd less than a 16–15 win.

You can't keep Ty Cobb's name out of this kind of discussion. It is only fair to the intelligent, flexible, and neurotic Cobb to say that if he had first appeared in 1925 instead of 1905 he would have been as great a player but a different kind.

As it was, the earlier game was the Cobb Game, the later was the Ruth Game. Cobb hit roughly as many home runs as Ruth stole bases, which is the simple formula of the change. Their value to their teams, on the scoreboard, was about equal. Cobb was worth 170 runs per season, Ruth 167.* But Cobb did his work coldly and craftily while Ruth played loosely and joyously, and the happy big bang sold a lot more tickets than Cobb's foxiness sold. Ruth was the first man who seemed always capable of breaking up the ball game every day he played. It became a national household question—Did he hit one today?

We often read that Babe Ruth "saved baseball" at the time of the 1919 Black Sox scandal (exposed in 1920) by reviving interest in the game. That is not quite accurate. His twenty-nine home runs of 1919 and his fifty-four of 1920 eclipsed the scandal, blocked it out of the minds of the people, so that the miscreants got about a tenth of the attention they would have had in, say, 1910. What he did for baseball was to enliven it so that the trend of attendance was reversed. From 1910 to 1918 baseball attendance did not increase as rapidly as the population. From 1919 to 1930 attendance increased at a much greater rate than the population. Until we know of some other cause we may credit the Ruth Game for turning the figures around.

Despite his relatively high salaries, Ruth was a bargain for the Yankees. At his peak he was worth from a third of a million to half a million dollars to the franchise. To baseball as an industry, his value is simply incalculable. We can only say that every club benefited from the greater popularity of the game. His presence with the Yankees, according to the Yankees' ablest scout, Paul Krichell, also had a good deal to do with the success of the Yankees in winning twenty-two pennants after Ruth left the team. In the days when the recruiting of beginners was an auction and not a kind of lottery, the Yankees found it easier to sign promising rookies because they wanted to be Yankees. The American League profited in the same way. By outdrawing the National League every club was better off, and therefore better able to outbid National League rivals for young

---

* Runs scored, plus runs batted in, minus home runs, divided by seasons of play. Figures from the *Baseball Encyclopedia* (1973).

Remembered on the seventeenth anniversary of death, August 16, 1965. (*National Baseball Library, Cooperstown, New York.*)

talent. (This advantage lasted until the National League earned the gratitude of blacks by breaking down the skin-color barrier.)

Babe Ruth is better remembered than contemporary Presidents Harding, Coolidge, Hoover, better than the contemporary ethical hero Lindbergh, better than the foxy hero Cobb. He needs no rescue from oblivion. Proofs of his lasting fame are everywhere, as a few instances will show.

—An organized baseball program for boys too old for Little League and too young for Legion Junior Baseball, called the Little Bigger League, changed its name in 1953 to the Babe Ruth League and, with Claire Ruth's help, has been flourishing ever since.

—As of this writing the city of Baltimore is renovating Pius Shamberger's house, where George Ruth was born and lived for a few days, in order to make it a Babe Ruth shrine.

—The National Commemorative Society, which commissions souvenir silver medals, polled its members in 1968 asking whose memory should be perpetuated on the 1969 medal. Babe Ruth won over Alexander Hamilton by a score of 760–724.

—*Der Sport Brockhaus; alles vom Sport von A-Z* (Wiesbaden, 1971), 575 p., gave Ruth seven lines (with three errors of fact) and a portrait.

—An ex-New Yorker named Jeff Shaya planted a tree in 1972 to memorialize Babe Ruth in the part of Israel's "youth woodland" called the "freedom forest for Soviet Jewry."

This list could be greatly lengthened.

Another kind of evidence is the interest of collectors. Dr. Helen Cripe of the American Antiquarian Society, studying the public sales of Americana, found seventeen pieces of Ruthiana listed in the years 1963–1973 in the catalogs of well-known dealers, at prices from $6.50 to $250.* Advertisements in the *Antique Trader* (Summer 1973) gave us a relative evaluation: three Mickey Mouse watches of 1931 from $95 to $135, and one Babe Ruth watch at $110.

Babe Ruth's fame is grounded on firm achievement. A baseball player can't hide mistakes or clumsiness; he stands alone and naked. There is no way to build up an ordinary player artificially into a great player for very long. A few "hot dogs" become well known, but their days of true popularity are few. Ruth was even more than a great player, he was a folk hero. He didn't have *all* of the qualities Thomas Carlyle insisted a hero must have (nor has Mickey Mouse), but he still gets from ordinary people most of the homage Carlyle said was due a hero.

His fame will last. Once a living legend crosses from the first generation into the third generation the legend is secure and durable. Captain John Smith made it; John Rolfe is rarely spoken of. Abraham Lincoln is remembered; Douglas, if recalled, is only Lincoln's foil. Babe Ruth's name draws crowds of small boys to the Ruth exhibit at Cooperstown; do many small boys urge visits to Lindbergh's trophies in St. Louis or to Grant's tomb in New York?

A man may be very imperfect and yet worth a good deal.
—Anthony Trollope, *Framley Parsonage*

Babe Ruth could not know the real world as obscure people know it. After living his formative years in a kind of monastery for boys he leaped into a heroic place as a winner on winning teams. He never saw anything anonymously; it was all shown to him as he

---

* See the Appendix: Ruthiana.

House of Pius Schamberger, grandfather of George
Ruth. George was born here and lived here for the
next several days. The scene is the 1969 dedication
of the house as a Ruth memorial. The two leftmost
ladies in the front row, seated, are Claire Ruth and
Mamie Ruth Moberly. The address is 216 Emory
Street, Baltimore. (*Weyman Swagger, Baltimore
Sunpapers.*)

stood on his pedestal. The ordinary person's world, how it worked,
what it looked like, what it did to people, he couldn't know. Which
may explain his fellow-feeling for people institutionalized in artificial
worlds—orphanages, hospitals, prisons.

He became a normal person by working to be normal. It was a
hard struggle for him to become an acceptable member of society,
partly because of his physical endowment. His appetites were strong
and his muscular urges even stronger. Driven by his makeup to
satisfy his gut and to use his muscles more than he used his mental
powers, he was initially out of balance. With effort he became
what we call normal by the age of thirty. If he had had less human
sympathy and even greater physical strength, he might have been in
a state of permanent emotional disturbance. But his generosity and

affections were as large as his hungers and his need to use his muscles.

It is rather sad that he never learned how typical a man he was. A reading of his memoirs and a study of his behavior raises the suspicion that he thought of himself as a kind of freak. Yet every American cigar store, pool hall, barber shop, bar, and grill during his glory times, had specimens much like him, lacking only the ability to play baseball well.

Ruth had all of our faults and had the material success most Americans would like to have. Never did he try to be anything he was not; he never spoke on a subject he was unqualified to speak on, except in reply to interviewers' questions, and even that was rare. The ballplayer was larger than the man. His mind was empty of practically everything but baseball, and packed tight with baseball. He never said a banal thing about baseball except in situations contrived by press agents, where he echoed the puritan bosh about the uplifting gifts of sport, platitudes he had heard others use, *pro forma*, with apparent success. Except when cornered in that way he was intellectually honest.

Did his manner of life hurt his play? The matter of keeping in shape for baseball has in it a deal of superstition. Inborn ability to make the catlike movements is far more important than precise weight. Only in long games and double-headers does overweight take its price. He may have neglected conditioning, but it wasn't that which killed him. Up to the age of thirty he tried hard to support the deathless belief of so many, that pleasure is happiness. Stories of the sins of popular heroes certainly grasp the attention of readers. There has been so much written about his very ordinary and rather tiresome hedonism (but never with names, places, dates), one is convinced there is a real need to believe Ruth a glutton who played best with a hangover. It reduces him to a smaller moral size so that some people can feel superior in some way to the otherwise titan figure, and, as John McCabe, in his life of George M. Cohan, well noted, America sees itself as "Peck's Bad Boy," rough and hard to rule but instinctively doing good because it knows what is right. Ruth *had* to be a bad boy to be the paramount American. As Tristram Coffin said, "The hero must have a bit of the fool in him."

The record contradicts the reputation of self-destructive gluttony. As of 1972 there were only sixty-one of ten thousand ballplayers who had played twenty full seasons in the major leagues. Ruth was one who played twenty full seasons and parts of two others. Whatever he did, it didn't destroy him as a player or a person.

Babe Ruth was driven by ambition and love. The ambition was to be the most successful baseball player, and the standard of success was the salary. Having money, he saw no reason not to enjoy it. He was driven by love in the sense of an urge to do good, which he saw in two ways—as being kind to the helpless, and not hurting people on purpose. He was good at both. The home runs and the dollars are famous, but we overlook the absence of permanent enemies and the number of people who knew him well and loved him.

With most professional athletes play is work. With Ruth play was play. And it was his life. Was his life trivial? Because the Greeks taught us that what is universally popular is literally vulgar and ignoble, we think the business leader, the statesman, and the soldier are really living while the athlete is wasting his and our time. (Euripides, for one, was *very* rough on athletes on this point; he had competing theaters to fill.) But there is a certain nobility in uniting mind and body in acts that demand their perfect harmony. There is no need to apologize for athletes. The body has disorganized stimuli, gnawing hungers, and some unsystematic goals. The athlete makes it over into something controlled and directed toward its own excellence. If the mind merely lives in the body as a fish lives in a bowl, it would be folly to spend much time and effort to perfect the bowl. But man is mind and body in one, and the great athlete is a complete man who has found the limits of adventure within the bounds of the rules of his kind of play. That is not trivial.

> **Only in constant action was his constant certainty found.**
> **He will throw a longer shadow as time recedes.**
> **—John Cornford, A Memoir**

Babe Ruth lived only fifty-three years, but not all shortened lives are unfinished lives. Some are well rounded off and end at a proper time. Since we have no reason to think he could have been a successful manager, and he had no other serious interest than baseball, we may say his was a finished, complete life. He was born at precisely the right time; it is hard to see how he could have been eminent if born earlier or unique if born later. In the judgment of the people, no ballplayer has succeeded him. More than that, all others have diminished while he has grown. At the first election to the Hall of Fame in 1936 he ranked third. At midcentury the Associated Press poll ranked him first over Cobb as the greatest in the previous fifty years. In 1969, the centennial year of professional baseball, the Baseball Writers Association of America and the baseball broadcasters voted him the best player in the history of the game. They were nearly all strangers to him personally. Somehow that fact seems to add credibility to Babe Ruth's history; one feels like saying, it really *did* happen.

A puzzled drama critic in 1948 asked Babe Ruth's close friend, the sportswriter Dan Daniel, why Ruth should have a funeral unlike any before in New York (or, one may add, since), and more obituary space than any New Yorker had ever had, more memorializing than proposed for Presidents or scientists or warriors. "Why all this? What did this man Ruth do, what did he have, to merit this?"

To answer, a generation later, he is our Hercules, our Samson, Beowulf, Siegfried. No other person outside of public life so stirred our imaginations or so captured our affections.

Appendix: Ruthiana

1963–1973

(compiled by Dr. Helen Cripe)

Item	Date of Sale	Price
Baseball autograph album, 125 signatures, 1933–34, including Ruth's	1963	$ 30.00
Printed colored playing cards, twice signed	1964	$ 10.00
Signature	1964	$ 12.50
Uncanceled check, $28.74, signed in 1948	1964	$ 25.00
Postcard addressed and signed, 1936	1964	$ 8.50
Last New York driver's license	1964	$ 22.50
Last New York auto registration	1964	$ 27.50
Same	1966	$ 30.00
Signature	1967	$ 15.00
Same	1967	$ 20.00
Early 8x10 signed photograph	1967	$ 6.50
Bank deposit slip	1969	$ 47.50
Small signed photograph, 1920s	1970	$ 75.00
Large card, signed	1970	$ 27.50
Postcard-size photograph, signed	1971	$ 75.00
Baseball autographed by all of the 1927 Yankees	1971	$250.00
Bat, signed	1972	$250.00*
Baseball autographed by Ruth and fourteen others	1973	$250.00*

* Asking prices. Sale prices unknown.

Appendix: Folklore and Fable

Much of the writing about heroes is intended to edify or amuse rather than to record the truth. There is a credulous hunger for such tales. As Roger Kahn put it, "There is an appalling shortage of genuine myth in this country's background." The sportswriters believe their job is to blend amusement and information. Following that principle they have done much to meet the need for myth. Babe Ruth, as their chief subject, is the central figure in a large part of the body of sports myth. No doubt most of the tales have some ground in fact, but they owe much to art and imagination. Many of the following may be literally true, but I haven't been able to confirm them. I also include here the stories which I simply cannot believe, as well as some I know, or at any rate firmly believe, to be false.

CHILDHOOD. I have described George Ruth's childhood as well as I can, but there is one matter yet to dispose of: *William (Bojangles) Robinson and Al Jolson were Ruth's schoolmates.* Maryland law barred race-mixture in the two Baltimore protectories for boys, which takes care of Bojangles (who was seventeen years older than Ruth). Al Jolson (Asa Yolson), son of a Washington rabbi, attended St. Mary's Industrial School for a few months in 1898, four years before George Ruth entered.

PERSONAL ECCENTRICITIES. It has been said *Babe Ruth never wore underwear* because he didn't wish to resume his sweaty underwear after the daily shower. Two independent news stories, years apart, mention him, in a manner incidental to the news, as wearing underwear. *He studied a posed photograph of himself and a woman and could not identify the woman, who was his sister Mamie.* That I simply can't believe. *Babe Ruth was in many fist fights.* He was in a very few; like most men, he wasn't very good with his fists. And he won fewer than he lost. *He was fragile, brittle, constantly ill.* From 1920 through 1934 his schedules called for 2,310 games. He appeared in 2,083, or more than 90 percent. Only once did a disability seriously damage his club's chances; that was his infection during the World Series of 1921. He liked the elder Mrs. Gehrig's pickled eels, and *he would mix a quart of pickled eels with a quart of chocolate ice cream* and eat the whole half-gallon. Perhaps he could swallow that, but I can't. *His eyes were in such bad condition in the summer of 1926 that he could not read because of "blurred vision."* (He was thirty-one; too young for presbyopia and bifocals.) Batting average .372, home runs 47.

THE SPENDTHRIFT. *Between batting practice and the start of a game he lost three thousand dollars shooting dice in the clubhouse.* That would be a very fast game. McCarthy didn't allow amusements in the clubhouse. In Huggins's day, Ruppert and Huston stayed out of the clubhouse. Most reporters didn't make that much in a year. Who would be there in those years to join Ruth in a game for such high stakes? *Babe Ruth owned nine automobiles of expensive make at one time.* He owned nine expensive automobiles altogether from 1914 to 1925. In his remaining life he bought fewer than nine. *Ruth smashed up a brand-new car in the country, told passing farmers they could have the remains, and returned to the dealer to buy another of the same model.* This story is given twice: two makes, two dates, two places. It is not an impossible story, but I think it dubious and suppositious. The gross estate of Ruth showed a balance on hand of about a fifth of his estimated lifetime gross earnings. By comparison with, say, Thomas Jefferson or Joe Louis, he was tightfisted.

BASEBALL. *A conspirator kept him up roistering all night before an important game. When Ruth played the next day, he hit two or three home runs.* I found three versions of this tale in which the night-life companion was (a) a Philadelphia boxing promoter, (b) Goose Goslin, (c) a Pittsburgh reporter. There will be others as time passes. *Babe Ruth hit two home runs into the center-field seats of the Polo Grounds on consecutive days.* The distance to the seats was 475 feet, and the wall was sixty feet high. My best information is that nobody ever hit one into those seats. *Ruth became a batter because he was beginning to fail as a pitcher.* His won-loss records for his full-time pitching years were 18–8, 23–12, 24–13. He never had a losing season. *A famous (pitcher, manager) said Ruth's only weakness was a base on balls.* This is probably true, but it is standard dugout humor. I have read it as applied to Honus Wagner, Ty Cobb, Al Simmons, and others as well as Ruth. *Ruth used a fifty-four-ounce bat.* His heaviest known bat weighed forty-seven ounces. At the end of his career his usual bat weighed 34½ ounces. *Ruth hit a high fly into a strong wind. It stayed up so long the fielders gave up on it. It landed near the shortstop for an infield home run.* The closest play resembling this was the previously noted two-base infield error by Jimmie Dykes, which Ruth thought should have been scored as a double. There was also a wind-blown inside-the-park home run in Yankee Stadium (against the Red Sox), but it landed behind the left-fielder, three hundred feet from home plate.

THE MIRACLE. *In Tampa a boy who had been unable to stand for two years was able to stand when Ruth passed.* Ruth claimed this himself (*The Babe Ruth Story*, p. 172).

BASEBALL ECONOMICS. Waite Hoyt put a common belief in words. "Wives of ball players, when they teach their children their prayers, should instruct them to say: 'God bless mommy, God bless daddy, God bless Babe Ruth! *Babe has upped daddy's home pay check by fifteen to forty percent!*'" In raw figures that is approximately true. (Trustworthy figures are scarce.) But baseball players' income as a share of club receipts has declined almost from the beginning of professional baseball. From 1883 to 1950 the gross receipts grew eighty times while salaries went up only seven times. From 1929 to 1950 the average baseball salary rose 84 percent. In the same years in other recreation industries (excluding the movies) the average went up 91 percent. In *all* industries the average went up 114 percent. We see this kind of information in the *American Economist* but not on sports pages. To bring a dry subject to an end, the proportion of club income spent for salaries is easily shown in a short table:

Year	Salaries as a percentage of club expenses
1878	68.0
1880	54.0
1929	35.3
1939	32.0
1950	22.1
1969	20.5

Babe Ruth may have increased the dollar income of players, but at best he only slowed the shrinkage of the players' cut of the baseball pie.

Stories which very likely came from the lives of other players have gathered around Babe Ruth like iron filings around a magnet. The same thing happened to all earlier folk heroes in the same way. Such legends have been well called "solidified rumor." If no busybody interferes, the fables blur the line between fact and fiction, and fiction finally gets the upper hand.

It may well be that many such fictions should win out because they embody human hopes, and, if they edify (George Washington and the cherry tree), they make good ethical symbols. But only the fictions of ethical heroes make useful ethical symbols. The folklore and fable of muscle heroes (Ruth and Hercules) and foxy heroes (Cobb and Bugs Bunny) seem to have little value except for amusement, and should pass as such, not as fact.

Appendix:
Some Record Performances

Some of Babe Ruth's records measure the player, some are merely curious (as, most home runs in September). Below is a selection in no particular order. Those which have been surpassed as of the beginning of play in 1974 are in italics (as is the home-run total bettered by Henry Aaron in the first days of the 1974 season).

The list could be lengthened to nearly seventy, taking in all the curiosities. A fairly complete record as of the end of the season of 1947 is an appendix to Babe Ruth and Bob Considine, *The Babe Ruth Story* (1948).

SEASON

Home Runs, 60 (1927)
Runs batted in, 170 (1921)
Slugging percentage, .847 (1920)
Home runs as a proportion of times at bat, 11.8 percent (1920)
Total bases, 457 (1921)
Extra-base hits, 119 (1921)
Runs scored (since 1900), 177 (1921)
Bases on balls, 170 (1923)

CAREER

Slugging percentage, .690
Home runs, 714
Extra-base hits, 1356
Home runs as a proportion of times at bat, 8.5 percent
Runs batted in, 2217
Bases on balls, 2056
Strikeouts, 1330

IN A SINGLE WORLD SERIES

Hits, four games, 10 (1928)
Home runs, six games, 3 (1923)
Home runs, seven games, 4 (1926)
Batting average, four games, .625 (1928)
Slugging percentage, six games 1.000 (1923)
Slugging percentage, seven games .900 (1926)

ALL WORLD SERIES

Most series, 10
Slugging percentage, .744
Home runs, 15
Total bases, 96
Home runs as a proportion of times at bat, 11.6 percent
Runs scored, 37
Runs batted in, 33
Bases on balls, 33
Strikeouts, 30

Note: The men who later broke Babe Ruth's career World Series batting records were all Yankees who played in more Series, except Duke Snider who briefly held the unsought World Series strikeout record.

WORLD SERIES PITCHING

Consecutive scoreless innings, 29⅔

Babe Ruth is also one of the dozen immortals who pitched 25 innings or more in World Series play without losing a game. He won three games; only four of the undefeated dozen won more games than he won.

A Note on Sources

While this book was being written there was no good book on Babe Ruth, a deficiency since remedied by the appearance of Robert W. Creamer's *Babe: The Legend Comes to Life* (New York, 1974). David Quentin Voigt will have an article on Ruth in the next supplement to the *Dictionary of American Biography*.

The only coherent printed primary materials are a few brief memoirs by close friends.

There is almost no "archival" material. The writer created a small archive by keeping notes of interviews and correspondence with informed baseball experts and veteran players, as mentioned in the preface, and of which more below.

The standard record books of baseball are widely available and annually in print.

The *International Index to Periodicals* lists nothing of use in this work. The *Essay and General Literature Index* has a few citations. But when the student comes to the *Readers Guide to Periodical Literature*, from 1915 to date, under "Ruth," "Baseball," "Baseballs," "Baseball Players," he finds hundreds of titles, of which a few are very valuable.

This book is based mostly on nearly two thousand news and feature stories in *The New York Times*, 1915 to date, the *Baltimore Sun*, 1914, the *Boston Globe*, 1915–19, the *Sporting News*, 1914 to date, and scattered stories in other papers. The method was to read every one of the roughly sixteen hundred relevant pieces entered in *The New York Times Index*. That *Index* led to specific stories, by dates, in the other newspapers.

The writer also followed every lead in the *Readers Guide* with mixed but occasionally good results.

The National Baseball Library at Cooperstown has the chief body of Ruthiana. At present it includes the Babe Ruth scrapbooks, a file drawer of Ruth materials (mostly from the daily press) in the

Major League Individual Player Files, another file drawer of photographs, and some unique Yankee materials. Its collection grows steadily.

Instead of listing a formal bibliography here, I have given a typescript copy of this book to the National Baseball Library together with my working bibliography, my correspondence and my notes of interviews with persons who knew Babe Ruth or have some unique knowledge of his life, a list of citations by chapters of the sources of all quotations which are not given at the point where quoted, and the small collection of documents and photographs I have brought together while studying and writing about Ruth.

Index

There is no independent entry for Babe Ruth. Where another reference includes his name the abbreviation BR is used. Incidental references to teams are not indexed. Where a statement about a major league team has some substance the name of the team is used, not the name of the city—thus, Indians, not Cleveland Indians.